Proud Heritage

Proud Heritage

PEOPLE, ISSUES, AND DOCUMENTS OF THE LGBT EXPERIENCE

Volume I

Chuck Stewart
Editor

ABC-CLIO

Santa Barbara, California • Denver, Colorado • Oxford, England

Library of Congress Cataloging-in-Publication Data

Proud heritage : people, issues, and documents of the LGBT experience / Chuck Stewart, editor.

    volumes cm

  Includes index.

  ISBN 978-1-61069-398-1 (hard copy : alk. paper) — ISBN 978-1-61069-399-8 (ebook)

 1. Homosexuality—United States.   2. Lesbians—United States.   3. Gays—United States.
4. Bisexuals—United States.   5. Transgender people—United States—History.   I. Stewart, Chuck, 1951–

  HQ76.3.U5P765   2015

  306.76'60973—dc23   2014023026

ISBN: 978-1-61069-398-1
EISBN: 978-1-61069-399-8

19 18 17 16 15   1 2 3 4 5

This book is also available on the World Wide Web as an eBook.
Visit www.abc-clio.com for details.

ABC-CLIO, LLC
130 Cremona Drive, P.O. Box 1911
Santa Barbara, California 93116-1911

This book is printed on acid-free paper ∞

Manufactured in the United States of America

Every reasonable effort has been made to trace the owners of copyright materials in this book, but in some instances this
has proven impossible. The editors and publishers will be glad to receive information leading to more complete acknowl-
edgments in subsequent printings of the book and in the meantime extend their apologies for any omissions.

Contents

VOLUME I

Preface, xiii
Chronology, xv

Part One: People, Events, and Issues, 1

Abbott, Steve (1943–1992), 3

ACT UP (AIDS Coalition to Unleash Power), 3

Activists, 6

Affirmative Action, 13

African Americans and LGBTQ Issues, 15

Africa's Gay Punishment Legislation: Involvement from U.S. Christian Factions, 21

AIDS and the Americans with Disabilities Act: *Bragdon v. Abbot* (1998), 24

AIDS History Project, 25

Ailey, Alvin (1931–1989), 28

Albee, Edward (1928–), 29

Alcohol and Drugs, 31

Alice B. Toklas Lesbian Gay Bisexual Transgender Democratic Club, 35

Allegra, Donna (1953–), 37

Allen, Mariette Pathy (1940–), 37

Allen, Paula Gunn (1939–2008), 39

American Civil Liberties Union (ACLU), 40

American Psychiatric Association (APA), 45

Amnesty International OUTfront, 47

Ancient Greek and Roman Sexuality and Philosophy and Impact on the American Legal System, 51

Angus, Patrick (1953–1992), 60

Anthony, Susan B. (1820–1906), 61

Antidiscrimination Statutes, 63

Arvin, Frederick Newton (1900–1963), 65

Asian Americans and LGBTQ Issues, 66

Asian Pacific Lesbian Bisexual Network, 71

Association of Gay and Lesbian Psychiatrists (AGLP), 72

Audre Lorde Project (ALP), 73

Baker v. Vermont (1999), 77

Baldwin, James (1924–1987), 81

Baldwin, Tammy (1962–), 82

Beam, Joseph (1954–1988), 84

BiNet USA, 84

Birch, Elizabeth M. (1956–), 85

Bisexual Health, 87

Bisexual Resource Center, 88

Boswell, John (1947–1994), 89

Bowers v. Hardwick, 106 S. Ct. 2841, 2843 (1986), 90

Boy Scouts, 91

Brown, Howard Juniah (1924–1975), 96

Brown, Rita Mae (1944–), 96

Bryant, Anita (1940–), 98

Buckmire, Ron (1968–), 99

Bunch, Charlotte (1944–), 99

Cameron, Paul Drummond (1939–), 103

Carpenter, Edward (1844–1929), 104

Center for Lesbian and Gay Studies (CLAGS), 105

Chinese American Queer History, 106

Chinese Early LGBTQ History in the United States, 113

Civil Service Reform Act of 1978, 122

Civil Union, 124

Combahee River Collective, 125

Committee on Lesbian and Gay History (CLGH), 127

Communications Decency Amendment (CDA) and Child Online Protection Act (COPA), 130

Crittenden Report, 131

Daughters of Bilitis, 133

Deaf Queer Resource Center, 134

Defense of Marriage Act (DOMA), 135

D'Emilio, John (1948–), 140

Disability Studies and LGBTQ Issues, 141

Domestic Partnership, 144

Don't Ask, Don't Tell: Homosexuality and the Military, 149

Duberman, Martin Bauml (1930–), 154

Endean, Steve (1949–1993), 157

Equal Access Act (EAA), 157

Exodus International, 159

Faderman, Lillian (1940–), 163

Falwell, Jerry L. (1933–2007), 165

Federal Employment Nondiscrimination Order, 166

Feinberg, Leslie (1949–), 167

Foucault, Michel (1926–1984), 169

Frank, Barney (1940–), 170

Full Faith and Credit Clause, 171

Gender-Motivated Violence Act (GMVA), 173

Gittings, Barbara (1932–2007), 174

Hall, Radclyffe (1880–1943), 177

Hay, Henry (Harry) (1912–2002), 178

Helms, Jesse (1921–2008), 179

Hirschfeld, Magnus (1868–1935), 180

Historical Overview of Gay Rights and Issues: From Pre-Columbian Times to the 1970s, 183

Historical Overview of Gay Rights and Issues: From the 1980s to the Present, 196

Hooker, Evelyn (1907–1996), 213

Human Rights Campaign (HRC), 214

Kameny, Franklin (1925–2011), 221

King, Billie Jean (1943–), 224

Kramer, Larry (1935–2008), 226

Lambda Legal Defense and Education Fund (LLDEF), 229

Latino/Latina Americans and LGBTQ Issues, 230

Lorde, Audre (1934–1992), 235

Lyon, Phyllis (1924–), 237

Mabon, Lon T. (1947–), 241

Martin, Del (1921–2008), 242

Matlovich, Leonard (1943–1988), 243

Mattachine Society, 245

Milk, Harvey (1930–1978), 247

Mishima, Yukio (1925–1970), 250

Moscone, George (1929–1978), 251

National Coming Out Day, 253

National Gay and Lesbian Task Force, 254

National Organization of Gay and Lesbian Scientists and Technical Professionals, Inc., 261

Native Americans and LGBTQ Issues, 265

Native Americans and Same-Sex Marriage, 269

Navratilova, Martina (1956–), 271

Near, Holly (1949–), 272

Obama, Barack, and Support for Same-Sex Marriage, 275

ONE, Incorporated, 276

Perkins, Will (1928–), 279

Perry, Troy (1940–), 280

Proposition 8 and the Mormon Church, 281

Proposition 8 Legal Analysis and the Impact of Judge Walker's Decision, 285

Rich, Adrienne (1929–2012), 289

Robertson, Pat (1930–), 290

Romer v. Evans (1996), 292

Rustin, Bayard (1912–1987), 294

Same-Sex Marriage in the United States, 299

Sappho (Sixth Century BCE), 304

Schlafly, Phyllis Stewart (1924–), 305

Sexual Orientation Change Efforts, 306

Signorile, Michelangelo (1960–), 311

Socrates (469–399 BCE), 313

Soulforce, 314

Stonewall Riot, 320

Symonds, John Addington (1840–1893), 322

Title VII, 325

Transgender Children, 327

Turing, Alan (1912–1954), 331

U.S. Department of Housing and Urban Development's Office of Fair Housing, 335

Ulrichs, Karl Heinrich (1825–1895), 336

Vaid, Urvashi (1958–), 339

Voeller, Bruce (1934–1994), 341

Waddell, Tom (1937–1987), 343

We'wha (1849–1896), 344

White, Dan (1946–1985), 345

White (Dan) Trial (1979), 346

Whitman, Walt (1819–1892), 350

Wilde, Oscar (1854–1900), 351

VOLUME 2

Part Two: Documents, from Biblical Times to the Present, 353

The Bible, 355

Sodom and Gomorrah, 355

The Abominations of Leviticus, 356

Ruth and Naomi, 358

David and Jonathan, 358

Jesus, 359

Paul, 361

Early America, 363

Navajo Sacredness for Nadleeh, 363

Indian Sodomy in Florida (1582 and 1702 Reports), 364

Virginia Sodomy Law (1610), 364

The Execution of Richard Cornish (1624–1625), 365

William Plaine Executed in New England for Teaching Masturbation (1646), 365

African American Jan Creoli Killed and Burned in Dutch Colony (1646), 366

Sara Norman and Mary Hammon Accused of Lewd Behavior (1649), 366

New Haven Law Prohibits Lesbianism (1655), 367

Puritan Sermon on the Cry of Sodom (1674), 367

Illinois Indian Transgender (1677), 368

Pirates in the Caribbean (1724), 369

Commentaries on the Laws of England (1765), 370

Spanish Priests Condemn Transgendered Yuma Indians (1775), 371

Spanish Colonial Suppression of Sodomites in California (1775–1777), 372

Early United States of America, 373

U.S. Declaration of Independence (1776), 373

U.S. Constitution and Bill of Rights (1791), 373

Bachelor Friendships of the Nineteenth Century, 375

National Women's Rights Convention (1852), 376

Walt Whitman and the Homoerotic Poetry of Democracy (1860), 377

Fourteenth Amendment to the Constitution (1868), 378

Walt Whitman's *Democratic Vistas* (1870), 378

Females Passing as Men (1894), 379

Turn of the Twentieth Century through World War I, 381

Anthony Comstock Seeks to Imprison Inverts (1900), 381

U.S. Navy Entraps Homosexuals (1919), 381

Society for Human Rights (1924), 383

The Well of Loneliness (1929), 386

World War II to 1950, 389

The German Criminal Code, Paragraph 175 (1935), 389

Sigmund Freud on Homosexuality (1935), 390

Lesbian Challenges Georgia's Sodomy Law (1939), 391

Lesbians in the Women's Army Corps (1945), 391

Psychiatrists Oppose Homosexual Rights Laws (1945), 393

Vice Versa Predictions (1947), 394

Employment of Homosexuals and Other Sex Perverts (1950), 395

1950s, 397

Formation of the Mattachine Society (1950), 397

Mattachine Society Meetings (1950), 398

Mattachine Protests Police Entrapment (1952), 399

Formation of ONE, Inc. (1952), 400

Jim Kepner's First Mattachine Meeting (1953), 401

Tampa Lesbian Bar Raid (1953), 402

Founding of ONE Institute of Homophile Studies (1956), 403

Allen Ginsberg and the Beatniks (1956), 406

The Crittenden Report on Homosexuality in the U.S. Navy (1957), 407

Evelyn Hooker's Psychological Research (1957), 409

Supreme Court Rules ONE Is Not Obscene (1958), 411

Mattachine National Convention (1959), 413

1960s, 415

"A Homosexual Bill of Rights" (1961), 415

Jose Sarria Runs for San Francisco City Council (1961), 417

ACLU Begins Gay Rights Cases (1963), 419

Bayard Rustin, Martin Luther King Jr., and the March on Washington (1963), 420

Mohave Indian Two-Spirit Person (1964), 421

Mattachine Pickets the White House (1965), 422

San Francisco Activism (1965), 423

Lesbian Activism and *The Ladder* (1966), 425

Supreme Court Excludes and Deports Homosexual Immigrants (1967), 426

Homophile Action League (1968), 430

A Gay Manifesto (1969), 431

Employment Rights: *Norton v. Macy* (1969), 432

Teacher's Rights: *Morrison v. State Board of Education* (1969), 441

1970s, 461

Gay Liberation Front and Gay Activists Alliance (1970), 461

"Gay Lib Zaps Psychologists" (1970), 462

Congress to Unite Women (1970), 463

"The Woman-Identified Woman" (1970), 464

Democratic Party Convention (1972), 465

Multiple Struggles for Lesbian Women of Color (1973), 465

Parents and Friends of Lesbians and Gays (1973), 466

Gay Rights to Organize: *Gay Students Org. v. Bonner* (1974), 466

Teachers' Rights: *Ancafora v. Board of Education* (1974), 480

The National Federation of Priests' Councils (NFPC) (1974), 485

Lesbian Child Custody Rights (1974), 486

Lesbians as the Vanguard of Feminism (1975), 486

Military Service: *Matlovich v. Secretary of the Air Force* (1976), 487

Union of American Hebrew Congregations Resolution (1977), 501

Teachers' Rights: *Gaylord v. Tacoma School Dist. No. 10* (1977), 501

Gay Men Harm Society (1978), 512

Civil Service Reform Act of 1978, 513

Harvey Milk on the San Francisco Board of Supervisors (1978), 514

Homosexuality Is Unnatural (1979), 517

Coming Out as Free Speech: *Gay Law Students Ass'n v. Pacific Tele. and Tel. Co.* (1979), 517

1980s, 521

Anita Bryant's Startling Reversal (1980), 521

Democratic Party and Gay Rights (1980), 522

Gay Students' Rights: *Fricke v. Lynch* (1980), 523

Child Custody by Lesbian Parents: *In re Breisch* (1981), 529

Wisconsin Antidiscrimination Law (1981), 536

Violence against Lesbians (1982), 537

Merle Woo Challenges the University of California (1982), 538

Lesbians of Color Conference (1983), 539

Teachers' Rights: *National Gay Task Force v. Board of Education of Oklahoma City* (1985), 540

Private Consensual Sexual Behavior: *Bowers v. Hardwick* (1986), 548

Dignity USA's Response to the "Congregation for the Doctrine of Faith—On the Pastoral Care of Homosexual Persons. . ." (1986), 551

AIDS as God's Punishment (1987), 552

ACT UP (AIDS Coalition to Unleash Power) (1987), 552

Old Lesbians Organizing for Change (OLOC) Mission Statement (1987), 554

AIDS Should Not Prevent Sexual Pleasure (1988), 555

National Coming Out Day (1988), 556

Congressman William Dannemeyer Opposes Gay Rights (1989), 557

A Jewish Rabbi's Acceptance of Gay and Lesbian Rights (1989), 558

Employment Rights: *Price Waterhouse v. Hopkins* (1989), 559

Family Issues: *Braschi v. Stahl Associates Co.* (1989), 575

1990s, 587

Queer Nation (1990), 587

Asylum from Torture: *Matter of Toboso-Alfonso* (1990), 588

Child Custody by De Facto Parents: *Alison D. v. Virginia M.* (1991), 594

Bisexuals and Gay Rights (1991), 600

Gays in the Republican Party (1991), 601

Democratic Party Pro-Gay Rights (1992), 601

Removing Prohibitions on Same-Sex Behavior: *Kentucky v. Wasson* (1992), 602

Colorado Amendment 2 (1992), 603

Oregon Measure 9 (1992), 604

Same-Sex Marriage in Hawaii: *Baehr v. Lewin* (1993), 607

Lesbian Attorney Appointed to High Federal Government Position (1993), 630

Military Working Group on Homosexuality (1993), 631

Barry Goldwater on Gays in the Military (1993), 632

March on Washington (1993), 633

Don't Ask, Don't Tell (1993), 635

PFLAG Supports Gay and Lesbian Children (1994), 639

Catholic Condemnation of Homosexuality (1994), 640

Ex-Gays Condemn Gay Rights (1994), 641

Sharon Bottoms Child Custody Court Case: *Bottoms v. Bottoms* (1994 and 1995), 642

Lesbianas Unidas (1994), 643

The Lesbian Avengers (1995), 644

Discrimination by Private Organizations: *Hurley v. Irish-American Gay, Lesbian, and Bisexual Group of Boston* (1995), 646

Communications Decency Act of 1996, 648

Brandon Teena Murder Trial (1996), 654

Protection from Discrimination for LGBT Citizens: *Romer v. Evans* (1996), 656

Harassment of Gay Students: *Nabozny v. Podlesny* (1996), 676

Defense of Marriage Act (DOMA) (1996), 688

Galluccio-Holden Adoption Lawsuit (1997), 691

Gay and Lesbian Alliance Against Defamation (1997), 693

Child Online Protection Act (COPA) (1998), 694

Transsexual Name Change: *In re McIntyre* (1998), 698

Same-Sex Sexual Harassment: *Oncale v. Sundowner Offshore Services, Inc.* (1998), 701

AIDS and the Americans with Disabilities Act: *Bragdon v. Abbot* (1998), 706

Same-Sex Marriage Equality: *Baker v. Vermont* (1999), 709

Overturning State Sodomy Laws (1999), 711

Gay Rights to Belong to a Group: *Boy Scouts of America v. Dale* (2000), 712

Student Rights to Form Gay Clubs: *East High Gay/Straight Alliance v. Board of Education* (1999), 716

Human Rights Campaign Statement on Why Reparative Therapy and Ex-Gay Ministries Fail, 728

Diversity Training: *Altman v. Minnesota Department of Corrections* (1999), 729

2000s, 735

The Westboro Baptist Church and Its Message of Hate, 735

Student Group Rights to University Funding: *Board of Regents of the University of Wisconsin System v. Southworth* (2000), 736

Gay Rights to Belong to a Group: *Boy Scouts of America v. Dale* (2000), 751

Transgender Rights and the ACLU (2000), 756

Transsexual Rights: *Schwenk v. Hartford* (2000), 757

Antigay Hate Crimes in High Schools (2000), 761

Millennium March on Washington (2000), 763

The Threat to Marriage from the Courts (2003), 765

The Supreme Court Rules That Anti-Sodomy Laws Are Unconstitutional: *Lawrence v. Texas* 539 U.S. 558 (2003), 773

Oregon Family Fairness Act (2007), 803

Uniting American Families Act (2007), 805

Matthew Shepard Act (2007), 807

In re Marriage Cases: Opinion (2008) California's Ban on Same-Sex Marriages Is Unconstitutional, 809

In re Marriage Cases: Dissent (2008), 814

The National Association for Research and Therapy of Homosexuality (NARTH) and Its Purpose (2014), 816

The Repeal of "Don't Ask, Don't Tell" (2010), 817

California's Law to Ban Sexual Orientation Change Efforts: Senate Bill No. 1172 (2012), 819

U.S. Supreme Court Lets Ban against Proposition 8 Stand, Allowing Same-Sex Marriage in California: *Hollingsworth et al. v. Perry et al.* (2013), 824

Supreme Court Rules That DOMA Is Unconstitutional: *UNITED STATES v. WINDSOR, Executor of the ESTATE OF SPYER, et al.* (2013), 838

Arizona's Attempted Legislation to Allow Discrimination Based on Religious Freedom: SB1062 (2014), 856

VOLUME 3

Introduction, xiii

Part Three: State Laws and Issues Concerning LGBT Rights, 859

Alabama, 861

Alaska, 864

Arizona, 874

Arkansas, 879

California, 885

Colorado, 895

Connecticut, 901

Delaware, 907

District of Columbia, 913

Florida, 919

Georgia, 926

Hawaii, 933

Idaho, 940

Illinois, 945

Indiana, 956

Iowa, 964

Kansas, 972

Kentucky, 982

Louisiana, 987

Maine, 992

Maryland, 998

Massachusetts, 1005

Michigan, 1013

Minnesota, 1021

Mississippi, 1034

Missouri, 1039

Montana, 1047

Nebraska, 1055

Nevada, 1068

New Hampshire, 1075

New Jersey, 1083

New Mexico, 1090

New York, 1101

North Carolina, 1115

North Dakota, 1123

Ohio, 1131

Oklahoma, 1136

Oregon, 1143

Pennsylvania, 1150

Puerto Rico, 1157

Rhode Island and Providence Plantations, 1164

South Carolina, 1169

South Dakota, 1180

Tennessee, 1186

Texas, 1191

Utah, 1199

Vermont, 1207

Virginia, 1211

Washington, 1217

West Virginia, 1226

Wisconsin, 1232

Wyoming, 1237

Recommended Resources, 1247
About the Editor and Contributors, 1263
Index, 1273

Preface

Proud Heritage: People, Issues, and Documents of the LGBT Experience is a comprehensive, three-volume work that illuminates the issues and hard-won rights of gay, lesbian, bisexual, and transgender people in the United States. From documents and historical accounts, the book also traces the historical cultural and legal antecedents that influenced the United States, ranging from the Bible, Native American culture, and early European colonial laws to the present-day struggles for same-sex marriage and complete equality. It will be of interest to all who wish to study the issues and challenges that members of gay, lesbian, bisexual, and transgender communities face, and this text provides models and contexts for students in high schools through college and all readers.

Gay and lesbian individuals have a long history in humankind, but they have long been denied rights, including the basic right to life. People convicted of homosexual acts were executed in the United States in the times of the early colonies and young republic. In following years, LGBT people were arrested, imprisoned, fired from jobs, and disowned by families and communities. It has primarily been only in the last 45 years that LGBT Americans have been able to persevere, asserting their rights and seeing laws slowly overturned that ensure their freedom to hold jobs, serve in the armed forces, hold political office, raise and have custody of their children, and currently, to be allowed to marry within same-sex unions, but only in some states.

Scope and Arrangement

Proud Heritage: People, Issues, and Documents of the LGBT Experience is a reference work focused on the issues that LGBT people in the United States have faced and continue to face, highlighting the milestones and the people who have led the way to ensure equality in their daily lives.

The three volumes include:

A detailed chronology, which provides historical context and an extensively annotated chronology of important events in LGBT history, from ancient Greek and Roman times to the present.

Part One (in Volume 1) is a section comprising 203 entries, or essays, in A-Z order, ranging from 300 to 7,000 words. They include two lengthy historical overviews of the main periods in LGBT history, profiles of people who have been important figures within LGBT rights, information on organizations that have been formed to fight for and against rights, accounts of key events, and articles on such controversial topics as the push to "repair" sexual orientation through sexual orientation change efforts and the efforts of some Americans to promote antigay legislation in Africa. Each entry provides a selected bibliography for further reading, allowing for more research and study on the topic.

Part Two (in Volume 2) is a section of 163 primary or historical documents highlighting controversial issues, legislation, and debates. Arranged chronologically from biblical times to 2014, these documents and excerpts proclaim the progress and lack of progress as people who are gay or lesbian or bisexual or transgender try to assert and claim their rights as human beings. These texts provide a sometimes-horrifying, disturbing but also inspiring text. Letters, reports, research, speeches, eyewitness accounts, official statements by organizations, court cases, and laws make up Part Two. Each document or excerpt begins with an introduction that gives the item as much context as necessary.

Part Three (in Volume 3) provides an introduction and 52 state-by-state (including District of Columbia and Puerto Rico) overviews of LGBT laws and issues and the status of current legislation. Each entry provides a historical introduction and information about state legislation, if any, related to the following topics: adoption and foster care, conversion therapy, custody and visitation law, donor insemination law, gender change on state issued id, hate crimes laws, health care laws, marriage and family law, nondiscrimination in employment, school laws, sodomy law, surrogacy law.

Volume 3 ends with an extensive and valuable section of recommended resources: books, journals, and websites, and organizations connected to lesbian, gay, bisexual, and transgender interests and rights. A comprehensive index completes this reference work.

There are 92 writers who have contributed to the richness of this work, including scholars, professors, lawyers, writers, and health professionals. Each brings keen interest, knowledge, and experience to writing about his or her topics. Their professional biographies are featured at the end of the book. We hope that readers of *Proud Heritage: People, Issues, and Documents of the LGBT Experience* will use this reference work as a springboard to their own research on the issues of lesbian, gay, bisexual, and transgender rights.

Acknowledgments

A writing project of this size includes the help of so many. So many academics and editors helped make this project possible. In particular, I would like to thank the ONE National Gay & Lesbian Archives at the University of Southern California for granting permission to many historical documents used in this encyclopedia. ONE has been at the center of the modern gay rights movement and is a treasure trove of documents and artifacts.

Chronology

Early Historical Events Concerning Lesbian, Gay, Bisexual, and Transgender People

Until recently, history courses amounted to little more than reading about the activities of wealthy white men who engaged in war against one another. Rarely did the histories and lives of people of color or women appear, and if they did, it was as a sidebar in textbooks and presented in relation to men. Homosexuality was completely ignored unless it pertained to particular "scandals."

The civil rights movement and women's rights movement in the 1960s and 1970s brought significant changes to historical textbooks. The process of consciousness-raising initiated by the women's movement included reclaiming its history—a process adopted by other marginalized groups including lesbians, gay men, and transgendered.

Even though people like American archivist Jim Kepner privately collected material on the early American gay movement (the world's largest collection with more than 1 million items contained in the ONE Institute and Archives located on the campus of the University of Southern California), many of the current lesbian and gay historical collections did not begin until the aftermath of the Stonewall Riots in 1969. The Lesbian Herstory Archives founded in 1973 and the San Francisco Lesbian and Gay History Project (1977) are examples of two new collections. Now lesbian and gay archives can be found on most universities, all around the country, and around the world.

Deciding on which events to include in this chronology is problematic. Before the twentieth century, there are virtually no writings of personal letters or books that include explicit sexual descriptions. Very little information exists about the actual lives of people in earlier times. Identifying someone as gay or lesbian is exceedingly difficult. The primary document created by older cultures is for the ownership, transfer, and taxation of property. With property ownership came the issue of inheritance. Only the wealthy were landowners and they wanted to guarantee that their property would go to their offspring. Religion and culture combined to create and reinforce heterosexual nuclear family norms. Thus, marriages and offspring were recorded to assure the legitimacy of heirs. Not all marriages and not all offsprings were recorded; the poor, slaves, and racial/ethnic outcasts were often ignored, so were same-sex relationships. The documents we have are biased toward wealthy landowners who formed heterosexual relationships and the resultant children.

A second source of documents related to human sexuality is legislation and court proceedings. Beginning in the 1600s America, colonies and states enacted laws to control sodomy. Vague terms were used to describe sodomy and generally meant any form of sexuality disapproved by those in power, who were white landowners. By the early twentieth century, states passed laws to sexually sterilize persons considered "deviant." With the development of psychology, psychopathic laws were passed to indefinitely incarcerate those convicted of illegal sexual crimes. These three categories of laws created a cache of documents that demonstrate how confused legislators were concerning human sexuality and morality. Court proceedings and decisions also help to shed light on the relationship between religion and sexuality in early America. Unfortunately, legislation and court proceedings only show the tip of the iceberg concerning homosexual behaviors and nothing about same-sex relationships—and what is shown is extremely negative.

Finally, we have the problem of identity. The *gay identity* is decidedly a modern term that cannot be properly applied to people of earlier cultures. Also, the gay-straight dichotomy is extremely limiting. How people express their gender, sexual orientation, sex roles, and more is extremely fluid. It seems that for most of human history and most places on this earth, conforming to gender roles was important but not with whom you had sex. Considering that there are no documents showing same-sex marriages, or the adoption of children by same-sex couples, or diaries that explicitly state homosexual behaviors or "gay" identities, it is problematic to tell a history that includes LGBT people.

Since Stonewall, and in particular the past 30 years, gay rights have come to the forefront of world politics. Every day there is some act of gay protest, opposition to gay rights, laws being passed or rescinded that specifically identify sexual orientation, and other events. Thus, any chronology, including this one, will be incomplete. Readers are encouraged to use this list as a starting point in their own research.

Homosexuality Prior to the Nineteenth Century

The Industrial Revolution caused major changes in most people's lives. The development of steam power, the use of fossil fuels, and the invention of electricity were technical developments that increased the ability of humans to communicate and be productive. These events occurred during the 1800s. Before that, most people worked on farms. A farmer in seventeenth-century England might be virtually indistinguishable from a farmer in 180 CE Rome or a farmer in Egypt or China or Africa in 2000 BCE. Cultures slowly evolved and most accepted homosexual behaviors. In general, as long as a person who owned property fulfilled his or her familial obligations of producing children, with whom they had sex was relatively immaterial.

What is rarely written about are what anthropologists call "all-male societies" (or societies made up of one gender). Jamestown, the first settlement in America by Europeans, was made up exclusively of men. Frontiersmen, the military, and the movement west were conducted mostly by men. The early settlement of the Midwest, mountains, desert regions, California, Oregon, and Washington was primarily by men. For example, in 1848, San Francisco had a population of 812 people, of whom approximately 74 percent were male. Within three years these numbers would become more male dominated as 25,000 Chinese men came to California through San Francisco to participate in the gold rush of 1851 and to build the cross-continental railroad. Whom did these men have relationships with? We can only conclude that same-sex relationships were, in fact, the norm, yet public documents will have no record of these lives.

First People (Native Americans), Polynesians, Indians, Asiatic Eskimos—Before the influence of Christianity, many of these societies saw sexuality as a gift from the spirit world. In general, it was unimportant with whom you had sex and homosexual behavior was accepted. Also accepted were transgendered people who adopted the behaviors and clothing of both men and women. *Two-spirited* people (previously termed *Berdaches* and also known as *yirka-la ul, mahu, hijras*) were thought to have two spirits and often held the position of teacher and shaman in these societies.

Amazons—When explorer Pedro de Magalhaes de Gandavo explored northeastern Brazil in 1576, he discovered women who imitated men, wore their hair like men, and had other women as their wives. At least 33 North American groups included Amazons in their societies. Other Amazon societies could be found around the world and in other times.

Institutionalized Homosexuality—Throughout history and into the modern age, many societies institutionalized homosexual behaviors and relationships. Such cultures included seventeenth-century Mayan society, Buddhist monks, the samurai class of early Japan, and Melanesia in southern New Guinea. In these societies, all members engaged in homosexual relationships for the majority of their lives.

Ancient Greece—Sex for the ancient Greeks was mostly value neutral. Exclusive homosexuality was discouraged. Sexual relationships between older men and young boys were considered a crucial part of the younger man's maturation process. Not much is known of lesbianism except for a limited number of poems written by Sappho extolling the virtues of love between women. Also, virtually nothing is known about the lives of slaves and the poor.

Ancient Rome—There is widespread evidence of homosexual behavior being accepted in the republic and early empire. Like the ancient Greeks, Romans did not identify homosexuality as a problem. A number of Roman and Greek leaders publicly took on male lovers going so far as to have public same-sex marriages. Around the third century CE, due to the influence of Christianity, Rome began to enact a series of laws regulating various aspects of homosexual relationships.

China—For 300 years beginning in the third century BCE, many historical documents show that homosexuality was accepted, particularly among the ruling class. It is from these stories that common euphemisms for male homosexual love, *fen tao zhi ai* (literally, "the love of shared peach") and *duanxiu* (literally, "the cut sleeve"), came.

The Catholic Church and the Twelfth-Century European Transformation—For most of the first thousand years of the Catholic Church, homosexual marriages were sanctioned by church ritual. The scholar John Boswell documented this in his groundbreaking work, *Christianity, Social Tolerance and Homosexuality: Gay People in Western Europe from the Beginning of the Christian Era to the Fourteenth Century* (Chicago: University of Chicago Press, 1980). Unlike heterosexual ceremonies that were mostly about property rights and were held outdoors, gay marriages were identified with love and held inside the church. But by the thirteenth century, the Catholic Church solidified its hold over Europe and Thomas Aquinas constructed the framework in which homosexual acts were classified less worthy than heterosexual ones. In 50 short years, from 1250 to 1300, homosexuality went from being completely legal in most of Europe to a behavior meriting the death penalty.

Ming Dynasty 1368 to 1644—Homosexuality was tolerated as long as it was not an exclusive sexual expression and as long as men fulfilled their familial procreative duties. When the Manchu entered the city in the summer of 1644 overthrowing the Ming dynasty, the first male homosexual rape law was enacted and male homosexuality was severely punished.

Russia—There is much evidence that male homosexuality was widespread and tolerated in all strata of Russian society prior to the Westernization reforms of Peter the Great (early eighteenth century). The first law penalizing consensual male homosexuality was enacted in 1706 and required burning at the stake. Peter the Great (who was bisexual) mitigated the penalty and there are no known instances of its application. The criminalization of male homosexuality came later under the brutal rule of Nicolas I, when article 995 was enacted in the legal code of 1832.

United States from 1607, by Years

The expansion westward of white Europeans brought with them various legal codes that included sodomy provisions. As territories and then states were formed, these codes were adopted into state charters and constitutions. Sodomy provisions were based on English or Spanish legal codes that were, originally, based on religious tenets formed during the many Catholic inquisitions that swept Europe in the twelfth through fourteenth centuries. Sodomy was not clearly defined and used as a catchall phrase to punish people for sexual transgressions (real or perceived). Often the penalty for committing sodomy was death.

1607   The initial reports back to England about the settlements at Jamestown (initially settled by all men) described sailors stealing food and trading for sexual favors. By 1610, sodomy had become so widespread that a military order was adopted stating, "[n]o man shal *[sic]* commit the horrible, and detestable sinnes of Sodomie upon pain of death[.]"

1610   The Virginia Colony passes the first sodomy law in America. It requires the death penalty for offenders and does not include women in its definition of "sodomites."

1625 The first known death sentence related to sodomy is carried out in the American colonies when Richard Cornish, master of the ship Ambrose, is hanged in Virginia Colony. He was convicted of forcibly sodomizing his indentured servant, William Cowse, ship steward. Cowse was referred to as a "rascally boy" and two other men claimed that Cornish was wrongfully accused. The two men were severely punished for their support of Cornish.

1629 Thomas/Thomasina Hall is proclaimed by the governor to be both "a man and a woman" and ordered to wear articles of clothing appropriate for each sex.

Rev. Francis Higginson discovers "5 beastly Sodomiticall boyes [*sic*], which confessed their wickedness not to be named" on a ship bound for New England. The incident is reported to the governor of the Massachusetts Bay Colony who sends the boys back to England for punishment. At that time, males over 14 years of age could be hanged for sodomy. It is not known what happened to the boys.

1632 Maryland adopts English common law in its charter. Sodomy as an "unnatural" and "perverted" sexual practice will remain in force for the next 161 years.

1639 Charter granted by King Charles I specifies that the laws of Connecticut authorities are to be consistent with the common law of England. As such, sodomy is a capital offense and applies only to males.

1641 The Massachusetts Bay Colony includes sodomy as a capital crime in its newly adopted code of laws. It defines sodomy as "man lying with mankind as he lies with a woman"—wording taken directly from Leviticus 20:13.

1646 "Jan Creoli, a negro" in New Netherland (New York) is executed by choking for engaging in sodomy. According to the records, sodomy was "condemned of God" yet there is no record of the specific criminal statute the sentence is based. He is choked to death and the body "burned to ashes." Ten-year-old Manuel Congo, whom Creoli allegedly sodomized, is flogged in public.

William Plaine of Builford Connecticut is executed for sodomy because he masturbated a number of the town's young men.

1647 Rhode Island makes sodomy a capital offense. The sodomy section of the law is entitled "Touching Whoremongers" and reads like a Christian sermon.

1648 Elizabeth Johnson is the first woman known to be prosecuted for sexual relations with another woman, in Massachusetts Bay Colony.

1649 Sarah Norman and Mary Hammond, two married women, are charged with lewd behavior. The charges are dropped against Hammond, who is younger. Norman receives a warning that her punishment will be greater if there are any subsequent charges.

1656 The New Haven Colony, which would later merge into Connecticut, becomes the first state in what would become the United States to specifically outlaw sex between two women.

1660 In the third sodomy case in New York, Jan Quisthout van der Linde (or Linden) is accused of sodomy with a servant. After being convicted, he is tied into a sack, thrown into a river, and drowns. The servant is flogged. There are no written details to determine why there is a difference in punishment. The widow petitioned for bankruptcy three years later.

1668 New Jersey enacts its own sodomy law that proscribes the death penalty except for those under the age of 14.

1673 to 1677 On his voyage down the Mississippi River, Father Jacques Marquette recounts that some Indians assume the garb of women, which they wear throughout their lives. Many other travelers to the American frontier make similar observations.

1676 Duke of York creates a set of laws used in colonial Pennsylvania and Delaware. The law includes a provision proscribing death for males over the age of 14 engaging in sodomy. The law is later modified in 1682 setting the maximum penalty at six-months in jail. This is the only sodomy law in colonial times not to specify death to all those convicted of sodomy. This lenient position ended when the Quakers lost control of the colony.

1700 Pennsylvania modifies its sodomy statutes to specify that blacks charged with buggery will also be punished by death. The preamble for the code states, "some difficulties have arisen" concerning blacks charged with crimes, indicating there are problems applying the law concerning free blacks or black slaves. Furthermore, the law establishes flogging every three months during the first year of imprisonment and, if the prisoner is married, he is to be castrated and his wife is allowed to divorce.

1704 Public discontent with the New Jersey legislature leads to the state pardoning everyone except those whose crime is 1 of 11 categories. Since sodomy is not 1 of the 11 categories, all sodomy convictions are overturned.

1712 South Carolina enacts a sodomy statute requiring a death sentence and forfeiture of property. The statute applied to males only who engaged in "the detestable and abominable vice of buggery."

1715 North Carolina adopts the common law of England thus making sodomy a capital offense and applies only to males.

1719 Delaware, an area that was subsequently under Swish, Dutch, and finally English control, enacts "An Act for the advancement of Justice, and more certain administration thereof" that clarified that sodomy is punishable under English common law and proscribes death for conviction.

1777 In anticipation of success of the American Revolution, Thomas Jefferson works with a committee to craft a new criminal code. Jefferson and other liberals argue to lift the death penalty for sodomy and, instead, advocate for the lesser penalty of castration for men and to bore a hole through the nose of women. Jefferson's ideas are rejected and the death penalty is retained.

1778 Baron Frederich von Steuben is the first soldier known to be dismissed from the U.S. military for engaging in homosexuality. Steuben was recognized as one of Europe's greatest military minds and was engaged by the U.S. military to train the disparate armies of the 13 colonies. He was discovered in bed with Lt. Gotthold Frederick Enslin.

1780 The first fellatio case in the United States is decided in Pennsylvania. Presiding judge Rice "cautioned the jury against allowing their abhorrence [*sic*] of this crime to prejudice them in considering the evidence against the defendant."

1782 Vermont adopts the Elizabethan buggery law of 1562 besides common law making sodomy a capital offense.

1786 Pennsylvania is the first state to abolish the death penalty for sodomy convictions.

1792 As one of the founding states of the new United States, Virginia enacts its first sodomy statute.

Kentucky adopts the laws of Virginia, including English buggery statutes that apply only to males.

1795 Illinois, as part of the Northwest Territory, adopts the English buggery law. The Northwest Territory ordinance applies sodomy only to males and makes it a capital offense.

Legislative Council of the Northwest Territories adopts English common law and statutory laws passed before 1607 for the newly formed state of Indiana. As such, the buggery law applied only to males and proscribed death for those convicted of sodomy.

Ohio adopts the common laws of England, including capital punishment for sodomy conviction.

1796 In adopting a new criminal code for New Jersey, it is the first in the nation to use the term *crime against nature* to describe sodomy.

1798 Rhode Island revises its criminal code and reduces the penalty for sodomy. Now, a second-time conviction for sodomy proscribes death, not the first conviction. No other state law was structured with a tiered conviction.

1801 While under Spanish law, California executes private soldier Jose Antonio Rosas for sodomy. The 18-year-old Los Angeles native confesses and pleads for mercy claiming that he was tempted by "El Demonio" (the devil). The viceroy sentenced him to be hanged, but there is no hangman available in California at the time. On February 11, he is executed by firing squad and his body purified by burning before burial at the Santa Barbara presidio cemetery in the presence of the whole garrison. He is the last person known to be executed for sodomy in the United States.

1802 Mississippi Territory is formed and enacts a new legal code. It includes common-law crimes, which criminalizing sodomy as a capital offense in Alabama. By 1822, the Alabama Supreme Court rules that common law is not in effect thereby nullifying the sodomy regulations. In 1830, the court reverses itself again making sodomy illegal. Mississippi has not repealed its sodomy laws.

1805 Although Louisiana was founded as a French colony with no sodomy law, its first criminal code enacted in 1805 lists sodomy as a criminal offense and requires a penalty of life imprisonment at hard labor.

1806 Ohio repeals its common-law reception statute thereby making sodomy legal. Surprisingly, sodomy would be legal for the next 60 years.

1807 An extremely harsh sodomy law is signed in Indiana, including flogging, and is signed by Governor William Henry Harrison, the only sodomy law ever signed by a future U.S. president.

1810 Maryland Court of Appeals publishes the first sodomy case in U.S. history.

1812 In the first case of its kind in the nation, Virginia Supreme Court decides that emission of semen is unnecessary for the completion of sodomy. This is a rejection of English law and most states follow suit with this approach.

Missouri receives laws from the Louisiana Territory that include life sentence for sodomy. It creates its own sodomy law in 1835 with the similar punishment and uses the term *crime against nature*.

1814 New York trial court publishes earliest known slander case in the United States involving the accusation of sodomy.

1816 A new legal code that criminalizes sodomy is adopted by Michigan. In the list of crimes prosecutable by the state by order of their perceived severity, sodomy was the fourth most heinous crime after murder, manslaughter and treason, and ahead of rape.

1817 Georgia was originally settled as a penal colony and its charters specifically stated that it was not to receive its laws from England. As such, Georgia is the only founding state not to have sodomy statutes thereby making sodomy legal. Finally, in 1817, 85 years after its founding, Georgia enacts a sodomy law with provisions similar to English common law.

1819 The Arkansas Territory receives Missouri law during its organization and includes antisodomy law requiring a compulsory life imprisonment sentence.

1820 Maine is formed and adopts the laws of Massachusetts making sodomy illegal, punishable by hard labor for a maximum of 10 years, and applies only to men.

1821 The nation's first obscenity case involving same-sex eroticism is heard by the Massachusetts Supreme Court.

1826 Delaware reduces the penalty for sodomy from death to a maximum of three years' solitary confinement, a fine of $1,000, and a public flogging of up to 60 lashes. The law had used different terms for "negroes" or "mulattoes" but these terms were eliminated.

1827 Illinois prohibits persons convicted of sodomy from voting and serving on a jury. This is the first state to impose such provisions limiting the civil rights of those convicted of sodomy.

1829 Tennessee adopts its own criminal code in which sodomy is defined as a "crime" against nature.

1833 Georgia's sodomy law is modified to define sodomy as "carnal knowledge and connection against the order of nature by man with man, or in the same unnatural manner with woman." Such wording totally ignored the possibility of women having sex with another woman. The mind-set of the time couldn't conceive of lesbianism.

1836 North Carolina is the last state in the Union to abolish reference to old English legal customs and laws to enact its own sodomy statute.

Texas adopts its own criminal code and recognizes common-law crimes. Although sodomy is not mentioned, the English penalty of death applies.

Wisconsin adopts the laws of Michigan Territory, including its sodomy provisions.

Abraham Lincoln enters into a four-year relationship with Joshua Fry Speed sharing the same bed. Both Lincoln and Speed were forced into their own marriages, but Lincoln never forgot Speed and wanted to name his first child after him (which Mary Lincoln forbade). As president, Lincoln shared his bed with men often when Mary was away.

1838 Iowa Territory receives the laws of Wisconsin Territory, which were based on Michigan laws and criminalizes sodomy with a penalty of up to three years in prison.

1840 Iowa abrogates all laws received from Michigan and Wisconsin, which means there are no sodomy statutes in effect. Iowa will operate without any sodomy laws in effect for almost a half century.

1841 Christian missionaries convert much of the population of Hawaii, including King Kamehameha III, in the 1820s and 1830s. A curious and puzzling edict is passed in 1841 that specifies "men and boys are forbidden to run in crowds after new things. Whosoever does this in an indecent manner shall be punished thus; he shall be taken to the house of confinement and remain till he pay a rial [unit of currency], and be sent at liberty."

1842 Florida enacts a sodomy statute that raised the penalty for sodomy conviction to death—an action that makes Florida the first state to raise the penalty for sodomy to death.

1843 Oregon adopts the laws of Iowa but it is unclear if this includes a sodomy provision. Oregon, in its early years, was settled almost exclusively by men and Portland, in particular, was seen as a new Sodom with open debauchery and immorality.

1845 Florida adds to its sodomy statute to state that persons convicted of sodomy are forbidden from being a witness in a trial.

1848 The first women's rights convention is held in Seneca Falls, New York. Susan B. Anthony and other women are ejected from the convention, propelling them into the national limelight.

1850 Sodomy provisions specifying five years to life are enacted in California under common-law definition. The law is passed just months before California becomes a state making it unclear if the law was valid.

1851 Minnesota Territory adopts common law from Wisconsin that criminalizes sodomy.

New Mexico Territory adopts common-law statutes that make sodomy a capital offense.

Utah is initially organized as the State of Deseret and adopts Iowa law that includes a prohibition for "any man or boy" from engaging in "any sexual intercourse with any of the male creation." The laws are modified the next year in 1852 and make no mention of sodomy, thus legalizing sodomy throughout the territory.

1853 Oregon passes a new criminal code that abrogates common-law crimes.

Washington Territory adopts the laws of Oregon. Because Oregon does not have sodomy provisions at the time, Washington, too, does not have a sodomy statute.

1854 Alabama enacts a law that allows a spouse to sue for divorce if the other spouse is found to have committed sodomy either before or after the marriage.

1855 Kansas enacts a criminal code that makes sodomy a felony and punishable with imprisonment for not less than 10 years.

Nebraska adopts the common law of England making sodomy a capital offense.

1857 A 21-year-old Mormon soldier is convicted of bestiality with his horse in Utah. The soldier is ordered to be shot but is not; however, the horse is shot.

1858 Half of the District of Columbia is controlled by Virginia law, and Maryland law controls the other half. The early criminal codes specified lengthy prison sentences for free men and death to slaves convicted of sodomy. By 1858, the entire criminal code is rescinded by the voters and, thereby, sodomy statutes are rejected—a first for the nation to have voters reject a sodomy statute.

1860 Colorado Territory is organized without explicit sodomy statutes but recognizes English common-law crimes thus requiring the death penalty for sodomy conviction.

Texas enacts its first explicit sodomy provision.

West Virginia adopts the "buggery" laws of Virginia proscribing a penalty of one to five years in prison.

The homoerotic *Leaves of Grass* is published by Walt Whitman to great controversy.

1861 Although Congress applies the organic law to the Nevada Territory, once it becomes a state later that year, it enacts a criminal code that adopts the common-law definition of sodomy requiring a penalty of imprisonment for five years to life.

1862 The territory of Dakota (which includes both North and South Dakota) enacts a common-law definition of sodomy in its criminal code and sodomy is punishable by one year to life in prison.

1863 Arizona Territory is formed and assigned the laws of New Mexico Territory, which included common-law statues proscribing life imprisonment for sodomy conviction.

The Connecticut Supreme Court rules that deadly force may be used to prevent acts of sodomy. This is the first such ruling and would influence courts for centuries to allow the "gay panic" defense.

1864 The territorial legislature of Idaho adopts a criminal common-law definition of sodomy that provides penalty from five years to life. Interestingly, females were included in the law, something most state laws failed to do.

1865 Montana territorial legislature adopts common-law definition in its criminal code making sodomy punishable by five years to life upon conviction.

1865 to 1935 At least 100,000 women formed a community and political movement that resisted marriage in the districts of Pearl River Delta, Hong Kong. The *sou hei* vowed to remain single and formed emotional and physical bonds only with her "sworn sisters."

1867 Alaska is purchased by the United States from Russia. Alaska Territory had, at the time, no laws at all and sodomy was legal for the next 17 years.

The Homophile Movement

The homophile movement is marked by the medicalization of homosexuality and an increase in public discourse on the topic.

1869 Karoly Maria Benkert (who used the pseudonym K. M. Kertbeny) is a Hungarian physician who coins the word *homosexual*. It would be another 10 years before the word *heterosexual* is defined. Heterosexuality initially is used to denote a sexual perversion.

Sodomy is made illegal in Wyoming with penalty of up to life in prison. Although sodomy was illegal until 1977 when the legislature repealed the statute, Wyoming is the only state in the Union with no published sodomy cases.

1873 Texas Supreme Court rules that the term *crime against nature* is vague and unenforceable since "vague" criminal statutes were forbidden under other criminal codes. This problem was solved in 1879 when, instead of revising or eliminating the vague language of the sodomy statutes, it repeals the "vague criminal" language statute instead.

1876 Ohio amends its obscenity statutes to make illegal the use of any instrument for "self-pollution." Ohio becomes the first state to make the possession of "sex toys" illegal.

The Utah legislature enacts a sodomy statute using the common-law definition and requires a penalty of up to five years in prison.

1879 Massachusetts prohibits the sale, exhibit, or lending of any "instrument or other article intended to be used for self-abuse", thus outlawing sex toys.

Pennsylvania becomes the first state in the Union to include *fellatio* in its sodomy statute. *Cunnilingus* is not mentioned.

1881 Washington Territory revises its criminal code and adopts common-law crimes, including sodomy.

1882 Louisiana Supreme Court is the first court in the nation to reject the argument that the language found in most sodomy laws is too vague to be constitutional.

1884 It had been reported that native Alaskans engaged in the appalling degradation and vice of sodomy. A Senate committee conducts an investigation verifying the behaviors. Congress enacts a statute that applies the laws of Oregon to Alaska, which include a sodomy law.

1885 Colorado enacts an obscenity statute that bans the use of foreign objects and instruments that could be used for "self-pollution" (meaning sex toys). Colorado would become only one of four states with such restrictions on sex toys and the only one located in the West.

Ohio criminalizes sodomy for the first time in 60 years. It is speculated that the Governor George Hoadly himself was gay. At the time, the governor of Ohio could not veto legislation. It is thought he was forced to sign the bill criminalizing sodomy to embarrass him.

Homosexual acts are recriminalized by the British Parliament.

1889 Washington is admitted into the United States and its constitution includes the explicit right to privacy. It is the first state constitution to mention privacy.

1890 Mississippi becomes the first and only state to adopt a unique legal provision that excludes the public from observing sodomy trials.

Oklahoma Territory adopts most of the laws of Nebraska. This includes common-law code making the punishment for sodomy one year to life in prison. The law explicitly permits the prosecution of married couples for acts of sodomy.

1892 Iowa enacts sodomy law that applies to any person. Surprisingly, the enabling legislation states it would become law upon publication in two newspapers. Technically, this gave either newspaper the right to veto the law by refusing to publish, but both papers comply.

1895 Louisiana prohibits the "promotion" of "obscene devices" (meaning sex toys). These included "an artificial penis or artificial vagina" and used for "stimulation of human genital organs." The term *promote* was detailed to mean the "manufacture, issue, sell, give, provide, lend, mail, deliver, transfer, transmit, distribute, circulate, disseminate, present, or exhibit" of such devices. Despite the lengthy wording prohibiting the selling or giving away of such devices, it did not restrict the right to purchase or use them.

South Carolina adopts a constitutional amendment to ban persons convicted of sodomy from voting. This is the first such law in the nation. South Carolina voters repeal the amendment in 1970.

1896 In the first such case in the nation, heterosexual defendants claim the sodomy laws don't apply to them. The Texas Court of Criminal Appeals rules against them, a precedent upheld by most future courts.

The 69th act to pass the Louisiana legislature in 1896 outlaws oral sex. Ironically, the law is officially known as Act 69.

The first periodical addressing the issue of homosexuality, *Der Eigene* ("The Community of the Special"), is published in Germany.

Two women hug and kiss for the first time on an American stage in the play *A Florida Enchantment*. The scene is so controversial (although the play is not lesbian in content), and ushers offer ice water during intermission to audience members who feel faint.

1897 The Scientific-Humanitarian Committee is founded by Magnus Hirschfeld, Max Sphor, and Eric Oberg in Germany.

Havelock Ellis, English sexologist, publishes *Sexual Inversion*. The publication is considered the first book in English to treat homosexuality as a natural condition and not as an illness or crime.

Even though the District of Columbia has no specific sodomy law, a district court rules that common-law crimes (e.g., sodomy) can still be prosecuted.

Illinois Supreme Court upholds a sodomy conviction based on an act of fellatio. It is decided that fellatio constituted a "crime against nature" and punishable under its sodomy statute. This is the first time a court in the United States upheld a sodomy conviction base on fellatio and, thereby, confirmed that there are many different sexual acts that could be considered criminal.

The "debauching" of boys by either males or females is made illegal in Michigan.

The first case in the United States dealing with sex in prison upholds a sodomy conviction by the California Supreme Court.

The Missouri Supreme Court reviews a sodomy case where the defendant is a police officer. This is the first such case in the United States.

1898 New Jersey, through its revised criminal code, makes it permissible to kill anyone who is "attempting to commit sodomy." The killer would be "guiltless, and shall be totally acquitted and discharged."

1899 Vermont Supreme Court rules that common-law statutes can be used to prosecute sodomy. This is never repealed and could be used today if local prosecuting attorneys decide to use it regardless of the *Lawrence* (2003) decision.

1901 New York politician Maury Hall dies and is discovered to have been a woman passing as a man.

1902 Puerto Rico enacts its own criminal code and outlaws sodomy with a penalty of not less than five years' imprisonment.

1904 Georgia Supreme Court is the first court in the nation to expand "crimes against nature" to include fellatio. The court states that fellatio was a "baser form of the abominable and disgusting crime against nature."

1905 Georgia Supreme Court decides the first case in the nation that finds a constitutional right to privacy. Although this had little impact for Georgia citizens, it was a concept that slowly influenced all other states and led to the eventual elimination of sodomy laws nationwide.

Sodomy convictions often required time spent in a pillory. Delaware is the last state in the union to eliminate such public pain and embarrassment.

1907 Indiana becomes the first state (and, in fact, the first government in the world) to enact a sterilization law. The law targets "confirmed criminals" including those convicted of sodomy. Controversy surrounding the law led newly elected governor Thomas Riley Marshall (who would become a U.S. vice president) to instruct state institutions to ignore the law.

1908 English writer Edward Carpenter publishes his book *The Intermediate Sex*. It is his most influential book on gay issues.

Edward Stevenson releases *The Intersexes,* the first review of gay issues within the United States.

1909 Washington adopts a sexual sterilization law. This makes Washington the second state, after Indiana, in the Union to adopt such law.

California becomes the first state to adopt laws requiring the sterilization of "sexual perverts." The law applies to persons convicted of two or more sexual offenses and exhibited evidence of being a "moral or sexual pervert" while incarcerated.

Washington is the first state to pass a law preventing newspapers from reporting on sodomy-related crimes. The law would stay on the books until 1982.

1911 Iowa enacts a sterilization law. Soon it is challenged in court and the U.S. District Court finds it unconstitutional in 1914. In 1929, Iowa again passes a sterilization law. It would not be until 1977 that the sterilization law would be repealed.

In quick succession, three more states adopt sterilization laws: Nevada, New Jersey, and New York.

1912 A group of "unorthodox women" begin to meet at Polly Halliday's restaurant in York City. The group, Heterodoxy, meets bimonthly and has among its membership many prominent lesbians, including Helen Hall, Katharine Anthony, Dr. Sara Josephine Baker, and Elisabeth Irwin. Heterodoxy continues to meet until the 1940s.

1913 Kansas enacts a sterilization statute. This is not repealed until 1965.

Nebraska outlaws oral sex in the 69th chapter of the newly adopted criminal law. It is unofficially known as Act 69.

North Dakota adopts a sterilization law stating that it can be applied to any prisoner whose "mental or physical condition" would be improved by the operation. The statute will be repealed in 1965.

Oregon legislature adopts a sexual sterilizations law that targets "sexual perverts" and those "addicted" to sodomy. A group of citizens force a referendum on the new law and it is repealed. Four years later, the legislature reenacts the law over the wishes of the people.

Wisconsin enacts a sexual sterilization law that could be used against homosexuals.

1914 A dictionary of criminal slang published in Portland, Oregon, describes the word *faggot* for the first time—referring to male homosexuals.

1915 California becomes the first state to specifically use the words *fellatio* and *cunnilingus* in sodomy statutes. A sex scandal in Los Angeles the previous year involving 500 gay men arrested as "social vagrants" prompts the expansion of the law. Within four years, the state Supreme Court rules that the law violated the requirement of the use of ordinary English in crafting laws as most citizens would not know the meaning of the words. The legislature responds by simplifying the terms to *oral copulation*.

1916 For the first time in the United States, the Articles of War make homosexuality and the intent to commit sodomy in the American military a capital crime.

1917 North Dakota court uses bizarre language in describing a heterosexual cunnilingus case. According to the judge, the girl involved "was not given even a peanut."

1918 Many courts in the nation make a legal connection between "solicitation to commit sodomy" with an "attempt to commit sodomy." A Delaware appellate court becomes the first in the nation to bifurcate this connection thereby making solicitation convictions more difficult to prove.

1919 The Institute for Sex Research is established by Magnus Hirschfeld in Berlin. It is one of the world's first organizations to explore sexual topics from a scientific standpoint. Hirschfeld becomes aware of the need to formally organize to help reform attitudes and laws concerning homosexuality. In 1921 he establishes the World League for Sexual Reform that grows to 130,000 members worldwide. It is through the League that Hirschfeld campaigns in German courts and legislature for the overturn of Paragraph 175—the legal code that criminalized homosexual behaviors.

The U.S. Navy, under orders from Assistant Secretary of the Navy Franklin Roosevelt, uses a squad of young enlisted men to search for "sexual perverts" at the Newport Rhode Island Naval Training Station. Sixteen civilians and 20 sailors are arrested on moral charges and prosecuted by naval and municipal authorities.

North Carolina adopts a sterilization law. This law is still in force.

1920 to 1935 The "Harlem Renaissance" was an unprecedented time in which African American culture flourished. Many lesbian and gay writers, artists, and musicians were central to this cultural explosion. These included Claude McKay, Bessie Smith, Langston Hughes, Countee Cullen, Ma Rainey, Bruce Nugent, Alain Locke, and Ethel Waters.

1921 Oregon court rules the sterilization law of 1917 unconstitutional. The legislature rewrites the law and reinstates the law in 1923.

Massachusetts Supreme Court decides the nation's first case concerning sexual relations in a bathhouse.

Florida Supreme Court issues a decision using extremely antigay language to describe sodomy: "A discussion of the loathsome, revolting crime would be of no edification to the people, nor interest to the members of the bar. The creatures who are guilty are entitled to a consideration of their case because they are called human beings and are entitled to the protection of the laws."

1923 The first attempt in the United States to use a "right to privacy" claim in a sodomy case is rejected by the New Jersey Supreme Court.

Sholom Asch's *God of Vengeance* opens on Broadway. It is the first play with a lesbian content to reach Broadway. It was originally written in Yiddish and first produced in Berlin in 1907.

1924 *Inversions,* the first gay French journal, is founded.

1925 Idaho enacts criminal statutes to force sterilization upon "habitual criminals, moral degenerates and sexual perverts."

Utah adopts a sterilization law applied to inmates of state institutions with "habitual sexual criminal tendencies."

Henry Gerber and others found the Society for Human Rights in Chicago. It is the first gay rights group in the United States and survives only a short time. It publishes two issues of *Friendship and Freedom,* its gay liberation magazine (the first in the country), before police confiscate them. The members of the Society are arrested by police and imprisoned.

1926 Bruce Nugent's narrative poem, "Smoke, Lilies and Jade," is published in the periodical *Fire!* The poem is considered to be the first published piece about homosexuality to be written by an African American.

1927 Mae West writes and produces *The Drag*, the first play produced in the United States with gay male content. It closes before reaching Broadway.

1929 The German Constitution is modified by the removal of Paragraph 175. This will prove to be a hollow victory for Magnus Hirschfeld and the World League of Sexual Reform as the Nazis would soon assume power and recriminalize homosexuality (in 1934).

Radclyffe Hall's lesbian novel *The Well of Loneliness* is published by Covici-Friede in New York. The publisher is convicted of obscenity; the conviction is later overturned.

1930 The Motion Picture Production Code is enacted by the Hollywood studios. It prohibits all references to homosexuality or "sexual perversion" in movies. The code is strengthened in 1934 under pressure from the Catholic-led Legion for Decency and is influential until its revision in the 1960s.

1933 Hirschfeld's Institute for Sex Research is ransacked by Nazi students and destroyed. Vast collections of library and artistic works are burned. *Note:* Two of the three famous photos used in history books showing Nazi book burning are photos of the destruction of Hirschfeld's collection. Ever wonder why our history books failed to tell you this?

A man asks if he can strip naked to prove he was "normal" to a Pennsylvania appellate court. The court upholds his sodomy conviction.

Oklahoma enacts a sterilization law.

1934 Lillian Hellman's play, *The Children's Hour*, opens on Broadway. It escapes the censors because of its moralistic ending: the lesbian character kills herself.

1935 Alabama state health officer, J. N. Baker, convinces the state legislature to pass an extremely antigay sterilization law. Baker and legislators are influenced by a similar law enacted earlier by Nazi Germany and consider it a "bold experiment" that could apply to 400,000 U.S. citizens.

Michigan is the first state to enact a psychopathic offender law. Such laws are adopted by many other states of the Union and are usually limited to sexual offenders including those involved in consensual sodomy. Often times, the offender faced years of incarceration in nightmarish state mental institutions.

Oklahoma Criminal Court of Appeals decides that "crime against nature" includes acts of cunnilingus.

1937 A sodomy conviction, which is based on letters opened by the U.S. Post Office, is upheld by the Minnesota Supreme Court.

1937 Puerto Rico is the last territory or state of the United States to enact a sterilization law that includes "sexual perverts." The law will be repealed in 1960.

1939 A wave of child molestations in St. Paul, Minnesota, influences the state legislature to enact the third psychopathic offender law in the nation. The law is still enforced and used for prosecution, unlike most states that have repealed such laws.

California enacts a psychopathic offender law, thus becoming the first state in the West to join the movement originating in the eastern states.

California enacts legislation requiring the revocation of a teacher's license if the teacher is convicted of oral copulation or sodomy. This is the first such law in the nation.

1941 to 1945 Almost 10,000 enlisted personnel in the U.S. military receive dishonorable discharges for homosexuality. They are called "blue discharges" because the orders are typed on blue paper.

1942 The U.S. military issues official prohibitions against homosexuality and homosexuals in the armed forces.

Washington repeals its sexual sterilization statute.

Jim Kepner begins his private collection of gay-related clippings, artifacts, books, and photographs in Los Angeles. The collection would later become the International Gay and Lesbian Archives and is now housed with the ONE Institute and Archives located on the campus of the University of Southern California. The collection contains more than 1 million items and is the largest in the world.

1943 Florida Supreme Court uses surprising language (both ungrammatical and injudicious) in the defense of a 76-year-old Indian War Veteran for sexually assaulting two 11- and 13-year-old girls, whom they claim solicited him. The court at one point seems to speak approvingly of his assault. He is released from charges of sodomy.

Vermont enacts a psychopathic offender statute that uses very broad language.

1944 The right to privacy is raised for the first time in any U.S. court in a sodomy case heard by the Arizona Supreme Court. The court ignores the claim.

1945 In an opinion written by the Colorado Supreme Court, the word *queer* is used for the first time in the nation in a sodomy conviction.

1946 U.S. Supreme Court refuses to review the first sodomy-related case to reach that level. The case involved a man trapped and solicited by military police in Hawaii.

1947 Building upon the growing antisodomy sentiments in the state, California pioneers a sex offender registration law. It requires anyone convicted of sex crime, including sodomy and oral copulation, to register as a sex offender with the local police or county sheriff. This is the first sex offender registration law in the nation.

Three more states enact a psychopathic offender law: Massachusetts, Washington, and Wisconsin.

The Modern Gay Movement Begins

World War II dislocated millions of people and brought large numbers of lesbians and gay men to the city. There, they began to organize, reject the medical deviancy label, and create the modern gay movement.

1948 The first U.S. lesbian magazine, *Vice Versa*, begins publishing in Los Angeles. From her desk at RKO Studios, Lisa Ben (anagram for "lesbian") typed each issue twice using four carbons, then circulated it among her friends who then circulated it to their friends.

Alfred Kinsey and the Kinsey Institute publish its groundbreaking study of sexual behavior in American men. Kinsey's book, *Sexual Behavior in the Human Male*, found that more than 50 percent of those surveyed admitted erotic responses to other men and that approximately 10 percent were exclusively homosexual. The Kinsey findings shook the heterosexual world and helped ground the fledgling gay community.

Congress enacts a psychopathic law to "provide for the treatment of sexual psychopaths in the District of Columbia." *The Washington Post* supported the measure and came about during one of the antigay witch hunts sweeping the capital.

1948 to 1953   McCarthyism purges homosexuals from federal government and thousands lose their jobs. More homosexual lose their jobs than those accused of being Communists. Ironically, Roy Cohn, McCarthy's right-hand man, is found to be gay.

1949   Three more states enact a psychopathic offender law: Indiana, Missouri, and New Hampshire.

The Utah Supreme Court is the first court in the nation to discuss the Kinsey Report as related to a sodomy case.

1950   In a surprising court case, an Arkansas case mentions the circumcision status of a partner in a male-male sodomy case. This is the only U.S. legal case to reveal such detailed personal information. Typically sodomy cases are vague about sexual behaviors and biological details of the defendants.

Two more states enact psychopathic offender laws: New York and Virginia.

New York reduces the penalty for consensual sodomy from a felony to a misdemeanor, the first state in the Union to make this change.

1951   Alabama enacts its own psychopathic offender law. The law would allow for anyone convicted of a sex offense to be referred for a psychiatric examination and, if found to be psychopathic, institutionalized for an indefinite period of time—including life.

California appellate court rules that gay men are automatically classified as vagrants, per se, and can be arrested and jailed without having engaged in any criminal behavior.

Utah enacts a psychopathic offender statute.

The Mattachine Society is founded by Harry Hay, Bob Hull, and Chuck Rowland in Los Angeles. It evolves into the ONE Institute and Archives located on the campus of the University of Southern California and becomes the most celebrated and long-lived gay rights organization in the United States.

Edward Sagarin, under the pseudonym Donald Webster Cory, publishes *The Homosexual in America*. It is one of the first books written by a gay author to describe gay life and ask for tolerance.

1951 to 1958   The International Conference for Sexual Equality is sponsored by the Amsterdam-based, The Cultaur-en-Ontspannings Centrum. The issue of gay rights is prominent on the agenda.

1952   "Sexual deviants" are barred from immigrating into the United States by the McCarran-Walters Act. The U.S. Supreme Court will extend this definition to lesbians and gay men in 1967.

1952   Dale Jennings is arrested in Los Angeles by an undercover officer and charged with lewd and dissolute conduct. Jennings claims that the officer accosted him and, with the support of the newly founded Mattachine Society, decided to fight the charges. This is the first known challenge to police abuse and solicitation. Jennings is probably the first person to ever stand up in court and unashamedly say that he is a "homosexual" and fight against the unfair and abusive law. The jury is deadlocked 11–1 for acquittal and the charges are dropped.

Pennsylvania enacts a psychopathic offender statute.

The word *homosexual* appears for the first time in a U.S. Supreme Court decision. An escape convict who fled to Ohio from an Alabama prison petitioned to stop extradition back to the Alabama prison claiming he had been abused by the "homosexuals" in the prison as they identified him as a "gal-boy." The Court rules against him.

1953 The Kinsey Institute publishes *Sexual Behavior in the Human Female*. This second historic study found that 28 percent of women surveyed responded erotically to other women and that between 2 and 6 percent identify their sex orientation as lesbian.

ONE begins publishing in Los Angeles as an adjunct to the Mattachine Society. This is the first national gay male publication.

Executive Order 10450, signed by President Eisenhower, makes "sexual perversion" grounds for being barred from federal employment.

Dr. Evelyn Hooker begins studying male homosexual personalities. It is this research that leads to her findings that there are no discernible psychosocial differences between homosexual and heterosexual men. It is her research that led to the overturn of the medical theories of homosexuality as a sickness.

Gay concentration camp survivors are rearrested by the German government for the offense of being "repeat offenders."

Two more states pass psychopathic offender laws: Colorado and Oregon.

1954 Copies of *ONE* magazine are seized by the Los Angeles postmaster who refuses to distribute them on the grounds they are "obscene, lewd, lascivious and filthy." *ONE* editors sue and are ruled against by two lower courts, but eventually prevail in 1958 in the U.S. Supreme Court decision (*One, Inc. v. Olesen*). Without this favorable decision, the gay rights movement would have been severely hampered.

Kentucky adopts the Uniform Code of Military Justice for its militia. It is the first state to do so which includes specific sodomy provisions. By 1970, Kentucky becomes the first state to repeal these specific sodomy provisions.

1955 The Daughters of Bilitis is founded by Del Martin and Phyllis Lyon in San Francisco. This is the first national lesbian organization in the United States and soon begins publication of *The Ladder*.

Florida and Iowa enact a psychopathic offender law.

The Maine Supreme Court rules that masturbating another person is not against the state's sodomy law. This is the first such ruling in the nation.

1957 Connecticut and West Virginia enact a psychopathic offender statute. Tennessee also enacts a psychopathic offender law; however, it is the last state to adopt this category of law.

Ohio court is the first in the nation to decide that married couples have a constitutional right to engage in sodomy.

The Crittenden Report, a 639-page navy document, concludes there is "no sound basis" that homosexuals posed a military security risk. The Pentagon denies the existence of this report for more than 20 years.

1959 Wisconsin is the only state to prohibit persons convicted of "sexual perversion" from obtaining a driver's license.

1960 The Florida attorney general considers the issue of sodomy on Indian reservations. It concludes that state law does not extend to sexual behaviors

The first national convention of the Daughters of Bilitis (the first national lesbian conference) is held in San Francisco.

1961 Illinois becomes the first state to decriminalized consensual homosexual sex conducted in private.

New Mexico House of Representatives introduces a new criminal code that repeals consensual sodomy law. This is the first state to consider the repeal of sodomy. However, the Senate does not agree and the bill fails to become law.

Illinois becomes the first state to completely revise its criminal code based on the recommendations of the American Law Institute and, as such, is the first state to repeal its law against sodomy.

1962 After five years of study, the United Kingdom's Committee on Homosexual Offenses and Prostitution (commonly known as the Wolfenden Committee) recommends the decriminalization of homosexual behavior.

1964 The "first" street protests for homosexual rights is conducted by the Homosexual League of New York and the League for Sexual Freedom in front of the Army Induction Center located at Whitehall Street, New York. The 10 members carry signs protesting the army's dishonorable discharges of lesbian and gay soldiers.

The Conference of East Coast Homophile Organizations (ECHO) in Washington, D.C. produces the first homosexual rights button.

Canada sees the formation of its oldest homophile organization, the Association for Social Knowledge (ASK), and its first gay magazine, *TWO*.

1965 The Mattachine Society New York leads the first protest demonstration in front of the White House. The seven gay men and three lesbians receive national TV coverage.

Kansas repeals its sterilization law.

New York is the first state in the Union to explicitly exempt married couples from the state's sodomy statutes.

1966   The SIR Center (Society for Individual Rights) opens in San Francisco and is the first gay community center in United States. Later, in the same year, ASK opens its community center in Vancouver, becoming the first such center in Canada.

The North American Conference of Homophile Organizations (NACHO) is created to coordinate protest efforts against the federal government's anti-gay discrimination policies.

1967   The *Advocate*, the oldest continuing national gay publication in the United States, begins publishing in Los Angeles.

The American Civil Liberties Union declares its opposition to state sodomy laws.

The first protest demonstration by gay activists against any police department in the world is held in front of the Black Cat and New Faces bars in Silver Lake, California. The demonstration is held to protest Los Angeles Police officers' treatment of bar patrons during a New Year's Eve party.

The British government acts upon the recommendations made by the Wolfenden Committee 10 years earlier and decriminalizes homosexual behavior between consenting adults.

The oldest gay bookstore in the United States, the Oscar Wilde Memorial Bookshop, opens in New York. Later, in 1973, the bookstore relocates to the junction of Christopher and Gay Street.

Alabama enacts a sex-offender registration law that applies to anyone convicted of "crimes against nature" and other sexual offense.

1968   Rev. Troy Perry in Los Angeles begins the first gay church, the Metropolitan Community Church.

Dr. John Money at John Hopkins University performs the first complete male-to-female sex-change operation in the United States.

The University of Sorbonne, Paris, is taken over by rioting gay French students led by David Cohn-Bendit.

Michigan, the state that pioneered psychopathic offender law, concedes the law is a failure and repeals it.

The Birth of Gay Liberation

1969   New York City police raid the Stonewall Inn on June 27. The bar patrons, including transvestites, butch lesbians, and gay teenagers, violently resist. This event is considered the birth of the modern gay liberation movement and is commemorated by parades and festivals around the United States.

Building upon the participants of the Stonewall Riots, the Gay Liberation Front (GLF) is founded in New York.

Time magazine contains articles on national gay rights and has on its cover "The Homosexual in America."

Canada amends its criminal code legalizing sexual acts, including homosexuality, between consenting adults.

West Germany repeals its antihomosexual sodomy laws.

Connecticut revises its criminal code leading to a repeal of its sodomy law and lowers the age of consent to 16.

Nebraska repeals its sterilization law.

1970   New York City's Gay Pride Parade, the first in the nation to commemorate the Stonewall Riots, draws about 10,000 marchers.

Three New York State assembly members convene the first legislative hearing on gay rights in United States.

The New York–based group of lesbian-feminist, Radicalesbians, publishes its manifesto "The Woman-Identified Woman," which defines lesbians as "the rage of all women condensed to the point of explosion."

Amazon bookstore in Minneapolis opens for business. It is the first lesbian/feminist bookstore in the United States. Later that year, A Woman's Place bookstore opens in Oakland, California.

Rita Hauser, U.S. permanent representative to the United Nations, advocates same-sex marriages as a tool for controlling world population growth.

Carl Wittman releases his "Gay Manifesto," which summarizes many of the goals of the gay rights movement.

A man convicted of sodomy is denied a driver's license in the state of Connecticut. John Tynan, commissioner of motor vehicles, states the man is an "admitted homosexual" and, as such, "makes him an improper person to hold an operator's license." In a tragic aftermath, the man denied the driver's license commits suicide.

Kansas repeals it psychopathic offender law.

1971   The Lesbian and Gay Community Services Center is founded in Los Angeles and becomes the world's largest such center.

The National Association of Women passes a resolution supporting lesbian rights. Just a few years earlier, Betty Friedan, president of NOW, had attacked similar resolutions and labeled lesbians "the Lavender Menace."

The American Library Association launches its annual Gay Book Award and gives the first award to Isabel Miller for her novel *Patience and Sarah*.

Ten years after Illinois repealed its sodomy law, Connecticut becomes the second state to do the same. Idaho attempted to do the same. It repealed the law but then, under pressure from religious and conservative leaders, reinstated the state's sodomy laws criminalizing homosexual behavior with felony punishment of up to five years in prison.

After years of meeting, the President's National Commission on Reform of Federal Criminal Laws recommends the repeal of all state sodomy laws.

Canadian gay groups call for legal reform and issue a "We Demand" brief to the federal government. The first gay public demonstration in Canada takes place shortly after in support of the brief.

Idaho becomes one of the earliest states to repeal its sodomy law, but outrage from the Mormon and Catholic churches causes alarm in the state. When the code is repealed, *The Advocate* ran a large headline celebrating the announcement. Some of the Idaho State legislators obtained copies of the newspaper and paraded them down the aisle of the Capitol building waving them in the faces of the other legislators. Fearfully, legislators repealed the newly enacted modernized code and reinstated the old code that included the sodomy provisions, making Idaho the first state ever to reinstate a repealed sodomy law.

Colorado repeals its sodomy statute while at the same time creating new language to "protect" the public from indecency and loitering "for the purpose of engaging or soliciting another person to engage in prostitution or deviate sexual intercourse." The Colorado Supreme Court later strikes down the "offensive solicitation" provisions in 1974. Colorado becomes the third state in the West to decriminalize sodomy.

Connecticut repeals its sodomy statutes.

Oregon legislature revises its criminal code and repeals the consensual sodomy law and at the same time makes 18 the age of consent.

Texas Court of Criminal Appeals is the first court to agrees that privacy exists in public restroom stalls when closed and locked.

The Alaska legislature removes surplus language form state law in a process of cleaning up the code. It accidently removed restrictions on oral sex. Even after the Alaska Supreme Court points out the oversight, the legislature fails to correct the effort and later repeals the entire anti-sodomy law.

1972 Beth Chayim Chadashim, the first gay synagogue in the United States, is founded in Los Angeles.

A U.S. district judge rules that the Civil Service Commission cannot discriminate against employees based on sexual orientation unless they can prove being gay impacts the workplace.

East Lansing, Michigan, becomes the first city in the United States to ban discrimination based on sexual orientation in city hiring.

The United Church of Christ, California, ordains William Johnson as the first openly gay minister of any major religious denomination.

Ann Arbor, Michigan, becomes the first city in the United States to officially proclaim Gay Pride Week.

Delaware revokes its sodomy statute during the revision of its criminal code. Fifteen years later in 1987, Speaker of the Delaware House, B. Bradford Barnes, attempts to resurrect the sodomy law only to be harshly condemned by health officials and fellow legislators. He makes a "tearful apology" on the floor of the House.

Hawaii revises its criminal code and repeals its sodomy law and lowers the age of consent to 14 years old—the lowest in the nation.

Ohio repeals its sodomy and solicitation statutes. The sex offender registration law, however, is not repealed.

Pennsylvania revises its criminal code and abrogates common-law crimes. It does not repeal its sodomy code but renames sodomy as "voluntary deviate sexual intercourse," reduces the penalty from a felony to a misdemeanor, and exempts married couples. The Pennsylvania Supreme Court later rules in 1980 the sodomy statute unconstitutional due to it being applied differently for married and unmarried people.

Two men are arrested at a Seattle, Washington, skating rink for holding hands while skating. The arresting officers were unsure what crime to charge the men that would hold up in court. The word got out and a protest by other same-sex couples skating and holding hands took place at the rink.

1973 The American Psychiatric Association removes homosexuality from its list of mental disorders.

The American Bar Association adopts a resolution supporting the repeal of all state laws regulating sexual acts between consenting adults.

Dr. Howard Brown declares at a medical convention that he is gay. As the former New York city commissioner of health, he is, at that time, the highest-ranked person to publicly declare his homosexuality. He will later be instrumental in the formation of the National Gay Task Force.

The National Gay Task Force, later renamed the National Gay and Lesbian Task Force (NGLTF), was founded in New York by activists Martin Duberman, Ron Gold, Barbara Gittings, Frank Kameny, Dr. Howard Brown, Bruce Voeller, and Nathalie Rockhill.

The front door of the UpStairs Lounge in New Orleans is doused with Ronsonol lighter fluid and lit on fire at 8 PM creating a massive fireball through the bar. At the time, the bar was packed with about 65 customers mostly from the Metropolitan Community Church (MCC), the nation's first gay church. Thirty-two people died including the pastors of MCC making it the largest massacre of gay people ever in the United States. No one was ever charged with the crime.

A lesbian-feminist collective begins Olivia Records.

Naiad Press is launched in Florida and is the oldest surviving lesbian book publisher.

Lambda Legal Defense and Education Fund is founded to help gay civil rights court action.

Although Florida Supreme Court ruled the state's statute that describes sodomy as a "crime against nature" is unconstitutionally vague and, therefore abrogated sodomy laws in 1971, just a few short years later it upholds the state's misdemeanor law that described sodomy as "unnatural and lascivious acts." Somehow the court, which consisted of the same membership, found "against nature" as being too vague but "unnatural and lascivious" being perfectly understandable.

North Dakota repeals its sodomy law.

1974 Massachusetts's Elaine Nobel becomes the first openly gay person ever elected to a state legislature.

New York City congresswoman Bella Abzug introduces a federal Gay and Lesbian Civil Rights Bill (HR-14752) to the U.S. House of Representatives. The bill fails and is reintroduced, without success, in subsequent sessions of Congress.

Halton Renaissance Committee is formed by fundamentalist minister Ken Campbell in Canada to oppose gay rights.

Lesbian Connection begins publishing in East Lansing, Michigan, and becomes the largest circulating lesbian periodical in the United States.

Puerto Rico revises its criminal code, keeps its sodomy statue, but clarifies that anal sex is illegal between any two persons but that oral sex is legal only between persons of the opposite sex.

1975 Santa Cruz County, California, becomes the first county in the United States to ban antigay discrimination.

Sergeant Leonard Matlovich is discharged from the U.S. Air Force because of his homosexuality. Matlovich wins his five-year court battle with the air force but chooses to accept a financial settlement of $160,000 instead of reenlisting.

The American Association for the Advancement of Science (AAAS) passes a resolution opposing discrimination based on sexual orientation.

A county clerk in Boulder, Colorado, issues a marriage license to six same-sex couples. The state attorney general later states the licenses are not valid but fails to legally revoke them.

Arkansas becomes the first Southern state to repeal its sodomy law. The repeal did not last long since antigay hysteria fueled by Anita Bryant's "Save Our Children" campaign influenced legislators to reinstate sodomy statutes between persons of the same sex only.

Maine revises its criminal code and abrogates common-law crimes including sodomy. It also establishes 16 as the age of consent.

Minneapolis, Minnesota, approves the first known law prohibiting discrimination against transgendered people.

New Hampshire repeals its sodomy law in 1975. Although the governor was outspokenly antigay and promised to veto the legislation, the section dealing with the repeal was not reviewed by the governor before he signed it.

New Mexico repeals its sodomy law.

The Washington legislature repeals the sodomy and vagrancy laws, and sets the age of consent for sexual conduct at 16.

1976 Montreal police launch many raids against gay bars to "clean up" the city before the opening of the Summer Olympics. The gay community fights back with many large demonstrations. Emerging from those demonstrations is the Association pour les droits des gai(e)s du Quebec (ADGQ).

The U.S. Supreme Court rules in *Rose v. Locke* that cunnilingus is covered by Tennessee's "crimes against nature" statute.

After having spent 26 years in a Florida state mental institution for having been convicted of "lewdness" (having sex with another man), Willard Eugene Allen is released.

"Tales of the City" by Armistead Maupin begins its serialized run in *The San Francisco Chronicle*.

California repeals its sodomy statute.

Indiana legislature revises its criminal code that repeals the consensual sodomy law and establishes 16 as the age of consent.

Iowa repeals its consensual sodomy law and establishes 16 as the age of consent.

South Dakota revises its criminal code and repeals its sodomy statute. It sets the age of consent to 13, the lowest in the United States. After much controversy, the age of consent is raised to 15.

Two gay men are arrested at the Fort Lauderdale Florida airport for kissing. It was claimed their actions created a public nuisance. The men were sentenced to probation.

West Virginia makes a complete revision of its sexual assault laws and repeals sodomy.

1977 Fundamentalist singer Anita Bryant and the "Save Our Children" campaign are successful at convincing voters in Dade County, Florida, to repeal a gay rights law.

Harvey Milk is elected as San Francisco's first openly gay supervisor.

Toronto police raid the offices of Canada's leading gay publication, *The Body Politic*, claiming "indecent" materials are being distributed. After a long and costly court battle and another police raid in 1982, the paper is acquitted but the financial strain pushes it under in 1987.

The National Gay Task Force meets with presidential assistant Midge Constanza at the White House to discuss gay rights issues. This is the first such meeting between a gay organization and the president's office.

Both the International Association of Chiefs of Police and the Fraternal Order of Police adopt resolutions opposing the hiring of lesbian and gay police officers.

The African American lesbian-feminist group, the Combahee River Collective, publishes "A Black Feminist Statement." The manifesto recognizes the interconnectedness of oppression based on race and sexual identity.

Ellen Marie Barrett is ordained as the first open lesbian priest of the Episcopal Church.

The province of Quebec passes a Charter of Human Rights that bans antigay discrimination in employment, housing, and public accommodations. This makes Quebec the first major city in North America to offer such protection.

Iowa repeals its sterilization law, which had originally allowed for the sterilization of "moral degenerates."

Nebraska repeals its sodomy law. Initially the governor vetoed the legislation but the legislature overrode his veto. This is the only repeal of a sodomy law in the United States that was achieved by overriding a governor veto. At the same time it lowered the age of consent to 15.

1978 Supervisors Harvey Milk and Mayor George Moscone of the city of San Francisco are shot to death at city hall by ex-supervisor Dan White. White has been a supervisor for the city of San Francisco but resigns for personal reasons. He quickly changes his mind but Moscone refuses to reappoint him to his old seat. Angry from what he considers a betrayal and a strong dislike for the liberals in the office and particularly openly gay Harvey Milk, he enters city hall through an open window to avoid the metal detectors and shoots and kills both Moscone and Milk. White is tried and convicted of involuntary manslaughter and given a light sentence (seven years, of which he serves only five), which offends the gay community and results in massive citywide riots. (After his release in 1984, White commits suicide in 1985.)

The Briggs Initiative (Proposition 6), which would have barred lesbian and gay men from teaching in state public schools, is defeated by California voters.

San Francisco's Gilbert Baker designs the rainbow flag, which will become the international symbol for gay liberation.

Ed Koch, the mayor of New York City, issues an executive order forbidding discrimination based on sexual orientation in government employment. The order is eventually overturned through efforts of the Roman Catholic Archdiocese.

In *Federal Communications Commission v. Pacifica Foundation*, the U.S. Supreme Court approves restrictions on broadcast material that is "indecent" yet not "obscene." Such a delineation of definitions affects future broadcasts of gay-themed programs.

New Jersey legislature repeals common-law crimes, including sodomy and establishes 16 as the age of consent. Senator Joseph Maressa crusades to reinstate the sodomy provisions, but he withdraws the bill due to much public criticism.

Wisconsin repeals its psychopathic offender statute.

1979 When Dan White is found guilty of involuntary manslaughter in the deaths of Mayor George Moscone and Supervisor Harvey Milk, lesbians and gay men take to the streets and riot on the night of May 21 in response to the light sentence. The "White Night" riots cause more than $1 million in property damage and more than a 150 people are injured.

The Moral Majority is founded by Jerry Falwell and his associates. It becomes one of the major opponents to gay rights in United States.

The First National March on Washington for Lesbian and Gay rights draws over 100,000 marchers.

Stephen Lachs becomes the first openly gay judge to be appointed to the Superior Court of Los Angeles.

The Japan Gay Center opens in Tokyo. It is the first center of its kind in Japan designed to educate the general public about homosexuality.

The first gay pride march in Mexico City is hosted by Frente Homosexual de Acción Revolucionaria (Homosexual Revolutionary Action Front).

San Francisco Police Department swears in its first openly lesbian and gay police officers.

Florida repeals its psychopathic offender law.

Texas outlaws the sale of possession for sale of artificial vaginas or dildos. Surprisingly, the law did not criminalize the purchase or usage of them. The Texas Court of Criminal Appeals upholds the constitutionality of the sex toy ban in 1985.

The 1980s to the Present: AIDS, the Gay Rights Movement, and Same-Sex Marriage

The Stonewall Riot in 1969 is considered by many as the beginning of the modern gay rights movement. For the next decade, the fledgling gay community focused mostly on community building. Gay student groups formed at many large colleges, community services centers were opened, cities and counties granted money for developing health service centers to serve the historically underserved LGBT community, theaters mounted more gay-themed plays, gay pride parades and festivals sprang up in most major cities, and more.

Much of this progress came to a halt with the advent of AIDS. The 1980s saw a tragic loss in life and leadership in the LGBT community from mounting AIDS deaths. But from this holocaust came discourse. Average Americans, politicians, the media, and religious organizations had to talk about homosexuality in ways they never faced before. With illness and death affecting so many, no one could claim not knowing someone who was LGBT. From this discourse developed policies to protect those with HIV from discrimination in the workplace, housing, and elsewhere. Realizing the overt discrimination LGBT people faced on a daily basis naturally led politicians to develop antidiscrimination laws to provide some level of protection. The 1990s saw incremental protections offered first by cities and then states.

The "cocktail" developed in the early 1990s helped transform AIDS from a death sentence to a manageable disease for many. LGBT organization took on greater political battles toward achieving equal rights. The 2000s saw major inroads with the reversal of the exclusionary federal policies of Don't Ask, Don't Tell (DADT), and the Defense of Marriage Act (DOMA). Marriage equality became a major issue and, as of 2014, 16 countries, more than 20 states and 8 Native American tribal jurisdictions of the United States had approved same-sex marriage statutes.

1980

International Events

—The Canadian Union of Postal Workers adopts a contract that includes nondiscrimination based upon sexual orientation. This is first such contract covering federal employees anywhere in the world.

National Events

—The Democratic Party National Convention accepts a plank supporting federal gay rights legislation. At the same convention, Mel Boozer, a gay black man, is nominated for vice president and is allowed to speak to the assembly.

—Sasha Alyson launches Alyson Publications, the largest gay press in the United States.

—Congressman Robert Bauman (R-MD), leading opponent of gay rights legislation and prominent member of the Moral Majority, is arrested for soliciting sex from a 16-year-old boy in Washington, D.C. Initially he disavows his homosexuality, but, by 1983, he appears before the American Bar Association recommending adoption of gay rights resolution.

State and Local Events

—The gay student group at Georgetown University, Washington D.C., is expelled and forbidden from using university facilities. It takes eight years for the student group to win its case and return to campus.

—Aaron Fricke sues his high school in Providence, Rhode Island, to allow him to bring his male date to the senior prom. He wins the suit and goes to the dance with Paul Guilbert. Fricke chronicles these events in the popular book, *Reflections of a Rock Lobster*.

—Missouri repeals its psychopathic offender law.

—New York Court of Appeals declares the state's sodomy laws unconstitutional.

1981

International Events

—More than 300 gay men are arrested by Toronto police in a massive raid on gay bathhouses. This was the largest mass arrest of gay men in Canadian history and in all of North America. A riot ensues from the arrest that has been called the Canadian Stonewall.

—All 20 participants in Finland's first gay pride parade are arrested in Helsinki for "encouraging lewd behavior."

—A cluster of men contract rare diseases associated with impaired immune system yet for no known reason. The only common characteristic between the men was that they were either intravenous drug users or homosexual or both. There was no known mechanism to explain the problem. Initially, the general press referred to the mysterious disease as gay-related immune deficiency (GRID).

National Events

—The U.S. Department of Defense revises its policy concerning lesbians and gays in the military and states that homosexuality is "incompatible with military service." Its new policy requires all recruits to be questioned about their sexual orientation.

—A group of mothers and fathers organize in Los Angeles and form the Parents and Friends of Lesbians and Gay Men (P-FLAG). It becomes the most influential parent group supporting gay rights in the United States.

—The first publishing house in the United States dedicated to women of color, Kitchen Table: Women of Color Press, is founded in New York.

—The Kinsey Institute releases a report showing that neither parental nor societal influences have much effect on a person's sexual orientation.

—The first cases of HIV-related illnesses are reported by the Centers for Disease Control and Prevention and *The New York Times*.

—The "Family Protection Act" is defeated in Congress. Its provision included withholdings social security, welfare, and pension benefits to anyone who is homosexual or who supports a homosexual lifestyle. Its sponsor, Congressman Roger Jepsen (R-Iowa), is later defeated for reelection when it is discovered that the "health spa" to which he belonged was actually a house of prostitution.

State and Local Events

—New York's Supreme Court overturned its state's sodomy laws as being unconstitutional.

—Mary Morgan is appointed to the State Supreme Court by Governor Jerry Brown of California, making her the first open lesbian judge.

—Wisconsin becomes the first state to pass antidiscrimination laws based on sexual orientation in the areas of employment, housing, and public accommodation.

—The New York City Gay Men's Chorus performs at Carnegie Hall. They are the first openly gay group allowed to perform there and are followed a year later by open lesbian singers Meg Christian and Cris Williamson.

—Florida's Governor Bob Graham signs the "Task Amendment" to the state constitution. It withholds money to any state institution that recognizes gay student groups. The state Supreme Court would later overrule this legislation.

—After gaining home rule from Congress, the District of Columbia repeals its sodomy law and makes the sexual assault laws gender-neutral. Congress steps in and disallows the new law to take effect due to a veto by the House of Representatives. Later, the U.S. Supreme Court rules against the veto striking down the law.

1982

International Events

—The first Gay Games are held in San Francisco with 1,300 people from 12 countries participating. Initially the Gay Games were called the Gay Olympics, but the USOC sued and blocked use of the word *Olympic* even though they allowed the use of the word *Olympic* in such events as the Rat Olympics and Dog Olympics.

—Bruce Voeller suggests that gay-related immune disorder (GRID) be renamed acquired immune deficiency syndrome (AIDS) as a better reflection of the characteristics of the disease. The medical community adopts the terminology.

—Quebec passes legislation that gives homosexual relationships status equal to heterosexual ones.

National Events

—A federal judge declares unconstitutional the U.S. Immigration and Naturalization Service policy of excluding homosexuals from entering the country.

—The 1,700 delegates to the National Convention of the American Federation of State, County, and Municipal Employees adopt, by unanimous vote, a resolution calling for laws to be passed prohibiting discrimination against lesbians and gay men at the federal, state, and local levels.

State and Local Events

—Wisconsin becomes the first state in the United States to pass statewide gay rights legislation.

—The voters in Austin, Texas, reject a ballot initiative designed to allow discrimination against lesbians and gay men.

—A social service and education agency, Gay Men's Health Crisis (GMHC), is formed in New York and serves as the model for other AIDS organizations throughout the nation.

—Texas sodomy law is ruled unconstitutional by a federal judge.

—The Philadelphia Board of Education establishes the first high school for gay and lesbian students at Byton High. A similar school, Harvey Milk School, is established three years later by the New York City Board of Education.

1983

National Events
—A man, whose partner of 27 years died, is awarded by the California Compensation Appeals Board $25,000 in survivor benefits. This appears to be the first such award by a governmental agency in the United States.

State and Local Events
—On the floor of the U.S. House of Representatives, Representative Gerry Studds (D-MA) states that he is gay.

—The Lesbian and Gay Community Services Center of New York is founded in a former public high school building.

—A West Virginia kindergarten teacher, Linda Conway, is fired because school administrators believe she looks like a lesbian.

—Kansas modifies its incest law to specifically include same-sex incest as a crime. Kansas is the first state to enact this unique law.

—Oklahoma repeals its sterilization law.

—Wisconsin repeals its "sexual perversion" statutes thereby making consensual sodomy legal.

1984

International Events
—Television evangelist Hans Bratterud is convicted of violating Norway's antidiscrimination law when he calls for the dismissal of gay men and lesbians from their jobs. The Norwegian Supreme Court upholds the conviction because his statements were of "an aggravated insulting nature . . . [against] homosexual tendencies, way of life or orientation."

National Events
—Charles O. Howard, 23, is attacked by three teenage boys in Bangor Maine and thrown into Kenduskeag Stream off the State Street Bridge. Howard could not swim, called for help, but was left to drown. The three boys, Daniel Ness (17), Shawn Mabry (16), and James Francis Baines (15), were arrested but released to their parents' custody. The boys were tried as juveniles, pleaded guilty, and sentenced to jail until their 21st birthday. The lenient sentence shocked the community and the nation. His death led to programs to reduce homophobia in public schools.

State and Local Events
—Mervyn Silverman, head of San Francisco's Health Department, closes 14 gay bathhouses because of high-risk behavior by patrons.

—Berkeley, California, is the first city in the United States to extend domestic partnership benefits to employees in same-sex relationships.

—The city of West Hollywood becomes incorporated as a separate municipality and elects a mostly gay city council with a lesbian mayor.

—A gay rights bill passes both houses in the California legislature, but Governor George Deukmejian vetoes the bill.

—Louie Welch loses a race for mayor of Houston when, days before the election, he is heard on an open microphone stating that the best way to contain the HIV epidemic is to "shoot the queers."

1985

International Events

—Margaret Roff is elected mayor of Manchester, England; she is the first open lesbian in British history to be elected to public office.

—A native Australian man, who was involved in a 10-year monogamous relationship with another man who was a U.S. citizen, faces being deported to his native country. He contests the deportation and receives an official notice from the U.S. Immigration and Naturalization Service stating, "A bonafide marital relationship cannot exist between two faggots." The court upheld the deportation ruling.

National Events

—The Gay and Lesbian Alliance Against Defamation (GLAAD) is founded in York City as a watchdog organization over the media's poor coverage of AIDS and gay and lesbian issues.

—The U.S. Food and Drug Administration (FDA) licenses a test for the HIV antibodies.

—Movie and television actor Rock Hudson, after repeated denials of being gay or having AIDS, issues a public statement that he had AIDS. He dies three months later.

—Hundreds of well-known women sign *Ms. Magazine* petition condemning government interference in the sexual lives of consenting adults.

—Dan White, murderer of Mayor George Moscone and Supervisor Harvey Milk of the city of San Francisco, commits suicide. White had been released from prison in early 1984 after serving five years of a seven-year sentence and kills himself in October 1985.

State and Local Events

—The Texas legislature adopts legislation that bans homosexual sodomy only, which is approved by the judiciary. This overcame Texas's Supreme Court 1982 decision that had invalidated its sodomy laws.

—Lesbian and gay men are prohibited from acting as foster parents by orders implemented by the Massachusetts House of Representatives.

1986

International Events

—Pope John Paul II issues a pastoral letter stating that homosexuality is intrinsically a disorder and forbids all Catholics from supporting civil rights legislation for lesbians and gay men.

—The province of Ontario, Canada, passes a gay rights ordinance.

National Events

—The U.S. Supreme Court, in the Georgia *Bowers vs. Hardwick* case, upholds the right of states to enforce sodomy laws.

—The experimental drug zidovudine (AZT) is released by the U.S. Public Health Services for people with pneumocystis carninii pneumonia (PCP).

—Outspoken opponent of homosexuality and prominent conservative Republican, Terry Dolan, dies from HIV-related illnesses and was believed to be gay.

—Fifteen-year-old Ryan White wins the right to return to school. Although he was healthy for most of his childhood, he became extremely ill with pneumonia when he was 13 years old. At that time medical doctors discovered he was infected with the AIDS virus. As a hemophiliac, it was determined he became infected when he was a baby and had a blood transfusion. Once the pneumonia cleared up he wanted to return to school. A large number of parents and teachers feared he was infectious and petitioned to keep him out of school. An eight-month legal battle forced the school to allow White to return. The publicity catapulted White to national attention and he became the "poster boy" for the AIDS crisis. Many celebrities and politicians publicly supported White. He finished high school but his health deteriorated rapidly. He died April 8, 1990 at age 19. Many charities were started in his name.

—For the first time in his presidency and six years into the epidemic, Ronald Regan mentions the word *AIDS* in public.

State and Local Events

—The Nevada Supreme Court upholds its state's sodomy laws. Ironically, Nevada is the only state with legalized prostitution.

—The voters reject an initiative on the California ballot that would have required the quarantine of people with AIDS.

—Kansas supplements its sodomy law by outlawing the manufacture, distribution, sale, or advertising of any "obscene device" (sex toys). This was achieved through modification of the state's obscenity laws.

—Oklahoma Court of Criminal Appeals rules that its sodomy statutes cannot be applied to people of the opposite sex.

1987

International Event

—AZT is approved in the United States and elsewhere for the treatment of AIDS.

National Events

—Approximately a half-million people attend the second National March on Washington for Lesbians and Gay Rights. At the event, 2,000 lesbian and gay couples participate in a mass wedding held on the steps of the IRS building. Also, sections equivalent to two football fields in size of the NAMES Project quilt are displayed on the Mall in front of the U.S. Capitol.

—*The New York Times*, for the first time in its history, uses the word *gay* in reference to homosexuality.

—Larry Kramer, along with other activists, begins the AIDS Coalition to Unleash Power (ACT UP). Its goal is to bring public and government attention to the need for AIDS funding and research.

State and Local Events
—Congressman Barney Frank (D-MA) becomes the second member of the House to announce he is gay.

—Vermont becomes the first state to distribute condoms to prison inmates.

—Mississippi enacts the "Sex Offense Criminal History Record Information Act." Its purpose was to create a centralized registry of persons convicted of certain sex crimes, including sodomy. The registry was available to state and private employers. By 1995, a sex offender registration law was passed requiring those convicted of sodomy (including consensual sodomy) to notify local police about their whereabouts.

1988

International Events
—The World Health Organization hosts its first World AIDS Day.

—Ireland is ordered by the European Court of Human Rights to eliminate its life imprisonment penalty for homosexual behavior.

—Clause 28, issued by the British government, prohibits all local governments from "promoting" homosexuality. This means all gay and lesbian groups are prohibited from obtaining local government funding for community centers, educational activities, health organizations, or other programs.

—Canada eliminates its sodomy laws.

—Homosexual acts between consenting adults are legalized in the state of Israel.

National Events
—The National AIDS Commission releases a report with more than 500 recommendations. An adviser to President Regan reduces this list to 10 items.

—The national lesbian and gay quarterly magazine, *Out/Look*, begins publication.

—Leonard Matlovich, who was discharged by the U.S. Army in 1973 after he announced that he was gay, dies from HIV-related illnesses. He had sued the army and won. Matlovich is buried at the Congressional Cemetery in Washington, D.C. where his tombstone states "When I was in the military, they gave me a medal for killing two men, and a discharge for loving one."

—October 11 is designated as the National Coming Out Day in honor of the historic 1987 Lesbian and Gay March on Washington.

—In response to the escalating national epidemic of violence against gay men and lesbians, the Campaign to End Homophobia holds its first conference in Washington, D.C.

State and Local Events

—The voters pass Measure 8, an amendment to the Oregon Constitution that repealed an executive order issued by the governor prohibiting discrimination in employment of gay men and lesbians. This paves the way for other antigay legislation to be passed in Oregon.

—After the District of Columbia enacts a gay rights ordinance, the U.S. Congress orders that it revoke the ordinance revoked or face losing all funding.

—In an interesting use of the law, Oklahoma enacts a state RICO statute that includes sodomy language in an attempt to target bathhouses.

1989

International Events

—Denmark enacts domestic partnership legislation that is just one step away from actual marriage for same-sex couples. Full marriage for same-sex couples is not granted until 2001.

—Poland forms its first national gay rights group (Lambda), launches an information center, and begins publishing a journal (*Filo*).

—The Gentlemen's Alliance is formed as Nigeria's first gay male organization.

National Events

—A federal court orders the reinstatement of Perry Watkins into the U.S. Army (*Watkins v. United States Army*). Changes in the military code make the precedence set in this case ineffective for future antigay discharges.

—The U.S. Supreme Court rules in *Price Waterhouse vs. Hopkins* that an accounting firm violated sex discrimination laws when it dismissed a woman for "masculine behavior."

—A retrospective of Robert Mapplethorpe's photographs is cancelled at the Corcoran Art Gallery in Washington, D.C. The exhibit is attacked by Senator Jesse Helms for its homoerotic content. The gallery director resigns and the ensuing media attention makes Mapplethorpe's name synonymous with artistic censorship.

—Artwork from gay artist Keith Haring is used by the U.S. Post Office to issue a commemorative stamp in honor of the 20th anniversary of the Stonewall Riots.

—When Larry Kramer's play, *The Normal Heart*, is scheduled to play at a local college in Springfield, Missouri, the residents react with animosity. Many believe the topic of the play, the early years of the AIDS epidemic, is not appropriate for public discussion. Efforts were made to close to show including bomb threats sent to the college and a student home being burned down. However, the play makes eight sold-out performances.

—Two internal Pentagon reports conclude that homosexuals posed no military security risks. Members of Congress release the reports after they are hidden for a number of years.

State and Local Events

—San Francisco passes domestic partnership legislation that includes lesbian and gay relationships.

—Massachusetts becomes the second state (after Wisconsin in 1982) to enact a gay rights law.

—Over 5,000 ACT UP members demonstrate in front of and inside New York's St. Patrick's Cathedral. They rally against the Catholic Church's antigay stance and policies on AIDS.

—A New York judge rules that a gay male couple constitutes a "family" for purposes of housing rules.

—Kansas Supreme Court decides that cunnilingus is not a criminal activity covered by the state's sodomy statutes. The Kansas legislature acts quickly to "rectify" the situation but uses a broad definition of cunnilingus that would include opposite-sex behavior. Again, the legislature steps in and redefines the law to re-legalized heterosexual cunnilingus.

—Montana enacts a sex offender registration statute.

1990

International Events

—Hong Kong repeals its sodomy laws.

—Twenty-seven percent of Russians interviewed for a survey conducted by the *Moscow News* support the death penalty for homosexuality.

National Events

—The Americans with Disability Act (ADA) is signed into law. It explicitly prohibits AIDS-based discrimination.

—Queer Nation is founded in New York City as a direct action, in-your-face, group with the rallying cry, "We're here, we're queer, get used to it!"

—Congress votes to end the national immigration policy that banned homosexual immigrants.

—The National Endowment for the Arts (NEA) revokes grants already awarded to four solo theater artists. This was unprecedented in the history of the NEA. The four—Karen Finley, John Fleck, Holly Hughes, and Tim Miller—soon become known as "The NEA Four." Senator Jesse Helms initiated their defunding. Three of the four artists are homosexual and their performance art is sexually explicit. They become a cause célèbre for the lesbian and gay community. The four artists sue the NEA in 1993 and settle out of court for $252,000.

—After ordaining two lesbians and a gay man as ministers, two Lutheran Churches in San Francisco are suspended from their national organization.

—The Hate Crime Statistics Act is approved by Congress and signed by President George Bush. It requires the Department of Justice to collect, maintain, and report statistics on hate crimes motivated by race, religion, national origin, or sexual orientation. It is the first federal legislation to include sexual orientation as a specific class. Senator Jesse Helms is instrumental in holding up the act. He believes it was a conspiracy initiated by "the radical elements of the homosexual movement."

—General Motors develops a promotional videotape in which it refers to Japanese-made trucks as "little faggot trucks." Later, the company apologizes for the statement.

—The lesbian and gay community boycott Miller beer and Marlboro cigarettes, products of the Philip Morris Company, when it is discovered that Philip Morris provided campaign.

State and Local Events

—The Michigan Supreme Court declares its sodomy laws unconstitutional.

—Dennis Barrie, director for Cincinnati Museum of Art, is charged with obscenity and then is acquitted when booking the homoerotic photographs of Robert Mapplethorpe.

—Polk County, Florida, jail officials discontinue the practice of requiring gay prisoners to wear pink bracelets. The practice was used to distinguish its gay from nongay prisoners in the mistaken hope of reducing the spread of HIV.

—Two men are sentenced to five years in prison by a judge in Adrian, Michigan, for having sex in a public park.

—When the local chapter of the Parents and Friends of Lesbians and Gays (P-FLAG) is asked to participate in the St. Louis adopt-a-roadway program, the St. Louis County Board of Highways and Traffic initially decides to cancel the entire program. Eventually it changes its mind and allows P-FLAG to participate.

—Kansas Supreme Court unanimously affirms a trial court's determination that the law banning sex toys is overly broad and unconstitutional.

—Maryland Court of Appeals decides that the state's sodomy laws do not and never have applied to heterosexual sexual activity.

1991

International Events

—The International Lesbian and Gay Association cancels its 13th Annual Conference in Guadalajara, Mexico, because the mayor threatens to use force to stop the function.

—For the first time, gay men and lesbians are included in Amnesty's International campaign to free individuals imprisoned because of sexual orientation and political crimes.

—Dr. Simon LeVay of Oxford, the United Kingdom, releases his findings suggesting a biological influence on brain structure and sexual orientation, otherwise known as "the gay brain."

—Because of the U.S. immigration policy banning the admission of HIV-positive visitors to the United States, the Eighth Annual International AIDS Conference is cancelled in Boston and moved to Amsterdam.

National Events

—Karen Thompson is awarded guardianship of her lover Sharon Kowalski (who laid in a coma due to a car accident) over the objections of Kowalski's parent.

—NOW's Executive Director Patricia Ireland discloses that she has a female lover besides being married to a man.

—Department of Defense spokesperson Pete Williams is outed by *The Advocate*.

—Marlon Riggs's documentary about African American gay men, *Tongues Untied*, is aired on PBS. The FCC receives many complaints from homophobic viewers.

State and Local Events

—In situations of domestic violence, an Ohio appellate court rules that lesbian and gay couples have a "spousal relationship."

—A request by the Irish Lesbian and Gay Organization (ILGO) to march in the annual New York City's St. Patrick's Day Parade is denied. The parade is protested by 1,000 members of ILGO.

—Baltimore's first Black Gay and Lesbian Pride March is held in Washington, D.C.

—Audre Lorde, an African American lesbian poet, teacher, and activist, is named Poet Laureate of New York State.

—Connecticut enacts a gay rights bill.

—The Milwaukee School Board approves a gay sensitivity training program for teachers and staff. It enrages conservative citizens and groups in the community who call for a recall of the board members.

1992

International Events

—Canadian country and pop singer, k.d. Lang, becomes the first major female recording artists to come out as a lesbian.

—The government of Argentina grants legal recognition to the gay and lesbian group, Comunidad Homosexual Argentina. It took three years of effort to get approved.

—Sodomy laws are abolished in the country of Estonia.

—Canada removes its ban on lesbians and gays in the military.

—For the first time in North America, the Canadian immigration service grants immigration status to an Irish lesbian whose partner is a Canadian citizen.

National Events

—The General Accounting Office reports that between 1981 and 1990, approximately 17,000 service men and women were discharged from the military for homosexuality at a cost of almost $500 million.

—At the Democratic National Convention, Bill Clinton becomes the first presidential nominee to mention gay people in his acceptance speech.

—Navy Airman Apprentice Terry Helvey beats to death sailor Allen Schindler, who had recently acknowledged he was gay and who was about to be discharged for that fact. The case receives national media attention due to its brutality and the fact that Schindler had reported these problems to his superiors months in advance. Schindler was so badly beaten his mother was unable to identify his body. Helvey stated during questioning, "I'd do it again." Helvey was sentenced to life in prison.

—For the first time at the Democratic National Convention in New York, an open lesbian, a gay man with AIDS, and an HIV-positive heterosexual woman are allowed to address the members.

—Levi Strauss, with 23,000 employees, becomes the largest company in the United States to grant health benefits to employee domestic partners.

—Lesbian Avengers is launched by a group of activists in New York City. Within two years, the organization grows to more than 35 chapters in North America and Europe.

State and Local Events

—Voters in the state of Colorado approve Amendment 2 to the state constitution prohibiting gay rights legislation. Similar legislation in the state of Oregon, Proposition 9, is defeated.

—The (San Francisco) Bay Area United Way publicly states that it will no longer support the Boy Scouts of America because of its antigay policies.

—New Jersey becomes the fifth state to pass a gay rights law.

—Massachusetts's becomes the first state to grant lesbian and gay state workers the same bereavement and family leave rights as heterosexual workers.

—Statewide bans on antigay discrimination are enacted by Vermont, California, and New Jersey.

—Kentucky Supreme Court declares its sodomy law unconstitutional as a violation of both privacy and equal protection laws. Furthermore, the court declares gay men and lesbians as a "suspect class." This is an important legal distinction that plays a role in obtaining protection from discrimination in employment and housing.

—Louisiana enacts a sex offender registration statute.

1993

International Events

—Ireland eliminates its 132-year-old law banning homosexual acts.

—Russia repeals its sodomy laws.

National Events

—Soon after taking office as president of the United States, Bill Clinton directs the secretary of defense to look into overturning the 1981 ban on gays in the military. Fierce opposition from conservative members of Congress and fundamental religious groups throughout the nation force Clinton to settle for the "don't ask, don't tell" compromise, which doesn't significantly change the current status of gays in the military.

—The March on Washington for Gay, Lesbian, and Bi Equal Rights draws a crowd between 300,000 (by the National Park Service) and 1,100,000 (by *The New York Times*). President Clinton, along with most legislators, leaves town. Surprisingly, or not so surprisingly, the three largest newspapers in the nation, *Time, Newsweek,* or *U.S. News and World Report,* fail to mention the march even though its size places it in the top 10 of such demonstrations in Washington, D.C.

—The First International Dyke March, organized by the Lesbian Avengers, holds its march the evening before the March on Washington.

—The Christian Right embraces findings of the Battelle Human Affairs Research Center that concluded that only 2.3 percent of U.S. men have had sex with other men and that only 1.1 percent considers themselves exclusively homosexual.

—Roberta Achtenberg is approved by the U.S. Senate as assistant housing secretary over the objections of many conservatives, including Senator Jesse Helms, who called her "a damned lesbian." She becomes the highest-ranked acknowledged lesbian in the U.S. government.

—President Clinton appoints the first "AIDS czar," Kristine Gebbie. She is widely criticized by AIDS activists and is forced to resign within a year.

—President Clinton restores the ban on HIV-positive visitors to the United States.

—The U.S. Post Office issues a red ribbon stamp depicting AIDS awareness.

—The U.S. Supreme Court rules Colorado Amendment 2 that limited homosexuals the right to participate in the political process and deny them many other rights is unconstitutional.

State and Local Events

—The Hawaii Supreme Court rules its lower courts improperly dismissed a challenge to the state's policy of same-sex marriage. They decide that denying same-sex marriage constitutes sex discrimination, which is prohibited by Hawaii's state constitution.

—Once again, the Irish Lesbian and Gay Organization (ILGO) is excluded from New York's Annual St. Patrick's Day Parade. Both Governor Mario Cuomo and Mayor David Dinkins, along with thousands of others, stay away from the parade. More than 200 people are arrested when they try to stage an alternative parade on the same day.

—The Nevada legislature votes to repeal its state's sodomy laws.

—The voters of Cincinnati, Ohio; Portsmouth, New Hampshire; and Lewiston, Maine approve antigay ballot measures.

—California becomes the sixth state to enact employment antigay discrimination provisions.

—The 10th Circuit Court of Appeals rules that Kansas's school officials may legally refuse to hire teachers suspected of being gay, regardless of whether a teacher/applicant is not gay.

—Three high school teachers are suspended after several lesbian mothers are allowed to speak to a parenting class in Meridian, Idaho. The teachers are reinstated two weeks later after vigorous protests by students.

—The adoption of the multicultural, gay-tolerant "The Rainbow Curriculum" causes much controversy in the New York City schools. Five of 32 local school boards refuse to adopt the curriculum. City Schools chancellor Joseph Fernandez does not have his employment contract renewed primarily over the "Rainbow" issue.

—The Wisconsin Supreme Court decides that landlords may refuse to rent to unrelated couples because it would undermine the stability of marriage and family.

—The Oregon Citizens Alliance is successful at getting the town of Cornelius to adopt a Proposition 9–like law banning civil rights protection for lesbian and gay men. This success leads them to affiliate with other groups and target 11 states for similar initiatives.

—Minnesota becomes the seventh state to pass gay rights legislation.

—Sharon Bottoms, 23-year-old lesbian mother, loses custody of her son Tyler to Sharon's mother. Henrico County (Virginia) Circuit judge Buford Parsons Jr. rules that Virginia's sodomy laws make Sharon Bottoms a criminal and, therefore by definition, unfit to be a mother. Judge Buford states that he fears the boy would grow up unable to distinguish between women and men. In 1997, the Virginia Court of Appeals overturns this decision returning Tyler to his mother.

—Nevada repeals its sodomy law.

1994

International Events

—Amnesty International mounts a six-month campaign in the United States to combat civil rights abuses against lesbians and gay men.

—The Academy Award for best actor is given to straight actor Tom Hanks for his portrayal of a gay man with AIDS in the movie *Philadelphia*.

—The United Nations Human Rights Committee decides that laws criminalizing consensual sex between adult men are a breach of privacy and that no nation should have such laws.

—Approximately 15,000 people from two dozen nations participate in Gay Games IV, New York City. This becomes the largest single athletic event in the world with more than 500,000 spectators.

—Randy Shilts, author of *And the Band Plays On* and *Conduct Unbecoming*, dies from AIDS-related causes in San Francisco. His funeral is picketed by Westboro Baptist Church members carrying signs that read, "Filthy Face of Fag Evil."

—Age of consent for homosexual acts is lowered by the British Parliament from 21 to 18. However, the age of consent for heterosexual acts is 16.

—The consultative status granted to the International Lesbian and Gay Association (ILGA) in 1993 is revoked by the United Nations based on the unsubstantiated claim that some of its members were affiliated with pedophile groups.

—The Brazilian newspaper *Folha de São Paulo* estimates that one antigay killing occurred every four days in the nation.

—In a vote of 159–96, the European Parliament recommends that lesbian and gay couples be allowed to marry and adopt children.

—With the end of apartheid in South Africa, its new constitution includes sexual orientation as a protected class—the only country in the world to do so.

—Germany revokes Paragraph 175. This law was enacted in 1875 and criminalized male homosexuality. It was used to incarcerate, torture, and kill gay men and lesbians during the Holocaust. Surprisingly, when the inmates of the concentration camps were freed by the Allies, men who were convicted under Paragraph 175 were returned to prison. The law persisted for over 100 years until East and West Germany were unified.

National Events

—The Boston St. Patrick's Day Parade is canceled by its organizers rather than comply with a court order allowing the Irish-American Gay, Lesbian, and Bisexual Group to participate.

—For the first time, the U.S. Immigration and Naturalization Service grants political asylum based on sexual orientation to a gay Mexican who claims his life would be threatened if he returned to Mexico.

—Surgeon General Joycelyn Elders, in an interview with *Advocate* magazine, says, "We have to be more open about sex, and we need to speak out to tell people that sex is good, sex is wonderful. It's a normal part and healthy part of our being, whether it is homosexual or heterosexual." Of course conservatives pressed President Clinton to "publicly disavow" Elders's views.

—The American Medical Association adopts policy to remove all references to "sexual orientation related disorders." By doing so, medical doctors are no longer justified in conducting "therapies" for "treating" homosexuality.

—In national midterm elections, Republicans obtain a majority in both houses of U.S. Congress and win many gubernatorial elections. Because these wins were made with major backing from the homophobic Christian Right, there is much fear within the lesbian and gay community about their future civil rights.

State and Local Events

—Massachusetts becomes the first state to provide protection from antigay harassment to public school children.

—An attempt is made by residents of Ovett, Mississippi, to close down Camp Sister Spirit because of their fear that the lesbian-run camp would be a haven for violent crime and transform unborn children in the community into lesbians. The Camp provides food, lodging, and support for women who are victims of abuse or homeless. Field marshals are sent to protect the lesbians by Attorney General Janet Reno when it becomes evident there is the potential for physical danger.

—Missouri enacts a new sodomy law that is so convoluted in its wording that most attorneys think that it applies to virtually all sexual conduct, even that engaged in by unmarried heterosexual couples.

—South Carolina enacts a sex offense registry statute.

1995

International Events
—Greg Louganis, four-time Olympic gold medalist in diving, reveals in a television interview with Barbara Walters on *20/20* that he has AIDS.

—Zimbabwe president, Robert Mugabe, says homosexuals are "lower than dogs and pigs."

—Protease inhibitors, a new generation of AIDS drugs, show considerable success and receive approval from the Food and Drug Administration.

—The Zimbabwe government forces Africa's biggest book fair to remove a gay exhibit and sparks antigay remarks from President Robert Mugabe.

—Dr. Dean Hammer releases a new study suggesting that genes inherited from the mother influenced whether a man becomes gay or not.

—Sweden legalizes domestic partnerships of same-sex couples.

National Events
—Congress passes the draconian Illegal Immigration Control and Immigrant Responsibility Act. The law deprived many binational couples and HIV-positive immigrants the opportunity to stay in United States on humanitarian "hardship" grounds.

—Jonathan Tyler Schmitz kills Scott Amedure by shooting him twice in the chest. Three days earlier, both men appeared on the "Jenny Jones Show" in which Amedure reveals his romantic feelings to an unsuspecting Schmitz. Schmitz was convicted of second-degree murder in 1996. His defense attorney argued that the humiliation on the talk show and his past mental problems reduced Schmitz's responsibility for the killings. *The Jenny Jones Shows* was sued by the Amedure family and was ordered to pay the family $25 million (in 1999). These events led "shock television" to reexamine its programming.

—Federal Judge Eugene Nickerson declares the "don't ask, don't tell" policy unconstitutional. By year's end, there are a number of conflicted rulings on this policy—some for, some against.

—When a group of gay and lesbian leaders come to meet with President Clinton, the White House security personnel put on latex gloves to meet the group. At the same time, Marsha Scott, a nongay woman, is appointed by Clinton as his liaison to the gay and lesbian community. Both incidences cause uproar in the gay community.

—The House approves the Ryan White Comprehensive AIDS Resources Emergency Act over delaying tactics by Senator Jesse Helms.

—President Clinton signs an executive order ending the policy of denying security clearances to gay men and lesbians.

—More than 100 transvestite, transgendered, and transsexual activist gather for the First National Gender Lobbying Day on Capitol Hill.

—Parents and Friends of Lesbians and Gay (P-FLAG) uses quotes from televangelist Pat Robertson's own television show to create television ads showing the impact hate speech has on gay and lesbian youth. Threats of lawsuits from Robertson keep most television stations from showing the spots.

State and Local Events

—In what would become the first of many, the state of South Dakota bans same-sex marriages as a preemptive strike against the potential of gay marriages being approved in Hawaii.

—Rhode Island becomes the ninth state to pass a statewide gay rights bill. In another ruling at year's end, the Rhode Island Supreme Court will uphold its state's sodomy laws.

—The Hawaii Supreme Court postpones until 1996 a decision on same-sex marriage in the state. It allows a special state commission to review the issue. The commission later recommends legalizing same-sex marriages.

—Penny Culliton, a schoolteacher in New Ipswich, New Hampshire, is fired when she uses the gay-themed books *Maurice* by E. M. Forster and *The Education of Harriet Hatfield* by May Sarton in her high school English class.

—New York's Supreme Court grants the right of unmarried couples, whether gay or not, to adopt their partner's children. This is a landmark ruling.

1996

International Events

—Stephen J. O'Brien and Michael Dean report finding that about 1 percent of the male population is resistant to HIV due to a defective gene.

—South Africa becomes the second country in the world to explicitly prohibit discrimination based on sexual orientation in its constitution.

National Events

—Magic Johnson returns to the National Basketball Association after a five-year absence since his announcement of being HIV-positive.

—The U.S. Olympic Committee decides to bypass Cobb County, Georgia, from its torch run for the Atlanta Summer Games because of an antigay resolution passed by the county.

—The U.S. Supreme Court declares Colorado's Amendment 2 (denies legal protection based up sexual orientation) unconstitutional. The Court stated, "We must conclude that Amendment 2 classifies homosexuals not to further a proper legislative end, but to make them unequal to everyone else. This Colorado cannot do."

—President Clinton signs the federal Defense of Marriage Act in which marriage is defined as the union of one man and one woman. Interestingly, no local, state, or federal law defines "man" or "woman."

—President Clinton boosts funding for the Ryan White AIDS CARE fund.

—The Virginia Federal Appeals Court upholds a ban on gays in the military.

—The last viewing of the complete AIDS Quilt (38,000 panels) is held at the National Mall in Washington, D.C.

State and Local Events

—Murder and assisting suicide charges against Keith W. Green are dropped after the gay community protests. Green helped reattach an auto exhaust hose being used by his AIDS-stricken lover to commit suicide in Los Angeles.

—District judge Jeffrey Sherlock rules Montana sodomy laws unconstitutional. The state appeals the ruling.

—The state of Utah passes two bills designed to eliminate gay-straight student unions at state-financed high schools. One bill prohibits teachers from promoting "illegal activities" (sodomy is illegal in Utah) and the second bill requires students to obtain parental approval before joining any club.

—Robert James Acemant admits killing Roxanne Ellis and Michele Abdill of Medford, Oregon, because they were lesbians. The bodies of the women were found bound and gagged in the back of a pickup truck and shot execution style. Acemant was convicted of the murders but not of a hate crime.

—Jamie Nabozny wins a $962,000 judgment against his Wisconsin high school for failure to protect him from antigay harassment while he was a student there. This ruling has significant impact for all gay and lesbian students and the nation's schools.

—Tennessee Supreme Court lets stand an appellate court's decision to strike down the sodomy statute privacy arguments. This is the first time a state Supreme Court allowed the decision of a lower court to stand regarding sodomy.

1997

International Events

—Russia decriminalizes homosexuality.

—The Centers for Disease Control and Prevention reports the first decline in the number worldwide AIDS-related deaths.

—International researchers confirmed that drug therapies using protease inhibitors are unable to completely eradicate HIV from all cells in the body.

—Lesbian actor Ellen DeGeneres comes out as a lesbian on her TV show *Ellen*. This is the first time the primary character on a commercial television program is openly gay.

—Many lesbians and gay men grieve over the death of Britain's Princess Diana. The community remembers her for her charitable activities, including helping in the fight against AIDS.

—While hiding out on a houseboat in Miami, Florida, fugitive Andrew Cunanan fatally shoots himself. He was wanted for a series of murders, was on the FBI's most-wanted list, and murdered gay fashion designer Gianni Versace on July 15.

National Events

—President Clinton makes a promise to find an AIDS vaccine within 10 years; however, activists are unimpressed by the promise since the initiative includes no new research funds.

—More than 500 AIDS activists converge on Wall Street and paralyze lower Manhattan by stopping traffic. ACT UP protests allege price-gouging by pharmaceutical companies.

—The Southern Baptist calls upon its 15.7 million members to boycott the Walt Disney Co. for ownership of "Ellen" and Disney's employee domestic partnership policy.

—Hundreds of AIDS activists protest in front of the Department of Health and Human Services against a federal ban on funding for needle-exchange programs.

—The National Conference of Catholic Bishops distributes the groundbreaking document titled "Always Our Children," which encourages parents to give first priority to love and support of their lesbian daughters and gay sons over church doctrine condemning homosexuality.

—The lesbian and gay community expresses concern over a rally of the Promise Keepers in Washington, D.C., that attracts more than 700,000 men. Although they claim to be apolitical, they have deep ties to the religious right and espouse antigay rhetoric.

—Openly gay businessman James Hormel is nominated to be the U.S. ambassador to Luxembourg. Acrimonious debate in the U.S. Senate delays his confirmation until 1998.

—President Clinton becomes the first sitting president to speak to a gay rights group. At a speech given at a dinner for the Human Rights Campaign, he calls for all Americans to overcome prejudice.

State and Local Events

—An Atlanta lesbian nightclub is attacked using a bomb laced with nails that injures five people. This was the third such attack in seven months and may have been related to the bomber responsible for the 1996 Summer Olympics bomb and a blast at the Family Planning Clinic.

—Hawaii becomes the first state to enact a domestic registry and, at the same time, passes a constitutional amendment limiting marriage to opposite-sex couples only.

—New Hampshire becomes the 10th state to ban discrimination against lesbians and gays in employment, housing, and public accommodations. Two days later, Maine becomes the 11th state to enact similar legislation.

—The city of San Francisco passes an ordinance requiring all companies doing business with the city to provide domestic partnership benefits to employees. The ordinance is challenged in court, but ultimately upheld in most situations.

—California places the names of approximately 64,000 men online who were convicted of sex offenses to make it easier for the public to learn if their neighbors and coworkers were sex offenders. It was quickly discovered the more than one-third of the listings were based on incorrect or dated information. Since gay men have historically been disproportionately discriminated against by police for engaging in "sexual deviancy," an effort was considered to modify the law to exclude consensual activity from the law's scope.

—New York is the first state in the Union to hear a sodomy case within its national guard unit as applied through the Universal Code of Military Justice (UCMJ).

1998

International Events

—In the Afghan city of Heat, 18-year-old Abdul Sami and 22-year-old Bismillah are placed beside a mud wall that is bulldozed on top of them. The men were found guilty of engaging in sodomy and were killed as part of a public execution.

—A Dutch man dying of pneumonia is granted the right to "marry" his partner of 40 years to become the first same-sex couple to marry in the Netherlands. Full marriage rights will not become effective in the Netherlands until 2001.

—The Cayman Islands give in to religious activists and prohibit a gay cruise ship from docking at their harbor.

—Pop star George Michael is arrested for lewd conduct in a Beverly Hill's public restroom. This leads to his coming out as bisexual and releasing a music video that spoofs his arrest.

National Events

—U.S. District judge Stanley Sporkin rules the navy went too far by illegally obtaining confidential information about dismissed Senior Chief Petty Officer Timothy McVeigh.

—The U.S. Supreme Court decides in *Oncale v. Sundowner* that sexual harassment laws apply to same-sex cases.

—Two court decisions in March concerning the Boy Scouts' ban on gays are conflicted. In the case of James Dale, the court finds that the Scouts must abide by New Jersey's antidiscrimination laws. In the Timothy Curran case, the California Supreme Court rules the Scouts are not a business and the states' discrimination laws do not apply.

—Nebraska minister Rev. Jimmy Creech is acquitted of misdeed by the United Methodist Church for performing a union ceremony between two lesbians. Although he wins, he is eventually forced out of the church.

—A Pentagon report confirms that discharges from the military for being gay skyrocketed 67 percent since "don't ask, don't tell" took effect in 1994.

—Although the Clinton administration issues a report showing that needle-exchange programs are effective at reducing the spread of AIDS, they still refuse to lift the ban on federal funding for these programs.

—African American leaders and the Congressional Black Caucus (CBC) declare there is a "state of emergency" in the United States with regard to HIV and help create the Minority AIDS Initiative.

—The United Methodist Church warns pastors that they will be tried, reprimanded, or defrocked if they perform same-sex union ceremonies.

—The 2nd U.S. Court of Appeal rules that Congress has complete authority to exclude gays from the military as part of its personnel policies.

—In a murder that shocked the nation, University of Wyoming freshman Matthew Shepard is found hanging spread-eagle on a fence post in subzero weather beside a remote road in Laramie, Wyoming. He had been abducted, beaten, burned with a cigarette, and left to die. His death a few days later became the springboard for many organizations to push for hate crime laws in their states. His funeral is picketed by Westboro Baptist Church members carrying signs that read "Matthew burns in Hell." His primary murderer, Aaron McKinney, is denied the right to use the "homosexual panic" defense and is sentenced to life in prison without parole (1999).

—A Cincinnati City Charter that banned any policies favorable to gays and lesbians is ruled constitutional by the U.S. Supreme Court. The ruling infuriates the gay community since the U.S. Supreme Court had decided in a similar case, Colorado's Amendment 2, that such prohibitions were not constitutional.

—Rev. Bob Moorehead steps down from the Overlake Christian Church in Seattle, Washington, after heading the church for 29 years, from allegations of sexual misconduct with underage boys. Moorehead is an evangelical preacher who had preached for the Promise Keepers, a conservative Christian revival movement. Eventually, many men joined in a common lawsuit against Moorehead.

State and Local Events
—The voters of Maine throw out a gay rights ordinance enacted the previous year.

—While addressing the Wisconsin State Assembly, Green Bay Packer Reggie White makes a speech full of homophobic comments and ethnic slurs that stun the audience.

—In response to the antiaffirmative action measure, California Proposition 209, the Los Angeles City Board of Education eliminates its Gay and Lesbian Education Commission along with six other minority education commissions.

—Lawmakers in the state of Rhode Island vote to eliminate the state's 102-year-old sodomy laws.

—Circuit Court judge Richard Rombow rules that Maryland's 1916 sodomy laws violated the state's constitution.

—The Georgia Supreme Court rules that the state's 165 year-old sodomy law violates its constitutional guarantee of privacy. This comes 12 years after the U.S. Supreme Court ruled that Georgia had the right to enforce its sodomy law (*Bowers v. Hardwick*).

—The Miami-Dade County Board of Commissioners votes to approve a new antigay discrimination ordinance. This is 21 years after Anita Bryant successively overturned a previous gay rights ordinance.

—Alabama joins a few other Southern states making it illegal to design or market devices used to stimulate human genital organs (otherwise known as sex toys).

—By judicial decision, the sodomy provisions of Maryland's criminal law are struck down.

—Rhode Island decriminalizes consensual sodomy.

1999

International Events

—The Canadian Supreme Court rules that same-sex couples must have the same rights as opposite-sex couples, including marriage.

—Rev. Robert Nugent and Sister Jeannie Gramick are ordered by the Vatican to end their 22-year-old ministry to gay men and lesbians.

—Britain is found to be in violation of the European Convention of Human Rights by the European Court in Strasbourg over its ban on gays and lesbians serving in the military. As a result, the British Defense Ministry draws up a new military code of conduct that allows gays to serve in the military.

—Israel's Supreme Court recognizes the rights of a lesbian partner to be one of the legal parents to the other partner's biological child.

National Events

—The 9th U.S. Circuit Court of Appeals rules that landlords in Anchorage, Alaska, can refuse to rent to unmarried couples if it is against their religious beliefs. This could have significant impact for gay and lesbian couples.

—Almost 13,000 people witness the holy union between long-time lesbian couple Jeanne Barnett and Ellie Charlton. This was an act of the ecclesiastical disobedient in Sacramento, California. Eighty United Methodist ministers attending the event may face formal charges from the church.

—Jerry Falwell outs Tinky Winky, the purple teletubby, in his *National Liberty Journal*. The national media and gay press have a field day with the absurdity of the accusation.

—A coalition of 18 religious right organizations launches Phase Two of its "Truth in Love" ad campaign, which urges gay men and lesbians to enter therapy to convert to heterosexuality.

—Pat Robertson's Christian Coalition loses its tax-exempt status from the IRS.

—Bill Clinton becomes the first president ever to proclaim June as Gay and Lesbian Pride Month.

— While asleep, army PFC Barry Winchell is attacked in his barracks with a baseball bat by Private Calvin N. Glover. Prosecutors acknowledge the killing is an antigay hate crime and Glover is convicted of premeditated murder. In 2000, Spc. Justin R. Fisher is sentenced to 13 years in prison for obstruction of justice in the murder investigation and for providing Glover with the murder weapon.

—Rev. Mel White leads a delegate of some 200 gay activists to meet with Rev. Jerry Falwell in an effort to get him to tone down his antigay rhetoric.

State and Local Events

—Both the states of New Hampshire and Connecticut remove barriers to child adoption by gay couples, whereas the states of Arkansas and Utah institute antigay policies against gay adoptions.

—Billy Jack Gaither, a 39-year-old man, is found burned to death on the banks of Pockerwood Creek in Alabama. He had been bludgeoned with an ax handle and his body was thrown on two burning tires. Two men are convicted of his murder and sentenced to life in prison without parole.

—Tracey Thompson, a 33-year-old transgendered woman, is found beaten to death with a baseball bat on a rural South Georgia road. No perpetrator is charged.

—New York City Police Officer Justin Volpe is convicted of sodomizing a Haitian immigrant, Abner Louima, with a broken broomstick handle while Louima was in custody.

—Gary Matson and Winfield Scott Mowder of Happy Valley, California, are killed by two white supremacists brothers who are connected to the antigay, racist World Church of the Creator. The two brothers, Benjamin Matthew Williams and James Tyler Williams, are charged with murder. They are also charged with setting fire to three synagogues and a medical clinic in Sacramento, California. Both men are convicted of their crimes and sent to prison. Matthew Williams commits suicide in prison. Tyler receives a life-imprisonment term.

—During the San Diego Gay Pride Parade, a tear-gas canister is thrown into the middle of a group of 70 children, parents, and grandparents. The parade is temporarily disrupted and approximately 15 people are treated for injuries.

—Dana Rivers, a transgendered woman ousted from her teaching position with Antelope School District, California, settles out of court for $150,000 not to seek her job back.

—The Orange County School District Board of Trustees, in a unanimous vote, denies the gay-straight alliance from meeting at El Modina High School. It is a surprising vote because the board members openly acknowledge they are in violation of federal law and that other high schools in the districts already had gay-straight alliance student groups meeting on campus.

2000

International Events

—Germany officially apologizes to lesbians and gay men for the persecution under the Nazi regime and subsequent discrimination under Paragraph 175.

—Hilary Swank wins the Oscar for best actress for her portrayal of transgendered murder victim Brandon Teena in *Boys Don't Cry*.

—Exodus International Chairman "ex-gay" John Paulk is removed from his position when he is discovered by three employees of the Human Rights Campaign sitting in a gay bar in Washington, D.C. At first he claims that he entered the bar to use the bathroom not knowing what kind of bar it was, but later admitted that he knew it was a gay bar. Paulk and his "ex-lesbian" wife, Anne, advocate "reparative therapy" for homosexuals wanting to be heterosexual.

National Events

—President Clinton calls upon Congress to pass the Hate Crimes Prevention Act and the Employment Nondiscrimination Act.

—Laura Schlessinger gets a $3 million contract from Paramount Studios to place her daily *Dr. Laura* radio talk show on TV. In response, the StopDrLaura.com effort is launched, due to her often voiced antigay opinions. Cincinnati-based Proctor and Gamble announces that it will not sponsor her upcoming television show and also pulls out of her radio show. Soon, most advertisers cease funding her show, and, as a result, it lasts a very short time on television.

—The U.S. Supreme Court rules the Boy Scouts of America has the right to ban gays from its ranks.

—The fourth national March on Washington attracts several hundreds of thousands of people. Instead of including "for gay and lesbian rights" in the title, the theme was absolute and total equality. Thus, the event was titled "March for Equality."

State and Local Events

—California enacts the first statewide domestic partnership registry in the nation.

—Proposition 22, the Knight Initiative that outlaws same-sex marriages, is passed overwhelmingly in California.

—The New Jersey Supreme Court makes a landmark decision when it declares the nonbiological parent of a same-sex couple who ended their relationship, the "psychological parent" of the twin girls she helped raise.

—The Vermont House approves the state's "civil union" law as a way of providing "marriage" to same-sex couples without calling it marriage.

—"J.R" Carl Warren Jr., of Grant Town in Marion County, West Virginia, is found dead on a lonely road. Two 17-year-old males confess that they were afraid he was going to reveal a sexual liaison he had with one or both of them. They beat and kicked him to death, then placed his body into the trunk of a car, drove to an isolated spot, placed his body on the ground, and ran over it several times to try and make it look like a hit-and-run accident.

—California State Board of Equalization votes to grant a nonbiological lesbian parent the tax status of "head of household."

—Two lesbians are ejected from Dodger Stadium, Los Angeles, California, for kissing to celebrate two home runs by their team. When the situation hits the news media, Dodger President and CEO Bob Graziano publicly apologizes to the women and the gay community—which were all the damages the women requested.

—Ronald Gay, 53, kills one and injures six patrons at a gay bar in Roanoke, Virginia. He defends his actions saying that he was made fun of his entire life because of his surname and that he wanted to get rid of "faggots."

—The Virginia Court of Appeals rejects a challenge to the state's sodomy laws.

—Kansas is the only state with discriminatory penalties for consensual sex by minors. Kansas law makes any sexual activity involving a person under 16 illegal. The 1999 "Romeo and Juliet" law, however, provides lesser penalties for consensual sex when one partner is 19 or under and the other partner's age is within four years. Convicted of sodomy for having sex in 2000 at age 18 with a 14-year-old boy, Matthew R. Limon was sentenced to more than 17 years in prison. Had Limon's partner been an underage girl, he could have been sentenced at most to one year and three months in prison.

—Louisiana Supreme Court interprets privacy amendment to mean that it provided for the legislature to make decisions about privacy, not that the citizenry had a right to privacy. As such, the court rebuked privacy challenges to its sodomy laws.

2001

International Events

—In April, the Netherlands becomes the first country in the world to legally sanctify same-sex marriage.

—The Chinese Psychiatric Association decides to drop all references to homosexuality as a pathological condition. This brings China's mental health establishment in closer line with Western nations.

—Police and the Egyptian State Security Intelligence raid the Queen Boat moored on the Nile in Cairo's Zamalek district. They arrest 55 men, many teenagers, while during a party. The arrests were made because the men were suspected of engaging in a gay sex party. As the months unfold and the matter is brought to trial, there is an international outcry over the proceedings and harsh sentences. U.S. Representative Barney Frank obtains signatures from 35 members of the House of Representatives and sends a letter expressing "strong disapproval" to Egyptian president Hosni Mubarak over the arrest of the men.

—Namibia President Sam Nujoma says, "The Republic of Namibia does not allow homosexuality [or] lesbianism here."

—The UN General Assembly issues a worldwide plan to fight the spread of AIDS and to provide better care for the approximately 36 million people currently infected.

—HIV/AIDS and prevention workers are arrested in India under sodomy and obscenity statutes.

—September 11, 2001, terrorists in northeastern United States hijack four airliners. Two airliners are used to crash into the World Trade Center towers destroying both. One crashes into the Pentagon, and, another believed to be headed for the White House, crashes into the countryside of Pennsylvania. The terrorist attacks are the worst ever experienced by the United States and it will be a day never forgotten. Many thousands of people die and the country is sent into a state of shock. A few days after the attacks, while on *The 700 Club* television program, Rev. Jerry Falwell blames gays and lesbians, among others, for the attacks. While Falwell makes these statements, Pat Robertson nods his head in agreement. There is a swift and furious outcry by liberals, conservatives, other religious leaders, and gay activist over their comments. Falwell and Robertson attempt damage control but without success. Also, there is continuing debate over whether to provide survivor funds to partners of lesbians and gay men who died in the attack.

—Germany comes close to legalizing same-sex marriages but is blocked at the last moment by conservative regional states.

—Switzerland's two largest banks agree to pay $1.25 billion in settlement to five groups of people, including lesbians and gay men. This represents more than 50,000 bank accounts placed with them in an effort to keep their assets out of the hands of the Nazis during World War II. After the war the banks failed to return the money to these people. Although other European governments have created funds to provide for victims redressed for Nazi crimes, this is the first time gays have been specifically mentioned and documented.

National Events

—The Permanent Partners Immigration Act is reintroduced to Congress by U.S. Representative Jerold Nadler (D-NY), which would offer same-sex couples the same privileges currently afforded to legal spouses under federal immigration law.

—*The Washington POST* reports that a Washington, D.C. Health Department's Administration AIDS pamphlet (paid for by the government) made statements such as "Jesus is our hope!" and contained a 15-page tract "A Christian Response to AIDS" in which the Bible is cited 30 times.

—The U.S. Supreme Court rules 8–0 that marijuana cannot be used for any debilitating diseases, including AIDS.

—The U.S. Census releases figures showing that the number of American households reporting same-sex couples has skyrocketed.

—Senator Jesse Helms is successful at getting the Senate to pass an amendment to deny federal funding to school districts that apply their antidiscrimination policies to the Boy Scouts.

—*The Washington Post* reveals that White House senior adviser Karl Rove brokered a deal with the antigay Salvation Army, which would receive between $88,000 and $100,000 a month in exchange for its support of President Bush's Faith-Based Initiative, HR 7. Initially, the White House vehemently denied the meetings took place, but only days later admitted that it had.

State and Local Events

—Seven gay and lesbian couples in Massachusetts apply for marriage licenses and are denied. They begin the process of suing the state.

—The James Byrd Jr. Hate Crimes Act is passed in Texas after a long, hard-fought battle. It is achieved when Lieutenant Governor Bill Ratliff and five other Republicans broke rank and voted along with all 15 Senate Democrats.

—Fred Martinez Jr., a two-spirit 16-year-old Native American, is beaten to death by Shaun Murphy, 18, near Cortez, Colorado.

—The firing of a lesbian because of her sexual orientation from the Kentucky Baptist Home for Children is upheld by a federal judge in Louisville, Kentucky.

—Openly gay Michael Guest is confirmed by the Senate to act as the U.S. ambassador to Romania. The antigay Family Research Council protests his appointment. Secretary of State Colin Powell presides over the swearing in and publicly acknowledges Guest's lover of six years.

—AB 25, California's Domestic Partnership bill, is signed into law by Governor Gray Davis making California second only to Vermont in the support of gay and lesbian relationships and families.

—Three antigay measures are defeated in Michigan while two pro-gay measures in Dade County Florida effectively erase the legacy of Anita Bryant.

—Los Angeles County Sheriff Lee Boca announces that condoms would be distributed in county jails as part of a HIV prevention program.

—Arizona and Minnesota repeal their sodomy laws.

2002

International Events

—On the first day of the New Year, Saudi Arabia in a public execution, beheads three men found guilty of "engaging in the extreme obscenity and ugly acts of homosexuality."

—The Australian High Court reaffirms the right of single and lesbian women to have invitro fertilization treatment (IVF).

—A controversial Jerusalem rabbi, David Batzri, states that gays should be "put to death."

—Besides the 52 men arrested in 2001, more homosexual men are arrested in Egypt in an apparent crack down.

—The Jamaican government rejects a recommendation by Parliament to decriminalize homosexuality.

—U.N. AIDS chief Peter Piot reports that Russia has the fastest-growing HIV infection rate in the world.

—Britain repeals its sex statutes that banned "gross indecency" between men, "soliciting for the immoral purpose," and "buggery." These were the same statutes used to prosecute Oscar Wilde.

—Romania bans discrimination based on sexual orientation and eliminates its sodomy laws.

National Events

—Two widowed domestic partners file claims with the New York State Workers' Compensation Board after their partner's life insurance companies denied them spousal benefits as an aftermath of the September 11, 2001, terrorist attack.

—Students at more than 1,900 high schools and colleges across the nation on April 10, 2002, choose not to speak in order to bring attention to antigay bias in schools in the first National Day of Silence.

—Pi Kappa Phi's national council removes all members of its Michigan State University fraternity for using antigay epithets and slogans during pledging rituals.

State and Local Events

—Alaska governor Tony Knowles signs an administrative order prohibiting discrimination based on sexual orientation in state employment.

—Bill Flanigan sues the University of Maryland Medical System in Baltimore City Circuit Court when he was refused the right to visit his dying life partner because only "family" members were qualified to visit. Flanigan and partner had a five-year California domestic partnership and the specified health care power of attorney, which the hospital refused to acknowledge.

—An Ohio lesbian couple goes to court to change their names so their children would have the same surname. The Ohio Supreme Court had not ruled but has affirmed Ohio's law not recognizing de facto parenting.

—The state of Washington enacts an antibullying bill in its public schools that prohibits bias-motivated harassment.

—Dallas, Texas, enacts an antidiscrimination ordinance that includes sexual orientation and gender identity.

—J'Noel Gardiner, a transgender woman, is denied the right to inherit her late husband's estate because the Kansas Supreme Court rules that he was not a woman under Kansas law and, thus, her marriage to Marshall Gardiner was not valid.

—A 37-year-old gay man, Clint Scott Risetter, is killed when gasoline is poured over him while he sleeps in Santa Barbara, California, and is set on fire. The killer, Martin Thomas Hartman, told the police that he "has a lot of hatred" toward gays.

2003

International Events

—Belgium and two provinces of Canada—Ontario and British Columbia—grant the right to same-sex couples to marry.

—Homosexuality is recriminalized in the country of Belize.

—Reuben Zellman is the first openly transgendered person accepted by the Hebrew Union College-Jewish Institute of Religion. Later, he becomes ordained in 2010. Also in 2003, the Committee on Jewish Law and Standards agrees that sex reassignment surgery (SRS) is permissible under Jewish law.

—The Major General of the Russian Medical Service concludes that homosexuals can serve in the military.

National Events

—U.S. Supreme Court in *Lawrence et al v. Texas* reverses Texas court support for sodomy and explicitly overrules the 1986 Georgia *Bowers v. Hardwick* decision. As such, sodomy laws as commonly constructed are struck down throughout the nation.

—Gene Robinson becomes the first bishop in the Episcopal Church in the United States to be openly gay.

State and Local Event

—Anitidiscrimination legislation is approved in Arizona (sexual orientation in public sector), Kentucky (gender identity and sexual orientation in public sector), Michigan (sexual orientation), New Mexico (sexual orientation and gender identity in private sector), and Pennsylvania (gender identity in public sector).

2004

International Events

—Canada approves same-sex marriage in the provinces of Quebec, Yukon, Manitoba, Nova Scotia, Saskatchewan, and Newfoundland.

—Australia bans same-sex marriage.

—New Zealand passes a civil union law.

National Events

—Massachusetts, by judicial decision, becomes the first state in the United States to approve gay marriage. By 2008, the Massachusetts legislature passes a bill to recognize marriages performed legally in other jurisdictions.

—Mississippi, Missouri, Montana, Oregon, and Utah ban same-sex marriage. Some states go even further to not only ban same-sex marriage but also civil unions. These include Arkansas, Georgia, Kentucky, Louisiana, Michigan, North Dakota, Ohio, Oklahoma, Virginia, and Wisconsin.

—Long-time lesbian activists Del Martin and Phyllis Lyon become the first same-sex couple to be legally married in the United States. For a brief time in early 2004, San Francisco mayor Gavin Newsom allowed city hall to grant marriage licenses to same-sex couples. Martin and Lyon were the first to have the honor. However, the California State Supreme Court annulled such marriages later that year. When the courts overturned Proposition 8 in 2008, same-sex marriages were again allowed in California. Martin and Lyon, again, were honored to be the first couple married in California under the new law. Del Martin died in 2008.

State and Local Events

—District of Columbia strikes down its adultery and fornication laws.

—Democratic governor James McGreevey, after being caught in a sex scandal with another man, comes out as a "gay American" at a press conference where he also announces his resignation effective later that year. As such, McGreevey has the distinction of being the first sitting governor to come out gay. The sex scandal involved him hiring his boyfriend, Golan Cipel (an Israeli citizen), as homeland security adviser for the state of New Jersey. This was ironic since Cipel could not gain a security approval from the federal government due to his citizenship status. After resigning from politics, McGreevey became a priest to work with prison inmates. His life history was detailed in the 2013 HBO documentary film, *Fall to Grace*.

—Ed Schrock, antigay-rights Republican politician who served as congressman from Virginia, aborts his reelection efforts for a third term when a videotape is released showing him soliciting sex from a male prostitute.

2005

International Events
—Both Latvia and Uganda ban same-sex marriages.

—Puerto Rico repeals its sodomy statutes.

—Spain and all of Canada enact same-sex marriage laws.

—Two teenagers Mahmoud Asgari (16) and Ayaz Marhoni (18) are executed by hanging in Iran. A series of graphic photographs on the Internet show the boys being loaded on to a pickup truck, being blindfolded, nooses placed around their necks, and the truck driving off. They were convicted of raping a 13-year old boy two years earlier. Although Sharia (Islamic Law) permits the death penalty for engaging in homosexual acts, Iran is a signatory of the Convention on the Rights of the Child, which forbids the execution of children and teenagers. Some English-language accounts of the execution suggested that the boys were actually killed for being gay and the rape conviction was a cover up. The hangings became a political issue between the United States and Europe, and Iran.

—South Africa's Supreme Court rules that the country's constitution made it illegal to ban gay marriages.

National Event
—The states of Kansas and Texas join many other states banning same-sex marriages.

State and Local Events
—Jim West, mayor of Spokane, Washington, and staunch antigay legislator, is investigated by the local newspaper, *Spokesman Review*, in relationship to leads that West had engaged in sexual activity with young boys. Although no evidence is found of the illegal activity, it does find that he used the alias Cobra82 and Right-BiGuy at Gay. com. The outing resulted in West being recalled by the voters. The FBI cleared West of all charges just five months before he died in 2006 of pancreatic cancer.

—Maine modifies its antidiscrimination laws to include sexual orientation and gender identity.

2006

International Events

—Russians attempt to hold its first gay pride march in Moscow. The event was condemned by most religious orders and Nikolai Kulikov, mayor of Moscow, banned the event. Only a few dozen Russian LGBT protestors along with a handful of foreign supporters walked down the street near the Tomb of Unknown Soldiers next to the Kremlin and were attacked by counter-protesters and the police. According to Human Rights Watch, there were hundreds of antigay protestors including skinheads and nationalists beating and kicking the participants while hurling antigay slogans and epithets. The subsequent marches in 2007, 2008, 2009, and 2010 were equally brutal and, again, held without permit because Moscow city officials denied them event permits. The organizers of the event took their complaints to the European Court of Human Rights. Although the court sided with the organizers, their opinion had no effect on Russian policy. Moscow officially banned all future gay events in 2011 for the next 100 years.

—South African becomes the first nation in Africa to approve same-sex marriage.

—The first gay pride parade held in Zabreb, Croatia, has participants coming from all over Eastern Europe.

National Events

—Florida Republican congressman Mark Foley resigns after it is revealed that he sent sexually inappropriate (and unlawful Internet messages) to underage male pages. Ironically, Foley was the chairman of the House Caucus of Missing and Exploited Children, which is charged with protecting Americans against sexual predators. Further investigation finds that he had had sexual relations with former pages who were over the age of consent and that was not illegal.

—Ted Haggard, evangelical pastor to the New Life Church in Colorado Springs, Colorado, is outed by professional masseur and prostitute Mike Jones. Haggard often preached about the immorality of homosexual sex and supported Colorado Amendment 43 (banning same-sex marriage) yet continued a three-year relationship with Jones for whom he paid for sex and crystal meth. Haggard was forced to resign from the church and move out of the area. He entered Christian counseling and within weeks was pronounced to be completely heterosexual. However, he was unable to resume his ministerial duties and years later declares that he is "bisexual." Surprisingly, he has been able to begin his own church that teaches that homosexuality is a sin.

—The U.S. Senate's fails in its attempt to pass a constitutional amendment banning gay marriage.

State and Local Events

—Illinois includes sexual orientation in its antidiscrimination statute.

—Tennessee becomes the next state to ban same-sex marriages. Alabama, Colorado, Idaho, South Carolina, South Dakota, Virginia, and Wisconsin ban not only same-sex marriages but also civil unions.

2007

International Events
—Nepal and the New Zealand territories of Tokelau and Niue decriminalize homosexuality.

—The first ever gay pride parade and festival in a Muslim country is held in Istanbul, Turkey.

—Kosovo is the first Eastern European country to include a mention of "sexual orientation" in its newly adopted constitution as an independent nation.

—Nicaragua and Panama decriminalize homosexuality.

National Events
—Human Rights Campaign co-hosts with the Logo cable channel the first American presidential forum that specifically focuses on LGBT issues. All presidential candidates were invited but only six Democrats participated including Barack Obama and Hillary Clinton. All Republican candidates declined the request.

—Former leader of the Young Republicans and one of the leading Republicans of Indiana, Glenn Murphy is reported to police for performing fellatio (without consent) on another Young Republican man while he slept. This was the second time Murphy was accused of this behavior. In 1998, he was charged with sexual battery when he accosted another man (while the victim's girlfriend was in the same room). Murphy was imprisoned in 2008 and forced to register as a sex offender.

—Jerry Falwell, founder of the Moral Majority, Liberty University and one of the major antigay leaders in the United States, dies of a heart attack.

State and Local Events
—Republican Washington State legislator Richard Curtis initially claims that Cody Castagna (a man he met at an erotic bookstore) stole his wallet. Later, Curtis admits to police that he had sex with Castagna but that the young man demanded money in exchange for staying silent about their encounter and Curtis's lifestyle. The local press got wind of the story and Curtis, who had voted against various gay-rights bills, resigned his legislative position.

—Robert "Bob" Allen, Florida State representative, is arrested by undercover police officer in a public park restroom for soliciting to perform fellatio. Allen offered $20 for the service to the officer and was charged with solicitation for prostitution. Allen had voted consistently against all gay rights legislation.

—U.S. senator Larry Craig is arrested by undercover police at the Minneapolis-St. Paul International Airport. The police claim Craig trawled for sex by peering through stall doors (for two minutes), tapping his toes, placing his foot against the officer's foot under the stall divider (what is termed *cottaging*), and running his hand under the stall divider a couple of times. Although Craig is an 18-year veteran in the U.S. Senate and holds antigay political beliefs (he voted in favor of "Don't Ask, Don't Tell" and other rights limiting legislation), he pleads guilty to the charges. Later he would change his mind and claim that the officer misinterpreted his "wide stance"—but the courts refuse to allow him to retract his guilty plead.

2008

International Event
—Bulgaria holds its first every gay pride parade and festival.

National Events
—Connecticut, by judicial decision, becomes the second state in the United States to approve same-sex marriage.

—Arizona, California (under Proposition 8), and Florida adopt laws banning same-sex marriages.

—Rachel Maddow begins hosting *The Rachel Maddow Show* on MSNBC. She is the first openly lesbian or gay to anchor a major prime-time news program in the United States.

—Stu Rasmussen is the first openly transgendered man to be elected mayor of an American city (Silverton, Oregon).

State and Local Events
—A transgendered woman, Angie Zapata, is murdered in Greeley, Colorado. The assailant, Allen Andrade, would be convicted of first-degree murder and committing a bias-motivated crime. He killed her after finding out that she was transgendered. This case is the first hate crime in the United States to obtain a conviction related to transgenderism. The story of Angie Zapata's life and murder were featured on Univision's *Aqui y Ahora* television show in 2009.

—Proposition 8 is passed by California voters. The ballot proposition amended the state's constitution to effectively ban same-sex marriage by defining marriage as the union of one man and one woman. Much of the financial support against gay marriage comes from outside the state and the Mormon Church. California, being the largest state in the Union by population and economy, garnered national attention from many gay-rights organizations and supporters in response to this act of discrimination and inspired the NOH8 campaign. The proposition came about because, for a short time in 2004, same-sex couples were allowed to marry. More than 18,000 same-sex couples legally married over a few short months. Proposition 8 was challenged in court and, as an amendment, ruled constitutional by the California Supreme Court in *Strauss v. Horton* in 2009. Immediately two same-sex couples filed suit in federal court against the amendment. Chief Justice Vaughn Walker ruled the amendment unconstitutional under the Equal Protection and Due Process Clauses of the Fourteenth Amendment since the amendment was used to re-remove rights of a class of citizens. The governor and state attorney general refused to defend the law. As such, proponents of the law appealed the decision to the U.S. Supreme Court. The Supreme Court ruled that the proponents did not have standing to defend the law and dismissed the appeal and directed the Ninth Circuit to vacate its decision. That left Walker's ruling intact. Governor Jerry Brown was empowered to allow same-sex marriages to resume in the state of California in 2013.

2009

International Events

—Norway and Sweden approve same-sex marriage.

—The High Court of Delhi strikes down much of S.377 of the Indian Penal Code (IPC) as being unconstitutional, thereby decriminalizing homosexuality.

—Uganda legislature considers a bill that will impose the death penalty for those engaging in homosexual behavior. The bill came about after years of antigay proselytizing by Scott Lively of the U.S.-based Abiding Truth Ministries with their outreach to Uganda. International outrage causes the bill to be withdrawn.

National Events

—Congress passes, and President Obama signs, the Matthew Shepard Act in recognition to the hate motivated murder of Matthew Shepard in 1998. The young man was tortured and brutally murdered because of his sexual orientation. The act expands the 1969 U.S. Federal Hate Crime Law to include crimes motivated by the victim's actual or perceived gender, sexual orientation, disability, or gender identity.

—President Barack Obama signs a Presidential Memorandum granting partners of federal employees in same-sex relationships to receive a few benefits excluding full health coverage. It is a start toward full recognition of gay and lesbian couples who work for the U.S. government.

—The NOH8 campaign is launched. In response to the passage of Proposition 8 in California that banned same-sex marriage, a distinctive logo made up of the letters N-O-H-8 representing "no hate" became a national symbol in support of gay marriage. During the 2009 Miss America Pageant, contestant Caroline Michelle Pregean Boller stated that she believed marriage should be between one man and one woman. This infuriated many and a photo shoot of some of the contestant and directors created the NOH8 logo placed on the face. The NOH8 effort has expanded to fight discrimination and bullying at all levels.

—The biographical movie of the life of Harvey Milk is nominated for eight Academy Awards, including Best Picture. It wins Best Actor in a leading Role (Sean Penn) and Best Original Screenplay (Dustin Lance Black). Harvey Milk was a San Francisco supervisor and gay activist who was murdered, along with Mayor George Moscone, by fellow supervisor Dan White.

State and Local Events

—Iowa (by judicial decision) and Vermont (through legislative action) adopt same-sex marriage. The Coquille Indian Tribe in Oregon also approves same-sex marriage.

—Maine bans same-sex marriage.

—Senator Barney Frank hires Diego Sanchez as a legislative assistant. Sanchez is the first transgendered person accepted on the Democratic National Committee's (DNC) Platform Committee and to work on Capitol Hill.

2010

International Event

—Portugal, Iceland, Argentina, and the Mexican Federal District approve same-sex marriage. The Mexican Supreme Court rules that marriages conducted in Mexico City are to be upheld throughout the country but that no other state is required to perform them.

National Events

—Eddie Long, a senior pastor at the New Birth Missionary Baptist Church and famed televangelist, is sued by four young men (in their early 20s) claiming that Long used his fame and money to coerce them into sexual relationships. Since the relationships occurred when the boys were over the age of 16, no consent laws were broken. Long took the boys on trips to Africa, gave them gifts such as cash, cars, and jewelry in exchange for oral sex, sensual massages, and mutual masturbation. Long had led a march with Bernice King (daughter of Martin Luther King) against same-sex marriage. The Southern Poverty Law Center had called Long one of the most virulently homophobic black leaders in the nation. Long settled the case out-of-court with the four men (plus a fifth one who joined in the suit) under undisclosed terms.

—President Obama's administration releases the first comprehensive national plan—*National HIV/AIDS Strategy*—for combating the disease in the United States.

—George Rekkers, American psychologist and ordained Southern Baptist minister, is photographed traveling with a 20-year-old male escort on a European vacation. Rekkers was a founding board member of the extremely antigay Family Research Council and officer and scientific adviser to the National Association for Research & Therapy of Homosexuality (NARTH). NARTH mission is to find ways to "treat" homosexuality including "reparative" or "conversion" therapy. Rekkers had been a high-paid court authority on homosexuality and had testified in Arkansas and Florida courts on the "harm" caused by LGBT people adopting children. Although he is virulently antigay, he hires "Lucien" (later identified as Jo-Vanni Roman) from RentBoy.com to provide daily nude massages that included genital touching while on the trip. He claims to have hired the young man to carry his luggage since he had back problems. However, the photo of Rekkers at the airport showed him carrying his own baggage. NARTH and other religious right organizations immediately distanced themselves from Rekkers.

—The "It Gets Better" project is launched by writer and advice columnist Dan Savage and his husband Terry Miller in response to the tragedy of gay teen suicide and antigay bullying. The goal of the project is to reduce gay suicide by encouraging gay and lesbian teens to reach out to appropriate support services—and advise teens that, over time, it will get better and not see suicide as a way out.

—Marshal McCurdy files rape charges against Bruce Barclay, the Republican commissioner of Cumberland County, Pennsylvania. When police search Barclay's home, they don't find evidence of rape but rather hundreds of videotapes of sexual encounters of Barclay with many men. The tapes were created through the use of hidden surveillance cameras mounted in his home. Some of these men later sue McCurdy over being filmed without their consent.

State and Local Events
—New Hampshire (by legislative action) and the District of Columbia (by legislative action) approve same sex-marriage.

—Proposition 8 is ruled unconstitutional by federal judge Vaughn Walker, thereby allowing same-sex couples the right to marry in California. The ruling is immediately appealed to the U.S. Supreme Court.

—Stanchly antigay California legislator Roy Ashburn is arrested for drunk driving. Ashburn and an unidentified man report they were coming from a gay bar. Later, Ashburn outs himself to KERN radio host Inga Barks and asks the public to pray for him. He defended his antigay voting record as representing his constituents and never runs for office again.

2011

International Events
—Elio Di Rupo becomes prime minister of Belgium. He is the first openly gay male to head a major government.

—Seventh version of the WPATH-SOC is released. The *Standards of Care for the Health of Transsexual, Transgender, and Gender Nonconforming People* by the World Professional Association for Transgender Health (WPATH-SOC) provides professionals working with transsexual, transgender, or gender variant people with psychiatric, psychological, medical, and surgical requirements or procedures information.

—Two women become the first same-sex couple to legally marry in India.

National Events
—"Don't Ask, Don't Tell" (DADT) policy banning gays and lesbians in the military is revoked. The policy (not law) prohibited homosexuals and bisexuals from being open about their sexual orientation meaning that they could not engage in homosexual behaviors nor share with others about the sexual orientation identity. The military was not supposed to conduct gay witch-hunts and only investigate a soldier if he or she were observed violating the code. However, since the enactment of DADT in 1993, over 13,000 military service personnel were discharged under the policy. Minutes after the repeal of DADT became official policy, U.S. Navy Lt. Gary Ross

married his partner of 11 years, Dan Swezy, making them the first same-sex couple in the military to be legally married.

—In the 13th season of the U.S. TV show *Dancing with the Stars*, Chaz Bono is the first openly transgender man to star in a major television network that has as its topic something other than transgenderism.

—The Defense of Marriage Act (DOMA) comes under judicial attack and President Obama states that his administration will no longer defend the statute.

—The TV show, *Dando Candela*, broadcasts nude photos of Roberto Arango, vice chair of the Bush/Cheney '04 campaign in Puerto Rico. The pictures were retrieved from the gay hook-up app Grindr and show Arango in various positions, including on all fours taking a photo of his ass. Arango had a clear antigay voting record and claimed he was taking photos to document his weight loss with no memory how they ended up on Grindr. He resigned his position with the Republican Party shortly thereafter.

—The U.S. Presbyterian Church votes to allow gay and lesbian ministers to be ordained.

State and Local Events

—The New York legislature legalizes same-sex marriage, thus becoming the largest state at this time to approve gay marriage.

—The Suquamish tribe in Washington State approves same-sex marriage.

—Antigay fundamentalist preacher, Grant Storms, is arrested after being viewed masturbating in his car while watching children play in a New Orleans public playground. Although he initially denies the accusations, the "self-styled Christian patriot" who often railed against gays and lesbians, later admitted that he was masturbating.

—Republican Indiana State representative Phillip Hinkle is uncovered by the local newspaper, *Indy Star*, offering an 18-year-old male prostitute a paltry $80 for a "really good time." The two met through an ad on Craigslist and the two met at an Indianapolis hotel. Once the story broke, many people called for Hinkle to resign. Hinkle refused to resign his position as legislator but decided not to run for reelection in 2012.

2012

International Events

—The countries of Denmark, Caribbean Netherlands, some Brazilian federal districts, and the Mexican state of Quintana Roo approve same-sex marriage.

—You Ya-ting and her partner Fish Huang are the first same-sex couple to be married in a traditional Buddhist wedding in Taiwan.

—Dr. Robert L. Spitzer recants his position that homosexuality can be "cured." His 2003 research into change therapies concluded that homosexuals could be made heterosexual if they were strongly motivated. As a respected world-class psychiatrist, his opinion and research had strong clout. The "reparative" or sexual orientation change efforts by religious organizations and conservative politicians pointed to his research to support their agenda. Ultimately, Spitzer realized this research was flawed and his findings were diametrically opposite to experience. Sexual orientation cannot be changed and efforts to do so cause emotional and mental harm. Spitzer officially apologizes to the gay community.

National Events

—Barack Obama becomes the first sitting U.S. president to publically announce his support for same-sex marriage. He explains that his views have "evolved" to accept gay marriage.

—The U.S. Department of Housing and Urban Development's Office of Fair Housing and Equal Opportunity issues regulations prohibiting discrimination in federally assisted housing programs based on sexual orientation and gender identity.

—Chief Operating Officer Dan T. Cathy of Chick-fil-A makes many public statements supporting "traditional" family and denouncing same-sex marriage. Considering a long history of the company donating money to many antigay groups and churches, a major media controversy ensued with some cities claiming to block the expansion of the company into their regions. The ACLU became involved and the Jim Henson Company ceased doing business with company. Protesters staged a same-sex "kiss day" whereas counterprotesters with a "Chick-fil-A appreciation day."

State and Local Events

—Longtime antigay activist and supporter of Proposition 8 in California (to ban same-sex marriages), Caleb Hesse is arrested for sexually abusing numerous underage boys. The first-grade teacher and volunteer youth leader for the virulently antigay Evangelical Free Church of Yucca Valley, CA confesses that he engaged in inappropriate sexual contact with young boys over a three-decade period.

—San Francisco becomes the first city in the United States to offer to cover the expenses related to transgender sex reassignment surgery for uninsured transgender residents.

—For the first time, voters approve same-sex marriage in Maine solely by ballot initiative.

—Tammy Baldwin is elected as senator for Wisconsin to the U.S. Senate. She is the first openly lesbian or gay politician to be elected to this high office. In the same year, Kyrsten Sinema (Democrat from Arizona), becomes the first bisexual elected to the U.S. Congress.

—The Maryland and Washington legislatures pass laws approving same-sex marriage. Anti-equality forces place initiatives on their ballots to overrule the legislature and block gay marriage. The initiatives fail. This is the first time in U.S. politics that same-sex marriage survives ballot efforts to overrule enabling legislation.

2013

International Events

—Brazil, France, Uruguay, New Zealand, and the Australian Capital Territory approve same-sex marriage.

—Russian president signs into law a ban on "homosexual propaganda" and a ban on foreign same-sex couples or single LGBT adults from adopting Russian orphans. The international community condemns Russia's action and the antigay policy threatens the success of the 2014 Winter Olympics.

—Exodus International announces that it is closing its doors and ceasing all worldwide activities. After three decades of operation trying to change people's sexual orientation through spiritual counseling, the board of directors apologized to the gay community for all the pain and suffering it caused. Exodus International planned to create a new ministry to help churches create safe and welcoming communities.

—A Ugandan LGBT group files suit against Abiding Truth Ministries founder Scott Lively for conspiring with political and religious leaders in Uganda to whip up antigay hysteria leading to a bill that imposes the death penalty for homosexual behavior. Under the Alien Tort Statute, American courts have the right to hear human rights case involving sexual orientation brought by foreign citizens. The lawsuit claims that Lively's actions resulted in the torture, arrest, and murder of Ugandan homosexuals.

—Germany becomes Europe's first country to allow babies to be registered as neither male nor female. On birth certificates a new category—"indeterminate sex"—will one of three available choices.

National Events

—Supreme Court justice Ruth Bader Ginsburg officiates at a same-sex wedding during the Labor Day weekend. This is believed to be the first time a member of the Supreme Court has officiated at a same-sex wedding.

—Daniel Lennox and Larry Choate III, both graduates of West Point, are the first male couple to be wed at the Cadet Chapel at the U.S. Military Academy. The two men met after their training at the academy. The first marriage between two women (Ellen Schick and Shannon Simpson) at West Point occurred a year earlier.

—The U.S. Senate votes to approve the Employment Non-Discrimination Act (ENDA). The law would outlaw workplace discrimination based on sexual orientation or gender identity. Although some states and cities have their own antidiscrimination statutes, this is the first time the federal government has taken on the issue at a national level. Considering that Republicans are a majority in the House, it is unlikely the bill will come to final vote.

—U.S. Supreme Court rules in *United States v. Windsor* that the Defense of Marriage Act (DOMA) is unconstitutional, which President Bill Clinton had signed into law in 1996. The Court found the act to be in violation of the due process clause of the Fifth Amendment.

—IRS announces that same-sex couples who are legally married will be treated exactly the same as opposite-sex couples regardless of the state in which they reside. The action was taken by the Obama administration to fully comply with the Supreme Court decision invalidating the 1996 Defense of Marriage Act.

State and Local Events

—2013 proves to be a banner year for gay marriage in the United States. Same-sex marriage is approved and weddings begin taking place in 13 states: Maryland (January 1 by voter approval), California (June 28 by judicial decision), Delaware (July 1 by legislative action), Minnesota (August 1 by legislative action; just six months after voters rejected an antigay marriage initiative the legislature passes enabling legislation), Rhode Island (August 1 by legislative action), New Jersey (October 21 by judicial decision), Illinois (November 20 by legislative action), Hawaii (December 2 by legislative action), a few counties of New Mexico (December 19 by judicial action) and Utah (December 2 by judicial action). Also, a number of First People nations approve same-sex marriage: Native American nations of Ceara & Little Traverse Bay Bands of Odawa Indians (Michigan), Pokagon Band of Potawatomi Indians (Michigan), Santa Ysabel Tribe (California), and the Confederated Tribes of the Colville Reservation (Washington).

—Sexual Orientation Change Efforts (SOCE) SB1172, a California bill prohibiting licensed mental health providers from attempting to change the sexual orientation of children and young adults under the age of 18, is to go into effect on January 1. However, religious right activists challenge the law on First Amendment claims and obtain a court-ordered stay. Later that year, the court ruled that the state has the right to establish professional standards and conduct for licensed therapist and reject the challenge. Governor Jerry Brown stated when he signed the law, that "reparative" or "change" therapy was to be consigned to the trash heap of medical quackery since SOCE does not work and only causes harm. New Jersey quickly picked up on the bill and enacted its own version of SB1172. The National Center for Lesbian Rights is coordinating a nationwide effort to enact similar legislation in all states.

—Tennessee debates the "Don't Say Gay" bill that would restrict public school teachers from discussing any sexuality other than heterosexuality in grades K-8. The bill also requires teachers to inform parents if they discover their child is gay or lesbian.

—California passes AB1266, a statue that requires schools to allow transgendered students to participate in "sex-segregated programs, activities, and facilities" based on their own self-perception of gender. Immediately, the National Organization for Marriage and other conservative groups mounted a legal attack on the bill.

—Georgia's Supreme Court upholds state law that bans the solicitation of sodomy. Since its law applies equally to homosexual and heterosexual sodomy, the *Lawrence* (2003) decision does not apply.

2014

International Events

—Same-sex marriage is approved in Scotland and will come into effect later in the year. Both England and Wales approved same-sex marriage in 2013 and how takes effect.

—The gay pride flag flies over the presidential palace in Costa Rica.

—Zakhele Mbhele of the South African Parliament comes out gay, making him the first openly gay black member of any African government.

—Carlos Bruce comes out as the first openly gay member of the Peruvian Congress.

—Giuseppe Chigiotti and Stefano Bucci marry in New York in 2012 and return to Italy which recognizes their overseas same-sex marriage in 2014.

National Events

—President Barack Obama signed an executive order on July 21 banning workplace discrimination based on sexual orientation and gender identity. It forbids discrimination in all federal employees and federal contractors. The order covers approximately 28 million workers and 24,000 companies. The order has two parts: (1) makes it illegal to harass or fire employees based on their perceived or actual sexual orientation or gender identity and (2) explicitly bans discrimination against transgender employees.

—Conner Mertens of Willamette University comes out gay, becoming the first active college football player (kicker) to do so.

—Derrick Gordon comes out gay, thus becoming the first openly gay player at UMass basketball and first openly gay player in college men's basketball.

—Michael Sam comes out gay and is drafted by the St. Louis Rams. He is the first openly gay player in the National Football League.

—David Bucher, U.S. Naval Academy graduate who works at the Pentagon, and his partner, Bruce Moats, are wedded at the Naval Academy Chapel; making it the first same-sex wedding held at the Chapel.

—The U.S. Department of Veterans Affairs bestows survivor benefits to Tracy Dice Johnsons when her wife, Donna Johnson, died from a bombing attack in 2012. This is the first time the agency awarded such benefits to a same-sex war widow.

—U.S. Supreme Court rejects challenge to California's ban on sexual orientation change effort (SOCE) therapy on persons under age 18. Senator Ted Lieu, sponsor of the bill, prided his efforts to stop the psychological abuse of California children by SOCE.

State and Local Events

—Tennessee lists a woman as the "father" on the birth certificate of Emilia Maria Jesty, thereby validating the lesbian couple's legal standing as co-parents.

—Illinois legalizes same-sex marriage.

—The federal courts in a number of states declare same-sex marriage bans unconstitutional. In some states, same-sex marriages begin immediately (Oregon, Pennsylvania). In other states same-sex marriages begin but the decision is appealed and the marriages are put on hold (Indiana, Michigan, Utah, Colorado, Kansas, Wisconsin, and Wyoming). Whereas in other states (Arkansas, Florida, Idaho, Kentucky, Oklahoma, Virginia, Texas), the decision is immediately stayed awaiting legal review. At this time, there are lawsuits pending in federal courts in all states that have not yet approved same-sex marriages. More than likely, the issue of including same-sex couples in legal marriage in all 50 states and territories will be addressed by the U.S. Supreme Court within the next couple of years.

—California elects its first openly lesbian speaker (Toni Atkins) of the Assembly.

—Alabama appeals court rules sodomy laws prohibiting consensual homosexual intercourse unconstitutional.

—Louisiana House votes to keep its unconstitutional sodomy ban in its criminal code under "crimes against nature."

—U.S. District judge Martin Feldman, appointed by President Ronald Reagan in 1983, declares Louisiana's ban on same-sex marriage to be constitutional. His ruling marks him as the only federal judge in the nation to uphold such discriminatory legislation.

—The U.S. 7th Circuit Court of Appeals issues a scathing, unequivocal position declaring same-sex marriage bans in Wisconsin and Indiana unconstitutional.

Further Reading

Blumenfeld, W. J. and D. Raymond, eds. 1993. *Looking at Gay and Lesbian Life,* rev. ed. Boston, MA: Beacon Press.

Duberman, M., M. Vicinus, and G. Chauncey, eds. 1989. *Hidden from History: Reclaiming the Gay and Lesbian Past.* New York: Meridian.

Frontiers Magazine. Year-end reviews for 1995–2001.

The Gay Almanac. 1996. Complied by the National Museum & Archive of Lesbian and Gay History. New York: Berkley Books.

Katz, J. 1976. *Gay American History: Lesbians and Gay Men in the U.S.A.* New York: Thomas Y. Crowell.

Marcus, R. 1990. "Powell Regrets Backing Sodomy Law." *Washington Post*, October 26, A3.

Newton, D. E. 1994. *Gay and Lesbian Rights: A Reference Handbook.* Santa Barbara, CA: ABC-CLIO.

Painter, G. 2001. "The Sensibilities of Our Forefathers: The History of Sodomy Laws in the United States. Available at: http://www.glapn.org/sodomylaws/sensibilities/delaware. htm. Accessed October 28, 2013.

Stewart, C. K. 2001. *Homosexuality and the Law: A Dictionary.* Santa Barbara, CA: ABC-CLIO.

Thompson, M., ed. 1994. *Long Road to Freedom: The Advocate History of the Gay and Lesbian Movement.* New York: St. Martin's Press.

United States v. Windsor, 570 U.S. ___ (2013) (Docket No. 12–307).

PART ONE

People, Events, and Issues

A

Abbott, Steve (1943–1992)

Born in Lincoln, Nebraska, Stephen (Steve) Eugene Abbott was a writer, publishing poetry, essays, and novels. He began his studies at the University of Nebraska but completed only one year before leaving to spend two years in a Benedictine monastery in Missouri. He returned to the University of Nebraska and, after meeting Allen Ginsberg, convinced the poet to do a reading at the university. In the fall of 1968, Abbott was drafted to serve in Vietnam but became a conscientious objector. In 1969, he married Barbara Binder after telling her he was bisexual. They had a daughter, but his wife died in a car accident in 1973. Abbott decided to move with his daughter to San Francisco, and two years later he had become active in the San Francisco poetry scene going by his nickname Steve. He published *Wrecked Hearts* in 1978, which contained both his poetry and comic drawings, and a year later he founded *Poetry Flash*, a monthly magazine about Beat poetry. In 1980 he founded *Soup* magazine, showcasing writers from the West Coast new narrative movement. In 1981, Abbott published another collection of poetry, *Stretching the Agapé Bra*, and organized the Left/Write conference, bringing together writers from various communities. The second half of the 1980s was Abbott's most prolific period: *View Askew: Postmodern Investigation* (1989), a collection of essays, interviews, and criticisms published between 1981 and 1988, but mostly consisting of pieces originally written for the San Francisco *Sentinel* between 1986 and 1988; *Lives of the Poets* (1987); *Skinny Trip to a Far Place* (1988); and his first full novel, *Holy Terror* (1989). These works made him a leading figure of the San Francisco literary scene. Abbott tested HIV positive in 1989 (which he revealed in *View Askew*) and died of AIDS complications three years later. His last novel, *The Lizard Club*, was published posthumously in 1993. His influence extends from and to the likes of Robert Glück, Dennis Cooper, and Kathy Acker.

T. Chandler Haliburton

See also: Duberman, Martin Bauml (1930–). Document: Allen Ginsberg and the Beatniks (1956).

Further Reading

Abbott, Alysia. 2013. *Fairyland: A Memoir of My Father*. New York: W.W. Norton.

Snider, Clifton. 1990. "Simple Truths: *Holy Terror* and *View Askew*." *The Advocate*, January 16, pp. 70–71.

Willkie, Phil. 1984. "Interview with Steve Abbott." *James White Review*, Summer, p. 11.

ACT UP (AIDS Coalition to Unleash Power)

ACT UP, a radical theatrical group of AIDS activists, first met in March 1987 in New York City. Their initial meeting came only a few days after Larry Kramer, a guest speaker at the Gay and Lesbian Community Center in New York City, gave a rousing speech deploring the growing number of deaths from AIDS (there were 35,000 in the United States at that point). Kramer blamed the government for neglecting the issue, as well as the pharmaceutical companies for acting as profiteers in the AIDS crisis. Days later, as many as 300 like-minded men and women met to establish a new organization, the AIDS Coalition to Unleash Power, or ACT UP. The group was mostly composed of "PWAs" (persons with AIDS) but was also supported by gay men without HIV, lesbian feminists, and heterosexual activists. It is important to note, however, that the formation of ACT UP was in the making long before Kramer gave his emotional speech. Members of GLAAD (Gay and Lesbian Alliance Against Defamation), the Gay Activist Alliance, The Gay Men's Health Crisis, and the members of the Advisory Committee of People Living with AIDS/ARC (AIDS-related complex) were all highly instrumental in bringing the critical social, cultural, political, and health issues regarding the AIDS crisis to the fore.

Early on, the group focused chiefly on pressuring the government and pharmaceutical companies for the early release of experimental drugs treating AIDS. Quickly, ACT UP members realized that it was not simply gaining access to new drugs that was important, but also making them more affordable for people living with the disease. The organization's first

political protest action was spawned in part by an announcement by Burroughs Wellcome, the makers of AZT (the only drug available to treat AIDS at that point in time), that the price for this medicine would cost a daunting $10,000 per year. On March 24, 1987, more than 250 people marched on Wall Street to demand speedy government approval for AIDS drugs as well as to demand reasonably priced AZT. Seventeen demonstrators were arrested for blocking traffic at the intersection of Broadway and Wall Street. They were charged with disorderly conduct and later released. Additional early protests included an effort to shut down the FDA (Food and Drug Administration) on October 11, 1988. At the FDA headquarters located in Rockville, Maryland, more than 1,000 activists staged "die-ins," lying down on the street and near the entrance to the FDA, holding cardboard tombstones with

American author, AIDS campaigner, and gay rights activist Larry Kramer in 1987. Kramer founded ACT UP and the Gay Men's Health Crisis group. (New York Times Co./Getty Images)

epitaphs such as "I Got the Placebo" or "I Died for the Sins of the FDA." More than 150 protestors were arrested, and the "demo" (ACT UP argot for "demonstration") received international attention.

The central tenets of ACT UP include disseminating information to persons living with AIDS regarding the newest medical studies and treatment options, challenging anybody deemed responsible for blocking AIDS treatment and prevention, and confronting discriminatory practices in the workplace or housing. In its literature, ACT UP made clear that it supports "direct action" or civil disobedience, in order to accomplish their goals. Holding regular weekly or biweekly meetings, ACT UP's ad hoc organization was shaped by democratic principles. Decisions about protests, political "zaps," and clarifying how best to articulate their cause were always made by consensus. Additionally, all ACT UP service positions were to be voluntary.

Although ACT UP's theatrical tactics were criticized by most, including many in the larger LGBTQ community, there is little doubt that the group challenged what may be called the assimilationist politics of the greater gay and lesbian community. In fact, less radical gay and lesbian organizations often argued that ACT UP undermined its important work toward liberation. But ACT UP was not interested in making a good impression. Because many of its members were sick and dying, ACT UP often claimed that it had little time for social niceties. Indeed, the ACT UP slogan, "Silence = Death," was taken quite literally by its members.

Between 1987 and 1995, ACT UP chapters emerged throughout the United States and abroad, and with its burgeoning membership came political clout. After the Wall Street protest and several other political actions regarding alleged price gouging by pharmaceutical companies, businesses like Burroughs Wellcome lowered the price of AIDS medicine. ACT UP took a nonpartisan approach to activism, equally challenging both Democratic and Republican politicians who did not actively engage in AIDS policy reform. As a result, local, state, and national officials, regardless of political affiliation, were often pressured to create AIDS task forces. These emergent AIDS organizations were often populated not only by health care administrators and politicians but also included persons living with AIDS.

While there is no way to concretely measure the political gains for persons living with AIDS (as they were then called) during ACT UP's early years, its theatrical protest tactics helped to shape future coalitions. Not only did emergent groups like Queer Nation use ACT UP members' street theater tactics to celebrate queer visibility, but also conservative liberation groups, such as the Human Rights Campaign Fund, may have shaped their image, at least in part, as a rejection of ACT UP's "in your face" rhetoric.

Although ACT UP still holds regular meetings and maintains an active website as well as an archive, by the mid-1990s, its confrontational tactics had stretched relations with the greater queer community almost to the breaking point. Critics of ACT UP claimed that the coalition was doing more harm than good and was, in fact, damaging the tenuous relationship between the queer and straight communities. A couple of political actions gone awry only deepened the rift between the "radical" members of ACT UP and the more moderate gays and lesbians. Additionally, great strides were made in drug policy and AIDS treatment, which offered ACT UP the opportunity to pursue other issues, but unsureness about exactly which concerns should remain at the center of the movement may have led to its dwindling support base.

Lorna Wheeler

See also: Activists; AIDS History Project; Historical Overview of Gay Rights and Issues: From the 1980s to the Present; Kramer, Larry (1935–2008).

Further Reading

ACT UP website. Available at: http://www.actupny.org/.

Miller, Neil. 2006. *Out of the Past: Gay and Lesbian History from 1869 to the Present*. New York: Advocate Books/Alyson Press.

Moore, Patrick. 2004. *Beyond Shame: Reclaiming the Abandoned History of Radical Gay Sexuality*. Boston: Beacon Press.

New York City Library's ACT UP archive. Available at http://www.actupny.org/documents/nyplPR.html.

Activists

Public activists are people who take on a cause and promote it in the public realm, through meetings, demonstrations, and local or national media. American society has always had its share of public activists: antislavery advocates, suffragettes, union organizers, pacifists, and so on. The gay movement also has had many public advocates, starting in the 1950s when Harry Hay, a member of the Communist Party in Los Angeles, started the first gay organization. The group called itself the Mattachine Society after a medieval clown who, in the guise of being a fool, could tell the truth. A few years later, the first lesbian organization, Daughters of Bilitis, was started. The name came from a poem, "Song of Bilitis," by Pierre Louys, in which he describes a group of lesbians living on a Greek Island with the world's most famous Greek lesbian poet, Sappho.

In the 1960s, individuals such as Harry Hay and his lifelong partner John Burnside; Washington, D.C. activist Frank Kameny; Cuban-born Philadelphian Ada Bello; D.C. activist Jack Nichols; New Yorkers Randy Wicker, Lilli Vincenz, and Rev. Robert W. Wood; Philadelphia couple Barbara Gittings and Kay Lahusen (then known as Kay Tobin); Philadelphia activist Clark Polak; and San Francisco couple Del Martin and Phyllis Lyon braved tremendous prejudice and intolerance to fight for basic civil rights for America's homosexual citizens. They did radio shows

One of the founders of the gay rights movement, Harry Hay, left, brushes the cheek of his partner John Burnside with his hand on July 19, 2002, at their home in San Francisco. Hay, a pioneering activist in the gay rights movement, died at 90. He devoted his life to progressive politics and in 1950 founded the secret network of support groups for gays known as the Mattachine Society. (AP Photo/Ben Margot)

and newspaper interviews. They published their own newsletters and magazines, among them *One, Drum,* and *The Ladder*. They held public meetings where topics of interest to gays were discussed and speakers (usually straight psychiatrists) were featured. One of their main goals was to educate the general public about homosexuality and demonstrate that America's gays were well-adjusted individuals. The only regular demonstration they organized was on July 4 of each year from 1965 to 1969: wearing proper clothing (men in suits and ties, women in dresses and heels), they picketed outside Independence Hall in Philadelphia carrying neatly printed signs that asked for acceptance of gays. While conservative by later standards, those pickets were considered radical in their day.

The role of gay public activists changed dramatically after the Stonewall Riots in New York's Greenwich Village in June 1969. Following three days of unrest after a popular gay bar was raided by police (as was the usual custom in those days), thousands of militant activists all over the country emerged from their closets to become part of a visible LGBTQ community. Though Stonewall is generally considered the beginning of the American queer resistance, there were other incidents. In August 1966 in San Francisco, transgenders and male hustlers started a scuffle after a police officer tried to arrest a drag queen in Compton's Cafeteria in the heart of the city's Tenderloin District, where many queens lived. What ensued was similar to what happened at Stonewall: transgenders fought back in anger against the police abuse they regularly endured. The night after the "Compton Cafeteria Riot," queens picketed the cafeteria. Many were members of a group of radical queer youth

Two hundred and fifty members of the Harvey Milk Gay Democratic Club from San Francisco parade down Market Street during the 1979 Gay Freedom Day Parade and Celebration in San Francisco on June 25, 1979. The parade celebrated the 10th anniversary of the gay rights movement. (AP Photo/Sakuma)

called Vanguard, which had been organized by the liberal Glide Memorial Church a block away.

Following the Stonewall Riots, the first Gay Liberation Front (GLF) formed in New York, then in Philadelphia, Boston, Chicago, Iowa City, Buffalo, Boulder, Kansas City, and many other places. Chapters eventually spread overseas to London and Paris. In New York City, many public activists emerged from those early meetings: Martha Shelley, Karla Jay, Arthur Evans, Arthur Bell, Vito Russo, Jim Owles, Bruce Voeller, Marty Robinson, Mark Segal, and Morty Manford, among them. Manford's parents, Jeanne and Jules, formed the first Parents, Families, and Friends of Lesbians and Gays (PFLAG). In Philadelphia, Kiyoshi Kuromiya called together the first gathering of

GLF in the City of Brotherly Love. A longtime peace activist, Kuromiya had been born in a Japanese detention camp in Wyoming in 1943. At Temple University, student Tom Ashe registered a GLF chapter with the administration and managed to gain official recognition. It was one of the first gay groups to be recognized on a college campus. In the Midwest, GLF and other organizations came together to sponsor an annual Midwest Gay Pride Conference in 1974 to 1976. Among those who organized it were Ames, Iowa activists Dennis Brumm, Joe Franko, and Allen Bell.

Those early 1970s activists, many of whom were 20-something students, took their lead from activists in other social justice movements, particularly the civil rights, antiwar, and women's struggles. Unlike

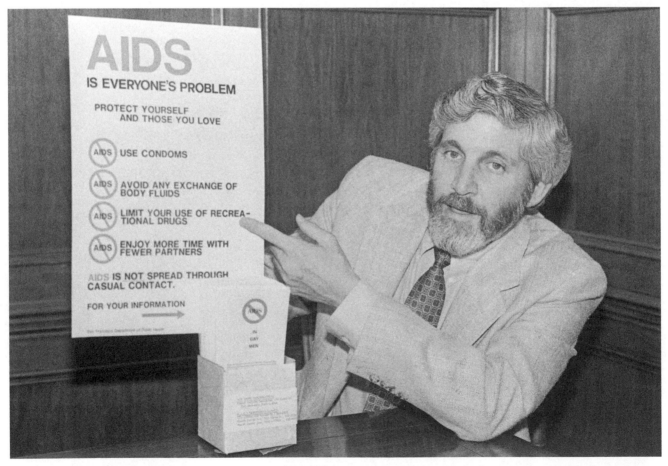

Dr. Mervyn F. Silverman, director of health for the city and county of San Francisco, displays a poster and leaflets meant to educate people to the health risks posed by Acquired Immune Deficiency Syndrome or AIDS. The disease was found in epidemic proportions among gay men in San Francisco in the 1980s. (Bettmann/Corbis)

the previous generation of activists who had often used fake names and were reluctant to reveal their identities in public, the new generation of activists were not afraid to use their own names and show their faces in the media.

Many of those activists had been involved in other social justice movements or were part of the counter-culture (including the famed Summer of Love) prior to coming out. Some had traveled south during the 1960s as part of the civil rights movement's Freedom Rides. Some had been mobilizing on campuses against the war in Vietnam, the draft, and ROTC (Reserve Officers Training Corps). Gay men such as Simeon Meadows White and Frank (Assunta) Femia were arrested and spent time in federal prison for refusing to serve in the military. Femia came out in prison and said that he was treated better there than in the South Philadelphia neighborhood where he grew up as an effeminate boy. As a 16-year-old black teen in Kingston, North Carolina, White organized sit-ins at lunch counters to protest segregation. He was denounced by then-radio host Jesse Helms, who went on to become a U.S. senator. White was a lifelong member of the American Friends Service Committee (AFSC), as were many other antiwar and social justice queers who came out into the movement in the early 1970s, George Lakey, Kay Whitlock, and Russell Silkey, among them. In Philadelphia, the national office of AFSC charged activists $15 a month for a space in an old storefront in an industrial part of town. From there, activists operated the first queer community center. Included in the services offered were a hotline, a counseling program, and a weekly gay male and a separate lesbian coffeehouse.

In order to counter the negative image of queers in the media and to get information out to other LGBTQ folks, the early gay liberation movement put out its own publications. They were much more radical than earlier homophile movement magazines. The new militant publications included *The Gay Alternative, Wicca, Amazon Quarterly, Hera, Off Our Backs, Lesbian Tide, Fag Rag, Big Mama Rag*, and *Gay Sunshine*. Philadelphia's *Gay Alternative* was founded by Jeffrey Escoffier and Matthew Grande, two gay men

Playwright, novelist, and journalist Larry Kramer poses at his home in New York's Greenwich Village in 1989. Kramer, who lost his lover to AIDS in 1984 and was himself infected with the virus, founded and is one of the principal voices in the AIDS Coalition to Unleash Power, or ACT UP. (AP Photo)

who also helped establish the local chapter of Gay Activists Alliance. Philadelphia's lesbian/feminist *Wicca* was penned each month by a collective of lesbians, among them Pat Hill. Boston's *Fag Rag* was edited by Charlie Shively, a professor of American Studies at the University of Massachusetts, Boston. San Francisco's *Gay Sunshine* was the work of writer Winston Leyland. Both *Fag Rag* and *Gay Sunshine* published books as well. With its literary bent, *Gay Sunshine* featured interviews with leading gay or bisexual writers of the day, such as Gore Vidal, Jean Genet, William Seward Burroughs, Tennessee Williams, and Allen Ginsberg. *Fag Rag*, meanwhile, took a more philosophical bent, with articles on topics such as gay sex "as an act of revolution." Lesbians of color had their own publishing ventures, including the best-known Kitchen Table: Women of Color Press, founded in 1980 by African American activist and writer Barbara Smith and internationally known lesbian poet Audre Lorde. Boston's *Gay Community News* was, for many years starting in 1974, the movement's radical gay newspaper, bringing together some of the leading writers of new gay Left: Eric Rofes, Cindy Patton, Scott Tucker, Daniel Tsang, Michael Bronski, Barbara Smith, and others. It stopped publishing in the early 1990s.

Activists also started bookstores, the first being in New York's Greenwich Village: Oscar Wilde Bookstore, founded by Craig Rockwell. In Philadelphia, Giovanni's Room was set up by three activists who were heavily involved in local gay politics: Tom Wilson Weinberg, Dan Sherbo, and Bernie Boyle. In Washington, D.C., it was Deacon McCubbin who got Lambda Rising going. In 1979, Canadian gay activist and bookseller Jearld Moldenhauer opened his second bookstore, Glad Day Books, in Boston. Lesbian bookstores also opened, including Alexandria Books in Philadelphia and Mama Bears in Oakland.

But the heart of this new gay liberation movement was, of course, the activism. That political organizing spread from the meeting rooms of the first post-Stonewall groups to every leftist happening in the early 1970s. At the Black Panthers Revolutionary People's Constitutional Convention, held at Temple University in Philadelphia on September 5, 1970, black, white, and Puerto Rican gay men conducted a workshop on gay rights. Hundreds of gays attended, including Ortez Alderson, a black gay man who helped mobilize the queer presence. Many Philadelphia GLFers of course were in attendance, including Kiyoshi Kuromiya, Basil O'Brien (aka Sweet Basil Razzle Dazzle), Dijon, and Ray Henry. The gay contingent was welcomed by a letter from then-Panthers chair Huey Newton, which called for support of the gay and women's liberation movements.

Post-Stonewall activists marched with Chicano migrant workers from the grape fields in California and backed their call for a farm workers' union, thus making a lifelong friend of Chicano leader Cesar Chavez. Many, including the city's first out supervisor Harvey Milk, stood with the low-income residents of the I-Hotel in San Francisco when that historic residence for Filipino war veterans was being demolished. Queer activists also spoke out in favor of women's rights and joined their sisters on many picket lines. Though initially out lesbians faced homophobia within the feminist movement, the "Lavender Menace," as dykes called themselves, soon became an accepted ally. "Lavender Menace" members included Rita Mae Brown, Lois Hart, Ellen Shumsky, Cynthia Funk, March Hoffman, and Barbara Love.

The new public activists soon began pushing hard for their own issues, including passage of gay rights bills, usually in the form of amendments to existing city human rights laws. In New York and Philadelphia, for example, gay rights bills were introduced into city council in the early 1970s, spearheaded by the successor to the GLF, the Gay Activist Alliance (GAA). The split-off occurred along ideological lines: GLF continued to work on various leftist causes; GAA dedicated itself to one issue: gay rights. Eventually, though, GAA expanded its scope. Many chapters, for instance, supported the Black Panthers and went on record against the Vietnam War.

Though gay rights bills initially went down in defeat, they eventually passed and became law in both New York and Philadelphia. In Dade County, Florida, in 1977, a former runner-up for Miss America, Anita Bryant, led a successful crusade against a gay rights bill pushed by two Dade County gay activists, Bob Kunst and Dr. Alan Rockway. The legislation passed. Because Bryant was spokeswoman for Florida orange juice, a national boycott against orange juice was organized and Bryant soon lost her job. Bisexual Rod McKuen, then the most popular poet in America, came out of the closet to denounce Bryant. Following Bryant's attack on the gay rights movement, ultraconservative California state legislator John Briggs placed on the ballot an amendment to ban gays from being schoolteachers. Activists mobilized throughout the state and managed to defeat it with a huge margin. It was the young movement's first show of political strength.

In San Francisco, a working-class Irish, Italian, and Latino neighborhood called Eureka Valley became transformed into a new gay ghetto, the Castro, with a bustling gay movement. Sylvester, a member of a group of gender benders called the Cockettes, soon became the Castro's enduring disco diva. African American GLFer Blackberri was a familiar face, singing folk songs at local venues. A school teacher, Tom Ammiano became school board president. He had come out while teaching in his Northern New Jersey hometown. Harvey Milk ran for office three times before becoming the city's first out gay supervisor. He was murdered a year later by former supervisor Dan White. Activist Harry Britt was appointed to replace Milk on the board, as per the assassinated leader's wish. Though Milk was the first out gay man elected to office in San Francisco, drag performer José Sarria had attempted to win that same office in 1961 and got an amazing 6,000 votes citywide.

As part of their modus operandi, activists conducted "zaps," unannounced actions against individuals or institutions that they felt were antigay. Sometimes those zaps took the form of sit-ins in offices or even disruptions of TV newscasts or conferences. When an offensive article was published in *The Philadelphia Inquirer*'s Sunday magazine, for instance, about 25 activists invaded the office of the editor and demanded more balanced coverage. The same thing happened in New York after a *Harper's Magazine* piece that gays found objectionable. When CBS News with Walter Cronkite refused to cover the gay liberation movement, Philadelphia gay activists got into the studio one night and Mark Segal walked onto the set with a banner, blacking out the news for about 30 seconds.

As could be expected, ideological differences did not take long to cause splits in the early movement. One major rift in the early 1970s involved transgenders, who felt the movement did not take their issues seriously. Cei Bell and Tommi Avicolli-Mecca formed Radicalqueens in Philadelphia. Sylvia Rivera and Marsha Johnson started Street Transvestite Action Revolutionaries (STAR) in New York. Those were among the first groups to call for inclusion of transgender issues within the gay rights movement. Iowa GLFer Ken Bunch (Sister Vicious Power Hungry Bitch) moved to San Francisco in the late 1970s and helped jump-start the Sisters of Perpetual Indulgence with fellow Iowa activist, Fred Brungard. A group of gay male nuns that mocked the Roman Catholic Church while mobilizing the community around queer issues, the Sisters were always controversial. At one point, Sister Boom Boom (Jack Fertig) ran against San Francisco mayor Dianne Feinstein and garnered some 23,000 votes. His campaign featured himself in nun garb riding on a broom like the Wicked Witch of the West. The slogan was also right out of *The Wizard of Oz:* "Surrender Dianne."

Turned off by sexism within gay groups, lesbians formed their own organizations. Lesbian Feminist Liberation in New York was a split-off of the GLF, founded by Jean O'Leary and others. In Philadelphia, Dyketactics emerged in the mid-1970s as the feminist alternative to the Gay Activist Alliance. It operated as a collective and took separatism seriously, not even allowing men into their households to read the gas meter. The collective included Cherrie Cohen, Paola Bacchetta, Julie Blackwomon, Kathy Fire, and Barbara Ruth. Cohen is the daughter of one of Philadelphia's oldest progressive council members, David Cohen, a prime mover of the city's gay rights bill. Blackwomon and Ruth were both well-known lesbian poets. Women also broke ground in bringing lesbian music to the forefront of the movement. Formed in Washington, D.C., in 1973, Olivia Records, which later moved to Los Angeles and then Oakland, presented lesbian music to the masses of women coming out. Meg Christian and Cris Williamson became the top sellers of the new label.

Various organizations for people of color formed, starting in the 1970s. The National Coalition of Black Lesbians and Gay Men was organized by Billy Jones of Washington, D.C., and Louie Hughes of Baltimore. Its first director was Gil Gerard. Board members included Darlene Garner, now a minister with the Metropolitan Community Church (MCC). Latino and Asian groups also formed. In San Francisco, Asian activists picketed a gay bar in the Castro that discriminated against Asians. Blacks held a similar protest against another bar in the Castro. In Philadelphia and New York as well, pickets appeared outside of gay bars that discriminated against women and blacks. By the end of the 1970s a group, Black and White Men Together, had formed to promote racial harmony within the gay male community. Its founder was San Francisco activist Michael J. Smith.

On the national level, old guard activists such as Barbara Gittings and Frank Kameny joined up with the newer public activists to successfully convince the American Psychiatric Association to reclassify homosexuality from a disease to a normal aspect of human sexuality. Air Force Sgt. Leonard Matlovich, a race relations specialist, came out in the military and was ousted. His famous quote, which appears on his gravestone, is: "When I was in the military, they gave me a medal for killing two men and a discharge for loving one." His case made the argument for gays in the military, though some activists felt that the military was problematic even if it were to accept queers.

Bruce Voeller of the Gay Activists Alliance New York helped establish the first national grassroots organization, the National Gay and Lesbian Task Force, to lobby for LGBTQ interests. Serving in various positions from 1986 to 2000, Urvashi Vaid gave the organization a more radical image. Other activists became involved in the Democratic Party. Black gay activist Mel Boozer spoke on gay rights at the 1980 Democratic National Convention. In 1979, activists organized the first-ever national march in Washington, D.C. Two others have followed, in 1987 and 1993.

The 1980s were dominated by activism around AIDS (Acquired Immune Deficiency Syndrome). The first cases were reported within the San Francisco gay male community in 1981. The indifference with which America treated the disease spawned a new breed of public activists who challenged the medical and pharmaceutical establishments like no other institution had ever been challenged. ACT UP (AIDS Coalition to Unleash Power) became the standard bearer of the new militancy. Under the banner of "Silence = Death," group members invaded offices, marched in the streets, and made demands of health departments,

the Centers for Disease Control and Prevention, even churches. They committed acts of civil disobedience and went to jail in great numbers. Their tireless mobilizing created a more comprehensive and compassionate response on the part of government and the medical establishment alike.

Randy Shilts, a reporter at *The San Francisco Chronicle*, wrote the story of the beginnings of the epidemic in *And the Band Played On*. Graffiti artist Keith Haring used his sudden fame to raise public awareness about AIDS. Playwright Larry Kramer staged *The Normal Heart*; Tony Kushner his *Angels in America*. Both works took critical looks at how the nation treated people with AIDS. In the end, it was only after closeted actor Rock Hudson and flamboyant entertainer Liberace came down with the disease that Americans began to show concern.

Also in the 1980s, the Boy Scouts of America was taken to task by Tim Curran for its antigay policy after he was ousted from a leadership position for being gay. Other Scouts were purged, including 16-year-olds Patrick Renner and Chris Strobel. Eventually school districts in San Francisco and other places prohibited the Scouts from using school space. Anti-queer violence made national headlines for the first time in 1984 after a Bangor, Maine, gay man, Charlie Howard, was thrown to his death into a river by three youths.

The 1990s saw the election of Bill Clinton, a president who promised to rid the military of its antigay policy. His unwillingness to sign an executive order outlawing discrimination, however, resulted in "Don't Ask Don't Tell," a policy that says the military won't ask someone's orientation and that person can't reveal it under penalty of being ousted. The decade also saw the advent of successful activist artists, among them: (Ron) Romanovsky and (Paul) Phillips, a nationally known folk-rock duo from San Francisco; Avalanche, a Philadelphia-based multiracial queer performance troupe; and the a cappella group the Flirtations (Michael Callan, Aurelio Font, Elliot Pilshaw, Jon Arterton, Cliff Townsend, and later Jimmy Rutland) who appeared in the film *Philadelphia*. Queer comedians emerged as well: Lea Delaria, Marga Gomez, and Kate Clinton, to name a few. Los Angeles ACT

UP member and performance artist Tim Miller made waves wherever he went with his activist-inspired theater pieces.

As the queer community entered the new millennium, same-sex marriage became a pet cause for many activists. At San Francisco City Hall in February 2004, Mayor Gavin Newsom authorized the marrying of queer couples until a court injunction put an end to it. Many notables joined the thousands exchanging vows. They included couples Del Martin and Phyllis Lyon, and Rosie O'Donnell and Kelli Carpenter. Also in San Francisco, the ugly issue of racism at a gay bar in the Castro resulted in a months-long picket line outside the bar on Saturday nights until a settlement was reached between complainants and the owner. In the queer community, as well as the nation at large, the public activist has become a household word.

Tommi Avicolli-Mecca

See also: ACT UP (AIDS Coalition to Unleash Power); Brown, Rita Mae (1944–); Daughters of Bilitis; D'Emilio, John (1948–); Faderman, Lillian (1940–); Gittings, Barbara (1932–2007); Historical Overview of Gay Rights and Issues: From Pre-Columbian Times to the 1970s; Historical Overview of Gay Rights and Issues: From the 1980s to the Present; Kameny, Franklin (1925–2011); Kramer, Larry (1935–2008); Lyon, Phyllis (1924–); Martin, Del (1921–2008); Mattachine Society; Milk, Harvey (1930–1978); National Gay and Lesbian Task Force; Same-Sex Marriage in the United States; Stonewall Riot.

Further Reading

D'Emilio, John. 1983. *Sexual Politics, Sexual Communities: The Making of a Homosexual Minority in the United States, 1940–1970*. Chicago: University of Chicago Press.

Faderman, Lillian. 1992. *Odd Girls and Twilight Lovers: A History of Lesbian Life in Twentieth-Century America*. New York: Penguin.

Gallo, Marcia M. 2006. *Different Daughters: A History of the Daughters of Bilitis and the Rise of the Lesbian Rights Movement*. New York: Carroll and Graf.

Stein, Marc. 2004. *City of Brotherly and Sisterly Love: Lesbian and Gay Philadelphia, 1945–1972*. Philadelphia: Temple University Press.

Teal, Donn. 1995. *Gay Militants*. New York: St. Martin's Press.

Affirmative Action

Affirmative action programs are designed to overcome the effects of past discrimination in the United States by allocating jobs, education, and other resources to members of historically stigmatized groups. The term *affirmative action* was first used by President John F. Kennedy when issuing Executive Order 10925 in 1961, which created the Committee on Equal Employment Opportunity. Later, President Lyndon Johnson signed into law the Civil Rights Act of 1964, which included provisions for affirmative action programs that were enforced through Executive Order 11246 in 1965.

President John F. Kennedy in 1961. (Library of Congress, Prints & Photographs Division)

Attorney General Robert F. Kennedy (right), using a hand amplifier and standing on a makeshift platform, addresses civil rights demonstrators in front of the Justice Department. Kennedy denied that there had been job discrimination at the Justice Department. (Bettmann/Corbis)

The Civil Rights Act provided protections for a few categories of people based on race, color, religion, sex, and national origin. These are categorized as "suspect class" for the purpose of strict court scrutiny. Affirmative Action measures are used to prevent discrimination against applicants for employment, discrimination against classes of employees, and even college admissions criteria. The next 30 years of affirmative action were tumultuous, with courts first approving, then disapproving the use of quotas, set-asides, and other techniques.

A backlash against affirmative action occurred from what some characterized as "angry white men." Some people claimed reverse discrimination, and, in *Regents of the University of California v. Bakke*, the

U.S. Supreme Court declared strict racial quotas unconstitutional, while at the same time supporting the concept of affirmative action. Eventually, conservative political forces were able to influence voters in the states of California and Washington to pass laws to abolish affirmative action in 1996.

These same conservative groups often attempt to block antidiscrimination statutes that protect lesbians and gay men. They claim that such legal protections are the first step toward affirmative action based upon sexual orientation. They further claim that affirmative action is the ultimate goal of gay activists. However, the claim is false because not one of the major national lesbian and gay organizations, college LGBT resource centers, local lesbian and gay community services centers, or professionally recognized academics on lesbian and gay culture advocates for affirmative action based upon sexual orientation.

Chuck Stewart

See also: Antidiscrimination Statutes; Federal Employment Nondiscrimination Order.

Further Reading

Anderson, Elizabeth S., John Rawls, and Arthur F. Thurnau. (2008, July). *Race, Gender, and Affirmative Action.* Ann Arbor: University of Michigan.

Anderson, Terry. 2004. *The Pursuit of Fairness: A History of Affirmative Action.* New York: Oxford University Press, pp. 39–40.

Douthat, Ross. June 15, 2009. *Affirmative Action. The New York Times.*

Executive Order 10925. 1961. *Establishing the President's Committee on Equal Employment Opportunity.*

Executive Order 11246. 1965. Overview. The Executive Order 11246 (E.O 11246) prohibits federal contractors and subcontractors and federally assisted construction contractors and subcontractors that generally have contracts that exceed $10,000 from discriminating in employment decisions on the basis of race, color, religion, sex, or national origin. It also requires covered contractors to take affirmative action to ensure that equal opportunity is provided in all aspects of their employment.

Regents of the University of California v. Bakke, 438 U.S. 265 (1978).

African Americans and LGBTQ Issues

African American gays have long walked a fine line between the two cultures in which they belong. While they are part of the black community as well as the gay and lesbian community, the tension felt between both groups has been palpable for many years. However, the tide has turned somewhat in the past few years as black gays in the United States have recently seen more acceptance from both groups. Yet, it is quite apparent more inroads are needed. Keith Boykin, well-known black gay activist who was a former president Clinton aid and former executive director of the National

Black Gay and Lesbian Leadership forum, talks about the unique dilemma faced by gay black men and women in his book, *One More River to Cross: Black and Gay in America* (1996). "Unable to determine my appropriate role in my biological family, I began to look for comfort in some alternative families. I looked to the gay community, the black community, and then to the gay black community for support. Independently, the first two groups could not fully accept me. I found racism and racial ignorance in the white gay community, and homophobia and heterosexism in the black community. Only in the black gay community did I find a group with which I felt at home" (p. 25).

Boykin's comments allude to the long-held belief that the black community is more homophobic than the white community. One area that greatly affects blacks' views on homosexuality is the community's strong adherence to religious traditions and the belief that homosexuality is against God's will. Horace Griffin in his book, *Their Own Receive Them Not: African American Lesbians and Gays in Black Churches* (2006), discusses this issue and theorizes that the higher percentage of African Americans affiliated with conservative Baptist, Methodist, and Pentecostal denominations, typically masculine and heteronormative, explains why many African American heterosexuals are more opposed to gays than whites or other groups. In recent years, many black religious leaders have reached out to the gay community and advocated for black churches to embrace their black gay and lesbian congregants. Black activist Reverend Al Sharpton is one vocal advocate, along with the Reverend Jesse Jackson, who was one of the first black civil rights leaders to openly embrace gay rights by welcoming homosexuals into his Rainbow Coalition. Although otherwise known for his antigay remarks, Nation of Islam leader Louis Farrakhan during the 2005 Million Man March invited black lesbians and gays to attend.

However, when looking at the behaviors and beliefs of those in the black community, mixed with numerous national surveys on gay issues, the results are still ambiguous. In 1993, CNN, *USA Today,* and the Gallup Poll conducted a public opinion survey about President

Trevor Project executive director Charles Robbins, left, and Keith Boykin, center, at the Trevor Project: Saving Young Lives New York Summer Gala at Capitale Restaurant in New York City on June 29, 2009. (Jeff Swartz/Retna Ltd./ Corbis)

Clinton's initiative to lift the ban on gays in the military. According to the results, the disapproval rate was 51 percent by whites but only 44 percent by blacks. When asked about other gay issues in the poll, 85 percent of blacks and only 79 percent of whites felt that homosexuals should have equal opportunities in terms of job opportunities. And lastly, on the issue of special rights vs. equal rights for gays, only 38 percent of blacks felt gays were asking for special rights, but 45 percent of whites felt homosexuals wanted special rights.

Some black gay activists have concluded that blacks are in fact no more homophobic than whites, but the issues occur when blacks feel that the gay community, with its white image, tries to take advantage of civil rights laws designed to alleviate discrimination against blacks. This has been a long-running point of contention between the black and gay communities, with some black civil rights leaders feeling that gay activists are trying to piggyback on the civil rights movement by saying it is the same exact struggle. Some black leaders have difficulty with this and are adamant that homosexuality is not the same as being black, because many consider being gay to be a choice, while being black is not. This again makes it difficult for black gay and lesbians, because they can identify with both struggles and they experience the oppression of being members of both groups.

Other evidence that indicates blacks are in fact less homophobic than whites are the actions of the Congressional Black Caucus (CBC). Voting records dating back 15 years reveal the strong support of the CBC for lesbian and gay rights issues, including the support of the efforts to change the gays in the military ban and the gay rights bill during the Clinton administration.

Yet even with such evidence, there is no denying there is a strong component of black intellectuals and public figures, such as Amiri Baraka, Eldridge Cleaver, Nathan Hare, Robert Staples, Haki Madhubuti, politician Alan Keyes, and NFL coach Tony Dungy, who do not support gays in their community. Many of them have theorized that homosexuality is a white disease and, under that rubric, assume black gays and lesbians have no connection to the black community. They also associate homosexuality with the decline of the black community. In her book, *The Isis Papers* (1991), Dr. Frances Cress Welsing argues that descendants of Africa are not predisposed to homosexuality.

There is still much debate over whether African tribes engaged in same-sex acts before European missionaries flooded the country. However, according to many historic accounts from explorers and colonizers, African colonies allowed for varied sexual activity among genders and even accepted those who were considered cross-gendered, especially in the Nubian, Moro, Nyima, Tira, and Otoro tribes. According to former Amnesty International official Cary Alan Johnson, African homosexuals played important spiritual roles in the Zulu, Zande, and Hausa cultures. It is also theorized that some of the practices were carried over

For the 45th Anniversary of the 1965 Civil Rights March from Selma to Montgomery, Alabama, Jesse Jackson and other dignitaries walk across the Edmund Pettus Bridge to re-create the event. (Library of Congress)

during the slave era, as there have been some firsthand accounts of same-sex behaviors. Also, there were numerous cases of black men being raped by their white male slave owners.

But the historical era in which black LGBTQ culture can unquestionably be seen is during the Harlem Renaissance. Occurring from the 1920s until the mid-1930s, the Harlem Renaissance was a historical moment in time created by the large urban migration of blacks fleeing the then broken South to the seemingly job-filled and more tolerant North. This period is known for the creation of numerous political essays, poems, novels, biographies, histories, paintings, sculptures, plays, musicals, dances, and blues and jazz compositions and performances, all by black Americans, which had a great influence on twentieth-century American popular culture and style. Not only were blacks looking for civil rights, but

black gays and lesbians were also looking for more acceptance and for others like them, which created quite the LGBTQ subculture during this time. Many of the leading figures included writers Wallace Thurman, Richard Bruce Nugent, Angelina Weld Grimké, Countee Cullen, Claude McKay, and possibly Langston Hughes; blues singers Bessie Smith, Ma Rainey, Alberta Hunter, Ethel Waters, and Gladys Bentley; and patrons Alain Locke and A'Lelia Walker.

The Depression ended the Renaissance, but black LGBTQ communities did not disappear. Harlem's drag balls became more popular and more explicitly gay during the 1930s. Drag balls were also held in Baltimore, Chicago, New Orleans, and other major cities and attracted large crowds and significant public attention from the 1930s through the 1950s, ultimately receiving coverage in black newspapers and magazines, including *Ebony* and *Jet*. These balls were actually the forerunners of the balls depicted in Jennie Livingston's 1990 documentary *Paris Is Burning*.

But by the 1950s and 1960s, the black community's attention turned to the civil rights movement. Many LGBTQ African Americans participated in the civil rights movement, but they usually could not be open about their sexuality. Bayard Rustin is the perfect example of this. He organized the 1963 March on Washington for Jobs and Freedom and served as a principal adviser to Martin Luther King Jr. However, because Rustin was known to be gay, he was often forced to work behind the scenes and did not receive significant credit at the time for his critical role in the civil rights struggle.

On the other hand, James Baldwin was widely recognized for his involvement in the civil rights movement. His poignant writings, including *The Fire Next Time* (1956), confronted racial issues that were sweeping the country. However, Eldridge Cleaver and other male leaders of the Black Power movement dismissed Baldwin, arguing that by engaging in same-sex sexual relationships, he had been emasculated and corrupted by whites.

Some LGBTQ African Americans were also involved in the gay rights movement during the 1950s and 1960s. But they often did not feel welcome in the predominantly white LGBTQ organizations, which rarely addressed members' racism and which focused exclusively on LGBTQ rights, ignoring the multiple struggles of black LGBTQ people. Feeling the LGBTQ organizations were dominated by whites and that they frequently failed to address the multiple ways in which LGBTQ people of color are oppressed, many LGBTQ African Americans began to organize independent groups in the 1970s.

A national LGBTQ movement began in 1978 with the formation of the National Coalition of Black Gays (later renamed the National Coalition of Black Lesbians and Gays—NCBLG). The organization drew to its ranks and nurtured some of the most significant African American lesbian and gay activists of the post–Stonewall era. NCBLG had chapters nationwide and was at the forefront of black and other people of color organizing for more than 10 years. The coalition greatly increased its membership following the first National Third World Gay and Lesbian Conference, held in conjunction with the First National March on Washington for Lesbian and Gay Rights, in 1979. By the mid-1980s, chapters existed in cities across the country, including groups in Philadelphia, New York, Norfolk, Minneapolis, New Orleans, Atlanta, Chicago, Portland, St. Louis, San Francisco, Washington, D.C., Boston, and Richmond. Unfortunately, many chapters could not sustain themselves and were dissolved by the 1990s. The National Black Lesbian and Gay Leadership Forum, begun in Los Angeles in 1988, briefly became a national voice for LGBTQ African Americans, but it too could not garner enough support to last.

Unfortunately, not feeling welcomed by the larger gay community was and continues to be a common theme among many black gays and lesbians. Historically, black gays and lesbians have been excluded from predominately white nightclubs and excluded from certain gay organizations; if they are included, they often feel their issues are not taken seriously and people of color are rarely in leadership positions. There has also been sexual exploitation of blacks in the gay community, reducing them to a fetish through body objectification, as in Robert Mapplethorpe's "Black Book."

In recent years, perhaps due to the greater acceptance of black gays and lesbians into the black community, more black LGBTQ public figures have been coming out. The most well known are singers RuPaul Charles and Me'Shell NdegéOcello; *Noah Arc*'s Doug Spearman and Darryl Stephens; *Saturday Night Live*'s Danitra Vance; directors and producers Lee Daniels *(Monster's Ball* and *The Butler)*, Paris Barclay *(NYPD Blue)*, and Rodney Evans *(Brother to Brother)*; editors Linda Villarosa *(Essence)*, Emil Wilbekin *(Vibe)* and Andre Leon Talley *(Vogue)*; supermodel runway coach J. Alexander; actress Raven Symone (of the Cosby Show and Disney's *That's So Raven)*; DJ Mister Cee; transgender B. Scott; and now-deceased actor Paul Winfield. Even in the sports world a few black players have had the courage to come out, including NBA former player John Amaechi; Australian snowboarder Belle Brockhoff; MMA fighter Fallon Fox; football star Kevin Grayson; WNBA star Britteny Griner; All-American Michael Sam, the first openly gay player in the NFL; and WNBA player Sheryl Swoopes. In 2013, Paris Barclay became the first openly gay African American president of the Director's Guild of America.

Politics has seen major changes in the last decade. Many more LGBT African American politicians have come out or been appointed to political positions. For example, in 2003, Rodney Oden became the first openly gay black mayor ever elected in an American city when he became mayor of Palm Springs, California, and E. Denise Simmons of Cambridge, Massachusetts, was the first African American lesbian mayor. Simone Bell became the first open lesbian African American elected in 2009 to serve in a U.S. state legislature. Governor Chris Christie nominated Bruce A. Harris to an open seat on the New Jersey Supreme Court in 2012. Had the nomination gone through, Harris would have been the first openly gay African American in that position. In 2014, President Barack Obama nominated Darrin Gayles, openly gay African American Florida circuit court judge, for two different U.S. district courts in Florida. Gayles would be the first openly gay black male on a federal bench (previously openly lesbian Deborah Batts was appointed by President Bill Clinton in 1994 for the District Court of New York and served in that capacity for many years). This represents the second time President Obama has nominated an openly gay African American male to a high court. His previous nominee, William Thomas, was blocked from being confirmed by Florida Republican senator Marco Rubio.

Yet pervasive rumors have been long heard about the sexuality of certain black celebrities, such as the late Michael Jackson, Missy Eliot, MC Lyte, Freddie Jackson, the late Whitney Houston, Queen Latifah, Carl Lewis, Tracy Chapman, Antonio Vargas, and Vin Diesel, but none of them has officially come out and some won't even discuss the issue, saying it is a private matter. Many black gay activists see this silence as a symptom of the denial found in the black community. According to Boykin and other black gay

activists, the black community knows homosexuality exists within their community, but they prefer not to speak about it or deal with the issues openly and honestly. According to Griffin, this has long been a practice within the black church, where gay men are very active in the choirs and musical direction but are not allowed to be open about their sexuality. A few heterosexual blacks have broken this code of silence and supported gay rights. Willie Brown, former mayor of San Francisco, has long been a supporter of gay rights. President Barack Obama, in his book *The Audacity of Hope* (2006), has made his support of gays and lesbians very clear. By 2013, his opinion concerning gay marriage evolved such that he called for full equality for every LGBT citizen in his second inaugural address. He stated, "Our journey is not complete until our gay brothers and sisters are treated like anyone else under the law—for if we are truly created equal, then surely the love we commit to one another must be equal as well" (Obama Inauguration 2013). It was historic to have a sitting U.S. president mention gay rights or the word *gay* in the inaugural address.

Unfortunately, this silence in the black community regarding homosexuality has created another phenomenon that has been linked to the community, which is the act of being "on the down low." This phrase was made popular in J.L. King's book, *On the Down Low*, and supposedly refers to black men, often married, who have sex with men but don't consider themselves gay. However, many black scholars, gay and straight, have suggested how racist this term has become, noting that many closeted gay men and women of all colors engage in secret sexual acts with members of the same sex—yet the phrase the "down low" has been specifically linked to African American men. It has also been conveniently deemed a cause of widespread of AIDS in the black community, which has increased in recent years, particularly among black females. Boykin discusses this in his book *Beyond the Down Low: Sex and Denial in Black America* (2004). "For closeted black gay and bisexual men, the down low is a way to validate their masculinity. For straight black women, the down low is a way to avoid the difficult issues of personal responsibility. For white America, the down low is a way to pathologize black lives. And for the media, the down low is a great way to sell papers" (p. 34).

Finally, another reason the black community has been perceived as being more homophobic than other cultures is because in some ways black popular culture has been in fact the worst offender when it comes to displaying negativity to the gay community. There have been many hip-hop artists who found nothing wrong with making disparaging remarks about gays and lesbians in their songs. Such offenders have been Tone Loc, Snoop Dogg, Chuck D, Ice-T, Ice Cube, Queen Latifah, and Shabba Ranks. Gay and lesbian stereotypes can also be found in some black movies and television shows (if they are even included at all), such as *Waiting to Exhale, In Living Color, Beverly Hills Cop*, and *School Daze*. Black comedians have also been known for telling jokes at the expense of gays and lesbians.

As in other parts of American society, attitudes in the black community have been changing for the better. There have been a few films and shows that have attempted to depict the life of black gays and lesbians in a more authentic, less stereotypical way, such as the work of Marlon Riggs, *Tongues Untied* and *Black Is . . . Black Ain't*; and Patrik-Ian Polk's cable comedy-drama, *Noah's Arc*, which centers around four male friends who are all black and gay.

Another area where black gays and lesbians have been quite prolific in celebrating their lives is in literature. In 1986 Joseph Beam edited *In the Life: A Black Gay Anthology*, the first collection of literature by and about black gay men ever published. The out and proud writers have included Melvin Dixon, Essex Hemphill, and Assotto Saint (Yves Francois Lubin). To date, nine such anthologies have been published and include the older writers as well as new ones, including James Earl Hardy, Brian Keith Johnson, and Tim'm T. West. It has also become quite popular during the twentieth and early twenty-first centuries in the black community to read novels featuring gay men, especially those by E. Lynn Harris, which have become quite popular among straight black women. The gay and lesbian black community has also been

very successful with their annual black pride events. The first Black Lesbian and Gay Pride celebration was organized in Washington, D.C. in 1991. As of 2014, black LGBTQ pride activities are held in more than 30 cities across the United States and in London and Toronto.

Although LGBTQ African Americans continue to experience racism in predominantly white gay organizations and homophobia in ostensibly heterosexual black organizations, some of these groups have begun to acknowledge and take steps to address the multiple oppressions faced by black gays and lesbians. This may lead to black and gay individuals being able to fully celebrate their complete identities within both the cultures in which they belong.

Victor Evans

See also: Allegra, Donna (1953–); Baldwin, James (1924–1987); Beam, Joseph (1954–1988); Buckmire, Ron (1968–); Lorde, Audre (1934–1992).

Further Reading

Baldwin, James. 1985. *The Price of the Ticket*. New York: St. Martin's/Marek.

Boykin, Keith. 2004. *Beyond the Down Low: Sex and Denial in Black America*. New York: Carroll and Graf Publishers.

Boykin, Keith. 1996. *One More River to Cross: Black and Gay in America*. New York: Anchor Books.

Carbado, Devon W. and Donald Weise, eds. 2003. *Time on Two Crosses: The Collected Writings of Bayard Rustin*. San Francisco: Cleis Press.

Davis, A. 1981. *Women, Race and Class*. New York: Random House.

Griffin, H. 2006. *Their Own Receive Them Not: African American Lesbians and Gays in Black Churches*. Cleveland, OH: Pilgrim Press.

Harris, E.L. 2005. *Freedom in This Village: Twenty-Five Years of Black Gay Men's Writing*. New York: Carroll and Graf Publishers.

King, J.L. and K. Hunter. 2004. *On the Down Low: A Journey into the Lives of "Straight" Black Men Who Sleep with Men*. New York: Broadway Books.

Mosley, W. 2006. *Life Out of Context*. New York: Nation Books.

Obama, B. 2006. *The Audacity of Hope.* New York: Crown Publishers.

"Obama Inauguration Speech Makes History with Mention Of Gay Rights Struggle, Stonewall Uprising." (2013, January). *Huffington Post.*

Welsing, Frances Cress. 1991. *The Isis Papers: The Keys to the Colors.* Chicago: Third World Press.

Africa's Gay Punishment Legislation: Involvement from U.S. Christian Factions

Scott Lively, founder and president of Abiding Truth Ministries, in Springfield, Massachusetts, traveled to Uganda, Latvia, and Moldova at the turn of the millennium to warn Christian church members and clergy there about what he says is the impending wave of Western gay rights activists. Lively is an antigay activist who runs a storefront mission and coffee shop (Holy Ground Coffee House) in Springfield, Massachusetts. He is the coauthor of *The Pink Swastika: Homosexuality in the Nazi Party*, which claims Nazism was inspired by homosexual thinking and further claimed the early Nazi Party was populated by many homosexuals (who were later purged from the party by murdering them during the "Night of the Long Knives"). He also publishes a guide sold through Abiding Truth Ministries to parents to protect against what he claims is pro-homosexual indoctrination (*Seven Steps to Recruit-Proof Your Child*).

Many conservative American evangelicals actively proselytized in Uganda in the 2000s. Lively was one of the most active speakers who addressed members of parliament, groups of lawyers, secondary schools, Christian leaders, universities, and at a multiple-day conference, warning Ugandans about the "gay agenda." These efforts made an impact on the country. Frank Mugisha of Sexual Minorities Uganda reported that as a result some citizens seemed to change their views about homosexuality after listening to these American speakers. He claimed that most Ugandans, until recently, had viewed homosexuals as being different but left them alone whereas after the antigay hate speeches, there was a major increase in persecution and violence toward homosexuals.

In 2009, Ugandan legislator David Bahati sponsored an "Anti-Homosexuality Bill" that would have imposed the death sentence for "aggravated homosexuality." Some Africans already held antigay beliefs and considered homosexuality to be unnatural and a remnant of European colonialism. More than half the countries comprising the African continent criminalized homosexuality to varying degrees. The Ugandan Parliament allowed Bahati to submit a private member's bill that divided homosexual behavior into two categories: "the offense of homosexuality" which included same-sex sexual acts and same-sex marriage, and required a life-imprisonment penalty; or "aggravated homosexuality" which included homosexual acts by someone who is infected with HIV, a parent or authority figure, acts committed with a minor, the use of intoxicating substances, and repeat offenders, and required the death penalty. Under Ugandan law, a private member's bill requires substantial financial support from the legislator making the request. It is unknown who is financing this effort.

Homosexuality and the support of homosexuality was already a crime in Uganda but the bill expanded persecution to include the death penalty. The bill came about within a month after an antigay conference was held in which Lively and two other American Christians (Caleb Lee Brundidge—a self-professed ex-gay man who promotes reparative therapy; and Don Schmierer—board member of Exodus International, an organization devoted to "curing" homosexuality through the "power of Jesus Christ") warned Africans about the "threat" faced by African families from radical homosexuals (Gettleman 2010; Rice 2009). Although Ugandan Stephen Langa organized the conference, it was strongly supported by Lively. In Lively's workshops, he asserted that homosexuality was akin to bestiality and child molestation, and that homosexuals were out to recruit African youth.

The basis for the antigay bill was announced at this 2009 conference and recommended parliament to take action. Lively met with several Ugandan legislators including James Buturo, minister of ethics and integrity. By April, the bill was announced and President Yoweri Museveni asserted his tentative

David Bahati, Ugandan Member of Parliament and the proposer of the Controversial antigay bill, in an interview with the Associated Press on April 20, 2011. The Ugandan parliamentarian was behind an anti-homosexual bill that attracted worldwide condemnation, though he said that the most controversial part of the proposed legislation—the death penalty provision—was being dropped from the bill. (AP Photo/Ronald Kabuubi)

support of the bill but thought it was too harsh. The Western world responded vigorously. Citizens; politicians; Christian religious leaders worldwide, including in the United States and in Uganda; and human rights organization in the United States, Europe, and South Africa actively spoke out against the bill for its mistaken claims and cruel and barbaric punishment. Considering these countries are major donors to Uganda, the bill was retracted by the legislature. Speaker of the parliament, Rebecca Kadaga, vowed to pass the bill in 2012. However, President Museveni suggested it would be necessary to cave to international pressure and veto the bill ("Why Uganda's anti-gay legislation is the world's business: View" 2011).

The public outcry influenced Lively and other antigay leaders to backtrack. Lively responded by

saying, "I agree with the general goal but this law is far too harsh. . . . Society should actively discourage all sex outside of marriage and that includes homosexuality. . . . The family is under threat . . . [Gay people] should not be parading around the streets" (Houreld 2009). Don Schmierer expressed his shock at the legislation and explained his only goal was to outline how gay people could repair their brokenness and become heterosexual. He thought the bill was "horrible, absolutely horrible. . . . Some of the nicest people I have ever met are gay people" (Gettleman 2010). Still, the damage was done. A decade of Christian interference led to the extreme legislation. When the bill was announced, a local Ugandan newspaper included articles about how to identify gay people and published the names of suspected homosexuals. Later that year in October, another newspaper named

Giles Muhame, managing editor of the Ugandan publication *Rolling Stone*, holds the latest issue of his newspaper on the streets of Kampala. This issue published the names and photos of 14 men it identified as gay in a country where homosexuality can lead to lengthy jail terms and has even prompted calls for the death sentence. (Marc Hofer/AFP Photo/Getty Images)

Rolling Stone (not affiliated with the American *Rolling Stone*) ran a story featuring the "top" 100 gays and lesbians along with their names, address, and photo. Next to the list was a yellow strip embedded with the words *hang them*. Of course the story created much fear and some people went into hiding or left the country.

On January 26, 2011, David Kato was beaten to death. He was Uganda's most prominent gay activist and had spoken at a conference sponsored by the United Nations concerning Uganda's antigay bill. His photograph and personal information had been published in *Rolling Stone* (Gettleman 2011). The high court ordered *Rolling Stone* to cease publishing the list.

President Museveni formed a commission to evaluate the bill's potential impact on Uganda's economy, culture, and politics. The Legal Affairs Committee recommended dropping the death provisions of the bill with reduced penalty to life in imprisonment. The bill was delayed until 2012 with a promise that it would be passed as a "Christmas gift" to its advocates (BBC News 2012). The bill passed in December 20, 2013, without the death penalty provision.

In 2012, Sexual Minorities Uganda brought suit against Scott Lively for crimes against humanity in a Massachusetts federal court. This is the first use of the Alien Tort Statute regarding sexual orientation discrimination. The statute allows U.S. courts to hear human rights cases brought by foreign nationals for conduct committed by U.S. citizens outside the United States that violate international law. The suit alleges that Lively conspired with political and religious leaders over a 10-year period to create antigay hysteria in Uganda that resulted in the persecution, arrest, torture, and murder of homosexuals and bisexuals in Uganda. The suit was brought to the United States because there is little support in Uganda for upholding international law protecting sexual minorities. Pamela C. Spees, lawyer for the Ugandan group and collaborator with the Center for Constitutional Rights in New York City, said the suit targets Lively's actions to deprive other people of their rights and not his beliefs. The Liberty Counsel, based in Virginia, announced that it would defend Lively and seek to have the suit dismissed.

In August 2013, Senior U.S. District Judge Michael Ponsor denied Lively's motion to dismiss the suit. The 79-page ruling stated that Lively's alleged planning and management of Uganda's repression campaign "are analogous to a terrorist designing and manufacturing a bomb in this country, which he then mails to Uganda with the intent that it explodes there" (Qualters 2013).

Chuck Stewart

See also: Proposition 8 and the Mormon Church; Sexual Orientation Change Efforts.

Further Reading

BBC News. 2012, November 14. "Uganda to Pass Anti-Gay Law as 'Christmas gift.' United Kingdom." *BBC News Africa*. Available at: http://www.bbc.co.uk/news/world-africa-20318436. Accessed November 30, 2013.

Gettleman, Jeffrey. 2010, January 3. "Americans' Role Seen in Uganda Anti-Gay Push." *The New York Times*. Available at: http://www.nytimes.com/2010/01/04/world/africa/04uganda.html?_r=0. Accessed December 1, 2013.

Gettleman, Jeffrey. 2011, January 27. "Ugandan Who Spoke Up for Gays Is Beaten to Death." *The New York Times*. Available at: http://www.nytimes.com/2011/01/28/world/africa/28uganda.html. Accessed December 1, 2013.

Houreld, Katherine. 2009, December 8. "Death Penalty for Gays? Uganda Debates Proposal. "*The Seattle Times*. Available at: http://politics.gaeatimes.com/2009/12/08/uganda-debates-death-penalty-for-gays-in-proposed-law-activists-say-bill-promotes-hatred-5883/. Accessed December 1, 2013.

Qualters, Sheri. 2013, August 18. "U.S. Lawyer-Minister to Face Trial for Uganda Anti-Gay Campaign." *The National Law Journal*. Available at: http://www.law.com/jsp/law/international/LawArticleIntl.jsp?id=1202616011403&slreturn=20131101192246. Accessed December 1, 2013.

Rice, Xan. 2009, November 29. "Uganda Considers Death Sentence for Gay Sex in Bill before Parliament." *The Guardian*. Available at: http://www.theguardian.com/world/2009/nov/29/uganda-death-sentence-gay-sex. Accessed December 1, 2013.

"Why Uganda's Anti-Gay Legislation Is the World's Business: View." *Bloomberg*, October 27, 2011.

AIDS and the Americans with Disabilities Act: *Bragdon v. Abbot* (1998)

Sidney Abbot went to the dental office of Randon Bragdon for an examination. She revealed that she was HIV-positive on the patient registration form. Dr. Bragdon performed a routine examination, determined that she had a cavity, and told her that he would not fill the tooth in his office because of his HIV policy. Rather, filling the tooth should be done in a hospital setting and at her expense. She declined his conditions and filed a complaint under Americans with Disabilities Act (ADA) and the Maine Human Rights Act (MHRA).

Both lower courts determined that Abbot's asymptomatic HIV was a physical impairment and that she was disabled as a matter of law under the ADA. The U.S. Supreme Court used the case-by-case method of analysis—first used in *Ennis v. National Ass'n of Business and Education Radio, Inc.* in 1995 where the Court decided that the plain language of ADA required each case to be analyzed by itself.

The Court decided HIV infection is an "impairment from the moment of infection" (*Bragdon v. Abbot*, 2203–04). Second, the Court agreed that HIV infection "substantially limits . . . [a] major life activit[y]" [42 U.S.C. § 12102(2) (1997)]. The Court noted this position was further supported by the Equal Employment Opportunity Commission (EEOC) regulation for Title

1, which states that a physical or mental impairment is "[a]ny physiological disorder, or condition, . . . affecting any one or more of [a number of listed body systems]" [29 C.F.R. §1630.2 (h)(1) (1997)]. The Court upheld Abbot's claim of discrimination under ADA.

The *Bragdon* decision is exemplary for finding asymptomatic HIV a disability under ADA. However, the Court failed to explicitly state that HIV infection is a disability per se. Although a few lower courts have accepted the argument that HIV infection is a disability per se (*Hoepfl v. Barlow*). Congress stepped in 2008 to clarify the situation and amended the ADA making it easier for people with HIV/AIDS to demonstrate that they are persons with disabilities and are covered under the statute. The ADA Amendments Act of 2008 gives specific guidelines that if an unmedicated HIV/AIDS person's immune system is substantially limited (often defined as a t-cell count under 200), they are, by definition, disabled and covered by all aspects of the ADA.

Chuck Stewart

See also: AIDS and the Americans with Disabilities Act: *Bragdon v. Abbot* (1998); AIDS History Project; Historical Overview of Gay Rights and Issues: From the 1980s to the Present.

Further Reading
"A Culture-Shifting Moment: *Bragdon v. Abbott and HIV Discrimination.*" n.d. GLAD (Gay and Lesbian Advocates and Defenders. Available at: https://www.glad.org/30years/case_apr.html. Accessed March 16, 2014.

AIDS History Project

In 1987, the same year that ACT UP (AIDS Coalition to Unleash Power) began organizing and President Ronald Reagan belatedly began addressing the AIDS epidemic in his public addresses, the AIDS History Project began to take shape in San Francisco, California. It is neither a place nor an organization, but rather a grant-funded collaboration between many groups and people for a specific purpose: to actively collect, catalog, and make available to interested publics the memories, histories, and voices of people who responded to the AIDS epidemic. The National

Historical Publications and Records Commission (NHPRC) has always been a primary sponsor for the AIDS History Project.

It is no coincidence that the AIDS History Project was born of the combined and continuing efforts of historians, archivists, and AIDS activists in San Francisco. While San Francisco is no different from other major cities in the United States in being devastatingly affected by the disease, it had become in the 1970s and 1980s an inviting place for many queers, particularly gay men, who came there from all across the country to experience the flourishing communities growing along Polk Street and in the Castro district. San Francisco differed from other major U.S. cities in its quick, organized, and diverse response to AIDS. At a time when the national political scene either ignored or demonized homosexuality (consider for example, Anita Bryant's "Save the Children" campaign and the financial punishment of queer artists, like Robert Mapplethorpe, Holly Hughes, John Fleck, and Tim Miller by the National Endowment for the Arts), San Francisco witnessed the development of efficacious and collaborative networks of city and state agencies, hospitals, community-based organizations (CBOs), and health care providers. San Francisco's approach to the onset of AIDS, particularly its medical approach, became known as "the San Francisco model" of AIDS care. Since its inception, the primary objective of the AIDS History Project has been to document the activities, organizations, and people that comprised the diverse network of collaboration that was and is the San Francisco model of AIDS care.

In the beginning, the AIDS History Project focused on getting records from local CBOs. Over 50 organizations were surveyed from 1987 to 1995, during which time the NHPRC provided crucial funding. In December 1995, the consecutive series of two-year projects came to completion. Some of the records from these early projects were deposited at the University of California, San Francisco (UCSF), the Gay, Lesbian, Bisexual, Transgender Historical Society (GLBTHS), also in San Francisco, and the San Francisco Department of Public Health AIDS Office. The records from the San Francisco Department of Public Health AIDS Office reside at the San Francisco Public Library.

Onlookers watch as almost 1,500 quilt panels bearing the names of New York area residents who have died of AIDS are unfolded on the Great Lawn in New York's Central Park on June 25, 1988. (AP Photo/Wilbur Funches)

UCSF has a long history with AIDS activism, AIDS care, and HIV prevention. Among its notable organizations are the AIDS Research Institute and the UCSF Center for AIDS Research. The UCSF Library and the Center for Knowledge Management, particularly the Archives and Special Collections unit, have also shown extensive support for AIDS research and AIDS activism, in which the AIDS History Project plays a prominent role. Among the most heavily used archival paper collections at UCSF are the San Francisco AIDS Project, the papers of Dr. Marcus Conant, and the Ward 86 collection donated by Dr. Paul Volberding. Conant is the medical director of the Conant Medical Group, one of the largest private AIDS practices in the United States. Volberding founded and directed one of the earliest AIDS clinics at San Francisco General Hospital (SFGH).

Originally called the San Francisco Gay and Lesbian Historical Society, the GLBTHS is a community-based public history organization founded in 1985 at a time when few other organizations were collecting GLBT material. One of the founding members of GLBTHS, Willie Walker, was also a project archivist for the AIDS History Project at UCSF in the late 1980s and early 1990s. Also a nurse who worked on Ward 5B (now 5A) at SFGH, the so-called AIDS Ward, Walker's dedication to caring for the LGBT community and preserving their histories provides an illustrative example of the collaborative and effective network of organizational efforts that went into the San Francisco model and the AIDS History Project.

Another early AIDS History Project goal was the collection of oral histories from physicians, nurses, and scientists instrumental to the development of the San

Francisco model of AIDS care. Some of these collections can be found in the Archives and Special Collections unit of the UCSF library, the Regional Oral History Office (ROHO) at the University of California, Berkeley (UCB), and in the San Francisco Public Library. This portion of the project was cosponsored by Evelyn and David Lennette (virologists), ROHO at the Bancroft Library, UCB, the Division of the History of Health Sciences, UCSF, and the Center for Knowledge Management.

ROHO's contribution to the AIDS History Project consists of a three-series oral history archive that focuses on the medical impact on the San Francisco AIDS epidemic. The first series included interviews with physicians at UCSF and SFGH who were prominent in AIDS medicine during its earliest phase between 1981 and 1984. The second series, also complete, documents the response of the nursing profession between 1981 and 1984. A third series that collects oral histories from physicians in private practice will also soon be available. Transcripts of all three series are available on the web.

An additional collecting component of the AIDS History Project in the late 1980s and early 1990s was the identification and cataloguing of relevant photographs, posters, newsletters, ephemera, and other graphical images that visually document the medical and activist response. These materials are primarily preserved at the UCSF Library's Archive and Special Collections Department.

The people organizing the AIDS History Project during these years selected and organized their body of research through a methodology described by archivist Joan Krizak in her book *Documentation Planning for the U.S. Health Care System*. The goal, as it was applied to the AIDS History Project, was to provide a concise overview of the activities and agencies of medical and activist AIDS organizations in San Francisco, while also offering detailed illustrative examples to contextualize and enrich this overview. The San Francisco AIDS Foundation, the oldest and largest multiservice organization, was chosen for comprehensive documentation.

In the summer of 2003, UCSF and GLBTHS teamed up to write a grant proposal in order to continue collecting AIDS history materials. After securing funding from the NHPRC, the project officially began in 2004 with an end date of 2006. GLBTHS primarily took the lead and slightly modified the name of the AIDS History Project to the AIDS Epidemic Historical Records Project. The purpose of this phase of the project is to create research tool resources for diverse publics like public policymakers, community activists, health professionals, journalists, and scholars attempting to understand the impact of the AIDS crisis today by considering the history of how it has been treated, discussed, and experienced in the past, particularly in the San Francisco Bay area.

The AIDS Epidemic Historical Records Project was carried out in two stages. During the first year, archivists processed collections already located at UCSF and GLBTHS. These collections focused on lobbying efforts, safer sex education, and the provision of social services for AIDS-related issues. The second phase of the project involved collaborating with four AIDS organizations to collect records that were in danger of being lost. Archivists worked with the San Francisco AIDS Foundation, Shanti (an organization working to enhance the quality of life, health, and well-being of people living with breast cancer and HIV/AIDS), the UCSF AIDS Health Project, and the UCSF Center for AIDS Prevention Studies to carefully archive and preserve these records for future scholars, activists, and medical practitioners. The AIDS History Project continues to focus on capturing the first 13 years of AIDS-related records, while also seeking to collect and catalogue records from institutions still in operation. Guides to the collections processed during the AIDS Epidemic Historical Records Project are available online.

Jennifer Tyburczy

See also: ACT UP (AIDS Coalition to Unleash Power); Activists; Historical Overview of Gay Rights and Issues: From the 1980s to the Present.

Further Reading

AIDS History Project at University of California, San Francisco (UCSF). Available at: https://www.library.ucsf.edu/collections/archives/manuscripts/aids.

Gay, Lesbian, Bisexual, Transgender Historical Society (GLBTHS). Available at: http://www.glbthistory.org/.

Ailey, Alvin (1931–1989)

Alvin Ailey was a giant figure in modern American dance and culture and created one of the most recognized dance companies in the world. Born in Rogers, Texas, Ailey grew up in the segregated, rural South, a milieu from which he drew a great deal in shaping his choreographies, and, as a result, he positioned centrally on the modern dance stage a Southern, African American idiom.

At 12, Ailey moved to Los Angeles, where his mother had found steady work at an aircraft factory. Although he sought out poetry and gymnastics as ways

Alvin Ailey with his dancers Marilyn Banks, left, and Masazumi Chaya in 1980. (AP Photo/Marty Reichenthal)

of expressing himself as an adolescent, it was not until he was 18, and under the influence of Lester Horton, that he first took up dancing. Ailey was quickly drawn to Horton, who, in addition to forming one of the first multiracial American dance companies, had created a technique that combined myriad styles—that is, classical ballet, modern, traditional Mexican, and Native American dances—and used corrective exercises to free up the body and add to its repertoire a wide range of movements.

Ailey quickly became a star dancer of the Horton Dance Theatre and assumed briefly the artistic directorship of the company after Horton's untimely death in 1953. The position was short-lived, but it offered Ailey the opportunity to stage his first choreographies. In 1954, however, Ailey moved to New York City along with his friend and fellow dancer, Carmen de Lavallade, to dance on Broadway in Truman Capote's *House of Flowers*, and he spent the next few years appearing in other musicals, including *Sing, Man, Sing* (1956) and *Jamaica* (1957), and in film, in *Carmen Jones* (1954). Ailey also used this time to study with modern dance pioneers Martha Graham, Doris Humphrey, and Anna Sokolow, who helped him expand his perspective on dance.

It was with *Blues Suite* (1958) that Ailey emerged as a talented choreographer. *Blues Suite*—a ballet set in a makeshift blues joint reminiscent of the Dew Drop Inn of Ailey's childhood in Navasota, Texas—is a rich exploration of the blues: its music, its drama, its archetypal figures, its sensuality, pathos, and joy. The dance was a critical success, and it was shortly after its premier at the famous 92nd Street YM-YWHA in New York City that Ailey formed the Alvin Ailey American Dance Theatre (AAADT), with the intention of providing an outlet for black modern dancers, who found very little opportunity on the American dance stage.

Both *Blues Suite* and his masterpiece *Revelations* (1960), Ailey once noted, were "a part of my blood memories." And if *Blues Suite* charted the contours of African American secular music and life, *Revelations* was a meditation on the sacred. As Judith Jamison, his longtime friend and collaborator, points out: "[*Revelations*] is one of Alvin's most personal works, reflecting as it does the long hours he spent on hard benches in rural Texas churches, all the Sundays of his childhood, discovering the beauty and power of gospel music and black faith in God and self." Divided into three sections—Pilgrim of Sorrow, Take Me to the Water, and Move Members Move—*Revelations* features altogether 10 suites, including a solo, duets, and ballets featuring the entire company. The first section begins with the Spiritual "I've Been Buked" and interprets the sorrow, forewarning, and yearning of that song with powerfully evocative gestures. When the curtain is raised, the dancers stand solemnly on the stage in a contracted, V-shaped formation, but slowly the formation expands as hips dip, torsos twirl, and arms are raised high (as if in supplication) or are arched and winged (as if in transport). Although *Revelations* begins on a weary note, the mood changes in subsequent sections: the second section theatricalizes a baptism on a lake, and the ballet ends ecstatically, dramatizing women and men, dressed in their Sunday best, at a revival.

Sponsored by the U.S. State Department, Ailey and his company made their first international tour in 1962 and were, in 1970, the first American dance company to perform in the former USSR since Isadora Duncan in the 1920s, their performance earning them standing ovations lasting more than 20 minutes in Leningrad and Moscow. In addition to choreographing for his company, Ailey was commissioned to create several works, including *The River* (1970), for the American Ballet Theatre. It was also in the early 1970s when Ailey founded both the Alvin Ailey American Dance Center to provide training to dancers and the Alvin Ailey Repertory Ensemble, a junior dance repertory.

The 1980s were years of turmoil for Ailey, as he suffered from manic depression and an addiction to cocaine. He also suffered a great deal from AIDS-related illnesses toward the end of the decade. Although the cause of his death was initially described as terminal blood dyscrasia, it was revealed years later that Ailey had died of AIDS-related complications but had not wanted his illness revealed for fear of stigma and shame. By the time of his death, Ailey had choreographed 79 works and had received numerous honors and awards, including an honorary degree from Princeton University, the Samuel H. Scripps American Dance Festival Award, and the Kennedy Center Honors.

Dagmawi Woubshet

See also: African Americans and LGBTQ Issues; Rustin, Bayard (1912–1987). Document: Bayard Rustin, Martin Luther King Jr., and the March on Washington (1963).

Further Reading

DeFrantz, Thomas F. 2004. *Dancing Revelations: Alvin Ailey's Embodiment of African American Culture*. New York: Oxford University Press.

Dunning, Jennifer. 1996. *Alvin Ailey: A Life in Dance*. Reading, MA: Addison Wesley.

Albee, Edward (1928–)

Edward Albee is considered one of the most influential American playwrights of the twentieth century. His plays explode the myth of the idyllic American family and explore the latent violence and angst that lurk in all human relationships. Edward Albee was born in Washington, D.C., and was adopted as an infant and raised in luxury in his adoptive parents' mansion in Larchmont, New York. His father, Reed Albee, was the son of Edward Franklin Albee, a powerful vaudeville tycoon. His mother, Frances, was a domineering woman who was unable to show Albee the love and affection he craved. Albee was a despondent young boy who felt at odds with his parents' lifestyle, and he often clashed with them. He attended various high schools, finally graduating from Choate School in Wallingford, Connecticut. He then took classes at Trinity College in Hartford, Connecticut, but left after a year and a half, never completing his degree.

Albee left home in 1949 and moved to Greenwich Village, where he began frequenting gay bars and socializing with the many other artists who had made New York City their home. At the time the Village had a thriving homosexual subculture and was considered a haven for many young men interested in the arts. During this period Albee held a series of odd jobs, none of which he was able to keep for very long. He paid the bills with the help of a small income from a trust that had been set up for him by his grandmother. At this point, Albee was writing primarily poems and was also working on a novel. Then, in 1953, he showed some of his poetry to Thornton Wilder, who subjected his work to careful criticism and then suggested that he try writing plays. This was a seminal moment for Albee and sparked his playwriting career.

In 1958 Albee penned his first successful play, *The Zoo Story*, a one-act that depicts the violence and absurdity of the world as it plays out in an encounter between two men in Central Park. *The Zoo Story* premiered in Berlin, Germany, and then had its American premiere at the Provincetown Playhouse (Massachusetts) in 1960. At about this same time Albee came into the remainder of the trust money from his

Edward Albee pays a sentimental visit to Provincetown Playhouse, where his *Zoo Story* had its American premiere on January 14, 1960. The Provincetown Playhouse helped launch the career of Eugene O'Neill decades earlier. (Bettmann/Corbis)

grandmother, and this allowed him the freedom to pursue writing full time. It also gave him the ability to sever all ties with his parents. He would remain estranged from his father and did not have any contact with his mother for the next 17 years.

Albee's second success, *The American Dream*, was produced in 1961. It is a comic indictment of the cold, unfeeling atmosphere that can pervade an American family. In it, Albee presents the characters of Mommy and Daddy, a humorous but threatening couple who has dismembered its first adopted child and decides to request a refund since he is still under warranty. The absurd tone of the play is similar to that exhibited in works of Eugène Ionesco, and Albee admits that parts of the play were directly inspired by Ionesco's *The Bald Soprano*. The characters of Mommy and Daddy are thinly veiled versions of Albee's own parents: the seemingly idyllic world that hides a vicious undercurrent reflects Albee's perception of his own home life.

Albee continued to explore the dysfunctional family in his plays and in 1962 produced his most significant work to date, *Who's Afraid of Virginia Woolf*. It is a biting satire that demonstrates the destructive power of language. The play focuses upon George and Martha, a married couple who are locked in a vicious love-hate relationship. George is a professor at the local university and Martha's father is president of the institution. Both characters have a deep-seated self-loathing but direct their hatred outward toward the world and each other. George and Martha get a sadistic satisfaction out of attempting to destroy each other and everything else in their wake, and on the night the play takes place a young professor and his wife become their unlucky targets. *Virginia Woolf* opened on Broadway in October 1962 to mixed reviews, but throughout its run it continued to gain respect from audiences and critics. It wound up winning five Tony Awards, including best production and best play. In 1966 it was made into a film starring Elizabeth Taylor and Richard Burton. *Who's Afraid of Virginia Woolf* is now considered one of the best American plays ever written, and it is still widely produced and studied to this day. In 2013, it won Tony Awards in the best revival of a play category, and Tracy Letts, as George, won the Tony for best actor in 2013. Some have suggested that George and Martha are really homosexual men thinly veiled in the play as a heterosexual couple. Albee adamantly disputes this claim, however, and has even stepped in to prohibit productions of *Virginia Woolf* with an all-male cast.

Albee followed *Virginia Woolf* with *The Ballad of the Sad Café* and then penned *Tiny Alice* in 1964. The latter was his most controversial play to date. The play deals with martyrdom, sexual hysteria, and man's relationship to God. Critics found it confusing and condemned him for what they considered self-indulgence. Albee was not deterred, however, and produced his next big success in 1966. The play was *A Delicate Balance*, another excoriation of the myth of the model American family. Albee was awarded the Pulitzer Prize for the play. Throughout the late 1960s, the 1970s, and much of the 1980s Albee struggled with alcoholism, a disease that hampered his writing career. He did have some new plays produced during this period, but most were nowhere near the quality of his earlier works. One exception, however, was *Seascape*, which Albee completed in 1975. It is his exploration of evolution and how difficult it can be for humans—and other species—to connect with one another. With it Albee won his second Pulitzer Prize.

After almost two decades of missteps and critical failures, Albee burst back onto the playwriting scene in 1991 with his Pulitzer Prize–winning play, *Three Tall Women*. It is Albee's most autobiographical work to date. In it he explores the human condition by having three actresses portray the same woman at three stages in her life. The woman that the three actresses portray is based on Albee's mother, Frances, and she exhibits many of the same opinions and prejudices: she uses ethnic slurs, she is vain and overbearing, and she is bitter about the estrangement of her gay son. The play thrust Albee back into the spotlight and revitalized his career. To this day Albee continues to write plays and win awards. In 2002 he had another success with *The Goat or Who Is Sylvia*, winning yet another Tony for Best Play, and in 2005 he was awarded

a special Tony Award for Lifetime Achievement in the Theatre.

Beth Kattelman

See also: Kramer, Larry (1935–2008).

Further Reading

Albee, Edward. 2005. *Stretching My Mind: The Collected Essays 1960 to 2005*. New York: Carroll & Graf.

Bloom, Harold. 1987. *Edward Albee*. New York: Chelsea House.

Bottoms, Stephen, ed. 2005. *The Cambridge Companion to Edward Albee*. New York: Cambridge University Press.

Gussow, Mel. 1999. *Edward Albee: A Singular Journey*. New York: Simon & Schuster.

Paolucci, Anne. 2000. *From Tension to Tonic: The Plays of Edward Albee*. Wilmington, DE: Griffon House Press.

Alcohol and Drugs

Alcohol and drug use are widely recognized to be common in contemporary queer culture. Accurate statistics about the prevalence of substance use by LGBTQ individuals are difficult to establish because of inconsistent study methodologies, the absence of questions about sexual orientation and gender identity in most epidemiological studies, and the lack of reliable figures about the size and demographics of the LGBTQ community in general. Nonetheless, the majority of existing scientific and social research concludes that there are disproportionately high rates of substance use and abuse among LGBTQ individuals as compared to the general population.

The onset of the public struggle for LGBTQ liberation in the United States is associated with an event at a bar, the Stonewall Inn, in Manhattan in 1969. In reaction to a police raid on the bar, a spontaneous street riot ensued as a form of public and communal resistance to a history of harassment by the police. With a bar as a venue for this critical event in the history of the modern queer liberation movement in the United States, it is not surprising that bars in general have an iconic status in contemporary LGBTQ culture and that the substance use that occurs in bars and clubs is a central and challenging issue for many LGBTQ individuals.

Many authors who have written about substance abuse in contemporary queer culture speculate about some of the reasons for the widespread problem. Among the most commonly noted factors contributing to substance abuse and addiction among LGBTQ individuals are the pain and shame of living "in the closet," the ongoing challenges of coming out, and the stresses of dealing with antigay prejudice, transphobia, internalized homophobia, religious intolerance, familial rejection, fear about HIV/AIDS, and the lack of many legal protections afforded to heterosexuals in the United States. These pressures can induce the

Bill Wilson was the cofounder of Alcoholics Anonymous. (AP Photo/Craig Line)

emotional and psychological problems that lead some individuals to use alcohol and drugs to cope or to escape. Others simply become a part of a social circle where drugs and alcohol are a social lubricant or an accompaniment to sexual activity.

Obviously, the substances that can become problematic for LGBTQ individuals are the same ones used by the general population: alcohol, nicotine, amphetamines, cocaine, "club drugs," inhalants, hallucinogens, opiates, sedatives, and cannabis. Because of the cultural history, social habits, and sexual practices of LGBTQ individuals, some substances have gained a higher profile in queer communities. Also the street names for these substances and the language associated with their use takes particular and idiosyncratic forms.

The most commonly used and abused substances are the legal drugs, alcohol and nicotine. Alcohol is a central nervous system depressant. Different alcoholic beverages vary considerably in their concentration of alcohol. Ingestion of alcohol can raise an individual's blood alcohol level to the point of getting drunk or "buzzed," an experience characterized by mood shifts, disinhibition, impaired judgment, slurred speech, unsteady gait, and memory lapses. The aftereffect of heavy consumption of alcohol can produce an unpleasant hangover marked by a headache, malaise, upset stomach, or more severe withdrawal symptoms such as sweating, tremors, racing heart, nausea and vomiting, anxiety, and other forms of psychomotor agitation. Repeated and prolonged intake of substantial amounts of alcohol can affect almost every organ system in the body and cause serious, life-threatening medical conditions. Despite all the potential harmful consequences, drinking alcohol is one of the most common social rituals among LGBTQ individuals. Bars and clubs sponsor shows, dances, and other events, especially on weekend nights. Additionally, some queer bars have "tea dances" where people gather to drink, socialize, and dance in the afternoon and early evening, sometimes after a previous night of partying.

Nicotine, another commonly used and highly addictive substance, is a central nervous system stimulant contained in all forms of tobacco. Scientific surveys have consistently found that LGBTQ people smoke at rates at least 40 to 60 percent higher than the general population. Tobacco smoking is very addictive because a decrease or cessation of nicotine use creates intense cravings and unpleasant withdrawal symptoms such as dysphoria, insomnia, restlessness, anxiety, and irritability. Tobacco smoking has been identified as a leading cause of physical ailments leading to serious medical conditions and death among LGBTQ individuals and society at large. With the discovery that prominent tobacco companies deliberately have targeted LGBTQ communities in their marketing efforts, queer activists and public health advocates have begun to promote smoking prevention and cessation campaigns directed at reducing cigarette use and hence nicotine consumption among queer individuals.

Among other drugs, crystal methamphetamine is arguably the most pervasive in the LGBTQ community. Some have suggested there is an epidemic of abuse of this chemical substance, commonly known as crystal meth. On the street, it goes by many other terms, including Tina, Crissy, Crank, Speed, Ice, or simply Crystal. Crystal meth got its name from its appearance as a crystalline substance. The crystals can be swallowed or smoked, crushed into a powder for snorting, or dissolved in a liquid before swallowing, injecting, or inserting in the anus. Crystal can be snorted in a small amount called a bump or a larger amount called a linc. Inserting crystal in the anus is called a booty bump.

Crystal meth is a powerful stimulant that induces a feeling of euphoria, a sense of power and stamina, heightened physical energy, changes in sociability, and increased verbal activity. Crystal meth also causes autonomic arousal, resulting in physiological changes such as increased blood pressure and body temperature, dilated pupils, heightened alertness, and decreased need for sleep. Those who get high on crystal are sometimes called tweakers. Users refer to getting high as tweaking or getting amped. A reduction or cessation of use often results in a withdrawal syndrome called a crash that is marked by depression, fatigue, and sleep problems. Sometimes excessive

or prolonged use can lead to cardiac arrhythmia, cardiac arrest, paranoia, panic disorder, or psychotic symptoms.

Crystal meth, the main party drug especially among many gay and bisexual men and queer sex workers, is strongly associated with heightened sexual activity. The term *party and play* (PNP) is an expression used widely in queer circles to refer to doing speed and having sex. On Internet sites designed for queer people to meet and find others for companionship, dating, and sexual encounters, individual profiles or ads often contain a reference to PNP or when an individual seeks an encounter that combines sex and speed use. Using crystal meth generally increases sexual arousal and stamina by delaying orgasm. Many people engage in hours of sexual activity while high. The prolonged sexual activity and decreased inhibitions can result in condom breakage or risky behaviors that can increase the chances of disease transmission. While crystal use increases sexual arousal, it can also cause impotence and the inability to maintain an erection, a condition usually referred to as "crystal dick."

Cocaine, though a different class of substance than speed, is a stimulant that produces similar feelings of euphoria, alertness, and confidence. Cocaine can be snorted, smoked, or injected. Because it is usually snorted, it is frequently called blow. When inhaled or ingested it causes an increase in heart rate, respiration, and blood pressure. While its effects are similar to crystal meth, it is much shorter-acting and usually more expensive. Nonetheless, in some queer circles, cocaine commonly accompanies partying. Like speed, people often crash with depressive symptoms after a run of using cocaine.

A host of different recreational drugs have become associated with clubbing, a social activity engaged in by large numbers of queer youth and young adults. Clubbing or dancing for hours on end, usually all night long, is a common weekend activity, and the club scene is often where people begin using drugs. Among the so-called club or dance drugs are ecstasy, gamma hydroxybutrate (GHB), and ketamine, as well as crystal meth and cocaine. Generally these drugs are readily available inside or outside dance clubs and many people enjoy the drugs' effects while dancing. It can be misleading, however, to classify these substances exclusively as club or dance drugs because they actually are used in all kinds of settings.

Ecstasy, often called E, is the popular name for methylenedioxymethamphetamine or MDMA. Although a chemical relative of speed, ecstasy belongs to a different class of drugs called enactogens and comes in pill form. MDMA acts as an acute antidepressant and mood elevator. By precipitating the release of the neurotransmitter serotonin, MDMA works within 20 to 30 minutes to create a relaxed, euphoric, exhilarated, positive emotional state. Users report feelings of happiness, self-acceptance, personal well-being, and heightened empathy and emotional warmth toward others. While ecstasy is not physically addictive, psychological addiction can form. Furthermore, exposure to high doses of MDMA can result in serotonin depletion, which causes long-term psychological problems such as anxiety and depression. Almost all medical emergencies involving ecstasy are caused by adulterated capsules containing other substances and by dehydration and heat stroke after long periods of dancing.

Two additional club drugs are GHB and ketamine, or K. GHB, classified as a sedative-hypnotic and originally developed as a sleep aid, comes in liquid or powder form. In clubs most users consume the liquid from small bottles. GHB has a similar effect to other club drugs. Within 20 to 40 minutes after ingestion, GHB induces feelings of relaxation, euphoria, and increased sociability. Overdose of GHB can lead to dizziness, drowsiness, slowed respiration, dehydration when dancing, and in some cases loss of consciousness.

Ketamine, commonly known as Special K or K, is a dissociative anesthetic, which comes as a liquid that is swallowed or injected, but more commonly is cooked into powder for snorting. Akin to nitrous oxide (laughing gas), it separates perception from sensation. Within a few minutes of ingestion, ketamine induces a dreamy, unreal feeling and, at higher doses, an out-of-body experience sometimes referred to as entering a K-hole. Low doses of K increase heart rate

and higher doses can cause loss of consciousness or slowed respiration that are dangerous in combination with other drugs. People can become addicted to ketamine. Because both ketamine and GHB can produce relaxation, drowsiness, and impaired perceptions, they have been implicated in drug-facilitated sexual assaults and other crimes.

As previously mentioned, the club drugs (especially crystal meth and ecstasy) are frequently associated with sexual activity. Another group of drugs commonly associated with sexual activity are poppers, the street name for various liquid alkyl nitrites that are bottled and sold for use during sex. Poppers are inhalants that within a few moments of being sniffed trigger vasodilation and smooth muscle relaxation. Users experience an almost instantaneous head rush, increased heart rate, and a relaxation of muscles in the anus or vagina. Among men who have anal sex with men, they are especially popular with the receptive partner. As a recreational drug, poppers are used primarily to enhance sexual experience. Some users experience headaches, dizziness, or erectile dysfunction. While poppers are not addictive, they can increase the risk of sexually transmitted diseases (STDs) and in combination with other drugs can cause cardiovascular problems.

Alcohol and several of the club drugs that have been reviewed can cause erectile dysfunction. With the advent of some prescription medications sold under the brand names of Viagra, Levitra, and Cialis, there are now pharmacological interventions available to treat erectile difficulties. These medications are now being sold via the Internet and in underground markets without a prescription. In the LGBTQ community, sexually active men have been known to abuse these substances. Use of any of these prescription medications in combination with poppers can produce a dangerous drop in blood pressure that could lead to a heart attack or stroke.

There are many other commonly abused drugs, including antianxiety medications like prescription Valium, Xanax, and Klonopin, that are highly addictive, hallucinogens like LSD and mushrooms that can cause perceptual disturbances, and pain-relieving opiates like heroin, methadone, and prescription Vicodin, Percoset, and OxyContin that are also highly addictive. There is no evidence that any of these substances are abused at a higher rate among LGBTQ individuals.

Among the LGBTQ population, cannabis or marijuana use has become a major political and health care issue. Marijuana is still considered an illegal drug. It is derived from the leaves, buds, and stems of the cannabis plant that are dried and called marijuana or weed. Marijuana is usually smoked by rolling it into a cigarette called a joint or by putting the leaves into a pipe or bong for inhaling the smoke. Marijuana can also be cooked into food, most often baked into cookies or brownies, or mixed with tea. Users describe marijuana as producing a "high" that includes some initial euphoria, distorted sensory perceptions, feelings of relaxation, and appetite stimulation. While there is little evidence that users develop any physiological dependence on cannabis, people may still develop a psychological dependence. Because marijuana has been used to treat some general medical conditions like the nausea and vomiting caused by chemotherapy or certain HIV medications, and the anorexia and weight loss caused by advancing HIV disease, LGBTQ activists have been at the forefront of efforts to legalize marijuana for medical use.

Individuals who acknowledge a problem with alcohol or drugs may seek treatment to support their recovery from the effects of a substance and the importance it has played in their lives. The most traditional recovery path is based on the spiritual principles outlined in the self-help, 12-step programs that are modeled on Alcoholics Anonymous (AA). Twelve-step programs such as AA and Narcotics Anonymous often have designated meetings for LGBTQ people, and such meetings can be located in many regions and in virtually every large metropolitan area in the United States.

Alternative self-help organizations such as the Secular Organization for Sobriety, Smart Recovery, and Moderation Management also exist. These groups employ more rational, scientific strategies to treat substance use problems and assist those interested in

curtailing the harm caused by their use who may not be interested in or ready for abstinence. Such self-help organizations are a part of the harm reduction movement that has been particularly popular in LGBTQ communities. The harm reduction approach seeks to help individuals minimize the harm or risks of their use of drugs. Individuals may also seek professional services through public health clinics or their health care providers.

Currently there are inpatient and outpatient treatment and recovery centers that work exclusively with LGBTQ clients. In clinics where treatment is provided to the general population, LGBTQ recovery groups or treatment tracks often exist to meet the specialized needs of queer clients. Consensus exists in the professional community that competent providers must be educated about and sensitive to the unique issues that affect LGBTQ individuals and that these issues must be addressed in any thorough and comprehensive treatment for substance use problems.

John Sauvé

See also: Historical Overview of Gay Rights and Issues: From the 1980s to the Present.

Further Reading

Borden, Audrey. 2007. *The History of Gay People in Alcoholics Anonymous*. Binghamton, NY: Haworth.

Center for Substance Abuse Treatment. 2001. *A Provider's Introduction to Substance Abuse Treatment for Lesbian, Gay, Bisexual and Transgender Individuals*. DHHS Publication No. (SMA) 01–3498. Rockville, MD: CSAT.

Guss, J. and J. Drescher, eds. 2000. *Addictions in the Gay and Lesbian Community*. Binghamton, NY: Haworth.

Kus, R., ed. 1995. *Addiction and Recovery in Gay and Lesbian Persons*. Binghamton, NY: Haworth Press.

Alice B. Toklas Lesbian Gay Bisexual Transgender Democratic Club

Born in San Francisco, Alice B. Toklas (April 30, 1877–March 7, 1967) was the lesbian lover and confidante of writer Gertrude Stein, whom she met in Paris in 1907. They lived together in Paris from 1909

Gertrude Stein sitting on a sofa in her Paris studio, with a portrait of her by Pablo Picasso, and other modern art paintings hanging on the wall behind her. (Library of Congress)

to 1946. Together they hosted a salon that attracted painters, including Picasso, Matisse, and Braque, and American writers Ernest Hemingway, Thornton Wilder, and Sherwood Anderson. Toklas died at the age of 89 and is buried in Paris.

In 1972 in the city of her birth, James Foster (1935–1990) founded the Alice B. Toklas Memorial Democratic Club (also known as the Alice B. Toklas Lesbian and Gay Democratic Club). Foster was dishonorably discharged from the army in 1959 because he was homosexual. He reported that this experience led him to become an advocate for gay rights in the United States, a mission that lasted for more than 25 years. He helped found the Society for Individual Rights in 1964, which focused on the concerns of lesbian and gay persons. Foster was also always active

in Democratic politics both locally and nationally. In 1972 in Miami he was one of the first openly gay speakers to address the National Presidential Convention for the Democratic Party. Madeline Davis, vice president of the Mattachine Society of the Niagara Frontier, also spoke. They urged the Democratic Party to adopt a gay rights plank in their platform. In the same year, while campaigning for Democratic presidential candidate George F. McGovern, Foster founded the Alice B. Toklas Memorial Democratic Club. Phyllis Lyon and Del Martin also participated in getting the club established. They had started the Daughters of Bilitis, the first lesbian organization in the United States, which was influential in local and national politics.

The club conducted registration drives among lesbian and gay persons. It also supported various candidates and/or issues in the city and county of San Francisco and promoted civil rights through endorsements in local, state, and national elections. And it sponsored events such as awards night for local heroes who had served the lesbian and gay community.

James Foster died of AIDS in 1990 at the age of 55. Robert Barnes became an influential person in the club and held numerous leadership positions in Democratic and LGBT community organizations. He was chair of the Lesbian and Gay Caucus of the state Democratic Party and was elected to the San Francisco Democratic County Central Committee. At one of the club's award ceremonies, Congresswoman Nancy Pelosi paid tribute to Barnes, who died the same year (2002) at the age of 42. She pointed out that his commitment to gay rights, social change, and political involvement began early. He founded one of the nation's first teenage gay clubs at San Francisco's Lowell High School. At the age of 18, through the encouragement of the late supervisor Harvey Milk, he worked as the youth coordinator for the "No on Proposition 6" campaign to defeat the antigay Briggs initiative. Barnes was responsible for electing more lesbian and gay candidates to office than any other political consultant in California. He also comanaged the first domestic partners initiative in San Francisco. As president of the club, he transformed it into one of the most influential local gay political organizations in the country.

Ski Hunter

Gertrude Stein, left, one of the world's foremost novelists, poses with Alice B. Toklas, and her dog, Basket, in front of her home in France. The grand lady of fiction lived in a chateau near Paris during the four years of Nazi occupation, but her identity was kept secret. (Bettmann/Corbis)

See also: Activists; Daughters of Bilitis; Mattachine Society.

Further Reading

Alice B. Toklas LGBT Democratic Club. Available at: http://www.alicebtoklas.org. Accessed January 15, 2014.

Armstrong, E. 2002. "Crisis, Collective Creativity, and the Generation of New Organizational Forms: The Transformation of Lesbian/Gay Organizations in San Francisco." *Social Structure and Organizations Revisited* 19: 361–95.

Allegra, Donna (1953–)

Prolific and often anthologized, and author of poetry, fiction, and essays, African American author Donna Allegra's work has appeared in over 30 mainly lesbian and feminist anthologies and woman-oriented magazines and collections. Much of her work features first-person narrators, and draws from aspects of her life and interests. Allegra's writing, usually focused on women, explores the lack of choices women face, various forms of oppression, racism, class perceptions, and the impact events and experiences have had on her consciousness and aesthetics.

A lifelong New Yorker, born in Brooklyn, she graduated from New York University in 1977 with a BA in dramatic literature, theater history, and cinema. She has variously worked as an electrician, yoga instructor, and African and jazz dancer. A member of Jemima, the first self-identified black lesbian writing group, along with Sapphire, Candace Boyce, and others, she was also involved in the Gap-Toothed Girlfriends Writers Workshop and the black lesbian performance group NAPS. She has also written theater, book, film, and dance reviews, and produced radio programs for WBAI FM (New York) from 1975 to 1981.

Winner of the Pat Parker Memorial Poetry Prize in 1992, Donna Allegra is the author of the fiction collection *Witness to the League of Blond Hip Hop Dancers: A Novella and Short Stories* (2000). A Violet Quill Award finalist, the collection explores desire between women, racism, and sexism, mostly set in or around dance classes.

Reginald Harris

See also: Abbott, Steve (1943–1992); Allen, Paula Gunn (1939–2008); Lorde, Audre (1934–1992).

Further Reading

Keller, Yvonne. 2005. "Was It Right to Love Her Brother's Wife So Passionately?": Lesbian Pulp Novels and U.S. Lesbian Identity, 1950–1965." *American Quarterly* 57(2): 385–410.

Walter, Kate. 2000. "Book Review: *Witness to the League of Blond Hip Hop Dancers: A Novella and Short Stories* by Donna Allegra." *The Advocate*, December 5.

Allen, Mariette Pathy (1940–)

For three decades photographer Mariette Pathy Allen has chronicled the lives of transgender individuals and the emergence of a transgender rights movement. Influenced by Margaret Mead's study of culturally diverse gender roles, in 1978 Allen stayed at the same hotel where a group of cross dressers were celebrating the last day of Mardi Gras and was immediately captivated by their struggles with gender stereotyping. Motivated to alter commonly held misperceptions of cross dressers, Allen spent 10 years building relationships with her cross-dressing subjects in order to capture some of their most intimate moments on film.

Her *Transformations: Crossdressers and Those Who Love Them* (1989) provides a unique view into the lives of mostly heterosexual, married men who cross dress. Composed primarily of black and white portraits, the book includes her interviews with many of her subjects. Allen photographed cross dressers in the daylight of everyday life, in relationships with their wives, children, and other family members, and thereby provided a humanizing portrait of a largely misunderstood and secretive community.

During the early 1990s, Allen became increasingly intimate—professionally and personally—with the emergent transgender movement. Like many other advocate-style photojournalists, Allen differs from strict documentary photographers by her abandonment of objectivity in exchange for personal immersion and empathy. In doing so, she has become an active participant in creating the change she documents. A frequent presenter, protester, lobbyist, and lecturer at transgender events, Allen's personal identification with her transgender subjects is captured in her photography and transmits the humanity of her subjects to viewers.

The Gender Frontier (2003)—which won a 2004 Lambda Literary Award—displays Allen's photographic exploration of the transgender community and

Mariette Pathy Allen, right, and others talk with other participants in the Easter Day parade along New York's Fifth Avenue on April 24, 2011. (AP Photo/Tina Fineberg)

political movement. Abandoning the static portraits of *Transmissions*, which were often taken in intimate and homey environments, the images of *Gender Frontier* are kinetic and captured in public spheres.

Allen was the still photographer for Lee Grant's 1984 documentary *What Sex Am I?*, Rosa von Praunheim's *The Transexual Menace*, and associate producer of the A&E documentary *The Transgender Revolution* (1998), Allen also consulted on and provided still photographs for the award-winning documentary *Southern Comfort* (2001). A frequent contributor to *Transgender Tapestry* magazine, Allen's photographs also grace the pages of books like Leslie Feinberg's *Transgender Warriors: Making History from Joan of Arc to Dennis Rodman* (1997) and Riki Wilchin's *Read My Lips: Sexual Subversion and the End of Gender* (1997).

Her photography has been exhibited in the United States and abroad and is included in the permanent collections of Bibliothèque Nationale of Paris, the Corcoran Museum in Washington, D.C., the Brooklyn Museum of Art, Houston's Museum of Fine Arts, and the New York Public Library. Her life's work, which includes more than the transgender material, is being archived at Duke University's Rare Book and Manuscript Library and the Sallie Bingham Center for Women's Studies.

Jacob Anderson-Minshall

See also: Historical Overview of Gay Rights and Issues: From Pre-Columbian Times to the 1970s; Transgender Children.

Further Reading

Allen, Mariette Pathy. 2003. *The Gender Frontier.* Heidelberg, Germany: Kehrer.

Allen, Mariette Pathy. 1989. *Transformations: Crossdressers and Those Who Love Them.* New York: E. P. Dutton.

Allen, Paula Gunn (1939–2008)

An American poet, novelist, essayist, and teacher, Paula Gunn Allen was born in Cubero, New Mexico. She was member of the Laguna Pueblo tribe. Her writings earned her the Native American Prize for Literature, as well as numerous other awards, including a Ford Foundation fellowship, a National Endowment for the Arts fellowship, and the 1990 American Book Award. Allen, who retired from the University of California–Los Angeles in 1999 as a professor of English and creative writing, was better known for her academic writings but was also recognized for her fiction and poetry. Central to Allen's work, both fiction and nonfiction, is the concept of the divided self, which emerges through her examinations of identity as it is affected by race, gender, and sexuality. Allen wrote from the viewpoint of the outsider who is alienated from the larger culture, due to her experiences as a Native American, woman, and lesbian. Many of her writings attempt to understand how to create wholeness within the self by reconnecting with tribal histories and knowledge, as well as accepting one's sexuality as a powerful source for identity. This desire for wholeness is driven by a need to voice Native American experience through stories, which stems from the Laguna belief in storytelling as a ceremony for curing. For example, in *The Woman Who Owned the Shadows*, her first novel, published in 1983, Allen's protagonist Ephanie Atencio, a young half-breed woman, struggles to come to terms with her Native American heritage and sexuality. After suffering a mental breakdown from the pressure of the dominant white culture, Ephanie regains her identity by reconnecting with tribal ways of knowing, as well as understanding her desire for women as she learns to voice her lesbian identity and tell her story.

Allen's other writings explore Native American literature and culture. Her most well-known work, *The Sacred Hoop: Recovering the Feminine in American Indian Traditions*, offers a feminist analysis of Native American history, the Native American narrative tradition, and women's experiences. The book covers a range of topics from female goddesses, to the power of the oral tradition, to feminism and women's issues in the Native American experience, as well as women's same-sex relationships in the Laguna tribal culture. In particular, *The Sacred Hoop* puts forth Allen's concept of the "ceremonial lesbian," an individual who has transformative powers. According to

Allen, same-sex relationships were most likely commonplace in the Laguna past and thought to hold special power.

Allen also edited collections that introduced readers to Native American literature, as seen in *Spider Woman's Granddaughters: Traditional Tales and Contemporary Writing by Native American Women*, and worked to preserve the importance of matrilineal heritage through a collection of creation myths about Native American goddesses in *Grandmothers of the Light*. Allen's later works include *Off the Reservation: Reflections on Boundary-Busting Border-Crossing Loose Canons* (1998), a collection of essays, and *Pocahontas: Medicine Woman, Spy, Entrepreneur, Diplomat* (2003), a biography that offers an unromanticized version of Pocahontas's life and influence. Paula Gunn Allen died of lung cancer in May 2008.

Jeannette E. Riley

See also: Lorde, Audre (1934–1992); Native Americans and LGBTQ Issues.

Further Reading

Allen, Paula Gunn. 1992. *The Sacred Hoop: Recovering the Feminine in American Indian Traditions*. New York: Beacon Press; Reissue edition.

Hanson, Elizabeth I. 1990. *Paula Gunn Allen*. Boise, ID: Boise State University.

Purdy, John. 1997. "'And Then, Twenty Years Later. . . .' A Conversation with Paula Gunn Allen." *Studies in American Indian Literatures: The Journal of the Association for the Study of American Indian Literatures* 9(3).

Van Dyke, Annette. 1990. "The Journey Back to Female Roots: A Laguna Pueblo Model." In *Lesbian Texts and Contexts: Radical Revisions*, ed. Karla Jay and Joanne Glasgow, pp. 339–54. New York: New York University Press.

Native American writer Paula Gunn Allen. (Christopher Felver/Corbis)

American Civil Liberties Union (ACLU)

Since its founding in 1920, the American Civil Liberties Union (ACLU) has come to permeate all aspects of society in that peculiarly American way—as a nonpartisan, nonprofit, nongovernmental agency that has an influence far exceeding its budget and the number of its paid staff and volunteers. Membership in the ACLU can be either a badge of honor or a brand of inequity, and, on occasion, can be both simultaneously. People with strong liberal social beliefs are often described as "card-carrying members of the ACLU."

Lesbians, gay men, bisexuals, and transgender people have received legal and grassroots organizational support from a number of people and organizations, but none more than the ACLU. Additionally, the ACLU has been intimately involved in the rights of every minority. It has represented Native Americans and other people of color; women; mental patients; prisoners; people with disabilities;

the poor; and Christians, Jews, Muslims, and atheists, among others, in seeking to defend and extend civil rights and civil liberties to those who would otherwise be excluded from constitutional and statutory protections.

When Roger Baldwin, Crystal Eastman, Albert DeSilver, and others formed the ACLU in 1920, the U.S. Supreme Court had never upheld a single free speech claim. Activists languished in jail for distributing antiwar literature. State-sanctioned violence against African Americans was routine. Women had won the right to vote only in August of that year. Workers were not allowed to organize unions. Immigrants whose activism put them at odds with the government were harassed and deported.

Since it was founded almost 94 years ago, the ACLU has tackled the thorniest issues confronting the United States—racism, sexism, homophobia, religious intolerance, and censorship. The representation of unpopular people or groups is the most controversial aspect of the ACLU's work. The organization, for example, has defended controversial and unpopular entities such as the American Nazis, the Ku Klux Klan, and the Nation of Islam not because they agree with the goals or methods of such organizations. The fact that the ACLU is willing to defend the right to free expression and free assembly of organizations that would destroy the ACLU is the essence of the organization. Historically, people whose opinions are the most controversial or extreme are the people whose rights are most often threatened. Once the government has the power to violate one person's rights, it can use that power against everyone.

The ACLU has provided legal counsel in tens of thousands of important and precedent-setting cases. It appears before the U.S. Supreme Court more than any other organization except the U.S. Department of Justice. A few of those cases are summarized.

- In 1920, the first year of its existence, the ACLU fought the campaign of harassment and deportation ordered by U.S. attorney general A. Mitchell Palmer. The ACLU championed such Palmer targets as politically radical immigrants and supported

the right of Industrial Workers of the World members and other trade unionists to hold meetings and organize. The ACLU also secured the release of hundreds of activists imprisoned for their antiwar views and activities.

- In 1925, the ACLU secured the services of celebrated attorney Clarence Darrow to represent biology teacher John T. Scopes, who was charged with violating a Tennessee ban on the teaching of evolution. Scopes was convicted and fined, but on appeal the Tennessee Supreme Court reversed Scopes's conviction (but upheld the constitutionality of the statute).

Crystal Eastman and Amos Pinchot in the early 1900s. (Library of Congress)

Roger Baldwin, the principal founder of the American Civil Liberties Union (ACLU) in 1920 and its director for 30 years, visits the U.S. Supreme Court in Washington, D.C., on January 20, 1970. (Bettmann/Corbis)

- In 1933, after a long anticensorship battle supported by the ACLU, a New York federal court lifted a Customs Service ban on the sale of James Joyce's novel, *Ulysses*, in the United States.

- In 1939, The ACLU argued successfully before the U.S. Supreme Court that a ban on union organizers' political meetings violated the First Amendment right to freedom of assembly.

- In 1942, the ACLU was one of the few organizations that denounced the federal government's round-up and internment in concentration camps of more than 110,000 Japanese Americans. In 1993, Congress officially apologized for the action.

- During the 1950s, the ACLU fought court battles against loyalty oaths, which a government gripped by Cold War fever demanded from federal workers. Many state legislatures also passed laws requiring that public schoolteachers, especially, swear their nonmembership in the Communist Party or in any "subversive organization," and the ACLU successfully fought many of these laws.

- In 1954, the ACLU joined a legal battle that began years before. The U.S. Supreme Court decision in *Brown v. Board of Education*, declaring racially segregated schools to be in violation of the Fourteenth Amendment, was the beginning of a decades-long fight against segregation in public schools. During the 1960s, from the first lunch counter sit-in through the Freedom Rides and mass marches, the ACLU supported the civil rights movement's goal of racial justice and equal opportunity and defended on First Amendment grounds its choice of peaceful demonstrations as the principal means for achieving that goal.

Westboro Baptist Church member Jacob Phelps of Topeka, Kansas, holds signs in front of the Supreme Court in Washington as the Court hears arguments in the dispute between Albert Snyder of York, Pennsylvania, and members of the Westboro Baptist Church. The case pits Snyder's right to grieve privately against the church members' right to say what they want, no matter how offensive. (AP Photo/Carolyn Kaster)

- In 1973, in *Roe v. Wade* and *Doe v. Bolton*, the Supreme Court held that the constitutional right to privacy encompasses a woman's right to decide whether she will terminate or continue a pregnancy. The ruling struck down all criminal abortion laws in the states. The ACLU remains in the forefront of the struggle to protect women's right to reproductive choice, and to achieve women's equality on all fronts.

- In 1983, 56 years after the Scopes trial, the ACLU challenged an Arkansas statute requiring that the biblical story of creation be taught as a "scientific alternative" to the theory of evolution. A federal court found the statute, which fundamentalists saw as a model for other states, unconstitutional.

"Creation science," said the court, was not science, but was actually religion and, therefore, could not be required by state law.

- Beginning in 1983, the ACLU and several other civil rights and civil liberties organizations began a systematic challenge to the nation's sodomy laws that made oral sex and anal sex activity between persons of the same (and sometimes the opposite) sex a crime. In 1986, the U.S. Supreme Court issued one of its most uniformly reviled opinions in *Bowers v. Hardwick* and held sodomy laws to be constitutional. The decision legitimized the entire legal system that regulated lesbian, gay, bisexual, and transgendered life in general (prohibiting relationships, restricting custody and child visitation rights, and justifying exclusion from certain jobs, for instance). *Bowers* was severely undermined by the *Romer* decision in 1996 and reversed by the *Lawrence* decision in 2003.

- In 1989, the U.S. Supreme Court invalidated a Texas statute punishing flag desecration, which the justices described as a form of political speech protected by the First Amendment.

- In 1996, in *Romer v. Evans*, the Supreme Court recognized for the first time the civil rights of lesbians and gay men by invalidating a state constitutional amendment, passed by public referendum in Colorado, that prohibited the state and its municipalities from enacting gay rights laws.

- In 1997, in *ACLU v. Reno*, the Supreme Court struck down the 1996 Communications Decency Act, which censored the Internet by banning "indecent" speech.

- In 1998, in *Bragdon v. Abbott*, the Supreme Court established that the antidiscrimination provisions of the Americans with Disabilities Act apply to people in the early stages of HIV infection, even if they did not have any overt symptoms of AIDS.

- In 1999, in *Chicago v. Morales*, the Supreme Court struck down Chicago's loitering law that disproportionately targeted African American and Latino youth and resulted in the arrest of 45,000 innocent people.

- In 2000, the ACLU was directly involved in the case of *Bush v. Gore*. The ACLU, participant in a national campaign to end felony disfranchisement, called "Right to Vote," and other civil rights groups filed lawsuits in Florida and elsewhere challenging the reliance on flawed electoral systems that not only failed to count every vote equally, but often operated in a racially discriminatory manner.

- In 2001, the Supreme Court in *Atkins v. Virginia* reversed itself and held that execution of the mentally retarded is unconstitutional cruel and unusual punishment.

- In 2001, after terrorists flew planes into the Pentagon and the World Trade Towers, the government responded by rounding up immigrants in new rounds of racial and ethnic profiling. The ACLU led the resistance to the actions of the Bush administration, fighting measures to roll back fundamental protections and jeopardize basic freedoms. Unfortunately, despite the efforts of the ACLU and other groups, the USA PATRIOT Act was rushed through Congress and gives the government expanded power to invade privacy, imprison people without due process, and punish dissent.

- In 2003, the U.S. Supreme Court in *Lawrence v. Texas* reversed its ruling in *Bowers v. Hardwick* (1986) upholding state sodomy laws. In striking down a Texas law that made same-sex intimacy a crime, the court expanded the privacy rights of all Americans and promoted the right of lesbians and gay men to equality. Beginning in 2004, the ACLU brought lawsuits in Oregon and New York and joined a case in California to fight for marriage equality for gay men and lesbians. Massachusetts became the first state in U.S. history to allow lesbian and gay couples to legally marry on the same terms as straight people. Numerous suits have been fought (and continue to be fought) in various judicial and legislative forums.

- In 2004, the Supreme Court made its most important statement in several decades on the balance between civil liberties and national security. By agreeing with the ACLU and ruling that foreign citizens detained at Guantánamo Bay and American citizens detained as "enemy combatants" in military brigs are entitled to at least some of the trapping of due process of law, the Court strongly repudiated of the Bush administration's arguments that the "war on terror" cannot be reviewed by American courts.

- In 2004, the Supreme Court revisited Internet censorship yet again and blocked enforcement of the Child Online Protection Act. Adopted by Congress in 1998, the act criminalizes sexually explicit speech on the Internet that is "harmful to minors" but does so in a manner that effectively deprives adults of access to constitutionally protected material.

It would be a mistake, however, to imply that the ACLU's impact is primarily in bringing and winning constitutional litigation cases in the U.S. Supreme Court. It also has an extensive public education program that publishes books and position papers on scores of controversial issues. It provides public speakers and news analysts on issues as they arise (or on old issues as they resurface). Representatives of the ACLU are well known in every state capitol. Most importantly, the organization provides inspiration for thousands of people every year who stand their ground in difficult situations in which they know their civil rights have been violated.

Although the ACLU has grown from a roomful of civil libertarians to more than 500,000 members, it still operates with a surprisingly small staff. Nevertheless, the ACLU today is the nation's largest public interest law firm, with a 50-state network of staffed, autonomous affiliate offices. It employs only 100 staff attorneys in those offices, but those lawyers coordinate the work of the 2,000 volunteer attorneys (handling close to 6,000 cases annually) who do the bulk of its work.

Because of a lack of resources, not every case with civil rights or civil liberties issues can be pursued. The ACLU pioneered the concept of "impact litigation," trying to select lawsuits that will have the greatest impact, cases that have the potential for breaking new ground and establishing new precedents that will strengthen American freedoms.

Perhaps most significantly, the ACLU has leveraged its expertise by establishing national projects to address specific civil liberties issues: AIDS, capital punishment, lesbian and gay rights, immigrants' rights, prisoners' rights, reproductive freedom, voting rights, women's rights, and workplace rights. In doing so, it has provided "think tanks" that keep it at the intellectual center of some of the most difficult developing issues in American culture. These national projects, and the quality and devotion of their staff members, provide the ACLU with the gravitas to convene conferences of similarly minded organizations and individuals.

Jim Kellogg

See also: Activists; Amnesty International OUTFront.

Further Reading

American Civil Liberties Union. Available at: http://www .aclu.org/. Accessed July 3, 2008.

Walker, Samuel. 1999. *In Defense of American Liberties: A History of the ACLU.* 2nd ed. Carbondale: Southern Illinois University Press.

American Psychiatric Association (APA)

The American Psychiatric Association (APA) is a professional organization that oversees ethical behaviors and other issues related to the profession of psychiatry. The APA also maintains the *Diagnostic and Statistical Manual of Mental Disorders* (*DSM*).

The APA initially classified homosexuality as a mental disorder in the first edition of the *Diagnostic Statistical Manual* (*DSM- I*). Research by Evelyn Hooker and others in the 1950s and 1960s demonstrated that homosexuality was as adaptive and psychologically sound as heterosexuality. President Johnson appointed Dr. Hooker to head the National Institute of Mental Health (NIMH) Task Force on Homosexuality, which in 1969 recommended the repeal of sodomy laws and better public education about homosexuality (Thompson 1994, p. 69).

A committee was formed within the APA in the early 1970s to investigate the belief that homosexuality was a mental illness. The NIMH report, along with the efforts of Dr. Charles Silverstein (founding editor of *The Journal of Homosexuality*) and other respected physicians and researchers, was able to convince the board of trustees of the APA in 1973 that homosexuality should be removed from the list of recognized disorders. A vote by the entire membership the next year

Rachel Sorrow, left, a transgender woman, attends a therapy session with Dr. Dan Karasic, a psychiatrist with the Center of Excellence for Transgender Health, at San Francisco General Hospital in San Francisco, on July 20, 2012. The psychiatric establishment is wrestling with questions on proper treatment of transgender people as it works to overhaul its diagnostic manual for the first time in almost two decades. (AP Photo/Marcio Jose Sanchez)

(1974) upheld the recommendation of the board and homosexuality was no longer listed as a mental disorder in the *DSM*.

Conservatives and members of the religious right have often portrayed the adoption of this change in the *DSM* as the result of scheming by a band of gay activists that pushed through their agenda. This is not true. Because the entire body of the APA voted on the change, it was the clear presentation of the research to the members that convinced them to change their position. The membership of the APA reflects society and is mostly heterosexual. Thus, it was primarily heterosexuals who reviewed the research and agreed that the change was needed.

Understanding this history helps explain one of the major tools used to maintain legal discrimination against homosexuals. Psychiatrists are often called upon by courts to give professional testimony. In the past psychiatrists provided support for the belief that homosexuals were mentally defective and thus unfit to have custody of their children, to teach or work with children, or to hold jobs that dealt with security and intelligence. They also supported the belief that heterosexuals would naturally respond with violence toward homosexuals who made passes at them.

Objective scientific research revealed that homosexuality is not a disorder. It is the poor treatment of homosexuals by society that is the problem. Psychiatrists now educate courts about homosexuality and support lesbian and gay parents during child custody cases. Their testimony helps to defeat attempts to use

Hundreds of gay rights activists crowd a San Francisco, California, plaza to demonstrate against a Supreme Court decision that upheld a Georgia law making sodomy a crime on June 30, 1986. The 5–4 decision meant consenting adults had no constitutional right to private homosexual conduct. (AP Photo/Norb Von Der Groeben)

the so-called homosexual panic defense and to counter negative stereotypes used to defeat lesbian and gay defendants.

The APA supports the American Psychiatric Association in its position that sexual orientation—whether it be homosexual, heterosexual, or bisexual—is innate for all human beings and one form of sexual orientation is not better or more psychologically healthy than another. The APA has issued position papers and a pamphlet contending that efforts to change sexual orientation violate ethical standards and that changing sexual orientation cannot be achieved.

Chuck Stewart

See also: Hooker, Evelyn (1907–1996); Sexual Orientation Change Efforts.

Further Reading

Diagnostic and Statistical Manual of Mental Disorders. 1994. 4th ed. Washington, DC: American Psychiatric Association.

Thompson, M., ed. 1994. *Long Road to Freedom:* The Advocate *History of the Gay and Lesbian Movement.* New York: St. Martin's Press.

Amnesty International OUTfront

OUTfront was a special program of Amnesty International USA's on LGBT human rights. The program was created in 1998 to advance Amnesty International's (AI) work to promote human rights standards for LGBT people around the world, increase awareness of

The two men who spent the night in jail in 1998 on sodomy charges, John Lawrence, right, and Tyron Garner, left, read a statement during a press conference in Houston, on June 26, 2003. The Supreme Court struck down a ban on gay sex, ruling that the law was an unconstitutional violation of privacy. (AP Photo /Michael Stravato)

abuses directed at LGBT people on a global level, and mobilize people in the United States and internationally to take action against such abuses. OUTfront was part of AI's International LGBT Network, a coordinating body of Amnesty Sections (country divisions) involved in LGBT human rights work (currently 37 in number). While many other AI Sections integrate LGBT rights work directly into their agendas, OUT-front was Amnesty's only full-fledged program with dedicated staff focused on LGBT projects, enabling it to play an important role within the amnesty movement. OUTfront is now fully integrated in the Amnesty International's LGBT Rights watch.

OUTfront follows AI's general format, premised on informed grassroots action. A key AI goal is to obtain the immediate and unconditional release of prisoners of conscience (POCs), anyone imprisoned because of his or her race, religion, color, language, sexual orientation, gender identity, or belief, so long as he or she

has not used or advocated violence. AI also works to end torture and executions worldwide, including torture of those subjected to these human rights abuses based on their sexual orientation or gender identity. Additionally, AI endeavors to end violence and other serious human rights abuses against LGBT people by government officials and nonstate actors and to ensure that the perpetrators of such abuses are held accountable. Finally, at the international, regional, and national levels, AI is working to ensure that human rights standards include protection from discrimination based on sexual orientation and gender identity. Amnesty's research and documentation is done primarily by the International Secretariat (IS) based in London. IS researches individual cases and relevant legal information, then compiles action guides distributed to national sections. Based on these guides, local and student groups and individual activists organize letter-writing and other campaigning activities.

"To Russia with Love" protesters on their way to the Russian embassy in Copenhagen, Denmark, on August 20, 2013. The organizers of the protest, Copenhagen Pride, Sabaah, Amnesty International, LGBT Denmark, and All Rights CPH, arranged the demonstration march from the Christiansborg Palace to the Russian embassy in Copenhagen. The march was a protest against the Russian Parliament's act that directly criminalized so-called homosexual "propaganda" to children and adolescents. (AP Photo/Polfoto, Politiken, Jens Dresling)

Along with its work coordinating campaigns on these issues, OUTfront has a more general informative role. AI produces regular reports on the status of LGBT human rights in countries around the world. These violations include the death penalty, torture, extrajudicial killing, and arbitrary arrest. OUTfront makes sure these reports are publicized in the United States. Additionally, OUTfront contributes to this effort by doing research on LGBT rights issues in the United States. Perhaps OUTfront's most important study to date is "Stonewalled: Police Abuse and Misconduct against Lesbian, Gay, Bisexual and Transgender People in the US." Released in 2005, this report draws on hundreds of interviews of advocacy organizations and testimonials from victims, as well as surveys of police departments in the largest cities in all 50 states, and documents human rights abuses by law enforcement officials against LGBT people. Besides describing persistent and widespread general misconduct, the report also concludes that within the LGBT community, transgender individuals, people of color, the young, immigrants, and sex workers suffer disproportionately due to increased vulnerability. The report provides recommendations on how authorities might resolve these problems.

AI's direct support of work on violations related to sexual orientation and gender identity has evolved over the last 20-plus years and through much international debate. Differences among sections arose due to the wide diversity of cultures and opinions on the work of the international movement. Progress began in 1979 when the biennial International Council Meeting (ICM), AI's key policy-setting process, affirmed that people imprisoned for advocating lesbian and gay rights would be considered for adoption as POCs. In 1982, the ICM condemned forced medical treatments carried out on people in detention to alter their sexual orientation. The next step occurred in 1985 when the AI Dutch Section undertook a study exploring future involvement on human rights violations and homosexuality, opening the doors for more organized efforts on behalf of LGBT human rights concerns.

In 1991, the ICM in Yokohama, Japan, passed changes that were seen as allowing AI to keep up with other social movements' priorities. Decisions were made that significantly expanded the scope of Amnesty's mission: AI would confront abuses by opposition groups, not just governments; rape carried out during military conflict would be considered a war crime; and people imprisoned "solely because of their homosexuality, including the practice of homosexual acts in private between consenting adults" would be considered POCs. Despite opposition from a number of AI sections, it was clear that the majority of the movement at large was in favor of the change supporting additional work on sexual orientation. Support for this decision, in large part, came from AI members and LGBT advocacy and lobbying on an international level.

The 1991 ICM became one of the most innovative in the organization's history and saw an overhaul of the statutes defining POCs (an entire section entitled "Taking on New Challenges" was included in its 1992 annual report describing the changes). While many amendments reflected practices already addressed unofficially by AI, others were largely new at AI's international level (such as the addition of sexual orientation). Also, while the language of the 1991 decision does not directly affirm the rights of transgender people, work on their behalf has

steadily been increasing as a natural extension of AI's efforts against both sexuality- and gender-based violence.

Although there was support for LGBT advocacy in a number of sections, AI members in the United States were among the strongest advocates for work on violations related to sexual orientation. In 1989, (AIUSA's volunteer-based Members for Lesbian & Gay Concerns (AIMLGC) formed to campaign for the development of AI's LGBT work. Similar groups in other Amnesty sections emerged soon after and LGBT rights became one of the most dynamic growth areas within AI throughout the 1990s. AIMLGC gained official status as a formally recognized volunteer group within AIUSA at its 1993 annual membership policy meeting in Los Angeles.

Frustrated by the slow progress on documentation of lesbian and gay human rights concerns coming from the London headquarters, AIUSA got approval to coordinate with LGBT groups in other sections and produced its own report in 1994. "Breaking the Silence: Human Rights Violations Based on Sexual Orientation" detailed abuses throughout the world and provided a comprehensive list of countries that criminalized homosexual relations. It was one of the first documents ever published by a mainstream human rights organization on sexual orientation and human rights. AIUSA sent the report, along with its research questionnaire, to all national sections of AI to help facilitate the integration of LGBT rights into the organization's existing concerns, which had been made possible by the 1991 ICM decision.

AIUSA has also been a leader in collaborating with other LGBT rights groups in advocacy and public education efforts. Amnesty OUTfront has partnered with a number of domestic and international LGBT nongovernmental organizations in lobbying, campaigning, and support of release of prisoners or repeal of discriminatory laws. As part of a global human rights movement, AI OUTfront has become a respected partner in a growing global effort to combat human rights abuses against LGBT people and to gain general recognition that LGBT people are entitled to the full range of human rights guaranteed to all the world's citizens.

Jon Hoffman

See also: ACT UP (AIDS Coalition to Unleash Power); Activists; Lambda Legal Defense and Education Fund (LLDEF).

Further Reading

Amnesty International USA. 2013. "Lesbian, Gay, Bisexual and Transgender Human Rights Homepage." Available at : http://www.amnestyusa.org/our-work/issues/lgbt-rights.

Amnesty International USA. 2001. *Crimes of Hate, Conspiracy of Silence: Torture and Ill-Treatment Based on Sexual Identity.* New York: Amnesty International Publications. Available at: http://www.amnesty.org/en/library/asset/ACT40/016/2001/en/c5792a3f-d961-11dd-a057-592cb671dd8b/act400162001en.html.

Amnesty International USA. 2005. *Stonewalled: Police Abuse and Misconduct against Lesbian, Gay, Bisexual and Transgender People in the U.S.* New York: Amnesty International USA. Available at:. http://www.amnesty.org/en/library/info/AMR51/122/2005.

Hopgood, Stephen. 2006. *Keepers of the Flame.* Ithaca, NY: Cornell University Press.

Ancient Greek and Roman Sexuality and Philosophy and Impact on the American Legal System

Greek men, skin glinting with olive oil, wrestling naked in the Mediterranean sunshine; entire island paradises populated by lesbians; steamy encounters in sultry bathhouses; Roman orgies of epic proportions: To a mainstream, homophobic, American mindset, no matter how impressive the Parthenon and the Colosseum may otherwise be, these "repugnant" images of sexual excess and debauchery only showcase the ancient Greco-Roman world as a backward, not-so-Golden Age that is better left lost in ruins and forgotten. At such a vantage point, ancient Greece and Rome must appear pejoratively *archaic*—and contemporary

LGBTQ individuals must surely seem like sorry vestiges of that backwardness. Modern American queers are, of course, not immune to seeing the worst stereotypes about themselves represented by the ancient Greeks and Romans either. From a twenty-first-century perspective, the practices and philosophies of ancient Greek and Rome might hardly resemble a bygone queer utopia; indeed, some iconographies of pederasty are likely to make even members of North American Man/Boy Love Association (NAMBLA) nervous.

Within this context of popular (mis)conception, any impact that ancient Greek and Roman sexuality and philosophy have had on the American legal system is bound to be seen as always already negative. It would thus seem all the more improbable that ancient ideals of "Greek love" should be particularly instrumental to challenging antihomophobic legislation in the United States. But they have been. At the same time, ancient evidence has also been deployed to bolster discriminatory legislation. Thus, appealing to Greco-Roman history is a double-edged sword for queer politics in the present.

Though potentially rewarding, such resignifying strategies are also fraught with several difficulties. First, when American lawmakers make recourse to archaic attitudes about sex or virtue, they sometimes reduce a contingent body of knowledge to stable foundation. Despite severe cutbacks in educational support, classical studies remain a vibrant field of scholarly inquiry. Each new discovery obliges a reassessment of what is known—or thought to be known—about peoples who lived over two millennia ago. The ancient Greeks and Romans may be long gone, but their legacy is a living, protean force. Thus, whatever self-validating interpretation of Plato's *Symposium* is *en vogue* today is sure to be contested or replaced by another tomorrow. And along those same lines, even a conscious, unbiased effort to excavate pro-queer sentiments from Greco-Roman culture is bound to meet with disappointing results at least some of the time.

For even when American queers look away from popular stereotypes and turn toward academic contexts for ways to demystify and historicize their

A Greek stele relief depicting a wrestling competition between athletes. From Kerameikos necropolis, circa 510 B.C. (DEA/ G. NIMATALLAH/De Agostini/Getty Images)

Greco-Roman heritage, there is no guarantee that they will like what they see. To illustrate, renowned classicist Eva C. Keuls, professor emeritus at the University of Minnesota, begins her landmark feminist revaluation of Ancient Greek culture and art, entitled *The Reign of the Phallus: Sexual Politics in Ancient Athens* (1985) in terms that one might hope are off-putting to anyone hoping to re-create the past in the present:

> In the case of a society dominated by men who sequester their wives and daughters, denigrate the female role in reproduction, erect monuments to the male genitalia, have sex with the sons of their peers, sponsor public whorehouses, create a mythology of rape, and engage in rampant saber-rattling, it is not inappropriate to refer to a reign of the phallus. Classical Athens was such a society. (p. 1)

She quickly qualifies this rather caustic characterization of Greek society, though, with a suggestion that acknowledging the phallocratic "nature" of ancient Greece "will have the effect, not of disparaging the achievements of Athenian culture but rather of enriching our sense of them" (p. 1). Obviously, her proposal that a *re*valuation need not be a *de*valuation of "the achievements of Athenian culture" must

be somewhat reassuring to an audience of traditional (and mostly male) classicists.

Far less obvious is what possible enrichment could be gained by modern members of the LGBTQ community in the United States, both within and outside academia, who might identify with Greek ancestors so eloquently presented as misogynists, prostitutes, pimps, phallus-worshippers, saber-rattlers, rapists, and pedophiles. Most assuredly, some people (queer and otherwise) might find more to desire than to disdain about "monuments to the male genitalia." The plethora of images posted online of enormous phalluses sculptured out of snow in front of fraternity houses may even attest to a quite literal remnant of the phallocratic Greek system. To what political or legal use such statues could be put is, however, perhaps difficult to conceive.

The ancient Romans would seem to be even less likely candidates for positive appropriation by American queers living two millennia and an ocean away from the amphitheaters. With their stereotypical reputation as a bloodthirsty, war-mongering, imperialist, gladiatorial culture, it is little wonder that they would seem to be chiefly remembered for the *dissolution* of their civilization rather than its lasting significance. Even the Roman bathhouse has become something of a doubly-lost ideal in queer communities. At the pinnacle of the empire, the baths "embodied the ideal Roman way of urban life" (Yegül 1992, p. 30). Their later American counterparts became staple features in many urban centers during the late nineteenth and early twentieth centuries. Now, though, in the wake of the AIDS epidemic, the comparatively few bathhouses that remain are often scorned as hotbeds of immoral, risky behavior (Cohler 2009).

Because specific instances of appealing to classical antiquity in recent American legal contexts occur within a wider web of identifications with Greco-Roman culture, it is instructive to briefly sketch some of the larger issues of identity politics that are also at stake. For example, in *How to Do the History of Homosexuality* (2002), David M. Halperin, W.H. Auden Distinguished University Professor of the History and Theory of Sexuality at the University of Michigan, articulates the crucial interplay between historicization and identification:

> Identification gets at something, something important: it picks out resemblances, connections, echo effects. . . . [T]he ability to set aside historical differences in order to focus on historical continuities is no less crucial to our personal, political, and cultural projects than is the ethical or ascetic determination to see in the documented experiences of other peoples something else besides self-confirming reflections of ourselves. (pp. 15–16)

For many LGBTQ Americans, the difficulty in finding "self-confirming reflections" in ancient artifacts is exacerbated by skewed accounts of those artifacts in the scholarly literature. For example, a variety of ancient representations suggest that many men and some women had sexual relationships with both females and males. Hence, contemporary bisexuals might reasonably be puzzled, if not completely alienated, by the way most historical studies, with the rare exception of Eva Cantarella's *Bisexuality in the Ancient World* (1994/2002), classify these relationships under the umbrella of *homosexuality*. They might then

A bust of Plato. First published in *Die Bildniskunst der Griechen & Rmer* by Anton Hekler. Published: J. Hoffmann Stuttgart, 1912. (Wellcome Library, London)

join their straight allies in gazing in bewilderment at the following sentence from the entry on "Heterosexuality in Ancient Greece" in the *Encyclopedia of the Ancient Greek World*: "Most men (we know less about the sexual habits and inclinations of Greek women) were bisexual" (Sacks 2005). What regrettably *is* accurate about such an otherwise bizarre statement is that most archaic cultural productions, from poetry to vases to mosaics to paintings, were produced by men. Thus, relics detailing the patriarchal "reign of phallus" abound; concrete examples of female sexuality generally and of woman-woman eroticism or bisexuality more specifically are comparatively rare. So deep are the depths of patriarchal thinking that the often virulent vilification of feminine men and masculine women in ancient art seems to tell us less about the history of crossdressing, intersexuality, or transgenderism than about codes of proper manliness.

However, just because instances of male sexuality are more readily located in the historical record does not mean that they easily invite or reward contemporary gay men's desirous identification with them. In *How to Do the History of Homosexuality* (2002), Halperin reflects on his motivations for writing his earlier and highly acclaimed monograph, *One Hundred Years of Homosexuality and Other Essays on Greek Love* (1990), stating: "it was not my intention to prevent anyone today from regarding the Greeks as positive gay role models, as sources of gay pride, or as points of reference for an anti-homophobic politics" (p. 14). "But at the same time," he continues, "I really *did* want to interrupt contemporary gay men's straightforward, uncritical identifications with the Greeks, in order to make the Greeks unavailable to us as vehicles of cultural chauvinism" (p. 14). As Halperin puts it: "There would be little point in promoting a new gay-affirmative practice of classical studies if the result of such gay affirmation was to affirm misogyny, class hierarchy, Eurocentrism, and racism (not to mention slavery) through an incautious return to Hellenism" (p. 14). Here, Halperin's unsavory description of "cultural chauvinism" echoes Keuls' "reign of the phallus." He goes on to affirm that "just because Greek paederasty differs in a number of crucial respects from contemporary metropolitan gay male identity, it doesn't follow that metropolitan gay men today cannot or should not identify with ancient Greeks" (p. 15). However, after reading such descriptions as Keuls's it is hard to imagine why gay men would *want* to do so. Indeed, the curious absence of any sustained discussion about Greek influences on contemporary queer culture in his recent study of *How to Be Gay* (2012) would seem to suggest that Halperin himself doubts the value of "going Greek" today.

These recent scholarly accounts would seem to reverse the terms from which orthodox Christian perspectives have long worried about their Greek heritage. If Christians ask, "how could the ancient Greeks, who had so many good things to say about virtue, be so thoroughly addicted to this vice" of homosexuality? (Davidson 2007, p. 1), historians and others looking for Greek role models might inquire: How could the ancient Greeks, who seem to embrace and accept homosexuality, act so repellently toward women, foreigners, and each other? If we dare to claim "Greek love" as virtuous rather than vicious, as an institution which could positively shape the relationship between the law and sexuality today, whose legal interests might such (re)claiming serve?

Faced with such difficulties in identification, it perhaps seems all the more incredible that ancient Greek evidence, in particular, should be cited in support of contemporary queer rights. Cataloging *all* of the ways in which Greek and Roman philosophy has influenced the treatment of LGBTQ people within the American legal system is necessarily beyond the scope of this encyclopedia topic. Instead, the stakes of interpreting the constitutionality of U.S. laws through ancient Greek lenses can be seen by focusing on pro-queer activities from the 1990s, a period bookended by two landmark and related Supreme Court decisions. In *Bowers v. Hardwick* (1986), the Supreme Court upheld as constitutional a Georgia anti-sodomy statute; in *Lawrence v. Texas* (2003), the Court not only deemed a Texas law against sodomy unconstitutional but actually overturned its own decision in *Bowers v. Hardwick*, effectively decriminalizing private, consensual homosexuality among adults nationwide.

Thus, as evinced by these decisions, the late 1980s to the early 2000s bracket a time of shifting attitudes toward homosexuality in the United States. Though many people might understandably prefer to forget *Bowers v. Hardwick* and the pall it cast on queer rights, to review the case is instructive. Supreme Court ruled that adults engaging in private acts of consensual sodomy are not protected under the "right to privacy" that is stipulated in the U.S. Constitution. As part of its ruling, the Court appealed to the history of anti-sodomy laws in the United States. Even before the signing of the Declaration of Independence, the 13 colonies had outlawed sodomy. All 50 states thereafter followed suit. Not until January 1, 1962, did Illinois become the first state to decriminalize sodomy.

By the 1980s, sodomy remained illegal in almost half of the United States—including Georgia. According to the Georgia Sodomy Statute, "a person commits the offense of sodomy when he performs or submits to any sexual act involving the sex organs of one person and the mouth or anus of another." Moreover, "a person convicted of the offense of sodomy shall be punished by imprisonment for not less than one nor more than 20 years." Hence, in 1982, when law enforcement inadvertently caught Michael Hardwick and another man in an act of oral copulation, the two men were arrested. Arguing that the anti-sodomy law was unconstitutional, Hardwick retaliated. However, Hardwick's ultimate loss when the case went before the Supreme Court in 1986 signified a major defeat for all queer Americans.

Significantly, in their efforts to combat the homophobia of the U.S. legal system, scholars and lawmakers turned to none other than the ancient Greeks for support. Then as now, within arguments defending homosexuality, Plato's *Symposium* (c. 385–380 bce) holds pride of place. Such a foregrounding of this text is perhaps unsurprising. For historians of Greek homosexuality, the *Symposium* has long been an invaluable resource. Within the text's Athenian setting, seven male attendees of the *symposium* (drinking party) deliver speeches about the nature and purpose of love (Eros): Phaedrus, Pausanias, Eryximachus, Aristophanes, Agathon (who also hosts the gathering), Socrates, and Alcibiades. Of special interest to students of "Greek love" are the speeches by playwright Aristophanes (c. 446 BC–c. 386 BCE) and philosopher Socrates (469–399 BCE). The former dramatist's oratory is sometimes taken as story of the origins and value of sexuality for all human beings, whereas the latter scholar defines and delineates a more specifically chaste "Platonic Love." To thank Plato for the greater freedoms extended to LGBTQ individuals in the wake of *Lawrence v. Texas* would, of course, grossly overstate the case. But the use to which the ancient Greek evidence was put in the years leading

up to the repeal of *Bowers v. Hardwick* can nevertheless shed light on how Greco-Roman philosophy has been—and may continue to be—a powerful force in the fight for queer rights.

Though obviously dated in their pre-*Lawrence v. Texas* outlook, scholarly and legalistic writings from the 1990s remain timely in their creative employment of Greek history in the service of advancing American LGBTQ rights. For example, in a fascinating chapter on "Platonic Love and Colorado Law: The Relevance of Ancient Greek Norms to Modern Sexual Controversies" in her book *Sex & Social Justice* (1999), Martha C. Nussbaum, the Ernst Freund Distinguished Service Professor of Law and Ethics, appointed in the Law School and Philosophy Department at the University of Chicago, provides both an informed summary and critique of recent appropriations of Greek history in legal cases and a spirited endorsement of Greek philosophy as a tool for American justice systems. Nussbaum delineates several ways in which timely debates about the morality and legality of sex can be enriched by the "radical and valuable" representations of sexuality in ancient Greece: by impelling us to reconsider the assumptions underlying juridical and moral practices, which only appear to be universal and timeless but are actually constructed, contingent, and thus susceptible to change; by enabling us to put to the test empirically based arguments, such as that family and societal structures will crumble in the face of increased tolerance for homosexuality; and finally, by both promulgating compassion for and offering compelling testimony to the human value of same-sex love and relations (p. 301).

Before explicitly articulating her position, Nussbaum prefaces her argument with a couple of telling anecdotes that led to her current stance. The first is a secondhand account of Richard Posner's self-tutelage in Greek philosophy. An "American judge, a Reagan appointee to the U.S. Court of Appeals for the Seventh Circuit," Posner in 1990 read "Plato's *Symposium* for the first time, in order to 'plug one of the many embarrassing gaps in my education'" (p. 300). She quotes Posner's reflection on this reading experience, as recorded in his book *Sex and Reason* (1992), at some length:

> I knew it was about love, but that was all I knew. I was surprised to discover that it was a defense, and as one can imagine a highly interesting and articulate one, of homosexual love. It had never occurred to me that the greatest figure in the history of philosophy, or for that matter any other respectable figure in the history of thought, had attempted such a thing. It dawned on me that the discussion of the topic in the opinions in *Bowers vs. Hardwick* was superficial. . . . (p. 300)

Nussbaum goes on to recapitulate Posner's argument that historical knowledge and empathetic attitudes toward homosexuals are two sides of the same coin: "he suggests that the 'irrational fear and loathing' expressed in the Georgia statute under which Michael Hardwick was prosecuted, and endorsed in the opinions, might have been dispelled by a study of history—beginning, it would appear, with a study of Plato" (p. 300). His book *Sex and Reason*, Nussbaum explains, "was his own attempt to advance this educational process, and 'to shame my colleagues in the profession' (p. 4) for failing to educate themselves in this area" (p. 300). She then analyzes how Posner's educative experience has subsequently shaped his judicial opinions, citing specifically the case of *United States v. Lallemand*, wherein Lallemand "deliberately set out to blackmail a married homosexual," and Posner's empathic response to the victim who had attempted suicide because of the ordeal (p. 300; 445).

The second anecdote is Nussbaum's first-person account of how "[o]n October 15, 1993, I found myself on the witness stand in a courtroom in Denver, Colorado, telling State District Judge H. Jeffrey Bayless about Plato's *Symposium*" (p. 300). Nussbaum explains that she concentrated on Aristophanes, not least because his speech is a mouthpiece for ideas Plato "wishes his reader to take especially seriously," a point she made in her earlier book on *The Fragility of Goodness: Luck and Ethics in Greek Tragedy and Philosophy* (1986). She continues: "I told the court the story of how human beings were once round and

whole—but now, cut in half for their overambitiousness, they feel a sense of lost wholeness and run about searching for their 'other half' (p. 300). Summarizing Plato's text, she notes that Aristophanes describes three different types of people who each search for a different type of completeness: "There are males whose 'other half' is male, females whose 'other half' is female, and people whose 'other half' is of the opposite sex" (p. 300). Other scholars have cited this classificatory schema as evidence of homosexual *persons* rather than just homosexual *acts* in the ancient world: a point Halperin cogently disputes (1990, pp. 20–21). For Nussbaum, at any rate, Aristophanes' speech underscores "the feelings of intimacy and joy" experienced when the pairs reunite and "sexual intercourse as a joyful attempt to be restored to the lost unity of their original natures" (p. 300). Each unified couple is seen as uniquely valuable to society, as their sexual desires reflect "a deep inner need," which nature has instilled in them (p. 300). By interpreting "[t]his text and many others," Nussbaum proposed that "a study of history" would help elucidate not only the "valuable array" of *what* has been said about homosexuality but also help clarify and assess the reasonable of more recent arguments (pp. 300–301).

Taken at face value, Posner's interpretation of the *Symposium* as a "defense . . . of homosexual love" and Nussbaum's subsequent defense of Posner's position make a compelling case. The Aristophanean imagery of lost halves coming together in wholeness must surely strike a chord in an American culture nursed on happy endings and romance plots about soulmates and "star-crossed lovers." Theirs, though, is something of a minority view. Regardless of how seriously we are to take Aristophanes's part, analyzing "many other" texts has led scholars to divergent conclusions about the nature and origin of Greek love. Philosophical, astrological, and literary works reference people who are said to prefer same-sex object choice "by nature," which has been construed as proof that the ancient Greeks recognized different "types" of people based on their inborn sexual preferences even though the terms *homosexuality, heterosexuality*, and *bisexuality* did not yet exist. As for origins, some scholars trace the beginnings of Greek "homosexuality" back to Crete or Sparta, others to Minoa and Indo-Europe (900–700 BCE), and yet others to texts by Plutarch, Homer, and other writers (cf. Hubbard 2003, pp. 14–15; Percy 1996, pp. 53–8).

When the implications of many historians' efforts are taken together, the picture that emerges is that, whatever their origins within ancient Greek culture, sexual desires were neither inherently "good" nor "bad." Rather, like all pleasurable urges and appetites, they were to be indulged in moderation and not abused to excess. Thus, there was no widespread disapproval of either same-sex or opposite-sex relations as such. Both were acceptably moral outlets for satisfying desire, such that even married Greek men customarily sought the services of sex workers, female and male alike, without censure. However, "Greek love" did not necessarily mean "free love," and increasingly notions of rightness and wrongness accrue around certain forms of sexuality, particularly pederasty.

Thus, it is crucial to note that in instances of sexual acts between free male citizens in classical Athens, the anatomical *sex* of the participants did not matter but their sociocultural *gender* roles absolutely did. The asymmetrical distinction in gender positions was especially pronounced in pederasty (*paiderastia*): a Greek term describing a socially recognized and sometimes celebrated homosexual relationship between an upper-class adult male "lover," known as the *erastês*, and a freeborn "beloved" youth, known as the *erômenos*. Though this description might conjure images of an aggressive grown "man" and a helpless prepubescent "boy," ancient visual evidence suggests that the *erômenos* would typically have been in his late teens and the *erastês* might not have been much older. Thus, the age gap between the partners could be bridged; however, their gender and social roles could not. According to Halperin, the "most salient erotic distinction" the ancient Greek made involved "the social articulation of power (superordinate vs. subordinate social identity)," not differences based upon sex or gender: "The result was a social/conceptual/erotic grid that aligned masculinity, activity, penetration, and dominance along one axis and femininity, passivity,

being penetrated, and submission along another. Those two axes corresponded to, but could function independently of, gender differences" (2002, p. 56). The older *erastês* was seen as the "active," penetrative partner, whose desire for, pursuit, and enjoyment of sex with the beautiful male youth were unproblematic to his superior masculinity and morality. Whether penetrating a male youth, woman, or prostitute of either sex, the older lover's active role was socially expected and encouraged, untainted by abnormality or unnaturalness. Meanwhile, viewed as "passive" and penetrated, the younger *erômenos* risked public condemnation for womanly behavior if he openly enjoyed his institutionalized subjugation *too* enthusiastically.

In other words, it was acceptable for the *erômenos* to delight in the nonsexual privileges he might gain from the fruits of his labor but not in the erotic sensations stimulated in being penetrated by his older lover. The role of the *erômenos* was properly transitory, a rite of passage on the way to adult manliness. Taking sexual pleasure in being penetrated risked developing a permanent proclivity for passivity that would impair his progression from passive, dominated *erômenos* to active, dominating *erastês*. By the same logic, however, the *erastês* had probably been an *erômenos* at one time, and satirists poke much fun at adult lovers who despite appearances still prefer the passive role.

Pederasty is an important chapter among many in the story of "Greek love," and recent reappraisals of ancient Greece are changing the way that story is told. Even the very *Greekness* of pederasty has been questioned (Williams 1999, pp. 64–72). From one direction, pederasty is to be distinguished from other contexts of male same-sex interactions such as legal prostitution and the bonds between warriors-in-arms (e.g., Halperin 1990, 2002). But from another, pederasty has been seen as just one gendered institution within a larger patriarchal paradigm, what Keuls calls "the reign of the phallus," whereby free adult Greek men had power and privilege over many "others": women, children, slaves, and foreigners. Novel interpretations of Greek art and literature further suggest that mutual affection was at least within the horizon of pederastic possibilities, that pederasty was an orthodox cultural practice and not simply a byproduct of men occupying close quarters away and apart from women, and that Greek loving encompassed a broader range of interactions beyond dynamics of domination and submission (cf. Davidson 2007).

While it now appears as though pioneering classicists exaggerated the importance of penetration in male same-sex relations, it is nevertheless the case that ancient Greek attitudes toward anal sex are mixed—and echoes of this ambivalence can be heard in contemporary views of sexuality and legal rights. If anal sex between men did occur in ancient Greek contexts, as was often assumed, it was nevertheless not to be spoken about in public: a stipulation that curiously resonates with one of the criticisms of *Lawrence v. Texas*. Since most sexual violence happens *in private*, the Court's decision has been seen by some feminist and queer detractors as implicitly sanctioning those violent acts committed behind closed doors.

At the same time, representations of anal sex flourish in some depictions of pederasty and, considering that some gay men still only reluctantly admit to bottoming because "playing catcher is seen as feminine—the woman's role," it might be tempting to see contemporary culture as *less* tolerant by comparison (Wilchins 2004, p. 18). Perhaps one reason why scholars and activists tend to look to ancient Greece rather than Rome is because, in Roman society, the equation of passive-penetrated-feminized became even more pronounced. According to Craig A. Williams, a Classics Professor at Brooklyn College and the CUNY Graduate Center: "The biographer Suetonius tells us that Julius Caesar was mocked for having had in his youth an affair with the Bithynian king Nicomedes in which he [Caesar] played the receptive or 'passive' role in sexual intercourse" (p. 9). Though Williams's account of Roman masculin*ity* has been accused of ignoring gradations between and among different Roman masculini*ties* (McDonnell 2006, p. 166), the parallels between anti-bottom sentiment then and now are unmistakably striking. *Lawrence v. Texas* may have decriminalized sodomy, but in the court of queer communities, gender injustices

certainly remain. The Greeks found their own way to avoid such gendered dangers: substitution. For example, many visual artifacts promote intercrural intercourse as an idealized alternative to anal sex. In these scenes, the problematic element of penetration is removed altogether, as the *erastês* is gratified by rubbing his penis between his younger lover's thighs. Additional concerns surrounding pederastic relationships include seeking casual sex that is not ensconced within larger cultural dynamics of politics, education, or friendship, buying or selling sexual favors, and committing rape (cf. Davidson 2007; Nussbaum 1999). Again, these ancient misgivings might serve as sobering reminders that a queer culture completely free of sexual exploitation and violence remains on a distant horizon.

Thus far this encyclopedia entry has focused on Greek influences in American legal contexts, but it would not be complete without some discussion of the surprising relationship between ancient Roman practices and current gay marriage. Williams may be right to assert that "'Greek love' is a modern invention"; however, his research also shows that male same-sex marriage was definitely a Roman affair (1999, p. 72). According to Williams, a variety of "evidence certainly suggests that some Roman men participated in wedding ceremonies with other men and considered themselves to be married to those men" (p. 246). Still, male-male marriages were "anomalous," and gender complications likely would have arisen: "In traditional Roman terms, a marriage between two fully gendered 'men' was inconceivable; if two males were joined together, one of them had to be 'the woman'" (p. 252). As noted earlier, the gendering of roles in male homosexuality remains a major point of contention in contemporary queer politics. In ancient Rome, one man acquired an infamous reputation, not only for having an incestuous relationship with his mother, but also for switch-hitting between the positions of husband and wife within his multiple same-sex marriages.

That man, of course, was Nero (37—68 CE): he reigned as emperor from 54 through 68 CE, and his infamy has, perhaps unsurprisingly, been appropriated by opponents to same-sex marriage. The following year after the U.S. Supreme Court decriminalized sodomy, Massachusetts became the first state to legalize gay marriage. In the eyes of many pundits, the bane of civilization was surely nigh. To counter these claims, Andrew Sullivan, a gay male and political conservative, argued on the pages of *Time* magazine that, because marriage is a conservative institution, extending marriage rights to gays and lesbians would actually buttress rather than destroy civilized society. Sullivan's controversial position inspired mixed responses.

One notable counter argument appeared, however, in *The New Oxford Review*: "Rump Rangers in Ancient Rome: A Rosy Future for Same-Sex Marriage?" (2005), by Leland D. Peterson, Emeritus Professor of English and Latin at Old Dominion University. Chiding Sullivan for his seeming ignorance of "precedents in the ancient world," Peterson asserts that Sullivan could, should if only he would take the time to do so, "find out easily that 'gay marriage' was a key element in the collapse of the Roman Empire. Something very much like the AIDS epidemic that has been the scourge of such 'gay' meccas as San Francisco, and is now a worldwide epidemic, can be identified in the second century A.D." At this point, Peterson commences an inflammatory account of Nero's sins, not the least of which is his alleged "invention" of "[s]ame-sex 'marriage,'" which is presented as of apiece of his murderous behaviors. Then follows a lengthy survey of other factors which contributed to the fall of the Roman Empire: homosexuality and pestilence chief among them. Homosexual and homicidal become synonymous terms. Yet, he qualifies his argument thusly: "Same-sex 'marriage' by itself did not bring about Roman decadence. But it signaled unmistakably the triumphant emergence of a society dominated by a homosexuality dedicated to insatiable sensual experiences without the responsibilities of producing and raising children." Sullivan had also claimed that because gay relationships typically tolerate "extramarital outlets," these open relationships might outlast heterosexual unions. To Peterson,

it sounds like Sullivan is advocating the ways of ancient Rome. The U.S. in the 21st century—with legalized abortion, readily available contraception, a consistently high rate of divorce, rampant adultery, and teenage fornication resulting in high rates of sexually transmitted diseases—has only to elect as its president a bachelor with same-sex partners who will have a wedding ceremony in the White House in which he wears the veil, and then to await its plagues, barbarian invasions, and epidemics to hasten its decline and fall. I predict the election of a president fulfilling those qualifications in A.D. 2068, two millennia after the death of Nero.

At the time of this writing, 2068 is still over half a century into the future, but Peterson might think that the United States has prematurely plunged into ancient Rome. Currently, 18 states and the District of Columbia recognize same-sex marriage in some fashion and 4 others acknowledge civil unions. Some queer scholars and activists judiciously question whether the rights afforded by same-sex marriage come at too high a cost to those who would still advocate for legal recognitions outside the bonds of matrimony. Those who cringe at the thought of being "normal" or "conformist," though, are probably also not likely to celebrate Nero as a model for queer praxis. In the words of Halperin: "The tendency to refashion past sexual cultures in the image of our own says a lot about our own historical situation, the functioning of contemporary sexual categories, our standard ways of thinking about the past. It is richly informative in its own right" (2002, p. 15). Peterson's appropriation of Roman history in an invective against same-sex rights is a powerful reminder that such refashioning cuts both ways, and that insisting upon the relevancy of the ancient past to contemporary sexual politics runs the risk of oppression as well as the potential for liberation.

To document all the ways ancient Greco-Roman sexuality and philosophy have had an impact upon the American legal system and on the LGBTQ citizens represented within it is impossible. Every landmark decision invokes different precedents, archaic and modern. What should be clear, however, is that more than just identification and a search for positive role models from the past are at stake. In popular parlance, people say "that is Greek to me" when they encounter ideas they cannot (or choose not to) understand. Making *Greek* a synonym for *incomprehensible* serves both sides of the battle for LQBTQ legal rights—indeed, it serves them both poorly. The homophobic legislator and the queer activist to whom each other's positions are "Greek" are not bound to make much headway in either direction. Similarly, the adage "when in Rome, do as the Romans do" is also misleadingly simplistic, implying as it does a kind of temporary conformity to "going Roman." Such a notion might fuel an oppressive agenda just as easily as a progressive one. Rome *fell*, after all, and whether its dissolution is a queer history to be repeated or a sign of portending doom remains to be seen. However, as difficult and contradictory as wrestling a usable past from our Greco-Roman heritage may be, the most egregious crime of all would be to wholly relinquish the project to those who would seek to make queers ancient history.

Christopher Lozensky

See also: Same-Sex Marriage in the United States; Sappho (Sixth Century BCE); Socrates (469–399 BCE).

Further Reading

Cohler, Bertram J. 2009. "Bathhouses and sex clubs." In *LGBTQ America Today: An Encyclopedia*, ed. John C. Hawley, pp. 106–111. Volume 1. Westport: Greenwood Press.

Davidson, James. 2007. *The Greeks and Greek Love: A Bold New Exploration of the Ancient World*. New York: Random House. Also published as *The Greeks and Greek Love: A Radical Reappraisal of Homosexuality in Ancient Greece*, London: Phoenix, 2008.

Halperin, David M. 2012. *How to Be Gay*. Cumberland: Harvard University Press.

Halperin, David M. 2002. *How to Do the History of Homosexuality*. Chicago: University of Chicago Press.

Halperin, David M. 1990. *One Hundred Years of Homosexuality and Other Essays on Greek Love*. New York: Routledge.

Hubbard, Thomas K., ed. 2003. *Homosexuality in Greece and Rome: A Sourcebook of Basic Documents*. Berkeley: University of California Press.

Keuls, Eva C. 1985. *The Reign of the Phallus: Sexual Politics in Ancient Athens*. New York: Harper & Row.

McDonnell, Myles. 2006. *Roman Manliness:* Virtus *and the Roman republic*. Cambridge: Cambridge University Press.

Nussbaum, Martha C. 1999. "Platonic Love and Colorado Law: The Relevance of Ancient Greek Norms to Modern Sexual Controversies". In *Sex & Social Justice*, pp. 299–331. New York: Oxford University Press.

Percy, William Armstrong, III. 1996. *Pederasty and Pedagogy in Archaic Greece*. Urbana: University of Illinois Press.

Peterson, Leland D. 2005. "Rump Rangers in Ancient Rome: A Rosy Future for Same-Sex Marriage?" *New Oxford Review*. Volume LXXII, Number 6. June 2005. Available at: http://www.newoxfordreview.org/article.jsp?did=0605-peterson&k=boBcQWfRJTYZpNmRNGy7Beh0qd7tLo&end=END. Accessed December 8, 2013.

Sacks, David. 2005. Heterosexuality in Ancient Greece. *Encyclopedia of the Ancient Greek World*, Revised Edition. Revised by Lisa R. Brody. New York: Facts On File, Inc. Retrieved from *Ancient and Medieval History Online*. Facts On File, Inc. http://www.fofweb.com/activelink2.asp?ItemID=WE49&iPin=EAGW0243&SingleRecord=True. Accessed October 1, 2013.

Wilchins, Riki. 2004. *Queer Theory, Gender Theory: An Instant Primer*. Los Angeles: Alyson Books.

Williams, Craig A. 1999. *Roman Homosexuality: Ideologies of Masculinity in Classical Antiquity*. New York: Oxford University Press.

Yegül, Fikret. 1992. *Baths and Bathing in Classical Antiquity*. Cambridge: MIT.

Angus, Patrick (1953–1992)

Born in North Hollywood, California, artist Patrick Morton Angus grew up in Santa Barbara. In 1974 he received a Santa Barbara Art Institute scholarship. Early influences were Picasso, Park, Diebenkorn and Wonner. But it was *72 Drawings* by David Hockney, in which Hockney celebrated his gay persona and the "good" gay life in Los Angeles, that inspired Patrick to move there in 1975. He soon learned the "good" gay life did not exist for poor people. In 1980, in New York City to see the Picasso Retrospective at the Museum of Modern Art (MOMA), Patrick observed the sexual autobiography inherent in Picasso's work, which liberated him to use his own life experience as subject matter. Patrick worked for a time at MOMA, which he contemptuously called "a retail establishment."

He realized realistic homoerotic art was not tolerated by the art establishment, but he made the decision to devote himself to painting the truth of his own life. He lived in poverty. After he was introduced to readers of *Christopher Street* by Robert Patrick, he began to make some sales. Patrick Angus had no recognition from his peers in the art world until David Hockney purchased six major works. Soon after, in 1992, he had shows at University of California-Santa Barbara, and in New York City at Ralph Park's Ganymede Gallery and the Leslie-Lohman Gay Art Foundation. Some of his canvases are epic in conception and are a major contribution to the legacy of American social realism as embodied in the work of Eakins, Homer, Hopper, Marsh, and Cadmus. Patrick was concerned that his work would end up in a dumpster. On his deathbed he saw the proofs for a book of his paintings and said, "This is the happiest day of my life." Patrick died of AIDS in St. Vincent's Hospital, at the age of 38.

Douglas Turnbaugh

See also: Historical Overview of Gay Rights and Issues: From the 1980s to the Present.

Further Reading

Patrick, Robert. 2003. "Patrick Angus." *Archive (The), The Journal of the Leslie-Lohman Gay Art Foundation* 11: 4–8.

Trent, Robert. 1990. "The Portraits of Patrick Angus: Love, Pain and the Whole Damn Thing." *Christopher Street* 147: 18–25.

Turnbaugh, Douglas Blair. 2003. *Patrick Angus: Los Angeles Drawings*. New York and Berlin: Leslie-Lohman Gay Art Foundation and the Schwules Museum.

Turnbaugh, Douglas Blair. 1992. *Strip Show: Paintings by Patrick Angus*. London: Editions Aubrey Walter.

Anthony, Susan B. (1820–1906)

Susan B. Anthony was one of the major activists behind the early suffragette movement. She was born to the family of a Quaker abolitionist on February 15, 1820, in Adams, Massachusetts. She was able to read at an early age and was sent to boarding school in Philadelphia to finish her education. She became a teacher at Eunice Kenyon's Quaker Academy in New Rochelle, New York.

Hailed as "the Napoleon of the woman's rights movement," Susan B. Anthony led the fight for woman's suffrage for more than 50 years. (Library of Congress)

Elizabeth Cady Stanton, right, and Susan B. Anthony were American pioneers in the women's rights movement. (Library of Congress)

By 1846, she moved to Rochester, New York, where she became headmistress of the female department at the Canajoharie Academy. She joined the temperance movement and began to identify the inequalities between the sexes. Soon, in 1851, she met Elizabeth Cady Stanton. They formed a 50-year-long personal and political partnership that significantly impacted nineteenth-century America.

Anthony discovered that male temperance leaders were not interested in the participation of women.

Thus, in 1852, she founded the Women's State Temperance Society of New York. The Civil War pushed the struggle for women's rights to the back burner. Once the war was over, Anthony spoke across the country on the issues of women's right to control property, to their guardianship of their children, and to divorce. When the debate on the Fourteenth Amendment was held in Congress in 1868, which granted all males the right to vote, she led an unsuccessful attempt to have women included.

One by one, the women Anthony associated with married. Her loneliness was swept away in 1868 when she met Anna Dickinson—a woman 20 years her junior and popular lecturer on women's rights.

In 1872 Anthony tested the legality of the right of women to vote in Rochester, New York. She attempted to vote and was arrested, tried, and fined. She refused to pay the fine on moral grounds garnering much publicity for the cause. Susan B. Anthony died on March 13, 1906, in Rochester, New York, 14 years before the passage of the Nineteenth Amendment to the U.S. Constitution—the so-called Anthony amendment that granted women the right to vote.

Chuck Stewart

See also: Document: National Women's Rights Convention (1852).

Further Reading

Faderman, Lillian. 1992. *Odd Girls and Twilight Lovers: A History of Lesbian Life in Twentieth-Century America.* Penguin Books.

Faderman, Lillian. 1999. *To Believe in Women. What Lesbians Have.* Houghton Mifflin Company: New York.

Gibson, Michelle and Deborah Meem, eds. 2006. *Lesbian Academic Couples.* New York: Routledge.

Marcus, Sharon. 2007. *Between Women: Friendship, Desire, and Marriage in Victorian England.* Princeton, NJ: Princeton University Press.

Stein, Gertrude. 1990. *The Autobiography of Alice B. Toklas.* Vintage.

Veaux, Alexis De. 2006. *Warrior Poet: A Biography of Audre Lorde.* W. W. Norton & Company.

Antidiscrimination Statutes

Just how effective are antidiscrimination statutes at protecting the rights of lesbian and gay people? Often it is claimed that antidiscrimination statutes are unnecessary and, in fact, counterproductive. Here, we review both the impact antidiscrimination statutes have on employment for LGBT people and the effectiveness in agencies who are charged with the responsibility to enforce the law.

The state of Texas is an example of a region that has no overriding state law providing employment protections for LGBT people, yet has some local protections provided by city ordinances. Laura Barron (U.S. Air Force Management Policy Division) and Michelle Hebl (Rice University) conducted three studies in 2013 in the Dallas-Fort-Worth-Arlington area. Texas can be used to test the efficacy of antidiscrimination laws since areas that have no law (e.g., Arlington) can be compared directly with areas that have law (e.g., Dallas-Fort-Worth) and see if there is a measureable difference.

Using phone interview of 111 households, they found that the existence of antidiscriminatory laws and awareness of such laws influenced people to be less inclined to discriminate based on sexual orientation and more open to sexual minorities. Surprisingly, a large portion of the population was unaware these kinds of laws existed in their area. Part two of the study had actors apply for employment in 295 retail jobs in cities that either had, or did not have, an antidiscrimination statute and their sexual orientation (gay, lesbian, or nongay) was openly presented. In cities that had antidiscrimination statute, there was less discrimination against LGBT applicants. Finally, part three of the study found that when employees and managers were informed of antidiscrimination laws, their attitudes changed to be less antigay (Barron and Hebl 2013).

Although it is often claimed that you cannot legislate morality, "research studies have consistently shown that this is not the case" (Vitelli 2013). The impact of antidiscrimination statutes is related to the amount of publicity the statutes receive when passed and implemented. As people become aware of the law, they modify their behaviors and eventually their attitude. This points out the importance of passing the federal Employee Non-Discrimination Act (ENDA) to establish a national law to protect LGBT employees from antigay harassment on the job.

Marsha Botzer, a board member of the gay advocacy group Pride Foundation, sits with foundation employees Jeffrey Hedgepeth, left, and Sara Elward as she displays a letter they received from Wal-Mart Stores, Inc., on July 2, 2003. After prodding by the Seattle organization, Wal-Mart is now one of the 10 largest *Fortune* 500 companies to extend its antidiscrimination policy to protect the rights of gay and lesbian workers. (AP Photo/Elaine Thompson)

But what about the agencies whose responsibility it is to enforce the laws? Very little research has reviewed the effectiveness of government agencies to protect the rights of LGBT people. A 1996 review of the Department of Labor Standards Enforcement (DLSE) in California found that 91 percent of all complaints were not successful (dismissed, abandoned, or withdrawn) (Stewart 1993, 1996). When the agency was contacted as to why only 9 percent of all cases were settled in favor of the complainant, there was no answer and no interest in inquiring why the success rate was so low. Considering it takes a rather gutsy lesbian or gay man to file a complaint, the success rate reveals that enforcing antidiscrimination laws is difficult and rarely successful. However, as Barron and Hebl demonstrated, the existence of such laws helps reduce discrimination against LGBT people in employment.

Chuck Stewart

See also: Affirmative Action; Federal Employment Nondiscrimination Order; Historical Overview of Gay Rights and Issues: From Pre-Columbian Times to the 1970s; Historical Overview of Gay Rights and Issues: From the 1980s to the Present.

Further Reading

Barron, Laura G. and Hebl, Michelle. 2013. "The Force of Law: The Effects of Sexual Orientation Antidiscrimination Legislation on Interpersonal Discrimination in Employment." *Psychology, Public Policy, and Law* 19(2): 191–205.

Stewart, C. 1993. "How Effective Is AB2601?" *Edge*, September 8, p. 12.

Stewart, C.. 1996. "How Effective Is the Department of Labor Standards Enforcement at Protecting Our Rights Under AB2601?" *Edge*, August , p. 30.

Vitelli, Romeo. 2013, August 13. "How Effective Are Laws against Sexual-Orientation Discrimination?" *Huffington Post*. Available at: http://www.huffingtonpost.com/romeo-vitelli/how-effective-are-laws-against-sexual-orientation-discrimination_b_3743297.html. Accessed February 2, 2014.

Arvin, Frederick Newton (1900–1963)

Born and raised in Valparaiso, Indiana, Newton Arvin was a writer and professor, one of three gay faculty members fired by Smith College in 1960 for their sexual orientation. He was the son of a domineering father who tried, unsuccessfully, to make his son into a "real man." Weak, sickly, and short-sighted, he received a BA from Harvard and began an academic career at Smith College, where he helped establish the study of American literature at a time when the subject was very rarely taught. Arvin published biographies of American authors, most notably Hawthorne, Melville, Whitman, and Longfellow. Although he was very much closeted, his biographies discover an undercurrent of unhappiness and loneliness in these writers that Arvin himself shared.

Arvin was aware at an early age of his difference from other boys and finally recognized his homosexuality in his early days at Smith. He had a large circle of gay friends, including Truman Capote, who dedicated his first novel to Arvin. Beginning in college, Arvin participated in leftist politics, campaigning for presidential candidate Robert La Follette in 1924. He failed to join the Communist Party, however, which helped him avoid being called before congressional committees during the "Red Scare." Conservative Smith alumnae, however, called unsuccessfully for the firing of leftist faculty.

In 1960, arrested for possessing obscene material (exposed by a search of his apartment by means later outlawed by the Supreme Court) and exposed to public scorn, Arvin gave the police the names of two instructors, who were gay friends. The Smith faculty and president supported all three, but the trustees of the college terminated them. The affair, which threatened all gay men at Smith, has come to be known as the "Pink Scare."

Truman Capote dedicated his novel *Other Voices, Other Rooms* to Newton Arvin. Capote, a fiction and prose writer who started a vogue for what he called the nonfiction novel, saw Arvin as a mentor. (Library of Congress)

Arvin suffered severe bouts of depression, complicated by alcoholism, much of his life. He received numerous electroconvulsive treatments in the 1950s. He died of pancreatic cancer.

Jack Turner

See also: Historical Overview of Gay Rights and Issues: From Pre-Columbian Times to the 1970s.

Further Reading

Arvin, Newton. 1950. *Herman Melville.* New York: Sloane.

Werth, Barry. 2001. *The Scarlet Professor: Newton Arvin, A Literary Life Shattered by Scandal.* New York: Doubleday.

Asian Americans and LGBTQ Issues

The question of how to consider gender, race, and sexuality in Asian America today is problematic, as the lives of both Asian American and LGBTQ people have historically been fraught with conflict. Asian Americans live in the shadows of a history of oppression, both in their countries of origin and in the United States, that includes legislation such as the Chinese Exclusion Act of 1882 and *Ozawa v. United States*, which restricted Asian American immigration to the United States through the mid-twentieth century. Sexual minorities are subject to discrimination by social, psychological, and legal methods, and Asian Americans might be assumed to share common interests with LGBTQ movements in opposing the white heterosexual social structure that serves as the norm in America. It is no surprise, therefore, that groups like Asian Americans for Equality organized to fight injustice in the 1960s and 1970s, the same period of political unrest during which the gay liberation movement grew.

Yet there are numerous obstacles to an alignment between those Americans who identify as Asian and those who identify as LGBTQ. First, the term *Asian American* can encompass a multitude of cultural practices and ethnic origins that includes the immigrants and descendants of East, South, and Southeast Asians, among others. Within the groups labeled "Asian" there exist tensions among citizens of different nationalities.

Additionally, the concept of homosexuality, along with Western notions of sexuality itself, have been problematic subjects for many of the Asian cultures from which Asian Americans come. As Eric C. Wat argues, a separation between Asian and LGBTQ identities has been created and upheld in Asian America. In many Asian communities, homosexuality is seen as a wholly Western sexual practice and identity or is seen to come from Western influences. The prevailing understanding in both gay and Asian communities has been one of mutual exclusion: one cannot be both Asian and gay.

As Wat observes, the intersection between two or more oppressed identity categories is difficult to navigate, so sexual minorities are largely excluded from the category of Asian America. Also, many queer Asians find that mainstream gay advocacy groups participate in an erasure of Asian voices and perspectives. For these reasons, Asian Americans often consider it necessary to reject one identity in favor of the other, either rejecting sexuality in favor of ethnic belonging or cutting ties with the cultures of their upbringing. These conflicts have prevented the full development of joint political action between Asian American and LGBTQ groups. In general, those who live in the interface or intersection between Asian and LGBTQ communities have not found their voice until relatively recently.

A few notable exceptions appeared in the 1970s. In 1979, Michiyo Cornell, a Japanese American lesbian mother, made an address before the Washington Monument as a representative of a newly formed group, the Lesbian and Gay Asian Collective. She made her short speech a rallying cry for Asian American lesbians and gays to recognize their histories and the unique intersection of oppressions they face. The same year, a California-based Asian American women's performance group called Unbound Feet formed. One of its members, a performance artist and writer named Canyon Sam, successfully lobbied the Chinese American Democratic Club to oppose Proposition 6, a 1977 California initiative that would have allowed the firing of any person who made positive references to gays and lesbians.

Efforts to reconcile Asian American and LGBTQ identities continued and intensified in the 1980s. Between 1986 and 1988, increasing numbers of documented AIDS cases among San Francisco Asians appeared. The epidemic had begun to ravage the gay community, including many Asian Americans. The confusion and horror that gripped the LGBTQ population during this time compelled alliances to form between Asian American lesbians and gays, especially in the metropolitan centers of California and New York. Filipino gay men in New York referred to AIDS as Tita Aida or Auntie/Aunt Aida. Many of them, some expelled from their homes, formed collective fund-raising efforts like drag shows to cover medical costs. AIDS figures also in many instances of Asian American literature, including poetry by Russell Leong and Timothy Liu. An awareness of AIDS and its impact on the gay Asian community makes an appearance in Amy Tan's 1989 novel *The Joy Luck Club*, one of the most successful Asian American novels ever published.

The familial connection to the individual is central in Asian cultures. Some gay Asian men came out to their families only when they or their friends were diagnosed with AIDS. A current study by Alice Y. Hom focuses on Asian American parents with lesbian or gay children. She finds that the immigrant parents who comprise most of her subjects were familiar with lesbian and gay sexualities before they came to the United States. She also finds that many of the parents in the study are aware of both essentialist and constructivist (nature versus nurture) arguments about their children's sexuality. Furthermore, she finds that the parents' accounts of the attitudes toward homosexuality differ by ethnicity. The views that Vietnamese parents express about homosexuality are not the same as those of Japanese parents, and neither are their stories of realizing or being told about their own children's sexuality. Though the parents Hom interviews are generally accepting of their children's homosexuality, she acknowledges that the perspectives of the parents she has selected are limited. One set of parents she describes attends a chapter of the Parents, Families and Friends of Lesbians and Gays (PFLAG),

In costume and makeup as a Chinese opera singer, B. D. Wong poses at the Broadway Theater in New York on April 12, 1988, where he starred in *M. Butterfly*, a play by David Henry Hwang. Wong's role was that of a man who impersonates a female opera singer. (AP Photo/Rene Perez)

where they are the only Asian family, and for that matter, the only people of color.

The literary world is a major site of the interface between Asian America and LGBTQ issues. Gay themes can be seen as early as the 1974 anthology *Aiiieeeee!* and a poem by Wallace Lin (Russell Leong), "Rough Notes for Mantos," published the same year. Implicitly lesbian- and gay-themed works appear even earlier. Several examples of Asian American LGBTQ literature take common or established works that many are already familiar with and refigure them. David Henry Hwang depicts a homosexual relationship between a French civil servant and a Chinese transvestite opera performer in his

Tony winners for the Broadway play *M. Butterfly*, from left, coproducer Eric Eisner, producer Stuart Ostrow, and playwright David Henry Hwang, pose with their awards at the 43rd Annual Tony Awards ceremony at the Minskoff Theatre in New York City on June 5, 1988. (AP Photo/Richard Drew)

1988 Tony Award–winning play *M. Butterfly*, a deconstructive adaptation of Puccini's opera *Madama Butterfly*. *M. Butterfly* explores cultural stereotypes between Europeans and Asians in addition to the intricacies of the secrecy surrounding homosexuality. Literary critic and scholar David L. Eng contends that Hwang created his drama around the suppression of homoeroticism. Willyce Kim, also author of a collection of poetry with lesbian themes, *Curtains of Light* (1971), revises the trope of the standard American Western in her novel *Dancer Dawkins and the California Kid* (1985). Kitty Tsui's 1982 poem "Why the Milky Way Is Milky" revises an ancient Chinese origin myth, "Spinning Girl and Shepherd Boy," toward a lesbian articulation of origins. Revision of the norm is a common theme among queer communities and

communities of color, and Asian American LGBTQ writers are no exception.

Several examples of literature by gay Asian men approach a controversial topic, "rice queens," or gay white men who seek Asian partners. Most Asian American accounts of these relationships attribute the attraction or "fetish" to a racist fantasy. Martin F. Manalansan IV's poem "Your Cio-Cio San" refers to Cio-Cio San from Puccini's *Madama Butterfly*, with whom many gay Asian men have felt unfairly aligned. Quentin Lee expands upon the problems of relations between "rice queens" and Asian men in "The Sailor and the Thai Boys," published in a 1999 issue of *Rice Paper*, by adding the figures of class difference and prostitution. He also addresses the infantilization of Asian men in pornography made to titillate white men. Justin Chin approaches his experiences with "rice queens" with humor in *Bite Hard* (1997).

Anthologies offer an opportunity for diverse voices to come together, an effort being forged by Asian American and LGBTQ writers. In *Between the Lines: An Anthology by Pacific/Asian Lesbians of Santa Cruz, California*, a 1987 collection, difficulties of reconciling sexual and ethnic differences among women are explored. Also in 1987, the Gay Asian Pacific Alliance started publishing *The Lavender Godzilla*. Some notable work by Asian American LGBTQ writers has also appeared in anthologies not specifically concerned with queer issues, such as *Charlie Chan Is Dead: An Anthology of Contemporary Asian American Fiction* (1994).

LGBTQ issues have figured largely in recent film and television made by and about Asian Americans. Ang Lee's acclaimed direction of *Brokeback Mountain* (2005) made his interest in gay-themed stories known to the general public, but he has approached LGBTQ issues before. The subject of his 1993 film *The Wedding Banquet* is the relationship between a Chinese American landlord, Wai-Tun Gao, and his white partner Simon. The tension between traditional familial expectations and the demands of one's own desires is made explicit when Gao's parents arrive in America to throw a wedding party for him and his tenant, a Chinese woman in need of a green card. The film skillfully uses a comedic structure to explore the emotions and intricacies caught up in the intersections between culture and sexuality.

Gregg Araki, one of the most prominent directors of independent film today, is part of a movement in film, *New Queer Cinema*, which also includes LGBTQ filmmakers Todd Haynes, Jennie Livingston, and Derek Jarman. He explores gay themes in all of his films, including issues of youth depression, homophobia, morality (or lack thereof), and HIV/AIDS. Some have criticized him for not casting Asian Americans. He has responded that he casts based solely on talent and fit, though he says he wishes to have an Asian character eventually.

Saving Face (2004), a recent film by Chinese American lesbian Alice Wu, presents parallel stories of a mother and daughter violating traditional cultural mores in different ways. A young surgeon, Wilhelmina Pang, must deal with her mother's moving in after becoming pregnant out of wedlock while simultaneously finding a way to come out to her mother in the midst of a difficult relationship with Vivian, a dancer. *Saving Face* has exposed the issues faced by many Asian American lesbians who have previously suffered a lack of representation in popular culture.

Openly gay actor B.D. Wong, who gained attention for his title role in Hwang's *M. Butterfly*, has gained national recognition on the television program *Law and Order: Special Victims Unit*, in which he plays a forensic psychiatrist, appearing in most episodes. He also appeared in HBO's *Oz* and the mid-1990s sit-com *All-American Girl*. Wong has committed to several LGBTQ activist causes, including AIDS charities and the Gay and Lesbian Alliance Against Defamation (GLAAD). His 2003 memoir, *Following Foo*, recounts his and his partner's becoming parents.

Comedian and actress Margaret Cho played the central character in *All-American Girl*, which gained significance as the first situation comedy on network television to focus on Asian Americans. In her comedy she deals frankly but humorously with race, gender, and sexuality. In 2004, Cho created "Love Is Love Is Love," a website for advocates of gay marriage, but since her beginnings in stand-up in the early 1990s, she has included gay humor in her repertoire. She addresses her own bisexuality in several of her shows, including *I'm the One That I Want* (2000). Cho discusses the humor of her affinity for gay men and "fag hags," and stereotypes of Asian Americans, but also addresses the damaging effects of prejudice.

Richard Fung, an independent video filmmaker, explores racialized stereotypes with respect to Asian sexuality in his essay "Looking for My Penis: The Eroticized Asian in Gay Video Porn." He argues that dominant attitudes concerning race and sexuality that arose during periods of European colonization have governed images of gay Asians, making them submissive "bottoms" and desexualized in relation to the white men who control the way their images are made and dispersed. The sexual excitement produced by gay Asian men in pornography, according to Fung, stems from their feminization (the lack of sexual agency of the feminine being an issue long explored by feminists) and being reminded of their lower social status. Writer Frank Chin terms the perception of the emasculated Asian American man the "Charlie Chan Sex Syndrome."

In 1991, the Asian Lesbians of the East Coast (ALOEC) and Gay Asian and Pacific Islander Men of New York (GAPIMNY) demonstrated in New York against the Lambda Legal Defense and Education Fund (LLDEF) and New York's Lesbian and Gay Community Services Center. This protest was organized when they found out that Cameron Mackintosh's popular Broadway musical *Miss Saigon* was to be used for the LLDEF and Lesbian and Gay Community Services Center's annual fund-raising events. *Miss Saigon*, like Hwang's *M. Butterfly*, is a modern adaptation of Puccini's opera *Madama Butterfly*. The protestors expressed anger over the content of the play, which they found racist, stereotyping Asian women as submissive and Asian men as asexual and hateful. They demanded that the two organizations recognize Asian issues and constituents as their own.

Thirteen years later, GAPIMNY joined with the Asian American Legal Defense and Education Fund, National Asian American Student Conference, and other groups to protest a feature that had appeared in an issue of *Details* magazine. Entitled "Gay or Asian?" the page in the magazine featured several stereotypical judgments or descriptions that could be attributed to both Asians and gay men, implicitly likening the two. The feature was intended to be tongue-in-cheek, but the protestors took great offense, seeing it as reinforcing cultural stereotypes. Dan Peres, editor-in-chief of the magazine, eventually made a public apology for the column.

GAPIMNY is only one of the organizations that are made up of members from the interface of Asian and LGBTQ America. Others include the Gay Asian Pacific Support Network, Q-Wave, Trikone, the Gay Asian Pacific Alliance, the South Asian Lesbian and Gay Association, and the Asian Pacific Islander Queer Women and Transgendered Coalition. The goal of API Family Pride, based in California, is to alleviate the isolation some families at the intersection of Asian America and LGBTQ feel.

Bryan Kim-Butler

See also: Activists; Historical Overview of Gay Rights and Issues: From the 1980s to the Present.

Further Reading

Eng, David L. 1994. "In the Shadows of a Diva: Committing Homosexuality in David Henry Hwang's *M. Butterfly*." *Amerasia Journal* 20 (1): 93–116.

Eng, David L., and Alice Y. Hom, eds. 1998. *Q and A: Queer in Asian America*. Philadelphia: Temple University Press.

Fung, Richard. 1991. "Looking for My Penis: The Eroticized Asian in Gay Video Porn." In *How Do I Look?: Queer Film and Video*, ed. Bad Object-Choices, pp. 145–60. Seattle, WA: Bay Press.

Hom, Alice Y. 1996. "Stories from the Homefront: Perspectives of Asian American Parents with Lesbian Daughters and Gay Sons." In *Asian American Sexualities: Dimensions of the Gay and Lesbian Experience*, ed. Russell Leong, pp. 37–40. New York: Routledge.

Leong, Russell, ed. 1996. *Asian American Sexualities: Dimensions of the Gay and Lesbian Experience*. New York: Routledge.

Manalansan IV, Martin F. 1994. "Searching for Community: Gay Filipino Men in New York City." *Amerasia Journal* 20 (1): 59–73.

Takagi, Dana Y. 1994. "Maiden Voyage: Excursion into Sexuality and Identity Politics in Asian America." *Amerasia Journal* 20 (1): 1–17.

Wat, Eric C. 1994. "Preserving the Paradox: Stories from a Gay-Loh." *Amerasia Journal* 20 (1): 149–60.

Woo, Jean M., George W. Rutherford, Susan F. Payne, J. Lowell Barnhardt, and George F. Lemp. 1988. "The Epidemiology of AIDS in Asian and Pacific Islander Population in San Francisco." *AIDS* 2: 473–75.

Asian Pacific Lesbian Bisexual Network

The story of the Asian Pacific Lesbian Bisexual Network began in an atmosphere of ferment and change within the Asian American queer population of the West Coast of the United States during the late 1970s and early 1980s, an era when Asian and Pacific Islander gay and lesbian people began to reclaim their own distinctive identity within the larger constellation of movement groups. While other groups had formed on a local level within America (the first appearing in Boston in 1979), many of them had been male-dominated or, at best, gave limited attention to issues raised by their lesbian members. The occasion of the second March on Washington for Lesbian and Gay Rights provided women who identified as Asian or Pacific Islander by heritage to form a distinctive contingent, although the first West Coast Asian Pacific Lesbian retreat, held in Sonoma, California, earlier in 1987, had begun the dialogue that would lead to the creation of the network. Headquartered in San Francisco, its purpose was to provide a bridge for Asian members of the lesbian, bisexual, and transgender communities residing both within and outside the United States. Its first national conference was held at the University of California at Santa Cruz in 1989 and was organized by three faculty members, Alison Kim, Cristy Chung, and A. Kaweah Lemeshewsky, who had compiled the groundbreaking collection *Between the Lines: A Pacific/Asian Lesbian Anthology*, the first such work published anywhere. In 1993, the name was expanded to the Asian Pacific

Yatin Chawatne dances as he marches in the Seattle 2004 Pride Parade with the group Trikone Northwest, an organization for differently oriented South Asians on June 27, 2004, in Seattle. Thousands gathered to take part in and watch the parade, which marked its 30th anniversary this year and was part of a worldwide celebration of gay pride. (AP Photo/Ted S. Warren)

Nancy Iskandar, right, a transgender and HIV/AIDS counsellor, talks to young transgenders at a clinic where many marginal groups receive medical treatment for HIV/AIDS in Jakarta on August 7, 2009. India, Indonesia, and Pakistan are key fronts in Asia's fight against HIV/AIDS. (ADEK BERRY/AFP/Getty Images)

Lesbian, Bisexual, and Transgender Network. The existence of the network stimulated regional Asian and Pacific Islander queer conferences and gatherings during the 1990s, culminating in its second national conference in Los Angeles in 1998. It also increased the visibility of this population of women at Pride parades and spearheaded the formation of the Asian and Pacific Islander Lesbian, Bisexual, Transgender and Queer Task Force, which provided recommendations to and testified at hearings held by the Presidential Commission on Asian American and Pacific Islanders in 2000. The organization is no longer active.

Robert Ridinger

See also: Asian Americans and LGBTQ Issues.

Further Reading

Eng, David L. and Alice Y. Hom, eds. 1998. *Q & A: Queer in Asian America.* Philadelphia: Temple University Press.

Association of Gay and Lesbian Psychiatrists (AGLP)

Association of Gay and Lesbian Psychiatrists (AGLP) is a community of psychiatrists that educates and advocates on lesbian, gay, bisexual, and transgender (LGBT) mental health issues. AGLP officially began as the "Gay Caucus of Members of the American Psychiatric Association" (APA) in 1978, five years after homosexuality was taken out of APA's diagnostic manual. AGLP's roots actually began in the late

1960s, when gay and lesbian members of the APA met quietly during the annual APA conventions. The members of this group informally referred to it as the "Gay-PA." Because homosexuality was classified as a mental illness during those years, gay and lesbian psychiatrists needed to be particularly discreet when finding each other at APA meetings.

The Gay Caucus, and AGLP, as it eventually came to be known, was never an official organization of the APA. In later years, APA would come to have its own committee on lesbian, gay, and bisexual issues, as well as a committee on AIDS and HIV, largely through lobbying efforts by members of AGLP. AGLP has been able to run its own educational programming as an independent organization but has also always had a role in educating and advising APA members on LGBT issues. Key issues that AGLP has worked on with APA have included the removal of the diagnosis "Ego-Dystonic Homosexuality" from the diagnostic manual, and issuing position statements supporting same-sex civil marriage and adoption and coparenting by same-sex couples. In 2006, AGLP established the John E. Fryer, MD, award, an APA award highlighting an individual who has made substantial contributions to LGBT mental health. The awardee gives a lecture at one of the APA annual meetings.

In recent years, AGLP has moved its advocacy and educational role outside the field of psychiatry to the general public. This has occurred through the organization's website, which generates frequent e-mails from the general public to members and contains informational fact sheets. In 2006 AGLP completed a documentary video, "Abomination: Homosexuality and the Ex-Gay Movement," which exposes the false promises and harm surrounding treatments that seek to change people from gay to straight. From its beginnings to the present, the organization has also served an important function as a support network for LGBT psychiatrists and other mental health professionals. AGLP's national office is in Philadelphia. The organization has had one executive director, Roy Harker, since the national office opened in 1995.

Mary Barber

Contributors to the new transgender reference book, *Trans Bodies, Trans Selves*, stand together at the offices of the Oxford University Press in New York. The encyclopedic new resource book written for and by transgender people was released in 2014. (AP Photo/ Bebeto Matthews)

See also: American Psychiatric Association (APA).

Further Reading

Association of Gay and Lesbian Psychiatrists. Available at: http://www.aglp.org.

Drescher, J., and J. P. Merlino, eds. 2007. *American Psychiatry and Homosexuality: An Oral History*. New York: Haworth Press.

Audre Lorde Project (ALP)

The Audre Lorde Project (ALP), located on 85 South Oxford Street, Brooklyn, NY 11217, is a community organizing center for lesbian, gay, bisexual, two spirit, and transgender (LGBTST) people of color. ALP addresses the distinct and diverse needs of LGBTST people of color in the New York City area, promoting community wellness and empowerment and progressive social and economic justice.

The project coalesced in 1994 around HIV/AIDS policy, as the Advocates for Gay Men of Color convened various networks of LGBTST people of color to establish a community center to meet the needs of LGBTST people of African/Black/Caribbean, Arab, Asian and Pacific Islander, Latina/Latino, and Native/Indigenous descent.

Named after Audre Lorde—in her words "a black, lesbian, feminist, mother, warrior, poet"—in her spirit, ALP is "committed to struggle across difference," an endeavor toward which it plays a critical role. Through its working groups, conferences, leadership retreats, and other daily events, ALP incorporates wellness promotion with other modes of empowerment, including cultural and political analysis and activism. For example, ALP developed and distributed the first Heath and Wellness Resource Guide for LGBTST people of color; it also organized "Arms Akimbo" and "TransWorld," conferences to mobilize, respectively, LGBTST women of color and transgender people of color—also the first of their kind.

ALP currently runs three working groups as part of its operation. One of the groups, TransJustice, is active in mobilizing trans and gender nonconforming people and pressing for equal access

People march during the 10th annual Trans Day of Action on June 27, 2014, in New York. Participants decried violence and discrimination while celebrating strides made by the lesbian, gay, bisexual, and transgender communities. (AP Photo/ Frank Franklin II)

to health care, employment, housing, and education. The Working Group on Immigrant Rights encourages network building for LGBTST immigrants of color in New York City and is committed to ensure that "all residents of the U.S. have access to the same rights and benefits regardless of immigration/migration status." The third group, the Safe OUTside the System (SOS) Collective, challenges various regimes of violence, including extralegal and state-sponsored violence directed at LBGTST people of color. The SOS Collective is active, too, in protesting America's violent actions internationally, as in the current occupation of Iraq, and seeks to show the connections between American violence domestically and abroad.

Since it found a home in Brooklyn, New York, in 1996, ALP has been crucial in providing space and other resources to buttress myriad cultural and political organizations, for example, Las Buenas Amigas (Lesbiana Latinas en Nueva York), South Asia AIDS Action, Gay Men of African Descent (GMAD), Domestic Workers United, and other groups. In addition to providing technical and material assistance to organizations committed to enhancing the lives of LGBTST people of color, ALP is home to *Color Life!* Magazine, which gives voice to LGBTST people of color and focuses on issues otherwise eclipsed in mainstream (straight or gay) media.

Dagmawi Woubshet

See also: Lorde, Audre (1934–1992).

Further Reading

Audre Lorde Project website. Available at: http://www.alp.org.

B

Baker v. Vermont (1999)

Although same-sex couples had attempted to sue for the right to marry in several states in the 1970s, those suits were quickly dismissed. No longer—today there is much legislative and judicial action around the issue of recognition of same-sex couples.

The case that led the Vermont legislature to create "civil unions," an institution offering within the state of Vermont all the benefits and responsibilities of marriage under another name, shows both how societal attitudes toward same-sex relationships have evolved and how state constitutions are being read in an inclusive fashion to include sexual minorities.

The plaintiffs in this case were three same-sex couples living in Vermont, each of whom had been in a committed relationship for periods ranging from 4 to 25 years; two of the couples were raising children together. Each couple filed for a marriage license with their local town clerk and was refused because state marriage law did not permit same-sex marriage. The plaintiffs then filed suit against the state of Vermont and the towns where they had been denied a marriage license—Milton, Shelbourne, and South Burlington.

The trial court dismissed the plaintiffs' complaint based on the defendants' motion for summary judgment. The trial court held that Vermont's marriage law could not be read to permit the issuance of a license to same-sex couples. It further held that the marriage statute was constitutional because it "rationally furthered the State's interest in promoting 'the link between procreation and child rearing'" (*Baker v. Vermont* [1999], 868).

The case was appealed to the Vermont Supreme Court, with the same-sex couples arguing that the trial court erred in concluding that the marriage statutes made them ineligible for a marriage license. But they further contended that, if those laws in fact do exclude them, the exclusion violates their right to the common benefit and protection of the law granted by the Vermont Constitution.

The Majority

The Vermont Supreme Court first analyzed the state's marriage statute using the common principle of statutory construction that "where a statute is unambiguous we rely on the plain and ordinary meaning of the words chosen" (p. 868). The court looked at other evidence that this was the intent of Vermont law, such as statutes that prohibited a man from marrying certain female relatives and a woman from marrying certain male relatives, and those referring to "husband" and "wife." Based on this analysis, the court agreed that, based on the plain meaning of the law and such terms as *marriage*, a marriage involves a partnership of one man and one woman.

Yet the plaintiffs in *Baker* had made an additional claim: that the "common benefits" clause in Vermont's constitution required giving them the rights and benefits of marriage, and that in excluding them from access to a civil marriage license, the state was depriving them and other same-sex couples from the entire array of benefits and protections provided through

Three gay and lesbian couples who are challenging Vermont's marriage laws watch arguments at the Vermont Supreme Court in Montpelier, Vermont, on November 18, 1998. From left are Stacey Jolles, Nina Beck, Peter Harrigan, Stan Baker, Lois Farnham, and Holly Puterbaugh. (AP Photo/Toby Talbot)

state recognition of a marital relationship. This was a much more difficult proposition to deny.

The Vermont Supreme Court first noted that Vermont's common benefits clause differed substantially from the U.S. Constitution's equal protection clause and that "[w]hile the federal amendment may thus supplant the protections afforded by the Common Benefits Clause, it does not supplant it as the first and primary safeguard of the rights and liberties of all Vermonters" (p. 870). Vermont courts, moreover, while sometimes making use of federal equal protection analysis, had adopted a different analytical framework, requiring that "statutory exclusions from publicly conferred benefits and protections must be 'premised on an appropriate and overriding public interest'" (p. 873).

The Vermont Supreme Court further distinguished itself from other courts in the way it interpreted its constitution. Unlike some legal strict constructionists, who favor looking at the plain language of the law and the intent of the drafters of the U.S. Constitution, the Vermont Supreme Court used a variety of means to construe its constitution.

These included the language of the provision in dispute, historical context, case law development, the construction of similar provisions in other state constitutions, and sociological materials. Moreover, declared the Vermont Supreme Court, "our task is to distill the essence, the motivating ideal of the framers. The challenge is to remain faithful to that historical ideal, while addressing contemporary issues that the framers undoubtedly could never have imagined" (p. 874).

The common benefits clause of the Vermont Constitution reads as follows: "That government is, or ought to be, instituted for the common benefit, protection, and security of the people, nation or community;

and not for the particular emolument or advantage of any single man, family or set of men, who are a part only of that community; and that the community hath an indubitable, unalienable and indefeasible right, to reform, alter or abolish government, in such manner as shall be, by that community, judged most conducive to the public weal" (Vt. Const. of 1777, ch. I, art. VI).

Reviewing this text, the Vermont Supreme Court noted that the common benefits clause evinced intent to provide government for the common benefit of the people and community as a whole. Moreover, the clause prohibited not only the denial of benefits to discriminated-against groups but also the granting of advantages to privileged groups. But the most important principle, concluded the justices in *Baker*, was the principle of inclusion. The prohibition in the common benefits clause against governmental favoritism toward any particular "family" or "single man" underscores the commitment of the drafters of Vermont's Constitution to avoiding favoritism of any kind, reflecting their objective "not only that everyone enjoy equality before the law or have an equal voice in government but also that everyone have an equal share in the fruits of the common enterprise" (744 A.2d at 875).

Next, turning to the historical context of the common benefits clause, the Vermont Supreme Court justices noted that the American Revolution had unleashed internal social pressures demanding freedom not only from the British but also seeking a more egalitarian society. The drafters of the Vermont Constitution were not against a societal elite per se, but demanded that such an elite be one based on talent, rather than birth or social connections. Once again, this was in contrast to traditional equal protection analysis of the purpose of the U.S. Constitution.

This difference between analysis under the common benefits clause of the Vermont Constitution and the federal equal protection clause lay at the heart of the Vermont court's reasoning. Under a common benefits analysis, one must first delineate the group being deprived of common benefits, a process that differs from the equal protection clause's drawing of suspect,

quasi-suspect, and nonsuspect classes. One next reviews the government's purpose in placing some persons outside the scope of a particular law. Finally, one must decide whether the omission of part of the community from a benefit under the challenged law "bears a reasonable and just relation to the governmental purpose." Factors to be considered, wrote the justices, can include: (1) the significance of the benefits and protections implicated by the challenged law; (2) whether the omission of members of the community from the benefits and protections of the challenged law promotes the government's stated goals; and (3) whether the classification is "significantly underinclusive or overinclusive" (p. 879).

Vermont contended in the litigation that its interest in excluding same-sex couples from the marriage statute was based on the government's interest in "furthering the link between procreation and child rearing." Because same-sex couples are unable to conceive children on their own, including them in the marriage laws would send a message to society, contended the state, that there was no connection between procreation and parental responsibilities. Yet the Vermont Supreme Court expressed skepticism about this rationale, noting that many married heterosexual couples either could not conceive children or did not wish to do so. Marriage laws advanced on the basis of a procreation rationale were significantly underinclusive, noted the court. Finally, the court took note that there were growing numbers of same-sex couples raising children, a fact that the Vermont legislature had noted and acted upon in removing barriers to same-sex couples adopting and rearing children born through new reproductive technologies. Vermont even had granted jurisdiction to family courts to safeguard the interests of same-sex couples and their children in the event that the couple broke up. Keeping same-sex couples outside of the scope of the marriage laws, the Vermont Supreme Court concluded, threatened the very interests that the state was attempting to assert by expanding the coverage of the family law statutes.

Having reviewed the state's asserted interest and found it wanting, the Vermont Supreme Court next turned to the question of whether the exclusion of same-sex couples from the marriage laws in fact violated Vermont's common benefits clause. The court first examined the history and significance of the benefits denied, noting that the U.S. Supreme Court, in *Loving v. Virginia*, a 1967 case challenging the constitutionality of Virginia's antimiscegenation law, declared that "[t]he freedom to marry has long been recognized as one of the vital personal rights" (*Loving v. Virginia* [1967], 12). The Vermont Supreme Court itself, 137 years prior to *Loving*, had stated that the rights and responsibilities of marriage were "the natural rights of human nature" (*Overseers of the Poor* [1840], 159). The Vermont Supreme Court further noted how the benefits and protections conferred by marriage have only grown in recent years, including inheritance rights, the right to various survivors' benefits, and hospital visitation rights. Thus, the court stated, "[t]he legal benefits and protections flowing from a marriage license are of such significance that any statutory exclusion must necessarily be grounded on public concerns of sufficient weight, cogency, and authority that the justice of the deprivation cannot be seriously questioned" (*Baker v. Vermont* [1999], 884). As the Vermont Supreme Court had already found the state's asserted interest in "furthering the link between procreation and child rearing" did not meet this test with respect to the exclusion of same-sex couples, it examined other asserted state interests for authority to act, including: "promoting child rearing in a setting that provides both male and female role models," discouraging marriages of convenience for tax or other benefits, maintaining uniformity with other states' marriage laws, and generally safeguarding marriage from "destabilizing changes."

The interest in assuring female and male role models in the context of raising children did not withstand analysis, declared the Vermont Supreme Court justices, as the legislature had passed, and the governor signed, a law removing all barriers to the adoption of children by same-sex couples. Nor did the interest in safeguarding uniformity with other states' marriage laws carry weight, because Vermont permits marriages between first cousins, which most states prohibit. The court further found Vermont's professed fears about possible marriages of convenience or destabilization of marriage to be "conjectures" that were not "susceptible to empirical proof before they occur" (p. 885).

The final interest that Vermont attempted to raise was the fact that society had a long history of animus toward same-sex relations and thus same-sex couples should not be deemed to deserve the benefits of marriage under the common benefits clause. The Vermont Supreme Court, citing *MacCallum v. Seymour's Administrator* (1996), stated that "equal protection of the laws cannot be limited by eighteenth-century standards" (p. 885). Moreover, recent Vermont legislation did not provide support for the state's contention. Vermont repealed its oral sodomy law in 1977 and was one of the first states to outlaw discrimination on the basis of sexual orientation. Vermont in recent years had also enacted laws against hate crimes, and removed adoption barriers for same-sex couples.

As the state had failed to assert any recognizable interest, the Vermont Supreme Court held that same-sex couples were entitled to all the benefits of marriage accorded to heterosexual couples. The court declined, however, to state how such equality of benefits could be ensured, arguing that this was for the Vermont legislature to decide. It suggested that domestic partnership or registered partnership (pioneered in Denmark) could provide such a solution, because they provide an alternate legal status for same-sex couples with similar licensing provisions, and extend most of the rights of marriage. However, the ultimate choice lay with the elected branches.

Lee Walzer

See also: Civil Union; Same-Sex Marriages in the United States.

Further Reading

Moats, David. 2005. *Civil Wars: A Battle for Gay Marriage*. New York: Mariner Books.

New Marriage Equality Bill. n.d. "State of Vermont." Available at: http://www.sec.state.vt.us/Marriage_Equality_FAQs.pdf. Accessed February 8, 2014.

Baldwin, James (1924–1987)

Essayist, novelist, short story writer, playwright, poet, and tireless civil rights activist, James Baldwin was born in Harlem on August 2, 1924. His mother, Emma Berdis Jones, worked as a domestic; his stepfather, whom she married shortly after the birth of her baby, was a day laborer and a fundamentalist Baptist minister. After graduating from high school in 1942, Baldwin held a variety of odd jobs—construction worker, busboy, waiter, elevator operator—and began to write book reviews, essays, and short stories. His promising early work won him a Rosenwald Fellowship, and with the money he received he moved to Paris in 1948. Thus he began his trans-Atlantic exile, which would continue on and off for the rest of his life. The early years he spent in France were crucial to his personal and artistic development: from afar Baldwin was able to reassess his country and define his relationship to

it; the cosmopolitan openness of Paris generally freed him from the humiliating daily encounters with racism he endured in the United States, and Europe afforded him a space where he could disregard American scripts of masculinity and chart the geography of his homosexual desire in greater freedom and anonymity.

Race and sexuality—two of Baldwin's primary preoccupations—became the central subjects of his work. In 1949 he published a little-known essay titled "The Preservation of Innocence"; it appeared in *Zero*, an obscure Moroccan journal, and was reprinted in the United States only in 1989. Here Baldwin defends the naturalness of homosexuality and daringly proposes that homophobia is often a consequence of heterosexual panic and an inability to acknowledge the fullness of one's own humanity. "Outing," a story of sexual awakening published in 1951, is the first fictional work in which Baldwin thematizes homoeroticism. He develops this theme more elaborately

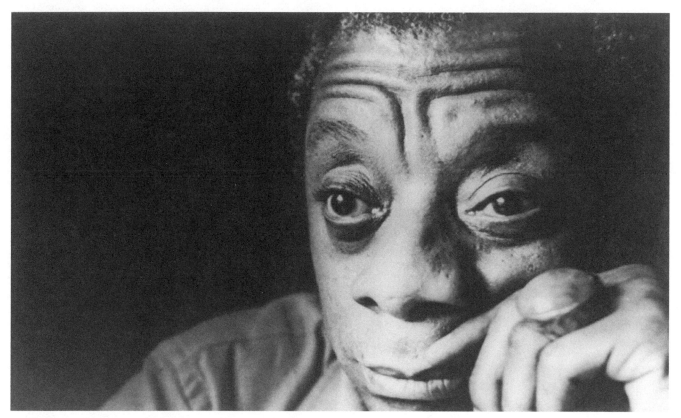

James Baldwin, author of the novel *Go Tell It on the Mountain* (1953), wrote about the effects of race, religion, and sexuality on personal identity. (Library of Congress)

in his first novel, *Go Tell It on the Mountain* (1953). A coming-of-age narrative, its main plot examines the familial and racial histories of its adolescent male protagonist; its subtle subplot, however, maps the incremental evolution of his homosexual consciousness.

This emergent gay identity is the defining theme of Baldwin's *Giovanni's Room* (1956), a modern classic. A Jamesian novel of expatriation and its discontents as well as a lyrical novel of remembrance and atonement, *Giovanni's Room*—a work set primarily in Paris—focus on a central crisis in the life of David, a young white American. On the one hand, he is faced with rigid social definitions of masculinity and cultural expectations of heterosexual conduct; on the other hand, he is forced to confront his sexual longing for other men, a desire that militates against all the belief systems that he has essentially internalized. The novel poignantly dramatizes David's dilemma. In *Another Country* (1962), Baldwin combines racial and sexual protests. Though an angry work, it nevertheless embodies Baldwin's vision of "another country"—a new Jerusalem, an imagined America—free of repressive racial boundaries and sexual categories.

Tell Me How Long the Train's Been Gone (1968) centers around the life of Leo Proudhammer, a bisexual black actor in his late 30s. Recuperating from a massive heart attack, Leo looks back at his complicated life; it is in his love for Christopher, a young black militant committed to revolutionary change, that he finds the redemptive meaning of his existence. Gay and bisexual themes resurface in Baldwin's sprawling post-Stonewall novel, *Just Above My Head* (1979). Here in his final major work of fiction, which chronicles the life of a gay black gospel singer, Baldwin elaborately treats a variety of themes he had explored earlier: the politics of identity, the maiming effects of racism, the alienation of the artist, the role of the black church, the interconnectedness between the past and the present, the relationship between self and community, and the salvific power of love. In contrast to his earlier works, here Baldwin handles the theme of transgressive sexualities less self-consciously and less polemically.

Baldwin is one of the most influential writers of the twentieth century. Simultaneously a racial and sexual outsider, he articulated a sustained intellectual challenge to the discourses of American racism and the dominant narratives of mandatory heterosexuality. By insisting on honest explorations of gay and bisexual themes, he made a sharp break from African American literary conventions; through such a pioneering departure from tradition, he helped create the space for a generation of young African American gay writers who succeeded him. Long before the Stonewall Riots of 1969 that helped liberate the gay literary imagination, Baldwin made his sexuality a central part of his artistic vision. He was, in the finest sense of the word, a revolutionary.

Emmanuel S. Nelson

See also: Stonewall Riot.

Further Reading

Field, Douglas. 2000. "Looking for Jimmy Baldwin: Sex, Privacy and Black Nationalist Fervor." *Callaloo* 27 (2): 457–80.

Miller, Quentin, ed. 2000. *Re-Viewing James Baldwin*. Philadelphia: Temple University Press.

Nelson, Emmanuel S. 1991. "Critical Deviance: Homophobia and the Reception of James Baldwin's Fiction." *Journal of American Culture* 14 (3): 91–96.

Powers, Peter Kerry. 2005. "The Treacherous Body: Isolation, Confession, and Community in James Baldwin." *American Literature* 77 (4): 787–813.

Baldwin, Tammy (1962–)

Tammy Baldwin is the first woman from Wisconsin and the first openly gay person in the nation to have been elected to the U.S. House of Representatives. In addition to concerns for the needs of her own constituents in Wisconsin's Second Congressional District, Baldwin is a strong advocate for health care reform, preservation of Social Security and Medicare/Medicaid programs, and programs in support of those with disabilities.

Baldwin was born in Madison, Wisconsin, on February 11, 1962. She was raised by her mother and

Senator Tammy Baldwin (D-WI), center, the Senate's first openly gay member, is surrounded by fellow Democrats just before a historic vote on legislation outlawing workplace discrimination against gay, bisexual, and transgender Americans on November 7, 2013, in Washington, D.C. From left are Senate Majority Leader Harry Reid of Nevada, Senate Majority Whip Richard Durbin of Illinois, Senator Tom Harkin (D-IA), Baldwin, Senator Jeff Merkley (D-OR), Senator Patty Murray (D-WA), and Senator Charles Schumer (D-NY). (AP Photo/J. Scott Applewhite)

her maternal grandparents. She graduated from Madison West High School in 1980 as class valedictorian. Baldwin continued her studies at Smith College, from which she received her bachelor's degree in 1984, and at the University of Wisconsin Law School, where she earned her JD degree in 1989. Even before completing her education, Baldwin had become politically active. She was elected to the Dane County Board of Supervisors in 1986, a post she held until 1994. She also served in the Wisconsin House of Representatives from 1993 to 1999. In 1998, she ran for the U.S. House of Representatives and was elected by a margin of 53 percent to 47 percent. She served seven terms in the House of Representatives, serving on Budget Committee, the Judiciary Committee, and the Energy and Commerce. In 2013, she was elected to the U.S. Senate. According to her website, she has been a strong advocate in Congress on the issue of bullying and suicide among LGBT youth, and helped lead efforts on hate crimes legislation, marriage equality, "Don't Ask Don't Tell," and the Employee Non-Discrimination Act.

David E. Newton

See also: Frank, Barney (1940–).

Further Reading

Senator Tammy Baldwin. Official website. http://www.baldwin.senate.gov/.

Beam, Joseph (1954–1988)

Joseph Beam was a black gay activist and writer best known for *In the Life* (1986), a first-of-its-kind collection of then-contemporary African American gay male writings. The African American expression "in the life" means "gay." His second collection, *Brother to Brother* (2007), was finished after his death by African American poet Essex Hemphill and Beam's mother Dorothy.

Born in Philadelphia, Beam attended Franklin College in Indiana, where he studied journalism and was influenced by the civil rights and black power movements. When he returned to Philadelphia in 1979, he found a job at Giovanni's Room, a queer bookstore named after the novel by James Baldwin, one of Beam's favorite authors. Almost immediately, Beam began writing for LGBT publications, including the local gay weeklies Philadelphia's *Gay News* and *Au Courant*, as well as national publications such as *The Advocate* and Boston's *Gay Community News*. He developed a style of writing that was as poetic as it was informative and analytical. He interviewed such black queer luminaries as James Baldwin and poet Audre Lorde.

His words in the introduction to *In the Life* still ring true: "Very clearly, gay male means: white, middle-class, youthful, nautilized, and probably butch; there is no room for Black gay men within the confines of this gay pentagon." Beam was also active in many social justice organizations, including the Gay and Lesbian Task Force of the American Friends Service Committee and the National Coalition of Black Lesbians and Gays. Beam died of AIDS complications in 1988 in Philadelphia.

Tommi Avicolli-Mecca

See also: African Americans and LGBTQ Issues; Baldwin, James (1924–1987); Lorde, Audre (1934–1992).

Further Reading

Beam, Joseph. 2007. *In the Life: A Black Gay Anthology.* Washington D.C.: Redbone Press.

Jackson, Isaac. 2004. *Freedom in This Village: Twenty-Five Years of Black Gay Men's Writing.* New York: Carroll and Graf.

BiNet USA

This national nonprofit organization was founded in 1990 under its original name, the North American Bisexual Network, which evolved from the first National Bisexual Conference, held in San Francisco in that year. It was officially incorporated as a nonprofit in 1993. An early accomplishment was in getting the word *Bi* added to the name of the 1993 March on Washington for Gay, Lesbian, and Bi Equal Rights and Liberation. BiNet USA is the oldest bisexual organization in the country and describes itself as "an umbrella organization and voice for bisexual people; BiNet USA will facilitate the development of a cohesive network of bisexual communities, promote bisexual visibility, and collect and distribute educational information regarding bisexuality. To accomplish these goals, BiNet USA will provide a national network for bisexual organizations and individuals across the United States, and encourage participation and organizing on local and national levels." Foci of BiNet USA projects have included AIDS education, training on bisexual issues to national gay and lesbian organizations, and actively addressing biphobia in the media. In 1995 and 1996, BiNet USA created the Bisexual Youth Initiative and the Bisexual Rural Initiative. In the late 1990s, in an effort to educate government leaders about bisexuality, BiNet USA met with White House staff and lobbied Congress. In the mid-2000s, BiNet USA leaders worked with the National Gay and Lesbian Task Force's Policy Institute to create a groundbreaking public policy publication about bisexual health. BiNet USA representatives also worked with the Lambda Literary Foundation to establish that group's first ever Bisexual Literature Award, in 2006.

Amy André

See also: Activists; Bisexual Resource Center; Historical Overview of Gay Rights and Issues: From the 1980s to the Present.

Further Reading

BiNet USA website. Available at: http://www.binetusa.org.

A group of friends embrace and celebrate during the first ever Gay and Lesbian Inaugural Ball, hosted by the National Gay and Lesbian Task Force on September 1, 1992, in Washington, D.C. (Mark Peterson/Corbis)

Lambda Literary Foundation website. Available at: http://www.lambdaliterary.org.

Birch, Elizabeth M. (1956–)

Elizabeth Birch served as president and executive director of the Human Rights Campaign (HRC) from 1995 to 2005. During that time, she was also head of the HRC Foundation, the organization's educational arm; founded HRC's WorkNet, a resource center for workplace advocacy for lesbian and gay concerns, and HRC's FamilyNet, a virtual online resource for gay, lesbian, bisexual, and transgendered families; launched HRC's National Coming Out Day Program; and created the Lesbian Health Project. She has authored a number of AIDS antidiscrimination policies that became law in California and is founder of AIDS Legal Services of Northern California.

Birch was born in September 1956 in Dayton, Ohio, to a Canadian Air Force officer stationed in the United States and his wife. She left home while still a teenager to join the cast of Up with People (an organization officially dedicated to developing young leaders with a global perspective, and which also presented a wholesome and conservative viewpoint). She entered the University of Hawaii at Manoa in 1979, where she earned a BA in political science and oceanography in 1983. Birch then continued her studies at the Santa Clara University School of Law, which awarded her a JD degree in 1985. She also returned to the University of Hawaii at Manoa from 2000 to 2004 to work on (and eventually earn) a PhD in humanities.

President Clinton greets Human Rights Campaign executive director Elizabeth Birch at the group's national dinner on November 8, 1997, in Washington. President Clinton, in a nod to the budding political clout of the gay rights movement, spoke before the nation's largest lesbian and male homosexual group—the first president to appear before such an audience. (AP Photo/Wilfredo Lee)

From 1985 to 1989, Birch was partner in the San Francisco law firm of McCutchen, Doyle, Brown, & Enersen (now Bingham McCutchen), where she specialized in high technology, intellectual property, securities, and antitrust issues. She then became general counsel at the Claris Corporation, a wholly owned subsidiary of Apple Computer. She left Claris in June 1989 to become director of litigation, worldwide and human resources at Apple, a post she held until being appointed president and executive director at HRC. After leaving HRC in January 2005, Birch established her own consulting firm, Birch and Company, where she now works. At the same time she hosts a talk show on *Here!* that has included guests Howard Dean, Pat Buchanan, Rosie O'Donnell, and John Lewis.

In recognition of her accomplishments, Birch was awarded an honorary doctorate of humane letters by the University of Hawaii in 2002 and the Hubert Humphrey Award of the Leadership Conference on Civil Rights in the same year. The latter award is the highest award for advocacy on behalf of lesbian, gay, bisexual, and transgender and HIV/AIDS communities in the United States.

David E. Newton

See also: Human Rights Campaign (HRC).

Reform Party presidential candidate Patrick Buchanan gives a thumbs-up prior to a postelection address at the National Press Club in Washington, D.C., on November 8, 2000. (AP Photo/Michael DiBari Jr.)

Further Reading

Dunlap, David. 1994. "Apple Lawyer Will Become New Director Of Gay Group." *New York Times*, November 21.

Bisexual Health

According to the Centers of Disease Control and Prevention, 50 percent of adults in the United States who identify as lesbian, gay, or bisexual, identify as bisexual. This means that bisexual people comprise the largest subgroup within the LGB (or sexual orientation minority) population. Research also shows that bisexual people have significantly poorer health than people of any other sexual orientation, including gays and lesbians.

Bisexual people are all those who use the term *bisexual* to describe/identify themselves. Bisexuality, in contrast to monosexuality, is typically defined as being able to experience attraction to other people, regardless of the gender(s) of those people. While monosexuals (gay men, heterosexuals, and lesbians) tend to describe being attracted to people of only one gender, bisexuals tend to disregard gender when assessing attractions to others. Bisexuals face enormous prejudice and stigmatization, or *biphobia*, based on their sexual orientation. Biphobia, which is proven to be more pervasive and virulent than homophobia, has a tremendous impact on health. This is the reason why bisexuals have worse health than other sexual orientation minorities.

In 2007, the National Gay and Lesbian Task Force (NGLTF), in association with BiNetUSA and the Fenway Institute of Boston, published *Bisexual Health: An Introduction and Model Practices for HIV/STI Prevention Programming*, a downloadable PDF e-book on the physical and mental health of bisexual people. This publication, a summary of over 100 different surveys, studies, reports, and research programs, represents the first time a national LGBT nonprofit organization has devoted resources of this kind to the topic of bisexual health. The book is available free from the NGLTF website, and is described on the NGLTF website here: http://www.thetaskforce.org/reports_and_research/bisexual_health.

The journal *Bisexual Health* reports on the current state of the bisexual health crisis, as well as outlining concrete steps for health care practitioners to follow, in order to improve the health of bisexual people. According to the existing research, bisexual people are experiencing the following—and in higher rates than lesbians, gays, and heterosexuals: depression and other mental illness, alcohol and drug abuse, smoking, intimate partner violence and physical assault, and stigma and phobia.

Notable findings include the fact that bisexual women are three times more likely than heterosexual women and two times more likely than lesbians to be heavy drinkers. Bisexual women also smoke slightly, but significantly, more than lesbians and two to three times more than heterosexuals. In addition, significantly higher numbers of bisexual women experience being punched or beaten, compared to lesbians and heterosexual women. And, in studies comparing attitudes toward groups such as Protestants, pro-lifers, people with HIV, African Americans, and so on, bisexuals are rated second only to IV drug users in level of stigma.

A large portion of research on sexual orientation minorities that includes bisexual people combines data on bisexuals with data on gays and lesbians, which skews public understanding of lesbian/gay health, as well as understanding of bisexual health. Only when identity groups are separated out do we see these significant differences in health between sexual orientation minorities. It is at that point that the bisexual health crisis becomes apparent.

There are several simple steps that health care providers, medical researchers, and the bisexual and LGBT communities can take in response to the bisexual health crisis. A 2007 report on bisexual health outlines some of the most critical, easiest, and most cost-effective health care practices needed at this stage. In particular, the bisexual health program at Boston's Fenway Community Health Center has been nationally recognized as a model for addressing the health care needs of bisexual people. The program at Fenway comprises several components, including bi-inclusive safer sex brochures, a support group for bisexual and bi-curious men, and a safer sex education team.

According to this 2007 report from the National Gay and Lesbian Taskforce (cosponsored by BiNet USA and the Fenway Institute), bisexual health experts recommend that health care providers "add new services or expand existing services to cater to bisexual people; ensure safe and accessible services for bisexual individuals; educate other providers about the special needs of the bisexual community" (p. 15). In addition, researchers and journalists are encouraged to "avoid sensationalizing stories/research, and . . .

include bisexual people's perspectives. Departments of public health, foundations, and other funding agencies need to fund programs like BiHealth at Fenway and recruit bisexuals to participate in advisory groups and to provide input on and/or write and review grant applications" (p. 17).

Amy André

See also: BiNet USA; Bisexual Resource Center.

Further Reading

The American Institute of Bisexuality. Available at http://www.americaninstituteofbisexuality.org/home.html.

The Health of Lesbian, Gay, Bisexual, and Transgender People: Building a Foundation for Better Understanding. 2011. National Academies Press. Available at http://www.iom.edu/Reports/2011/The-Health-of-Lesbian-Gay-Bisexual-and-Transgender-People.aspx.

Kerr, Shelly, and Robin Mathy, eds. 2007. *Preventive Health Measures for Lesbian and Bisexual Women.* New York: Haworth Medical Press.

National Gay and Lesbian Taskforce. 2007. "Report on Bisexual Health." Available at: http://www.thetaskforce.org/press/releases/prBI_031407.

Shankle, Michael. 2006. *The Handbook of Lesbian, Gay, Bisexual, and Transgender Public Health: A Practitioner's Guide to Service.* New York: Harrington Park Press.

Bisexual Resource Center

This international nonprofit organization is based in Boston and operates with two specific organizational goals: to educate about bisexuality and to provide support for bisexuals and the allies of bisexuals, on an international level. Leaders of the Bisexual Resource Center state that they "believe in a world that acknowledges people as whole and indivisible and where they should not have to leave any part of their heritage and identity at the door." The Bisexual Resource Center coordinates a speaker's bureau and facilitates the connections of bisexual public speakers with students, agencies, and media in need of information.

In 2005, the Bisexual Resource Center published *Getting Bi: Voices of Bisexuals around the World*, an anthology of essays edited by Tufts University professor and leading bi activist Robyn Ochs. The center offers pamphlets that cover topics such as safer sex, bisexual politics, bisexual history, bisexual visibility, biphobia, polyamory, bisexual support group formation, and bisexuality and religion.

A current project of the center is the Bisexual Archives. Staff and volunteers work to collect bisexual-related memorabilia and other archival materials pertinent to the history of the bisexual community. The archives are available for public perusal upon request and are housed in the center office. Additional services of the Bisexual Resource Center include accessibility services for bisexuals with disabilities; political and organizational support for bisexual people of color; consultation with researchers doing work in bisexuality studies; grant writers who are raising funds for bisexual-related causes and other bisexual organizations; bisexual conference organizing; and providing resources, referrals, and counseling. Bisexual Resource Center representatives also worked with the Lambda Literary Foundation to establish that group's first ever Bisexual Literature Award, in 2006.

Amy André

See also: BiNet USA; Bisexual Health.

Further Reading

Bisexual Resource Center website. Available at: http://www.biresource.org. Accessed March 16, 2014.

Lambda Literary Foundation website. Available at: http://www.lambdaliterary.org. Accessed March 16, 2014.

Ochs, Robyn, ed. 2005. *Getting Bi: Voices of Bisexuals around the World*. Boston: Bisexual Resource Center.

Boswell, John (1947–1994)

John Boswell, a prominent gay historian, influenced medieval studies, religious studies, and queer studies throughout his 20-plus-year career. Boswell was born into a military family in 1947 and during his undergraduate studies converted to Roman Catholicism. A talented scholar who read over a dozen ancient and modern languages, Boswell completed his doctorate from Harvard University and joined the history faculty at Yale in 1975, served as A. Whitney Griswold Professor of History, and helped create Yale's Gay and Lesbian Studies Center in 1987.

A celebrated lecturer, teacher, and scholar, Boswell is most famous for his 1980 text, *Christianity, Social Tolerance and Homosexuality: Gay People in Western Europe from the Beginning of the Christian Era to the Fourteenth Century*, in which he argued that although religious belief and practice is blamed as the cause for intolerance of sexual difference for much of modern history, up until the twelfth century the Roman Catholic Church did not condemn love between men. This controversial interpretation of Western history earned him the 1981 American Book Award and sparked a debate over whether or not gay people could be found throughout history, and about the nature of sexual categories and identities throughout history. Social constructionists challenged his methodology for its essentialist postures, but Boswell rejected identifying himself as an essentialist. In 1994, Boswell published *Same-Sex Unions in Pre-Modern Europe*, in which he investigated manuscripts from the eighth to the sixteenth century that made reference to love, friendship, and marriage, concluding that same-sex emotional—perhaps erotic—relationships were liturgically celebrated in the Middle Ages.

Boswell remained a devoted Roman Catholic throughout his life, although he disagreed with the Church's official position on same-sex love—instead participating in Catholic lesbian and gay movements such as Dignity. Much of Boswell's academic work investigated historical actors who also attempted to reconcile sexuality and religious belief. Thus, his work was not without controversy or critics. Boswell died of AIDS-related complications in December 1994.

Howell Williams

See also: Historical Overview of Gay Rights and Issues: From Pre-Columbian Times to the 1970s; Historical

Overview of Gay Rights and Issues: From the 1980s to the Present.

Further Reading

Boswell, John. 1980. *Christianity, Social Tolerance and Homosexuality: Gay People in Western Europe from the Beginning of the Christian Era to the Fourteenth Century*. Chicago: University of Chicago Press.

Duberman, Martin Bauml, Martha Vicinus, and George Chauncey Jr., eds. 1989. *Hidden from History: Reclaiming the Gay and Lesbian Past*. New York: Nal Books.

Bowers v. Hardwick, 106 S. Ct. 2841, 2843 (1986)

Michael Hardwick was a 28-year-old white gay man who worked at one of the well-known gay bars in Atlanta, Georgia. After a long night at the bar, he left at 7:00 AM with a beer in hand. He decided he did not want the beer and disposed of it in a trash can outside the bar before getting in his car to drive home. Police officer Torick pulled Hardwick over to the side of the highway. He asked Hardwick where he worked. Hardwick's answer indirectly indicated to the police officer that Hardwick was gay. Torick suspected Hardwick of drinking and asked where he disposed of his beer. Hardwick was placed in the rear of the police car while Torick drove to where the beer was discarded. They did not find the trash receptacle and Torick issued a ticket to Hardwick for drinking in public.

The ticket Hardwick was given required him to appear at court. There was a discrepancy as to whether the court appearance was on a Tuesday or Wednesday. Two hours after the Tuesday court date, a warrant for the arrest of Hardwick was issued. Officer Torick came to Hardwick's home to arrest him, but he was not there. When Hardwick returned home later that day, his roommate informed him about the officer's visit. Hardwick went to the county clerk. The clerk said that was impossible since it usually takes at least 48 hours for such a warrant to be issued. Later it was discovered that Torick personally processed the

warrant, the first time this was done in over 10 years. Hardwick paid the $50 fine and thought the case was closed.

About three weeks later, officer Torick returned to Hardwick's home at 3 AM with the arrest warrant. The door was open and Torick was allowed to enter the home by a houseguest who was half-asleep on the couch. He did not know Hardwick and his companion were together in Hardwick's bedroom. Torick walked to the bedroom and discovered Hardwick engaged in oral sex with another man. Torick proceeded to enter the bedroom and arrested Hardwick and his companion for violating Georgia's sex statute. Hardwick was entitled to bail within an hour after arriving at the jail, but, instead, he was held for 12 hours and was subjected to harassment by the other prisoners because they had been informed of the charges against him.

Hardwick was charged. Gay activists saw this as a perfect test case and Hardwick decided to challenge the Georgia statute in federal court. Because the Georgia sex statutes do not refer to the gender or marriage status of an offender, a married heterosexual couple attempted to join Hardwick's action, but the court dismissed the married couple's claim.

Hardwick lost his claim in federal court, but won on his appeal to the U.S. District Court for the Eleventh Circuit. The case was appealed to the U.S. Supreme Court by Attorney General Michael J. Bowers for Georgia in 1986. The Court ruled against Hardwick in a five to four decision. The Court ruled that claims for "homosexual sodomy" as a protected right to privacy are "facetious, at best." The Court therefore established that lesbians and gay men have no right to sexual expression under the federal constitution. Soon after his retirement, Justice Lewis Powell conceded that he "had made a mistake" and should have voted to strike down Georgia's sex statute (Marcus 1990).

Since *Hardwick*, many within and without the lesbian and gay legal community have written scathing critiques of the ruling. If the Court had ruled in favor of Hardwick, all state sex statutes would have been overturned. Instead, the battle continued state by state for almost another two decades. For example, the Kentucky Supreme Court decision in *Commonwealth v. Wasson* (1992) rejected many of the arguments made by the majority in *Hardwick*. Instead, the court held the privacy protections contained within the Kentucky Constitution were more comprehensive than those provided by the U.S. Constitution. Since many states have constitutions similar to Kentucky with regards to privacy, this decision has been instrumental in the overturning of other state sex statutes. Eventually, the U.S. Supreme Court would overturn same-sex sodomy in *Lawrence et al v. Texas* in 2003.

Interestingly, Georgia's sodomy law would later play a role in ending Georgia attorney general Bowers's public career. In 1998, Bowers resigned as attorney general to seek the Republican nomination for governor. He was presented as a moral crusader who helped defend Georgia against homosexual sodomy. However, during the campaign, it came to light that Bowers was involved in a long-term extramarital affair—a violation of Georgia's archaic sex law against adultery. The hypocrisy that Michael J. Bowers defended Georgia against homosexual sodomy yet himself was an adulterer derailed his political career and he lost the race.

Chuck Stewart

See also: Historical Overview of Gay Rights and Issues: From the 1980s to the Present; *Romer v. Evans* (1996).

Further Reading

Cohen, Jean L. 2002. *Regulating Intimacy: A New Legal Paradigm*. Princeton, NJ: Princeton University Press.

Glenn, Richard A. 2003. *The Right to Privacy: Rights and Liberties under the Law*. Santa Barbara, CA: ABC-CLIO.

Irons, Peter H. 1990. *The Courage of Their Convictions: Sixteen Americans Who Fought Their Way to the Supreme Court*. New York: Penguin.

Marcus, R. 1990. "Powell Regrets Backing Sodomy Law." *Washington Post* (325), October 26, A3.

Signorile, Michelangelo. 2003. *Queer in America: Sex, the Media, and the Closets of Power*. Madison: University of Wisconsin Press.

Boy Scouts

The Boy Scouts of America has sustained many legal challenges for its policy of excluding homosexual members. Until 2013, when the organization decided to allow gay members, but not as troop leaders, the Boy Scouts had claimed that it had a First Amendment legal right to promote their belief that homosexuality was immoral and inappropriate. Many school districts, cities, counties, nonprofit organizations, and religious groups then severed their relationships with the Boy Scouts over this issue. Some school districts, cities, and counties had decided that they could not allow their facilities to be used by, and they cannot provide other government support to, an organization that excludes particular groups of people because this violates antidiscrimination policies and equal access laws. The Boy Scouts organization thus became the legal focal point over the debate between freedom of association and equal access. The Boy Scouts was founded by Robert S. S. Baden-Powell in England in 1907. He was a decorated war hero and, it is ironic to learn, he was gay (Greif 1989; Halsall 1994). He promoted the Boy Scouts as a "character factory" to help young men find honor and learn to be helpful to society. The Boy Scouts has become an institution in American life. The policies of the Boy Scouts, embodied in over a hundred years of actions, teachings, positions, and documents, neither provide directives on nor condemn homosexuality. It was only the recent leadership that had become steadfast against homosexuality. In the United States, there are more than 5 million Boy Scouts, of whom 55 percent are in troops sponsored by churches. The Boy Scouts contends that it has an overarching objective to reach "all eligible youth."

Boy Scouts of America v. Dale (2000)

Over the past decade courts had often ruled against the Scouts for removing openly gay troop leaders, only to see these decisions overruled by higher courts. The crucial issue of whether the Boy Scouts could discriminate against homosexual members and leaders was finally reviewed by the U.S. Supreme Court in *Boy*

Sir R. Baden was the founder of the Boy Scouts. (Library of Congress)

Scouts of America v. Dale (2000). James Dale was involved with the Boy Scouts for 12 years. He obtained the rank of Eagle Scout, was elected to the Order of the Arrow, and became assistant troop leader in 1990 at age 20. He never made his homosexuality known to the Scouts, nor did he mention or discuss the topic of homosexuality. That same year he was interviewed in a college newspaper and was identified as the copresident of a lesbian and gay student group at Rutgers University. The paper ran a photo of him marching in the local gay pride parade. When the Scouts' Monmouth, New Jersey, council discovered this fact, they sent him a letter stating that the Boy Scouts "specifically forbid

membership to homosexuals" and expelled him from the organization (*Boy Scouts of America v. Dale*, 137). Dale was not expelled for inappropriate conduct "on" or "off-duty," but rather for simply being identified as a homosexual.

Dale sued the Monmouth council and the national organization in 1992. He contended that their actions violated New Jersey's antidiscrimination law. The state court threw the case out, stating that the Boy Scouts was not a public accommodation and therefore was not bound by state antidiscrimination laws. The case was appealed and the New Jersey Supreme Court ruled in Dale's favor. The court rejected the Scouts' position that allowing homosexuals to participate would violate the Scouts' Oath's promise to remain "morally straight" and "clean." The court decided that the Boy Scouts was a public accommodation and was subject to state regulation.

The New Jersey Supreme Court made the following points:

- The Boy Scouts is a public accommodation because of its enormity and entanglement with governments and public entities.

- The Boy Scouts' policy of expelling openly gay members violated the state's law prohibiting places of public accommodation from discriminating on the basis of sexual orientation.

- To recognize the Boy Scouts' First Amendment claim would be tantamount to tolerating the expulsion of an individual solely because of his status as a homosexual—an act of discrimination unprotected by the First Amendment freedom of speech.

- The state's interest in prohibiting invidious discrimination outweighs the rights of nonsectarian organizations to exclude individuals simply because of who they are.

The issue polarized many in America. Together, 71 organizations filed briefs in this case. Every major civil rights organization including the NAACP and the American Bar Association joined with states, cities, deans of divinity schools, youth organizations, mental health and social services organizations, and

Rap mogul Russell Simmons, left, speaks with former Eagle Scout James Dale, center left, as New York City public advocate Mark Green, center right, speaks with Tony Award–winning actress Mary-Louise Parker before the 2001 Lesbian, Gay, Bisexual, and Transgender Pride Awards Ceremony at New York's City Hall, Thursday, June 21, 2001. Green presented Advocate Awards to Dale, Parker, and Simmons, among others. (AP Photo/Tina Fineberg)

rabbinical institutions in lobbying the Supreme Court in Dale's favor. The religious right, including Orthodox Jewish groups, supported the Boy Scouts.

The Boy Scouts argued the following in Court:

- No one has the "right" to be a Boy Scout leader. The Boy Scouts has the right to determine the qualifications of its leaders. Because it believes homosexuality is immoral, it has the right to disallow homosexuals from being troop leaders. It contends that Boy Scouts policy is promoted through its leadership and attempts to control its leadership is, in fact, control of its speech.

- Homosexuals cannot teach "true manliness" and a boy's ultimate responsibility to women, children, and religious belief.

- Boy Scouting espouses family values, which emphasize marriage and fatherhood—neither of which homosexuals stand for.

- Requiring the Boy Scouts to accept homosexual leaders would, by word and deed, put leaders in place who disagreed with the organization's moral code.

- Applying the New Jersey law to the Boy Scouts violates the members' constitutional right to intimate and expressive association. The Boy Scouts is a private, voluntary organization and should have the freedom to "create and interpret its own moral code."

- The Boy Scouts is being forced to condone homosexuality against its will.

Dale's lawyers made the following arguments to the U.S. Supreme Court:

- The Boy Scouts does not have a history of actions or policy that excludes homosexuals. If anything, the Boy Scouts teaches tolerance and encourages an end to bigotry and hate.

- The U.S. Supreme Court has repeatedly rejected the notion that the First Amendment gives groups the right to discriminate. The First Amendment right to freedom of association and its corollary, the freedom not to associate, has never been regarded as an absolute free-floating right.

- Dale was expelled from the Scouts solely because he was gay and not for misconduct. In New Jersey, discrimination based upon sexual orientation is illegal. The Boy Scouts illegally discriminated against Dale.

There were two basic arguments to this issue.

For the Boy Scouts: The Boy Scouts have a First Amendment right to determine and promote the moral goals of a private organization. This includes the right to choose leaders who reflect the organization's goals. A few court cases back this position. For example, in *Hurley v. Irish-American Gay, Lesbian, and Bisexual Group of Boston*, the court upheld the First Amendment right of the organizers of the Boston St. Patrick's Day Parade to exclude gays from their event. The gay marching contingent was not barred from participating because of its gay identity, but rather because it intended to express a message in the parade contrary to that of the parade organizers.

For James Dale: Because of the size and institutional nature of the Boy Scouts, it is a public organization subject to state laws. As such, if state laws prohibit discrimination based upon sexual orientation, then the Boy Scouts should not be allowed to exclude lesbian or gay members or leaders. This position is supported by three recent cases, all dealing with all-male organizations. In *Roberts v. United States Jaycees*, the Supreme Court allowed the state of Minnesota to require that females be accepted as members into the once all-male Jaycees. In general,

the courts found the clubs existed for commercial purposes and that the exclusion of women was not part of their self-described mission.

The Boy Scouts asserted that by donning the Scout uniform, James Dale would celebrate his identity as an openly gay scout leader precisely as did the gay Irish marchers who attempted to conscript the Boston St. Patrick's Day Parade for their own purposes. However, Dale argued that "learning that someone is gay tells you nothing about his or her political party, religious beliefs, lifestyle, or moral code." Thus, his exclusion from the Boy Scouts is the same discrimination based on status that the court rejected in the all-male club cases.

The balance between First Amendment rights to free speech and association and government regulation of discrimination is distinguished between identity-based and speech-based discrimination. The Boy Scouts is free to express its point of view in pamphlets, speeches, and other ways.

However, it has chosen not to do so. Heterosexual troop leaders have publicly stated that discrimination against homosexuals is wrong and that homosexuality is moral; yet the Boy Scouts has not acted against these leaders (*Boy Scouts of America v. Dale* 2000, 2455). Only those who are openly gay have been expelled. This is conduct discrimination that the courts have held to be unconstitutional for private nonsecular organizations that are deemed public accommodations.

On June 28, 2000, the U.S. Supreme Court reversed the New Jersey Supreme Court decision. The Court held that requiring the Boy Scouts to include Mr. Dale in their ranks would violate the organization's First Amendment right of "expressive association." The Court said, "We are not, as we must not be, guided by our views of whether the Boy Scouts' teachings with respect to homosexual conduct are right or wrong. Public or judicial disapproval of a tenet of an organization's expression does not justify the state's effort to compel the organization to accept members where such acceptance would derogate from the organization's expressive message" (*Boy Scouts of America v. Dale.*). Because Boy Scouts leaders are drawn from the ranks of young scouts, it is inferred that gay people are forbidden in the Scouts at any level. The dissenting justices, John Paul Stevens, David Souter, Stephen Breyer, and Ruth Bader Ginsburg, said that the scouting precept of being "morally straight and clean" was not related to homosexuality. However, the Boy Scouts' lawyer George Davidson stated that being openly homosexual communicates the concept that this is acceptable and is against the Scouts' policy.

The U.S. Supreme Court failed to force an overall change in the Boy Scouts' policy. It is expected that more cities, local governments, school districts, and others will withdraw their support of the Boy Scouts because of the Boy Scouts' intransigent ban on allowing gay members to participate. For example, the day after the announcement by the Supreme Court, the mayor of Philadelphia was asked to withdraw all city support for the Boy Scouts of America (Center for Lesbian and Gay Civil Rights 2000). Some tax scholars have queried whether the Boy Scouts should have their tax-exempt status revoked by the IRS ("Does Boy Scouts' Policy" 2000). This is based on the law that charitable institutions must demonstrably serve and be in harmony with the public interest to qualify for tax-exempt status. In *Bob Jones University v. United States* (1983), the Supreme Court upheld the revocation of the university's tax-exempt status because it had a policy forbidding interracial dating. By 1983, the social, political, and legal climate of the United States was such that this policy violated community conscience. The Court respected the right of the university to have this policy, but ruled that the government could not provide financial support by granting tax-exempt status. At this time there is no clear public position concerning the acceptance of sexual orientation–based discrimination. Consequently, the Boy Scouts will probably retain its tax-exempt status. However, this will probably change in the future as lesbians, gay men, bisexuals, transgendered, and intersexed people gain greater social and legal acceptance.

A decade of bad publicity and major loss of funding influenced the Boy Scouts to modify its antigay position. On May 23, 2013, the Boy Scouts of America's national governing body voted to rescind its long-standing position against allowing gay boys to participate as members. Beginning January 1, 2014, all boys regardless of sexual orientation may join and participate in all aspects of scouting. However, it maintains its ban on LGBT adults from being troop leaders. A new scouting organization (not affiliated with the Boy Scouts) called Trail Life USA was formed in September 2013 that will not allow gay boys or adults to join. Several Baptist congregations and other fundamentalist Christian denominations have severed their ties with the Boy Scouts and replaced them with Trail Life USA.

Chuck Stewart

See also: Antidiscrimination Statutes.

Further Reading

Boy Scouts of America. Membership Resolution Points of Clarification. Available at: http://www.scouting.org/MembershipStandards/Resolution/FAQ.aspx. Accessed March 16, 2014.

Center for Lesbian and Gay Civil Rights. 2000, June 28. "Gay Group Demands City Withdrawal of Support for Boy Scouts." Press release, Available at www.center4civilrights.org.

"Does Boy Scouts' Policy on Homosexuals Preclude Tax-Exempt Status?" 2000. *Tax Analysts' Tax Notes Today*, December 11.

Greif, M. 1989. *The Gay Book of Days*. New York: Lyle Stuart.

Halsall, P. 1994. *Queers in History*. Available at www.dezines.com/rainbow/queers.htm.

Koppelman, Andrew and Tobias Barrington Wolff. 2009. *A Right to Discriminate?: How the Case of Boy Scouts of America v. James Dale Warped the Law of Free Association*. New Haven, CT: Yale University Press.

Perry, Rick. 2008. *On My Honor: Why the American Values of the Boy Scouts Are Worth Fighting for*. Macon, GA: Stroud & Hall Publishers.

Volokh, Eugene. 1919–1968. "Freedom of Expressive Association and Government Subsidies." *Stanford Law Review* (UCLA) 58.

Brown, Howard Juniah (1924–1975)

Brown served as the city of New York's first health services administrator in the administration of Mayor John Lindsay. In that position, he was in charge of coordinating programs of the Departments of Health and Hospitals, the Community Health Board, and the Office of the Chief Medical Examiner. He held that post slightly more than a year before resigning in December 1967, afraid that his being a gay man would soon become public knowledge. He then went on to become director of community medicine at Fordham University and, later, professor at New York University's School of Public Administration and its School of Medicine. In October 1973, after years of leading a double life, Brown announced at a meeting of 600 physicians that he was gay. At that moment, as he points out in his autobiography, *Familiar Faces, Hidden Lives*, he became "the most prominent self-confessed homosexual in America."

Howard Juniah Brown was born on April 15, 1924, in Peoria, Illinois. His father's occupation as a civil engineer forced the family to move frequently. In *Familiar Faces, Hidden Lives*, he remembers having his first homosexual feelings when he was about 18, but made no attempt to act on them. He was sure, he said, that "I must be the only homosexual in northern Ohio" (Brown 1976, p. 32). It took him five years to discover he was very much wrong on this point.

Brown entered Hiram College on a prelaw scholarship, but decided in his senior year to switch to medicine because he believed that a law career would be too risky, given his sexual orientation. He was accepted by Cleveland's Western Reserve Medical College in 1943, but was drafted before he could enroll. After serving in the army for a year, he was discharged and began his medical training at Western Reserve. After earning his medical degree, Brown moved to Detroit to do his residency. He worked at Jennings Memorial Hospital and the UAW-CIO Clinic until 1954, when he moved to New York City. There he took a job as director of professional services for the Health Insurance Plan of Greater New York. He held that position until 1961, when he was appointed head of the Gouverneur Ambulatory Care Unit on New York City's Lower East Side.

The notoriety that Brown received after his "coming-out" announcement encouraged him to become active in a variety of gay and lesbian causes. In October 1973, he was one of the founding members of the National Gay Task Force (now the National Gay and Lesbian Task Force). One of his major activities at the Task Force was an effort to convince the American Psychiatric Association to change its classification of homosexuality as a mental disorder, an effort that was eventually successful. After suffering from coronary problems for many years, Brown died of a heart attack on February 1, 1975. An alternative health care clinic founded in Chicago in 1974 was later named in his honor, the Howard Brown Memorial Clinic. Today, the Brown Clinic is widely recognized as one of the nation's leading centers for gay, lesbian, bisexual, and transgendered health care problems.

David E. Newton

See also: American Psychiatric Association (APA); National Gay and Lesbian Task Force.

Further Reading

Brown, Howard. 1976. *Familiar Faces, Hidden Lives*. New York: Harcourt Brace Jovanovich.

Brown, Rita Mae (1944–)

Born to an unwed mother, Rita Mae Brown was adopted by Ralph and Julia Brown of York, Pennsylvania. The family lived in Pennsylvania for Brown's first 11 years and then moved to Florida, where Brown eventually entered college. In 1964, Brown was dismissed from the University of Florida for civil rights activism and lesbian relationships. She moved to New York City, where her political activism continued as she formed the Student Homophile League at New York University and Columbia University in 1967 and helped open a women's center on the Lower East Side. Brown was an early member of the National Organization for Women, which she left after protesting the group's racism, classism, and homophobia. After briefly working with the Redstockings, a radical feminist group, Brown joined Gay Liberation, a radical gay/lesbian group. At the same time, she was writing essays for feminist journals, many of which are collected in *A Plain Brown Rapper*, and working on her first novel, *Rubyfruit Jungle*, which was rejected by mainstream presses for its lesbian content and was published by Daughters Press, a small feminist organization. Recognized as one of the first novels in America to reject cultural representations of lesbianism as perverse, the story focuses on the coming of age of tomboy protagonist Molly Bolt as she steps into her identity as both a woman and a lesbian. Through Bolt's experiences, Brown's novel confronts the social stigmas associated with homosexuality.

Brown followed this novel with *In Her Day*, another work with lesbian issues at the center. Drawing up the relationship between lesbian protagonists Carole Hanratty, a professor of art history, and Ilse James, an undergraduate student at Vassar, the novel examines political and social issues stemming from homosexuality and its effect on the couple's relationship. The purchase of *Rubyfruit Jungle* in 1977 by Bantam Books made that novel a best seller, a turn of events that enabled Brown to begin her career as a full-time writer. She followed this success with *Six of One*, her first work to be published with Harper and Row, which established Brown as a mainstream author. Her next novel, *Southern Discomfort*, turned to issues of racism and classism in its portrayal of a relationship between a wealthy Southern socialite and a black teenager. With *Sudden Death*, Brown returned to lesbian relationships through her portrayal of the professional women's tennis tour and the experiences of tennis player Carmen Semana and professor of religion Harriet Rawls, a novel drawn from her own two-year relationship with Martina Navratilova during the 1980s.

These novels were followed by, among others, *Venus Envy*, which argues for gays and lesbians to overcome internalized homophobia and accept themselves, as well as *Dolley: A Novel of Dolley Madison in Love and War*, a historical novel, and *Riding Shotgun*, a work where a woman from the present travels

Author Rita Mae Brown uses an electric typewriter from her floor in 1982. (Roger Ressmeyer/Corbis)

to the seventeenth century. In 1990, Brown expanded her writing to the mystery genre with her Sneaky Pie Brown series, which she pretends to coauthor with her cat, a shift that has firmly established Brown with a mainstream readership. Her most recent book in the Mrs. Murphy series (featuring a crime-solving cat, Mrs. Murphy, along with other animals and humans), and also coauthored with Sneaky Pie Brown (published in 2014, *Nine Lives to Die*).

In addition to her fiction writing, she has published collections of poetry, written for television, and narrated the groundbreaking documentary on gay and lesbian history, *Before Stonewall*. In interviews, she often stresses that she is a Southern woman writer rather than a lesbian writer. Yet, she admits that sexuality is a central factor, as her writings confront the dominant heterosexual culture, while also addressing issues of gender, race, and class as her characters strive to find happiness and remain true to themselves.

Jeannette E. Riley

See also: Navratilova, Martina (1956–).

Further Reading

Chew, Martha. 1983. "Rita Mae Brown: Feminist Theorist and Southern Novelist." *The Southern Quarterly* 22 (1): 61–80.

Ward, Carol M. 1993. *Rita Mae Brown.* New York: Twayne Publishers.

Bryant, Anita (1940–)

Anita Bryant launched the Save Our Children organization to stop gay and lesbian rights in Dade County, Florida. This became the galvanizing force behind what would become the religious right.

Singer Anita Bryant in her home in Miami Beach, Florida, on June 7, 1978. (AP Photo/Kathy A. Willens)

Born into a devoutly Southern Baptist family in Barnsdall, Oklahoma, Anita Bryant accepted Jesus Christ as her savior when she was eight. In 1958 she was chosen Miss Oklahoma and later runner-up Miss America. She was a talented singer and was chosen by Bob Hope in 1961 to participate in his Christmas junket entertaining GIs in the Caribbean. For seven years, Anita traveled with Bob Hope to the Arctic, the Pacific, and the Far East, including Vietnam, to sing in his Holiday Troupe.

Her trademark song was a rousing rendition of the "Battle Hymn of the Republic," which she sang at the 1976 Super Bowl halftime, Bob Hope's Christmas specials, and presidential performances. From 1960 to 1980, Bryant was a spokesperson for the Florida Citrus Growers. She became known as the Sunshine-Tree Girl. During those 20 years she made 76 television commercials and orange juice sales climbed from 382 million gallons to more than 800 million gallons a year.

In 1977, the Miami-Dade County Commission passed an ordinance making it illegal to discriminate on the basis of sexual orientation. Upset by this development, Bryant organized a group called Save Our Children. She obtained sufficient signatures to place a referendum on the ballot to overturn the ordinance. It was passed overwhelmingly by the county citizens. Her crusade galvanized the gay pride movement to organize and coordinate a national protest and spurred conservative religious groups into what is today known as the religious right. A successful boycott by the gay community of orange juice resulted in the termination of her contract with the Florida Citrus Growers. At the same time, her marriage dissolved.

Her activism adversely affected her career. Her divorce caused some fundamentalists organizations to stop inviting her to perform and speak, thus losing a major source of income. With the marriage to her second husband, Charlie Hobson Dry, in 1990, she attempted to reestablish her music career by launching "Anita Bryant's Music Mansion"—reviews where she mixed performances of her more successful songs with preaching Christian beliefs.

The venture failed and she filed for bankruptcy in 2001 leaving a trail of unpaid creditors and unpaid employees. This was her second bankruptcy in just a few years.

Twenty-one years later, in 1998, a new law outlawing discrimination based on sexual orientation was approved by the Miami-Dade County Commission. Bryant made no comments about this new law, as she was preoccupied with the bankruptcy of the Anita Bryant Theater. Plans were announced in 2013 to produce a biographical film based on Bryant's life to star Uma Thurman.

Chuck Stewart

See also: Falwell, Jerry L. (1933–2007); Schlafly, Phyllis Stewart (1924–).

Further Reading

Bryant, Anita. 1977. *The Anita Bryant Story: The Survival of Our Nation's Families and the Threat of Militant Homosexuality.* Tappan, NJ: Fleming H. Revell.

Bryant, Anita and Green, Bob. 1978. *At Any Cost.* Grand Rapids, MI: Fleming H. Revell.

Jahr, Cliff. 1980, December. "Anita Bryant's Startling Reversal." *Ladies Home Journal* (Charter Company): 60–68.

Buckmire, Ron (1968–)

Ron Buckmire is an African American professor of mathematics who is the creator of the Queer Resources Directory—the largest and oldest source of gay/lesbian/bisexual/transgender and AIDS/HIV information on the Internet. Born May 21, 1968, in Grenville, Grenada, Buckmire was recognized early as having strong mathematical skills. He was three-time Barbados Junior Chess Champion (1983–1986) and three-time Barbados Senior Chess Champion (1983–1986). He was accepted to Rensselaer Polytechnic Institute in Troy, New York, where he completed his bachelor of science degree, magna cum laude, in mathematics in 1989. He continued on to receive his master's degree (1992) and then his PhD in applied mathematics (1994). While at Rensselaer, Buckmire designed and launched the Queer Resources Directory (www.qrd.org).

In 1991, Buckmire met his life partner, Dean Elzinga. They both moved to Los Angeles when Buckmire accepted a teaching position at Occidental College in 1996. Besides teaching, Buckmire continues his chess playing and is currently ranked in the top 250 of the United States. He is also a board member of PlanetOut Corp., on the steering committee of the Los Angeles Freedom to Marry Coalition, cofounder of Digital Queers Los Angeles (1995), and manager of numerous Internet mailing lists, such as Queerlaw, Marriage, GLBPOC, Queer Politics, and NA-teach. In 1996, *Out* magazine named Buckmire as one of the Top 100 Gay and Lesbian Activists of the Year and for the 30th anniversary issue *The Advocate* named Buckmire as one of those from "Generation Q," 30 activists under-30 who had made a difference in LGBTQ rights.

Chuck Stewart

See also: Historical Overview of Gay Rights and Issues: From the 1980s to the Present.

Further Reading

Queer Resources Directory. Available at: http://www.qrd.org/qrd/. Accessed March 16, 2014.

Bunch, Charlotte (1944–)

Charlotte Bunch is widely regarded as one of the most important and articulate theorists of the gay and lesbian movement, particularly with regard to feminism. She has written and lectured extensively on feminist theory and its relationship to lesbianism. She has authored, coauthored, edited, and coedited a dozen books and more than 250 scholarly papers and popular articles on feminist theory and related topics.

Bunch was born in West Jefferson, North Carolina, on October 13, 1944, but she grew up in Artesia, New Mexico. After graduating from Artesia High School in 1962, she returned to North Carolina for her college education, earning her BA degree in history and political science from Duke University in 1966. Strongly influenced by the turmoil surrounding the Vietnam War in progress at the time, Bunch decided to make political activism a career.

During a White House ceremony to present the 1999 Eleanor Roosevelt Human Rights Awards on December 6, 1999, President Clinton and First Lady Hillary Rodham Clinton applauded the work of Charlotte Bunch of New Brunswick, New Jersey. Bunch founded and was the executive director of the Center for Women's Global Leadership at Rutgers University. She has led efforts to have gender and sexual orientation included in the U.N.'s human rights agenda. (AP Photo/J. Scott Applewhite)

In 1967, Bunch married Jim Weeks, a man who shared many of her interests in political activism. Over the next four years, however, the two grew apart, and in 1971, Bunch came out as a lesbian. She later wrote that this decision was "not a reaction against my husband but a response to the power of sexual self-discovery" (Bunch 1987, p. 102). She rapidly became involved in the young lesbian-feminist movement and was one of the founding members of the Furies collective, a group committed to the development of a lesbian-feminist political analysis, culture, and movement.

From her days at Duke to the present, Bunch's life has been a whirlwind of political activity. Following her work in the civil rights and antiwar movements,

she has been involved at one time or another in the National Organization for Women, the University Christian Movement, the National Council of Churches Conference on Church and Society, the National Gay and Lesbian Task Force, the President's National Advisory Committee for Women, the National Women's Program of the American Friends Service Committee, the New York City Commission on the Status of Women, the Organizing Committee for the Decade for Human Rights Education, and the National Council for Research on Women.

In 1989, Bunch founded the Center for Women's Global Leadership at Rutgers University, and was for many years its executive director, and is now founding director and senior scholar at the Center for Women's

Global Leadership, as well as a Board of Governor's Distinguished Service Professor in the Women's and Gender Studies Department at Rutgers University. In 2007, she was awarded an honorary doctor of laws degree by the University of Connecticut.

Chuck Stewart

See also: Historical Overview of Gay Rights and Issues: From the 1980s to the Present.

Further Reading

Bunch, Charlotte. 1987. *Passionate Politics: Feminist Theory in Action.* New York: St. Martin's Press.

C

Cameron, Paul Drummond (1939–)

Paul Cameron is the primary source of antigay "research." Cameron was born on November 9, 1939, in Pittsburgh, Pennsylvania. He received his bachelor's degree from Los Angeles Pacific University in 1961, obtained a master's degree from California State University Los Angeles in 1962, and earned his PhD from the University Colorado in 1966. He was affiliated with various colleges and universities until 1980, including Wayne State University (1967–1968), University of Louisville (1970–1973), Fuller Graduate School of Psychology (part of the Fuller Theological Seminary, 1976–1979), and the University of Nebraska (1979–1980).

In 1980, his teaching contract with the Department of Psychology of the University of Nebraska was not renewed. At that time, he began publishing hysterical pamphlets alleging that gays were disproportionately responsible for serial killings, child molestation, and other heinous crimes. In these pamphlets, Cameron misrepresented the findings of respected academic researchers. Many of these researchers formally petitioned Cameron to retract his claims but he refused. Complaints were filed, and the American Psychological Association investigated Cameron and found that he not only misrepresented the works of others but also used unsound methods in his own studies.

For this ethical breach, he was expelled from the association in 1983. Cameron has also been expelled from the Nebraska Psychological Association and the American Sociological Association. In *Baker v. Wade* (the case in which a Texas court found the state's prohibition against consensual sodomy between homosexuals to be unconstitutional), Judge Buchmeyer of the U.S. district court in Dallas states, "Dr. Paul Cameron . . . has himself made misrepresentations to this court" and "there have been no fraud or misrepresentation except by Dr. Cameron" (p. 536).

Gregory M. Herek, University of California at Davis psychologist specializing in prejudice against sexual minorities, has performed extensive research into the works of Paul Cameron. According to Herek, there are at least six serious errors in Cameron's studies. Herek stated, "An empirical study manifesting even one of these six weaknesses would be considered seriously flawed. In combination, the multiple methodological problems evident in the Cameron group's surveys mean that their results cannot even be considered a valid description of the specific group of individuals who returned the survey questionnaire. Because the data are essentially meaningless, it is not surprising that they have been virtually ignored by the scientific community" (Herek 2007).

Cameron conducted a large research study in the early 1980s from which he has made outrageous claims—such as the short life expectancy of gay men. The professional censure of Cameron has not stopped his antigay agenda. In 1987, Cameron founded the Family Research Institute (FRI) and has been a virtual one-man propaganda press, periodically revising his brochures and distributing them to policymakers. The Southern Poverty Law Center has classified the FRI as a hate group. Yet with all these problems of poor science, the religious right latched onto and helped fund Cameron's work to substantiate its religious agenda. When challenges concerning Cameron's ethical

Paul Cameron of the Family Research Institute listens to testimony against the civil-unions bill during the House Judiciary Committee, at the state capitol in Denver, Colorado, on March 31, 2011. Senate Bill 172, which would give same-sex couples many of the rights and responsibilities of marriage, included child support and hospital visitation. (Craig F. Walker/The Denver Post/Getty Images)

breach, unsound research methodology, and misinformation are made, the religious right dismisses the problems, holds him up as a martyr, and continues to promote his work.

Chuck Stewart

See also: Sexual Orientation Change Efforts.

Further Reading

Baker v. Wade, 106 F.R.D. 526 (1985-07-01).

Bialik, Carl. 2005. "Debate over Gay Foster Parents Shines Light on a Dubious Stat." *Wall Street Journal*, April 28, 2005. Available at: http://online.wsj.com/news/articles/SB111461604615918400.

Herek, Gregory M. 1997–2007. "Critique of Surveys by the Paul Cameron Group." Available at: http://psychology.ucdavis.edu/faculty_sites/rainbow/html/facts_cameron_survey.html. Accessed February 9, 2014.

Carpenter, Edward (1844–1929)

Carpenter was one of the first authors to write about homosexuality in a positive light. He took great chances with his writing at a time when people such as Oscar Wilde were being imprisoned for homosexual acts.

Born in Brighton, England, on August 29, 1844, Edward Carpenter grew up in a home dominated by his retired naval officer father. Carpenter was educated in Brighton College and then studied for the priesthood at Trinity Hall at Cambridge in 1864. He was ordained in 1869 and appointed to the parish of St. Edward's in Cambridge in 1870.

Soon, he developed serious doubts about the church. He resigned from the priesthood in 1874 and supported himself teaching classes on astronomy in northern England. At the same time, he became active in the socialist movement and wrote a half-dozen books exploring change in society.

Carpenter became aware of his own sexual awakening and was influenced by Walt Whitman's homoerotic poetry. In April 1877, Carpenter traveled to the United States to speak with Whitman and found the poet reluctant to discuss social and political issues as they related to his work. Carpenter was disappointed by these meetings with Whitman but began to integrate a positive homosexual view into his socialist writings. Carpenter saw the Uranian (homosexual) spirit to be more enlightened than that of the common man and believed that Uranians were the new prophets of the coming social revolution.

Carpenter inherited a large sum of money on the death of his father in 1882, which allowed him to build a home isolated on seven acres in Millthorpe, Chesterfield. He lived there for the next 40 years. In 1891, Carpenter met and fell in love with George Merrill, with whom he lived until the latter's death in 1928.

Heartbroken, Carpenter moved to a small cottage in nearby Guilford and died a year later.

Chuck Stewart

See also: Symonds, John Addington (1840–1893); Whitman, Walt (1819–1892); Wilde, Oscar (1854–1900).

Further Reading

Tsuzuki, Chushichi. 1980. *Edward Carpenter 1844– 1929: Prophet of Human Fellowship*. Cambridge, UK: Cambridge University Press.

Center for Lesbian and Gay Studies (CLAGS)

Founded in 1991, Center for Lesbian and Gay Studies (CLAGS) is the first university-based research center in the United States whose mission was dedicated to the study of historical, cultural, and political issues of central concern to lesbian, gay, bisexual, and transgender individuals and communities. Located in the Graduate Center of the City University of New York, in Manhattan on Fifth Avenue between 34th and 35th Streets, CLAGS sponsors conferences, offers fellowships to individual scholars, and functions as a conduit of information on and about LGBT issues.

Part of the mission of CLAGS is to promote scholarship that fosters social change and to advance inquiry on LGBT topics by bringing together scholars, writers, and activists from New York, the United States, and around the world. CLAGS also seeks to foster social change by sponsoring public programs and conferences that CLAGS strives to make accessible, providing American Sign Language interpretation and wheelchair accessibility, and making its events affordable or free of charge.

CLAGS was founded by Martin Duberman, Distinguished Professor of History at Lehman College and the Graduate Center of the City University of New York (CUNY). He chaired a preliminary group of scholars, artists, and activists in 1986 as an exploratory committee that eventually evolved into CLAGS; he then became its first official director in 1991. One of the country's foremost historians, Duberman is the author of numerous books, articles, and essays, winner

of the Bancroft Prize for *Charles Francis Adams*; recipient of two Lambda awards; and recipient of a special award from the National Academy of Arts and Letters.

The idea for CLAGS came out of Duberman's frustration at the consternation with which he was met in post-Stonewall academic New York when, in his desire to explore gay history, he offered to teach a course on sexuality in history. His proposal was rejected on the grounds that gay studies was not a recognized discipline. It took 15 years, a shift in the attitudes of the administrations within academia, and some generous financial donations for the idea of CLAGS finally to become a reality in 1991. In 1992, CLAGS received its first endowment fund with a donation of $100,000 from Dr. David Kessler. This fund supports the annual Kessler Lecture, which honors individuals who have made "an outstanding contribution to the expression and understanding of lesbian and gay life." Also in 1992, CLAGS received a $250,000 grant from the Rockefeller Foundation. This three-year grant, which was renewed for another three years, allowed 12 scholars-in-residence to come to the Graduate Center of CUNY between 1993 and 2000.

CLAGS offers a number of fellowships and student awards, including CLAGS Fellowship Award; the Martin Duberman Fellowship; the Joan Heller-Diane Bernard Fellowship; the Robert Giard Fellowship; the Kessler Award; the Passing the Torch Award; the Sylvia Rivera Award in Transgender Studies; the Paul Monette-Roger Horwitz Dissertation Prize; Graduate Student Paper Award; Undergraduate Student Paper Award; Student Travel Award.

In 1995, the CLAGS initiative to foster LGBTQ pedagogy nationally resulted in a systematic collection of college syllabi that was subsequently made available online. These syllabi are now in demand around the country, as evidenced by calls coming to the CLAGS office. The year 1999 saw CLAGS initiate an e-mail discussion listserv for the dissemination of the work in LGBT studies.

In its ongoing commitment to providing a public forum for intellectual discussion and debate, in 1998 CLAGS initiated the Seminars in the City program. In this program CLAGS acts as a bridge, connecting activists, academics, and the larger community, enabling all to share their knowledge about lesbian and gay lives. Seminars in the City is a monthly series offered in partnership with the Lesbian and Gay Community Services Center. The seminars provide an informal but intellectually charged forum for addressing major issues and works of LGBTQ studies, with the aim of engaging nonacademic readers in the often complex issues presented.

Mária I. Cipriani

See also: Committee on Lesbian and Gay History (CLGH); Duberman, Martin Bauml (1930–).

Further Reading

Center for Lesbian and Gay Studies (CLAGS). Available at: http://www.clags.org/ Accessed March 16, 2014.

Duberman, Martin B. 1994. *Stonewall*. New York: Plume.

Duberman, Martin B. and George Chauncey, eds. 1990. *Hidden from History: Reclaiming the Gay and Lesbian Past*. New York: Penguin.

Halberstam, Judith. 2005. *In a Queer Time and Place: Transgender Bodies, Subcultural Lives*. New York: New York University Press.

Jakobsen, Janet R. and Ann Pellegrini. 2003. *Love the Sin: Sexual Regulation and the Limits of Religious Tolerance*. New York: New York University Press.

Ross, Marlon B. 2004. *Manning the Race: Reforming Black Men in the Jim Crow Era*. New York: New York University Press.

Chinese American Queer History

Sensationalist stories about Asian Americans and the pathologies of "Asian cultures" are so common that more complex stories seem inauthentic to American audiences, so pervasive that even most Asian Americans believe that they are true. But the perception of how Asian Americans relate to people who are LGBT and their culture holds a special place in these mainstream narratives to the point where it becomes inconceivable that Asians, with their supposedly rigid and backward beliefs, can be anything but homophobic. Pop culture loves to paint images of queer[1] Asian Americans forcibly hidden under a veil of shame, held tightly in place by a static, repressive culture that immigrated to America with traditional parents. These racist and oversimplified tropes treat being Asian, being American, and being queer as static, adversarial, and ultimately separate identities.

Academic works are not immune to falling into similar traps. Asian American scholars Sau-ling Wong and Jeffrey Santa Ana observed that "in academic investigations, each of these [identities] has a history of serving as a discrete analytic category, but it is in fact impossible to separate their workings" (Wong 1999, p. 171). Countless research has framed the experience of queer Asian Americans as being "trapped" between two (separate, unrelated) worlds, Asian and American, which is further complicated by the Asian world's apparent homophobia. This type of scholarship not only legitimizes the "pathological culture" approach but also neglects historical context, societal/systemic impacts like racism, and the influence of crossing national boundaries. This encyclopedia topic exploring Asian Americans, and in particular, Chinese Americans, and attitudes to homosexuality and queerness seeks to avoid these deficiencies by providing a contextualized historical overview that acknowledges the ways that race, ethnicity, gender, and sexuality have dynamically interacted and informed each other, within the borders of United States and between the borders of the United States and China.

In "Asian American History and Racialized Compulsory Deviance," historian Judy Tzu-Chun Wu

---

1. Editor's Note: In this encyclopedia entry, the term *queer* is primarily used as a synonym for the term *lesbian, gay, bisexual, and/or transgender*, or *LGBT*. Many in the LGBT community use the term *queer*, partly to replace the clumsy LGBT; partly to reclaim for themselves and defuse a term that has often been thrown at non-heterosexual people as a slur; and sometimes to suggest a more activist and academic orientation, as in *queer studies*.

(2003) demonstrates that the relatively recent field of "Asian American History" had itself been pressured to conform to heteronormative narratives as a "critique of racially motivated intrusions on the construction of family" (p. 59). During the 1960s and 1970s, scholars seeking to draw attention to racism that Asian communities faced throughout U.S. history developed historical accounts of nineteenth-century exclusionary immigration policies targeting Asians (Wu 2003). Starting with the Page Act of 1875, these policies enforced quotas for "undesirable" immigrants, which included anyone who "could be classified as convicts, contract laborers, and Asian women coming to work in prostitution" (Luibhéid 2002). Scholar Eithne Luibhéid (2002) observed that the Page Act's linking of race and sexuality created the beginnings of a pattern of "sexuality based immigration exclusions," a pattern which came to shape how sexuality was defined and negotiated in immigrant communities (Luibhéid 2002, p. 31). The targeting of Asian women, particularly Chinese women, was no coincidence. While women of all nationalities were involved in sex work, anxieties about the "immoral and [. . .] heathen" Chinese immigrants were sexualized (Luibhéid 2002, p. 33). "Fears about white lives, cultural norms, and nation" were translated in the white American public as fears about the sexuality of Chinese women, who were scapegoated "in strategies officials devised to try to identify and exclude Chinese prostitutes" (Luibhéid 2002, p. 31).

Focusing on the extreme gender imbalance beginning with predominantly male early immigrants and worsened by immigration policies, early scholars in Asian American History used the term *bachelor society* to describe resulting "lonely" communities of Chinese men, a characterization that "draws attention to the lack of conjugal families on American soil" (Wu 2003). The argument that exclusionary policies like antimiscegenation laws also created a "racial barrier that prevented the predominantly male Asian population from developing nuclear families" gave rise to the field's "[tendency] to celebrate the creation of 'normative' families" (Wu 2003). The centering of Chinese men, heterosexuality, and normative families came

Director Ang Lee attends a forum in Hong Kong to promote his new movie, the gay love story *Brokeback Mountain* on Saturday, January 21, 2006. Lee said he found Chinese audiences more accepting of gay subject matter than U.S. viewers. (AP Photo/Lo Sai-hung)

at the exclusion of real attention to the sexual policing of Chinese women, but also of non-normative relationships in Chinese communities. In *Contagious Divides: Epidemic and Race in San Francisco's Chinatown*, historian Nayan Shah uses the term "queer domesticity" to describe the range of "space[s] and social relations" that "countered or transgressed [. . .] normative expectations" (Shah 2001).

As evidenced by the effort officials put into defining and policing sexuality, the dominant ideology in the nineteenth century was the belief that "modern, healthy society" was built from white "heterosexual married couples and their children [. . .] who perpetuated the race and enriched the nation" (Shah 2001, p. 78). Consequently, there were strong societal

Washington State Supreme Court justice Mary Yu is applauded by current court members behind as she acknowledges the gallery after being sworn in to the bench on May 20, 2014, in Olympia, Washington. Yu, a former King County Superior Court judge, was sworn in as the newest member of the court, marking the first time the high court has had an openly gay justice. Yu, whose mother is from Mexico and father is from China, is also the first Asian American and first female Hispanic member of the court. (AP Photo/Elaine Thompson)

expectations to live up to "respectable domesticity," which was "increasingly defined by a self-contained household that had at its center the [white] married couple's pursuit of reproduction" (Shah 2001, p. 78). Chinese immigrants threatened this paradigm, not only through the menace of nonwhiteness but also in the social structures that developed within their communities. Queer domesticity in Chinese communities offered alternatives to the nuclear family structure in the form of "emotional relations between men and women that upset normative heterosexual marriage, as well as homosocial and homoerotic relations" (Shah 2001, p. 78).

Though queer domesticity is related to how U.S. society conceives of homosexuality today, it would be an oversimplification to map "queer" versus "respectable" domesticity onto a "homosexual" versus "heterosexual" binary (Shah 2001, p. 79). In fact, as Shah explains, the categories of "heterosexual" and "homosexual," including the sharp distinction between them, was "an emerging binary" that had only been "invented and [popularized]" in the late nineteenth and twentieth century (Shah 2001, p. 78). He further notes that "sexuality was not a fixed set of acts, behaviors, and identities, but rather, a set of formations that encompassed a variety of social relations and sites." In order to reinforce the nuclear family as primary, government officials, politicians, and other influential voices in society had to clearly define what types of sexuality belonged in respectable domesticity (heterosexuality) and which ones were deviant (homosexuality). As a result, it would be counterproductive to frame accounts of queer domesticity in Chinese communities as gay or homosexual, taking for granted the binary terms imposed by nineteenth- and twentieth-century society. Defining queer domesticity along such lines ignores the complex, "sexual, social, and gender relations that could not be easily slotted into the [. . .] binary of 'heterosexual' and 'homosexual'" (Shah 2001, p. 78).

According to Southeast Asia scholar Tamara Loos in "Transnational Histories of Sexualities in Asia," historians concerned with sexuality have repeatedly observed, "how the practices, norms, and meanings of sexuality were recalibrated over time" (Loos 2009, p. 1312). These recalibrations happen through the interaction of multiple contexts in historical moments. One of the pioneers of Queer Marxist thought, Petrus Liu, adds that "no account of sexuality is complete without a consideration of geopolitics—how nations are formed and their borders policed, and how these institutions sustain and constrain the possibilities of lives" (Liu 2010, p. 292). Consequently, queerness and queer identities "are as much about private sexuality as they are about the political tensions, cultural exchanges, and economic inequalities" between China and America (Liu 2010). These complexities cannot be more relevant in considering queerness in Chinese American communities today. Unfortunately, mainstream narratives portray Chinese American communities' attitudes about queerness as direct, unchanging imports from a backward, repressive China, even as the preceding account demonstrates that American society's racialization of Chinese immigrations and related sexual policing played a powerful role in how sexuality comes to be defined.

Mainstream narratives attempt to reduce Chinese immigrants' relationship to queerness as a simple "import," a story that assumes immigrants brought their homophobia from a traditional and backward China. This narrative is ironic in light of the impact that European and U.S. imperialism had on these attitudes. Loos references several studies that "reveal how colonial encounters transformed 'local' moral hierarchies" in Asia (Loos 2009, p. 1310). European and U.S. colonial regimes, like their U.S. domestic counterparts, "[enforced] 'civilized' sexual and gender norms through law, coercion, or moral pressure backed by economic and political infrastructures." These norms were unsurprisingly parallel to those imposed on Chinese immigrants in America as they were extremely effective "weapons in the imperial arsenal" in regards to maintaining social control. Among the norms imposed were "the polarization of gender roles in the late-nineteenth century 'Victorian' era, the elevation of monogamous heterosexual marriage as the 'civilized' conjugal standard, and the construction of a heterosexual/homosexual binary" (Loos 2009, p. 1315). At the same time, local "culture-bound practices" were "removed from their local religious and historical context" and delegitimized as "backward and patriarchal." By depicting Asian women as victims, imperial governments could justify their colonialism to "intervene to rescue women from such 'traditions.'" In semi-colonial China, "an influx of translations of Western sexological texts [. . .] in the early twentieth century 'liberated' sexual pleasure from the constraints of what it categorized as repressive patriarchal tradition" (Loos 2008, p. 1317).

The imposed norms sought to redefine sexuality through "sex and genitalia," whereas "studies of the erotic in Asian history reveal that gender played, and arguably still plays, a more significant role in determining sexual morality of participants" (Loos 2008, p. 1317). Before the imperial-influenced redefinitions of sexuality, in most of Asia, erotic acts between same-sex participants were "unremarkable, if not normative" as long as they were "hetero-gendered" with one partner masculine and the other feminine. Western definitions of sexuality, by contrast, define sexuality exclusively through "vaginal-penile and same-genitalia acts, and obfuscate the hetero-gendered aspect of erotics" (Loos 2008, p. 1320). These historical conflicts and forcible interventions have complicated definitions of sexuality in postcolonial Asia. Unlike in the United States, where mainstream narratives ignore or are ignorant of the history of colonialism and the damage it has caused, in China, there is not only an awareness of Western imperialism's history and continued presence, but also an intense backlash against Western imposition of ideas and values (Loos 2008, p. 1318). This backlash has manifested in one-dimensional narratives that blame the West and "(neo) imperialism for the existence of homosexuality, prostitution, and human trafficking," which, given the history of imperialist norms imposed in Asia, is not necessarily inaccurate (Loos 2008, p. 1318).

In the United States today, sexual and gender norms are still imposed on communities of color, but are so pervasive that they are almost invisible and usually taken for granted as universal fact. As with imperialist influences in China and the corresponding policing of Chinese immigrants' sexualities, these norms are explicitly racialized, even when they shift toward supposed "progress." The United States believes itself to be progressive in how it regards gender and sexuality, a descriptor that has replaced the outdated "civilized" but nonetheless serves the same purpose. "Americanized" brings to mind a spectrum of beliefs that connect proximity to American whiteness with "progressive," whereas Chinese brings to mind "traditional," "repressive," and "conservative," direct antonyms.

This type of "civilizing" narrative has a long history of serving to create useful impressions of the liberated West in contrast to the backward East through the policing of gender norms as described earlier through Loos's work. The same narrative continues today, but has taken on queerness along with gender to further racialize Chinese communities and other communities of color. As the United States increasingly views itself as exceptionally progressive on gay and lesbian issues, it depicts the opposite in all non-Western nations while forcefully privileging its own conceptions of what it means to be queer and what it means for a society to be progressive ("civilized") in relating to queerness. Any other model is labeled *homophobic*,

creating pressure to adopt U.S. progressive gay and lesbian politics through condemnation, economic constraints, and military intervention.

These false contrasts are especially effective at labeling U.S. communities of color. U.S. media and scholarship constantly lament the supposed homophobia in communities of color and their "cultures." The result is often increased racism in wider society as well as in mainstream, predominantly white queer communities and a solidifying of normative definitions of sexualities.

One example of this mechanism in action is the adoption of the label "transgender" in mainstream queer politics. In anthropologist David Valentine's (2007) ethnography *Imagining Transgender*, he highlights how the imposition of "transgender" as a category enforces a strict distinction between experiences of gender and sexuality that frequently ignores the varying ways that many gender nonconforming people of color frame their experiences. The black and Latino/a participants that Valentine (2007) interviews frequently call themselves "gay" even when mainstream definitions of gender and sex would label them "transwomen" with separate sexual orientations. He notes that many of his colleagues who are "social service providers and activists" approaching identity from mainstream perspectives would believe that these participants' framing of their own identities are not just "alternative" but "false" categorizations, "using an outmoded view of gendered and sexual identity which conflates or confuses her transgender identity with homosexual desire" (p. 4). These patronizing attitudes are often leveled at communities of color, who are seen as lacking access to "the conversations and historical developments" that created the supposedly superior and more accurate "transgender" categorization (Valentine 2007, p. 4), further playing into racist tropes about communities of color being less advanced or progressive about queerness. This pervasive perception of "backwardness" goes hand in hand with the news stories that blamed black communities in California for the passing of Proposition 8, a ballot measure banning gay marriage (see Vick and

Surdin 2008). As a result, white queer communities often label black communities as especially homophobic, an implicitly racist justification for more overt racism that targets all communities of color.

Many queer Asian/Americans have criticized this racism in the queer community. Staff attorney for AALDEF (Asian American Legal Defense and Education Fund) Glenn Magpantay points to a study by the National Gay and Lesbian Task Force Policy Institute that found that "82 percent of LGBT APA respondents had experienced racism within the white LGBT community, with more than one in three strongly agreeing" (Magpantay 2006). Racism in mainstream queer communities has been well documented but "problems" of homophobia in communities of color are prioritized, urging queer people of color to choose a queer identity that is tied to whiteness (since being a person of color is tied to homophobia and silence).

Uncomplicated assumptions of homophobia in Chinese American communities erase their histories of queer domesticity in the United States, disregard the *tongzhi* (Liu 2010, p. 296) movement in China, and ignore the role of the United States in creating those same homophobic narratives that continue to benefit white Americans (even those who are queer-identified). The narratives that the United States uses to celebrate its own progressivism, which is attributed to mainly white queer communities, require the contrasting tropes that pathologize people of color as homophobic and backward. Lauded traditions in mainstream queer communities have developed similar racial connotations. For example, "coming out" is assumed to be universal to the queer experience and is often celebrated as a vocal assertion of queer identity in defiance to silencing. However, while those who are white and queer can have good, bad, or mixed experiences coming out to family members, Asian Americans are always assumed to have bad experiences and, if he or she has not told their family members, it's assumed that that person is ashamed and/or silenced by their traditional family members. Accordingly, the notion that telling one's family members (or anyone else) is an essential part of one's queer identity is rarely, if ever, questioned.

Queer Asian Americans often frame their own experiences through these narratives and take on the associated beliefs that their "Asian culture" (or Asian parents' "culture") is causing problems with their queer identities.

In higher education, scholar Mitsu Narui's (2011) study, "Understanding Asian/American Gay, Lesbian, and Bisexual Experiences from a Poststructural Perspective," she interviews Korean American college student Carrie, who is concerned about coming out as pansexual to her "very conservative" parents (p. 1221). Narui (2011) interprets this situation through the lens of a power differential between Carrie and her parents, where her parents "enforced [. . .] norms and expectations" that "promoted intolerance of [Carrie's] GLB identity" through "a position of power" (p. 1221). Regardless of the "truth" of Carrie's parents' conservatism, Narui's analysis treats the parents as an unchanging relic defined only by "conservatism," power, and homophobia, while Narui (2011) contextualizes Carrie and the other students' experiences by referring to the impact of racism, the model minority myth that stereotypes Asians as model citizens, and their interactions with peers (conditions that their parents presumably also face).

Based on the study and perhaps how it is written, it appears that both Narui (2011) and the students interviewed follow this pattern, where they viewed Asian parents, the implicit carriers of backward culture, as "conservative" without explanation or further definition: Does conservative mean Republican? Are they fiscally and/or socially conservative? Or are they "Asian conservative" (also known as "traditional")? Narui (2011) concludes that the students practiced agency through "coming out": "As the students revealed their orientation to more individuals, they were able to achieve a higher degree of agency within hegemonic, discursive regimes and better understand themselves as Asian/American GLB individuals" (p. 1223). Since the study positions parents most strongly as the barrier to "coming out," the narrative suggests that the students' agency should be at the expense of their parents. However, as Narui (2011) herself observes, queer-identified Asian Americans must navigate many different contexts in order to "come out," unlike those who are white. A more critical reading of the interviews demonstrates that one requires power and agency to come out, which systemically privileges those who are white, yet the "coming-out" narrative ignores these power differences to demand equally that everyone who does not fit cleanly into the category of heterosexual comes out, lest they be labeled "ashamed." Instead of questioning a narrative that ignores differences in power, privilege, and agency to enforce a norm of "disclosure," Narui and, to a lesser extent, the students further valorize it. These students are not afforded the privileges in coming as their white peers, but instead of considering these as structural/systemic barriers, their decision whether to come out is often read as a symptom of their "Asian-ness," further racializing them. However, Narui (2011) ignores the negative impact of this narrative, contending that the students' "decisions regarding disclosure or concealment [. . .] allowed [them] to shape and reshape their subjectivity and to further assert their agency" (p. 1223).

A closer look at the coming-out narrative reveals that it encapsulates nearly all of the early imperial attempts to socially control Chinese immigrants and colonial territories in Asia. Coming out requires that one categorize himself or herself as some category that is not heterosexual, reinforcing a strict heterosexual-homosexual (or queer) binary, and how one categorizes himself or herself is dependent upon attraction by "sex and genitalia." Since people of color are usually viewed as hostile to the coming-out process, the narrative is also used to label entire communities as uncivilized and repressive to people who are LBGT and, much like imperial labeling of Asian women as victims in "patriarchal" Asian societies. Mainstream queer communities have come to resemble the imperial conditions of early nineteenth and twentieth centuries, not only through the coming-out narrative, but also in the emerging prioritization of gay marriage. The arguments for gay marriage eerily echo the ideology of "respectable domesticity," valuing monogamous family units and conjugal child-rearing

or adoption. Magpantay (2006) notes that there was "ambivalence toward same-sex marriage" among queer identified Asian/Americans, partially because the campaigns rarely feature people of color, but also because they ignore urgent issues that impact Asian/Americans, such as "immigrant rights and racism" (p. 115). Additionally, though Asian Americans often value "coming out," Narui's study reveals that they find their experiences and contexts at odds with the narrative. Rather than pathologize Asian culture as the culprit for these disconnects or simply attempt to include more Asian voices to drown out the ambivalence toward marriage, perhaps it is time we examine the racism embedded in mainstream queer narratives, historically and currently.

Silvena Chan

See also: Asian Americans and LGBTQ Issues; Chinese Early LGBTQ History in the United States.

Further Reading

Hsu, M.Y. 2012. "The Disappearance of America's Cold War Chinese Refugees, 1948–1966." *Journal of American Ethnic History*: 12–33.

Liu, P. 2010. "Why Does Queer Theory Need China? *Positions: East Asia Cultures Critique*, 291–320". From Liu, 296: Some Chinese scholars assert that "China has a unique tongzhi community that cannot be conflated with 'queer,' which is supposed to be a description of U.S.-style sexual politics." Chou Wah-Shan asserts that "Chinese tongzhi are different from 'gays and lesbians' because these English-language concepts have no equivalent in the Chinese tradition of same-sex erotic relations, which is characterized by cultural tolerance and harmony."

Loos, T. 2009. "Transnational Histories of Sexualities in Asia." *American Historical Review*: 1309–1324.

Luibhéid, E. 2002. *Entry Denied: Controlling Sexuality at the Border*. Minnesota: University of Minnesota Press.

Magpantay, G.D. 2006. "The Ambivalence of Queer Asian Pacific Americans toward Same-Sex Marriage." *Amerasia Journal*: 109–117.

Narui, M. 2011. "Understanding Asian/American Gay, Lesbian, and Bisexual Experiences from a Postructural Perspective." *Journal of Homosexuality*: 1211–34.

Shah, N. 2001. *Contagious Divides: Epidemics and Race in San Francisco's Chinatown*. Berkeley and Los Angeles: University of California Press.

Valentine, D. 2007. *Imagining Transgender: An Ethnography of a Category*. Durham, NC: Duke University Press.

Vick, K., and A. Surdin. 2008, November 7. "Most of California's Black Voters Backed Gay Marriage Ban." *The Washington Post*. Available at: http://articles.washingtonpost.com/2008-11-07/politics/36807003_1_marriage-issue-gay-rights-advocates-civil-rights.

Wong, S.-l. C., and J. J. Santa Ana. 1999. "Gender and Sexuality in Asian American Literature." *Signs*: 171–226.

Wu, J. T. 2003. "Asian American History and Racialized Compulsory Deviance." *Journal of Women's History*: 58–62.

Chinese Early LGBTQ History in the United States

"We are all prisoners of our time and place": This pessimistic platitude is proffered by Rene Gallimard, the French diplomat and antihero of David Henry Hwang's Tony Award–winning play *M. Butterfly* (1988), as he begs the audience to "try to understand it from my point of view," where "it" means the ignominious fact that he had an affair for over two decades with a Chinese woman who turned out to be a spy—and *a man* (p. 38). In his "Playwright's Notes" presented before the text of the play, Hwang includes an excerpt from the 1986 *New York Times* article that called international attention to the true story of "mistaken sexual identity" upon which *M. Butterfly* is loosely based (p. 4). As Hwang himself insists: "This play does not purport to be a factual record of real events or real people" (p. 4). However, because the plot spans from 1960 to the late 1980s, and the characters knowingly reenact scenes from Giacomo Puccini's famous Italian opera *Madame Butterfly* (1904), Hwang quite literally situates his satirical tragedy within a broader historical and cultural context reaching back at least as far as the nineteenth century while offering a (still) timely (if

perhaps problematic) critique of Orientalist sexual politics during the twentieth century. "Exploring the ideology of Orientalism that Hwang negotiates in his play," affirms Eileen Chia-Ching Fung, the associate dean for Arts and Letters at the University of San Francisco and an associate professor of English and Asian American Studies, "one must study the long history of colonial and imperial contexts between the East and the West" (2010, p. 16). Hence, Hwang's interweaving of past and present, East and West, as well as complicating of heterosexual/homosexual, masculine/feminine, white/Chinese, among other binary oppositions, makes his work a useful point of entry into the early history of Chinese LGBTQ individuals in the United States—and its lasting significance.

In the scene immediately following Gallimard's pathetic plea for understanding, opera diva Song Lilin's true identity as a male Communist spy dressed in a female disguise is not all that is revealed. Rather, the scene is set in 1961 Beijing, and the ensuing dialogue between Comrade Chin and Song Liling not only explains why Gallimard has become the laughing stock of France but also comments suggestively on the suppression of homosexuality in modern China:

CHIN. You're not gathering information in any way that violates Communist Party principles, are you?

SONG. Why would I do that?

CHIN. Just checking. Remember: when working for the Great Proletarian State, you represent our Chairman Mao in every position you take.

SONG. I'll try to imagine the Chairman taking my positions.

CHIN. We all think of him this way. Good-bye, comrade. (*She starts to exit.*) Comrade?

SONG. Yes?

CHIN. Don't forget: there is no homosexuality in China!

SONG. Yes, I've heard.

CHIN. Just checking. (*She exits.*)

SONG. (*To us.*) What passes for a woman in modern China. (p. 39)

Chinese laborers at work with picks, shovels, wheelbarrows, and one-horse dump carts filling in under the town trestle on the present Southern Pacific Railroad lines of Sacramento in 1877. (Bettmann/Corbis)

Here, the obvious humor and irony of Song Liling's last line stands in marked contradistinction to the unfunny condemnation—and, indeed, disavowal—of homosexuality under the repressive reign of the Chinese Communist Party.

"Our Chairman Mao" to which Chin refers is Mao Zedong (or Tse-tung) (1893–1976), a founding member and leader of the Chinese Communist Party after 1935 until his death, and chairman (chief of state) of the People's Republic of China (1949–1959). In an oft-quoted phrase, Mao condemned homosexuality as a Western indulgence, a product of the "moldering lifestyle of capitalism"—and that sour note echoes throughout other scenes of *M. Butterfly*. For example, in a mini play-within-the-play set in 1966, Song Liling appears in a Mao suit while Comrade Chin brandishes a banner reading "*The Actor Renounces His Decadent Profession!*" Within the dialogue that follows, Song

says he has "shamed China by allowing myself to be corrupted by a foreigner," and that he "engaged in the lowest perversions with China's enemies!" When Chin admonishes him to "Be more clear!," Song exclaims: "I let him put it up my ass!" Other dancers on the stage then "*look over, disgusted.*" Emphasizing the alleged patriotism of his motivations, Song repeatedly shouts: "I want to serve the people!" (p. 54). The dancers then "*unveil a banner: 'The Actor is Rehabilitated!'*" (p. 54). While Song's cries of self-abnegation and patriotic protestation may seem comically incongruous and disingenuous, inviting the audience to ponder over just who or what is rehabilitated by these actions, the hostile atmosphere of Mao's China evoked around them is hardly a laughing matter.

For many Chinese, irrespective of sexual orientation, Mao's legacy is controversial. The founding of the Communist Party of China (CPC) in 1949 meant

HARPER'S WEEKLY.

MINING LIFE IN CALIFORNIA.

CHINESE MINERS.

Chinese miners at work in California in 1857. (Library of Congress)

the repression not only of non-normative sexuality but "a denial of romantic love" in favor of "the affirmation of the absolute role of the collective over the individual as a basic tenet toward which one should direct any affections" (Gil 1992, p. 570–71). Two particularly ruinous political movements Mao spearheaded have permanently tarnished his name. First, during what he called the Great Leap Forward (1959–1961), Mao "demanded, in communist parlance, the 'renunciation of the heart.' Party policy deliberately constructed an altruism which sought (for every man and woman) hard work through the day, without being 'deflected or confused' by love, sexual desire, or any strivings for private happiness" (Gil 1992, p. 571).

Meanwhile, at least 20 million people perished in a famine—achieving the exact opposite of the movement's intended effort for increased industrial and agricultural productivity.

Then, millions more suffered, were imprisoned, tortured, or lost their lives during the Cultural Revolution of 1966. What is also known as the Great Proletarian Cultural Revolution began when Mao closed schools and impelled the youth of China to revolt against a government he characterized as bourgeois, complacent, and "impure." Maoist paramilitary groups such as the Red Guard wreaked havoc and violence, nearly bringing the entire country to state of anarchism and economic ruin. The chaos subsided after

Mao's death but the scars it left ran deep. Millions of marriages were dissolved, untold numbers of couples separated. Elaborating on a point made by Peter Stafford in *Sexual Behavior in the Communist World: An Eyewitness Report of Life, Love, and the Human Condition behind the Iron Curtain* (1967), Vincent E. Gil, a medical anthropologist and HIV epidemiologist, Division of Social and Behavioral Sciences, and Human Sexuality Professor at Vanguard University, recounts how "life had become hard and all but hopeless in mainland China": by the late 1950s/early 1960s, "there were few escapes except in the pleasures and delights men and women could give each other bodily" (1992, p. 571). Hence, in the minds of many Chinese, the Cultural Revolution understandably represents a time of unspeakable horror, some wounds from which have never fully healed.

Though cast as a great revolution, Mao's call for the purification of China resembled nothing so much as a return to the past. In an insightful *Time* magazine piece, Jonathan D. Spence, who holds the position of Sterling Professor of History, Emeritus, at Yale University and has authored several famous books on China's history, remarks on Mao's "ruthlessness," the ironic origins of which are to be found in the fourth-century BCE writings of a draconian administer named Shang Yang:

> Rejecting his former party allies, and anyone who could be accused of espousing the values of an older and more gracious Chinese civilization, Mao drew his sustenance from the chanting crowds of Red Guards. The irony here was that from his youthful readings, Mao knew the story of how Shang Yang late in life tried to woo a moral administrator to his service. But the official turned down Shang Yang's blandishments, with the words that "1,000 persons going 'Yes, yes!' are not worth one man with a bold 'No!'" (1998, p. 2)

As Spence's report makes clear, even the ancient past has had a palpable influence on modern politics in China. Along these lines, Spence also relates how "Mao took Shang Yang's experiences as emblematic

of China's crisis," and further explains that "Shang Yang had instituted a set of ruthlessly enforced laws, designed 'to punish the wicked and rebellious, in order to preserve the rights of the people.' That the people continued to fear Shang Yang was proof to Mao they were 'stupid,'" and, as Spence points out, "Mao attributed this fear and distrust not to Shang Yang's policies but to the perception of those policies: 'At the beginning of anything out of the ordinary, the mass of the people always dislike it'" (1998, p. 1). Taking this broader historical context of oppression, ancient and modern, into account, the ironic tone of Comrade Chin's incessant rejoinders to the sexually degenerate Song Liling regarding Communist principles and *"Our* Chairman Mao" perhaps sounds especially bitter. On another level, to the LGBTQ individuals who attended Hwang's play in America when it first opened at the National Theatre in Washington, D.C., Chin's Maoist dictum that "there is no homosexuality in China!" must have been all too ironically and eerily reminiscent of the silencing of AIDS discourse during the Ronald Reagan Republican administration (1981–1989).

But there is a further irony still, one less openly remarked upon in *M. Butterfly* yet well known to historians: that ancient China, despite the selective and repressive purposes to which Maoists put its history, was apparently far more tolerant—even accepting—of homosexuality than modern China (even arguably more so than, for much of its history, the United States). Synthesizing research by numerous scholars, Gil explains that prior to "the Revolution of 1949, China had a long history of dynastic homosexuality":

> This tolerance for male sexual diversity throughout much of Chinese history was accumulated in a well[-]developed literature, which allowed the male homosexual a modicum of introspection and self-reflection about his orientation, particularly if the person was literate. The surviving literature of the Spring-Autumn Period (770–745 [BCE]), the Warring States Period (475–221 [BCE]), and of the Chou and Han dynasties (206

[BCE–CE] 220) indicates that homosexuality was accepted by the royal courts and its custom widespread among the nobility. . . . The dynastic record is one, then, of general tolerance for the male homosexual, and an amoral if not moral construction of the lifestyle itself. (p. 570)

Of course, Gil is hardly claiming that ancient China was a queer utopia for everyone; nevertheless, within this portrait of tolerance, his repetition of "the male homosexual" is crucial to note.

Where in this tradition, one might ask, are the lesbians? A Harvard alum and professor in the department of History at Fo Guang University, Taiwan, Bret Hinsch asserts in his magisterial study of *Passions of the Cut Sleeve: The Male Homosexual Tradition in China* (1990) that "[s]ince lesbianism remained separate from the male homosexual tradition, it would have been an imposition to have integrated lesbianism into the body of this study. Nevertheless, it is a subject that deserves investigation" (p. 173). Indeed, Hinsch does investigate it in his later monograph *Women in Early Imperial China* (2011), which offers a richly nuanced account of women's roles during the Qin (221–206 BCE) and Han (202 BCE–220 CE) dynasties. Hinsch notes in *Passions* that there are several reasons why the evidentiary written record of lesbianism does not constitute a "sustained literary tradition such as that associated with male homosexuality": these reasons include women's seclusion within the home of their husbands, lack of male interest in "women's affairs," and the patriarchal control of textual production (1990, p. 174). Regrettably, the voices of everyday women and lesbians in China's history have been comparatively muted with respect to men, though not completely silenced. In his famous book *Sex in China: Studies in Sexology in Chinese Culture* (1991), Fang Fu Ruan of Shu-Te University, Taiwan, argues: "In ancient times Chinese culture was characterized by a very tolerant attitude toward lesbianism" (p. 135). Ruan offers a provocative account of lesbianism in ancient and modern China, drawing in part on interviews "conducted in 1985 with young women incarcerated in the Shanghai Women Delinquents

Correction Institution," while still emphasizing the dearth of scholarly information on Chinese lesbianism (p. 135). A decade later witnessed the first book-length study of *The Emerging Lesbian: Female Same-Sex Desire in Modern China* (2003), in which Tze-Lan Deborah Sang, associate professor of Chinese at the University of Oregon, charts an overall shift from "innocence to sensitivity about female-female intimacy" in Chinese culture (p. 5). Sang's work is an exception which proves the rule of scholarly attention to male (homo)sexuality, and these lingering silences speak volumes in the ongoing efforts of contemporary Chinese feminists and lesbians who must contend with patriarchy in China and the United States.

Whereas Sang's work documents the (re)emergence of lesbianism in Chinese literature, popular culture, and queer activism, Hinsch describes the androcentric context from which these representations emerge. The variegated nature of the male homosexual tradition in China resists overgeneralizations within and across dynastic periods: a point Hinsch rightly stresses. Nevertheless, the ancient image from which the titular phrase *Passions of the Cut Sleeve* is derived has become symbolic of the tradition as a whole. The story of the *Cut Sleeve* pertains to the love between youthful emperor Ai, who ruled during the Han dynasty from 6 BCE to 1 CE, and his male favorite, Dong Xian. Hinsch quotes the influential tale as told by Ban Gu, a first-century Han historian:

Emperor Ai was sleeping in the daytime with Dong Xian stretched across his sleeve. When the emperor wanted to get up, Dong Xian was still asleep. Because he did not want to disturb him, the emperor cut off his own sleeve and got up. His love and thoughtfulness went this far. (p. 53)

Upon seeing the emperor attired in such a fashion, the members of Emperor Ai's court reportedly cut their sleeves in celebration, as well. "The complete integration of homosexuality into early Chinese court life, as reported in *Memoirs of the Historian* and *Records of the Han*, was alluded to repeatedly in later literature and gave men of subsequent ages a means for situating their own desires within an ancient tradition. By seeing their feelings as passions of the 'cut sleeve,'" Hinsch states, "they gained a consciousness of the place of male love in the history of their society" (p. 53). Though the story of the *Cut Sleeve* seems to have been especially influential, other significant literary representations of male same-sex love that shaped this cultural "consciousness" include stories of the Shared Peach and of Long Yang and the Fish.

Compared to this tender, ancient imagery of "love and thoughtfulness" among Chinese men, the brutal reception of Chinese immigrants in America, decades before Mao's procrustean politics in mainland China and continuing long after, seems all the more shocking. Though the plot of *M. Butterfly* begins long after the first Chinese immigrants arrived in the United States, traces of this early history are embedded in the play. As Fung observes, the representation of Orientalist stereotypes in *M. Butterfly* is drawn in significant part from the "early presentation of Asian sexual identity of men and woman—desexualization of men and hyper-sexualization of women" (2010, p. 18). Both of these long-standing stereotypes are invoked during Song Liling's testimony at Gallimard's espionage trial near the end of the play. When the judge demands to know just *how* he could have deceived the French diplomat for so long, Song Liling, with characteristic irony, responds: "One, because when he finally met his fantasy woman, he wanted more than anything to believe that she was, in fact, a woman. And second, I am an Oriental. And being an Oriental, I could never be completely a man" (Hwang 1988, p. 62). By invoking the stereotypical images of the Chinese "fantasy woman" and the emasculated "Oriental" man, Song Liling also interpolates into the play a long history of oppression that reified such imagery as facts of nature.

Addressing the image of men first, Liling's oddly self-deprecating comments confirm that Chinese American men have long been subjected to what David L. Eng, Richard L. Fisher Professor of English and professor in comparative literature, literary theory, and Asian American Studies at the University of Pennsylvania, has termed a "racial castration." In his brilliant reading of *M. Butterfly*, Eng argues that "[t]he white diplomat's racial castration of Song exemplifies

a distinct psychic process through which whiteness and heterosexuality work collectively to articulate and secure their universal status in relation to a devalued Asian racial positioning" (2001, p. 152). Whether Liling has internalized his own devaluation, is merely playing a part he think the French judge wants to hear, or both, is open to interpretation. In any event, while Eng helpfully contextualizes his argument within the play's engagement with Western Cold War rhetoric whereby homosexuals and "Orientals" represented a double threat to the "health" of civilization, Fung's article on "Deconstructing the 'Butterfly': Teaching David Henry Hwang's *M. Butterfly* in Cultural and Socio-Political Contexts" (2010) historicizes the point even further by linking the "gendered political relationships" depicted in the play with the (mis)treatment of Asian Americans in the nineteenth and early twentieth centuries (p. 16).

From its inception during the first half of the 1800s, the migration of Chinese people to the United States had gendered as well as racialized ramifications. While some women migrated to America to be workers like their far more numerous male counterparts, the vast majority of them were coerced into prostitution by men, for men. In this way, "the transit of Chinese prostitutes reflected the nature of the Chinese migration to America: it was mainly the movement of men" (Takaki 1989, p. 42). Thus writes Ronald Takaki, a professor emeritus at the University of California-Berkeley before his suicide in 2009, in the first edition of his controversial book *Strangers from a Different Shore: A History of Asian Americans* (1989). Takaki's magnum opus sketches the history of a sexist and racist division of labor among female and male immigrants to the United States.

According to Takaki's account, the perceived need for Chinese workers originated on a proposed Hawaiian sugar plantation during the 1830s and was exacerbated by the railroad industry in the following decade. Takaki relates how, on a fateful 1835 visit to a sugar mill on the island of Kauai, Bostonian William Hooper, who had been sent to "establish the first sugar plantation in Hawaii," noted that the Chinese workers not only toiled for six days a week but that "[t]hey have to work *all* the time—and no regard is paid to their complaints for food, etc., etc. Slavery is nothing compared to it" (p. 21). Takaki does not remark upon it as such, but it is difficult not to see Hooper's dismissive "etc., etc." as adding insult to the inhumane treatment of the Chinese workers. At any rate, when Hawaiian laborers proved to be intolerably slow and stubborn, Hooper started putting Chinese workers on the payroll and, in 1838, so as to facilitate more timely completion of the plantation, recommended to his own employer, Ladd and Company, that more laborers be imported from China (p. 22). Ten years later, Aaron H. Palmer beseeched Congress to establish San Francisco as *the* major trading hub between the United States and China by importing Chinese workers to build railways. As Takaki observes, "Hooper and Palmer shared a peculiarly white-American world view. . . . Their vision of Chinese cultivating cane in Hawaii and building railroads and clearing lands in the West reflected a significant theme of American history—what the perspicacious scholar Perry Miller described as 'the errand into the wilderness'" (p. 23). On its ideological "errand," this "white-American world view" also brought along stereotyped notions of race and gender.

While the sugar industry boomed, planters sought to supplement their indigenous Hawaiian labor force with workers from China, Japan, the Philippines, and other regions. The intermixing of laborers from different racial backgrounds was deliberate: "In their orders for laborers, planters systematically developed an ethnically diverse work force as a mechanism of control. During the 1850s, they used Chinese laborers to set an 'example' for the Hawaiian workers. Managers hoped the Hawaiians would be 'naturally jealous' of the foreigners and 'ambitious' to outdo them" (Takaki 1989, p. 25). Lest any single group of "foreigners"—or even high-minded white workers—congregate in numbers significant enough to unionize or strike, the practice of maintaining a diverse workforce continued for decades and in other industries, too. However, the annexation of Hawaii to the United States in 1898 held the state accountable to federal legislation prohibiting Chinese immigration, forcing planters to import workers not only from other Asian countries but also African Americans from southern states (Takaki 1989, p. 26).

Another major motivation for Chinese immigration to the continental United States was the California gold rush: a time of opportunity upon which many Chinese actively sought to capitalize. While it is true that in Peru Chinese forced laborers or "coolies" numbered in the thousands, the same cannot be said, despite pervasive stereotypes, of Chinese migrant workers in the United States (Takaki 1989, p. 34). As Takaki demonstrates, "Beginning in the 1840s and 1850s, they departed [China] by the tens of thousands—about 46,000 to Hawaii in the second half of the nineteenth century and about 380,000 to the U.S. mainland between 1849 and 1930" (p. 31). Due to perpetual civil unrest and severe economic hardships in Guangdong (known in English as Kwangtung/Kwongtung or Canton Province), it is unsurprising that most Chinese immigrants to the United States came from that region in the hopes of finding better livelihoods on American soil. Fantastic tales of the "gold hills" enflamed the imagination, and not always misleadingly so. "During the 1860s," says Takaki, "a Chinese laborer might earn three to five dollars a month in South China; in California, he could work for the railroad and make thirty dollars a month" (p. 34). The keyword in that sentence, though, is *he*.

For a number of reasons, men comprised the vast proportion of Chinese migrant workers. Of these reasons, cultural concepts of gender in China played a significant role. Many male laborers were married. Traditional notions of proper femininity for Chinese women, however, discouraged them from joining their husbands' travels. A Chinese wife belonged in the family home, tending to both her own children and her husband's parents. The practice of foot binding would in any case have probably rendered an upper-class woman physically incapable of working alongside her husband even if she wanted to. Meanwhile, the perceived expense, if married couples travelled together, was too steep for most Chinese to pay—for able-bodied peasant women, such a price would nevertheless have been unthinkable. Unmarried women would not have journeyed overseas unaccompanied and thus would have faced the same fiscal limitations. Furthermore, a Chinese man's employment in America was supposed to be impermanent. To return to his family in China having earned enough money to ensure a more comfortable life was the common goal. Some parents fretted, moreover, that if a son took his wife with him he might not return to China—and not send any money back home, either (Takaki 1989, pp. 36–37).

That is not to say, though, that *no* Chinese women migrated to the United States. Obviously, they did: but both the places they migrated to and their reasons for doing so interestingly differ along axes of ethnicity and gender. Takaki writes:

> Significantly, sons migrating to Hawaii were more likely to take their wives with them than their counterparts leaving for California. In 1900, of the 25,767 Chinese in Hawaii, 3,471 or 13.5 percent were female, but of the 89,863 Chinese on the U.S. mainland, only 4,522, or 5 percent, were female. (1989, pp. 37–38)

Contemplating the reasons for these disparities between Chinese migrants to Hawaii and California, Takaki suggests that ethnic differences in China influenced which Chinese women *could* migrate whereas gender differences in the United States affected the demand for female migrants. Most Chinese migrants to California were Punti, who practiced foot binding and thus restricted women's physical and travel capabilities; however, most Chinese migrants to Hawaii were Hakka, who did not observe this practice, making female migration more feasible.

Moreover, in California, single Chinese men comprised the desired labor force because of their mobility. Without wives and children, these male laborers could move swiftly from place to place, jobsite to jobsite. Employers in California cared more about the labor than the laborer. Such was not the case in Hawaii, where a migrant worker might be employed at a single plantation for years.

While Takaki's account illuminates the influential role of gender and ethnicity in early Chinese migration to the United States, what remains obscured are issues of sexuality. However, if one reads between the lines of a historical record which has been set *too* straight, the potential queerness of early Chinese American migrants, female and male alike, can be glimpsed. To be sure, such a queer rereading of history is not without its risks, as it forces historians to retrieve trace evidence from a context of exclusion and oppression. Asian women were barred from entering the United States almost entirely, as stipulated by legislation like the Page Act (1875) and the Chinese Exclusion Act (1882). Even into the early twentieth century, anti-immigration laws and anti-Asian sentiments made traveling from Asia to the United States precarious and often impossible.

Thus, before it even clearly enters the picture, sexuality is further obfuscated by damaging and enduring stereotypes, the cultural origins of which stem from these earlier periods of Chinese migration to America. The lingering image of Asian men as effeminate and homosexual, captured by Hwang's portrayal of Song Liling in *M. Butterfly*, can be linked to the ways they were barred from becoming husbands and fathers in "bachelor societies." As Fung observes: "A large number of Chinese and Filipino men formed 'Bachelor Societies' where they would literally live and die among only men. Since the late 19th century, this cultural phenomenon of Asian men denied [who are] the chance to become husbands, lovers, and fathers has created the image of Asian men as emasculated" (2010, p. 18). Though Takaki does not press the issue, his account nevertheless bears witness to American fears that the homosociality of all-male migrant communities could degenerate into homosexuality. For example, Takaki quotes the following plea from missionary Frank Damon, who urged plantation owners in Hawaii to seek Chinese women to accompany the male workers: "No surer safeguard can be erected against the thousand possible ills which may arise from the indiscriminate herding together of thousands of men! Let the sweet and gentle influence of the mother, the sister, and the daughter be brought to bear upon the large and yearly increasing company of Chinese in our midst, and we shall soon see a change wrought, such as police regulations cannot produce" (quoted. in Takaki 1989, p. 38). That Damon proposes importing women as a curative "safeguard" to a "thousand possible ills," one of which is most assuredly homosexuality, is telling. On the one hand, Damon's statement attests to the homosexualization of the always already feminized Oriental man. But on the other, it also gestures toward nineteenth-century Western notions of woman's role as the "angel of the house": the moral regulator of hedonistic male behaviors, presumably including what scholar Jennifer Ting (1995) in her study of bachelor societies refers to as "deviant heterosexuality."

Such an angelic view of women both supports and contradicts other double-edged stereotypes of Asian women as either sexless Butterflies or sexually rapacious Dragon Ladies. Once again, *M. Butterfly* provides a useful touchstone. In his "Author's Notes," Hwang describes how Bernard Bouriscot, the actual French diplomat upon which the fictional Rene Gallimard is based, claimed "that he had never seen his 'girlfriend' naked" because, in Bouriscot's own words, "I thought she was very modest. I thought it was a Chinese custom." To this notion, Hwang remarks: "Now, I am aware that this is *not* a Chinese custom, that Asian women are no more shy with their lovers than are women of the West" (1988, p. 85). The playwright further surmises that "the diplomat must have fallen in love, not with a person, but with a fantasy stereotype" (Ibid.). By "continu[ing] to impose an image of the sacrificial Asian woman in the name of love for a Western man," the manner in which by the end of the play Gallimard becomes "Butterfly" and commits suicide has incited an ongoing debate over whether Hwang's play successfully challenges or harmfully perpetuates the very stereotypes he ostensibly intended to resist (Fung 2010, p. 23). In any event, such a vision of the self-sacrificing "Butterfly" harkens back, and quite paradoxically so, to a historical moment that also constructed Chinese and other Asian woman as sexually voracious beings.

Far from the moral regulator of the home, many Chinese women were seen as immoral and in need of regulation: a negative stereotype associated with women's employment as prostitutes. As Fung (2010) points out, only after alterations to immigration policies in the mid-1960s were Chinese women able to become a substantial part of the Asian American population. A century earlier, most of the Chinese women in the United States worked as prostitutes: a major contributing factor to their derogating portrayal. Fung quotes the following statistic from Takaki: "In the 1870 census manuscripts, 61 percent of the 3536 Chinese women in California had occupations listed as 'prostitute'" (Takaki 1989, p. 123; quoted in Fung 2010, pp. 18–19). She further notes that "[t]he image of the women as prostitutes—sexually available and immoral—set the stage for the popular and 'believable' role of the hypersexualized Oriental woman" (p. 19). It is worth adding that Hwang's portrayal of Song Liling intersects this historical narrative in an interesting way: through Song's mother. During Gallimard's espionage trial, Liling claims that "it wasn't all that hard" to fool Gallimard into thinking he was a woman because "my mother was a prostitute along the Bundt before the Revolution. And, uh, I think it's fair to say she learned a few things about Western men. So I borrowed her knowledge. In service to my country" (Hwang 1988, p. 61). These lines invoke and inflect several historical timeframes and settings. If what makes Song's performance of womanliness "believable" is his borrowed maternal/carnal knowledge, then at least part of what makes his mother's role as a prostitute "believable" to the audience is the history of Chinese women as prostitutes in the United States. In every instance, "believability" hinges upon stereotypes of Chinese women as two-faced and duplicitous. The Butterfly and the Dragon Lady are two sides of the same stereotypical coin.

For LGBTQ Chinese Americans, then, a work such as *M. Butterfly* is perhaps as likely to erase queer histories as it is to inscribe them. After all, the representation of Rene Gallimard arguably "coming out" as a straight "Oriental" woman precisely in order to kill "herself," Song Liling merely prostituting himself out of patriotism rather than sexual desire, the absence of woman-woman relations and overall marginalizing of the biologically female characters leaves gay and bisexual men, transgender individuals, and women of all sexual proclivities with little cause to celebrate. Substituting the literary context with a more conventionally historical one might seem equally unpromising. The repressions of Maoism; the androcentrism of the "cut sleeve" tradition; the indelibly heterosexist iconography of Chinese migrant fathers, husbands, and sons woefully separated from their daughters, wives, and sisters; the twin stereotypes of the sacrificial Butterfly and sensuous Dragon Lady, paragon and prostitute: the force of this history of oppression, exclusion, and silence might seem hopelessly crushing. But though the work has barely just begun, new—and queerer—histories of Chinese Americans *are* being written. From these narratives, queerness becomes not only a fantastic possibility but a documental *fact*. The need for such histories is pressing. In our own historical moment, the politically incompatible contradictions of ostensibly pro-queer celebrities who perform in yellow face to the ambivalent reception of self-proclaimed "rice queens" within queer communities might seem paralyzing at best and self-mutilating at worst. However, by filling in the blanks and silences of a past that has always been queerer than heteropatriarchal histories have acknowledged, LGBTQ Chinese Americans today can perhaps see that they, like their forebears, can *make history queer*—and therefore need not subscribe to the fatally erroneous, ahistorical assumption that "[w]e are all prisoners of our time and place."

Christopher Lozensky

See also: Asian Americans and LGBTQ Issues; Asian Pacific Lesbian Bisexual Network; Historical Overview of Gay Rights and Issues: From Pre-Columbian Times to the 1970s.

Further Reading
Eng, David L. 2001. *Racial Castration: Managing Masculinity in Asian America*. Durham, NC: Duke University Press.

Fung, Eileen Chia-Ching. 2010. "Deconstructing the 'Butterfly': Teaching David Henry Hwang's *M. Butterfly* in Cultural and Socio-Political Contexts." *Asian American Literature: Discourses and Pedagogies* 1:16–26.

Gil, Vincent E. 1992. "The Cut Sleeve Revisited: A Brief Ethnographic Interview with a Male Homosexual in Mainland China." *The Journal of Sexual Research* 29(4): 569–77.

Hinsch, Bret. 1990. *Passions of the Cut Sleeve: The Male Homosexual Tradition in China*. Berkeley: University of California Press.

Hinsch, Bret. 2011. *Women in Early Imperial China*, 2nd ed. Lanham: Rowman & Littlefield Publishers, Inc.

Hwang, David Henry. 1988. *M. Butterfly*. New York: Dramatists Play Service, Inc.

Ruan, Fang Fu. 1991. *Sex in China: Studies in Sexology in Chinese Culture*. New York: Plenum Press.

Sang, Tze-Lan D. 2003. *The Emerging Lesbian: Female Same-Sex Desire in Modern China*. Chicago: University of Chicago Press.

Spence, Jonathan D. 1998, April 13. "Mao Zedong: His Ruthless Vision United a Fractured People and Inspired Revolutions far beyond China's Borders." *Time Magazine*. Available at: http://content.time.com/time/magazine/article/0,9171,988161-1,00.html. Accessed October 17, 2013.

Takaki, Ronald. 1989. *Strangers from a Different Shore: A History of Asian Americans*. Boston: Little, Brown and Company.

Ting, Jennifer. 1995. "Bachelor Society: Deviant Heterosexuality and Asian American Historiography." In *Privileging positions: The Sites of Asian American Studies*, ed. Gary Y. Okihiro, Marilyn Aquizola, Dorothy Fujita Rony, and K. Scott Wong. Pullman: Washington State University Press.

Civil Service Reform Act of 1978

Government employers are subject to constitutional requirements to act fairly toward all individuals and not act capriciously or irrationally. The issue of homosexuality and federal employment came before a federal court of appeals in 1969. Clifford Norton was employed by the National Aeronautics and Space Administration. He was arrested by officers of the District of Columbia Police Department's morals squad in Lafayette Square (directly across from the White House) for a traffic violation after they saw him attempt to make the acquaintance of another man. He was fired from his job. He sued and the court agreed that the government failed to show a specific connection between the employee's potentially embarrassing conduct and any reduction in the efficiency of the department for which he worked (*Norton v. Macy*). On the basis of this and related decisions, the Civil Service Commission issued a directive to federal supervisors in December 1973 that stated that "you many not find a person unsuitable for Federal employment merely because the person is a homosexual or has engaged in homosexual acts" (*Civil Service Bulletin* 1973). Later this concept was expanded by the enactment of the Civil Service Reform Act of 1978. Supervisors were directed not to discriminate against employees on the basis of conduct that does not adversely affect the performance of others. Finally, in 1998 President Clinton signed Executive Order 13087, specifically banning

President Lyndon B. Johnson is applauded as he finished his speech in the White House in Washington on July 2, 1964, over a radio-TV network prior to signing the 1964 Civil Rights Bill. Front row from left: Attorney General Robert F. Kennedy, Senator Everett M. Dirksen (R-IL); Senator Hubert H. Humphrey (D-MN); Representative Charles Halleck (R-IN); and Representative Emanuel Celler (D-NY). Second row: Whitney Young, behind Dirksen, executive director, National Urban League; Representative Richard Bolling (D-MO); Dr. Martin Luther King, Southern Christian Leadership Conference; and Senator Thomas H. Kuchel (R-CA). (AP Photo)

discrimination based on sexual orientation in the federal civilian workforce.

Chuck Stewart

See also: Kameny, Franklin (1925–2011).

Further Reading

Civil Service Bulletin. (1973, December 21). Quoted in *Aston v. Civiletti*, 613 F.2d 923, 927 (D.C. Dir. 1979).

Civil Service Reform Act of 1978, 5 U.S.C. § 2302(b)(10).

Norton v. Macy, 417 F.2d 1161 (D.C. Cir. 1969).

Civil Union

Civil union is the legal recognition of same-sex couples in marriage-like relationships. In April 2000 Vermont became the first state to give full legal rights to same-sex couples without the use of the word *marriage*. The civil union status confers upon same-sex couples the identical state law protections and responsibilities that are available to heterosexual spouses in a marriage. This includes preferences for guardianship of, and medical decision making for, an incapacitated partner; automatic inheritance rights; the right to leave work to care for an ill spouse; hospital visitation rights; control of a partner's body upon death; the right to be treated as an economic unit for tax purposes under state law, including the ability to transfer property to each other during life without tax consequences; greater access to family health insurance policies; the ability to obtain joint policies of insurance and joint credit; parentage rights; and the right to divorce (called a "dissolution") with an ordered method for ascertaining property division as well as child custody and support. Because civil unions are not marriage, the 1,049 protections afforded to married couples under federal law are not in effect.

Civil union legislation is the outcome of the decision by the Vermont Supreme Court in *Baker v. Vermont* (1999), which concluded that same-sex couples in Vermont were entitled to the same protections and benefits provided by law for opposite-sex married couples. The Vermont Constitution contains an "equal protection" clause that guarantees all citizens the same treatment under the law. These clauses are similar to the equal protection provision of the U.S. Constitution's Fourteenth Amendment, which was used to secure civil rights for racial minorities, women, and other groups. The court did not specify how this was to be done, rather leaving it to the Vermont legislature to devise a method to achieve this end. Marriage was considered, but ultimately the Vermont legislature created the civil union program in 2000. Immediately, the religious right and conservative representatives called for the impeachment of the judges making this decision and a reversal of the decision. However, many powerful Vermont politicians took great pride in the fact that Vermont was the first state to outlaw slavery in 1777 and believed that lesbians and gay men deserved to be treated fairly and equitably. Governor Howard Dean stated, "We will remain in the forefront of the struggle for equal justice under law" (Dean 2000).

By constructing a parallel institution to marriage for lesbians and gay men, Vermont created a super domestic partnership that is legally identical to marriage without invoking the "m" word. A term that comes from the civil rights movement describes this arrangement as "separate but equal." The U.S. Supreme Court found in *Brown v. Board of Education* (1954) that separate is inherently unequal. Many legal scholars predict that domestic partnership will be untenable and only full marriage will be achieved for same-sex couples.

A number of other states enacted civil union/domestic partnerships (e.g., California, Oregon, Vermont, D.C., Maine, New Jersey, Connecticut, Washington, New Hampshire, Wisconsin, Colorado, Nevada, Rhode Island, Illinois, Delaware, and Hawaii). The inherent inequalities of the domestic partnership arrangement have been recognized by the courts and, in some states, the courts have rejected the status and either thrown the issue back to the legislature or supported same-sex marriage. With the acceptance of same-sex marriage in Massachusetts in 2003 and 16 other states embracing same-sex marriages

Carolyn Conrad, right, and Kathleen Peterson sign their civil union license at the town clerks' office at midnight on July 1, 2000. They were the first couple to enter a civil union in Vermont. (AP Photo/Toby Talbot)

by 2014, the issue of civil unions/domestic partnership as an alternative to full-blown marriage has become moot.

Chuck Stewart

See also: Baker v. Vermont (1999); Same-Sex Marriage in the United States.

Further Reading

Baker v. Vermont, 744 A.2d 864 (Vt. 1999).

Dean, H. 2000. State of the State Address. January 5, at Montpelier, Vermont governor's website: www.state .vt.us/governor/0002.htm.

Combahee River Collective

Originally a chapter of the National Black Feminist Organization, the Combahee River Collective began meeting under its new name in 1977. Referencing a Civil War battle at the Combahee River in South Carolina that Harriet Tubman planned and led (the first U.S. military campaign planned and led by a woman) and centering an unapologetic focus on black lesbian subjectivity, the collective began a series of retreats for black lesbians in and around the Boston area.

Founding members Barbara and Beverly Smith and Demita Frazier, among others, convened the first

Audre Lorde was a prominent African American poet and political activist during the twentieth century. (Library of Congress)

official retreat on July 8, 1977, in South Hadley, Massachusetts. Radical black lesbian figures such as Lorraine Bethel, Cheryl Clarke, Yvonne Flowers, Gloria Joseph, and Audre Lorde consistently attended these retreats. The collective was organized in response to the racism that the members experienced as they worked in the second-wave feminist movement, and the sexism and homophobia they encountered while working in mainstream black-nationalist organizations. Out of these critiques of the limits of the liberation movements of the 1970s the collective developed what would come to be known as an "intersectional" analysis of oppression. In their foundational and oft-cited *Combahee River Collective Statement*, they explain that "we are actively committed to struggling against racial, sexual, heterosexual and class oppression, and see as our particular task the development of integrated analysis and practice based on the fact that the major systems of oppression are interlocking."

The collective founded Kitchen Table Press, based on the need that they saw for publishing venues for critical work by feminists of color, after white-run feminist venues let their work go out of print. In November 1980, Smith held meetings in her Roxbury apartment with a group of predominantly African American and Afro-Caribbean women, including Audre Lorde and Cherríe Moraga, who decided to make "an autonomous publishing resource for all women of color." A year later the press was officially founded and named "Kitchen Table" in order to represent the way women of color had often done their organizational, creative, and critical work, without traditional resources and in private and informal spaces. In addition to a number of groundbreaking anthologies, the press published the "Freedom Organizing Series" pamphlets with essays and speeches by Angela Davis, Audre Lorde, Barbara Smith, and others, along with organizational resources and political buttons.

In addition to the impact it has made through its political analyses and publishing practices, the Combahee River Collective was firmly grounded in local grassroots organizing in Roxbury, a predominantly black neighborhood in Boston where the collective's founders were based. They supported black people wrongfully accused of violent crimes and picketed for black construction labor to build a high school in a black community. In 1979, when in the course of four months 12 black women were found murdered in black neighborhoods, they created a powerful coalitional response that included the mobilizing of feminist activists and artists throughout the region to raise money and awareness for the ongoing movements against domestic violence and rape. This remains a model for feminist struggles against gendered violence to this day.

Alexis Pauline Gumbs

See also: Lorde, Audre (1934–1992).

Further Reading

DeVeaux, Alexis. 2004. *Warrior Poet: A Biography of Audre Lorde*. New York: W. W. Norton.

Smith, Barbara, and Gloria T. Hull, eds. 1982. *All the Women Are White, All the Blacks Are Men, but Some of Us Are Brave: Black Women's Studies*. New York: Feminist Press.

Committee on Lesbian and Gay History (CLGH)

The Committee on Lesbian and Gay History (CLGH) is an affiliated society of the American Historical Association (AHA), one of the leading professional organizations of historians, and has nearly 300 members, many of whom are history professors, graduate students, librarians, and independent scholars. The committee focuses on the study of homosexuality in the past and fosters interdisciplinary and intercultural exchange between scholars working in this field; it also guards against homophobic discrimination within the history profession. In addition to sponsoring sessions on LGBTQ history at the annual meetings of the AHA, the CLGH promotes the inclusion of LGBTQ topics in the general history curriculum and supports public history groups and activities that pursue LGBTQ-oriented projects. The CLGH also awards four prizes for outstanding work in the field of LGBTQ history. The John Boswell Prize for books and the Joan Nestle Prize for undergraduate work are awarded in odd-numbered years, while the Audre Lorde Prize for articles and the

From left, Diversity Committee chair and Children's Programming Peer Group governor Daniel Evans III, actor Laverne Cox, and Diversity Committee member and Casting Directors Peer Group governor Howard Meltzer attend the Academy of Television Arts & Sciences Presents "10 Years after the Prime Time Closet—A History of Gays and Lesbians on TV," on October 28, 2013, at the Leonard H. Goldenson Theatre in North Hollywood, California. (Frank Micelotta/Invision for Academy of Television Arts & Sciences/AP Photo)

Gregory Sprague Prize for graduate student work are bestowed in even-numbered years. Additionally, the CLGH maintains a website with an archive of syllabi for LGBTQ history courses and publishes a newsletter twice a year.

The CLGH was founded in 1979 by Walter L. Williams, then an assistant professor at the University of Cincinnati and later renowned for his 1986 work, *The Spirit and the Flesh: Sexual Diversity in American Indian Culture*. While pursuing research in Chicago, Williams met Gregory Sprague, a professor at Loyola University who had started the Chicago Gay History project (which would become in 1981 the Gerber-Hart Library and Archives, a repository of queer historical materials). The two commiserated over their displeasure with the absence of queer topics at the annual AHA meetings. Although some relevant panels had been held during these convocations, they were largely few and far between, both because LGBTQ history was not considered by many mainstream academics to be a topic worthy of serious study and due to a paucity of resources for scholars who would pursue it. However, Carroll Smith-Rosenberg's groundbreaking essay "The Female World of Love and Ritual" appeared in a 1975 issue of *Signs*, a feminist academic journal, and Jonathan Ned Katz's book *Gay American History: Lesbians and Gay Men in the U.S.A.*, a collection of documents pertaining to queer life in the United States, was published in 1976. Katz, along with fellow historians John D'Emilio, Joan Nestle, and Martin Duberman, had founded the national Gay Academic Union (GAU) in 1973, but, nonetheless, scholars of the queer past were still without any professional organization that would address concerns specific to their work.

While attending the 1979 convention of the AHA, Sprague and Williams approached the organizers and asked for space to hold a meeting of gay and lesbian historians. Their request was granted, and after hastily advertising with handmade signs, Williams and Sprague welcomed 15 historians to their meeting. Dubbing themselves the "Committee on Homosexuality in History" and helmed by Sprague, the group proceeded to make plans to hold another meeting at the next annual convention of the AHA. Within the next year, it gained a new moniker, the Committee on Lesbian and Gay History, at the suggestion of Williams and Lesbian Herstory Archives cofounder Deborah Schwartz and Walter Williams, then serving as cochairs. In 1982, the CLGH applied for, and received, recognition as an affiliated society of the AHA. The association's 1984 presidential address by Arthur Link approvingly referred to the AHA's commitment to welcome and honor, encourage, and defend its members without regard to gender, race, politics, religion, or "lifestyle," which, despite Link's unfortunate choice of terminology, suggests that the AHA was fully aware of the presence and importance of its queer members, likely due to the increased visibility resulting from the CLGH's activities. The acceptance of the AHA stood in marked contrast to Williams's experience at the national convention of the Organization of American Historians (OAH) around the same time; scheduled to deliver a paper on same-sex relationships in Native American culture, Williams was surprised to learn that conference organizers had received a death threat against him. Over the objections of conference organizers, he proceeded to present his paper, which was warmly received. The episode illustrated the resistance with which the field of LGBTQ history was met in its formative years.

The establishment and early years of the CLGH coincided, not surprisingly, with a vital period of growth in the field of queer history. Throughout the 1980s, a number of scholars explored LGBTQ history, and many exciting and innovative works appeared during this period of discovery and reclamation. Lillian Faderman's *Surpassing the Love of Men: Romantic Friendship and Love between Women from the Renaissance to the Present* (1981) and John Boswell's *Christianity, Social Tolerance, and Homosexuality: Gay People in Western Europe from the Beginning of the Christian Era to the Fourteenth Century* (1980) were well received, and historian John D'Emilio in 1983 parlayed his Columbia University doctoral dissertation into what has come to be a touchstone work for scholars of LGBTQ history, *Sexual Politics, Sexual*

Communities: The Making of a Homosexual Minority in the United States, 1940–1970. Topics explored ranged widely, from an art historian's exploration of LGBTQ life in sixteenth-century Europe—James Saslow's *Ganymede in the Renaissance: Homosexuality in Art and Society* (1986)—to a look back at LGBTQ political involvement in the United States from the 1940s to the 1970s in Toby Marotta's *The Politics of Homosexuality* (1981).

CLGH members contributed to the burgeoning number of works in LGBTQ history that saw publication in the 1990s, notably *Boots of Leather, Slippers of Gold: The History of a Lesbian Community* (1993) by Madeline Davis and Elizabeth Lapovsky Kennedy, Allan Bérubé's *Coming Out under Fire: The History of Gay Men and Women in World War Two* (1990), and George Chauncey's *Gay New York: Gender, Urban Culture, and the Making of the Gay Male World* (1994), which was widely lauded and won several awards, including the CLGH's own John Boswell Prize. This period also saw the development of much of the "queer theory" whose resonations would be felt in scholarly treatments of LGBTQ history to come. In 1990 alone three particularly influential books were published. Eve Kosofsky Sedgwick's work, *Epistemology of the Closet*, explores the tensions inherent within the multiple historical understandings of the "hetero-/homosexual" binary, while David Halperin's *One Hundred Years of Homosexuality: And Other Essays on Greek Love* posits that the category "homosexual" is anachronistic and inadequate for use in the study of queer sexuality before the late nineteenth century. Philosopher Judith Butler's innovative book, *Gender Trouble: Feminism and the Subversion of Identity*, advances the notion of gender "performativity" and challenges the supposed naturalness of biological sex.

The CLGH continues to unite historians of LGBTQ history, encouraging them to expand the boundaries of their field. The influence of the CLGH may have also played a role in the controversial decision by the AHA to move the location of their 1995 annual meeting from Cincinnati to Chicago after the former passed an antigay city ordinance. Though the financial ramifications of this choice were significant, it demonstrated the AHA's stance against homophobic discrimination. Furthermore, the organization developed new guidelines for selecting sites of its annual meeting, which specified that they would refuse to hold their conventions in any location where state or city laws would permit discrimination on the basis of race, gender, sexual orientation, and physical ability, among other things. Another watershed moment illustrating the widespread acceptance of the legitimacy of academic studies in LGBTQ history occurred in 2003, when a group of LGBTQ historians, many of them CLGH members, filed an amicus curiae brief in relation to the case of *Lawrence v. Texas*. The brief is considered to have been instrumental in determining the outcome of the landmark case, which overturned the 1986 decision of *Bowers v. Hardwick* and invalidated all other laws in the United States that criminalize consensual homosexual acts between adults occurring in private.

More recently, the CLGH has focused on issues pertaining to its nature and its membership. There has lately arisen some discussion of the CLGH changing its name to more clearly reflect an inclusion of bisexual, transgendered, transsexual, and queer history, although at the present time no decision on this issue has been made. In its ongoing efforts to abet the status of LGBTQ historians in the profession at large, the CLGH is also presently attempting to ensure that AHA publication's listing job opportunities clearly note whether the institution's advertising positions have nondiscrimination policies covering sexual orientation. The committee also conducted a survey in 2001 to assess the academic climate for queer historians. The findings were disheartening, indicating that many historians whose graduate work focuses on LGBTQ history have difficulty finding tenure-track employment in higher education; former CLGH chair Marc Stein noted in a 2006 speech at the AHA convention that while there have been small signs of improvement in this regard, the study of LGBTQ life in the past is still considered by many academics to be a marginal field with only limited claim to being "real" history. Lamentable as this condition is, it only serves to underscore the continued need for the CLGH and demonstrates that its mission to firmly establish LGBTQ history as an integral facet of the landscape of the past is just as relevant and urgent in its third decade as in its first.

Christianne Anastasia Gadd

See also: Center for Lesbian and Gay Studies (CLAGS); D'Emilio, John (1948–); Faderman, Lillian (1940–).

Further Reading

Chauncey, George. 1994. *Gay New York: Gender, Urban Culture, and the Making of the Gay Male World.* New York: Basic Books.

D'Emilio, John. 1982. *Sexual Politics, Sexual Communities: The Making of a Homosexual Minority in the United States, 1940–1970.* Chicago: University of Chicago Press.

Faderman, Lillian. 1981. *Surpassing the Love of Men: Romantic Friendship and Love between Women from the Renaissance to the Present.* New York: Morrow.

Katz, Jonathan Ned. 1976. *Gay American History: Lesbians and Gay Men in the U.S.A.* New York: Crowell.

Communications Decency Amendment (CDA) and Child Online Protection Act (COPA)

Many parents, Congress members, conservatives, and others wish to censor information from the Internet in the belief that some material is harmful to minors. To achieve this aim, Congress passed the Communications Decency Act in 1996, which was struck down in *ACLU v. Reno I* (1997) as being an unconstitutional restriction of the First Amendment. Congress tried again in 1998 and created the Child Online Privacy

Senator Jay Rockefeller (D-WV), left, and Federal Trade Commission chairman Jon Leibowitz, right, confer at the start of a meeting on the new Children's Online Privacy Protection Act, COPPA, which regulates Internet websites that collect information from children under the age of 13, on Capitol Hill in Washington, D.C., on December 19, 2012. (AP Photo/ J. Scott Applewhite)

Protection Act (COPPA). Even though it was more narrowly focused, U.S. district judge Lowell A. Reed Jr. issued a preliminary injunction barring COPPA from going into effect after he determined that the ACLU was likely to win the case against COPA (*ACLU v. Reno II*).

Court discussion showed that there were major questions about enforcing the act. For example, the act claimed to protect children from "harmful" materials, yet no one could give a clear definition of what constituted "harmful" or give evidence that such material actually harmed. Second, the act required adults to divulge personal information such as credit card numbers to gain access to adult sites. The judges recognized that this would produce a "chilling effect" and radically reduce the usage of the sites since some people would be reluctant to give that information. Third, the act specified that "contemporary community standards" would be used to delineate "offensive" material. However, the government could not clearly indicate which community and which standards would be used, given that the Internet is worldwide. Judge Reed concluded that the government was relatively helpless in trying to solve the problem of children's access to material that might be harmful to them on the Internet. Any kind of censorship of the Internet has impact for the gay rights movement because historically LGBT materials and discussion were automatically deemed obscene and censored.

Nonetheless, the act did pass into law by Congress, and the Federal Trade Commission (FTC) in late 2012 adopted final amendments to it to ensure that the law kept up with technology, including the increased use of mobile devices and social networking (Federal Trade Commission 2012).

Chuck Stewart

See also: American Civil Liberties Union (ACLU): Historical Overview of Gay Rights and Issues: From the 1980s to the Present.

Further Reading

Federal Trade Commission. 2012. "FTC Strengthens Kids' Privacy, Gives Parents Greater Control over Their Information by Amending Children's Online Privacy Protection Rule." Available at: http://www.ftc.gov/news-events/press-releases/2012/12/ftc-strengthens-kids-privacy-gives-parents-greater-control-over.

Crittenden Report

The Crittenden Report was a U.S. Navy report that concluded that there was no sound basis for the belief that homosexuals posed a security risk. In 1957 the secretary of the navy put together a board chaired by Captain S. H. Crittenden Jr. The findings, known as

Col. Margarethe Cammermeyer of the National Guard speaks to reporters in Tacoma, Washington, on May 28, 1992, after being officially notified that her 26-year military career is over because she admitted that she is lesbian. Cammermeyer, 50, a Vietnam veteran, was one of the highest-ranking soldiers to be removed from the service for being gay. (AP Photo/Matt Todd)

the Crittenden Report, examined the antigay stereotype that homosexuals are easy targets of blackmail by enemy agents who might threaten to expose their sexuality. The board found that "the number of cases of blackmail as a result of past investigations of homosexuals is negligible. No factual data exists to support the contention that homosexuals are a greater risk than heterosexuals" (Dyer 1990, p. xvi).

The 639-page report so threatened the navy that it refused to release it. It took 20 years and a court order to pry the report loose from the grips of the navy. Thirty years after the initial Crittenden research, two more studies were conducted. These too were buried, but were forced out through leaks in Congress. These reports also reinforced the Crittenden findings that homosexuals do not pose a security risk because of sexual orientation and, thus, the belief that homosexuals should not serve in the military because of the threat of potential blackmail remained unsupported.

Chuck Stewart

See also: Don't Ask, Don't Tell: Homosexuality and the Military.

Further Reading

Dyer, K. 1990. *Gays in Uniform: The Pentagon Secret Report*. Boston: Alyson Press.

D

Daughters of Bilitis

Daughters of Bilitis (DOB) was the first national lesbian organization in the United States. In 1955, eight women, including Phyllis Lyon and Del Martin, formed DOB in San Francisco. In 1894, Pierre Louys had published the poems *The Songs of Bilitis* and claimed a Greek woman, Bilitis, had written these overt lesbian erotic poems about Sappho circa 600 BCE. The poems were later found to be forgeries, but Bilitis remained an important signifier to lesbians.

In the 1950s, the homophile movement in the United States, which DOB was a part of, aimed to educate the public about homosexuality and offer an alternative to gay bar culture. DOB was unique compared to other homophile organizations because it was lesbian-focused. Although founding members agreed on this concentration, they argued over the direction of the club, whether it should include political and educational elements or remain strictly social. In 1956, the original group splintered, and the new DOB, headed by Martin and Lyon, developed its statement of purpose as a women's organization that promoted the integration of homosexuals into society through education, participated in research projects by experts aiming to further understand homosexuality, and investigated and proposed changes to discriminatory legislation and codes.

Publishing was at the center of DOB's activities. DOB's magazine, *The Ladder* (1956–1970), included poetry, biographies, political news, and fictional stories pertinent to lesbians. This journal gave a vital voice to the lesbian experience in America, attempted to change the status quo of lesbian representation, and

inspired the growth of DOB during the 1950s and 1960s. By 1970, DOB had local chapters throughout the country in places such as New York, Los Angeles, Denver, Chicago, Boston, and New Orleans.

By extending their membership to include heterosexual women, DOB had more influence on social movements during the 1960s in comparison to other homophile organizations. DOB inspired the women's movement by organizing consciousness-raising groups they had called "Gab 'n' Javas." The structure of these gatherings provided the framework for feminist groups. DOB's success was short-lived in part because of the development of the modern women's movement. The organization dissolved in 1970 at a national level when the editor Barbara Grier and the national president Rita Laporte decided to publish *The Ladder* as an independent lesbian review, stripping it from DOB's control. The national board disbanded rather than fight over ownership of the magazine. Still, DOB's influence continued. Ex-DOB members remain active participants in the struggle for LGBTQ and women's rights. On February 12, 2004, Phyllis Lyon and Del Martin celebrated their 51st anniversary by becoming the first same-sex couple married by U.S. government officials at San Francisco's City Hall. Although their marriage would soon be voided by the California Supreme Court later that year, in 2008, the California Supreme Court legalized same-sex marriage, and they were again wedded in June 2008. Del Martin died in August 2008.

Aimee Klask

See also: Alice B. Toklas Lesbian Gay Bisexual Transgender Democratic Club; Lyon, Phyllis (1924–); Martin, Del

Phyllis Lyon, left, and her partner Del Martin, right, sit at their home in San Francisco on December 17, 2004. Lyon and Martin, who were together for over 50 years and were the first same-sex couple married at city hall in San Francisco, are one of 12 gay and lesbian couples suing the state to have its marriage laws declared unconstitutional. (AP Photo/Eric Risberg)

(1921–2008); Same-Sex Marriage in the United States; Sappho (Sixth Century BCE).

Further Reading

D'Emilio, John. 1983. *Sexual Politics, Sexual Communities: The Making of a Homosexual Minority in the United States, 1940–1970*. Chicago: University of Chicago Press.

Meeker, Martin. 2006. *Contacts Desired: Gay and Lesbian Communications and Community, 1940s–1970s*. Chicago: University of Chicago Press.

Streitmatter, Rodger. 1995. *Unspeakable: The Rise of the Gay and Lesbian Press in America*. London: Faber and Faber.

Deaf Queer Resource Center

Historically, members of the gay and lesbian community whose hearing abilities were limited or nonexistent found themselves marginalized within their own population, as most activist groups made only rare provision for sign language interpreters in either their meetings or at public demonstrations, while cruising in gay bars posed for the deaf a unique set of obstacles. Awareness of deaf queer people as a distinct community of their own within the gay rights movement began to become more common in the early 1990s in some of the larger American cities, with programs and institutions created to address their needs, while the publication in 1993 of Raymond Luczak's groundbreaking *Eyes of Desire: A Deaf Gay and Lesbian Reader* further raised their visibility. But despite the proliferation of Internet sites related to gay and lesbian people, little was done to provide an electronic forum for data on the deaf.

The first major website created to bring information to a geographically unlimited LGBT deaf population is the Deaf Queer Resource Center, formally launched on September 1, 1995, by San Francisco deaf transsexual activist Dragonsani Renteria. The Deaf Queer Resource Center represents one of the first effective applications of the interwoven technology of the web to the challenge of constructing an enduring identity for segments of the LGBT community whose needs for recognition, peer acceptance, and information had not been adequately addressed by mainstream activism.

Renteria had previously published the first newspaper for deaf LGBT people, *CTN (Coming Together Newsletter)*, in 1991, which would give rise in time to *FLASH*, the first national e-zine for deaf queer discussion and postings affiliated with the center, whose subscription figures worldwide had passed 11,000 by late 2003. From 1992 to 1995, he served as the director of San Francisco's Deaf Gay and Lesbian Center, an outreach program of an agency that provided a number of programs for the general deaf community of San Francisco and adjoining communities. The impetus to create an online national nonprofit information center and resource clearinghouse for the deaf members of the LGBTQ community came out of the variety of calls the center received from deaf people across the United States requesting data and assistance. The Deaf Gay and Lesbian Center's mandate was to serve only the deaf LGBT population of the Bay Area, but the rising possibilities offered by the Internet offered a solution to filling the need for coherent information for the national deaf lesbian and gay communities. Online resources include the full texts of a sample of a collection of coming-out stories of deaf queer people begun in 1997 and made available on the web on National Coming Out Day, October 11, in 2006, advice and documents relating to coming out as a member of the deaf queer population, a busy chat room serving as

a forum for both discussion and networking, and a calendar of local gatherings for LGBT deaf people in the United States, Canada, England, and Spain.

Robert Ridinger

See also: African Americans and LGBTQ Issues; Latino/Latina Americans and LGBTQ Issues. Documents: Mohave Indian Two-Spirit Person (1964); Multiple Struggles for Lesbian Women of Color (1973).

Further Reading

Barr, Billy. "DQRC's Eight Year Anniversary Special Issue [and interview with Dragonsani Renteria]." Available at: http://www.deafqueer.org/411/about/interview.html. Accessed January 21, 2014.

The Deaf Queer Resource Center. Available at: http://www.deafqueer.org/411/about/index.html.

Defense of Marriage Act (DOMA)

The federal Defense of Marriage Act (DOMA), signed into law in 1996, had two purposes: (1) it prevented states from being forced by the full faith and credit clause of the U.S. Constitution to recognize same-sex marriages validly celebrated in other states; and (2) it defined marriage for federal purposes as the union of one man and one woman.

At the time of its adoption, experts believed that the act was probably unconstitutional because: (1) it was the antithesis of the full faith and credit clause; (2) it lacked sufficient generality; (3) it was constructed without adequate justification; (4) it encroached upon an area of law that had been within the traditional power of the states; (5) it restricted interstate travel; and (6) it was motivated by animus toward a disfavored group.

The state has a fundamental interest in protecting the predictability, security, and stability of marriage. For couples who marry in one state (state of celebration) and live in another, the home state (domicile state) recognizes marriages from other states as long as they are not polygamous and incestuous, and do not violate a strong public policy of the domicile state. There is a long history of courts accepting valid marriages from other states that otherwise would be prohibited or odious to the public policy of the domicile state.

Plaintiffs in *Hollingsworth v. Perry*, the California Proposition 8 case, react on steps of the Supreme Court in Washington, D.C., on June 26, 2013. The justices had just cleared the way for the resumption of same-sex marriage in California. (AP Photo/J. Scott Applewhite)

Choice-of-law procedures are used to determine the acceptance of out-of-state marriages, not the full faith and credit clause. The validity of a marriage is determined by the laws of the state of celebration and the laws of the state of domicile at the time of the marriage. If both the state of celebration and the state of domicile recognize the marriage, it is valid everywhere except those states that have declared such marriages void or have passed some kind of evasion statute. Because the DOMA did not address the issue of choice of law, the DOMA does not affect this procedure. Thus, if a same-sex couple were married in one state and their domicile state also accepted the marriage as valid, no other state could refuse to accept their marriage as valid unless it was proved to be obnoxious to that state's law.

One reason this choice-of-law procedure has developed is to stop people from so-called forum shopping. For example, assume a couple create a marriage that is valid in their home state but is void in other states. Then, one partner moves to one of these other states in which the marriage would not have been allowed. Here, the person could claim that he or she was never in a valid marriage and therefore was not responsible for child support or other claims. "Because the interstate recognition of marriages involves choice of law and because of how each state's choice-of-law rules operate, only the exception involving obnoxiousness to the domiciliary state's law may invalidate a marriage" (Strasser 1997, p. 130).

Currently, *according to each state's law*, the only state laws potentially applicable to determine the

Members of the LGBT community and their supporters gather to celebrate two decisions by the U.S. Supreme Court, one to invalidate parts of the Defense of Marriage Act and another to uphold a lower court ruling that struck down California's controversial Proposition 8, during a rally in New York's Greenwich Village on June 26, 2013. (AP Photo/Jason DeCrow)

validity of a marriage are the laws of the states of celebration and domicile. A state which is not the domicile at the time of the marriage will be forced by its own law to recognize a marriage validly celebrated in another state as long as the domicile at the time of marriage would recognize it. Thus, because DOMA did not affect state law, the act had *no* effect on which marriages are recognized by the various states (Strasser 1997, p. 133).

Surprisingly, DOMA may have more of an effect on divorce than on marriage. Divorce decrees are not subject to choice-of-law rules. Thus, divorce decrees are legal judgments that are subject to the DOMA. Thus, for example, if a state's own choice-of-law rules require it to recognize all nonincestuous, nonbigamous marriages that do not violate public policy

of the domiciliary state at the time of marriage, it may have to recognize a same-sex marriage and yet will retain the right not to recognize a same-sex divorce.

The DOMA did not increase the number of states allowed to refuse to recognize same-sex marriages validly celebrated in other states. States already have that right through their choice-of-law procedures. However, the DOMA may act as a destabilizing effect on the full faith and credit clause. Congress is opening itself up to demands for other exceptions to be made to the clause.

The exception Congress created to the clause with the DOMA is highly specific. Court interpretations of the clause demonstrate a reluctance to allow the federal government to make a change to one category of the clause or to target a subgroup within a category.

Family Research Council president Tony Perkins, center, with, from left, Representative Katherine Harris (R-FL), Senator Wayne Allard (R-CO), and Bishop Harry Jackson, delivers his remarks during a news conference on Capitol Hill to support the Marriage Protection Amendment on June 6, 2006, in Washington, D.C. (AP Photo/Manuel Balce Ceneta)

The DOMA lacks generality. It is unclear whether Congress had the power to differentiate between different types of judgments as covered by the clause.

The right to interstate travel is fundamental to the concept of a federal union and is virtually unqualified (*United States v. Guest*, 1966). The DOMA would have a chilling effect on the right to travel to a state or migrate to a state. For example, if a validly married same-sex couple traveled through a state that did not recognize same-sex marriage, a situation could occur in which a hospital would not let the partner of an injured person give consent for medical treatment for

life-threatening injuries sustained in an automobile accident. Same-sex married couples would be justified in being reluctant to travel through or migrate to states that were hostile to their relationship.

This scenario also points out the problem that the state through which the couple was passing would essentially invalidate their valid marriage. Currently, domestic relations law does not allow a state to invalidate a previously valid marriage without the consent of one or both partners. The DOMA would overrule this. Enforcing the DOMA would result in federal intrusion into state law. The Supreme Court has made

Former representative Bob Barr (R-GA), left, with other panel witnesses, Vincent P. McCarthy, center, of the American Center for Law and Justice and John Hanes, chairman, Wyoming Senate Judiciary Committee, testifies before the House Judiciary Committee regarding the proposed Federal Marriage Amendment that would define marriage as only the lawful union between a man and a woman on Capitol Hill on March 30, 2004. Barr, who is not a supporter of the same-sex marriage and opposes a constitutional amendment, authored the Defense of Marriage Act commonly known as DOMA, which was signed into law by President Clinton in the fall of 1996. (AP Photo/Manuel Balce Ceneta)

it clear that state law can be overridden when the law causes "major damage" to "clear and substantial" federal interests (*Rose v. Rose*, 1987). The discussion in Congress shows a concern over extending federal benefits to same-sex couples. It is left to future courts to decide if this concern constitutes major damage to federal interests.

Congress overreached its power without adequate justification. Congress is displacing state law with the DOMA. Marriage, divorce, child adoption, and family law have historically been left to the states to regulate. The DOMA will interfere with that long history. It is difficult to believe that Congress had any legitimate justification for offering this act. It is very clear from the debate in Congress that animus was the motivation behind its adoption. Courts have consistently viewed the disfavoring of a disadvantaged minority as an illegitimate role of government.

By 2000, 29 states passed preemptive laws similar to the DOMA that exempt them from having to recognize same-sex marriages from other states. Many lawsuits were filed. By 2013, the U.S. Supreme Court ruled DOMA unconstitutional (*United States v. Windsor*, 2013). The Court decided that Section 3 of DOMA violated the Due Process Clause of the Fifth Amendment. Also, by 2014, 17 states, the District of Columbian, and 8 First People nations had approved same-sex marriage. This means a majority of the population in the United States now lives in states that endorse same-sex marriage.

Chuck Stewart

See also: Civil Union; Domestic Partnerships; Same-Sex Marriage in the United States.

Further Reading

Carter, W. Burlette. 2013. "The Federal Law of Marriage: Deference, Deviation and DOMA." *American University Journal of Gender, Social Policy & the Law*, 70.

Feigen, Brenda. 2004. "Same-Sex Marriage: An Issue of Constitutional Rights Not Moral Opinions." *Harvard Women's Law Journal*, 345.

Litigating the Defense of Marriage Act: The Next Battleground for Same-Sex Marriage. (June, 2004). *Harvard Law Review* 117 (8): 2684–2707.

Manning, Jason. 2004, April 30. "Backgrounder: The Defense of Marriage Act." *The Online News Hour*. The News Hour with Jim Lehrer.

Rose v. Rose, 481 U.S. 619 (1987).

Same Sex Marriage Passage. (2005, May 2). *CQ Weekly. Congressional Quarterly*.

Strasser, M. 1997. *Legally Wed: Same-Sex Marriage and the Constitution*. Ithaca, NY: Cornell University Press.

United States. 104th Congress. Defense of Marriage Act. House of Representatives Committee Report. 1996.

United States v. Guest 383 U.S. 745 (1966).

United States v. Windsor, 570 U.S. ___ (2013) (Docket No. 12–307).

Wardle, Lynn D. 1996. "A Critical Analysis of Constitutional Claims for Same-Sex Marriage." *Brigham young University Law Review, 1*.

D'Emilio, John (1948–)

John D'Emilio is one of the preeminent historians of the gay and lesbian rights movement. He is the author of six major books on the subject: *Sexual Politics, Sexual Communities: The Making of a Homosexual Minority in the United States, 1940–1970* (University of Chicago Press, 1983); *Intimate Matters: A History of Sexuality in America* (with Estelle B. Freeman; Harper and Row, 1988); *Making Trouble: Essays on Gay History, Politics, and the University* (Routledge, 1992); *Creating Change: Sexuality, Public Policy and Civil Rights* (St. Martin's Press, 2000; with William Turner and Urvashi Vaid); *The World Turned: Essays on Gay History, Politics, and Culture* (Duke University Press, 2002); and *Lost Prophet: Bayard Rustin and the Quest for Peace and Justice in America* (The Free Press, 2003).

D'Emilio was born in New York City on September 21, 1948. He attended Columbia University, from which he received his BA in 1970, his MA in 1972, and his PhD in 1982, all in history. He then accepted an appointment at the University of North Carolina at Greensboro, where he served as assistant professor (1983–1988), associate professor (1988–1992), and professor (1992–1998). From 1988 to 1993, he was also director of graduate studies. In 1995, D'Emilio was named founding director of the National Gay and Lesbian Task Force Policy Institute, generally regarded as the movement's primary "think tank" on ways of advancing equality for gay men and lesbians. In 1999, he was named Professor of History and Gender and Women's Studies at the University of Illinois at Chicago, a post he continues to hold.

In addition to his books, D'Emilio has written a number of articles, book chapters, and policy papers dealing with the history and philosophy of the lesbian and gay rights movement, including "The Military and Lesbians during the McCarthy Years" (1984), "The Homosexual Menace: The Politics of Sexuality in Cold War America" (1989), "Power at the Polls: The Gay/Lesbian/Bisexual Vote" (1996); "Cycles of Change, Questions of Strategy: The Gay and Lesbian

Movement after Fifty Years" (2000); and "Placing Gay in the Sixties" (2001). Among the more than 30 awards received by D'Emilio are nominee for the 1983 Pulitzer Prize in history; Best Book Award of the Task Force on Gay Liberation of the American Library Association (1984); David R. Kessler Lecturer, Center for Lesbian and Gay Studies, City University of New York (1999); Editor's Choice, Best Book Award, Lambda Literary Foundation (2003); American Library Association, Stonewall Award, Best Gay and Lesbian Nonfiction Book (2004); a "Chicagoan of the Year" award (*Chicago Tribune*; 2004); Brudner Prize from Yale University, for lifetime contribution to the development of lesbian and gay studies (2005); and induction to the City of Chicago Gay and Lesbian Hall of Fame (2005). He has been a fellow at the Center for Advanced Studies in the Behavioral Sciences in Stanford, CA.

David E. Newton

See also: Boswell, John (1947–1994); Duberman, Martin Bauml (1930–).

Further Readings

D'Emilio, John. 2002. *The World Turned: Essays on Gay History, Politics, and Culture*. Durham, NC: Duke University Press.

D'Emilio, John and Estelle B. Freedman. 2012. *Intimate Matters: A History of Sexuality in America*, 3rd ed. Chicago: University of Chicago Press.

Disability Studies and LGBTQ Issues

Disability studies examine the histories and experiences of people with disabilities, as well as cultural understandings of disability, able-bodiedness, and normalcy. The field has grown exponentially since the founding of the Society for Disability Studies in 1982, extending its reach into university programs, publishing houses, and conferences. As the field has developed, scholars have forged connections with LGBTQ movements, arguing that disability and able-bodiedness exist not in isolation, but in relation to other categories of difference, including race, class, gender, and sexuality. Disability studies and queer studies share an interest in building connections among scholars, artists, and activists working toward social change.

This work involves a critique of the ways in which queer, disabled, and queer disabled people have been marked as abnormal, unnatural, or pathological; disability studies and queer studies trace the histories and effects of such representations, highlighting the ways in which nondisabled, straight, "normal" bodies are produced through the exclusion of "others." Queer and disability studies scholars analyze these histories, highlighting their ableist and heteronormative biases.

This joint project is hindered by historical practices associating homosexuality with sickness, particularly mental illness. Although homosexuality was removed from the *Diagnostic and Statistical Manual of Mental Disorders* in 1973, representations of LGBTQs as "sick" continue to circulate; during the 1980s and 1990s, depictions of AIDS as the "gay plague" fostered understandings of queer sexual and relational practices as pathological, dangerous, and contagious. In an attempt to counter such representations, and to facilitate assimilation into mainstream culture, some LGBTQs have disassociated themselves from disabled people, denying any linkages between the two movements. Similarly, some disabled people have tried to distance themselves from LGBTQs by insisting on their own "normalcy" in the realm of sexuality and gender identity.

Queers with disabilities, however, are becoming more vocal in both disability and LGBTQ communities, and the field of queer disability studies is developing rapidly. The 2002 Queer Disability Conference at San Francisco State University marked the first time that an international group of queers with disabilities and their allies gathered to discuss linkages among ableism, homophobia, transphobia, and heteronormativity; organizations such as the Deaf Queer Resource Center and Bent (an online community of disabled gay men) continue to foster community building among deaf and disabled LGBTQs. This kind of queer disability organizing is accompanied by anthologies exploring the personal experiences of LGBTQ people with disabilities in the United States, including

While in front of the Rainbow flag, Palomar College interpreting student Kali Jensen signs for the hearing impaired as a video showing speakers and music is played during the PC3H Rally to remember gay and lesbian students who have taken their lives because of bullying. (North County Times/ZUMA Press/Corbis)

Raymond Luczak's *Eyes of Desire: A Deaf Gay and Lesbian Reader* (1993), Victoria Brownworth and Susan Raffo's *Restricted Access: Lesbians on Disability* (1999), and Bob Guter and John Killacky's *Queer Crips: Disabled Gay Men and Their Stories* (2004).

Disability studies' interface with LGBTQ movements and issues takes several overlapping forms: highlighting the similarities between disabled people and LGBTQs; mapping the experiences of people living with both disability and queerness; tracing the ways in which disability studies uses and extends the insights of queer studies, and vice versa; and highlighting the ways in which ideologies of able-bodiedness and heterosexuality/heteronormativity are mutually constitutive.

First, disabled people and LGBTQs face similar issues of discrimination, marginalization, and abuse.

Members of both groups have been characterized as "unfit" parents: many disabled women report being discouraged by their doctors and families from becoming parents, while some fertility clinics have refused to assist same-sex couples in having children. Advances in genetic medicine have also led to a fixation on etiologies of queerness and disability; scholars have been particularly concerned with increases in prenatal testing and selective abortion in order to "cure" alleged "defects."

Violence and hate crimes mark another point of connection between LGBTQ communities and disability. Evidence suggests that people with disabilities and LGBTQs are at an increased risk for abuse by medical and social service professionals; some lesbians report being sexually assaulted by doctors and therapists in an effort to "cure" them of their lesbianism, while disabled people, particularly those who are institutionalized, have been abused by caregivers, service providers, and fellow patients. Domestic violence shelters and hotlines have often been unresponsive to the specific needs of LGBTQs and people with disabilities, failing to train counselors about same-sex abuse or to provide disability accommodations.

Second, queer disability studies explore the specific experiences of disabled LGBTQs, with sexuality as a key site of analysis. People with physical impairments are often represented in contemporary culture as asexual, while those with cognitive impairments or mental illnesses are seen as hypersexual perverts. Queerness only serves to magnify such representations. Same-sex desire or interest in nonnormative sexual practices such as BDSM is seen as a symptom of one's impairment; same-sex relationships are cast as signs of either mental/cognitive confusion or failure as a heterosexual. For disabled people living in institutions or relying on attendants, these problems are exacerbated by homophobic administrators, parents, or attendants who prevent disabled people from acting on their desires or compel them to remain quiet for fear of provoking abandonment or abuse.

Attention to the experiences of disabled queers also highlights the inaccessibility of LGBTQ and disability communities. Bars often feature stairs or inaccessible restrooms; in locations where smoking is still permitted, smoke and perfume make it impossible for those with asthma or chemical sensitivities to participate; and protests and demonstrations frequently lack American Sign Language (ASL) interpreters, aren't advertised in Braille or large print, and require the ability to stand for long periods or walk long distances. Similarly, disability communities have been slow to include LGBTQs in their projects; centers for independent living often failed to provide for the needs of gay men during the early days of the AIDS crisis, while histories of disability rights frequently overlook the presence of LGBTQs in the movement. Thus, disability studies' interface with LGBTQ movements and issues involves not merely mapping connections but also highlighting disjunctures between movements.

Third, disability studies and queer studies share methodological and theoretical concerns. Central among them is a focus on language and self-identification. Refusing to be reduced to diagnostic categories, many disabled people choose instead to identify under broader rubrics such as "disabled people" or "people with disabilities"; echoing moves among LGBTs to reclaim pejorative labels such as "dyke," "fag," and "queer," many within disabled communities have worked to reimagine epithets such as "crip," "spaz," and "crazy." There are also moves within disability studies and activism to articulate notions of pride and disability culture akin to gay pride and queer culture.

This focus on identity and community, combined with widespread assumptions that "disability" means only wheelchairs and other visible markers of difference, leads many people with invisible disabilities (such as chronic fatigue immune deficiency syndrome or learning disabilities) to partake of the coming-out discourse common among LGBTQs. Because their impairments are not marked on their bodies, their claims to disability status are often ridiculed or denied; they repeatedly have to "come out" as disabled to friends, family, or experts acting as gatekeepers for accommodations and disability-related benefits. As in LGBTQ contexts, the impulse to come out is directly related to the phenomenon of passing. Those whose impairments are not readily legible on the body or in one's behaviors often pass as nondisabled. Such passing can translate into more privileged positions in mainstream society than those afforded more apparently disabled people but is often accompanied by exclusion from disability communities and a lack of support and resources.

Due in part to the difficulties of establishing fixed definitions of disability, and to the wide range of experiences and histories that fall within the realm of disability, many people involved in disability studies have built on the challenges to identity politics put forth by LGBTQ scholars and activists. Rather than positioning all people with disabilities as the same, and thereby erasing differences in class, race, gender, and impairment, some disability studies scholars have focused instead on the conditions producing "disabled people" as a discrete group. Part of this project involves a commitment to coalition politics rather than strict identity-based movements, encouraging, for example, collaborations between disabled people and genderqueer or transgender people around the need for safe, gender-neutral, accessible restrooms.

Finally, queer disability studies aim to show how heterosexuality and able-bodiedness are inseparable parts of a larger system of compulsory normativity. Just as queer theorists have argued that heterosexuality can never fully be attained, queer disability theorists such as Robert McRuer argue that able-bodiedness likewise represents an impossible, unattainable ideal. Both rely on the containment or disavowal of queer, disabled bodies, a disavowal that is taken to be natural, unquestionable, and common sense.

Both disability studies and queer studies face criticism from people of color and antiracist scholars for ignoring issues of race; for failing to recognize the role of whiteness; and for marginalizing the work of people of color. Both have also been called to task for their imposition of Western concepts of identity, progress, and individualism on other cultures and communities. Critics argue that queer disability studies must recognize that questions of globalization, imperialism, nationalism, and racism are inextricably bound up with questions of heterosexuality and able-bodiedness.

Alison Kafer

See also: Deaf Queer Resource Center.

Further Reading

Clare, Eli. 1999. *Exile and Pride: Disability, Queerness, and Liberation*. Cambridge, MA: South End Press.

Kafer, Alison. 2003. "Compulsory Bodies: Reflections on Heterosexuality and Able-Bodiedness." *Journal of Women's History* 15 (3): 77–89.

McRuer, Robert. 2006. *Crip Theory: Cultural Signs of Queerness and Disability*. New York: New York University Press.

McRuer, Robert, and Abby L. Wilkerson, eds. 2003. "Desiring Disability: Queer Theory Meets Disability Studies." Special issue of *GLQ: A Journal of Lesbian and Gay Studies* 9 (1–2).

Sherry, Mark. 2004. "Overlaps and Contradictions between Queer Theory and Disability Studies." *Disability and Society* 19 (7): 769–83.

Domestic Partnership

Couples who have formed relationships but are unmarried sometimes gain legal recognition for their relationships, which are termed *domestic partnerships*. Increasingly, governmental entities and private businesses are formally recognizing domestic partnerships.

The acceptance of domestic partnerships arises from two cultural forces. First, the social construction of the family is changing. The traditional nuclear family consisting of a married heterosexual couple with children under the age of 18 represents a minority of families in the United States. The April 2012 report from the U.S. Census finds that married straight couples with families now make up less than half of U.S. households (Nhan 2012). There are approximately 6.8 million unmarried-partner households in the United States of which 593,000 are same-sex households (U.S. Census). Domestic partnership programs recognize and address the issue of fairness to nontraditional families. Second, the gay civil rights movement has brought to the attention of Americans the need for equity between same-sex couples and the rights and responsibilities opposite-sex couples are given through marriage. For example, it is estimated that benefits comprise approximately 40 percent of a worker's employment compensation. Opposite-sex couples who marry are able to obtain benefits for their spouses. This, in effect, gives heterosexual married employees a significantly higher rate of pay as compared with lesbian and gay employees. Domestic partnership benefits help equalize the workplace, thereby helping to attract and retain qualified employees in a competitive market.

Definition and Verification

Just as there are many definitions of what constitutes a family, there are wide variations in how domestic

Paula Long, right, and Rosalind Heggs in their Camden, New Jersey, home on July 7, 2005. The women drove their red Ford Mustang convertible to Vermont for their civil union ceremony on September 8, 2001. Long and Heggs are among many gay couples who pushed to make same-sex marriage legal in New Jersey. (AP Photo/Mel Evans)

partnerships are defined and implemented by states, cities, and private businesses. Domestic partnership programs sometimes use other words, such as "life partner," "spousal equivalent," "functional marriage equivalent," "alternative family," and "family-type unit." In general, domestic partnership is defined as an ongoing relationship between two adults of the same or opposite sex who are over the age of 18, are sharing a residence, are emotionally interdependent, and intend to reside together indefinitely.

Some domestic partnership programs specify same-sex couples only. The rationale for doing so is that opposite-sex couples have the ability to marry, whereas same-sex couples do not. Some civil libertarians argue that this is appropriate because domestic partnership policies are an attempt to right an injustice toward lesbian and gay couples. Also, heterosexuals who choose not to marry by obtaining domestic partnership status are undermining legal and social marriage norms. Most lesbian and gay legal organizations, including the National Gay and Lesbian Task Force, recommend including both same- and opposite-sex couples in domestic partnership policies. Some courts have struck down same-sex only domestic partnership policies as being discriminatory based on sexual orientation or on marital status. More and more employers are designing domestic partnership programs that allow both same- and opposite-sex

Domestic partners Rick Sipe, left, and Dan Neish put away their wedding bands after taking a first look at them as they sit in their home in Seattle in 2014. Neish, 57, said that he was disappointed to learn that the domestic partnership they've had since 2007 wouldn't automatically be converted to marriage, as were thousands of others on June 30, because Sipe is 64. A provision of the same-sex marriage law, approved by voters in 2012, converted all same-sex domestic partnerships—in which both partners are under 62 years of age—to marriage. (AP Photo/Elaine Thompson)

couples to register. Some domestic partnership programs are all-inclusive. For example, Bank of America allows employees to designate any member of their household to be a recipient of their health benefits. This may include a married spouse, unmarried domestic partner, or relative (e.g., a sibling or parent). Few employers have adopted such programs, but they are ideal to fit the wide range of family arrangements. Surprisingly, unmarried opposite-sex couples are the primary people who sign up for domestic partnership benefits (Donovan 1998). Also, some, but not all, domestic partnership programs extend benefits to the children of domestic partners.

Verifying domestic partnerships involves a number of strategies. In some cities and one state (California), couples may register their relationship. Sometimes they only need to swear to the accuracy of their statement: other times they must show proof, such as living together (rental agreements or home mortgages), having joint bank accounts, and other examples of joint ownership and financial interdependence. Requiring such documents may be discriminatory because married couples often either do not need to show any proof of marriage or simply need to show their marriage certificate. To be fair, businesses should require similar documentation for married couples and for domestic partners enrolling in employee benefit programs.

Benefits Provided

Workplace benefits are often divided into two categories. "Soft" benefits usually include bereavement and sick leave, adoption assistance, relocation benefits, child resource and referral services, access to employer recreational facilities, participation in employee assistance programs, and inclusion in employee discount policies. "Hard" benefits usually include medical benefits, dental and vision care, dependent life insurance, accidental death and dismemberment benefits, tuition assistance, long-term care, day care, and flexible spending accounts. It is important to note that more than a substantial number of benefits in the public and private sector extended to married couples are denied domestic partners.

Governmental Programs

Domestic partnerships are recognized by governmental bodies in one of two forms. First, some cities and one state allow couples who live together to "register" their status as domestic partners. Usually, this opens the door to soft benefits for government employees who register. California's registry is symbolic and does not confer any rights. In the second form, some cities extend to domestic partners of city employees the same health care and other benefits as are extended to spouses of married employees. In some cases, both a registry and extension of benefits are available, in other cases, one or the other form exists.

In 2000, Vermont became the first state to provide a same-sex equivalent to marriage. This "civil union" is designed to provide all the same rights and responsibilities as opposite-sex marriage without using the word "marriage." In many ways, civil unions represent a domestic partnership policy.

Private Employment

Thousands of companies include sexual orientation as a protected category in their nondiscrimination policies. Only a few hundred of these companies provide domestic partnership benefits. For example, in June 2000, General Motors, Ford, and DaimlerChrysler announced that health care benefits would be extended to same-sex domestic partners. This action affected more than 465,000 employees around the country. Program definitions vary as to what constitutes a domestic partnership, who qualifies, and what benefits are conferred.

Many reasons can be cited as to why businesses have a vested interest in providing domestic partnership benefits. First, it is a matter of equality for all employees. By participating in benefit programs, married employees are, in fact, receiving significantly higher salaries. Lesbian and gay employees feel less valued and second rate if they do not receive the same benefits. Second, comprehensive benefit packages are one way to attract and retain talented employees. In our competitive world, employers cannot ignore the power antidiscrimination policies and domestic partnership programs have in influencing lesbian and gay employees to maintain company loyalty. Third, many of the leading companies in technology, entertainment, financial, legal, medical, academic, and computer companies provide domestic partnership programs. They find that doing so boosts employee morale and attracts customers.

In many ways, the extension of benefits to same-sex couples by businesses is more important than governmental recognition. Registries provide few real benefits, whereas company benefits affect the everyday life of employees and their families.

Concerns

When domestic partnerships are considered for businesses and cities, a number of common issues are voiced as concerns.

First, there is the fear that the program will cost too much to implement. The experiences of other cities and businesses have found this to be untrue. Part of the fear is the antigay stereotype that gay people are mostly infected with HIV and, thus, will impose significant health care costs. As of the year 2006, the lifetime costs for HIV care were approximately

$354,100—which is equal to or less than the cost for cancer care or organ transplants (Schackman et al. 2006). The cost for premature birth can exceed $1 million. For example, Home Box Office has found that its health care program for gay partners cost 17 percent less than for heterosexual partners because there were no pregnancy costs. The city of Seattle found that domestic partners had lower overall claim costs and fewer medical visits than married employees. The city of West Hollywood found that claims ran lower than for married couples and there were negligible increased costs. Likewise, Berkeley and Santa Cruz found domestic partner costs to be equivalent to adding an equal number of married spouses (Becker 1995). Although insurance companies initially added surcharges to their premiums to companies providing domestic partnership programs, most have reduced or eliminated these charges once they learned that costs were no higher than they were for spouses of married employees (*Report of the CUNY Study Group on Domestic Partnerships* 1993).

Typically, enrollment in domestic partnership programs is low because: (1) many lesbian and gay employees are reluctant to come out of the closet at work for fear of experiencing discrimination; (2) domestic partnership benefits are considered taxable income by the IRS; and (3) most adults work, therefore the partner of a same-sex couple is often covered under his or her own employer's benefit program.

To claim costs as a reason to deny domestic partnership benefits is not fair. Employers do not bar employees from getting married or having children—both of which raise health care costs. Companies that care for their employees should treat all employees equitably.

Besides cost, a second major concern is that domestic partnership programs are open to abuse and fraud. Some believe that employees may attempt to exploit the system by enrolling sick friends or relatives. There are no reported cases of this happening. The process of registration helps preclude such a scenario. Employees also run the risk of reprisal or dismissal from employment for engaging in such practices. Finally, the act of registering for domestic partnership creates legal documents that can be used in tort actions for damages caused by fraud. Thus, fraud is not a real problem.

A third concern involves the fear of a potential backlash from other employees and customers, which is sometimes thought to be sufficient reason to deny domestic partnership programs. Experience has shown that there are usually positive reactions to the implementation of domestic partnership programs that far outweigh the negatives. One of the most visible examples of this was when the Walt Disney Company adopted domestic partnership benefits in 1996. The Southern Baptist Convention announced a boycott of Disney's products and services. Ultimately the boycott failed, as 70 percent of Americans rejected the idea of the boycott and fewer still actually participated (Morganthaus 1997).

A fourth obstacle to domestic partnerships is that many employers do not believe they have lesbian or gay employees and, therefore, do not believe they need to provide domestic partnership benefits. This is not true. Lesbians, gay men, and bisexuals, and transgendered, transsexual, and intersexed people are everywhere.

Tax Consequences

There are negative tax consequences to domestic partnership programs. Federal tax law does not recognize such relationships. Domestic partners who do not receive more than 50 percent of their support from their partners do not qualify as "dependents." Therefore, the benefits they receive become taxable income to the employee because the benefits are not excludable from the employee's gross income. Furthermore, the nonexempt benefits may be taxed at "fair market value." Health care costs are often very high and this could result in a significant amount of calculable income for which the employee would have a tax liability.

Legal Consequences

Domestic partnership registration creates an enforceable contract for partners to be jointly responsible for basic living expenses. The precise nature of this obligation is dependent upon the wording of state and city ordinances. It is unknown how this will be enforced. Creditors may be able to enforce agreements between domestic partners. For example, the city of San Francisco specifically requires domestic partners to be jointly responsible for basic living expenses that can be enforced by anyone to whom the expenses are owed.

Termination of the domestic partnership needs to be made with formal notice to the state or city if it has a registry, with the employee's company, and with any third party who may have relied upon the existence of the partnership. San Francisco requires couples to give written notice to a third party under penalty of perjury. In the event of failure to give notice, anyone who suffers a loss from the dissolution of the partnership may sue to recover actual damages.

The domestic partnership and civil union landscape has changed drastically with the advent of same-sex marriage. A number of other states enacted domestic partnerships (e.g., California, Oregon, Vermont, D.C., Maine, New Jersey, Connecticut, Washington, New Hampshire, Wisconsin, Colorado, Nevada, Rhode Island, Illinois, Delaware, and Hawaii). Many courts have recognized the inherent legal conflicts domestic partnership arrangement create and have either thrown the issue back to the legislature or supported same-sex marriage. With the acceptance of same-sex marriage in Massachusetts in 2003 and 16 other states embracing same-sex marriages by 2014, the issue of civil unions/domestic partnership as an alternative to full-blown marriage is becoming moot.

Chuck Stewart

See also: Civil Union; Same-Sex Marriage in the United States.

Further Reading

Becker, L. 1995. "Recognition of Domestic Partnerships by Governmental Entities and Private Employers." *National Journal of Sexual Orientation Law* 1(1): 91–104.

Donovan, J. M. 1998. "An Ethical Argument to Restrict Domestic Partnerships to Same-Sex Couples." *Law and Sexuality* 8: 649–670.

Kohn, S. 1999. *NGLTF Domestic Partnership Organizing Manual for Employee Benefits*. Washington, DC: National Gay and Lesbian Task Force.

Morganthaus, T. 1997. "Baptists vs. Mickey: Why the Boycott against Disney Faces Steep Odds." *Newsweek*, June 30, p. 51.

Nhan, Doris. 2012, May 1. Census: More in U.S. Report Nontraditional Households. *National Journal*.

Report of the CUNY Study Group on Domestic Partnerships, The. 1993. New York: City University of New York.

Schackman, B. R. et al. 2006. "The Lifetime Cost of Current Human Immunodeficiency Virus Care in the United States." National Center for Biotechnology Information, National Institute of Health. Available at: http://www.ncbi.nlm.nih.gov/pubmed/17063130. Accessed February 10, 2014.

United States Census. 2012, July 31. "Unmarried and Single Americans Week September 16–22, 2012." Profile America Facts for Features. Available at: http://www.census.gov/newsroom/releases/archives/facts_for_features_special_editions/cb12-ff18.html. Accessed February 9, 2014.

U.S. General Accounting Office. 1997. *Defense of Marriage Act Report*. OGC 97–16: 58. Washington, DC: Government Printing Office.

Don't Ask, Don't Tell: Homosexuality and the Military

The history of homosexuals in the military has a long and storied past. Starting back in the days of Greeks, it was traditionally known and accepted that there was not only homosexuality in the military, but it was also encouraged as it raised morale and emotional bonds between men so they would fight better on the battlefield (Hanson 2009, p. 124).

In the United States, that history is a little less affirming and progressively became oppressive, leading up to Don't Ask, Don't Tell (DADT) legislation in 1993. In fact it was argued that homosexuality was bad for unit cohesiveness and morale, which led to the first institutionalized ban on homosexuality in 1982. Prior to World War II, it was a more complex issue as

Former Army National Guard Lt. Dan Choi, an Arabic-speaking specialist dismissed through the "Don't Ask, Don't Tell" policy, comments on Proposition 8 outside the Beverly Hills hotel, where President Barack Obama attended a benefit dinner in Beverly Hills, California, on May 27, 2009. (AP Photo/Damian Dovarganes)

sodomy was illegal in most states and homosexuality was considered a mental illness.

From 1982 until DADT was signed into law, the military policy at the time was based off the Article 125 of the Uniform Code of Military Justice (UCMJ) enacted by the Department of Defense (DOD). This policy is still in the books but interpreted for cases of rape and sexual assault.

This policy reads:

(a) Any person subject to this chapter who engages in unnatural carnal copulation with another person of the same or opposite sex or with an animal is guilty of sodomy. Penetration, however slight, is sufficient to complete the offense.

(b) Any person found guilty of sodomy shall be punished as a court-martial may direct. (Article 125)

This policy was to dissuade homosexuals from serving in the military and would punish those who were caught in the act of sodomy with a court-martial. During this period, the chain of command would often participate in "witch hunts" where, if someone was even just suspected of being homosexual or engaging in homosexual acts, they were investigated, charged, and discharged from the service. There are several manners this could have been handled administratively: court-martials, Article 15s (very serious offenses in military law), and discharged with less than honorable or dishonorable discharges.

In 1993, DADT was implemented as a compromise by President Clinton with Congress. He had promised during his presidential campaign to eliminate the barriers for homosexual men and women to serve in the military and to end the witch hunts. He was quick to create the legislation, which was strongly supported by Americans and pro-gay activists, but it was met by opposition quickly, primarily from top officials in the military branches as well as by Senator Sam Nunn, a Democrat from Georgia who was head of the Senate Armed Services Committee. The legislation President Clinton brought up in Congress didn't have the steam to pass and he was afraid they would veto his executive order. So Clinton's administration and Congress worked together and came up with "Don't Ask, Don't Tell" policy that Clinton signed in to law on November 30, 1993.

The military didn't create or implement "Don't Ask, Don't Tell" policy, but it was created by Congress and written into law by an executive orders directed by the commander-in-chief (the president), at the time President William Clinton. DADT specifically directs that the military "don't ask, don't tell, don't pursue, and don't harass" and became effective October 1, 1993. Though this was supposed to liberate homosexuals in the military, it didn't offer full protection and acceptance in the military. It was a compromise that confirmed the military's stance that same-sex acts creates an unacceptable risk to the morale, order, and unit cohesion and thus continues to be a danger. But it was okay for gay and lesbian service members to continue to serve, as long as they do not engage in such acts or discuss their orientation to anyone. Technically it ordered the military to never ask if a soldier was gay nor could a serviceman or woman admit their sexual orientation, as was permitted under previous Article 125. It was intended to stop the witch hunts and allow a transition to a more affirming environment. Thus the name "Don't Ask, Don't Tell" came into existence.

Instead of the intended "liberation" of homosexuals to be able to serve in the military, instead, it created

Marine Staff Sgt. Eric Alva, center, then-House Speaker Nancy Pelosi of California, right, Commander Zoe Dunning, and others watch as President Barack Obama signs the Don't Ask, Don't Tell Repeal Act of 2010, at the Interior Department in Washington, D.C., on December 22, 2010. (AP Photo/Pablo Martinez Monsivais)

a hostile environment where homosexuals were forced to go into hiding and cover up their personal lives. It also fostered an environment where chain of commands had a written policy that could be used to persecuting gays in greater numbers. From 1993 until the Repeal of DADT, more than 14,500 service men and women were discharged from the military under DADT (Servicemen Legal Defense Fund). Ironically, prior to 1993, the discharges from the military for homosexuality were declining (Burrelli 2010).

Legal challenges from discharged service men and women continued with renewed intensity following the implementation of DADT in 1993.

Navy Lt. Gary Ross, right, and Dan Swezy exchange wedding vows on September 20, 2011, in Duxbury, Vermont. The two men recited their vows at the first possible moment after the formal repeal of the military's "Don't Ask, Don't Tell" policy. (AP Photo/Toby Talbot)

Despite large amount of legal cases nationwide, the Supreme Court of the United Stated directly never considered a challenge to any military policy about homosexuality, not even DADT (Feder 2013). However, it did consider several cases where discrimination against homosexuality was addressed that indirectly affected military policy. In 1986, in *Bowers v. Hardwick*, the Court held that there was no fundamental right to engage in homosexuality. This was upheld until the *Lawrence v. Texas* case in 2003 where "the Court held that the 'liberty' interest in privacy guaranteed by the due process clause of the Fourteenth Amendment protects a right for adults to engage in private, consensual homosexual conduct, expressly overruling Bowers's contrary conclusion.

In particular, the community's moral disapproval of homosexuality was no 'rational' justification for deploying the power of the state to enforce those views" (Feder 2013).

The reason the Supreme Court did not directly deal with DADT was that the Constitution directly assumes command of the military forces to the executive branch and also grants Congress the ability to raise and monetarily support an army. But nowhere does the Constitution designate the judicial arm of the government to deal with military affairs, so that is left to the military to self-govern with direction and input from the executive and legislative branches.

Despite their deference to overturning DADT, it is cases like *Lawrence v. Texas* that further embolden the legislative branch to introduce bills to amend or strike down DADT. In all cases, proposed bills either were struck down or never made it to the floor for a vote.

On January 27, 2010, in his State of the Union address, President Barack Obama publically acknowledged that he wanted to work with Congress "to finally repeal the law that denies gay Americans the right to serve the country they love because of who they are" (President Barack Obama 2010). This then started a chain reaction from all levels of the government. Shortly, several committees on Capitol Hill held hearing to discuss DADT, to include the House Military Personnel Subcommittee on March 3, 2010, and the Senate Armed Services Committee (SASC) on February 2 and March 18, 2010. During the SASC hearing, Secretary of Defense Robert Gates and the chairman of the Joint Chiefs of Staff, Admiral Michael Mullen, called for allowing homosexuals to serve openly without fear of recriminations. They then ordered a review by the Department of Defense (DOD) (McMichael 2010).

On September 9, 2010, Federal Judge Virginia A. Phillips ruled that the 1993 law was unconstitutional. In her statement, she exclaimed "the 17-year-old policy 'infringes the fundamental rights of United States service members and prospective service members' and violates their rights of due process and freedom of speech" (Schwartz 2010). Under judicial and White House pressure, DADT was repealed by the House of Representatives and Senate in December 2010 and signed into legislation by President Barack Obama on December 22, 2010. This policy became effective September 20, 2011.

With the repeal of DADT, all servicemen and woman are free to serve in the military openly, regardless of their sexual orientation. The culture in the military still stigmatizes homosexuality but commanders no longer have tools to punish gays and the freedom afforded to those who serve their country openly is encouraging.

The repeal of DADT has farther reaching effects beyond those for active-duty homosexual service members. A result of this repeal is that servicemen and women who were discharged previously can re-enlist into the military if they so choose. Veterans who were separated from the military with a "less than honorable" or "dishonorable" discharge because of DADT as well as the pre-DADT era can have their discharge upgraded to "honorable" status, their records amended, and receive VA benefits. There are two ways to do this:

(1) If they have been discharged due to Homosexual Conduct within the last 15 years, veterans can apply to the Army Discharge Review Board (ADRB) and have their case reviewed. (2) If it has been more than 15 years, veterans can apply to the Army Board for Correction of Military Records (ABCMR) to have their discharge reviewed. Based on the outcome of the review, their Re-entry code (RE) may be amended and remedies will be suggested such as correcting records, restoration to a grade, credit for time lost, and/or an increase in pay from no separation pay to half or full separation pay (Army Review Board Agency). Such remedies are to compensate for lost pay and time as a result of DADT being regulation at the time of discharge. Additionally, since the repeal of DOMA, legal spouses of veterans, regardless of sexual orientation or gender, can now enjoy VA medical, death, and burial benefits, when eligible.

Thanks in part to the many servicemen and women who fought legal, social, and emotional battles after discharge, and those who openly fought DADT while still serving, DADT is now earmarked for the dusty pages of history books. While some will remember First Lieutenant Daniel Choi who publically "outed" himself on national television on the *Rachel Maddow Show* and challenged DADT, many others names are lost (Maddow 2009). But their sacrifices will always be remembered and their hard work has paid off.

The military to this day is slowly integrating homosexual servicemen and women, most of whom were already serving their country with pride, albeit with only a part of their lives shared. The most intimate and personal aspects of their lives were "closeted" and oppressed. Those who braved being openly homosexual, or were caught physically or emotionally, were shamed, disciplined, and discharged. Gay men and women can now openly serve without fear of being targeted or harassed just for being who they are and their families can be openly proud of their spouses, partners, or parents without fear of losing a career and can no longer be denied benefits bestowed upon any dependent and spouse of military personnel.

Katiuscia O'Brian

See also: Historical Overview of Gay Rights and Issues: From the 1980s to the Present; Matlovich, Leonard (1943–1988).

Further Reading

Army Review Board Agency. n.d. DADT. Available at: http://arba.army.pentagon.mil/dadt.cfm. Accessed November 17, 2013.

Article 125. Uniformed Code of Military Justice. Available at: http://www.ucmj.us/sub-chapter-10-punitive-articles/925-article-125-sodomy. Accessed September 2, 2013.

Burrelli, David F. 2010. "'Don't Ask, Don't Tell': The Law and Military Policy on Same-Sex Behavior." Congressional Research Service. (2010). Available at: https://www.fas.org/sgp/crs/misc/R40782.pdf. Accessed November 18, 2013.

Feder, Jody. 2013. "'Don't Ask, Don't Tell': A Legal Analysis." Congressional Research Service.

Hanson, Victor Davis. 2009. *The Western Way of War: Infantry Battle in Classical Greece.* Oakland: University of California Press.

Maddow, Rachel. 2009, March 20. "'The Rachel Maddow Show' for Friday March 20, 2009 (Transcript)." MSNBC. Available at: http://www.nbcnews.com/id/29836340/. Accessed November 18, 2013.

McMichael, William H. "Mullen: Dropping 'Don't Ask' Is the Right Thing to Do." *Navy Time,* February 15, 2010, pp. 11, 14.

President Barack Obama. 2010, January 27. Remarks of the President in the State of the Union Address. White House Office of the Press Secretary.

Schwartz, John. 2010. "Judge Orders U.S. Military to Stop 'Don't Ask, Don't Tell'." *New York Times,* October 13, p. 1.

Servicemen Legal Defense Fund. n.d. "About Don't Ask Don't Tell." Available at: http://www.sldn.org/pages/about-dadt. Accessed September 13, 2013.

Duberman, Martin Bauml (1930–)

Duberman is a highly respected historian and gay rights activist. He has taught at Yale, Princeton, and the City University of New York (CUNY), where he has been distinguished professor of history since 1971, a post he now holds as emeritus distinguished professor. Duberman has written more than 20 books on a variety of historical topics, specializing in the struggles of minority groups, including blacks and gay men and lesbians. He was a founding member of the National Gay Task Force, the Gay Academic Union, and the Center for Lesbian and Gay Studies at CUNY.

Martin Duberman was born in New York City on August 6, 1930, the son of Joseph M. Duberman and the former Josephine Bauml. He earned his BA at Yale in 1952, and then an MA in 1953 and a PhD in history at Harvard in 1957. Duberman reports that he was sexually attracted to other men as far back as he can remember, but did not act on this feelings until his freshman year at Yale. He then entered a long period during which he tried to understand and deal with his homosexual feelings, an experience he has eloquently recounted in his 1991 book *Cures: A Gay Man's Odyssey.*

Duberman has held a series of increasingly prestigious academic appointments: instructor at Yale; Morse Fellow, bicentennial preceptor, and assistant professor of history at Princeton; and associate professor, professor, and now Distinguished Professor of History Emeritus at City University of New York (CUNY). In addition, he has been a prolific author, biographer, and playwright. His books on gay-related themes have included *Hidden from History: Reclaiming the Gay and Lesbian Past* (1989), coedited with Martha Vicinus and George Chauncey Jr., an anthology on gay and lesbian history; *About Time: Exploring the Gay Past* (1986), a collection of his essays on the young gay and lesbian movement; *Stonewall* (1994), Duberman's own account of the early years of the gay liberation movement; and *Midlife Queer: Autobiography of a Decade* (1996), a memoir dealing with the gay and lesbian movement during the 1970s. Duberman's book, *The Worlds of Lincoln Kirstein*, was one of two finalists for the 2007 Pulitzer Prize. His play *In White America* won the Drama Desk Award for Best Off-Broadway Production in 1963. Publishing Triangle granted Duberman the Bill Whitehead Award for Lifetime Achievement in 2009. In 2012, his book *Howard Zinn: A Life on the Left*, was published by the New Press. In May 2012, Amherst College awarded him an Honorary Doctorate in Humane Letters at its annual convention.

David E. Newton

See also: Activists; Center for Lesbian and Gay Studies (CLAGS).

Further Reading

Duberman, Martin Bauml. 2013. *The Martin Duberman Reader: The Essential Historical, Biographical, and Autobiographical Writings*. New York: The Free Press.

Duberman, Martin Bauml. 1993. *Stonewall*. New York: Dutton.

A female college student, one of more than 400 who moved into Mississippi to work in the Mississippi Project, a summer-long campaign whose main goal is to increase voter registration, holds the book *In White America* by Martin B. Duberman. (Bettmann/Corbis)

E

Endean, Steve (1949–1993)

Stephen R. Endean was born in Minneapolis, Minnesota, in 1949 and became interested in politics at an early age. He had hoped to pursue a career in politics but became convinced that such an option was not available to an openly gay man, as he intended to be. Instead, encouraged by the Stonewall riots of 1969, he chose a career in the gay rights movement.

Endean founded the Minnesota Committee for Gay Rights in 1971. Its first campaign was an effort to have an antidiscrimination bill passed by the Minnesota legislature. He supported himself for many years on a salary of about $300 a month as a lobbyist, supplemented by the income from a night job in a gay bar. Endean's efforts finally paid off two decades later when the Minnesota legislature adopted a gay rights bill in 1993.

Building off his efforts in Minnesota, Endean moved to Washington, D.C., and served as co-chair of the board of directors of the National Gay Task Force (later NGLTF). In 1978 he became executive director and lobbyist for the Gay Rights National Lobby. *The New York Times* reported in his 1993 obituary that when he took charge, "the struggling group had a single desk in another organization's office, a disconnected telephone and a pile of unpaid bills." Two years later, Endean's work had made possible a staff of 10 with an annual budget of $300,000.

In 1980 Endean founded the Human Rights Campaign Fund, an organization whose purpose was to lobby Congress on gay rights issues. By 1993, the fund had more than 75,000 contributors and a budget of $5 million.

Endean was present (albeit in a wheelchair) at the Minnesota State Capitol when the legislature passed the Minnesota GLBT Equal Rights law—an effort he started more than 20 years earlier. Endean died a few months later in Washington on August 4, 1993, at the age of 44 of HIV-related complications.

David E. Newton

See also: Human Rights Campaign (HRC); National Gay and Lesbian Task Force.

Further Reading

Griffin, Jr., Carl. 1975. "'No Compromise' Gay Coalition May Sink Rights Bill." *The Advocate*, May 7, p. 4.

Equal Access Act (EAA)

The goal of the Equal Access Act (EAA), passed by Congress in 1984, is to allow equal access to federally funded public secondary school facilities by all student groups. The law was initially lobbied by religious groups that wanted to ensure Bible study programs by students could be held on school grounds during lunch and after school. Ironically, EAA has been the major tool used by gay-straight alliances to organize in public schools—often to the displeasure of some religious groups.

The debate in Congress demonstrated that lesbian and gay student groups were considered a possibility and that they were to be given access to public schools equally with other groups. The bill, in its original form, addressed only the problem of schools barring religious groups. The bill was amended to include all extracurricular groups without preference. Debate

A student opens her arms to Will Uznanski, center, at Stratford High School in Connecticut during a Gay Straight Alliance meeting in 2002. About 20 students from Stratford High School met weekly with an advisor to talk about sexuality and antigay bigotry. (AP Photo/Douglas Healey)

in Congress showed an understanding that: (1) high school students are sophisticated enough to understand that having equal access does not imply governmental support or encouragement for a particular religion or thought; (2) an open policy does not turn schools into "battlegrounds for souls"; (3) schools may try to thwart the limited open forum aspect, but evaluation of their attempt to bypass the EAA will be conducted upon a review of their actions; and (4) claims by schools that "hecklers" would give schools the right to veto a particular group would be unacceptable. As Senator Denton stated:

Can students be prohibited from expressing their views if those who hold opposing views become angry and boisterous? No. . . . Can school officials keep students from forming an after-school club having a dissident point of view? No. . . .

Can the school prevent students from inviting a speaker to their club meeting because he or she is too controversial? No. (130 Cong. Rec. 19211–52)

Schools cannot deny equal access to students who wish to conduct a meeting if the reason for the denial is objection to the speech of the meeting. The EAA is triggered when secondary public schools that receive federal financial assistance offer a "limited open forum." A "limited open forum" is created when a school provides access to any (even just one) "noncurriculum-related student group to meet on school premises during non-instructional time" (Equal Access Act § b). The EAA does not define "noncurriculum-related student group," but the U.S. Supreme Court found in *Board of Education of Westside Community School v. Mergens* that Congress intended the act to have a reading and a low threshold for triggering its requirements. The justices concluded that the EAA is triggered if any student group is allowed access that is not directly related to the body of courses offered by the school.

The *Mergens* Court found four factors that defined "directly related":

1. The subject matter of the group is actually taught, or will soon be taught, in a regularly offered course;
2. The subject matter of the group concerns the body of courses as a whole;
3. Participation in the group is required for a particular course; or
4. Participation in the group results in academic credit.

Thus, the connection to the curriculum must be strong.

A number of clubs have not triggered the EAA. These include the French club, student government, school band, vocational clubs, and computer clubs (with some limits). Clubs that courts have determined to be noncurriculum related and, therefore, trigger the EAA have included a scuba diving club, chess clubs, the Peer Advocates (a service group with special education classes), the Key Club (a civic service club), the Pep Club, the Girls' Club, ski clubs, bowling clubs, the Special Kiwanis Youth Club, international clubs, varsity clubs, minority student unions, dance squads, and the Future Business Leaders of America.

A number of strategies have been attempted to circumvent the EAA:

- A school claimed that all clubs were school sponsored, not "student initiated," and, therefore, that the EAA did not apply. In *Pope v. East Brunswick Board of Education* the Third Circuit Court of Appeals found that the requirement of "student initiation" is not in that part of the statute that sets forth what causes the act to apply to a school. Thus, such a ploy does not circumvent the EAA.

- A school attempted to restrict student groups meeting during lunchtime. The Ninth Circuit Court of Appeals in *Ceniceros v. Board of Trustees of the San Diego Unified School District* determined that lunch time was "noninstructional time" and if one group was allowed to meet at lunchtime, then all groups must be allowed the same access.

Students at one school attempted to distribute religious materials to other students on one occasion. One court found that the EAA does not apply to this situation because a one-time effort does not constitute a "meeting."

Chuck Stewart

Further Reading

Kern, Alexander and Alexander, M. David. 2012. *American Public School Law*, 8th ed. Independence, KY: Wadsworth Cengage Learning, p. 258.

Macgillivray, Ian. 2007. *Gay-Straight Alliances: A Handbook for Students, Educators, and Parents*. New York: Harrington Park Press, pp. 37–53.

Murray, Joe. 2007. "Michigan High School Slams Door on Christian Student Group." *The Evening Bulletin*, May 23.

Public High School Prevents Student Christian Bible Club, Thomas More Law Center Sues. 2007, May 21. Thomas More Law Center.

Stewart, Chuck. 2001. *Homosexuality and the Law: A Dictionary*. Santa Barbara, CA: ABC-CLIO, pp. 14–15.

Exodus International

Since the advent of the field of psychiatry, there have been efforts by some therapists to effect a change in a client's sexual orientation—from LGBT to heterosexual (never the other way around). Exodus International was a large and influential organization formed in 1976 by Christian ministers who promoted sexual orientation change. The techniques for such change range from simple talk therapy, cognitive behavioral techniques, spiritual counseling, to medical shock therapy, surgeries, or outright torture. Sometimes heterosexual rape is used with the belief that having a heterosexual experience is all that is needed to turn someone straight. Some therapists who believe in sexual orientation change efforts (SOCE) claim they are "curing" or "repairing" the homosexual's sexual orientation. Medical experts as well as the foremost group that had promoted changing people's sexual orientation, Exodus International, have come to renounce and apologize for inaccurately interpreted research and harmful attempts to force people to change.

Exodus International was the most prominent SOCE organization in the world with a very large membership and fund-raising. From its founding in 1976, it grew to include over 120 local conservative Christian ministries in the United States and 150 ministries in 17 other countries. Since the 1970s, mental health and medical professional organizations have concluded that all sexual orientations are normal and that there is nothing to "cure." A large body of academic research has shown that homosexuality and, in fact, all variations of human sexual orientations and identities are healthy and contribute to healthy families. Every professional organization in the United States—the American Medical Association, the American Psychiatric Association, the American

Psychological Association, the American Pediatric Association, and hundreds more besides thousands of sex researchers—agrees with these findings.

Dr. Robert L. Spitzer was one of the spokespersons claiming that sexual orientation could be changed through psychological counseling. Spitzer was a mainstream psychiatrist and widely regarded Princeton University professor, often referred to as the "father" of modern psychiatry. With the removal of homosexuality from the *Diagnostic and Statistical Manual of Mental Disorders (DSM)* in 1973, published by the American Psychiatric Association, he and his team were tasked with rewriting the *DSM* in 1980. In doing so, homosexuality was treated as equal to heterosexuality.

Between 1970 and 1990, the religious Right and political conservatives teamed up. Promoting anti-gay laws proved successful at the voting box and with fund-raising. The National Association for Research & Therapy of Homosexuality (NARTH) in the United States became the primary source of "academic"

A billboard along I-64 in St. Louis announces that "Change Is Possible" for homosexuality on February 16, 2006. A conference aimed at helping Christians address homosexuality or change their lifestyle was held in St. Louis, on February 25. The event was sponsored by Focus on the Family and Exodus International, two Christian organizations. (AP Photo/James A. Finley)

Alan Chambers, president of Exodus International, answers a question during an interview inside a conference center near Black Mountain, North Carolina, on July 20, 2005. Chambers describes himself as someone who overcame unwanted same-sex attraction. (AP Photo/Alan Marler)

research that condemned homosexuality and actively promotes sexual orientation change. Similar organizations sprung up in many places in the country and world. Exodus International became the largest faith-based organization to claim success with SOCE and received significant backing from religious right organizations.

Self-described "ex-gay" protesters demonstrated at the AMA annual meeting in 1999. They were outraged that psychiatry was denying their experience and sought a change in the *DSM*. Dr. Spitzer heard their concerns and conducted a large research study

in 2000 with 200 men and women, some from Exodus International. Because of his work on the *DSM* years before, he was considered authoritative and unbiased. However, the research was flawed and he was warned not to publish it. In the study, he did not claim that sexual orientation was a choice nor that anyone could change. He did, however, claim that those who were highly motivated could change their sexual orientation.

The SOCE industry and conservatives jumped on Spitzer's research to prove their contention that SOCE was possible. Conservative politicians used the research to argue against antidiscrimination legislation and argue against same-sex marriage. The research was misused for political reasons.

Many academic researchers were critical of Spitzer's findings. For almost a decade he reflected on his work and heard the parade of legitimate researchers who found SOCE to be emotionally damaging and hurtful—sometimes leading to suicide in gay patients. Finally, in 2012, Spitzer, then in his 80s, issued a formal retraction and apology of his research. He admitted that he had misinterpreted his data.

Although Exodus International was a prominent sex-orientation change group, there had been controversies within the organization. Michael Bussee and Gary Cooper, two of the original founders, left the group in 1979. They divorced their wives and formed a loving same-sex relationship. They were critical of the hypocrisy perpetrated by the SOCE industry and maintained that no one was ever changed. Later, in 2000, Chairman John Paulk was seen in Washington, D.C., drinking and flirting at Mr. P's, a gay bar, and using the alias "John Clint." While working his way up in responsibility at Exodus International, Paulk would often give testimony describing himself as a drag queen and homosexual prostitute who had turned his life around. The name he used while working as a prostitute was John Clint. Paulk's picture was taken at Mr. P's and revealed to the press. Paulk was immediately expelled from Exodus International. Years later in 2013, Paulk renounced his former cause and stated that sexual orientation change cannot be achieved and such efforts are fraudulent.

After years of failure and secrets, Alan Chambers, president of Exodus International, addressed the Gay Christian Network in 2012 and stated the "99.9%" of all conversion therapies were unsuccessful and that participants in reparative therapy do not experience a change in their sexual orientation (Throckmorton 2012). He also apologized for misleading the public with the Exodus slogan "Change Is Possible." He further stated that conversion therapy was potentially harmful and does not work. In June 2013, Chambers released a notice to the press that the board of directors of Exodus International had voted to shut the organization down and apologized to the gay community for "years of undue judgment by the organization and the Christian Church as a whole." Now they want Exodus International to create a new ministry to work with other churches to create "safe, welcoming and mutually transforming communities" (Lopez 2013).

Chuck Stewart

See also: Africa's Gay Punishment Legislation: Involvement from U.S. Christian Factions; Sexual Orientation Change Efforts.

Further Reading

Lopez, Robert. 2013, June 19. "Exodus Ministry to Shut Down after Apology to Gay Community." *Los Angeles Times*. Available at: http://www.latimes.com/local/lanow/la-me-ln-exodus-ministry-to-shut-down-20130619,0,2132827.story. Accessed November 17, 2013.

Throckmorton, Warren. 2012, January 9. "Alan Chambers: 99.9% Have Not Experienced a Change in Their Orientation." *Patheos: Hosting the Conversation on Faith.* Available at: http://www.patheos.com/blogs/warrenthrockmorton/2012/01/09/alan-chambers-99–9-have-not-experienced-a-change-in-their-orientation/. Accessed November 17, 2013.

F

Faderman, Lillian (1940–)

Lillian Faderman received her BA and PhD from the University of California, Berkeley, and currently serves as a Distinguished Professor of English at California State University, Fresno. A pioneer in the field of lesbian history, Faderman's work has generated considerable controversy among historians of sexuality, primarily because of her argument that, prior to the rise of sexology, women's relationships with women, while undeniably emotionally intense and physically intimate, may not have been genitally sexual. In her 1979 article "Who Hid Lesbian History?" Faderman takes historians and literary scholars to task for having overlooked and suppressed evidence of women's love for other women, clearly expressed in the diaries and letters of women such as Emily Dickinson and Amy Lowell. Faderman continued the work of restoring to the historical record women's relationships with women in her 1981 monograph *Surpassing the Love of Men: Romantic Friendship between Women from the Renaissance to the Present*. Focusing on white middle- and upper-class women's romantic friendships during the eighteenth and nineteenth centuries, Faderman demonstrates the omnipresence of intense emotional relationships between women in American and European society. She documents the widespread cultural acceptance of these relationships prior to the rise of sexology, with women's emotional and romantic connections to other women being frequently lauded in fiction and the popular press.

Acceptance of love between women only went so far, however, as Faderman's 1983 monograph *Scotch Verdict* makes clear. In this work, she examines the 1811 case of two Scottish schoolmistresses, Jane Pirie and Marianne Woods, who sued the grandmother of one of their pupils for libel, after that pupil accused Pirie and Woods of having

Some of Lillian Faderman's article "Who Hid Lesbian History?" emerged from her study of Emily Dickinson, a mid-nineteenth century lyric poet. Faderman contended that Dickinson's diaries and letters show love between women. (Library of Congress)

Author Lillian Faderman attends Outwrite! 2013: A Celebration of LGBT Literary Pioneers at the West Hollywood Library on April 27, 2013, in West Hollywood, California. (Beck Starr/FilmMagic/Getty Images)

a sexual relationship. Although the case's male judges were clearly incredulous at the notion of female sexuality that existed independently of men, their pupil's accusation nonetheless ultimately cost Pirie and Woods both their school and their reputations. Faderman's 1991 monograph *Odd Girls and Twilight Lovers: A History of Lesbian Life in Twentieth Century America* focuses on the experience of lesbians from the rise of sexology through the sex wars of the 1980s. By creating the category of the lesbian, Faderman argues, sexologists at once pathologized women's relationships with women and gave women a new identity that enabled those who self-identified as lesbians to seek one another out and form lesbian-centered communities. Faderman details how women's conceptions of themselves, their sexuality, and their relationships with women altered over the course of the twentieth century, paying particular attention to how class shaped women's experiences. Throughout the monograph, Faderman maintains that there is nothing constant about lesbian identity, but rather that women's sense of sexual identity is profoundly and inevitably shaped by changing historical circumstances. *Odd Girls and Twilight Lovers: A History of Lesbian Life in Twentieth Century America* was reissued in 2012 by Columbia University Press.

In 1998, Faderman coauthored *I Begin My Life All Over: The Hmong and the American Immigrant* and followed this work with *To Believe in Women: What Lesbians Have Done for America* (1999), which argues that lesbian women made considerable, and largely neglected, contributions to the suffrage movement, the development of female universities, the rise of settlement houses, workers' rights campaigns, and the establishment of a female presence in the medical profession during the late nineteenth and early twentieth centuries. In 2003, Faderman published *Naked in the Promised Land: A Memoir*, which details her troubled relationship with her mother, who immigrated to America from Latvia in the 1920s, and Faderman's own coming-out process in the years prior to the gay liberation movement. Faderman coauthored *Gay L.A.: A History of Sexual Outlaws, Power Politics, and Lipstick Lesbians* (2006), an account of Los Angeles's lesbian and gay communities from Spanish settlement through the present. In addition to these works, she has co-edited two collections of American ethnic writing, *Speaking for Ourselves* (1969) and *From the Barrio* (1973), and a collection of lesbian writing: *Chloe Plus Olivia: An Anthology of Lesbian Literature from the 17th Century to the Present* (1994). In 1991, she published an important history of lesbian life in the twentieth century: *Odd*

Girls and Twilight Lovers: A History of Lesbian Life in Twentieth-Century America.

Holly M. Kent

See also: Committee on Lesbian and Gay History (CLAGS); Historical Overview of Gay Rights and Issues: From the 1980s to the Present.

Further Reading

Faderman, Lillian. 2012. *Odd Girls and Twilight Lovers: A History of Lesbian Life in Twentieth-Century America.* New York: Columbia University Press.

Faderman, Lillian. 1999. *To Believe in Women: What Lesbians Have Done for America: A History.* Boston: Houghton Mifflin.

Faderman, Lillian. 1995. "What Is Lesbian Literature? Forming a Historical Canon." In *Professions of Desire: Lesbian and Gay Studies in Literature*, ed. George E. Haggerty and Bonnie Zimmerman, pp. 49–59. New York: Modern Language Association of America.

Falwell, Jerry L. (1933–2007)

Jerry Falwell founded the Moral Majority and was one of the major forces representing fundamentalist Christian principles in U.S. politics. Falwell was born on August 11, 1933, in Lynchburg, Virginia. He received a bachelor's degree from the Baptist Bible College of Springfield, Missouri, in 1956 and was married two years later to Macel Pate (with whom he had three children).

Falwell founded the Thomas Road Baptist Church in Lynchburg in 1956, where he continued

Rev. Jerry Falwell speaks during the Christian Coalition of America Road to Victory 2000 conference in Washington, D.C., on September 29, 2000. (AP Photo/Stephen J. Boitano)

as pastor until his death in 2007. He saw the need for a Christian-based school of higher education and founded Liberty University in Lynchburg in 1971. Recognizing the power of radio and television, he hosted the *Old-Time Gospel Hour* television program for many years. Falwell condemned homosexuality and regularly claimed AIDS pandemic to LGBT issues. He stated, "AIDS is not just God's punishment for homosexuals, it is God's punishment for the society that tolerates homosexuals" (Press 2007).

In 1979, as a reaction to the political battle over homosexuality in Florida and elsewhere, he branched out into political action and founded the Moral Majority. Unlike the church or university or television programs, the Moral Majority allowed Falwell to directly participate in local and national elections. The Moral Majority was one of the major opponents of gay rights legislation in the United States. In 1989, the Moral Majority changed its name to the Liberty Federation.

Falwell wrote many books, with the most influential being *Listen, America!* (1980); *The Fundamentalist Phenomenon* (1981); *Champions for God* (1985); and his autobiography, *Strength for the Journey* (1987).

A national outcry occurred when Jerry Falwell blamed feminists, lesbians, and gays as well as others on national television for the bombing of the World Trade Center on September 11, 2001. Two days after the attack, Falwell was interviewed on Pat Robertson's *700 Club* TV show and stated,

> ACLU's got to take a lot of blame for this. And, I know that I'll hear from them for this. But, throwing God or successfully with the help of the federal court system, throwing God out of the public square, out of the schools. The abortionists have to bear some burden for this because God will not be mocked. And when we destroy 40 million little innocent babies, we make God mad. I really believe that the pagans, and the abortionists, and the feminists, and the gays and the lesbians who are actively trying to make that an alternative lifestyle, the ACLU, People For the American Way, all of them who have tried

to secularize America. I point the finger in their face and say " 'you helped this happen."

Pat Robertson nodded his head in agreement. There was an outcry from both conservatives and liberals condemning their actions. Both Falwell and Robertson made public corrections and apologized for their comment, but it only intensified the controversy.

Chuck Stewart

See also: Robertson, Pat (1930–); Schlafly, Phyllis Stewart (1924–). Documents: Homosexuality Is Unnatural (1979); AIDS as God's Punishment (1987); Congressman William Dannemeyer Opposes Gay Rights (1989); The Westboro Baptist Church and Its Message of Hate.

Further Reading

For a day-by-day accounting, see GLAAD New Pop, September 21, 2001, at http://h-net.msu.edu/cgi-bin/logbrowse.pl?trx=vx&list=H-Radhist&month=0109&week=d&msg=q%2BZKBco6NqiGhE8FFFWUwg&user=&pw=.

Press, Bill. 2007. "The Sad Legacy of Jerry Falwell." *Milford (Mass.) Daily News*, May 18.

Williams, Daniel K. April 2010. "Jerry Falwell's Sunbelt Politics: The Regional Origins of the Moral Majority." *Journal of Policy History* (Cambridge University Press) 22(2): 125.

Federal Employment Nondiscrimination Order

On May 28, 1998, President Clinton signed Executive Order 13087 that amended Section 1 of Executive Order 11478 (1969). The order reaffirmed the executive branch's long-standing internal policy that prohibits discrimination based upon sexual orientation within executive branch civilian employment. This was the first time a specific directive from any president prohibited discrimination based on sexual orientation. The order did not create any additional enforcement rights, such as the ability to proceed before the Equal Employment Opportunity Commission (EEOC), nor did it authorize affirmative action programs.

Chuck Stewart

White House senior adviser George Stephanopoulos, left, listens to Representative Barney Frank (D-MA) prior to addressing the National Lesbian and Gay Journalists Association on October 20, 1995, in Washington. The White House officials said that President Clinton would back legislation in Congress that would prohibit job discrimination against homosexuals. (AP Photo/Denis Paquin)

See also: Antidiscrimination Statutes.

Further Reading

Newton, David E. 2009. *Gay and Lesbian Rights: A Reference Handbook*, 2nd ed. Santa Barbara, CA: ABC-CLIO.

Feinberg, Leslie (1949–)

Leslie "Les" Feinberg is an internationally renowned transgender author and activist. Feinberg has worked consistently throughout hir life as an advocate for transgender people, building stronger alliances among lesbian, gay, bisexual, and transgender communities. Identifying as lesbian and transgender, ze has dedicated hir life and work to questioning societal structures based on an assumption of binary gender.

Perhaps Feinberg's most important contribution has been hir ability to draw connections between fighting against transphobia and struggles against all forms of oppression including classism, racism, sexism, homophobia, and imperialism.

Feinberg was born in Kansas City, Missouri, to Jewish working-class parents. One of hir early childhood memories is hearing about and identifying with Christine Jorgenson, a transsexual woman who garnered international notoriety when she traveled from the United States to Sweden for a sex-change operation. Feinberg's family moved to Buffalo, New York, where he grew up as a butch lesbian in the factories and bars of New York and Canada before the 1969 Stonewall riots. During the economic depression of the early 1970s, Feinberg took hormones and

Christine Jorgensen, formerly George W. Jorgenson, Jr., in 1952. Jorgensen's transformation played an influential role in Feinberg's early life. (Bettmann/Corbis)

lived as male. While in Buffalo, Feinberg became active in the Workers World Party. Today, Feinberg is a sought-after speaker and managing editor of *The Workers World* newspaper.

Feinberg's first novel, *Stone Butch Blues* (1993), received national and international acclaim, winning the American Library Association Gay and Lesbian Book Award and the Lambda Literary Award. The novel has been translated into Chinese, German, Italian, Dutch, Slovenian, and Hebrew. Feinberg's intent in writing *Stone Butch Blues* was to help readers comprehend oppressions they may not have experienced directly by witnessing them through the life of the protagonist. The novel is a poignant and unflinching portrayal of a working-class butch, Jess Goldberg, as she struggles to survive and build community during the post–McCarthy era. Contrary to popular belief, *Stone Butch Blues* is not autobiographical.

Feinberg's second publication, *Transgender Warriors* (1996), is a sweeping historical documentation of gender variance and a treatise on the origins of transgender oppression. Mixing personal narrative, history, and images, *Transgender Warriors* argues that the current oppression of transgender people is tied directly to the rise of patriarchy and class divisions within society. *Trans Liberation*, Feinberg's third book, is a compilation of hir speeches and written portraits of transgender, intersexed, and allied activists. Written for a general audience, this book frames transgender liberation as part of a larger political movement to end all forms of identity-based oppression. Feinberg's most recent novel, *Drag King Dreams* (2006), is reminiscent of *Stone Butch Blues*, featuring gender queer protagonist Max Rabinowitz coming to political consciousness in post–September 11 New York City. Most significantly, this novel connects antiwar and anti-Arab discrimination to working-class and queer struggles for greater freedom.

Feinberg, June Arnold, and some other writers choose either to avoid the use of pronouns, or to invent non-gendered ones. This is part of their strategy to engage readers in a deconstruction of the stereotyping dependent upon gender roles in American society.

Lena McQuade

See also: Transgender Children.

Further Reading

Abolishgender. Available at: http://community.livejournal.com/abolishgender/profile. Accessed July 5, 2008.

Califia, Patrick. 2003. *Sex Changes: The Politics of Transgenderism*. San Francisco: Cleis Press.

Edwards, Mac, ed. 1999. *The Construction of Gender* (SIECUS Report) 28(1). Available at: http://www.iiav.nl/ezines/email/SiecusReport/1999/Oct-Nov.pdf.

Halberstam, Judith. 1998. *Female Masculinity*. Durham, NC: Duke University Press.

Transgender Warrior. Leslie Feinberg. Available at: http://www.transgenderwarrior.org/

Foucault, Michel (1926–1984)

Michel Foucault brought academic research and language concerning sexual deconstruction to queer theory and AIDS activism. Foucault was born in Poitiers, France, on October 15, 1926. He was the son of an eminent surgeon and excelled in school. In 1946 he attended Ecole Normale Supérièure and was the fourth-highest-ranked student. There he received his *license* in philosophy in 1948 and in psychology in 1950; he was awarded diplomas in psychopathology in 1952. He taught in France, Sweden, Poland, and Germany and returned to France in 1960 as head of the Philosophy Department at the University Claremont-Ferrard. There he published his landmark work *Madness and Civilization* (1965). For this book he won the *doctorate d'état*. He argued that "madness" is an invention of the age of reason.

In that same year, Foucault met Daniel Defret, a philosophy student 10 years his junior. They formed a relationship that lasted more than 18 years. It would be Defret's political activism that influenced Foucault's future theoretical work.

In 1966, Foucault's second major work, *The Order of Things*, became a best-seller in France and made Foucault a household name. The combination of economics, the natural sciences, and linguistics in the eighteenth and nineteenth centuries was, in his opinion, coming to an end. He predicted that "man" (the construct) would be "erased, like a face drawn in sand at the edge of the sea" (Russell 1995, p. 132).

Foucault's influential work that has impacted gay and lesbian thought was his monumental unfinished project *The History of Sexuality. Volume 1: An Introduction*, which caused much controversy when it was released in 1976. The second and third volumes—*The Uses of Pleasure* and *The Care of the Self*—came out just before his death in 1984.

It was Foucault's experiences in San Francisco during 1975 when he was teaching at the University California, Berkeley, that influenced the development of *The History of Sexuality*. He was impressed by liberated gay sexuality, particularly in the bathhouses. He wrote: "I think that is politically important that

Michel Foucault at the radio broadcast studio Europe 1 in Paris, France, on December 16, 1981. (AP Photo/Alexis Duclos)

sexuality be able to function as it functions in the bath houses. You meet men there who are to you as you are to them: nothing but a body with which combinations in production of pleasure are possible. You cease to be imprisoned in your own face, in your own past, in your own identity" (Russell 1995, p. 133).

The History of Sexuality articulated what is known as the theory of social constructionism. It states that sexuality is far from being "natural" and unmediated. Rather, it is a cultural construction that varies considerably from culture to culture and over time. Our modern notions of gay and lesbian, of homosexual and heterosexual, are comparatively recent inventions. Michel Foucault died on June 25, 1984, in Paris from complications resulting from AIDS.

Chuck Stewart

See also: Duberman, Martin Bauml (1930–); Rich, Adrienne (1929–2012).

Further Reading

Foucault, Michel. 1990. *The History of Sexuality*. 3 vols. New York: Vintage.

Frank, Barney (1940–)

Barney Frank was an openly gay Democratic Congress member from the state of Massachusetts who wielded significant power in the House of Representatives from 1981 to 2013. Born in Bayonne, New Jersey, on March 31, 1940, Frank earned his bachelor's degree from Harvard College in 1962 and then entered a doctoral program in political science. He left graduate school in 1967 to become involved in Kevin White's campaign for mayor of Boston. White was elected and appointed Frank as his executive assistant. That allowed Frank an inside look at the workings of politics in Boston and in Massachusetts.

Frank won election to the Massachusetts House of Representatives in 1972 and earned a reputation as being very outspoken, extremely liberal, and sometimes one of the most abrasive personalities in the state. He easily won reelection in 1974 and 1976. Frank weathered a number of very close elections, each time improving his winning margin. Frank ran for the U.S. House of Representatives for the 4th congressional district in 1980 and won by a small margin. Frank was known for his quick wit and liberal/progressive stance.

Representative Barney Frank (D-MA) gestures during his news conference on his retirement on Capitol Hill in Washington, D.C., on November 29, 2011. Frank, a gay pioneer in Congress, married Jim Ready, his longtime partner from Maine in 2012. (AP Photo/Pablo Martinez Monsivais)

In 1989, the conservative *Washington Times* discovered and reported on a male prostitute, Steve Gobie, who was living in Frank's home at the time. *The Times*' investigation discovered that Gobie had used Frank's apartment to operate a bisexual prostitution business. Frank claimed not to know anything about the illegal behavior, but he nevertheless came under investigation by the House Ethics Committee. The House officially reprimanded Frank by a vote of 408–18. Ironically, Larry Craig, Republican, led the attempt to expel Frank from the Congress. Larry Craig would be arrested and convicted in 2007 for soliciting gay sex in an airport bathroom.

After the incident, Frank spoke out more often on gay and lesbian issues. In the early years of Frank's political activism, he said very little about his own personal life other than he lived with Herb Moses (who was an economist and LGBT activist). Their relationship ended amicably in 1998. Disclosure of his homosexuality has had little effect on his career. In 2006, incoming House Speaker Nancy Pelosi and Barney Frank were accused by Representative John Hostettler (R-IN) of having a "radical homosexual agenda"; Frank quipped, "I do have things I would like to see adopted on behalf of LGBT people: they include the right to marry the individual of our choice; the right to serve in the military to defend our country; and the right to a job based solely on our own qualifications. I acknowledge that this is an agenda, but I do not think that any self-respecting radical in history would have considered advocating people's rights to get married, join the army, and earn a living as a terribly inspiring revolutionary platform" (News Release from Barney Frank 2008).

Although Frank is openly gay and promotes gay rights legislation, he has sometimes been chastised by lesbian and gay civil rights leaders. For instance, the debate over President Bill Clinton's promise to revoke the ban on gays and lesbians in the armed forces resulted in Frank supporting Clinton's compromise. Frank explained this as being an expedient decision. Frank continues living in Newton, Massachusetts, with his husband, Jim Ready, whom he married in 2012. Their marriage was the first same-sex marriage by a sitting Congressman.

Chuck Stewart

See also: Baldwin, Tammy (1962–).

Further Reading

Frank, Barney. 2008, August 1. News release from Barney Frank. U.S. House of Representatives.

Full Faith and Credit Clause

The U.S. Constitution, Article IV, Section 1, reads, "Full Faith and Credit shall be given in each State to the public Acts, Records, and judicial Proceedings of every other State." This has been interpreted to mean that each state must treat the judgments of other states as the judgment would be treated in the state in which it was made. The clause is a "nationally unifying force" (*Magnolia Petroleum Co. v. White*) that recognizes that states are required to "sacrifice particular local powers as the price of membership in a federal system" of government (*Sherrer v. Sherrer*, 356).

However, there are limits to the power that the federal government can exert over states to accept one another's laws. Judgments of other states do not need to be respected if they are (1) "obnoxious" to the public policy of the state or (2) if the state can show that there are important, rather than merely legitimate, state interests for rejecting the other state's claim. When courts are faced with competing state interests and laws, this becomes a choice of law.

Choice of law is a notoriously murky area. It is sometimes difficult to determine which state's laws apply to a particular situation. In general, the Hague court explained that "if a state has only an insignificant contact with the parties and the occurrence or transaction, application of its law is unconstitutional" (*Allstate Insurance Co. v. Hague*, at 310–11). Furthermore, courts have recognized that frequently the laws of one state and the contrary laws of another state may apply equally. Unfortunately, the U.S. Supreme Court has not stepped in to help clear up the

Margaret Mueller, right, and Charlotte Stacey at their home in Norwalk, Connecticut, in 2006. Connecticut's highest court then ruled that some legal rights of same-sex couples predate the state's approvals of civil unions in 2005 and gay marriage in 2008, a decision that gay rights supporters call the first of its kind in the country. The case involved Mueller and Stacey who had a civil union in Connecticut in 2005 and got married in Massachusetts in 2008 after 23 years together under that state's gay marriage law, shortly before the Connecticut Supreme Court approved gay marriage. (AP Photo/ Douglas Healey)

confusion over the Full Faith and Credit Clause. The Court believes such conflicts are "unavoidable" and has left it for other courts to "determine for [themselves] the extent to which the statute of one state may qualify or deny rights asserted under the statue

of another" (*Allstate Insurance Co. v. Hague*, at 547). The Court has decided that the alternative to this confusion is worse.

The prospect of same-sex marriages set off a storm of controversy nationwide. Confusion over the Full Faith and Credit Clause led Congress to enact the Defense of Marriage Act (DOMA) in 1996. It was clear, however, from the debate in Congress that there was no clear understanding of how the current system works. DOMA (as well as legislation enacted in many states) defined marriage as the union between one man and one woman and allowed states to not recognize same-sex marriages of couples who move into their state. This was unnecessary since states already possessed this power. When federal DOMA was enacted, many lawsuits were filed. Some courts supported DOMA, whereas other found it in violation of the Due Process Clause of the Fifth Amendment. Almost 17 years later, in 2013, the U.S. Supreme Court invalidated Section 3 of DOMA specifically because it violated the Due Process Clause (*United States v. Windsor*). This decision affects only federal DOMA and not the individual state law. Now that the federal government is out of the picture for enforcing discriminatory laws against same-sex couples; it will be left to states to see how they interpret and enforce the Full Faith and Credit Clause.

Chuck Stewart

See also: Defense of Marriage Act (DOMA); Same-Sex Marriage in the United States.

Further Reading

Allstate Insurance Co. v. Hague, 449 U.S. 302, 310–11 (1981).

Magnolia Petroleum Co. v. White, 320 U.S. 430, 439 (1943).

Sherrer v. Sherrer, 334 U.S. 343, 355 (1948).

United States v. Windsor, 570 U.S. ___ (2013) (Docket No. 12–307).

G

Gender-Motivated Violence Act (GMVA)

The Gender-Motivated Violence Act (GMVA) is a subsection of the federal Violence against Women Act (VAWA) of 1994. The VAWA was signed into law by President Bill Clinton and codified into 42 U.S.C. sections 13701 through 14040. It provided $1.6 billion toward investigation and prosecution of violent crimes committed against women besides setting prison and mandatory restitution against those convicted. The law established the Office on Violence against Women within the Department of Justice. The act was drafted by the office of Senator Joe Biden (D-DE) with broad support from both Democrats and Republicans. The act was modified in 2000 when the U.S. Supreme Court ruled part of the act unconstitutional (the provision allowing women the right to sue their attackers in federal court) as a violation of state rights. VAWA was reauthorized by Congress in 2000, 2005, and, after long legislative battles mostly concerning the inclusion of LGBT people, in 2013.

The section on Gender-Motivated Violence has caused legislators and courts the most confusion. They often conflate the concepts of sex, gender, and gender identity. Until recently, courts have interpreted Title VII of the Civil Rights Act of 1964 as *not* applying to cases involving people between the sexes (intersexed) or transitioning from one sex to another (transsexuals).

Douglas Schwenk, a self-identified preoperative transsexual who went by the name of "Crystal" and dressed as a woman, received repeated unwanted sexual overtures from prison guard Robert Mitchell. Mitchell attempted to rape Crystal anally in her prison cell. She filed a federal lawsuit claiming violation of her civil rights under the Eighth Amendment ("cruel and unusual punishment") of the Constitution and the GMVA (*Schwenk v. Hartford*, 2000).

Judge Stephen Reinhardt of the Ninth Circuit Court of Appeals concluded that Schwenk was protected under the Eighth Amendment because precedent had been set in prior transsexual prisoner cases (*Farmer v. Brennan*, 1994). He also rejected Mitchell's argument that the GMVA did not apply to the case because it was part of the VAWA and Schwenk was a man. Reinhardt noted that members of Congress made statements that supported the interpretation of the GMVA as protecting all residents of the United States from gender-motivated violence.

Reinhardt went on to consider if "gender identity" came within the meaning of gender-motivated violence. Reinhardt reviewed the previous cases testing Title VII. He believed the limitations transsexuals faced in achieving standing to sue were effectively swept away by the Supreme Court's 1989 decision in *Price Waterhouse v. Hopkins*. In that case, a woman was denied a partnership in an accounting firm because she was perceived to be inadequately feminine in her appearance and behavior. The Supreme Court ruled that discrimination using sexual stereotypes about gender roles violated the ban on sex discrimination. Reinhardt found that the Supreme Court had, in fact, collapsed the concept of sex and gender into one broad category—gender identity.

Because Title VII had treated sex and gender separately, this was a groundbreaking conclusion. Reinhardt concluded that under Title VII, and, by extension, under the GMVA, discrimination or violence aimed at a person because of his or her gender identity would violate those statutes. In effect, this decision gives transsexuals and the issue of gender identity federal protection—something lesbians and gay men have failed to achieve.

Because Schwenk's case was brought on grounds of the Eighth Amendment and the GMVA, Reinhardt's discussion on Title VII is not technically binding, but it has alerted the courts under the Ninth Circuit that discrimination against transsexuals in employment and other areas may violate Title VII. Likewise, this decision makes it unnecessary to add "gender identity" to the Employment Nondiscrimination Act (ENDA) as it will already be covered under Title VII. It is expected that Mitchell's lawyers will appeal the decision and other judges will look closely at this controversial extension of Title VII. Also, this decision does not address people who do not conform to gender roles.

Chuck Stewart

See also: Title VII.

Further Reading

Farmer v. Brennan, 511 U.S. 825 (1994).

Harris, Sheryl I. n.d. "Employment Discrimination Protections for Transgender People in California." The Legal Aid Society. Available at: http://www.transgenderlaw.org/resources/caoverview.htm. Accessed February 11, 2014.

Price Waterhouse v. Hopkins, 490 U.S. 228 (1989).

Schwenk v. Hartford, 204 F. 3d 1187—Court of Appeals, 9th Circuit 2000.

Gittings, Barbara (1932–2007)

Gittings was a pioneer activist in the young lesbian and gay rights movement of the 1950s. She founded the New York City chapter of the Daughters of Bilitis (DOB) in 1958 and served as editor of the organization's magazine, *The Ladder*, from 1958 to 1966. During the 1950s and 1960s, Gittings was visible at virtually every public protest on the behalf of gay and lesbian rights.

Although not a librarian herself, she found herself at home in the gay and lesbian caucus of the American Library Association founded in 1970. She was particularly interested in developing positive images of lesbians and gay men in literature available to the general public. In 1972, she was a leader in the effort to have the American Psychiatric Association remove homosexuality from its list of mental disorders, an effort that was eventually successful.

Barbara Gittings was born in Vienna, Austria, on July 31, 1932. Her father was a member of the diplomatic service, stationed in Austria at the time. Upon returning to the United States, she attended high school in North Carolina and Maryland. After graduation, she entered Northwestern University to study drama. Her experience at Northwestern was a disaster as she discovered her erotic interest in other women. She became so engrossed in attempting to learn more about homosexuality, spending endless hours at the library, that she eventually dropped out of college and moved to Philadelphia, where she continued to look for additional information—especially positive information—about homosexuality.

During a visit to California in 1956, Gittings met Del Martin and Phyllis Lyon, founders of the DOB. Martin and Lyon convinced Gittings to return to New York to form a local chapter of DOB. For many years, she supported herself in a variety of jobs, including 10 years as a mimeograph operator for an architectural firm, while devoting her real energies to the gay and lesbian movement. In addition to her local efforts, Gittings was involved in national organizations, such as the East Coast Homophile Organization (ECHO) and the North American Conference of Homophile Organizations (NACHO).

Gittings met her partner, Kay Tobin Lahusen, in 1961, and they lived together until Gittings's death on February 18, 2007. In her later years, she continued her activist efforts, working to get the American Association of Retired Persons to provide health insurance to same-sex couples at the same price as for opposite-sex couples. The American Library Association has named its award for the best gay or lesbian novel of the year for her, and the Gay and Lesbian Alliance Against Defamation has established the Barbara Gittings Award to honor organizations and individuals that develop positive media images of gay men and lesbians.

David E. Newton

See also: Daughters of Bilitis; Historical Overview of Gay Rights and Issues: From Pre-Columbian Times to the 1970s; Lyon, Phyllis (1924–); Martin, Del (1921–2008).

Further Reading

Bullough, Vern, ed. 2002. *Before Stonewall: Activists for Gay and Lesbian Rights in Historical Context.* York, UK: Harrington Park Press.

Gallo, Marcia. 2006. *Different Daughters: A History of the Daughters of Bilitis and the Rise of the Lesbian Rights Movement.* New York: Carrol & Graf Publishers.

Katz, Jonathan. 1976. *Gay American History: Lesbians and Gay Men in the U.S.A.* New York: Crowell (now HarperCollins).

Marcus, Eric. 2002. *Making Gay History: The Half-Century Fight for Lesbian and Gay Equal Rights.* New York: Perennial Press (now HarperCollins).

Tobin, Kay and Wicker, Randy. 1975. *The Gay Crusaders.* San Francisco: Arno Press.

Kay Tobin Lahusen, 82, an early photographer of the gay rights movement, poses for a photograph with a portrait of her late partner Barbara Gittings on May 10, 2012, in Kennett Square, Pennsylvania. (AP Photo/Matt Rourke)

H

Hall, Radclyffe (1880–1943)

Radclyffe's Hall's book *The Well of Loneliness* (1928) was banned in Britain and caused far-ranging discussions of the topic of lesbianism in the United States. Hall was born Margaret Radclyffe-Hall Bournemouth in Hampshire, England, on August 12, 1880. She came from a very wealthy family and was educated at King's College, London. She wore very short hair and men's clothing and was known to her friends as John. By age 27, she is reported to have "probably loved more women than she had read books" (Russell 1995, p. 114). At that time, she met Mabel Batten (a woman 20 years her senior), fell in love, and moved in with her.

At a London tea party in 1915, they met Una, Lady Troubridge, an admiral's wife. Batten unexpectedly died a few months later from a heart attack. This facilitated the development of a close relationship between Hall and Troubridge that lasted for the next 30 years.

Hall wrote and published a considerable volume of poetry and a set of short stories with lesbian themes in 1924. Soon after she won a number of coveted prizes for her writing. In 1928 *Covici-Friede (New York)* published *The Well of Loneliness*. For its time, it was a sexually explosive story of a masculine girl who loves and loses women. Although the book seems very tame by today's standards, it was declared obscene by London magistrate Chartres Biron. He stated, "The better an obscene book is written, the greater is the public to whom it is likely to appeal. The more palatable the poison, the more insidious it is" (Russell 1995, p. 115). He ordered the police to destroy all copies of the book.

The book was initially withheld in the United States but eventually was published and distributed. For many women, *The Well of Loneliness* was a

Radclyffe Hall in her garden with her dog Colette. Hall won the Prix Femina and the James Tait Black Memorial Prize for her novel. (Bettmann/Corbis)

beacon of light in an otherwise dark time for lesbians. For years it was known as "the lesbian Bible." Today, the book is difficult to read, couched as it is in old terminology and early-twentieth-century vernacular.

Chuck Stewart

See also: Carpenter, Edward (1844–1929); Daughters of Bilitis; Historical Overview of Gay Rights and Issues: From Pre-Columbian Times to the 1970s; Wilde, Oscar (1854–1900).

Further Reading

Russell, Paul. 1995. *The Gay 100: A Ranking of the Most Influential Gay Men and Lesbians*. New York: Kensington Books.

Hay, Henry (Harry) (1912–2002)

Harry Hay is considered by many to be the founder of the modern gay rights movement. Hay was born on April 7, 1912, in Worthing Sussex, England. His family was American and returned to Los Angeles in 1917. He graduated from Los Angeles High School with honors in 1929 and worked as an apprentice for a local attorney's office. At the age of 17, he enticed older gentlemen for sex at the notorious Pershing Square in downtown Los Angeles.

From one of these older men, Hay learned of the Society for Human Rights formed in Chicago many years earlier. The society was the earliest gay rights group in the United States. Hay found the idea of men getting together for anything other than sex "an eye opener of an idea" (Newton 1994, p. 69).

He enrolled in the Drama Department at Stanford University in 1930. Hay was tired of hiding his sexual orientation and told his friends. Many avoided contact with him, but his closest friends were not perturbed by the information. Hay quickly realized that acting was unlikely to provide a living for him, so he became active in guerrilla theater productions focused on workers' rights and demonstrations. From there he joined the Communist Party, working as union organizer and a developer of cultural projects for the next 15 years. The party was decidedly antihomosexual, however, and under its pressure, Hay married another

party member, Anita Platky. Their marriage lasted for 15 years, producing two daughters.

In 1948 during a "beer bust" at the University of Southern California, Hay and a group of gay friends developed the idea of an organization named Bachelors for Wallace in support of presidential candidate Henry Wallace of the Progressive Party. Hay realized that gay men needed to organize themselves to combat the rising tide of Senator Joseph McCarthy's anticommunist and antihomosexual campaign. Two years later, Bob Hull, Chuck Rowland, and Dale Jennings, along with Hay, founded the International Bachelors Fraternal Order for Peace and Social Dignity. Later the organization was renamed the Mattachine Society. The Mattachine Society grew and became the longest-lived homophile organization in the United States. It has been at the forefront of activism on behalf of freedom of the press and archiving gay history.

Hay was instrumental in organizing the first gay pride parade in Los Angeles (and perhaps the nation) and other political actions that put Los Angeles at the forefront of gay liberation in the 1960s. He and his lover John Burnside, with whom he formed the Circle of Loving Companions, opened a kaleidoscope factory. The Stonewall Riots in New York in 1969 did not impress Hay. As far as he was concerned, the East Coast was finally catching up with Los Angeles. But Hay got caught up in the excitement of the times and was elected chair of the Southern California Gay Liberation Front in 1969 and hosted "Gay-In" and "funky dances" despite police warnings against such activities since same-sex couple dancing was illegal under California law at the time.

In 1970, Hay and Burnside moved their mail-order kaleidoscope factory to New Mexico. The area had always enchanted Hay ever since traveling there in the 1950s on his research into berdache. He became increasingly interested in spiritual issues and formed the Radical Faeries—a movement devoted to spiritual truth, ecology, and gay life. The first gathering of the Radical Faeries was held in the Arizona Desert in 1978 with more than 200 men in attendance. The Radical Faeries movement grew, but, like the Mattachine experience, Hay's politics came in conflict with many of the Faeries and he was ousted from its leadership.

Spirit of Stonewall (SOS) leaders talk to reporters during a news conference inside the Stonewall Inn in New York's Greenwich Village on June 24, 1994. From left are drag queen activist Glenn Belverio, who goes by the name Glennda Orgasm; Bill Dobbs, a New York gay activist; Harry Hay of Los Angeles, founder of Mattachine Society and the Radical Faeries; and Charley Shivley of Boston, editor of *Fag Rag*. (AP Photo/Marty Lederhandler)

In their later years, Hay and Burnside were provided housing and care as a tribute for his pioneering work by the gay community. Hay died in San Francisco, October 24, 2002.

Chuck Stewart

See also: Historical Overview of Gay Rights and Issues: From Pre-Columbian Times to the 1970s; Mattachine Society.

Further Reading

D'Emilio, John. 1983. *Sexual Politics, Sexual Communities: The Making of a Homosexual Minority in the United States, 1940–1970*. Chicago: The University of Chicago Press.

Hay, Harry, with Will Roscoe, ed. 1996. *Radically Gay: Gay Liberation in the Words of Its Founder*. Boston: Beacon Press.

Katz, Jonathan. 1977. "The Founding of the Mattachine Society: An Interview with Henry Hay." *Radical America* 11(4): 27 40.

Miller, Neil. 1995. *Out of the Past: Gay and Lesbian History from 1869 to the Present*. New York: Vintage Books.

Timmons, Stuart. 1990. *The Trouble with Harry Hay*. Boston: Alyson Publications.

White, Todd. 2009. *Pre-Gay LA*. Chicago: University of Illinois Press.

Helms, Jesse (1921–2008)

For more than 30 years, Jesse Helms had been the most outspoken opponent of gay and lesbian rights in the U.S. Senate.

Senate Foreign Relations Committee chairman senator Jesse Helms (R-NC) makes his opening statement at Richard Holbrooke's confirmation hearing on June 17, 1999. (AP Photo/Joe Marquette)

Born on October 18, 1921, in Monroe, North Carolina, Helms received his bachelor's degree from Wake Forest University. He served in the U.S. Navy during World War II and after the war took a job with *The Raleigh North Carolina Times*. He later became city editor. From 1948 to 1970 he was the administrative assistant to a number of U.S. senators, executive director of the North Carolina Bankers Association, and an executive vice president and vice chairman of the Capitol Broadcasting Company.

He became disenchanted with the Democratic Party and switched to the Republican Party in 1970. He was elected U.S. senator in 1972 and became one of the most powerful conservative voices in the U.S. Senate.

Helms consistently blocked gay and lesbian rights legislation in the Senate. For example, in 1990 he was one of only four senators to vote against the Hate Crime Statistics Act. He believed the U.S. Congress was being "hoodwinked" into adopting legislation that would promote homosexuality. Helms was also a major opponent of AIDS research and education. In 1990, he attempted to persuade the U.S. Senate to amend the Americans with Disabilities Act (ADA) to permit restaurant owners to discharge HIV-infected individuals, but he was unsuccessful. Helms retired from politics in 2002, announcing that he had had a change of heart with regard to AIDS funding but not homosexuals. He died in 2008 in Raleigh, North Carolina.

Chuck Stewart

See also: Frank, Barney (1940–).

Further Reading

Clarke, Patsy, Eloise Vaughn, Nicole Brodeur, and Allan Gurganus. 2001. *Keep Singing: Two Mothers, Two Sons, and Their Fight Against Jesse Helms*. New York: Alyson Books.

Furgurson, Ernest B. 1986. *Hard Right: The Rise of Jesse Helms*. New York: Norton.

Levy, Alan Howard. 1987. *Government and the Arts: Debates over Federal Support of the Arts in America from George Washington to Jesse Helms*. Lanham, MD: University Press of America.

Link, William A. 2008. *Righteous Warrior: Jesse Helms and the Rise of Modern Conservatism*. London: St. Martin's Press.

Najafi, Yusef. 2005. "Helms Regrets AIDS Stance: Former Senator 'Wrong' on AIDS Funding Because Families Hurt." *The Washington Blade*, June 17.

Hirschfeld, Magnus (1868–1935)

Hirschfeld was a physician, sex researcher, and early advocate for the rights of gay men and lesbians. In 1897, he and two friends, Max Spohr and Erich Oberg, founded the *Wissenschaftlich-humanitäres Komitee*

(Scientific-Humanitarian Committee) in Berlin. The purpose of the organization was to work for social recognition of gay men, lesbians, and transgendered persons and against their persecution by the government and its agencies. It was the leading voice for gay and lesbian rights in Germany until it was suppressed by the Nazi Party in 1933. Hirschfeld seemed possessed of limitless energy, devoting every moment of his life to writing, speaking, and organizing for the rights of lesbians, gay men, and transgendered persons. In 1913, he was one of the founders of the Medical Society for Sexual Science and Eugenics. Five years later he established the Magnus Hirschfeld Foundation for Sex Research and then, a year later, the Institute for Sexual Science.

Hirschfeld was born in Kolberg, Germany, on May 14, 1868, the son of the esteemed Jewish physician Herman Hirschfeld. After graduating from the *Domgymnasium* in Kolberg in 1887, he studied philosophy and philology at the University of Breslau and then medicine in Berlin, Heidelberg, Munich, and Strasbourg. In 1892, he received his doctoral degree from the University of Berlin. In the early 1890s, Hirschfeld set out on the first of what was to become numerous foreign travels. His initial goal was the 1893 Chicago World's Fair, after which he traveled across the United States and then on to Asia, Africa, and Europe. In 1895, he established a medical practice in Charlottenburg, where he remained until 1909. He then transferred his practice to Berlin, where he specialized in problems of the nervous system and in human sexuality.

A gay man himself, Hirschfeld believed that sexual orientation was a "deep, inner-constituted natural instinct," not a conscious choice that one makes (Adam 1987, p. 231). Gay men and lesbians cannot,

Professor Magnus Hirschfeld with a visiting Chinese doctor in Brunn 1929. (Wellcome Library, London)

Mark Segal, director of the Dr. Magnus Hirschfeld Fund and publisher of the *Philadelphia Gay News*, at the site of a planned, gay-friendly affordable housing facility on December 14, 2011, in Philadelphia. (AP Photo/Matt Rourke)

therefore, be accused of being ill or sinful, Hirschfeld wrote. The goal of the medical profession, he went on, should be to help lesbians and gay men adjust to their condition, not to try to change that condition.

An important focus of Hirschfeld's work was the attempt to have Paragraph 175 of the German Constitution, outlawing same-sex acts, revoked. After three decades of struggle, that objective was achieved when the Reichstag removed homosexual acts from the nation's penal code in 1929. But it was a pyrrhic victory for Hirschfeld and his allies. The Nazi Party was already on the rise in German politics, and it strongly opposed those who were engaged in homosexual acts, as it opposed other groups such as Jews, gypsies, and non-Aryans. By 1932, Hirschfeld found it necessary to flee first to Switzerland and later to France to escape Nazi oppression. He spent the last few years of

his life in France and died in Nice on May 15, 1935. He left behind his domestic partner of many years, Kurt Giese, who committed suicide in Prague in 1936.

The accomplishments of the Scientific-Humanitarian Committee were rapidly obliterated in the early years of National Socialism. The climatic event in that purge occurred on May 6, 1933, when hundreds of students from a nearby Nazi school for physical education attacked Hirschfeld's Institute for Sexual Science, sacked its contents, and burned the building. About 12,000 books and 35,000 photographs, most of them irreplaceable, were destroyed.

David E. Newton

See also: Historical Overview of Gay Rights and Issues: From Pre-Columbian Times to the 1970s; Ulrichs, Karl Heinrich (1825–1895).

Cold-fetishism. From *Sexualpathologie* by Magnus Hirschfeld. (Wellcome Library, London)

Further Reading

Adam, Barry D. 1987. *The Rise of a Gay and Lesbian Movement.* Boston: Twayne Publishers.

Blasius, Mark and Shane Phelan, eds. 1997. *We Are Everywhere: A Historical Source Book of Gay and Lesbian Politics.* New York: Routledge, See chapter: "The Emergence of a Gay and Lesbian Political Culture in Germany."

Gordon, Mel. 2000. *Voluptuous Panic: The Erotic World of Weimar Berlin.* Los Angeles: Feral House.

Grau, Günter, ed. 1995. *Hidden Holocaust? Gay and Lesbian Persecution in Germany, 1933–45.* New York: Routledge.

Historical Overview of Gay Rights and Issues: From Pre-Columbian Times to the 1970s

There always have been and always will be people who engage in homosexual activities and relationships. Being "gay" is a modern political concept. It reflects the efforts made by homosexuals to fight against a heterosexist society that tells them they are deviant and not deserving of full human rights. Gay rights is the process of claiming the respect due all people.

The Americas were populated for many thousands of years before the arrival of Europeans. Hundreds if not thousands of languages were spoken and only a few nations in South America used limited written symbols. In North America, no language group had a written language. As such, we have no original documentation about the lives of First People residing in what is now the United States. We have no specific information about family structure, marriage, same- or other-sexual relationships, or more. What do exist are some of the diaries and reports from the first European explorers who were confused and shocked by the amount of gender and sexual nonconformity they witnessed within the indigenous population. Considering the many reports of "sodomitical" behaviors observed within First People, it could be assumed that "sodomy" was common.

But what is sodomy? A review of historical documents, court cases, legislation, and religious treaties shows a wide variance as to what it means. Sometimes it was defined as any sexual behaviors (regardless of same- or other-sex) outside of wedlock. Many laws vaguely referred to sodomy as a crime so heinous that it could not be named, the public was not allowed to observe the trials, and newspapers were forbidden to report on the outcome of the trials. Other times it was concisely defined as to where vaginas, anus, penises, and mouths were used and the location the sexual behavior occurred. Often the gender, age, or status of the person changed the definition. For example men could be convicted of sodomy but not women. For centuries, lesbianism was not identified since sex between women was thought to be inconceivable. Also, slaves faced greater punishment for the same behavior. The European explorers most likely identified any behavior that did not conform to Catholic gender and sexual norms as "sodomy."

In a sense, most First People nations were not antigay. Most tribes respected the innate spirit they

Timucua men cultivating a field and Timucua women planting corn or beans, 1588. (Library of Congress)

believed resides in all things. They looked for the benefits each person brought to the tribe. A two-spirited person was truly special as he or she contained the spirit of both women and men and, as such, often held a respected position in the tribe as spiritual leader, teacher, and counselor. Creation myths often told the stories of how god created a two-spirited person to help men and women in the world. Being central to their creation myths helped nurture tolerance between different sexual relationships, gender expressions, and sex roles.

But all that would change with the invasion of Europeans. The English sent initial settlements to Jamestown and the Virginia colonies as business ventures. The sailors, soldiers, and farmers were all men. It was reported that men were stealing food and trading for sexual favors. Sodomy was so widespread that

the military implemented rules against its practice under pain of death. As the English established more colonies, English common laws were applied—and this included sodomy provisions meting out the death penalty. In the Spanish- and Portuguese-controlled areas, Catholic rules were applied. The Catholic world had experienced centuries of religious inquisitions and, as such, was ruled by mysticisms and fear. The form of Catholicism that came to the Americas was fundamental, extremely antigay, and paranoid. Colonies set up under Spanish and Portuguese rule applied Catholic rules, and sodomy was punishable by death.

As can be imagined, the spread of Europeans throughout the Americas brought with them antigay beliefs, sentiments, and legal systems. Homosexuality and same-sex relationships not only were illegal but also couldn't be spoken about. The idea of gay rights had not entered the American psyche.

Rise of the Modern Gay Rights Movement

The modern gay rights movement began in Germany during the mid-1800s. The rise of Nazism crushed the fledgling movement. But the idea of equal rights for homosexuals did not die with World War II. Instead, it rose again in the United States paralleling the civil rights movement that began in the 1950s.

The German Homosexual Emancipation Movement

Karl Heinrich Ulrichs published many social and juridical studies in Germany concerning same-sex love between men. His 12 books represented the largest body of work on homosexuality in the 1860s and were collectively known as *Researches on the Riddle of Love between Men*. He used the term "Uranian" in reference to male homosexuality, a term taken from Plato's *Symposium* in which love between two men was referred to as a beautiful love that belonged to the heavenly "Muse Urania." Ulrichs is recognized as the "grandfather of gay liberation."

The word *homosexual* was coined in 1869 by Hungarian doctor Karoly Maria Benkert (who went by the pseudonym K.M. Kertbeny). The term *heterosexual* was not used publicly until 11 years later in 1880. Initially heterosexuality meant sexual deviancy and was used in defense of homosexuality. In 1871, the newly united Germany enacted the New Prussian Penal Code. It included Paragraph 175 outlawing "unnatural sexual acts between men, and men and beast" and specified imprisonment for up to four years (Plant 1988, p. 33).

British doctor Havelock Ellis continued with the medicalization of homosexuality and coin the phrase "sexual inversion" to characterize homosexual behavior. Freud was influenced by the work of Ellis and further characterized homosexuality as an "immature" stage of development. It is important to realize that Freud and early psychologists did not base their theories on any scientific evidence, but instead cast social and cultural norms and prejudices into the new field of psychology. Unfortunately, these theories would influence psychology for the next 100 years.

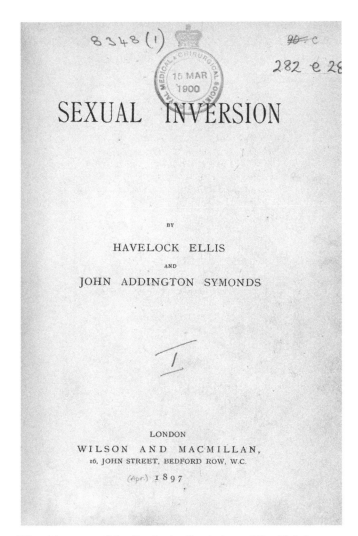

The title page of *Studies in the Psychology of Sex*, Vol. 1. *Sexual Inversion* by Havelock Ellis and John Addington Symonds, 1897. (Wellcome Library, London)

Heterosexuality was medicalized as the norm and homosexuality as "deviant." However, not everyone accepted this. Magnus Hirschfeld founded the Scientific Humanitarian Committee in Germany in 1897 to overcome antigay prejudice and to change the law. He worked tirelessly for three decades for homosexual emancipation. The committee distributed over 50,000 copies of the pamphlet *What People Should Know about the Third Sex*. Although there were 40 gay bars in Berlin by World War I, he had little success organizing the many homosexual groups in Germany.

Hirschfeld opened the Institute for Sexual Research in 1919. The library contained more than

Havelock Ellis in 1923. (Wellcome Library, London)

12,000 volumes of rare anthropological, medical, legal, and social documents. It employed four physicians and several assistants and included over 35,000 photographs.

German brownshirts and police often physically beat Hirschfeld. One month after Hitler was named chancellor of Germany on January 30, 1933, all homosexual rights organizations and pornography were banned. Four months later on May 6, 1933, approximately 100 students surrounded and entered the Institute for Sexual Research. They smashed and carried everything out. A public ceremony was held four days later where these materials, along with a bust of Hirschfeld, were burned. (History books contain the infamous pictures of the

Nazi burning books. They imply that Nazis were "bad" for destroying books. However, what books were being burned? The first fires contained the institute's collection on sexuality and homosexuality. Why do history books fail to mention this? Perhaps our own culture wants to suppress all references to homosexuality.)

For the next two years, the Nazis staged a campaign against homosexuals. Bars were closed, groups and meetings were banned, and homosexuals were arrested by the thousands. On July 3, 1934, the leader of the Brown Shirts (SA) and a known homosexual, Ernst Roehm, was executed along with hundreds of other members (known as the "Night of the Long Knives"). By 1935, the entire homosexual reform movement was extinguished and thousands of homosexuals were thrown into concentration camps where at least 50,000 of them died. They were identified with a lavender triangle sewn onto their clothes. Tragically, some legal-minded Allied commanders forced those who survived the camps to return to prison to serve out their sentences as sexual deviants.

The American Homosexual Emancipation Movement

There is very little evidence of efforts toward homosexual emancipation in the United States in the nineteenth century and early twentieth century. The Chicago Society for Human Rights was the first group in the United States to advocate for gay rights. Henry Gerber, a German American immigrant, along with a number of working-class homosexuals, launched the Society in 1929 and were granted nonprofit corporate status from the state of Illinois. They created a newsletter and were able to distribute only two issues before law enforcement arrested (without warrant) all members of the board. The men were jailed, brought to trial, but ultimately set free. Gerber lost his job with the Post Office and the Society disbanded (Katz 1976).

The early 1920s saw an increase in the number of novels with lesbian and gay themes published in the United States, although not without great controversy.

A growing underground developed in Harlem in New York and in other major cities such as San Francisco and New Orleans. Homosexuals were fairly free to associate with each other, yet still under the fear of police entrapment and harassment.

World War II and the Migration of Lesbians and Gays to the Cities

Family patterns, social networks, and entire cultural systems were disrupted by World War II. Millions of men and women left their homes to enter the military or to work in factories to help make war supplies. Many of these settings were segregated by race and sex. Soldiers often had to share bunks and men were often seen sleeping in each other's arms at train depots while waiting to ship out. Men often danced with each other at army canteens. Women lived together in company-provided housing at war factories. Homosexuality was a criminal act in the military in the 1920s and 1930s, but the war provided an excuse for these behaviors. Under these conditions, lesbians and gay men were able to find each other without bringing undue attention (Blumenfeld and Raymond 1993, p. 291; D'Emilio and Freedman 1988, pp. 25–26).

An effort was made to reduce the number of personnel in the military after the war. One way was to enforce the 1943 regulations banning homosexuals from all branches of the military. Approximately 10,000 men and women were dishonorably discharged from the military for homosexuality during the war and immediately afterward (known as "blue-discharges" because the document was printed on blue paper). Many did not return home, but rather flocked to New York, Los Angeles, and San Francisco to form gay enclaves. The gay community found relative safety and, eventually, its identity within these enclaves.

A number of factors led to the development of the modern gay movement after World War II. In 1948 Alfred Kinsey, American biologist and sexologist who founded the Institute of Sex Research at Indiana University, released his study of American male sexual habits—*Sexual Behaviors in the Human Male*, and

Biologist and zoologist Dr. Alfred Charles Kinsey in New York City on March 18, 1948. (AP Photo)

in 1953 his corresponding study of American female sexual habits—*Sexual Behaviors in the Human Female*. The reports sent shock waves through American culture, forever shattering stereotypes and myths concerning American puritanical codes of sexual conduct. The reports showed, besides other things, that many Americans had sex out of wedlock, engaged in sex in their teens, and had participated in a variety of sexual behaviors, including bisexuality and homosexuality.

Another factor was McCarthyism. Joseph McCarthy led a campaign to purge Communists and homosexuals from the federal government. Although many Communists lost their jobs, many more homosexuals (thousands) lost theirs. (Interestingly, our history books constantly refer to "McCarthyism" as the period in which Communists were routed out with the question "Are you now or have you ever been a Communist?" Yet, the plight of homosexuals is barely mentioned. Have history books purposely ignored this inequality in an effort to continue keeping homosexuals hidden?) However, the hearings gave unprecedented exposure to homosexuals and homosexual oppression. Homosexuality was discussed and written about in the press in new ways. Much of what was written was negative, but it allowed closeted and isolated homosexuals to know that there were many others like them.

The Homophile Movement

The homophile movement is a period in which people who engaged in homosexual behavior and relationships began to self-identify and cast off the deficit label put on them by early sexologists. They began to overcome their own homophobia and find love for themselves and other homosexuals. This is the period of *homo* (same) *phile* (love) identity formation.

Harry Hay (previously known as Henry Hay) was one of the key founders of the modern gay movement. He was a Communist organizer in Los Angeles and a sought-after teacher of Communist theory. In 1950, he assembled friends from the University of Southern California and launched the International Bachelors Fraternal Orders for Peace and Social Dignity (sometimes referred to as Bachelors Anonymous). The group was structured as a secret society with underground guilds separated so that no one would know all other members—a method used by the Old Left to keep members safe.

In 1951 Bachelors Anonymous incorporated in California as the Mattachine Society. The name *Mattachine* was inspired by the *Société Mattachine*, a secret fraternal organization in thirteenth- and fourteenth-century France and Spain of unmarried townsmen who performed music, dances, and rituals while wearing masks, sometimes in protest against oppression. The Society wanted to unify homosexuals and educate people about gay issues. At the same time, the Mattachine Foundation was established to provide a legal front for the Society.

In the same year the Mattachine Society was formed, Edward Sagarin (under the pen name Donald Webster Cory) published *The Homosexual in America*. Sagarin was an American professor of sociology and criminology at the City University of New York. He argued that the problems experienced by homosexuals stemmed from societal disapproval rather than from homosexuality itself. This was an important perspective, but American society was not ready for it. The publisher was ordered to cease publishing books with homosexual themes.

America was a very dangerous place for lesbians and gay men during the 1940s, 1950s, and 1960s. Bars were almost the only place gays and lesbians could meet, and often they were unmarked and required patrons to enter through a backdoor so no one could see them entering from the street. Police regularly entrapped men for lewd conduct, raided bars and baths, and suspended business licenses of gay establishments with no provocation or legitimacy. For example, in some cities and states there were laws that required bar patrons to wear clothing conforming to their gender. Police would enter a lesbian bar and seek out the manliest-looking patron. They would take her outside to the sidewalk and make her strip. They were making sure that she wore at least three items of clothing that were "feminine." If she wore boxer shorts she could be arrested.

In 1952, Dale Jennings, one of the members of the Mattachine Society, was arrested and charged with lewd conduct. He claimed that a man he was not overly interested in came home with him. When Jennings went to make him coffee, the man moved to the window and played with the blinds. Police immediately entered the apartment and arrested Jennings. Jennings felt this was entrapment, a very common practice by police at that time (and unfortunately, still a problem).

Most people charged with vagrancy and lewd conduct pleaded guilty and paid the fine so as to avoid jail (where they could be raped and beaten) and to keep it quiet so employers and families would not find out. Jennings convinced the Mattachine Society to help with the fight. At the trial, Jennings admitted being a homosexual (probably the first time anyone stood in a court of law and made that pronouncement) and insisted that he was neither lewd nor criminal. He helped educate the jury about the process of entrapment and how homosexuals were targets of police abuse. The defense attorney caught the arresting officer lying on the witness stand. They jury was hung (11 wanted acquittal, 1 wanted conviction) and the judge dismissed the case. Although this was the first successful defense against police entrapment, none of the mainstream news media carried the story.

The Mattachine Society set up another organization to publish a newsletter—*ONE, Incorporated*. It began publication in January 1953 and was the voice of the homophile movement. The U.S. Postmaster seized copies of *ONE* on grounds that it was "obscene, lewd, lascivious and filthy" and refused to allow the newsletter to be sent by U.S. mail. *ONE* sued, eventually winning an U.S. Supreme Court decision (*One, Inc. v. Olesen*, 1958). The Court ruled that homosexual materials were not automatically deemed "obscene" and could be sent via the mail. This was a very important decision. Without the right to send materials through the mail, the fledging gay rights movement would have been significantly hampered.

In 1953, Joseph McCarthy called Mattachine Foundation legal adviser Fred M. Snyder to testify before the House Un-American Activities Committee. McCarthy considered Snyder an unfriendly witness and attempted to defame and humiliate him. At the same time, the Mattachine Society held a convention in Los Angeles. With over 500 representatives, it was the largest such gathering of homosexuals in U.S. history. A power struggle ensued between the founders, who were leftist, and those who wanted a more moderate, liberal organization. The liberal factions won out and the old Mattachine Foundation board resigned.

Over the next 40 years, the Mattachine Society/ *ONE*, Inc., evolved, changed names a number of times, floundered, regrouped, but survived. Currently, it is mostly a library and archive collection located on the campus of the University of Southern California (USC) and is named ONE Institute and Archive. It contains the largest collection of homosexual books, magazines, articles, paintings, and memorabilia in the world with more than 1 million items catalogued.

Soon after the formation of the Mattachine Society in California, homosexuals in New York began meeting informally in a group called the League. Sam Morford and Tony Segura were frustrated by the flimsy nature of the League and decided in December 1955 to launch *The Mattachine Review* and *Mattachine Society New York* (MSNY). Approximately 30 persons attended the first meeting of MSNY at the Diplomat Hotel. The organizers had to work with extreme caution because homosexuality was a felony in New York State and punishable by up to 20 years in prison.

Women were always involved with the Mattachine Society, although they constituted a very small percentage of the membership. However, inspired by its success, Del Martin and Phyllis Lyon in 1956 transformed their lesbian social club into a lesbian activist organization named the Daughters of Bilitis (DOB): the first national lesbian organization in the United States. The name came from Pierre Louÿs's narrative "Song of Bilitis," in which Bilitis is a lesbian poet and disciple of Sappho who lived in ancient Greece on the isle of Lesbos. Chapters of DOB were established in major cities around the country and in Australia. They produced a newsletter called *The Ladder*. DOB was well connected with the Mattachine Society and other early gay rights organizations.

The early 1960s was a turning point for the homophile movement. The Mattachine Society and DOB were conservative in their actions and avoided direct politics. For example, when they were involved in official business, they required members to dress conservatively—suits and ties for men, dresses and heels for women. They excluded members who were overly effeminate or ultramasculine. They wrote polite letters, planned scholarly publications, and invited experts to lecture on "sexual variation" before serious audiences in respectable halls. Most members were secretive and even the leaders often used pseudonyms. Because of the fears and inhibitions of these organizations, few members were attracted. As such, many homosexuals felt left out and resented professionals who told them they were deviants and immoral. They wanted an organization that would take direct political action to reduce police harassment and to change laws.

Frank Kameny, Harvard astronomer, was an activist who took direct political action. He was dismissed from his army post in 1957 for being a homosexual. He contested the dismissal all the way to the U.S. Supreme Court. The Court would not review the case and let stand his dismissal. The betrayal he felt toward a legal system that denied his right to employment led him to form the Mattachine Society of Washington (MSW). He wanted the group to take direct political action. He rejected the deviancy label and coined the phrase "Gay Is Good" to paraphrase African American militants whose motto was "Black Is Beautiful." He argued:

that discrimination was squarely to blame for the homosexual's problems and that boldly challenging discriminatory policies was the most effective way to make progress . . . [and we should take] a militant homophile approach to gay political activity. (Marotta 1981, p. 25)

The activist approach for MSW threatened Mattachine leadership in New York, San Francisco, and Los Angeles who wrote:

that Mattachine cannot pursue any path but the educational and research. . . . Our charter is placed in jeopardy whenever we try to influence legislation through any other means publicly. . . . We can endorse the action of other agencies working in this field, and "ride on their shirttails," so to speak, with relative safety. But we cannot lobby on our own, and must be careful how we recommend changes of law so that our charter and the right to solicit funds through the mail is not in danger. ("Letter from Hall Call" 1956)

Other groups formed outside of Mattachine were more activist oriented. In 1964, 10 participants from the Homosexual League of New York and the League for Sexual Freedom picketed along the street in front of the Army Induction Center on Whitehall Street. In this "first" gay demonstration, they protested the army's dishonorable discharges of gay soldiers.

The next year, 1965, the Mattachine Society held its first public demonstration in front of the White House to protest government discriminatory employment practices. Before they went, they agreed that the men would wear suits and ties and the women would wear conservative dress. That same day, 20,000 antiwar protestors were at the Washington Monument. The coincidence of media being there for the antiwar protestors got national TV coverage for this gay demonstration.

In spring 1966, the police began "Operation New Broom" in New York City in which they "cleaned up" Times Square and Greenwich Village areas. They raided and closed gay bars, restaurants, bookstores, and taverns. Many men were entrapped and charged with solicitation and lewd conduct. Seven members of the Mattachine Society attended a public meeting at Judson Memorial Church where the chief inspector for the police was holding a community hearing. Randy Wicker and Craig Rodwell from Mattachine spoke and explained how previous efforts by New York police to "crack down" on gay bars left homosexuals with no social outlet and led to underworld elements opening illegal operations for homosexuals. The illegal bars were sources of police corruption and bribery. The chief inspector responded by saying that gay bars were illegal because of "illicit activities." Wicker pointed out these illicit activities were mostly undercover policemen soliciting bar patrons for entrapment. The chief inspector denied the allegations. Wicker was shocked by the naïveté of the chief inspector and said, "It's alarming to think that the Chief Inspector doesn't know that a large number of police spend their duty hours dressed in tight pants, sneakers, and polo sweaters . . . to bring about solicitations" (Marotta 1981, p. 36). The audience at the meeting shouted out "Bravo!" Soon after, the mayor of New York issued a memorandum ordering the police to cease engaging in entrapment.

It is important to understand the process of overcoming stigmatization and oppression. Initially, those who engaged in homosexual behaviors had no identity concerning their sexual orientation. In much of history and in many cultures today, as long people meet their familial obligations by marrying and having children, society does not care if they engage in homosexual behaviors. In these cultures, homosexuality is not spoken. Only if the homosexual relationship interferes with the family or becomes too "obvious," does the culture crack down, often seeking the death of the offender.

As the science of psychology developed, homosexuality was identified as a "sexual inversion" that was deviant. These characteristics were not based on science but rather the codification of social and cultural norms. Still, it influenced psychologists, legislators, judges, police, schools, universities, churches, and others in power and enabled them to justify the persecution of homosexuals. Those who engaged in homosexual behaviors began to see an identity, albeit one that was negative and enforced feelings of worthlessness. This is called internalized homophobia.

But not all homosexuals felt they were mentally ill or deviant. Instead, they recognized that society put this label on them. It was society that expressed homophobia. The Mattachine Society took an educational approach. It believed that if accurate information got out, it could dispel stereotypes and influence society. It issued newsletters and pamphlets, held educational seminars, and challenged the medical establishment. Its demonstrations were meant to bring attention to problems the media and society refused to face or even name.

The Mattachine Society was the right organization for its time. If gay activists had engaged in direct political action in the 1950s, they would have been jailed and their message would have been obliterated. But by the late 1960s the Mattachine Society proved to be too conservative and few outside the gay community heard their message. Many homosexuals did not accept the negative stereotypes of society and wanted immediate relief from the oppression of police and laws. They wanted to be able to keep their jobs, homes, and families without having to stay in the closet. Thus, they took more political action, such as

the public meeting at Judson Memorial Church. They wanted a public hearing with the chief inspector of police to bring the issue of entrapment to his attention. As described earlier, the chief inspector denied entrapment occurred, yet the gay community knew otherwise and brought it to the attention of the media, the surrounding community, and the mayor.

Bringing the problem to the attention of the community is the first step toward overcoming oppression. Homosexuality was hidden, but no more. Now the arrests, beatings, firings, and more were brought to everyone's attention. Homosexuals were overcoming their internalized homophobia, but so were heterosexuals. The U.S. Constitution and civil religion emphasize fair and equitable treatment. The entrapment of gay men by New York City police was brought to the attention of the mayor and city council, who saw the unfairness of these actions and stepped in to stop the abuse. It was heterosexuals who understood the oppression of heterosexism and took action. Heterosexuals were overcoming their homophobia.

The next 30 years of gay activism reflect this process. Heterosexuals controlled the laws and institutions of the United States. Gay activists, especially in the early years, were few in numbers. Yet the truth of their message of equity between homosexuals and heterosexuals was strong enough to convince heterosexuals to intervene and change the power structure. This is a recurring pattern for overcoming injustice.

Another major change occurred during the 1950s and 1960s. Psychologists engaged in academic research into homosexuality. Their work would forever change the social and cultural norms that depicted homosexuality as a mental illness.

The early investigations into homosexuality were performed on a skewed sample of people who visited gay bars, patients in psychiatric hospital, and prison inmates. Not surprisingly, these studies confirmed the societal beliefs and stereotypes that homosexuals are alcoholics, crazed, and criminal. In the mid-1950s, Dr. Evelyn Hooker (1963) at UCLA carried out the first rigorous studies using nonclinical gays and discovered that psychiatrists could not identify lesbians and gay men using psychological testing. Psychiatrists who made money "curing" allegedly insane gays now could not even identify them (Hooker 1963). Evelyn Hooker (who was heterosexual) and other respected academic researchers showed every antigay stereotype to be incorrect. With this evidence, the American Psychiatric Association (APA) dropped homosexuality as a mental illness from the *Diagnostic and Statistical Manual of Mental Disorders* (*DSM*) in 1973 (Bayer 1981).

The Stonewall Riots and Gay Liberation

There are junctions in history at which many forces come together to mark the creation of a major shift in the social paradigm. The riot at Stonewall Inn in New York's Greenwich Village was such an event.

On the night of June 27, 1969, officers from the Public Morals Section of the New York City Police Department attempted to shut down the Stonewall Inn—a small local bar. The bar was a favorite place to meet for drag queens, street kids, dope heads, speed freaks, and other marginal people. As people were dismissed by the police and allowed to leave, they gathered across the street. Each time someone appeared in the doorway that the crowd knew, they applauded, which encouraged the brassy individual to pose and make some flippant remark. This infuriated the police even more. When the paddy wagon came to take away the drag queens, bar owner, and bartender, a cry went up from the crowd to overturn the paddy wagon. The wagon drove off, but then the crowd exploded by throwing bottles and stones at the police. The police had to retreat into the bar. A battle cry was heard through the Village and hundreds came out to participate. A small fire began in the window of the Stonewall. Soon after, more police arrived and the crowd scattered.

For the next couple of nights, there were street demonstrations that were more political in nature. Groups of people milled around the streets yelling "gay power," holding hands, and kissing in public. A group of gay cheerleaders was heard singing "We are the Stonewall girls/We wear our hair in curls/We have no underwear/We show our pubic hairs" (Marotta

1981, p. 75). After the first two days of disturbances, the Mattachine Society of New York handed out flyers in the Village capitalizing on the "Christopher Street Riots" as the "Hairpin Drop Heard around the World" (Marotta 1981, p. 77).

Michael Brown was a New Left homosexual who was thrilled to see homosexuals fight against the police. Days after the riots, he met with Dick Leitsch of MSNY to discuss sponsoring more demonstrations. When Leitsch adamantly insisted that MSNY could not engage in such activity, Michael Brown set up an independent action committee that became the Gay Liberation Front (GLF).

Before Stonewall, about a dozen gay organizations existed. Within three months after the riot, more than 50 lesbian and gay organizations formed throughout the United States. These organizations become more radical with many cities hosting marches and festivals in June to commemorate the anniversary of the Stonewall Riots. It is these events, more than any other, that helped bring unity to the gay community and influenced political and legal progress.

GLF was composed of a series of small groups in the United States and other Western countries. It never became a formal organization. GLF represented an important transitional phase for the homophile movement. It built coalitions with other disenfranchised groups and attempted to dismantle oppressive economic, political, and social structures. Many of its participants had been members of the New Left, such as the Students for a Democratic Society (SDS), and others who rejected strict social norms such as pacifists and "hippies." GLF was responsible for the beginnings of many college lesbian and gay student groups. It believed that a total transformation of society was needed to obtain equality and freedom for all marginalized people. Primarily, they engaged in consciousness-raising sessions in people's living rooms, church basements, and storefronts. These groups were nonhierarchical in structure and often did not have a leader. They built upon the belief that the "personal is the political" and launched a number of small newsletters and engaged in demonstrations.

The ideological differences between the revolutionaries, social radicals, and reformers were too great to maintain and GLF soon broke apart. Many, if not most of the reformers, felt alienated by the radical politics of GLF. Although they had outgrown the conservative homophile groups, they did not want to overthrow the entire political and social system as advocated by radicals and revolutionaries. Instead they sought a more activist organization that would bring about political change to eliminate discrimination against homosexuals. It was these GLF reformers who created the Gay Activists Alliance (GAA).

GAA engaged in petition drives, political "zaps," and street theater. "Zaps" are demonstrations in which politicians are directly confronted in public and asked pointed questions or chastised for antigay statements. Street theater included "gay-in" or "kiss-in" in which members of the same sex would hold hands or kiss in public, something that heterosexuals are able to do but was (and still is) "shocking" when done by same-sex couples. GAA was successful at obtaining media attention and brought gay issues to the forefront of public discussion. In New York, these actions informed Mayor Lindsay and the city council, all of whom were heterosexual, about gay issues. Seeing how government was unfair toward gay people they ended entrapment, police harassment, and public employment discrimination. GAA was able to educate those in power about homophobia, and it was heterosexuals who changed the power structure.

Many groups formed in the early 1970s. They reflected the identity of their members. Separatism was advocated by some as the solution to heterosexual oppression. The National Organization of Women (NOW) was challenged by lesbian feminist over women's fears of being identified as dykes. Bisexuals made their needs known and became a voice within the lesbian and gay liberation movement. The 1969 Eastern Regional Conference of Homophile Organizations (ERCHO) proposed a national celebration each June 28 to commemorate the Stonewall Riots. Now, most major cities and many smaller ones hold Gay Pride festivals and parades to which tens of thousands, and sometimes hundreds of thousands, people attend and participate.

Equal Rights and Community Building

After Stonewall, there was a decline in radical activism. Gay reformers aimed at community building and political activism. They worked to educate and overcome oppressive laws, not to overthrow the system. There were over 1,100 organizations nationwide devoted to lesbian and gay concerns by 1973. This number would more than double by the 1980s and again more than double by the 1990s. There are support organizations for every conceivable group—businesses, students, schools, scientist, lawyers, academics, artists, religious organizations, racial and ethnic minorities, recreation, and more. There was also a flood of publications, media, and more devoted to lesbian and gay concerns.

Government agencies were made aware that homosexuals underutilized their social services. Many cities developed entire centers providing services for lesbians and gay men. Some of the services included mental and physical health clinics, vocational services, counseling, lesbian advocacy, telephone hotlines, roommate referral, rap groups, medical services, legal help, and more. Often these centers provided professional advice to cities and governmental agencies about the needs, opinions, and concerns of the gay community.

One of the most influential political groups formed in the United States is the National Gay and Lesbian Task Force (NGLTF). Founded in 1973 as the National Gay Task Force (NGTF), it blended the old homophile movement with the newer reformist strategies of GAA. Lambda is a national organization that promotes the civil rights of lesbians, gay men, bisexuals, transgendered, and AIDS sufferers through litigation, education, and public policy work. When the secretary of state rejected its application for incorporation, Lambda took the case to the New York Supreme Court where the decision was overturned.

Again, we see the process of a handful of gay activists educating heterosexuals to overcome their homophobia. Lambda argued that the U.S. Constitution explicitly allows people to come together to advocate for legal change (otherwise known as the right of assembly guaranteed in the First Amendment); and this was Lambda's goal concerning gay rights. The New York Supreme Court agreed and rejected the unfairness inherent in denying their application for incorporation. It was heterosexual judges who changed the prohibition against gay groups forming in the state of New York.

Later in 1974, similar arguments were made at the U.S. Supreme Court level in *Gay Students Organization v. Bonner*. Here, gay activists educated the Court about the right of lesbians and gay men to come together and form organizations qualifying for federal tax-exempt status. Again, heterosexual judges found the arguments convincing and ruled that homosexual groups were to receive the same treatment by the IRS as any other qualifying group.

One of the most significant decisions came from the APA in 1973–1974. The APA formed a committee in the early 1970s to review the research on homosexuality as related to its classification as a mental illness. It reviewed the works of Dr. Evelyn Hooker and many other researchers, along with the 1969 recommendations by the National Institute of Mental Health (NIMH) Task Force on Homosexuality, to repeal sodomy laws and educate the public about homosexuality (Thompson 1994, p. 69) The committee, along with the APA's Council on Research and Development, Reference Committee, and Assembly, made recommendations to remove homosexuality from its list of mental illness. The APA board unanimously passed a resolution removing homosexuality from the *DSM*. A group of psychoanalysts filed a petition against the resolution. A referendum was held during which more than 58 percent of the 10,000 voting members supported (with 37.8% against) the board action. Future challenges to the resolution have been rejected by even larger margins.

Conservatives and members of the religious right often considered that this change in the *DSM* was accomplished by a band of scheming gay activist that pushed through their agenda. This is not true. It was a multiyear review of academic and government research combined with a clear presentation of the findings to the members that convinced the APA to change its position. The membership of the APA reflects society and is mostly heterosexual. It was primarily heterosexuals who reviewed the research and agreed that the change was needed. It was heterosexuals who overcame their bias and homophobia and made a rational decision based on objective research. In the intervening 30 years, no academic research has found any evidence suggesting that homosexuality is a mental illness. If anything, the research has affirmed that there are no differences in psychosocial measures related to sexual orientation.

Gay rights grew nationwide during the 1970s with individual cities and counties (but no states) adopting antidiscrimination statutes. However, there was a conservative backlash. For example, in 1977 the Miami-Dade County Commission passed an ordinance making it illegal to discriminate on the basis of sexual orientation. This came about because local gay groups brought their concerns about employment and housing discrimination to the Commission. The Commission, which was comprised of heterosexuals, understood the need for such an ordinance. It understood that it was not giving homosexuals additional rights, but rather was providing the city with the legal power to enforce rights already enjoyed by all Americans but denied homosexuals due to historical and social reasons.

Upset by this development, singer and Florida Orange Juice representative Anita Bryant organized a group called "Save Our Children." It used scare tactics claiming homosexuals molest children and are mentally ill. It obtained sufficient signatures to place a referendum on the ballot to overturn the ordinance. The county citizens passed it overwhelmingly. The "Save Our Children" campaign is an example of emotional hysteria caused by religious conservatives and based on false information and stereotypes that overruled decisions made by heterosexuals who were educated on the issue. Twenty years later, Dade County passed the same ordinance and, this time, religious conservatives were unsuccessful in overturning it.

The very next year, 1978, a similar battle occurred in California. Senator John Briggs collected signatures and placed Proposition 6 on the ballot. It would have barred homosexuals from teaching in public schools. The "Save Our Children" slogan and methodology were used to promote the proposition. Despite this, every teacher and labor union, Democrats, many Republicans, and many others including Governor Ronald Reagan came out against the proposition. It failed to pass.

It seems that many Americans were not ready to give antidiscrimination protection to lesbians and gay men (as we saw in Dade County), but were not ready to outright discriminate against them (as in California's Briggs Initiative).

Tragedy hit in 1978. Dan White gunned down the mayor of San Francisco and Supervisor Harvey Milk in city hall. White was a conservative supervisor on the San Francisco City Council who held much animosity toward openly gay supervisor Harvey Milk. In November 1978, White resigned his position on the council. He changed his mind and asked the mayor for his position back. The mayor refused. A week later, White entered city hall and shot Harvey Milk and Mayor George Moscone to death. The murder of the two men resulted in one of the most impressive memorial services ever seen in San Francisco in which more than 40,000 men, women, and children marched by candlelight to city hall.

At the trial, White's lawyers claimed that White was addicted to junk food and the sugar affected his judgment (what has since become known as the "Twinkie Defense"). White was not convicted of first-degree murder but, rather, voluntary manslaughter and was sentenced to seven years in prison. The gay community exploded at the lenient sentence and took to the streets of San Francisco. That night in 1979, in what is referred to as "White Night," police cars were overturned, fires set, and thousands of people marched to city hall. More than 150 people were injured and property damages in excess of $1 million

resulted. White was released after serving just five years of his sentence. He committed suicide in 1985.

Anita Bryant's crusade, Briggs effort, and the murder of Harvey Milk and George Moscone galvanized the gay movement. But it also galvanized conservative religious groups into what is today known as the religious right. In 1979, Rev. Jerry Falwell launched the Moral Majority (renamed the Liberty Federation in 1989). In the same year, Beverly LaHaye founded Concerned Women for America. Pat Robertson, who began the Christian Broadcast Network (CBN) in 1961 and has hosted *The 700 Club* since 1968, opened CBN University in 1977 making his operation one of the best-financed conservative religious organizations in the nation. These three groups would become, and are the most power antigay organizations in the United States.

As disco receded in the late 1970s, a new scourge swept the gay community in the 1980s forever changing the face of gay liberation. The cause was AIDS. Unknown and unnamed in the 1970s, AIDS would kill tens of thousands of young men in the coming decade. Gay rights organizations, political parties, and cultural groups saw major shifts in their membership as young men died from the mysterious disease. Many gay men faced their greatest fears with the AIDS epidemic—that antigay moralizing was right and that God was judging gay men.

See also: ACT UP (AIDS Coalition to Unleash Power); American Psychiatric Association (APA); Boswell, John (1947–1994); Bryant, Anita (1940–); Daughters of Bilitis; Falwell, Jerry L. (1933–2007); Hay, Henry (Harry) (1912–2002); Hirschfeld, Magnus (1868–1935); Hooker, Evelyn (1907–1996); Kameny, Franklin (1925–2011); Lambda Legal Defense and Education Fund (LLDEF); Lyon, Phyllis (1924–); Martin, Del (1921–2008); Mattachine Society; Milk, Harvey (1930–1978); National Gay and Lesbian Task Force; Native Americans and LGBTQ Issues; ONE, Incorporated; Stonewall Riot; Ulrichs, Karl Heinrich (1825–1895); We'wha (1849–1896); White, Dan (1946–1985).

Chuck Stewart

Further Reading

Bayer, R. 1981. *Homosexuality and American psychiatry.* New York: Basic Books.

Berlet, C. 1998. "Who Is Mediating the Storm? Right-Wing Alternative Information Networks." In *Media, Culture, and the Religious Right*, ed. L. Kintz and J. Lesage, pp. 249–74. Minneapolis, MN: University of Minnesota Press.

Blumenfeld, W.J., and D. Raymond, eds. 1993. *Looking at Gay and Lesbian Life*, rev. ed. Boston, MA: Beacon Press.

Boy Scouts of America v. Dale, No. 99–699 U.S. (2000).

Childers v. Dallas Police Dept., 513 F. Supp. 134 (N.D. Tex. 1981).

D'Emilio, J., and E.B. Freedman. 1988. *Intimate Matters: A History of Sexuality in America*. New York: Harper & Row.

Gay Students Org. v. Bonner, 367 F. Supp. 1088 (D.N.H.), *aff'd*, 509 F.2d 652 (1st Cir. 1974).

Hooker, E. 1963. "The Adjustment of the Male Overt Homosexual." In *The Problem of Homosexuality*, ed. H.M. Ruitenbeed, pp. 141–61. New York: Dutton. (Reprinted from *Journal of Projective Techniques, 21*, 18–31, 1959.)

Hurley v. Irish-American Gay, Lesbian and Bisexual Group of Boston, No. 94–749, (1995, June 19).

Katz, J. 1976. *Gay American History: Lesbians and Gay Men in the U.S.A.* New York: Thomas Y. Crowell.

Keen, L., and S.B. Goldberg 1999. *Strangers to the Law: Gay People on Trial*. Ann Arbor, MI: The University of Michigan Press.

Khan, S. 1998, October. *Calculated compassion: How the Ex-Gay Movement serves the Right's attack on democracy*. A report from Political Research Associates, the Policy Institute of the National Gay and Lesbian Task Force, and Equal Partners in Faith.

Letter from Hall Call to Dwight Huggins, Sam Morford, Tony Segura, et al., August 30, 1956; appended to Segura's letter to Huggins in MSNY files. Reported in Marotta, T. 1981. *The Politics of Homosexuality* (p. 15). Boston: Houghton Mifflin Company.

Loth, Renee. 1992. "Buchanan Calls AIDS 'Retribution.'" *Boston Globe*, February 28.

Marcus, R. 1990. "Powell Regrets Backing Sodomy Law." *Washington Post*, (325), October 26, A3.

Marotta, T. 1981. *The Politics of Homosexuality*. Boston: Houghton Mifflin Company.

Mookas, I. 1998. "Faultlines: Homophobic Innovation in Gay Rights/Special Rights." In *Culture Media, and the Religious Right*, ed. L. Kintz and J. Lesage. Minneapolis, MN: University of Minnesota Press.

Nabozny v. Podlesny, 92 F.3d 446, 7th Cir. 1996).

One, Inc. v. Olesen, 355 U.S. 371 (1958).

Plant, R. 1988. *The Pink Triangle*. New York: New Republic Books/Henry Holt.

Shilts, R. 1987. *And the Band Played On: Politics, People, and the AIDS Epidemic*. New York: St. Martin's Press.

Stewart, C.K. 2001. *Homosexuality and the Law: A Dictionary*. Denver, CO: ABC-CLIO.

Thompson, M., ed. 1994. *Long Road to Freedom: The Advocate History of the Gay and Lesbian Movement*. New York: St. Martin's Press.

"We've Come a Long Way. . . Maybe." 2000, March 3. *Frontiers* 18(22): 12.

White, M. 1997. *The Justice Report* (Special Edition). Selected quotes from the *700 Club*. Soulforce, P.O. Box 4467, Laguna Beach, CA 92652, journey@soulforce.org.

Young, P.D. 1982. *God's Bullies: Native Reflections on Preachers and Politics*. New York: Holt, Rinehart, & Winston.

Historical Overview of Gay Rights and Issues: From the 1980s to the Present

As the 1970s came to a close and disco faded away, a new terror struck the gay community—AIDS. The period from 1980 to the present day is an era that ranges from the days that the community thought it would literally die to a time that many began to gain the right to marry. A recurring theme to notice is that the advances in gay rights are the result of heterosexuals overcoming any of their own internalized homophobia and cultural heterosexism. Laws and customs are created by the larger society and heterosexuals dominate that society. Only by heterosexuals learning and overcoming their own prejudices against those who do not conform to their heterosexual bias are able to change laws and cultural norms. The last fifty years of U.S. history demonstrate how local city councils, state government and

Thousands of gays and lesbians march down Pennsylvania Avenue to act out their plea for equal rights on October 14, 1979. The march was organized by the National March on Washington for Lesbian and Gay Rights. (Bettmann/Corbis)

eventually federal government have changed due to changes in heterosexuals championing equal rights for all—including LGBT people. Without straight allies, the gay rights movement would not advance.

1980s—AIDS, Political Organizing, Political Backlash, Sodomy, Same-Sex Marriage, and Gay "Cure"

Seeing the need to coordinate pro-gay political efforts, the Human Rights Campaign (HRC) was founded in 1980. It focuses on fighting antigay ballot initiatives and supports candidates who promote antidiscrimination policies based on sexual orientation. Its political action committee (PAC) provides financial support for candidates and typically raises and donates more than $1 million a year to candidates at the federal level. For example, by 1998, of the 200 political candidates to

whom it contributed money, 91 percent won their respective races.

The 1980s saw a continuation in the trend toward greater recognition and equality for lesbians and gay men. For example, over 200,000 people participated in the first March on Washington in 1979. In 1981, a court case in Dallas banned police from discriminating against lesbians and gays in employment as police officers (*Childers v. Dallas Police Department*). In 1982, Wisconsin became the first state to pass a wide-reaching law prohibiting discrimination against lesbians and gay men. A high school support program for lesbian and gay children was established in 1984 (Project 10, Los Angeles). In 1987, the second March on Washington took place with over 600,000 people attending. The National Education Association in 1988 adopted a resolution calling for every school

Dr. Robert Gallo, right, chief of the National Cancer Institute laboratory of Tumor Cell Biology, along with Health and Human Services secretary Margaret Heckler, talks to reporters in Washington, where they announce that the probable cause of Acquired Immune Deficiency Syndrome (AIDS) has been found, a cancer virus called HTLV-3, in 1984. (AP Photo/Lana Harris)

district to provide counseling for students struggling with their sexual orientation.

The U.S. Supreme Court handed down the most significant antigay ruling in 1986. Michael Hardwick was charged with engaging in sodomy in Georgia. Hardwick sued and the case reached the U.S. Supreme Court. The Court ruled against Hardwick in a five to four decision stating that claims for "homosexual sodomy" as a protected right to privacy are "facetious, at best." The Court established that lesbians and gay men have no right to sexual expression under the

federal constitutional. This ruling would hinder the civil rights gains by lesbians and gay men for decades. Interestingly, soon after his retirement, Justice Lewis Powell conceded that he "had made a mistake" and should have voted to strike down Georgia's sex statute (Marcus 1990).

AIDS

The 1980s also marked the advent of AIDS. The first cases were reported in 1981 in the United States and exclusively involved gay men. Doctors were unsure what caused this "Gay Plague" and initially called it gay-related immune deficiency (GRID). As more nongays came down with the disease (Haitians, intravenous drug users, hemophiliacs, and heterosexuals), it became obvious that it was not related to being gay, but rather was an immune deficiency caused by a virus spread through bodily fluids. Bruce Voller, a biological researcher, coined the terms *acquired immune deficiency syndrome* (AIDS) to better reflect the nature of the disease.

There was much hysteria about AIDS. People who developed AIDS were often fired from their jobs, forced out of their apartments and housing, lost their health insurance, and more. Children who were asymptomatic but infected with human immunodeficiency virus (HIV) were expelled from schools. Public swimming pools were emptied, scrubbed, disinfected, and refilled after a person with AIDS used the pool. Mortuaries refused to handle the bodies of people who died from AIDS. Airlines refused to allow people with AIDS to fly. And even health professionals sometime refused to care for those with AIDS. Massive discrimination resulted and the government initially ignored the severity of the problem.

The religious right used AIDS to reignite its antigay crusades. They claimed AIDS was "God's punishment" for the "immoral" gay "lifestyle." They called for a general quarantine of people with AIDS, the firing of lesbian and gay teachers, and even more draconian measures. Even the mainstream media refused to cover the AIDS epidemic until the first heterosexuals were reported to be infected (Shilts 1987).

Police officers detain gay right activist Yury Gavrikov in St. Petersburg, Russia, on July 7, 2012. Russian police detained several gay rights activists for holding an unsanctioned protest rally against a law of prohibition of homosexuality propaganda made by the St. Petersburg's city parliament that year. (AP Photo/Rex Features)

It was seven years into the epidemic before President Ronald Reagan publicly spoke the word AIDS. Yet Patrick Buchanan, Reagan's Chief of Communications, was very outspoken, claiming that AIDS was "God's awful retribution" for homosexual behavior and that AIDS patients did not deserve help ("Buchanan calls AIDS 'retribution'" 1992). AIDS, unfortunately, is still tied to antigay sentiments in many people's minds even though it was never a gay disease.

President Reagan appointed a 13-member AIDS panel in July 1987. Although there was much in-fighting between the members, it made remarkably progressive recommendations including the call for massive governmental funding for research and care. The panel also recommended legislation to prevent discrimination against people with AIDS (PWA) and people infected with the virus. These recommendations impacted the 1990 adoption by Congress of the American with Disabilities Act (ADA).

The frustration in the gay community over overt discrimination and government inaction compelled Larry Kramer and other activists to form AIDS Coalition to Unleash Power (ACT UP) in 1987. ACT UP was a group of individuals united in anger and committed to ending the AIDS crisis through direct action. The slogan "Silence = Death" originated with ACT UP. It engaged in a number of high-profile demonstrations that brought significant media attention to the problem. For example, in 1989, over 5,000 ACT UP members demonstrated in front of and inside New York's St. Patrick's Cathedral rallying against

Marcia Hams, left, and her partner, Susan Shepherd, right, take an oath administered by city clerk D. Margaret Drury, foreground, during the application process for a marriage license just after midnight on May 17, 2004, at city hall in Cambridge, Massachusetts. Hams and Shepherd were the first couple to complete the application process as Massachusetts became the first state to legalize same-sex marriage in the United States, and were wed later that day. (AP Photo/Steven Senne)

the Catholic Church's antigay stance and policies on AIDS.

There was one "good" that came from the AIDS crisis—it compelled the media, government, and average citizen to talk about homosexuality and gay issues in ways they never did before. For example, *The New York Times* used the word *gay* in reference to homosexuality for the first time in 1987. AIDS brought more attention to gay rights than the previous 30 years of educational efforts and public demonstrations.

By 1993, the "cocktail" was developed to treat AIDS. Various drugs had been created using different biological strategies in the 1980s to combat HIV. It was discovered that mixing the drugs proved to be effective at reducing viral infection to undetectable levels at the same time reducing side effects from taking the drugs and reducing viral resistance. The Highly

Active Antiretroviral Therapy (HAART) methodology was quickly adopted by most physicians, resulting in a dramatic drop in deaths caused by opportunistic infections. Although a few people were unable to sustain taking the cocktail, it was effective for most people who were infected. Infection from AIDS went from being an automatic death sentence within two to three years to being a manageable disease through the use of life-long treatment. Slowly, Christian groups' claim that AIDS was god's retribution against gay people lost its sting and by the 2010s only the most fundamentalist groups still used the old bromide.

Anti-Gay Backlash

To counter the political progress lesbian and gay rights were making and the successes of the Human Rights Campaign (HRC), Pat Robertson formed the Christian

Coalition in 1989. It was a political organization that works to elect conservative Christians to political office. Formed as a nonprofit religious organization, it violated its tax-exempt status by issuing voters guides and engaging in other direct political action. By 1999, the IRS revoked its tax exemption.

Many other antigay groups were formed in the 1980s and 90s. These included the Family Research Council, Focus on the Family, Moral Majority, Traditional Values Coalition, Truth in Action Ministries, Exodus International, Westboro Baptist Church, National Association for Research & Therapy of Homosexuality (NARTH), MassResistance, and others. Many of these organizations have been racked by internal scandal when leaders were found in same-sex sexual relationships or were in violation of their nonprofit status. A few of the organizations crossed the line into advocating violence and have earned a listing with the Southern Poverty Law Center and the Anti-Defamation League as recognized hate groups. These included the Family Research Institute, Family Research Council, Traditional Values Coalition, MassResistance, and Westboro Baptist Church. The Westboro Baptist Church is infamous for picketing funerals of American military personnel or other high-profile deaths with slogans such as "God Hates Fags," "Thank God for Dead Soldiers," and similar. The outrageousness of Westboro Baptist Church actions has produced many counter demonstrations and brought divergent groups together in support of their gay and lesbian families and friends.

World Politics

The gay rights movement in Europe and the world has paralleled a similar path. Some countries were at the initial stages of simply trying to form support organizations. For example, when 20 gay Finish citizens attempted to host the first gay pride parade in Helsinki in 1981, all were arrested for "encouraging lewd behavior." In 1989, Nigeria formed the Gentlemen's Alliance and Poland formed its national gay rights group, Lambda.

Other countries were much further along in the process of affirming gay rights. For example, Canada gave postal workers an antidiscrimination contract in 1980, yet conducted a massive raid arresting 300 gay men in Toronto the very next year. The ensuing riot has been called the Canadian Stonewall. Later, in 1988, Canada repealed its sodomy laws. Ireland was compelled in 1988 by the European Court of Human Rights to eliminate its life imprisonment penalty for homosexual behavior. Britain elected its first openly lesbian mayor in Manchester in 1985 and Israel legalized homosexual acts between consenting adults in 1988.

Norway was further along, having enacted a national antidiscrimination statute that included sexual orientation. In 1984, television evangelist Hans Bratterud was convicted of violating the law. Denmark enacted domestic partnership legislation in 1988 that was just one step away from full marriage for same-sex couples. Full marriage for same-sex couples would finally be granted in 2001, placing Denmark ahead of all other countries in recognizing gay rights.

However, with every step forward there often was a backlash. Uganda, other African nations, the Middle East, and Russia saw an increase in antigay sentiments and legislation in the 2000s. Scott Lively, founder and president of Abiding Truth Ministries, traveled to Uganda in early 2000s to spread his gospel of hatred for gays. By 2009, the Ugandan legislator David Bahati sponsored the "Anti-Homosexuality Bill" that would have imposed the death sentence for anyone convicted of being a homosexual or supporting human rights for homosexuals. World leaders spoke out against the law and it was shelved for a while. Finally, in late 2013 the Ugandan legislature passed a modified bill that eliminated the death provision but still imposed life imprisonment. As expected, violence against lesbians and gays increased significantly in Uganda.

In early 2000s, Saudi Arabia publicly executed a number of men by beheading and Iran hung two teenage boys for engaging in homosexuality. Russia also cracked down on homosexuals. In 2006, the first gay pride march took place in Moscow. Counter-protesters and the police attacked the marchers. Even though the event was banned by the city of Moscow, the march was held the next four years with the same results—brutal beatings from thugs and police. Moscow officially banned all future gay events for the next 100 years. Although same-sex relations were decriminalized in 1993 and homosexuality declassified as a mental illness in 1999, Russian president Vladimir Putin signed into law in 2013 a nationwide ban against the promotion of "nontraditional" sexual relation. This effectively bans any gay pride events, speaking in defense of gay rights, and more. The law specifies large fines against citizens and corporations supporting gay rights and foreigners will be fined and deported within 15 days. The international community strongly condemned the Russian law and calls were made to boycott the 2014 Winter Olympic Games being held in Sochi (located near the Black Sea).

The end of the twentieth century and the beginning of the twenty-first saw a continuation of this process: a forward march toward greater equity for lesbians and gay men, with an occasional step backward. Many more U.S. cities and states enacted hate crime statutes and antidiscrimination statues that included sexual orientation. The U.S. military dropped homosexuality as a trait identifying spies and eventually dropped "Don't Ask, Don't Tell." President Clinton signed an executive order banning discrimination based on sexual orientation in the federal civilian workforce. And the third March on Washington in 1993 attracted an estimated 1.2 million participants.

Marriage Equality

Lesbians and gay men want their relationships to be safe and stable, and as valued by society as heterosexual relationships. Sodomy laws made the idea of same-sex marriage inconceivable since merely being homosexual classified them as "criminal." Still, some brave gays and lesbians filed for marriage licenses in the 1960s, 197070s, and 1980s without success. Many states updated their criminal codes and revoked or rescinded their sodomy statutes besides including language granting privacy and equality clauses. By 1990, three couples in Hawaii tested their state's constitution's equal protection clause by petitioning to marry. The court sided with the couples in *Baehr v. Lewin*. This sent shock waves through the cultural and political landscape of the United States. The prospect of same-sex couples having the right to marry was

incomprehensible to many Americans. For Hawaii, the same-sex marriage case was tossed between lower courts, the legislature, committees and more for the next nine years only to have it blocked by a constitutional amendment in 1999 defining marriage as the union between one man and one woman.

The prospect of same-sex marriage united conservatives and the religious right in efforts to block such marriages. At the federal level, Georgia representative Bob Barr (Republican) introduced the Defense of Marriage Act (DOMA) in 1996. The bill modified the legal code to enable states to: (1) prohibit same-sex marriages, (2) refuse to recognize same-sex marriages legally performed elsewhere and, (3) to make same-sex couples ineligible for a host of state and federal rights and benefits. The bill was fast tracked through Congress and approved with a veto-proof margin. Although President Bill Clinton was not in favor of same-sex marriage at that time, he did not think the bill was needed since marriage is traditionally a state function. Regardless, he thought the prospect of Congress overruling his veto could set off a call to change the U.S. Constitution to restrict marriage to opposite-sex couples only. The prospect of a constitutional amendment battle would divert the country from more important problems. So, he signed the bill in September 21, 1996, but did not hold a traditional bill-signing ceremony nor allow photographs to be taken of his signing. Many states also passed their own versions of DOMA. Four states passed statutes prohibiting same-sex marriages and 29 states passed amendments to their state constitutions banning same-sex marriages and the recognition of same-sex marriages legally performed elsewhere.

From the very beginning, many legal analyst and government attorneys predicted both federal and state DOMAs would not survive court challenges. At the state level, preventing civil rights based on a characteristic such as sexual orientation would be in conflict with due process and equality clauses. At the federal level, DOMA would violate the Tenth Amendment of the U.S. Constitution since it would be overreaching into state legal territory. Lawsuits were quickly filed against both federal and state DOMAs.

Vermont saw the next legal challenge for same-sex marriage. As with Hawaii, the Vermont court sided with same-sex couples and declared that same-sex couples must have the same rights as opposite-sex couples (*Baker v. Vermont*, 1999). The court pushed the problem back to the Vermont legislature to solve. In 2000, Vermont created "civil unions" for same-sex couples that conferred all the rights and responsibility of marriage without the use of the word *marriage*. This was an obvious attempt to placate religious opposition to same-sex marriage. As soon as civil unions were adopted, same-sex couples sued in court for this "separate but equal" approach to balancing the rights of LGBT citizens and religious fundamentalist. California also implemented a statewide domestic partnerships registry—the first in the nation—to provide the benefits of marriage to same-sex couples without calling it *marriage*. This approach, too, was challenged in court.

Finally, in 2004, Massachusetts became the first state in the United States to approve same-sex marriage. The Massachusetts Supreme Judicial Court ruled in 2003 (*Goodridge v. Department of Public Health*) that nothing short of full marriage would fulfill the equality clause of the state constitution.

From the Hawaii case in 1990 and for the next 20 years, many states faced the challenge of same-sex marriage. Gay and lesbian couples sued for the right to marry while legislatures wrestled with ways to either accommodate the relationship without using the word *marriage* or outright blocking them by legally defining marriage in ways to exclude same-sex couples. Many conservatives and religious fundamentalist did not trust their state legislators or courts and successfully amended their state constitutions to exclude same-sex marriage through the use of DOMA.

Importantly, the overturning of state sodomy statutes by the U.S. Supreme Court in 2003 (*Lawrence v. Texas*) effectively made homosexuals equal, under the law, to heterosexuals. By decriminalizing homosexuality, local, state, and federal governments now faced questions of how to fully integrate homosexuals and their relationships into their legal frameworks that often were constructed with a heterosexual bias.

The fight for same-sex marriage in California became an extended struggle between those favoring equal rights for all and those wanting to keep LGBT people as second-class citizens. In 2000, Proposition 22 was passed by the votes to limit marriage to one man and one woman. It added language to the Family Code and was not a constitutional amendment. In 2004, San Francisco mayor Gavin Newsom instructed city employees to grant marriage licenses to same-sex couples. He believed he had the right under the U.S. Constitution. Approximately 4,000 same-sex couples obtained their licenses before the state attorney ordered Newsom to cease and desist from issuing further license. In August, the State Supreme Court annulled the marriages. The fiasco in San Francisco encouraged State Assembly member Mark Leno in 2005 to introduce a bill legalizing same-sex marriage. At the same time, some of the couples who had their marriages annulled sued the state and antigay forces were crafting a state-wide initiative to modify the state constitution to ban same-sex marriages. Leno's bill made no progress with the legislature whereas the suits—*In re Marriage Cases*—made it to the state Supreme Court. In 2008, the California Supreme Court ruled against Proposition 22 and same-sex marriages resumed in June 16, 2008. Months before the ruling, Proposition 8 gathered sufficient signatures to be placed on the November ballot. Proposition 8 was designed to modify the state constitution to ban same-sex marriages. Between June and November 2008, approximately 18,000 same-sex marriages were performed. Proposition 8 was narrowly approved by the voters which brought an immediate cessation to same-sex marriages. Proposition 8 was challenged in court and the California State Supreme Court ruled it to be a valid amendment to the constitution. That put California in the unique position of having thousands of legal marriages that other citizens could no longer obtain the same right. American Foundation for Equal Rights (AFER) took the case to federal court to challenge Proposition 8 under the U.S. Constitution. U.S. District Court for the Northern District of California judge Vaughn R. Walker conducted a full trial and ruled Proposition 8 unconstitutional in August 12, 2010, because it violated both the due process and equal protection clauses of the U.S. Constitution (*Perry v. Schwarzenegger* renamed *Hollingsworth v. Perry*). Neither the governor nor attorney general wanted to defend the state against the ruling. However, supporters of Proposition 8 appealed the case to the U.S. Supreme Court. On June 26, 2013, the Court ruled that the petitioners did not possess legal standing, which reverted to Judge Walker's ruling. Same-sex marriage resumed in California on June 28, 2013.

Much happened throughout the country during the 10 years of legal skirmishes in California. In 2008, Connecticut became the second state to approve same-sex marriage. Many more states enacted same-sex marriage laws: Iowa (2009 by judicial decision), Vermont (2009 by legislative action), New Hampshire (2010 by legislative action), District of Columbia (2010 by legislative action), New York (2011 by legislative action), Maine (2012 by ballot initiative), Maryland (2012 by ballot initiative), Washington (2012 by ballot initiative), California (2013 by judicial decision), Delaware (2013 by legislative action), Minnesota (2013 by legislative action; just six months after voters rejected an antigay marriage initiative the legislature passed enabling legislation), Rhode Island (2013 by legislative action), New Jersey (2013 by judicial decision), Illinois (2013 by legislative action taking effect in 2014), Hawaii (2013 by legislative action), a few counties of New Mexico (2013 by judicial action), and Utah (2013 by judicial action). Also, a number of First People nations approved same-sex marriage: Native American nations of Ceara & Little Traverse Bay Bands of Odawa Indians (Michigan), Pokagon Band of Potawatomi Indians (Michigan), Santa Ysabel tribe (California), and the Confederated Tribes of the Colville Reservation (Washington).

Importantly, in 2013 the U.S. Supreme Court ruled the DOMA to be unconstitutional (*United States v. Windsor*). The Court decided that Section 3 of DOMA violated the due process clause of the Fifth Amendment. The case clearly demonstrated the inequality DOMA imposed on LGBT citizens. Here, Edith "Edie" Windsor and Thea Spyer, residents of New York, married in Toronto, Ontario, where same-sex

marriages were legal. The women had been together for 40 years and built up significant assets. Spyer died in 2009 and Windsor was required to pay $363,053 in federal estate taxes on her inheritance of her wife's estate. If they had been an opposite-sex couple, there would have been no inheritance tax. The court agreed that Section 3 of DOMA, which specified that the term "spouse" only applied to opposite-sex marriage, denied due process to same-sex couples.

By 2014, 19 states, the District of Columbia, and eight First People nations have approved same-sex marriages in the United States. In late 2014, legal reviews in Arkansas, Idaho, Illinois, Kentucky, Michigan, Ohio, Oklahoma, Oregon, Pennsylvania, Texas, Utah, Virginia, and Wisconsin resulted in permanently establishing same-sex marriage rights in those states. This means a majority of Americans now reside in states that respect marriage equality. For the first time, a sitting president—Barack Obama—voiced his support in 2012 for same-sex marriages. Likewise, for the first time a U.S. Supreme Court judge—Ruth Bader Ginsburg—officiated at a same-sex marriage in 2013. It is expected that these trends will continue and eventually, the U.S. Supreme Court will rule that same-sex marriage must be allowed everywhere and treated equally to opposite-sex marriage.

Sodomy

Beginning with the revision of Illinois criminal code in 1961and the repeal of its statutes against consensual sodomy, the number of states with sodomy laws reduced significantly over the next 50 years. Gay activists and attorneys brought attention to state legislatures and courts about the unfairness of these laws. Sodomy laws are a violation of the modern concept of privacy and result in the unequal application of the law (a violation of the equal protection clause of the U.S. Constitution). Many courts revoked their state's sodomy laws. Less than one-third of the states by 2002 still had them on the books. Still, the shadow cast by the 1986 U.S. Supreme Court decision in *Hardwick* held influence over many sodomy statutes.

In 2003, the U.S. Supreme Court revisited the issue of sodomy in *Lawrence v. Texas*. John Lawrence and Tyron Garner were arrested in their home for engaging in consensual anal and oral sex. Police had entered John Lawrence's home investigating a possible crime when they witnessed the acts. Under Texas "Homosexual Conduct" it was a Class C misdemeanor crime if someone "engages in deviate sexual intercourse with another individual of the same sex" (Chapter 21, Sec. 21.06 of the Texas Penal Code). Lawrence pleaded not guilty and his attorneys argued that the charges violated the Fourteenth Amendment of equal protections since the law applied only to same-sex couples and not opposite-sex couples. The three- judge panel of the Texas Fourteenth Court of Appeals ruled the Texas law was unconstitutional and violated the 1972 Equal Rights Amendment to the Texas Constitution. The full Court of Appeals reversed the decision. Ultimately, the case was taken to the U.S. Supreme Court. The Court ruled that the Texas statute was unconstitutional since it violated due process and equal protection guarantees. The Court affirmed that sexual behaviors conducted in the privacy of the home between consenting adults could not be restricted. Also, sexual conduct laws had to apply equally to opposite-sex couples as they do to same-sex couples. There is a misconception that *Lawrence* declared sodomy unconstitutional throughout the country. Some states still have sodomy statutes on the books, which are used to prosecute public sex, forced sex, prostitution, and sex with minors. The net effect of *Lawrence* was to require states to recognize same-sex sexual activity on the same footing as opposite-sex sexual activity. This concept of equality would help pave the way toward recognizing same-sex marriages. It is important to recognize that it has been predominantly heterosexual judges who came to understand that sodomy laws are discriminatory and invasive and ruled them invalid.

Another consequence of sodomy provisions has been the impact on forced sterilization and psychopathic incarceration. In 1907, Indiana became the first state (in fact, the first government in the world) to enact a sterilization law. It targeted "confirmed criminals" including those convicted of sodomy. Soon, more than half the states enacted similar legislation.

Similarly, in 1936 Michigan enacted the first psychopathic offender law. The goal was to protect the public from criminals who were "psychopathic"—a broad term that includes sexual offenders. In a short time, more than half the sates enacted similar laws. Both the sterilization and psychopathic laws were used against "sexual deviants." Sodomy laws classified all same-sex sexual behavior as "deviant." LGBT citizens fared poorly because they were, by legal definition, deviant and criminal. Being defined as "criminal" by default prevented many LGBT people from being able to adopt children, hold specific jobs (like teachers, police officers, military personnel), marry, and exposed them to legal persecution with imprisonment and forced medical treatment and torture. As the sodomy laws were revised and repealed beginning in the 1960s, so were the psychopathic and sterilization laws rescinded. Sodomy would not be effectively repealed until 2003. In many ways, the explosion in gay rights seen in the 2000s to now is the result in lifting the stigma related to automatically being defined as "criminal." This is a prime example where defining a particular group (here LGBT citizens) as "criminal" impacted their employment, family, safety, health, and welfare.

Don't Ask, Don't Tell

In 1983, the Uniform Code of Military Justice (UCMJ) was modified to formally ban homosexuality by classifying all forms of "unnatural carnal copulation" to be "sodomy" and punishable by court-martial. The definition applied to both same- and opposite-sex couples (and with animals). The vagueness of the code allowed it to be applied capriciously and facilitated "witch hunts" against LGBT personnel.

When Bill Clinton became president of the United States in 1992, one of the first issues he took up was the presence of gays in the military. The fierce response by many legislators and the religious right resulted in a compromise bill entitled "Don't Ask, Don't Tell" (DADT) being approved in 1993. It did not radically change the UCMJ but rather added words that directed military personnel to not inquire as to a person's sexual orientation, not to share if known, and if rumors were heard to not pursue or harass. Instead of liberating LGBT military personnel, it created a hostile environment of whispers and court-martial. From 1993 through its repeal 17 years later, more than 14,500 service men and women were discharged from the military under DADT (Servicemen Legal Defense Fund n.d.). Ironically, prior to 1993, the discharges from the military for homosexuality were declining (Burrelli 2010).

When Barack Obama was sworn in as president in 2010, he promised to work with Congress toward the repeal of the law. Soon, a number of congressional committees along with the secretary of defense reviewed DADT. At the same time, federal judge Virginia A. Phillips ruled the 1993 law unconstitutional. Under pressure from the court and the White House, the House of Representatives and Senate passed legislation repealing DADT. President Barack Obama signed the policy into law September 20, 2011. Minutes after the repeal of DADT became official policy, U.S. Navy Lt. Gary Ross married his partner of 11 years, Dan Swezy, making them the first same-sex couple in the military to be legally married. The impact of the law's repeal is to allow LGBT personnel to serve openly, previously discharged personnel can re-enlist if they choose to, and a "less than honorable" discharge due to DADT could be upgraded to "honorable" status thereby opening up right to VA benefits.

Restricting Rights

Colorado's Amendment 2 was one of the watershed decisions made by the U.S. Supreme Court concerning gay rights. Early in the 1990s, a number of cities and counties in the state of Colorado enacted antidiscrimination statutes that included sexual orientation. This angered a number of conservative residents. Colorado for Family Values (CFV) was formed and successfully placed an amendment to the Colorado Constitution on the ballot. Amendment 2 sought to repeal any existing law or policy that protected persons with "homosexual, lesbian, or bisexual orientation" from discrimination in the state and to prohibit future adoption or enforcement of any such law or policy. CFV claimed the amendment provided "special rights" to lesbians, gay men, and bisexuals that they neither "deserved" nor "needed."

The "special rights" argument has a long history. Originally used by opponents of laws prohibiting discrimination based upon race, the slogan implies that a particular class of people will be given rights or privileges beyond what the majority have. "In truth, the laws simply ensured that minorities would have the same rights the majority already had, to participate in society without fear of discrimination" (Keen and Goldberg 1999, p. 10). Brain McCormick, staffs counsel for Pat Robertson's National Legal Foundation, coached CFV to keep the term *special rights* out of the initiative, but to use it in all campaign promotions. As McCormick explained, "If language denying special privileges to homosexuals is in the amendment it could possibly allow homosexuals to argue that they are not asking for special privileges, just those granted to everyone else. [However] I believe that 'No Special Privileges' is a good motto for the amendment's public campaign" (Keen and Goldberg 1999, p. 11). It is important to realize the religious right knows the expression "special rights" is not valid, but that it uses the slogan to influence voters and raise money.

In November 3, 1992, the voters passed the amendment with 53 percent in favor and 46percent against. A temporary injunction was granted and six months later Judge Bayless of the Colorado District Court for Denver heard the case. He rejected all state claims. The state appealed to the State Supreme Court, which upheld Judge Bayless's decision.

In 1995, the U.S. Supreme Court agreed to review the Colorado Supreme Court's decision. The Court characterized Amendment 2 as "unprecedented in our jurisprudence" in that it identified "persons by a single trait and then denies them protection across the board. . . . A law declaring in general that it shall be more difficult for one group of citizens than for all others to seek aid from government is itself a denial of equal protection of the laws in the most literal sense." Also, Amendment 2 "inflicts on [gay people] immediate, continuing, and real injuries that outrun and belie any legitimate justifications that may be claimed for it."

The Court ruled (six to one) that Amendment 2 appeared to violate the fundamental right of lesbians, gay men, and bisexuals to participate in the political process on a basis equal to other Coloradans. Justice Kennedy stated, "We conclude that Amendment 2 classifies homosexuals not to further a proper legislative end but to make them unequal to everyone else. This Colorado cannot do. A state cannot so deem a class of persons a stranger to its laws."

The Court made a number of findings important to the rights of lesbians and gay men. First, the Court agreed that homosexuals have a long history of being persecuted. Second, the Court accepted the medical, psychological, social, and scientific evidence that homosexuality is not a medical disorder and equivalent to heterosexuality. These two findings have significantly impacted other courts and administrative decisions nationwide. For example, at the trial of the two men who brutally murdered Matthew Shepard in 1998, the judge refused to allow the "homosexual panic" defense—a completely discredited stereotype. Likewise, fewer judges are willing to allow antigay stereotypes to be used as the basis for taking children away from gay and lesbian parents during child custody and adoption proceedings.

Schools and Anti-Bullying Programs

Another major development occurred in the public schools. Many schools faced having to accept a gay-straight alliance (GSA) student group on campus. A number of schools refused to accept these groups, but courts consistently upheld the Equal Access Act (EAA), which requires schools to accept all noncurricular student groups on an equal footing. This trend should continue with many more, if not most, schools having gay supportive programs on campus.

Schools have traditionally been a dangerous place for gay and lesbian students. One celebrated case has changed this completely. Jamie Nabozny experienced terrible abuse from other students while attending an Ashland, Wisconsin, high school. He was attacked by other students, mock raped, urinated upon, and kicked so badly he required surgery to stop internal bleeding. His parents complained to school officials who told

them he "had to expect that kind of stuff" because he was a homosexual. He sued and a jury found the school officials violated Jamie's rights under the Fourteenth Amendment's Equal Protection Clause and the District was forced to pay $900,000 in damages (*Nabozny v. Podlesny*).

The Gay and Lesbian Independent School Teachers Network (GLSTN) was founded in 1990. Its goal was to help organize local volunteer groups of lesbian and gay educators and Gay-Straight Alliances (GSAs). In 1997 it changed its name to Gay, Lesbian and Straight Education Network (GLSEN) to broaden its appeal to include straight allies. By 2010, it coordinated more than 3,600 GSAs and had a staff of approximately 40 full-time employees. It has hosted more than eight national conferences. The Trevor Project was founded in 1998 and focused specifically on young (13–24-year-old) LGBTQ people to provide crisis intervention. The GLSEN has set up a nationwide network of telephone hot lines to help youth with their questions and issues surrounding their sexuality, coming out, and bullying. Trevor Project is named after the 1994 Academy Award winning film named *Trevor* about a gay teen boy considering suicide.

A number of tragic suicides made the news in late 2000s. Many centered on gay kids who experienced extreme bullying about their sexual orientation. School districts around the country began implementing anti-bullying campaigns. The suicide by 18-year old Tyler Clementi influenced syndicated columnist Dan Savage to launch the "It Gets Better Project" in 2010. The goal was to compile 100 or so videos from individual contributors to post on YouTube that would convey the message to gay and lesbian kids that life would get better as an adult and to "hang in there." By February 2011, more than 10,000 people had submitted videos watched more than 30 million times. The "It Gets Better Project" gained overwhelming support from politicians, school districts, and LGBT support organizations like GLSEN and Trevor Project. Savage published a hard copy book entitled: *It gets better: Coming Out, Overcoming Bullying, and Creating a Life Worth Living* by Dutton in 2011 besides audio materials. The book reached spot 16 on *The New York Times* best-seller list in 2011.

Public Access

The 1990s also brought to the forefront the potential conflict between antidiscrimination statutes and the desires of private organizations. Two U.S. Supreme Court decisions illustrate this problem. Each year the Boston St. Patrick's Day Parade is sponsored by the South Boston Allied War Veterans Councils. They refused to allow a gay marching group to participate. The gay group sued and the court initially sided with the gay group. The parade organizers canceled the event and appealed to the U.S. Supreme Court. In *Hurley v. Irish-American Gay, Lesbian and Bisexual Group of Boston* (1994), the Court upheld the First Amendment right of the organizers to exclude gays from their event, not because they were gay but rather because the "private" organizers of the event had the right to control the message of the event. The Court said parades are a "form of expression" and private sponsors cannot be forced to include groups that "impart a message the organizers do not wish to convey."

Similarly, the U.S. Supreme Court upheld the right of the Boy Scouts to exclude openly gay men from serving as troop leaders or participating as members (*Boy Scouts of America v. Dale*, 2000). They held that requiring the Boy Scouts to include Mr. Dale in their ranks would violate the organization's First Amendment right of "expressive association." The Court said, "We are not, as we must not be, guided by our views of whether the Boy Scouts' teachings with respect to homosexual conduct are right or wrong. Public or judicial disapproval of a tenet of an organization's expression does not justify the state's effort to compel the organization to accept members where such acceptance would derogate from the organization's expressive message."

Although many lesbians and gay men saw the St. Patrick's Day Parade and Boy Scout cases as losses, some civil libertarians believe they were the right decisions. Private organizations need to retain the right to select their members and promote their cause. However, the dividing line between public and private

is not clear. The aftermath of the Boy Scouts case has been a withdrawal of support for the Boy Scouts by many cities, school districts, and local governments. They often have nondiscrimination conditions for use of facilities and the Boy Scouts are open about their discrimination. Many of these agencies have withdrawn their support of the Boy Scouts in favor of organizations that do not discriminate (e.g., the Indian Guides, Police Cadets, Girl Scouts, Camp Fire Girls). The Boy Scouts ultimately lifted its ban on gay scout members in 2014 yet retained its ban on gay adult leaders.

The Culture Wars

Some political analysts believe lesbians and gay men have already won the culture wars and that the complete elimination of sodomy laws, the right to marriage, and so on, are mopping up activities, albeit ones that may take another generation or two to achieve. They point to the fact that more and more cities, counties, and states are enacting antidiscrimination statutes and hate crime reporting procedures and enforcement, businesses are extending domestic partnership benefits to their employees with same-sex partners, and more. Television has gay characters on many programs, from MTV's *The Real World* to ABC's *Will and Grace* to ShowTime's *Queer as Folk* and many more. Every bookstore has a gay and lesbian section. And schools nationwide have to accept gay-straight student groups on campus and are incorporating lesbian and gay educational materials into their curriculum from kindergarten to high school level.

The knowledge that homosexuals are virtually indistinguishable from heterosexuals and that both orientations are equally valid has gradually filtered into society. It was scientist in the 1950s to 1970s, most of whom were heterosexual, whose studies influenced the APA to recognize that homosexuality is as valid as heterosexuality. The predominately heterosexual membership of APA supported removing homosexuality as a mental illness. This knowledge spread to city councils, state legislatures, courts, places of religious service, schools, and more. Public attitude has also shifted significantly, with most Americans accepting the idea of gay adoption, gays in the military, and support for nondiscrimination laws. Changes in laws and policies have come about because heterosexuals understood that discrimination against homosexuals was unfounded and unfair.

The religious right has always recognized homosexuality as an issue that generates significant funds. For example, Robert Billings, the first executive director of the Moral Majority, stated, "I know what you feel about these queers, these fairies. We wish we could get in our cars and run them down when they march. . . . We need an emotionally charged issue to stir up people. . . . I believe that the homosexual issue is the issue we should use" (Young 1982, p. 78). Throughout the 1990s, the religious right increased the use of homophobic rhetoric to raise money and recruit followers (Berlet 1998; Mookas 1998).

Sexual Orientation Change Efforts (and Exodus)

By the late 1990s, there was a shift in the tactics of the religious right, claiming that homosexuals are child molesters and mentally ill just did not have the impact that it used to have. Likewise, "No Special Rights" is still used, but it too is losing its impact. Too many people, courts, and politicians know these stereotypes and slogans are completely untrue. A new tactic was used to raise funds from conservatives and the religious right and that was the claim homosexuals could change their sexual orientation. Their logic was that since they believed homosexuality was a sin, then not changing his or her sexual orientation was proof that LGBT persons were not deserving of equal rights.

From the earliest days of the gay rights movement, there have been organizations and persons who claimed sexual orientation could be changed. One of the earliest organizations was founded in 1973 in San Francisco called Love in Action. It was an "ex-gay" ministry that provided spiritual counseling for gay men wishing to reduce their homosexual feelings and become heterosexual. Often referred to as "reparative" therapy (i.e., to "repair" their "broken" sexual orientation), an international organization formed to help coordinate worldwide change efforts. Exodus

International would grow to include over 270 ministries. Various psychological techniques were used to attempt to change a person's sexual orientation including shock therapy, talk therapy, behavioral modification, aversion therapy, and prayer (often humorously referred to as "pray away the gay").

Many religious leaders and some academic researchers jumped on the Sexual Orientation Change Effort (SOCE) bandwagon. Paul Cameron, a discredited psychologist and sex researcher, founded the Institute for Scientific Investigation of Sexuality (renamed the Family Research Institute [FRI] in 1982) to promote his materials. The academic materials produced by FRI are used extensively by the religious right to support their antigay beliefs. FRI is identified as a hate group by the Southern Poverty Law Center. Similarly, the National Association for Research & Therapy of Homosexuality (NARTH) was founded in 1992 to provide clinically based sexual orientation conversion therapies and too produced academic-looking materials used by the religious right.

Regardless that most of these ex-gay programs experienced major scandals (e.g., leaders found preying on their homosexual clients, use of same-sex prostitutes, and more), the money poured in during the 1980s and 1990s. In July 1998, full-page paid advertisements were placed in major national newspapers promoting the "ex-gay" movement. The ads were purchased through a coalition of 15 Christian Right organizations. They condemned homosexuality as a sin but emphasized curing homosexuality as an act of prolife. They hope to plant the idea that homosexuality is a chosen lifestyle and is alterable. Logically this would imply that homosexuals have chosen a lifestyle that is stigmatized and "criminal" with legal restrictions, discrimination, and pain. They claimed that all homosexuals need to do is choose heterosexuality to receive full rights. Accepting the ex-gay movement's position would undermine lesbian and gay men's claim to civil rights. "The ex-gay movement poses a significant new threat to efforts to secure civil rights legal protections for gay/lesbian/bisexual/transgender people. Potentially, it is the most damaging manifestation of an ongoing backlash against this community. . . .

The long-term goal of the Christian Right in using the ex-gay movement to convince people that lesbian, gay, and bisexual people can become heterosexual is to create a restrictive legal environment in which equal rights are only accorded to heterosexual men and women" (Khan 1998, pp. 17–18).

In 2003, Dr. Robert Spitzer published an article that claimed "highly motivated" homosexuals could change their sexual orientation. This was significant because Dr. Spitzer was a highly regarded expert and considered "unbiased" since he was part of the effort in 1973 to have the American Psychological Association declassify homosexuality as a mental disorder. Immediately the religious right held up his work as proof that homosexuals could change if they really wanted to. However, therapists were hearing more and more horror stories about SOCE therapy from their clients. For example, a friend of John Evans (one of the founders of Love in Action) committed suicide due to his inability to change. Evans stated in a 1993 interview with *The Wall Street Journal* that SOCE destroyed people lives and proponents are living in a fantasy world. Every major psychology organization came out against SOCE claiming that it not only didn't work but that it also caused emotional harm in those attempting to change. Between 2012 and 2013, the SOCE industry collapsed. Alan Chambers, president of Exodus International, told the Gay Christian Network in 2012 that all efforts to change sexual orientation were failures and potentially harmful. Exodus International publicly apologized for all the harm it caused and disbanded. Similarly, Dr. Spitzer published a letter in *Archives of Sexual Behavior* in 2012 apologizing to the gay community. He acknowledged that his 2003 research was flawed, that sexual orientation cannot be changed, and SOCE harmed clients.

California senator Ted Lieu became concerned about the terrible toll SOCE was taking on its citizens and, in particular, its teenagers. He authored a bill to prohibit the use of reparative therapy on children under age 18. It passed and was signed into law in 2013 by Governor Jerry Brown who stated, "These practices have no basis in science or medicine, and they will now be relegated to the dustbin of quackery"

(Shapiro 2013). The law was challenged but the court concluded that the state has the right to regulate specific industries and create standards. SOCE was proven to not work and harm clients and, thus, the state could require licensed therapists to not engage in such activity or risk losing their license. New Jersey has passed a similar law and many other states are considering the same. The National Center for Lesbian Rights is the primary organization spearheading the national effort to ban SOCE.

Theocratic State

It is important to remember the religious right's goal is to create a theocratic state, a "nation whose laws are based on fundamentalist's interpretation of the Bible" ("We've come a long way. . . maybe" 2000). Founder and director of the Christian Coalition, Pat Robertson, stated, "The country was founded by Christians. It was founded as a Christian nation. They're trying to sell us this nonsense about separation of church and state. And that's what it is, it's a fanatical interpretation of the First Amendment. . . . We're going to win this battle but we've got to stand together, all the Christians in America need to join hands together and say we've had enough of this utter nonsense" (White 1997). Similarly, Dean Wycoff, director of the Moral Majority of Santa Clara County, California, stated, "I agree with capital punishment and I believe that homosexuality . . . could be coupled with murder. . . . It would be the government that sits upon this land who will be executing the homosexuals" (Young 1982, p. 77). The agenda of the religious right is to take control of the United States and use state power to discriminate, incarcerate, and kill those who do not agree with them—particularly homosexuals.

Separate but Equal

The gay rights movement parallels the civil rights movement. The process of overcoming prejudice is the process of deconstructing a social bias. For example, we have seen African Americans move from being nonpersons and property when slavery was legal to gaining citizenship through the adoption of the Fourteenth Amendment to the U.S. Constitution. But there was a backlash by Christian conservatives who influenced state and local authorities to enact Jim Crow laws that kept the races separate. For almost 100 years, separate-but-equal was the law of the land and terror perpetrated by white supremacists was used to keep blacks in their place. Then, in 1954, the U.S. Supreme Court ruled that separate-but-equal was inherently unequal. Only then was America faced with fully integrating African Americans into the society. Still, the Civil Rights Act of 1964 and other legislative acts were required to ensure the equal participation of people of different races. This process deconstructed the allocation of rights and privileges associated with race.

Lesbians and gay men are entering the second phase of overcoming the stigmatization associated with their sexual orientation. Until the beginning of the civil rights movement, homosexual behavior was illegal and lesbians and gays were often arrested, prosecuted, imprisoned, and killed, and were constantly at risk of losing their jobs, homes, and children. Slowly, cities and states have removed antigay laws and replaced them with antidiscrimination laws aimed at providing some protection in the areas of employment and housing. With the possibility of same-sex marriages being recognized, there has been a terrible backlash by Christian conservatives who have influenced federal and state governments to define and defend marriage as an exclusive heterosexual institution. Some states are attempting to ameliorate the situation by providing domestic partnership for same-sex couples while retaining marriage for heterosexuals. Vermont implemented a "civil union" program that confers all the same legal rights and responsibilities associated with marriage without having to call such unions "marriage." As such, lesbians and gay men are entering the separate-but-equal phase of civil rights.

But civil unions are still not the full equivalent of marriage; other states do not recognize them. This is similar to the recognition by courts that separate schools for blacks still do not confer all the same benefits that whites enjoy in segregated schools. It is expected that the courts will eventually rule that any scheme that attempts to give lesbians and gays the same rights enjoyed by heterosexuals without giving them exactly the same right is inherently unequal. Ultimately, gay liberation will deconstruct sexual orientation much as African American liberation deconstructed race and the women's movement deconstructed gender.

The major impediment to African Americans gaining equal rights has been white supremacists and Christian fundamentalists. The major impediment to women's rights has been male supremacists and Christian fundamentalists. The major impediment to gay rights has been heterosexist people and Christian fundamentalists. In each case, the arguments used by bigots and Christian fundamentalists—such as blacks and women are naturally inferior, a position they support by quoting scientists of the time and scripture from the Bible—have been shown to be false. The stereotypes used against homosexuals have all been proven false. More than anything, this demonstrates that discrimination against a class of people is never justified and that the real issue is not science or scripture, but a *culture war* involving those in power and those who are stigmatized. The way a culture is changed is through education. As more people, courts, and politicians learned homosexuals are virtually indistinguishable from heterosexuals, bias and discrimination were reduced. Heterosexuals overcame their homophobia and heterosexism and changed society to make it safe for people of differing sexual orientations to exist together. Heterosexuals are an important and necessary ally for lesbians, gay men, bisexuals, transgenders, transsexuals, and intersex people.

Chuck Stewart

Further Reading

Baehr v. Lewin, 74 Haw. 530, 852 P.2d 44 (1993), reconsideration and clarification granted in part, 74 Haw. 645, 852 P.2d 74 (1993).

Baker v. Vermont, 744 A.2d 864 (Vt. 1999).

Bayer, R. 1981. *Homosexuality and American psychiatry*. New York: Basic Books.

Berlet, C. 1998. "Who Is Mediating the Storm? Right-Wing Alternative Information Networks." In *Media, Culture, and the Religious Right*, ed. L. Kintz and J. Lesage, pp. 249–74. Minneapolis, MN: University of Minnesota Press.

Blumenfeld, W. J. and D. Raymond, eds. 1993. *Looking at Gay and Lesbian Life*, rev. ed. Boston, MA: Beacon Press.

Boy Scouts of America v. Dale, No. 99–699 U.S. (2000).

"Buchanan Calls AIDS 'retribution.'" *Boston Globe*, February 28, 1992.

Burrelli, David F. 2010. "'Don't Ask, Don't Tell': The Law and Military Policy on Same-Sex Behavior. Congressional Research Service". (2010). Available at: https://www.fas.org/sgp/crs/misc/R40782.pdf. Accessed November 18, 2013.

Childers v. Dallas Police Dept., 513 F. Supp. 134 (N.D. Tex. 1981).

D'Emilio, J. 2004. *Lost Prophet: The Life and Times of Bayard Rustin*. Chicago: University of Chicago Press.

D'Emilio, J., and E. B. Freedman. 2012. *Intimate Matters: A History of Sexuality in America*, 3rd ed. Chicago: University of Chicago Press.

Gay Students Org. v. Bonner, 367 F. Supp. 1088 (D.N.H.), *aff'd*, 509 F.2d 652 (1st Cir. 1974).

Goodridge v. Dept. of Public Health, 798 N.E.2d 941 (Mass. 2003).

Hollingsworth v. Perry (formerly *Perry v. Brown* and *Perry v. Schwarzenegger*), 570 U.S. ___ (2013) (Docket No. 12–144).

Hooker, E. 1963. "The Adjustment of the Male Overt Homosexual." In *The Problem of Homosexuality*, ed. H. M. Ruitenbeed, pp. 141–61. New York: Dutton. (Reprinted from *Journal of Projective Techniques, 21*, 18–31, 1959.)

Hurley v. Irish-American Gay, Lesbian and Bisexual Group of Boston, No. 94–749, (1995, June 19).

In re Marriage Cases, 43 Cal.4th 757 (2008).

Katz, J. 1976. *Gay American History: Lesbians and Gay Men in the U.S.A.* New York: Thomas Y. Crowell.

Keen, L. and S. B. Goldberg. 1999. *Strangers to the Law: Gay People on Trial*. Ann Arbor, MI: The University of Michigan Press.

Khan, S. 1998, October. *Calculated compassion: How the Ex-Gay Movement serves the Right's attack on democracy*. A report from Political Research Associates, the Policy Institute of the National Gay and Lesbian Task Force, and Equal Partners in Faith.

Lawrence v. Texas, 539 U.S. 558 (2003).

Letter from Hall Call to Dwight Huggins, Sam Morford, Tony Segura, et al., August 30, 1956; appended to Segura's letter to Huggins in MSNY files. Reported in Marotta, T. 1981. *The Politics of Homosexuality* (p. 15). Boston: Houghton Mifflin Company.

Marcus, R. 1990. "Powell Regrets Backing Sodomy Law." *Washington Post*, (325), October 26, A3.

Marotta, T. 1981. *The Politics of Homosexuality*. Boston: Houghton Mifflin Company.

Mookas, I. 1998. "Faultlines: Homophobic Innovation in Gay Rights/Special Rights." In *Culture Media, and the Religious Right*, ed. L. Kintz and J. Lesage. Minneapolis, MN: University of Minnesota Press.

Nabozny v. Podlesny, 92 F.3d 446, 7th Cir. 1996.

One, Inc. v. Olesen, 355 U.S. 371 (1958).

Plant, R. 1988. *The Pink Triangle*. New York: New Republic Books/Henry Holt.

Servicemen Legal Defense Fund. n.d. "About Don't Ask Don't Tell." Available at: http://www.sldn.org/pages/about-dadt. Accessed September 13, 2013.

Shapiro, Lila. 2013, June 25. "Straight Talk: How Mathew Shurka and His Conversion Therapist Renounced the 'Gay Cure'." *Huffington Post*. Available at: http://www.huffingtonpost.com/2013/06/25/mathew-shurka-conversion-therapy_n_3466943.html. Accessed January 1, 2014.

Shilts, R. 1987. *And the Band Played On: Politics, People, and the AIDS Epidemic*. New York: St. Martin's Press.

Stewart, C. K. 2001. *Homosexuality and the Law: A Dictionary*. Denver, CO: ABC-CLIO.

Thompson, M., ed. 1994. *Long Road to Freedom: The Advocate History of the Gay and Lesbian Movement*. New York: St. Martin's Press.

United States v. Windsor, 570 U.S. ___ (2013) (Docket No. 12–307).

"We've Come a Long Way. . . Maybe." 2000, March 3. *Frontiers* 18(22): 12.

White, M. 1997. *The Justice Report* (Special Edition). Selected quotes from the *700 Club*. Soulforce, P.O. Box 4467, Laguna Beach, CA 92652, journey@soulforce.org.

Young, P. D. 1982. *God's Bullies: Native Reflections on Preachers and Politics*. New York: Holt, Rinehart, & Winston.

Hooker, Evelyn (1907–1996)

Evelyn Hooker's research in psychology in the early 1950s opened the door to scientific demonstration that homosexuals are not mentally ill. Born on September 2, 1907, Hooker was the sixth of nine children. She lived next door to Buffalo Bill's home in North Platte, Nebraska. Her parents were extremely poor. They had lived in a sod house in Sand Hills just months before her birth. Her family lived on a succession of small farms, and she attended one-room schoolhouses.

She entered the University of Colorado on a tuition scholarship in 1924. She chose the Psychology Department because, in part, it allowed her to work in the department and pay her own way through college. In her senior year, Hooker accepted an instructor position that enabled her to work on a master's degree. In 1930 Hooker was determined to go to an eastern university for her doctoral degree. She wanted to attend Yale University, but the chair of the department refused to recommend a woman. She went to Johns Hopkins University instead. She completed her PhD in 1932 at the height of the Depression. There was no academic position for her other than a teaching position at a small women's college near Baltimore.

In the fall of 1934, she came down with tuberculosis and went west to a sanitarium in California. She recovered, and after two years of convalescence she obtained a part-time teaching position at Whittier College. There she received an anonymous fellowship that allowed her to travel to Germany and Russia in 1937 and 1938. Experiencing these totalitarian states intensified her feelings that she wanted to do something important with her life to help correct social injustices.

Soon, she was offered a research associate position in the Psychology Department of the University California, Los Angeles (UCLA), where she remained until 1970. She enjoyed teaching, and it was at the suggestion of some of her students that she decided to conduct research with homosexuals. She conducted exploratory research, but her divorce in 1947 and subsequent remarriage in 1951 postponed the project.

In 1953, Hooker applied to the National Institute of Mental Health for a six-month grant to study the adjustments of nonclinical homosexual men and to compare them to a similar group of heterosexual men. This had never been done. All previous research had included only homosexuals who either were in prison or were mental patients. John Eberhart, chief of the grants division of the institute, explained that her application was quite extraordinary considering this was the height of the McCarthy witch-hunt era. Even so, she received the grant, which was continually renewed until 1961. In her 1957 research, Hooker found that expert clinical judges could not distinguish the projective test protocols of nonclinical homosexual men from those of a comparable group of heterosexual men, nor were there differences in adjustment ratings. Her findings were soon validated by other academic investigators. Research by Hooker and others directly led to the American Psychiatric Association deleting homosexuality from the *DSM* in 1973. Hooker gained great satisfaction from contributing to the freedom of and lifting of the stigma from this marginalized group.

Hooker entered private practice in the 1970s and was appointed chair of the National Institute of Mental Health Task Force on Homosexuals. She won many awards and acclaims. She died at her home in Santa Monica, California, on November 19, 1996, at the age of 89.

Chuck Stewart

See also: American Psychiatric Association (APA); Historical Overview of Gay Rights and Issues: From Pre-Columbian Times to the 1970s.

Further Reading:

Ball, L. 2010. "Profile of Evelyn Gentry Hooker." In *Psychology's Feminist Voices Multimedia Internet Archive*, ed. A. Rutherford. Available at: http://www.feministvoices.com/evelyn-gentry-hooker/. Accessed February 2, 2014.

Hooker, Evelyn. 1965. "An Empirical Study of Some Relations between Sexual Patterns and Gender Identity in Male Homosexuals." In *Sex Research: New Development*, J. Money (cur.), pp. 24–52. Holt, Rinehart & Winston, New York 1965.

Hooker, Evelyn. 1957. "The Adjustment of the Male Overt Homosexual." *Journal of Projective Techniques* 21(1): 18–31.

Hooker, Evelyn. 1961. "The Homosexual Community." Proceedings of the XIV International Congress of Applied Psychology, Munksgaard, Copenhagen.

Marmor, J., 1997. "Evelyn Hooker: In memoriam (1907–1996)." *Archives of Sexual Behavior* 25(5): 577–78.

Shneidman, E.S. 1998. "Evelyn Hooker (1907–1996)." *American Psychologist* 53(4): 480–81.

Human Rights Campaign (HRC)

The Human Rights Campaign (HRC) is the largest gay and lesbian political organization in the United States. In 2014, the HRC had an annual budget of $32 million and a staff of more than 240 people. It is estimated that the HRC has an active membership of around 1.5 million people throughout the United States. The primary work of the HRC happens in Washington, D.C., on Capitol Hill; however, many collateral activities of the HRC are focused in the 25 communities around the United States where the organization has steering committees.

The HRC is made up of three related organizations: the Human Rights Campaign Foundation, a nonprofit, tax-deductible, educational organization; the HRC, a nonprofit organization that lobbies the U.S. Congress; and the HRC PAC, an organization that endorses and funds federal, state, and local candidates for elective office.

History

The Human Rights Campaign Fund (HRCF) was founded in 1980 by Steve Endean to raise money for gay-supportive congressional candidates. Endean was already working in Washington, D.C., as the director of the Gay Rights National Lobby (GRNL), an organization with a mission to lobby Congress on behalf of gay and lesbian people. The HRCF incorporated in

1982 with the mission to "advance the cause of lesbian and gay civil rights by supporting and educating candidates for federal elective office." In 1982, former vice president Walter "Fritz" Mondale spoke at the HRCF fund-raising dinner at the Waldorf-Astoria in New York City. At the time, he was the highest-ranking elected official to address a gay and lesbian audience.

From its inception, HRCF was part of Endean's vision for a three-prong strategy to advance and mainstream gay liberation. First, GRNL would lobby Congress; second, HRCF would make political contributions to congresspeople; and third, Endean would organize another grassroots mobilization program to generate constituent mail. Although Endean's vision would be ultimately implemented through the HRCF, conflict between Endean and the board of directors prompted his departure from the organization in 1983.

Vic Basile became the next executive director of the HRCF. In addition to political savvy, Basile brought greater fund-raising capacity to the organization; in 1983, the first direct mail fund-raising appeal was done, signed by literary luminary Tennessee Williams. In 1985, under the leadership of Basile, the Gay Rights National Lobby and the HRC merged their operations. Later that year, the new organization, still called the HRCF, merged with the Fairness Fund, a grassroots program founded and run by Endean to generate constituent mail to congresspeople. The main program of the Fairness Fund was retained and renamed "Speak Out." "Speak Out" operated as an autonomous program under the penumbra of the HRCF well into the 1990s; today the HRC continues to generate constituent communications to congresspeople, now relying mostly on electronic communication tools.

In 1986, HRCF thwarted efforts to diminish a District of Columbia law that barred insurance firms from denying coverage to people testing HIV-positive. It was the first victorious roll call vote on Capitol Hill for the gay and lesbian community. It was one of many legislative initiatives relating to HIV and AIDS, ultimately leading to the Ryan White CARE Act, on which the HRCF worked.

HRC president Chad Griffin speaks during a rally celebrating the historic rulings from the Supreme Court that Prop 8 is unconstitutional, alongside attorneys Ted Olson and David Boies, Prop. 8 plaintiffs Kris Perry and Sandy Stier, and Paul Katami and Jeff Zarrillo and thousands of other marriage equality supporters on June 26, 2013, in West Hollywood, California. (Bret Hartman/AP Photo for Human Rights Campaign)

When Vic Basile departed as executive director in 1989, Tim McFeeley was hired. McFeeley, an activist from the Boston area, expanded the strategy of city-based, black-tie fund-raising dinners dramatically. From a few gala dinners along the Eastern seaboard to nearly 20 by the end of his tenure in 1994, the revenue from these events enabled the substantial growth of the organization during this period.

While comprehensive gay rights legislation was the focus of the HRCF's lobbying activity throughout the 1980s, the first affirmative bill to pass was the Hate Crimes Statistics Act in 1990. HRCF representatives, at the invitation of President George H. W. Bush, attended the signing ceremony for the

Hate Crimes Statistics Act. It was the first successful piece of legislation the organization passed and reflected a partnership with the National Gay and Lesbian Task Force and a number of other national and local gay and lesbian organizations. Later that year, the Ryan White CARE (Comprehensive AIDS Resource Emergency) Act was passed in August 1990. The act was designed to improve the quality and availability of care to people with HIV/AIDS and their families.

The fall of 1992 brought the election of William Jefferson Clinton as president. As a candidate he distinguished himself by speaking directly to the hopes and dreams of the gay and lesbian community and

Rosie O'Donnell, left, listens on stage as Elizabeth Birch, right, makes her comments at a rally for the Human Rights Campaign on August 27, 2004, in Fort Lauderdale, Florida. (AP Photo/Rick Silva)

promising to "end discrimination with the stroke of a pen" through an executive order to lift the ban on gays and lesbians in the military. The ensuring national debate about military service energized and emboldened the gay and lesbian community.

While the HRCF was gaining political clout in Washington, D.C., there was increasing organizing at a grassroots level across the United States dating from the 1987 March on Washington on October 11. From that March a new organization, National Coming Out Day, emerged to celebrate the anniversary of this historic march. In 1993, National Coming Out Day merged with the HRCF. Combined efforts of these two groups brought new action and visibility to National Coming Out Day, including celebrity spokespeople.

Tim McFeeley departed from HRCF at the end of 1994, just as the Republicans swept into Congress with their regressive "Contract with America." Elizabeth Birch began as executive director in January 1995. A former attorney for Apple Computer and an activist as the cochair of the National Gay and Lesbian Task Force, Birch led the organization through a revamped marketing campaign resulting in dropping the name "Fund" and the introduction of the now iconic equal sign logo. She was responsible for significant expansion in the fund-raising and programmatic work of the institution as well as overseeing the successful capital campaign.

In 1996, Congress came within a few votes of passing the organization's then cornerstone legislation, the Employment Non-Discrimination Act, which

Human Rights Campaign president Chad Griffin takes the stage at the Human Rights Campaign Dinner Gala on March 22, 2014, in Los Angeles, California. (Josh Edelson/AP Photo for HRC)

would provide workplace protections to gay and lesbian people; however, the act came a few votes short of success, and instead, the Defense of Marriage Act (DOMA) passed the House and the Senate and was signed by then president Bill Clinton. The failure to prevent the passage of DOMA may be the greatest defeat suffered by the organization.

Despite this defeat, the work of the HRC continued. In 1997, President Bill Clinton spoke at HRC's National Dinner in Washington, D.C., the first sitting president to address a gay and lesbian organization. In 1998, the endorsement of then senator Alfonse D'Amato in the New York Senate race brought controversy anew to the HRC and created a rift for the organization in the state of New York. It forced the organization to reconsider its endorsement criteria.

In early 1999, the HRC turned its efforts to organizing a Millennial March on Washington in April 2000, gathering hundreds of thousands of marchers on behalf of gay and lesbian equality. Organizing for the march was politically challenging, with a variety of political factions on all sides criticizing the organizing model, the timeliness of the march, and the proposed political platform. The march eventually attracted hundreds of thousands of people and featured a rock concert titled "Being Out Rocks." From the Millennial March on Washington, the HRC moved into a $25 million capital campaign to purchase the current headquarters at 1640 Rhode Island Avenue in northwest Washington, D.C. The capital campaign was successfully completed at the end of 2003. At that time, Elizabeth Birch departed as executive director.

Moderator Hilary Rosen, director of the Human Rights Campaign (HRC) Family Project Ellen Kahn, and senior director of Communications of ESA Dan Hewitt speak at Electronic Arts' LGBT Full Spectrum Event on March, 7, 2013, in New York City, New York. (Photo by Amy Sussman/Invision for EA/AP Photo)

Cheryl Jacques, a former state senator from Massachusetts, succeeded Birch. Jacques's tenure began shortly after the court in Massachusetts ruled that gay and lesbian people must have the right to marry. During Jacques's tenure, HRC focused on civil marriage for gay, lesbian, bisexual, and transgender people. Jacques served for nine months as the president and executive director. Hilary Rosen, Elizabeth Birch's long-time partner, was the acting director of HRC upon the departure of Cheryl Jacques. Long known in the gay and lesbian community in Washington, D.C., and the former head of the Recording Industry Artist Association (RIAA), Rosen is recognized consistently as a key thinker behind HRC strategies and tactics. Joe Solmonese was appointed president and executive director of HRC in April 2005 from his long-time position at EMILY's List, a political organization dedicated to electing prochoice Democratic women to the House and the Senate.

In 2008, President Barack Obama was the keynote speaker at HRC's 13th Annual National Dinner. After 11 years of hard work by HRC and other organizations, President Barack Obama signed the Matthew Shepard and James Byrd, Jr. Hate Crimes Prevention Act in 2009. HRC's national strategy helped overturn the military discriminatory "Don't Ask, Don't Tell." HRC remains at the forefront of the marriage equality efforts nationwide. For example, in the fight for marriage equality in New York, HRC dedicated 30-full time field organizers who generated over 150,000 constituent contacts. HRC spent years advocating for the passage of the Employment Non-Discrimination Act (ENDA), which makes it illegal, in companies employing 15 people or more, to refuse to hire people based on their sexual orientation or gender identity. Finally, in November 2013 the U.S. Senate voted 64 to 32 to pass ENDA, but the legislation is languishing in the House of Representatives (as of 2014). HRC continues major fund-raising to influence elections for progressive pro-gay candidates.

Organizational Description

Today, the organization continues to be the lead lobby on Capitol Hill on gay, lesbian, bisexual, and transgender issues, addressing fair employment practices, domestic partner benefits, and HIV/AIDS policy, as well as working to defeat anti-GLBTQ legislation. Each year the organization coordinates thousands of personal communications from constituents to federal officials as well as hundreds of lobby visits to congresspeople in Washington, D.C. and in their home districts.

Each election cycle, the HRC releases a "Congressional Scorecard" that rates all congresspeople based on votes over their careers. In addition, the HRC and the affiliated HRC PAC contributed over $1.5 million to GLBTQ-supportive candidates during the last election cycle. Recently, the HRC has expanded its PAC contributions from exclusively focusing on federal candidates to also focusing on state and local candidates in races of strategic significance.

The HRC is governed by a board of governors, which includes people elected from each of the organization's steering committees around the country and numbers in excess of one hundred people, as well as by a smaller board of directors. Each steering committee has at least a dozen members engaged in the local work of the organization, including fund-raising through the black-tie dinners, "Federal Club," and community events, as well as political work and diversity work. Hundreds of notable lesbian and gay leaders have served as members of the organization's boards as well as on the staff.

The affiliated HRC Foundation, governed by an independent board of directors, is an educational component of the organization. The HRC Foundation sponsors programs focusing on workplace issues, National Coming Out Day, issues of religion and faith

that effect the GLBT community, outreach to students at Historically Black Colleges and Universities, and family issues. Through the HRC Foundation, the Corporate Equality Index, as well as a variety of other educational publications, is published.

Praise and Critique

Throughout the lifetime of the organization, the HRC has been criticized and become the focus for internal debates of policy and strategy for the gay and lesbian movement. From its beginning in 1980, gay activists questioned Endean's "mainstream" approach, particularly in light of the radical and liberatory politics of the 1970s. Many activists found these values embodied more effectively by the work of the then National Gay Task Force. Critiques of the HRC as being "too mainstream," not "radical" enough, and not "inclusive" enough have been a regular part of the discourse about the organization throughout its 25-year history.

The reliance on black-tie fund-raising dinners and its visible history of predominately white gay men in leadership roles have led critics to label it the "Human Rights Champagne Fund" or the "Highly Rich Campaign Fund." Periodic efforts to diversify the board and staff of the organization, particularly in terms of gender and race, have addressed these concerns in various ways at different times.

Throughout the late 1990s, when many gay and lesbian organizations were amending their work and mission statements to be more transgender inclusive, the HRC was reticent with regard to the inclusion of transgender people in either the public presentation of the organization or in its programmatic work and advocacy. Eventually, it did amend its mission statement to include transgender people and gender identity and has in recent years included transgender people in central legislative initiatives.

The HRC has also been criticized for its focus on marketing to and merchandising for gay and lesbian people—some believe to the exclusion of working on a legislative agenda. The pervasive use of the equal sign logo and the organization's retail outlets are two visible examples of actions that raise these concerns.

Praise for the HRC has been as voluminous as critique. The organization has been praised by numerous politicians and Capitol Hill insiders for its savvy legislative and political work to advance the rights of gay and lesbian Americans. Many credit the HRC with helping to create an environment of greater political acceptance of gay and lesbian people and gay and lesbian issues at federal and state levels. Others attribute to the work of HRC greater political understanding and insight among people in the gay, lesbian, bisexual, and transgender communities throughout the United States. The historical archives of the organization are available at Cornell University.

Julie R. Enszer

See also: National Coming Out Day; National Gay and Lesbian Task Force.

Further Reading

Brelin, Christa. 1996. *Strength in Numbers: A Lesbian, Gay and Bisexual Resource*. Detroit, MI: Visible Ink Press.

Chasin, Alexandra. 2000. *Selling Out: The Gay and Lesbian Movement Goes to Market*. New York: St. Martin's Press.

Endean, Steve, with Vicki L. Eaklor, ed. 2006. *Bringing Lesbian and Gay Rights into the Mainstream: Twenty Years of Progress*. New York: Harrington Park Press.

HRC Home. Available at: http://www.hrc.org. Accessed July 8, 2008. (The historical archives of the organization are available at Cornell University.)

S.815—Employment Non-Discrimination Act of 2013; 113th Congress (2013–2014). Available at: http://beta. congress.gov/bill/113th-congress/senate-bill/815.

K

Kameny, Franklin (1925–2011)

Kameny has been described by a historian of gay and lesbian rights as "[o]ne of the most significant figures" in the American gay rights movement (Bullough 2002, p. 207). Trained as an astronomer, Kameny became active in the gay and lesbian rights movement when he was fired from his job with the Army Map Service (now the Defense Mapping Agency) in January 1958 for being gay. He has spent the rest of his life working for gay and lesbian rights, largely in response to this action. Throughout his career, he had taken a strong, confrontational approach in an effort to obtain equal rights for gay men and lesbians. In 1965, for example, he and Jack Nichols organized the first picket line around the White House in pushing for gay and lesbian rights. He is also credited with having created the slogan "Gay is good" in 1968. In 1971, Kameny

Buttons from Franklin Kameny's collection of gay rights memorabilia seen at an exhibit in Washington on June 3, 2009. (AP Photo/Jacquelyn Martin)

became the first openly gay man to run for national public office when he ran for the post of nonvoting delegate to the U.S. House of Representatives from the District of Columbia.

Kameny was born in New York City on May 21, 1925. His parents were Polish and Austro-Hungarian Jews. He taught himself to read by the age of four, and two years later had decided that he wanted to become an astronomer. He entered Queens College at the age of 15, but his education was interrupted by World War II. At the war's conclusion, he returned to Queens and earned his BS in physics in 1948. He then continued his education at Harvard College, from which he received his master's degree in astronomy in 1949 and his PhD in astronomy in 1956. After a year of teaching at Georgetown University, Kameny

took a position with the Army Map Service. He served in that position for only a brief period of time before being fired for being gay. Not given to yielding on matters of principle, Kameny then began a long series of court battles to regain his job. His fundamental premise throughout this fight was that his employer (the U.S. government) had no right to inquire into his personal life unless it interfered with his work, a claim the government never made. No organization, including the American Civil Liberties Union, was willing to support Kameny's position, and when his case finally reached the Supreme Court, he had to write his own brief. The Court declined in March 1961 to hear Kameny's case, and he decided that his life thenceforward would have a new direction—he was going to become a gay activist.

President Barack Obama is congratulated by Franklin E. Kameny, right, after delivering brief remarks and signing a presidential memorandum regarding federal benefits and nondiscrimination during a ceremony in the White House Oval Office on June 17, 2009, in Washington, D.C. Applauding from left to right are Vice President Joe Biden, Representative Barney Frank (D-MA), and Senator Joseph Lieberman (I-CT). (AP Photo/Haraz N. Ghanbari)

One of his first acts was to organize (with Nichols) a Washington chapter of New York City's Mattachine Society. Kameny began to put into practice his attitudes about the gay rights issue. It was necessary not for gays to change and adapt to an oppressive society, he argued, but to help educate the non-gay world and help them to recognize the legitimacy of the gay rights cause. He outlined his position in an article he wrote for *The Ladder* in 1965 when he said, "We ARE right; those who oppose us are both morally and factually wrong. . . . We must DEMAND our rights boldly, not beg cringingly for mere privileges, and not be satisfied with the crumbs tossed to us" (Blasius and Phelan 1997, p. 335).

In the last decade of his life, Kameny received many awards and, most important, a formal apology from the U.S. government. In 2002, the Harvard Gay and Lesbian Caucus gave its lifetime Achievement Award to Kameny for his contributions to the gay and lesbian rights movement. In February 2009, Kameny's home was recognized by the District of Columbia's Historic Preservation Review Board and designated as a D.C. Historic Landmark. Later, on June 29, 2009, Kameny received a formal apology on behalf of the U.S. government for being fired from his position as astronomer in 1958. John Berry (director of the Office of Personnel Management), who is openly gay, presented Kameny with the Theodore Roosevelt Award—the department's most prestigious award—for his untiring efforts to protect the rights of LGBT employees from unwarranted discrimination in

John Berry, left, director of the Office of Personnel Management, talks with Representative Barney Frank (D-MA), right, and LGBT activist Rick Rosendall, center, before the start of memorial service in honor of gay rights pioneer Franklin Kameny on Capitol Hill in Washington, D.C., on November, 15, 2011. (AP Photo/Pablo Martinez Monsivais)

federal employment. When President Barack Obama signed the Don't Ask, Don't Tell (DATA) Repeal act of 2010, Kameny represented the Triangle Foundation's Board of Advisors and was honored to be seated in the front row of witnesses to the signing. Kameny died at home from heart disease on October 11, 2011 (Dunlap 2011).

David E. Newton

See also: Federal Employment Nondiscrimination Order; Historical Overview of Gay Rights and Issues: From Pre-Columbian Times to the 1970s; Mattachine Society.

Further Reading

Bianco, David. 1999. *Gay Essentials: Facts for Your Queer Brain*. Los Angeles: Alyson Books.

Blasius, Mark and Shane Phelan. 1997. *We Are Everywhere: A Historical Sourcebook of Gay and Lesbian Politics*. New York: Routledge.

Bullough, Vern L., ed. 2002. *Before Stonewall: Activists for Gay and Lesbian Rights in Historical Context*. New York: Haworth Press.

Dunlap, David. 2011, October 12. "Franklin Kameny, Gay Rights Pioneer, Dies at 86." *New York Times*. Available at: http://www.nytimes.com/2011/10/13/us/franklin-kameny-gay-rights-pioneer-dies-at-86.html?_r=0. Accessed February 2, 2014.

Gambone, Philip. 2010. *Travels in a Gay Nation: Portraits of LGBTQ Americans*. Madison: University of Wisconsin Press.

Kisseloff, Jeff. 2007. *Generation on Fire: Voices of Protest from the 1960s*. Lexington: University Press of Kentucky.

Murdoch, Joyce and Deb Price. 2001. *Courting Justice: Gay Men and Lesbians v. The Supreme Court*. New York: Basic Books.

King, Billie Jean (1943–)

Although best known as the top-ranked athlete on the tennis courts of the world for over 10 years, Billie Jean King also served as a role model for the empowerment of women to *make it in a man's world*. She was a women's rights pioneer in sport, outspoken against

Tennis star Billie Jean King at the Los Angeles premiere of TV movie *When Billie Beat Bobby* in 2001. (Featureflash/Dreamstime.com)

sexism in both sport and society, and an activist for gay rights.

Billie Jean Moffitt was born on November 22, 1943, in Long Beach, California. Her parents were conservative and traditional; her father, Bill, served as a fireman in the community and her mother stayed at home. Athletic ability was obviously in the family genes, however, for her brother, Randy, also entered professional sports as a major league pitcher for various baseball franchises.

While attending Long Beach Polytechnic High School, Billie Jean won the women's doubles title at Wimbledon in her first effort and met her future husband, attorney Lawrence King. In 1970, King was the first woman athlete to demand and receive prize monies topping $100,000 and helped to found the Virginia Slims professional tour for women. Three years later, she organized a union for women tennis players, the Women's Tennis Association, which she served as first president. Over her athletic career, she took home 20 Wimbledon titles and turned women's tennis into not only a media event but also a legitimate sport. She was the first woman to receive *Sports Illustrated*'s coveted "Sportsperson of the Year" award.

As a radical feminist, King became a symbol for gender equality in sport. Although her initial focus was to secure equal prize money for women, her efforts extended beyond the financial into areas of self-esteem for and empowerment of young women athletes. In 1981, King was the first prominent American athlete to come out as openly gay and, in 2000, she received an award from the Gay and Lesbian Alliance Against Defamation, a group whose mission was to reduce discrimination against homosexuality. The award was presented to her for "furthering the visibility and inclusion of the community in her work" and for her activities with several AIDS charities.

Although that one particular event paled beside her other accomplishments, King gained a universal reputation for her participation in "The Battle of the Sexes." Tennis hustler Bobby Riggs announced that he wanted "to take down a noted libber" and invited King to a match. She turned down his first offer but when he bested his second choice, Margaret Court, Billie Jean knew she had no choice but to recoup for her gender. By the appointed date in 1973, the Houston Astrodome was packed with over 30,000 spectators and television coverage added more than 90 million viewers in 37 countries, producing the largest audience ever to witness a tennis match. Always the proverbial showman, Riggs staged the event: Billie Jean was carried into the arena on a Cleopatra-type Egyptian litter lifted by several muscular men; Riggs entered in a drawn rickshaw. At center court the two exchanged gifts; King received a Sugar Daddy and she presented Riggs with a live baby pig, both symbols

Retired tennis champion Bobby Riggs challenged Billie Jean King to a battle of the sexes tennis match in 1973. King beat Riggs in three sets and helped female athletes gain ground in matters of pay and recognition on September 20, 1973. (Bettmann/Corbis)

of the slang of the era. King smashed through three sets, winning each by at least two points. She said if she had not won, it would have set women back 50 years and affected the self-esteem of all women. Thus, considered a win for equality and women's rights, the match produced a trickle-down effect in various areas of society as well as enhancing the image of women's sports. The bottom-line message was that a woman could succeed in a man's world where it was then safe to be a feminist.

In 1974, King worked as the player/coach of the Philadelphia Freedoms of World Team Tennis, a team she founded with her former husband, Larry King.

She also created tennis clinics for children from impoverished neighborhoods and set up a foundation to aid in building self-esteem for women through sports. In addition, she served as the first woman commissioner in the history of professional sports.

For her work in empowering women and educating men, King received the 1998 Elizabeth Blackwell Award presented to one whose life exemplified outstanding service to humanity. She was named one of the one hundred most important Americans of the twentieth century by *Life* magazine.

Joyce D. Duncan

Further Reading

King, Billie Jean with Christine Brennan. 2008. *Pressure Is a Privilege: Lessons I've Learned from Life and the Battle of the Sexes*. New York: LifeTime Media.

Roberts, Selena. 2005. *A Necessary Spectacle: Billie Jean King, Bobby Riggs, and the Tennis Match That Leveled the Game*. New York: Crown Publishers.

Ware, Susan. 2011. *Game, Set, Match: Billie Jean King and the Revolution in Women's Sports*. Chapel Hill: University of North Carolina Press.

Kramer, Larry (1935–2008)

Larry Kramer was a founder of AIDS Coalition to Unleash Power (ACT UP) and was one of the earliest AIDS activists. Kramer was born in Bridgeport, Connecticut, on June 25, 1935. He grew up in a middle-class household, received his bachelor of arts degree from Yale, and served a brief stint in the army. He found work as an agent with the William Morris Agency in New York City. Within a year, he began working for Columbia Pictures as an assistant story editor and then production executive. United Artists hired him to be the assistant to the president in 1965.

By 1969, he was a respected screenwriter and wrote the screenplay for and produced Ken Russell's film *Women in Love*. For his effort, Kramer was nominated for an Academy Award. The movie was famous for its homoerotic elements, something unseen at the time.

In 1978 Kramer published his first novel, called *Faggots*. It was a satire of a gay man's search for love in bathhouses and bars. Many in the gay community denounced the work but Kramer argued that it was meant to be a serious critique of the excesses of certain people within the gay community.

Kramer was one of the first to write essays on what we now know as AIDS. In his famous "1,112 and Counting" article, he wrote: "If this article doesn't scare the shit out of you, we're in real trouble. If this article doesn't rouse you to anger, fury, rage, and action, gay men may have no future on this earth. Our continued existence depends on just how angry you can get" (Russell 1995, p. 187).

Seeing the potential devastation from AIDS, Kramer, along with five other men, founded the Gay Men's Health Crisis (GMHC) in 1982. Kramer's combative personality forced him to resign one year later. He used that experience to frame his 1985 drama, *The Normal Heart*. Although many agents and directors initially turned the drama down, eventually it was produced and won the 1986 Dramatists Guide Marton Award, the City Lights Award, and the Sarah Siddons Award for best play of the year. It was later made into a movie. The purpose of the play was to make people see gay men as men who love men and are supportive during the dying process.

In 1987 Kramer was the primary force behind the creation of the ACT UP. Its purpose was to encourage public disobedience to draw attention to the AIDS crisis. Its first demonstration was held on March 24, 1987, on Wall Street in New York City. Almost 300 men and women tied up traffic for several hours chanting for AIDS reform. Many were arrested, and the story garnered widespread media attention. ACT UP spread across the country, with chapters found in every major city.

Kramer learned he was HIV-positive and infected with Hepatitis B in 1988. He responded by writing the critically acclaimed 1992 play, *The Destiny of Me*. The play ran off-Broadway for a year at the Lucille Lortel Theatre by the Circle Repertory Company. It continues to be produced throughout the world.

Larry Kramer's brother, Arthur Kramer, was a very financially successful attorney and founder of the law firm Kramer Levin. In 2001, Arthur gave Yale University $1 million to establish the Larry Kramer Initiative for Lesbian and Gay Studies. In later years, Arthur was a staunch gay rights advocate and helped with many high-profile gay cases in the U.S. Supreme Court, including *Lawrence v. Texas* (2003). Arthur Kramer died in 2008 from a stroke.

Hepatitis B took its toll on Larry Kramer and was told in 2001, at the age of 61, that he needed a liver transplant. He was initially turned down because of his HIV status. At that time patients with HIV were routinely turned down for transplants due to the perception that they had short lifespans. Eventually the Thomas E. Starzl Transplantation Institute at the University of Pittsburgh accepted Kramer on its waiting list. He received a new liver on December 21, 2001.

Five days after George W. Bush was reelected as president in 2004, Kramer published the speech "The Tragedy of Today's Gays." The speech contrasted Bush's claim to be the president of "moral values" while at the same time condemning LGBT people. He stated, "Please note that a huge population of the United States hates us" (Kramer 2005, 3, pp. 6–37). He concludes that gay men and lesbians need to take more urgent action, not less.

On July 24, 2013, Kramer married his life-long partner architectural designer David Webster. His in-your-face activism has made Kramer one the most influential gay men in America today.

Chuck Stewart

See also: ACT UP (AIDS Coalition to Unleash Power); Albee, Edward (1928–).

Further Reading

Johansson, Warren and William A. Percy. 1994. "The Making of an AIDS Activist: Larry Kramer." In *Outing: Shattering the Conspiracy of Silence*, ed. John Dececco and William Percy, pp. 162–64. New York and London: Haworth Press.

Kramer, Larry. 2005. *The Tragedy of Today's Gays*. City of Westminster, London: Penguin.

Russell, Paul. 1995. *The Gay 100*. New York: Kensington Books.

Specter, Michael. 2002. "Public Nuisance, Larry Kramer the Man Who Warned America about AIDS, Can't Stop Fighting Hard and Loudly." *The New Yorker*, May 13.

L

Lambda Legal Defense and Education Fund (LLDEF)

In 1971, several attorneys incorporated the Lambda Legal Defense and Education Fund in New York State. The organization was based on the model of the National Association for the Advancement of Colored People (NAACP) Legal Defense Fund and, like it, intended to provide legal support for political groups fighting for the rights of gay men and lesbians. The Stonewall Riots had occurred in 1969, and the Gay Activists Alliance was providing the grassroots organizational skills for pressing the demands of the movement. The plan was that Lambda would provide necessary legal assistance by finding volunteer lawyers to litigate on behalf of the movement.

When Lambda was organized, LGBT people had few legal rights. Most states made gay sexual activity a felony, and those laws were the lynchpins for judicial decisions prohibiting adoptions by gays, upholding exclusion of LGBT people from various professions, and outlawing gay student groups, and for the entire range of homophobic legislation.

Until the early 1980s, Lambda had only one paid lawyer on staff and had to depend on volunteer litigators. Nevertheless, quite a bit was accomplished in those years. The federal government was forced to stop giving gay service members dishonorable discharges (which denied them housing and GI benefits). Cities were forced to allow gay pride parades. Gay community services were required to be listed in phone books. Prisons were required to allow inmates access to gay publications.

With the onset of the HIV epidemic in the 1980s, Lambda expanded its staff and its volunteer base dramatically. The organization was directly involved in a wide range of cases on behalf of people who were fired from their jobs, refused services at restaurants, and evicted from their homes because they were infected with HIV. Lambda was also directly involved in litigation requiring medical coverage by insurance companies and helped establish the right to keep medical records confidential.

Lambda was a leading force in the two most significant U.S. Supreme Court victories relating to LGBT people. *Romer v. Evans* (1996) successfully challenged a voter-enacted amendment to Colorado's constitution that prohibited cities from enacting gay rights laws. *Lawrence v. Texas* (2003) overturned all remaining sodomy laws in the United States.

Lambda staff members and volunteer attorneys have been in the forefront of the difficult fight to provide protections for lesbian and gay families. They have won cases that require that committed same-sex couples be given the same rights as heterosexuals, and have fought voter initiatives to outlaw same-sex marriages. Lambda's record is not perfect on these issues, nor is the battle over. But in almost any gay or lesbian litigation, Lambda is not only involved but is also a central player.

Lambda continues to shape public policy and litigate when necessary on the whole range of issues related to LGBT people. In 30 years, it has grown from a few volunteers to a staff of more than 80 with a national headquarters and four regional offices across

Susan Sommer, lead attorney from the Lambda Legal Defense and Education Fund, speaks outside the Arkansas Supreme Court in Little Rock on June 27, 2002. Sommer, who represented seven gay plaintiffs, argued that the Arkansas law banning sex between people of the same sex violates citizens' constitutional rights to privacy and equal treatment under the law, thus making it unconstitutional. (AP Photo/Mike Wintroath)

the country, supplemented by cooperating attorneys in every state.

Jim Kellogg

See also: ACT UP (AIDS Coalition to Unleash Power); American Civil Liberties Union (ACLU); Stonewall Riot.

Further Reading

Lawrence v. Texas, 539 U.S. 558 (2003).

LLDEF website. Available at: http://www.lambdalegal.org.

Romer v. Evans, 517 U.S. 620 (1996).

Latino/Latina Americans and LGBTQ Issues

The presence and contributions of Latinos/Latinas in the U.S. gay rights movement have been largely ignored in spite of their active involvement in the Stonewall Riots of 1969, which began the modern movement. Transgender activist Sylvia Ray Rivera was but one leader in the famous riots and their aftermath. The exclusion of Latinos/Latinas from the homophile movement results in what author-historian Emma Pérez calls the necessity to create a *sitio y lengua*, our own place and language. By creating and building spaces of recognition, Latinos/Latinas are able to discuss the effects of homophobia and address the needs specific to the Latino LGBTQ community.

The first significant large-scale organization of the gay community began in 1951, with the founding of the Mattachine Society in Los Angeles, California. Although the Mattachine Society did a great deal for the homosexual community, its members were mostly upper-class European American men. The group portrayed itself as representing the gay community as a whole; however, it served only white men. With the 1955 formation of the Daughters of Bilitis (DOB), lesbians attempted to educate women to live without the presence of men. The formation of this group was predicated on the "different experiences and concerns of gay women and men" (D'Emilio 1983, p. 105). Although the group tried to focus on the needs of *all* lesbians, it, too, failed, in the sense that the DOB attracted mostly European American women of semiprofessional status. The membership of the DOB distanced itself from the working-class bar culture that badly needed organizing. Exclusion of poor, working-class women inherently meant that participation by women of color in the DOB would be lacking.

The 1950s and 1960s, however, became decades of multiple civil rights movements, from African American to Chicano and Native American. The rise in activism led to the abandonment of an accommodationist standpoint by gay and lesbian organizations in favor of an activist approach. By 1965 a collective identity had been formed among gays and lesbians, resulting in greater and more explicit militancy. The culmination of two decades of activism was visibly

Stonewall veteran Sylvia Rivera leads the ACT UP march past New York's Union Square Park on June 26, 1994. The march was one of two held to commemorate the 25th anniversary of the riot at the Stonewall Inn, a Greenwich Village bar that erupted in violence during a police raid in 1969. (AP Photo/Justin Sutcliffe)

expressed in the often-cited major event in gay history, the Stonewall Riots of 1969. This event is important not only because it birthed the modern gay rights movement, but also because the Stonewall was a drag bar frequented mostly by minorities, Puerto Ricans, and other low-income patrons. These Puerto Rican drag queens, lesbians, and gay men continued the rioting throughout the first night and after (Adam 1987, p. 75). Embodying a colonized relationship to the United States, Puerto Rican activists had a long history of resisting U.S. encroachments on their island and of migration to New York City because of U.S. capitalism, which drove many off their lands at home and into impoverishment. Other Latino organizers and groups would think about the meaning of Puerto Rican drag queens, often the most despised members of a minority population, standing up to the New York Police Department. Latinos' involvement in the Stonewall Riots was a call to action for

the Latino LGBTQ community and prompted the subsequent creation of Latino gay and lesbian organizations in the 1970s.

The large number of independent gay and lesbian organizations that arose following Stonewall dealt not only with homophobia and sexism but also with discrimination and prejudices encountered among European American gays. Latinos/Latinas most often sought to highlight the overlapping issues that affected them, such as race, national origin, ethnicity, color, and gender. Some of the organizations that were formed in the early 1970s were *El Comite de Orgullo Homosexual Latinoamericano* (COHLA), *Comunidad de Orgullo Gay*, Greater Liberated Chicanos, and the Gay Latino Alliance (GALA). Some existed on either the East Coast (COHLA) or the West Coast (GALA).

The Latino groups that were formed in the 1970s brought attention to a distinctly Latino gay agenda. The basic rights that European American gays desired,

Transgender activist and prominent AIDS leader Diego Sanchez talks about his work as a legislative assistant to Representative Barney Frank (D-MA) on Capitol Hill in Washington, D.C. Sanchez became the first transgender person named to the Democratic Party's national platform committee in 2009. (J. Scott Applewhite/Corbis)

health care, and protection of equal voting privileges. "Gay and lesbian rights are human rights, which are in fact, Latino civil rights" (M. Ornealas-Quintero, personal communication, July 1999).

Although the leadership of gay organizations such as the large group originally known as the National Latina/o Lesbian and Gay Organization (LLEGO—an acronym that, when translated, means "arrived"), but finally designated the National Latina/o Lesbian, Gay, Bisexual & Transgender Organization, recognizes the link between gay rights and Latino rights, many Latino organizations treat gays as invisible members of the community. Groups formed after and during the U.S. civil rights movement (post-1964), including the Mexican American Legal Defense and Education Fund (MALDEF), initially placed gender and sexuality low in the categories of cases or causes they would represent. Instead, they decided to prioritize supporting educational equity and property rights or fighting job discrimination; as a result, sexual identity or orientation was rarely the key issue at play in the cases these financially pressed organizations advanced.

One of the primary mobilizing points for the Latino gay movement was also the most difficult one it tackled in the twentieth century: HIV and AIDS. The LGBTQ community rallied to design programs to educate and inform Latinos/Latinas about the prevention of HIV and AIDS when it became clear that poor Latino and African American men comprised one of the fastest-growing segments of the population dying from the disease and were also the least likely to be able to afford the attendant expensive and exploratory treatments.

Formed during the crisis and intended to help educate the community about HIV disease, the Gay and Lesbian Latinos Unidos de Los Angeles (GLLU) also represented an important new and significant change in political organizations at the urban level: both gay men and lesbians, as well as bisexuals of all genders, organized to promote education and social services and to draw attention to the extreme conditions of poverty and neglect that tended to exist, especially among immigrant Latinos/Latinas and poor communities of color.

such as full and equal citizenship, the right to live happily and openly, the right to the material benefits society gives to preserve families, and the right to serve in the military, were driven by middle-class aspirations or middle-class status, along with a healthy dose of liberalism and belief in the American doctrines of equal protection under the laws (Nava and Dawidoff 1995, pp. 135–36). These desired rights reflect Latinos' aspirations as well. In addition, however, to these basic demands or interests, Latino gays and lesbians had other views that proved particular to their community, including those related to the realities of race, class, and gender oppression (Martinez 1998, p. 102). Examples of these would be educational equity, access to

GLLU was instrumental in forming the program Bienestar through community outreach. Through it, *Queers Understanding Education, Power and Solidarity = Advancement*, or *QUE PAS = A* (translation: What's happening?), has been an important part of HIV and AIDS education in the Los Angeles area. By providing free HIV screenings, safer-sex instruction, and a dedicated space to discuss questions about sex and sexuality, the program has reached many people in the Latino LGBTQ community. Programs like *QUE PAS = A* exist throughout the country now, intended to meet the needs of Latinos.

In 1986, various Latino/Latina gay and lesbian organizations attended the International Lesbian and Gay People of Color Conference in Los Angeles. There, the Latino caucus met to discuss the need to create a national organization that could help smaller local groups to better serve the Latino LGBTQ community. The following year, during the Lesbian and Gay Rights March on Washington, D.C., the need for such an organization was again raised and LLEGO was created (LLEGO, Cornell holdings 2003).

LLEGO was formed at the Primer Encuentro Conference in 1987, as the national clearinghouse that would represent gay and lesbian Latinos/Latinas in the United States and Puerto Rico. The purpose of the organization was to:

- organize the LGBTQ Latina/o communities from grassroots to national and international levels through mobilization and networking in a culturally sensitive environment in order to overcome social, health, and political barriers faced due to sexual orientation, gender identity, and race/ethnicity.

- advance community and individual self-determination and empowerment among Latina/o LGBTQ individuals; to develop and obtain access to culturally appropriate health and wellness services; and facilitate the development of cultural, political and community resources.

- work within the mainstream Latino/Hispanic community in addressing deep-rooted homophobia, sexism, and discrimination through culturally and linguistically appropriate capacity-building assistance and

training designed to sensitize that community. (1994 LLEGO Mission Statement, in Cornell holdings)

LLEGO forums served as an opportunity to identify resources within and outside the community. One forum was held in San Diego, California, on October 10 and 11, 1999, and others followed into the new century as more and more Latino/Latina gays and lesbians linked in causes that helped serve their communities, first at the global or international level, and then at home.

Congreso Internacional was one "gathering of grassroots activists designed to teach, inform and create social change" (LLEGO-Final Report 1999, in Cornell holdings). The inclusion of grassroots organizations and activists in this forum ensured that the concerns and issues of people at all levels would be heard and addressed. Representatives from over 20 Latin American and Caribbean countries attended the *Encuentro*. The program format was designed to "address the challenges that we face as Lesbian, Gay, Bisexual, and Transgender Latinas/os as well as giving an opportunity to customize training programs to the needs of the Latino LGBTQ community" (LLEGO-Final Report 1999, in Cornell holdings).

Reviewing the components of the *Encuentro*, or *congreso*, suggests some new developments in terms of interactions with mainstream but also global LGBTQ movements. First, many derive from younger people's increasing identification with the term *queer*, whereby racial and ethnic identity are subsumed under this larger umbrella. Second, whether or not such identification is accurate or historically negligent is less an issue than the fact that the global or international approach derives from an interest in linkages beyond the borders or boundaries of the United States. In other words, what Latino LGBTQ organizations, congresses, or gatherings have to offer gay and lesbian movements in the United States is a healthy dose of the way the world increasingly moves beyond borders and in coalitions formed around specific issues. Such broachings of difference and understanding, especially when funding is at stake, suggest new ways of allowing LGBTQ Latinos/Latinas to retain a distinctiveness while also helping support global and human rights.

The goals set for the forum reflect issues of the Latino community as a whole, not just ones specific to the LGBTQ community. The lack of education in relationship to HIV/AIDS, for example, resulted in a high infection and transmission rate among poor Latinas/Latinos with the disease (Alonso and Koreck 1993, pp. 110–25). The gap in public health education resulted in a low access to preventative medicine. Community mobilization, similarly, is beneficial to all Latinos, regardless of sexual orientation. The concerns of the gay and straight Latino communities are similar, even when the exclusion of Latino LGBTQs is based on stigma and negative images. The belief that gay rights are also Latino rights was the basis for the work of LLEGO and similar groups in trying to improve the image of Latino gays and lesbians. As such, whether or not they advance an agenda in concert with other mainstream HIV organizations is beside the point: they seek justice and a place for Latino/Latina LGBTQ issues.

Many authors focus on the homophobia that is considered traditional to Latino/Latina cultures. But as Latinos/Latinas are no more and no less homophobic than European Americans or other ethnic minority groups, it is difficult to generalize perceptions across the divisions existing within the group, divisions of class, race, ethnicity, color, or social status, as well as of gender. In Latino culture, gays are sometimes erroneously rendered as invisible. "Homosexuality is another repressed ghost in our closet," writes Ilan Stavans. "Since ours is a galaxy of brute macho types and virginal devoted women, gays represent another facet. . . . they are repressed and silenced" (Stavans 1995, pp. 107–9). The values of manliness and of strict gender roles historically created cultures driven by the necessity of heterosexuality, endorsed by most organized religions and certainly by laws and the military as utter necessities, perhaps especially for immigrants (Herdt 1997, pp. 139–42).

Ostracization of Latino gays is sometimes justified by producing negative images, with representa- tions of them ranging from pedophiles to prostitutes. Recently, the Christian Right has forged a tie with various Latino groups. "Family values" groups such as La Amistad use negative images of Latino gays to justify their discrimination and harassment. In an interview with *The Los Angeles Times* the group's executive director, the Reverend Martin Garcia, stated that Amistad is "out to promote family values. Meaning the mama and papa. Not two mamas and two papas" (Olivo 1999, p. 2). When the Christian Right's outreach to Latino organizations was revealed, LLEGO quickly put in place strategies to counter the efforts. By emphasizing La Amistad's ties to the antigay Traditional Values Coalition, Martin Ornealas-Quintero, director of LLEGO, hoped to derail an alliance between the two that is seen by many Latinos/Latinas as a ploy to gain the influential Latino vote. The Christian Right (including the Traditional Values Coalition) was one of the biggest supporters of Proposition 187 in California, calling for the denial of access to public school and government services for undocumented immigrants. LLEGO hopes it can change the minds of members of groups such as La Amistad. In the new century, LLEGO began a media campaign to redefine *family*, using pro-gay advertisements in Spanish-language newspapers to showcase Latino LGBTQ as members of the Latino family.

Despite LLEGO's success in organizing the Latino LGBTQ community as well as its tremendous impact on Latino politics, the organization was unable to overcome the financial difficulties often faced by nonprofit organizations. Due to a $700,000 deficit resulting from heavy reliance on federal funding and further exacerbated by internal divisions on how to resolve financial issues, LLEGO announced its dissolution in late August 2004 (Crea 2004). In 2005, with an approach that focused more on cultural arts and awareness, health, and advocacy, LLEGO was reestablished as a nationwide organization for queer people of color. ALLGO lessened its reliance on government funding and redirected its energy toward creating change in the community rather than "satisfying bureaucratic government contract expectations"

(ALLGO website). By continuing to create and provide a space for the Latino LGBTQ community, ALLGO expanded the work begun by LLEGO more than 20 years before.

Representation and an end to the silence, along with safety and a place for socializing, a space, and a language were what transgender and transvestite activists at Stonewall sought. Slowly, among Latino gay organizations, as well as among arts groups and elected leaders, the movement is achieving human dignity without having to forsake culture, language, or orientation. The many writers and artists involved in these developments are represented in Maria Dolores Costa's timely volume (2003). Prominent among them, and representative of the humor that is often laced with some anguish, is Dan Guerrero, son of Chicano music icon Lalo Guerrero. Guerrero's *Gaytino!* Was a critically acclaimed musical stage performance in 2006. He is considered one of the 25 most powerful Latinos/Latinas in Hollywood.

Yvette Saavedra and Deena J. González

Further Reading

Adam, Barry D. 1987. *The Rise of a Gay and Lesbian Movement*. Massachusetts: Twayne Publishers.

ALLGO (A Statewide Queer People of Color Organization). Available at: http://allgo.org/history07.htm.

Alonso, Ana Maria and Maria Teresa Koreck. 1993. "Silences: 'Hispanics,' AIDS and Sexual Practices." In *The Lesbian and Gay Studies Reader*, ed. Henry Abelove, Michèle Aina Barale, and David M. Halperin, pp. 110–26. New York: Routledge.

Apontes-Parés, Luis and Jorge B. Merced. 1998. "Paginas Omitidas: The Gay and Lesbian Presence." In *The Puerto Rican Movement: Voices from the Diaspora*, ed. Andrés Torres and José E. Velázquez, pp. 297–315. Philadelphia: Temple University Press.

Costa, Maria Dolores, ed. 2003. *Latina Lesbian Writers and Artists*. New York: Harrington.

D'Emilio, John. 1983. *Sexual Politics, Sexual Communities: The Making of a Homosexual Minority in the United States, 1940–1970*. Chicago: University of Chicago Press.

Herdt, Gilbert. 1997. *Same Sex, Different Cultures*. Boulder, CO: Westview Press.

Martinez, Dorie Gilbert. 1998. "Mujer, Latina, Lesbiana—Notes of the Multidimensionality of Economic and Sociopolitical Injustice." *Journal of Gay and Lesbian Social Services* 8: 99–112.

National Gay and Lesbian Organization (LLEGO). 1996. In Guide to the National Latino/a Lesbian And Gay Organization (LLEGO), And Names Project AIDS Memorial Quilt Ephemera, 1996 Collection Number: 7610, Division of Rare and Manuscript Collections Cornell University Library. Available at: http://rmc.library.cornell.edu/EAD/htmldocs/RMM07610.html. Accessed July 12, 2008.

National Latino/a Lesbian and Gay Organization (LLEGÓ) Records, 1987–2004. Available at: http://www.lib.utexas.edu/taro/utlac/00273/lac-00273.html.

Nava, Michael and Robert Dawidoff. 1995. *Created Equal: Why Gay Rights Matter to America*. New York: St. Martin's/Griffin.

Olivo, Antonio and Joseph Trevino. 1999. "Foes Find Common Cause against Gay Rights. Activism: The Issue Brings Latino Evangelical Parties Together with Conservatives They Had Opposed on Prop. 187." *Los Angeles Times*, August 18, p. 2.

Rotello, Gabriel. 1998. "Gay and Lesbian Rights." *Social Policy* 28 (3): 56–59.

Stavans, Ilan. 1995. *The Hispanic Condition: Reflections on Culture and Identity in America*. New York: HarperCollins.

Lorde, Audre (1934–1992)

Audre Lorde was an African American poet whose book of essays *Sister Outsider* has become a feminist classic and is used as a staple in women's studies courses. Lorde was born in Harlem, New York, on February 18, 1934. Her parents were from Granada and believed they were going to return to their Caribbean home. As such, Lorde had a profound nostalgia for her lost "home."

She picked up languages easily and memorized poems voraciously. She attended Hunter College High School and in 1954 attended the National University of

Caribbean American writer, poet, and activist Audre Lorde lectures students at the Atlantic Center for the Arts in New Smyrna Beach, Florida. Lorde was a Master Artist in Residence at the Central Florida arts center in 1983. (Robert Alexander/Archive Photos/Getty Images)

Mexico for a year. "For the first time in my life," she wrote, "I walked down the streets of the city where most of the people were brown-skinned, everywhere I went. It was like coming into sunlight" (Russell 1995, p. 201).

She returned to the United States and entered the "gay-girl" scene in Greenwich Village. However, she was distressed to find only three or four black women in the lesbian community. At Hunter College she worked as a librarian and continued to write poetry. She attempted to become part of the Harlem Writers Guild, but was driven away by the groups' homophobia. In 1959 she received a bachelor of arts degree in literature and philosophy and went on to Columbia University School of Library Services where she earned a master's of library science in 1960.

She published her first book of poems, *The First Cities*, in 1968. Because of its success, she spent six weeks as a writer-in-residence at Tougaloo College in Mississippi. It was there that she met Frances Clayton, the woman who would become her life partner.

Lorde returned to New York City and taught courses for the SEEK program at City College. There she met writers Alice Walker and Adrienne Rich, an enriching experience for Lorde. Through their encouragement, Lorde publicly read a lesbian love poem for the first time in 1971. Although it was later published in *Ms.* magazine, her book editor rejected it for inclusion in her third volume of poetry, *From a Land Where Other People Live*. That book was nominated for a National Book Award in 1974.

A day of action initiated by the TransJustice Audre Lorde Project, a lesbian, gay, bisexual, two spirit, trans, and gender nonconforming people of color and allies, is held in lower Manhattan. The protesters, many of whom were transgender, demanded the end of profiling, harassment, and brutality at the hands of the police. (Scott Houston/Corbis)

Lorde contracted breast cancer in the late 1970s, which later recurred. She wrote about her mastectomy and decision to forgo additional surgery in her autobiographical *Cancer Journals* (1980). In 1984 she wrote *Sister Outsider*, a collection of essays on feminism and race. She died on November 17, 1992.

Chuck Stewart

See also: Allegra, Donna (1953–); Allen, Paula Gunn (1939–2008); Rich, Adrienne (1929–2012).

Further Reading

Birkle, Carmen. 1996. *Women's Stories of the Looking Glass: Autobiographical Reflections and Self-Representations in the Poetry of Sylvia Plath, Adrienne Rich, and Audre Lorde*. München, Germany: W. Fink.

De Veaux, Alexis. 2004. *Warrior Poet: a biography of Audre Lorde*. New York, New York: W. W. Norton.

Keating, AnaLouise. 1996. *Women Reading Women Writing: Self-Invention in Paula Gunn Allen, Gloria Anzaldúa, and Audre Lorde*. Philadelphia, Pennsylvania: Temple University Press.

Lorde, Audre, Rudolph Byrd, Johnnetta Cole, and Beverly Guy-Sheftall. 2009. *I Am Your Sister: Collected and Unpublished Writings of Audre Lorde*. Oxford, United Kingdom: Oxford University Press.

Lorde, Audre and Joan Wylie Hall. 2004. *Conversations with Audre Lorde*. Jackson, Mississippi: University Press of Mississippi.

Lyon, Phyllis (1924–)

Lyon's name is inextricably linked with that of Del Martin, her domestic partner of 56 years. Lyon and Martin founded the Daughters of Bilitis in 1955, the first political and social organization in the United States designed specifically for lesbians. Throughout their lives, Lyon and Martin were involved in a number of gay, lesbian, and feminist organizations, including the Council of Religion and Homosexuality, whose goal it was to encourage religious leaders to include gay men and lesbians in church activities, and the Alice B. Toklas Memorial Democratic Club, the first gay and lesbian political organization in San Francisco, and still one of the most influential such groups in the city.

Phyllis Lyon was born in Tulsa, Oklahoma, on November 10, 1924. She grew up in Seattle, Southern

State senator Mark Leno (D-San Francisco) escorts Phyllis Lyon from the Assembly Chambers after she and her late partner, Del Martin, were honored for their contributions to the lesbian, gay, bisexual, and transgender community, at the capitol in Sacramento, California, on June 14, 2010. (AP Photo/Rich Pedroncelli)

California, and San Francisco, graduating from Sacramento High School in 1943. She then attended the University of California at Berkeley, from which she received her BA in journalism in 1946. Like many women of her day, Lyon felt that her life would eventually have to center on a man. As she told historian John D'Emilio, "If you were a woman, you had to have a man. There was no other way" (D'Emilio 1983, p. 102). By the 1950s, however, she learned otherwise. After a stint as a general reporter for *The Chico Enterprise-Record*, Lyon moved to Seattle to work on a trade magazine. There she met Del Martin and fell in love. In 2004, they were the first same-sex couple to be married in San Francisco after Mayor Gavin Newsom issued an order permitting same-sex marriage licenses in the city. Four years later, after the California Supreme Court ruled that same-sex marriages were legal in the state, the couple was married a second time.

In 1972, Lyon and Martin coauthored *Lesbian/Woman*, a book that discussed lesbian lives in a strongly positive tone, an approach that was virtually unknown at the time. *Publisher's Weekly* called the book one of the 20 most important women's books of its generation. In the last three decades, Lyon has been especially interested in the topic of human sexuality in general and, in 1970s, cofounded the Institute for Advanced Study of Human Sexuality in San Francisco, from which she received her EdD in 1976. She also served on the San Francisco Human Rights Commission for more than a decade, acting as chairperson for two of those years.

The Lyon-Martin Health Services was founded in 1979 to provide medical services for lesbians in a nonjudgmental setting at affordable prices. The clinic soon became a model for other culturally sensitive community-based health care. The clinic expanded into case management and primary health care programs in 1993 for very low-income and uninsured women with HIV. In 1989, Lyon and Martin joined the Old Lesbians Organizing for Change and named delegates to the White House Conference on Aging in 1995. For a short time in 2004, San Francisco mayor

Gavin Newsom ordered the city clerk to issue marriage licenses for same-sex couples. This was a first in the nation, and Lyon and Martin were the first same-sex couple to be married in the United States. Unfortunately the California Supreme Court voided the several thousand marriages that occurred between February and August. However, once Proposition 8 was nullified by the U.S. Supreme Court on June 16, 2008, the couple was the first married in San Francisco. Her partner of more than 50 years, Del Martin died August 27, 2008, just months after their second legal marriage.

David E. Newton

See also: Daughters of Bilitis; Historical Overview of Gay Rights and Issues: From Pre-Columbian Times to the 1970s; Martin, Del (1921–2008); Proposition 8 Legal Analysis and the Impact of Judge Walker's Decision; Same-Sex Marriage in the United States.

Further Reading

Bullough, Vern L., ed. 2002. *Before Stonewall: Activists for Gay and Lesbian Rights in Historical Context.* New York: Harrington Park Press.

D'Emilio, John. 1983. *Sexual Politics, Sexual Communities: The Making of a Homosexual Minority in the United States, 1940–1970.* Chicago: University of Chicago Press.

Gallo, Marcia M. 2006. *Different Daughters: A History of the Daughters of Bilitis and the Birth of the Lesbian Rights Movement.* New York: Carroll & Graf.

M

Mabon, Lon T. (1947–)

Lon Mabon founded Oregon Citizens Alliance (OCA), which was instrumental in the passage of Measure 8 (which revoked the governor's executive order giving equal legal protection based on sexual orientation). Mabon was born on May 12, 1947, in Minnesota. As an adult, he lived in southern Oregon with his wife, Bonnie, and their three children. He and his wife owned an adult retirement home. Lon Mabon is a Bible teacher involved in his local church.

In 1986, Mabon was the southern Oregon regional director for fundamentalist Baptist preacher Joe Lutz in his challenge for Robert Packwood's Senate seat. From that experience and his religious teachings, Mabon launched OCA and the No Special Rights Committee. Their goal was to overturn Governor Neil Goldschmidt's executive order giving equal legal protection based on sexual orientation. OCA collected the necessary signatures to place Measure 8 on the ballot, and the measure won by an overwhelming majority. Thus, the executive order was revoked. OCA has been instrumental in developing other initiatives and political movements in Oregon with the goal of preventing antidiscrimination laws based on sexual orientation, stopping abortions, and prohibiting public schools from "promoting the homosexual lifestyle." Most of these other efforts were unsuccessful. By 1993, the Oregon Legislative Assembly passed a law prohibiting local governments from considering ordinances with LGBT provisions. The Oregon Court of Appeals upheld the law in 1995. As such, any headway OCA made toward limiting the rights of LGBT citizens was blocked. In 1996, Lon Mabon ran for position as U.S. senator from Oregon. His candidacy split the Republican ticket allowing Democrat Tom Bruggere to win.

Gay rights activist Catherine Stauffer, left, leaves court as antigay rights crusader Lon Mabon, right, stands handcuffed with a county sheriff after Mabon was arrested during his appearance in Multnomah County circuit court in Portland, Oregon, in 2002. Stauffer was awarded more than $30,000 in 1992 after she was roughed up during an Oregon Citizens Alliance antigay event. Mabon, who runs the OCA, was arrested after the judge ruled he was in contempt of court for failing to attend a debt hearing. (AP Photo/Don Ryan)

During a 1991 antigay event, gay rights activist Catherine Stauffer was roughed up by OCA spokesman Scott Lively. She sued and won a $30,000 judgment against OCA. The Mabons refused to pay, and the case went back to court a number of times. The Mabons claimed that OCA did not have the $30,000 to make restitution, even though it is estimated that more than $1 million went through the organization in a few years. The court required the Mabons to produce OCA's financial records. Lon Mabon refused to comply with the court order and was jailed in 2002 for contempt of court. Bonnie Mabon avoided going to jail when she agreed to bring the records in. Stauffer continued suing Lon Mabon, claiming he fraudulently transferred money out of OCA to avoid paying the 1992 judgment to her. After getting out of jail, Mabon crafted together two more antigay ballot initiative for 2008. However, they failed to secure enough signatures to be placed on the ballot.

Chuck Stewart

See also: Cameron, Paul Drummond (1939–).

Further Reading

Kidd, Joe. March 23, 1994. "Voters Pass Anti-Gay Law for 2nd Time." *The Register-Guard* (Eugene: Guard Publishing), pp. 1, 4A.

Wentz, Patty. 1999. "Homophobia Hits Home." *Willamette Week* (Portland: City of Roses Newspapers).

Martin, Del (1921–2008)

With her longtime domestic partner, Phyllis Lyon, Martin was deeply involved in the gay and lesbian political rights movement for more than half a century. In 1955, Martin and Lyon founded the Daughters of Bilitis, the first organization created to push for political rights of lesbians in the United States. A year later, they also founded and edited the nation's first lesbian periodical, *The Ladder*. The two women were also involved in creating the Council on Religion and the Homosexual in 1964 and San Francisco's Alice B. Toklas Memorial Democratic Club in 1972.

Martin was born Dorothy L. Taliaferro in San Francisco on May 5, 1921. Early in life, she became better known as Del. She attended George Washington High School in San Francisco before matriculating at the University of California at Berkeley. She later transferred to San Francisco State College (now San Francisco State University), where she met her future husband, James Martin. She then left San Francisco State, gave birth to a daughter, Kendra, and moved with her family to the suburbs. Before long, she realized that her long-standing attraction to women made her marriage impossible, and she was divorced from Martin (although she did keep her husband's surname).

In 1950, Martin moved to Seattle to take a job with a publisher of construction trade information. There she met Lyon, who was working with the same company. They made a commitment to each other in 1952 and, in 1955, moved to San Francisco. There they bought a house where they continued to live for more than 50 years.

In addition to her political activities, Martin wrote two important books, *Lesbian/Woman* (with Lyon) and *Battered Wives*, a book that became critical in the development of a national movement against domestic violence. The Lyon-Martin Health Services was founded in 1979 to provide medical services for lesbians in a nonjudgmental setting at affordable prices. The clinic soon became a model for other culturally sensitive community-based health care. The clinic expanded into case management and primary health care programs in 1993 for very low-income and uninsured women with HIV. In 1989, Lyon and Martin joined the Old Lesbians Organizing for Change and named delegates to the White House Conference on Aging in 1995. For a short time in 2004, San Francisco mayor Gavin Newsom ordered the city clerk to issue marriage licenses for same-sex couples. This was a first for the nation and Lyon and Martin were the first same-sex couple to be married in the United States. Unfortunately the California Supreme Court voided the several thousand marriages that occurred between February and August. However, once Proposition 8

Phyllis Lyon, center left, and Del Martin, center right, longtime gay rights activists, are married by San Francisco mayor Gavin Newsom, center, in a special ceremony at city hall in San Francisco on June 16, 2008. Lyon and Martin became the first officially married same sex couple after California's Supreme Court declared gay marriage legal. (AP Photo/Marcio Jose Sanchez, Pool)

was nullified by the U.S. Supreme Court on June 16, 2008, the couple was the first married in San Francisco. Del Martin died August 27, 2008, just months after their second legal marriage.

David E. Newton

See also: Daughters of Bilitis; Lyon, Phyllis (1924–); Historical Overview of Gay Rights and Issues: From Pre-Columbian Times to the 1970s; Proposition 8 Legal Analysis and the Impact of Judge Walker's Decision; Same-Sex Marriage in the United States.

Further Reading

Bullough, Vern L., ed. 2002. *Before Stonewall: Activists for Gay and Lesbian Rights in Historical Context.* New York: Harrington Park Press.

Gallo, Marcia M. 2006. *Different Daughters: A History of the Daughters of Bilitis and the Birth of the Lesbian Rights Movement.* New York: Carroll & Graf.

Matlovich, Leonard (1943–1988)

Leonard Matlovitch may well have been the best-known American gay man in the early 1970s. His picture appeared on the cover of *Time* magazine on September 8, 1975, with the caption: "I Am a Homosexual: The Gay Drive for Acceptance." Matlovich was featured in the story because, in spite of a spotless personnel record, he had been discharged from the U.S. Air Force for being gay. After his discharge, he devoted most of his life to activities related to gay and lesbian rights issues.

U.S. Air Force Sergeant Leonard Matlovich holds his Honorable Discharge papers at Langley Air Force Base in Virginia. Even after significant legal battles, Sgt. Matlovich was discharged from the service because he was gay. (Bettmann/Corbis)

Matlovich was born in Savannah, Georgia, on July 6, 1943, to a career air force sergeant. He grew up on air bases in the United States and England as, according to his own account, an ultraconservative, flag-waving racist grounded in a very traditional Roman Catholic house. After graduating from high school in England in 1962, Matlovich immediately joined the air force at least partly, he later said, because he had long been aware of his homosexual feelings and felt that he had to prove that he was a real man. He immediately volunteered to serve in the Vietnam conflict, eventually serving three tours of duty there. When he returned to the United States, he had been awarded a Bronze Star, a Purple Heart, and an

Air Force Meritorious Service Medal for his service in Vietnam.

After the war, Matlovich was assigned to a new kind of duty as a race-relations instructor at Virginia's Langley Air Force Base. At the time, Matlovich was still a virgin, very much uncertain and considerably appalled about his own sexuality. Only after exposure to gay bars in Florida, where he was later stationed, did he realize that he was hardly the only gay man in the world, and that others like him that he met were decent, successful members of society. As a result of this experience, he decided to inform his military superiors of his sexual orientation, which he did in a letter written in March 1975. Although Matlovich had a spotless military record including a number of commendations for his work, the U.S. Air Force began proceedings to release him with a general discharge. (A general discharge ranks below an honorable discharge, but above a dishonorable discharge, permitting the recipient to receive some, but not all, military benefits after leaving the service.)

Matlovich refused to passively accept the air force's decision and began a long battle to gain reinstatement to the military services. After four years, the air force offered Matlovich a cash payment of $160,000, a promotion, and an honorable discharge. By that point, Matlovich no longer wanted to return to the air force, and he accepted the settlement. In the remaining years of his life, Matlovich was popular as a speaker on issues of gays and lesbians in the military and on AIDS, which he had contracted. He ran unsuccessfully in 1978 for a seat on the San Francisco Board of Supervisors. Matlovich died in San Francisco on June 23, 1988, of complications of AIDS. The epitaph he selected for his tombstone reads: "When I was in the military, they gave me a medal for killing two men, and a discharge for loving one." He was buried at the Congressional Cemetery in the same row with FBI director J. Edgar Hoover.

His gravesite has become a mecca for many gay rights activists. Activists Army Lt. Dan Choi, Army Staff Sergeant Miriam Ben-Shalom, and members of GetEQUAL held vigil at the gravesite on November 10, 2010, before proceeding to the White House fence where they chained themselves (and subsequently arrested) protesting Don't Ask, Don't Tell (DADT). Gay Iraq veteran Captain Stephen Hill and his partner Josh Synder were married at the gravesite in July 2011. Captain Hill later became famous when he was booed by audience members at a Republican presidential candidate debate when he asked if any of the candidates would attempt to restore Don't Ask, Don't Tell.

David E. Newton

See also: Don't Ask, Don't Tell: Homosexuality and the Military.

Further Reading

Castañeda, Laura and Campbell, Susan B. 2005. "No Longer Silent: Sgt. Leonard Matlovich and Col. Margarethe Cammermeyer." In *News and Sexuality: Media Portraits of Diversity*, ed. Laura Castaneda and Susan Campbell, pp. 198–200. Sage; Newbury Park, CA.

Hippler, Mike. 1989. *Matlovich: The Good Soldier*. New York: Alyson Publications Inc.

Miller, Neil. 1995. "Leonard Matlovich: A Soldier's Story." In *Out of the Past: Gay and Lesbian History from 1869 to the Present*, ed. Neil Miller, 411–14. Virginia: Vintage Books.

Sergeant Matlovich vs. the U.S. Air Force, made-for-television dramatization directed by Paul Leaf, written by John McGreevey, starring Brad Dourif in title role. Originally aired on NBC, August 21, 1978.

Shilts, Randy. 1993. *Conduct Unbecoming: Gays and Lesbians in the US Military*. Darby, PA: Diane Publishing Company.

Mattachine Society

The Mattachine Society is considered the founding organization of the gay civil rights movement. Harry Hay (previously known as Henry Hay and who wrote under the pseudonym Eann MacDonald) spearheaded the Mattachine Society and the homophile movement. When Hay was 17 years old in 1930, he came to Los Angeles and met Champ Simmons who had recently been involved with one of the members of the Chicago Society for Human Rights—the first homophile organization in the United States. Simmons spoke about the Society, which encouraged Hay to begin a similar organization.

Hay was a Communist organizer and sought-after teacher of Communist theory in Los Angeles in the 1930s. He realized his homosexuality after being married, and in 1948 conceived the idea of organizing a gay group. He believed political organizing was the key to political power and self-protection. He discussed the idea with friends at the University of Southern California (USC). Two years later he assembled enough friends to launch the group—International Bachelors Fraternal Orders for Peace and Social Dignity (sometimes referred to as Bachelors Anonymous). The goals of the group included the following: to fight encroaching American fascism, to help save employment of "androgynous civil servants" (androgynous was Hay's term for gay and lesbian), to protect and improve conditions for the "androgynous minority," and to collaborate and help attain full-class citizenship for all minorities. The group was initially set up as underground separate guilds. This way no one would know everyone involved. A secret society structure was thought to be necessary in light of the police harassment that lesbians and gay men faced in the Los Angeles of the 1950s. Also, a secret society structure was a method used by the old Left and was employed by Algeria in its successful liberation from France.

In April 1951 the group refocused and incorporated itself in California as the Mattachine Society. The goals of the group were to unify homosexuals, to educate homosexuals and heterosexuals about how the homosexual rights movement would parallel other minority rights movements, and to lead the "whole mass of social deviants" (Katz 1976, p. 412). The name *Mattachine* was inspired by the *Société Mattachine*, a secret fraternal organization in thirteenth- and fourteenth-century France and Spain of unmarried townsmen who performed music, dances, and rituals while wearing masks, sometimes in protest against oppression. At the formation of the Mattachine Society, Hay severed his 18-year tie with the Communist Party to devote himself completely to homosexual

From left to right are Roy M. Cohn, David Schine, Joseph R. McCarthy, and Karl E. Mundt, during Senator McCarthy's Senate Investigating subcommittee hearing on July 1, 1953. (George Skadding/The LIFE Picture Collection/Getty Images)

emancipation. The Mattachine Society was seen as a vehicle to assist homosexuals to explore in discussion groups basic questions such as "Who are we?" "Where have we come from?" and "What are we here for?" A separate entity, the Mattachine Foundation, provided a legal front for the Society.

Several members of a discussion group within the Mattachine Society decided to publish a monthly newsletter to be distributed nationally. The new organization, ONE, Incorporated, began publication in January 1953. Soon, the newsletters were seized by the U.S. Post Office on grounds that they were "obscene, lewd, lascivious and filthy." ONE editors went to court, and ultimately, the U.S. Supreme Court overturned the lower courts in 1958 (*One, Inc. v. Olesen*). This was a "legal and publishing landmark" (*Gay Almanac* 1996, p. 13). Homosexual materials were no longer automatically deemed obscene and the mail service could be used to distribute them.

In 1953 a number of forces came together to change the direction of the homophile movement. Joseph McCarthy called Fred M. Snyder, Mattachine Foundation legal adviser, to testify before the House Un-American Activities Committee. McCarthy branded Snyder an unfriendly witness and attempted to defame and humiliate him. The investigation caused grave concern for Mattachine members. At the same time, President Dwight Eisenhower issued Executive Order 10450, which expanded President Truman's loyalty and security program to exclude from government employment those who engaged in "sexual perversion." Historian John D'Emilio estimated that approximately 1,000 homosexuals were fired from federal employment each year during the 1940s, approximately 2,000 per year during the 1950s, and over 3,000 per year during the 1960s.

Within this climate, the Mattachine Society held a convention in Los Angeles on April 11, 1953. More than 500 representatives participated in the largest such gathering of homosexuals in U.S. history. A power struggle ensued between the founders who were leftist and those who wanted a more moderate, liberal organization. The liberal factions won out and the old Mattachine Foundation board resigned.

The newly incarnated Mattachine Society was open and democratic. Its goals were primarily educational. It believed that legal change could be accomplished through education, not necessarily political action. The organization was increasingly concerned with being "respectable" and adhered to a basic homophile outlook.

As the years passed, a multitude of people and forces helped shape the Mattachine Society and ONE, Incorporated. Jim Kepner, one of the leaders of the Mattachine Society after the resignation of the board in 1953, went on to found the International Gay and Lesbian Archives. ONE Publication was the premier homophile newsletter until 1972 and continues to this day. By the mid-1990s, the Mattachine Society had been completely enveloped by ONE, Incorporated and merged with the International Gay and Lesbian Archives (ONE/IGLA). ONE/IGLA is now located on the campus of the University of Southern California with over 1 million items in the collection—making it the largest collection in the world of homophile art, books, articles, and other items and the premier academic research facility of queer history.

Chuck Stewart

See also: Daughters of Bilitis; D'Emilio, John (1948–); ONE, Incorporated.

Further Reading

Gay Almanac, The. 1996. Complied by the National Museum and Archive of Lesbian and Gay History. New York: Berkley Books.

Hay, Harry. 1996. *Radically Gay: Gay Liberation in the Words of Its Founder*. Ed. Will Roscoe. Boston: Beacon.

Katz, J. 1976. *Gay American History: Lesbians and Gay Men in the U.S.A.* New York: Thomas Y. Crowell.

Sears, James T. 2007. *Behind the Mask of the Mattachine: The Hal Call Chronicles and the Early Movement for Homosexual Emancipation*. Binghamton, NY: Haworth.

Milk, Harvey (1930–1978)

Harvey Bernard Milk was born in Woodmere, New York, on May 22, 1930. In 1951, Milk earned a degree from New York State College for Teachers in Albany, New York. After graduating from college, Milk served in the navy during the Korean War. In 1955, Milk was honorably discharged from the navy after earning the rank of junior lieutenant. Milk considered himself to be fairly conservative in terms of his political views during the 1960s. In 1968, Milk moved to San Francisco, California, with his gay partner, Jack Galen McKinley, who was involved in theater productions. At this time, Milk was employed in the area of finance, but he was fired from his job after he demonstrated against the U.S. invasion of Cambodia in 1970. In 1972, Milk opened a camera shop on Castro Street in the predominately gay district of San Francisco (Ernst, "The Dan White [Harvey Milk Murder] Trial: 1979").

By the early 1970s, Milk had grown disillusioned by the political corruption of the Nixon administration, particularly the Watergate scandal. Therefore, he decided to become politically active by running for a seat on the San Francisco Board of Supervisors. While Milk lost his first two attempts at winning a seat on the board, he finally won on his third try and became the first gay person elected to a citywide office in the history of San Francisco. Milk became so popular that he was nicknamed "the Mayor of Castro Street" (Ernst, "The Dan White [Harvey Milk Murder] Trial: 1979").

Together with Mayor George Moscone, Milk was instrumental in passing a law to protect gays from discrimination in the areas of housing and employment. He also gained national attention for helping to defeat a bill in the California legislature that would

Gay activists gathered on San Francisco's city hall steps in protest of a voluntary manslaughter verdict for former supervisor Dan White for the killings of Mayor George Moscone and Supervisor Harvey Milk in 1979. (AP Photo/Paul Sakuma)

have banned gays from teaching in the public schools. While Milk is recognized today as a symbol of civil rights for homosexuals, he also was a key figure in bringing about social change in such areas as education, public transportation, housing for the poor, and health care for children (Ernst, "The Dan White [Harvey Milk Murder] Trial: 1979").

On November 27, 1978, Milk and Mayor Moscone were shot to death at the city hall by Dan White, a former supervisor who had opposed the gay rights legislation. White was convicted on a reduced charge of manslaughter and sentenced to less than eight years in prison for the murders, which outraged members of the gay community. White was released on parole after serving only five years of his sentence (Law Library, "Dan White Trial").

Milk's memory is honored today in a number of ways, including the Harvey Milk Gay and Lesbian Democratic Club, the Harvey Milk Memorial Plaza, the Harvey Milk Memorial Community Center, and the Harvey Milk Branch of the San Francisco Public Library, all in San Francisco. His life was memorialized in two acclaimed movies. The first was the 1984 documentary, *The Times of Harvey Milk*, directed by Rob Epstein, and the 2008 motion picture *Milk*, directed by Gus Van Sant, and starring Sean Penn (who won an Oscar for his performance as Harvey Milk), Emile Hirsch, and Josh Brolin as Dan White. In August 2009, President Obama honored Harvey Milk posthumously with America's highest civilian medal, the Presidential Medal of Freedom, where the president stated the following:

Harvey Bernard Milk dedicated his life to shattering boundaries and challenging assumptions. As one of the first openly gay elected officials

San Francisco supervisor Harvey Milk, left, openly gay, talks with Gwenn Craig and Bill Kraus, co-coordinators of the San Francisco No on Prop 6 program in San Francisco, on November 7, 1978. Milk was awaiting the first results from California on the controversial proposition that would see homosexual teachers fired from schools. (AP Photo/Sal Veder)

in this country, he changed the landscape of opportunity for the nation's gay community. Throughout his life, he fought discrimination with visionary courage and conviction. Before his tragic death in 1978, he wisely noted, "Hope will never be silent," and called upon Americans to stay true to the guiding principles of equality and justice for all. Harvey Milk's voice will forever echo in the hearts of all those who carry forward his timeless message. ("Announcing Harvey Milk Champions of Change" 2013)

The medal was presented to Harvey Milk's nephew, Stuart Milk.

Scott P. Johnson and David E. Newton

See also: Historical Overview of Gay Rights and Issues: From Pre-Columbian Times to the 1970s; Moscone, George (1929–1978); White, Dan (1946–1985); White (Dan) Trial (1979).

Further Reading

"Announcing Harvey Milk Champions of Change." 2013. President Obama and the LGBT Community. The White House, April 8. Available at: http://www.white-house.gov/blog/2013/04/08/announcing-harvey-milk-champions-change.

Ernst, Cindi. 1979. "The Dan White (Harvey Milk Murder) Trial: Selected Links & Bibliography." *Famous Trials*. Available at: http://www.law.umkc.edu/faculty/projects/ftrials/danwhitelinks.html.

Law Library–American Law and Legal Information. "Dan White Trial: 1979—Double Execution, Unique Defense."

Notable Trials and Court Cases—1973 to 1980. Available at: http://law.jrank.org/pages/3303/Daniel-James-White-Trial-1979.html.

Shilts, Randy. 1982. *The Mayor of Castro Street: The Life and Times of Harvey Milk*. New York: St. Martin's Press.

Mishima, Yukio (1925–1970)

Yukio Mishima was a charismatic Japanese writer who was nominated for the Nobel Prize three times. Born on January 14, 1925, in Tokyo, Hiraoka Kimitake was the son of a high-level civil servant. He was slight and sickly by nature and allowed to be raised as a girl by his grandmother. He wrote and published his first short story under the pseudonym Yukio Mishima when he was 16.

He worked in a factory during World War II and after the defeat studied law at the University of Tokyo. His second novel, *Confessions of a Mask*, was published in 1949 and brought immediate fame. Although the story revolves around a young boy recognizing his homosexuality and the need to conceal it behind a mask, Japanese audiences seemed to miss the homosexual theme and saw the story as a coming-of-age tale. After the success of the novel, Mishima wrote numerous books and plays, including the famous *Madame de Sade*.

Famous Japanese novelist Yukio Mishima reviews a parade of Tatenokai (Shield association), a militant youth group he had organized in 1968 with the purpose of reviving the old Japanese way of life, on the first anniversary of the society's foundation. (Bettmann/Corbis)

He became obsessed with the military samurai past of Japan and saw it as a solution to the materialism and isolation of the modern world. Through exercise, karate, and kendo (a traditional Japanese form of swordsmanship), he transformed himself physically into the samurai he wanted to be. Although dutiful as a husband and father, his main sexual attraction was to male "rough trade." He celebrated and engaged in the tradition of homosexual love between samurai warriors.

His writings and beliefs attracted many followers. He built his own private army, the Shield Society, to defend the emperor in the event of a leftist uprising. On November 25, 1970, Mishima and his followers took an army general hostage in Tokyo's Ichigaya military headquarters and encouraged an assembly of 1,500 soldiers to reject Japan's democratic constitution and restore worship of the emperor. The soldiers were unimpressed with the demand. Two hours later, Mishima had himself beheaded and his devoted young collaborators committed hara-kiri.

Chuck Stewart

See also: Historical Overview of Gay Rights and Issues: From Pre-Columbian Times to the 1970s.

Further Reading

Inose, Naoki and Hiroaki Sato. 2013. *Persona: A Biography of Yukio Mishima.* Berkeley, CA: Stone Bridge Press.

Moscone, George (1929–1978)

George Moscone was born on November 24, 1929, in San Francisco, California. Moscone grew up in a working-class family with a Catholic background. After graduating from the University of the Pacific where he played basketball on an athletic scholarship, Moscone earned a law degree from the University of California's Hastings College of Law. After a brief stint in the navy, Moscone started a law practice in 1956 and also married his childhood sweetheart, Gina Bodanza (Ernst, "The Dan White [Harvey Milk Murder] Trial: 1979").

At the suggestion of a college friend, John Burton, Moscone decided to enter into politics. As a Democratic candidate for political office, he was elected to a seat on the San Francisco Board of Supervisors in 1963 and then, in 1966, won a seat in the California State Senate where he eventually served as the Majority Leader of the Senate. During his tenure in the state senate, Moscone joined an alliance of progressive Democrats who were successful in repealing a sodomy law in California that prohibited homosexual behavior. Moscone also was viewed as a champion of the poor, racial minorities, and the interests of small business (Sward 1998).

Labor leaders began preparations for a general strike by all union workers in San Francisco, in a showdown over voter-approved pay limitations on city workers. Mayor George Moscone, shown here at a news conference, said he did not want to dare them to have a general strike, but predicted it would not get off the ground. (Bettmann/Corbis)

In 1975, Moscone was elected the mayor of San Francisco. During his first year in office, Moscone was successful at preventing the San Francisco Giants baseball team from moving to Toronto and helped to institute citywide elections for the board of supervisors. He also became the first mayor to appoint women, gays, and minorities to various positions within city government. In 1977, the district elections for the supervisor positions resulted in a number of Moscone's allies winning seats on the board. Among the newly elected supervisors was Harvey Milk, the first openly gay person elected to citywide office (Sward 1998).

When a conservative member of the board of supervisors, Dan White, resigned in 1978, Moscone had the opportunity to appoint a replacement in order to secure a liberal majority for the mayor and his allies. However, when White asked to be reinstated to his position as a supervisor, Moscone declined his request. On November 27, 1978, after making a final plea to be reinstated, White shot and murdered Moscone and Harvey Milk at San Francisco City Hall. White was eventually convicted on reduced charges of manslaughter and given a light sentence in a controversial trial in which defense attorneys and the media focused upon the homosexual lifestyle of Milk and virtually ignored the fact that Moscone, a happily married man with four children, was also a victim in the double murder (Law Library, "Dan White Trial").

Today, Harvey Milk and George Moscone are regarded as significant figures in the battle over equal rights for homosexuals. However, Milk has received far more attention from the media as a heroic figure who died for the cause of gay rights. In 2008, Moscone was portrayed by actor Victor Garber in the award-winning film *Milk*, which highlighted the political career and assassination of Harvey Milk.

Scott P. Johnson

See also: Historical Overview of Gay Rights and Issues: From Pre-Columbian Times to the 1970s; Milk, Harvey; White, Dan (1946–1985).

Further Reading

Ernst, Cindi. 1979. "The Dan White (Harvey Milk Murder) Trial: Selected Links & Bibliography." *Famous Trials*. Available at: http://www.law.umkc.edu/faculty/projects/ftrials/danwhitelinks.html.

Law Library–American Law and Legal Information. "Dan White Trial: 1979—Double Execution, Unique Defense." *Notable Trials and Court Cases—1973 to 1980*. Available at: http://law.jrank.org/pages/3303/Daniel-James-White-Trial-1979.html.

Sward, Susan. 1998. "Moscone's Time Was Anything but Quiet: His Election, Style Reflected S.F.'s Changing Demographics." *San Francisco Chronicle*. November 26, p. A1.

N

National Coming Out Day

The Human Rights Campaign designated October 11 as National Coming Out Day in 1988. This day has grown into thousands of events held nationally to encourage people to come out to family, friends, neighbors, and fellow employees about being lesbian, gay, bisexual, transgendered, transsexual, or intersexed. It has been found that visibility—that is, being seen and known to be homosexual—is the most effective way to effect societal changes toward the acceptance of homosexuality. However, there are many

Atlanta's Gay Pride Parade, one of the largest in the United States, coincides with National Coming Out Day celebrations. Thousands gathered at Piedmont Park in the city's predominately gay midtown for the festival. (Robin Nelson/ZUMA Press/Corbis)

legal questions about what constitutes being openly gay and what behaviors are legally protected.

Chuck Stewart

See also: Human Rights Campaign (HRC).

Further Reading

Human Rights Campaign. National Coming Out Day. Available at: https://www.hrc.org/resources/entry/national-coming-out-day.

National Gay and Lesbian Task Force

Bruce Voeller, Howard Brown, Ron Gold, Martin Duberman, Frank Kameny, and Nathalie Rockhill conceived a new kind of political organization, founded on October 15, 1973, in New York City. Called the

National Gay Task Force, its founding board of directors envisioned the country's first *national* political organization dedicated to ending oppression of gay and lesbian people by securing positive change in social policies and practices within branches of government and major public institutions. They believed that strong leadership shared by women and men on the board of directors and among professional staff would be integral to abolishing social and governmental discrimination against gay and lesbian people and to securing full equality under the law and complete social acceptance.

Like other social visionaries before them, Voeller, Brown, Gold, Duberman, Kameny, Rockhill, and other founders embarked on a path that would take them, and all lesbians, gay men, bisexual, and transgender people in the United States, through largely

Participants in a march sponsored by the National Gay Task Force file past the White House in Washington, D.C., on October 14, 1979. Demonstrators were supporting a federal ban against discrimination in federal jobs. (AP Photo/ Dennis Cook)

unexplored terrain. The National Gay Task Force (in 1985, its name was changed to National Gay and Lesbian Task Force), since its founding in 1973, has established an astonishing record of achievement and innovation and has charted the political course for a significant social movement. The story of the National Gay and Lesbian Task Force, in many important ways, is the story of the LGBT political movement.

Over the past three and a half decades, the Task Force's portfolio of progress has included nondiscrimination laws and policies to protect lesbians, gay men, bisexual, and transgender people; combating hate violence against LGBT people; effective federal responses to the HIV/AIDS epidemic; repeal of sodomy laws that criminalized private adult consensual sex; rescinding/repealing policies and laws that called for discharges of lesbian, gay, and bisexual service members; family and relationship recognition; student and campus organizing; advocacy by, for, and about old and young LGBT people; securing federal funding for LGBT social service projects; organizing within communities of faith; and fighting back against right-wing anti-LGBT movements, especially when the rights and lives of LGBT people are put up for a popular vote by the electorate.

The Task Force brought the voice of LGBT people into a lively and rambunctious public discourse about the rights of those Americans whose opportunities had been limited by bigotry and prejudice, particularly African Americans and women. The Civil

President Barack Obama, right, with Betty Byrd Boatner, center, and Louvon Harris, left, after delivering remarks at the enactment of the Matthew Shepard and James Byrd, Jr., Hate Crime Prevention Act in a ceremony in the East Room of the White House in Washington, on October 28, 2009. Both women are sisters of James Byrd, Jr., the man who, in 1998, was dragged to death down a three-mile stretch of country road in Jasper, Texas. (AP Photo/Pablo Martinez Monsivais)

Representative Nanci Pelosi (D-CA) holds up a copy of a report on gay violence during a news conference at the National Press Club in Washington on March 19, 1992. The report by the National Gay and Lesbian Task Force Policy Institute claimed that antigay violence surged 31 percent in 1991. (AP Photo/Barry Thumma)

Rights Act of 1964, a crowning achievement of the black civil rights movement, provided equal access to public facilities and to private businesses serving the public and prohibited discrimination in the workplace based on race, sex, religion, or national origin. The Equal Rights Amendment, a proposed amendment to the federal constitution stating that "equality of rights under the law shall not be denied or abridged by the United States or by any State on account of sex," had been passed by Congress and sent to the states for approval in 1972. The momentum of social justice movements seemed unstoppable and the aspirations of gay rights activists for legal protections on the basis of sexual orientation seemed destined to rise on this incoming tide of equality under the law.

Four years after the Stonewall Riots in 1969, gay rights issues were receiving unprecedented media exposure and the organized opposition, although noticeable, was as embryonic as that era's gay rights movement, as it was called. The National Gay Task Force, in its first year of life, scored a major victory when the American Psychiatric Association declassified homosexuality as a mental illness. A strong push to win employment rights for lesbians and gay men in the U.S. civil service system was under way, much due to the visionary work of Task Force founder Frank Kameny.

In collaboration with Congresswoman Bella Abzug (D-NY) and Congressman Edward I. Koch (D-NY), the National Gay Task Force leaders initiated a project to enact federal nondiscrimination law to protect people on the basis of sexual orientation. Abzug and Koch introduced the Equality Act of 1974 on May 14, 1974, a sweeping federal bill to ban

David Fleischer of New York, director of organizing and training for the National Gay and Lesbian Task Force, points at a tally of voters while talking to volunteers in Boston on March 27, 2004. Volunteers went door-to-door in Boston neighborhoods to talk to voters about gay and same-sex marriage and ranked the level of support from individual voters on a scale of 1 to 5, with 1 being highest. (AP Photo/Stanley Hu)

discrimination against lesbians, gay men, unmarried persons, and women in employment, housing, and public accommodations. Abzug and Koch's bill stands as the first ever national legislative proposal to end discrimination against lesbians and gay men.

Jean O'Leary and Bruce Voeller, coleaders of the Task Force staff in 1977, organized the nation's first ever, historic meeting between lesbian and gay activists and staff at the White House, in part to make the case for federal nondiscrimination law. On March 26, 1977, they led a group of 15 women and men into the Roosevelt Room to brief the staff of the White House Office of Public Liaison on a portfolio of issues for which they demanded attention from federal authorities. President Jimmy Carter's Public Liaison, Midge

Costanza, received the group, meeting with them for three hours and poring over carefully prepared briefing books. The Task Force representatives educated White House staff about discrimination against gay men and lesbians in the military, Internal Revenue Service (IRS) regulations, and immigration law and policy. They sought federal funding for community projects from agencies within the Department of Health, Education, and Welfare. They pointed out that the U.S. Civil Rights Commission did not address discrimination on the basis of sexual orientation in hiring, education, and public accommodations. Representatives of the Metropolitan Community Church and Parents and Friends of Lesbians and Gays talked about the need for greater understanding of the LGBT community in religious circles and within family configurations. Following the historic meeting, Task Force representatives met with officials of pertinent federal agencies and succeeded in reversing an IRS policy that categorically denied tax-exempt status to groups arguing that homosexuality was acceptable.

But hopes for swift action by federal entities to ensure equal justice for lesbian and gay people were dashed almost as soon as Jimmy Carter left the White House in 1980. Unforeseen by the activist leaders, three social and political dynamics converged to create a perfect storm that swamped their early optimism:

- increasingly well-organized antipathy toward LGBT people that the movement did not have the capacity to address,

- the AIDS crisis into which a critical portion of the LGBT community's political energy was necessarily diverted and which fueled fear of gay men and gay sexuality, and

- the steady takeover of the federal government by a Republican Party beholden to socially conservative voters who demanded opposition to equality claims of LGBT people, women, racial minorities, and immigrants in exchange for their votes.

Against this rising tide of anti-LGBT political fervor, the Task Force set about building the political strength and power of LGBT communities by working directly with community leaders and activists in cities, towns, and states. Recognizing that enduring political and social change could only be won on a firm foundation of gains at the local and state levels, the Task Force turned its attention and energies to community-based organizing strategies throughout the 1980s and 1990s.

In 1982, the Task Force launched its Anti-Violence Project to research and document the heretofore hidden reality of hate violence against LGBT individuals. Working with (and often helping start) local antiviolence programs, the project produced widely publicized national statistical reports on antigay violence throughout the 1980s, which were critical factors in

winning enactment of a federal law to collect statistics on hate violence in 1990. This victory was the first in the federal arena. In 1994, responsibility for producing the annual national reports shifted to the newly formed National Coalition of Anti-Violence Programs, which continues the annual reports to this day. This pattern of specific LGBT issues being developed by the Task Force, then becoming freestanding entities, is an integral and essential role of the Task Force within the movement.

As the AIDS epidemic swept through LGBT communities in the early 1980s, the Task Force mounted the first ever federal lobbying campaign to demand a full and effective response to the crisis, including the hiring of Jeff Levy, the nation's first lobbyist focused on HIV/AIDS. By securing funding for research and direct care, the Task Force and its allies in Congress directed resources to local community-based organizations that dispensed much-needed care to people with AIDS and much-needed prevention information to staunch the spread of the epidemic. The Task Force was instrumental in founding a coalition of AIDS advocates, National Organizations Responding to AIDS (NORA), that led many of the early funding battles. Along with allies in NORA, the Task Force unsuccessfully opposed a series of congressional proposals to restrict AIDS education funding that "promoted homosexuality," sponsored in 1987 by the notoriously antigay U.S. senator from North Carolina, Jesse Helms.

When the U.S. Supreme Court handed down its devastating 1986 decision in *Bowers v. Hardwick* that declared there would be no constitutionally recognized right to engage in private, adult consensual sex, the Task Force responded by launching the Privacy Project. The Privacy Project, standing alongside the community organizing of the Anti-Violence Project, was a groundbreaking campaign to mobilize and inspire LGBT people in 25 states to challenge the laws criminalizing same-sex sexual behavior. Just as the Anti-Violence Project built local organizations to combat hate violence, the Privacy Project birthed a dozen statewide political organizations to initiate sodomy law repeal efforts.

The Creating Change conference, an innovative and unique skills-building and movement-building annual gathering for those working on behalf of LGBT people and issues, was founded by the Task Force in 1988. Following the historic 1987 March on Washington for Lesbian and Gay Rights, staffers at the Task Force were deluged with requests for assistance, advice, and support by LGBT organizers who had attended the march. Seeking a way for the movement to teach itself and to sharpen skills among its leaders, the Task Force convened the first Creating Change conference in October 1988 in Washington, D.C. From the first, relatively small gathering of 300 people, Creating Change has developed into the movement's preeminent strategy and training event. Thousands of attendees have learned the essential skills of organizing, media relations, lobbying and advocacy, electoral and campaign tactics, message development, creating alliances with non-LGBT groups, and building a more fully inclusive movement. Creating Change has been the site of emerging constituencies, such as bisexual and transgender advocacy, LGBT people of color, old and young LGBT people, and people who work within communities of faith. The annual conference has also seen the launch of many important new organizations, for example, the 1992 Boycott Colorado project that followed the passage of Colorado's Amendment 2 and Southerners on New Ground, which brings together lesbians, both white and nonwhite, to work for social justice. The Creating Change conference, organized and sponsored by the Task Force, serves as the movement's incubator for new ways of accomplishing its overarching goals.

The National Consortium of Directors of LGBT Resources in Higher Education, also launched at the Creating Change conference in 1997, was an outgrowth of the Task Force Campus Organizing Project. The Campus Project published the nation's first organizing manual for campus activists, a comprehensive training guidebook that is still in use today.

Continuing into the 1990s, the Task Force dispatched organizers and trainers into communities and states that faced hostile ballot questions on a range of LGBT-related issues. The virulently anti-LGBT right-wing organizations, working under the guise of "family values" and "traditional values," discovered that voters, if left uneducated about the reality of LGBT lives, were likely to agree to strip away rights from LGBT people. The Task Force created the Fight the Right Project in 1992, the country's first project to educate and energize voters to defend the rights of LGBT people when under attack at the ballot box. The Fight the Right Project later became the Organizing and Training department of the Task Force and trained local and state campaign leaders to win at the ballot box by talking with voters one-on-one.

Almost from its inception, the Task Force broke ground by committing itself to being an organization with both male and female leadership, which at the time was unheard of in "gay" politics. Ten of the organization's 14 executive directors have been women, including three women of color.

The Task Force has consistently championed a movement of LGBT people that is fully inclusive. This enriching of the LGBT movement has been a particular focus of the Task Force Policy Institute, founded in 1995. The Policy Institute, the movement's preeminent independent think tank, has published a series of research reports and papers that focus on LGBT communities of color, including African Americans, Latinos/Latinas, and Asian American LGBT people. Policy Institute publications have also focused on the health needs of bisexual people, the needs of old and aging LGBT people, the needs of young LGBT people, and the political aspirations of transgender people. This body of research and scholarly work serves two purposes: to gather and analyze information about a range of LGBT populations and to bring their needs to the attention of the broader movement for LGBT equality with the expectation that the movement would more fully integrate these underserved groups.

Thirty-three years after Congresswoman Abzug and Congressman Koch introduced the first version of a federal bill to outlaw discrimination on the basis of sexual orientation, only modest progress has been made toward the enactment of federal protections. But much progress has been made to include transgender people in nondiscrimination and hate crime laws, due to the leadership of the Task Force. Beginning in 1999, the Task Force was the first national LGBT political organization to insist on the inclusion of transgender people in federal legislation protecting against discrimination and bias violence. By 2007, two major pieces of federal legislation concerning nondiscrimination and hate crimes had explicit language inclusive of gender identity. In 2001, the Task Force established its Transgender Civil Rights Project, which has worked with local organizers to secure trans-inclusive nondiscrimination law in over a dozen states and the District of Columbia.

Working for equality from the ground up has been a guiding principle of the Task Force strategy. In March 1998, the Task Force planned and sponsored Equality Begins at Home, a nationwide initiative for political actions in all 50 U.S. states to focus attention on the importance of local organizing and political power. Up to this time, the vast majority of the movement's resources had flowed to national work, with scant results at the federal level. The Task Force made small grants to organizers in every state and over 250 actions took place within one week, bringing LGBT people to their state capitol buildings and drawing attention to hate crimes, employment discrimination, the need for safe schools, and the need for relationship recognition for same-sex couples. During this time, the Task Force took a leading role in coordinating the work of statewide LGBT organizations and founding the Federation of Statewide LGBT Advocacy Organizations. Like the antiviolence programs before them, the statewide groups formed their own stand-alone group, renamed the Equality Federation in 2002.

In 2004, the state of Massachusetts became the first state in the United States to legally marry same-sex couples, which set off a firestorm of political activity by right-wing opponents who sought to amend the state's constitution to ban these marriages. The Task Force was a founding member of MassEquality, the coalition formed to protect marriage rights for same-sex couples. As the battle heated up, Task Force organizers led grassroots efforts to increase constituent lobbying contacts with legislators whose job it was to approve the proposed amendment before it could go to the ballot. The Task Force organizers succeeded in turning the votes of a handful of key legislators, including one of the sponsors of the amendment, resulting in the amendment's defeat in a 2007 legislative session.

Since 1973, the National Gay and Lesbian Task Force has spoken boldly and consistently on behalf of LGBT people who face a myriad of obstacles that impede their contributions to society. Task Force executive directors have provided the LGBT movement with vision, leadership, and uncompromising advocacy. Virginia Apuzzo led a project to bring LGBT issues into the 1984 Democratic National Convention and was in the first rank of a huge demonstration at the convention demanding action on AIDS. Urvashi Vaid in 1989 attended President George Bush's first ever speech about the AIDS epidemic and challenged him from the floor of the auditorium to fully fund the fight against AIDS. Kerry Lobel spoke eloquently in the mid-1990s about full inclusion of bisexual and transgender people in the Task Force agenda for change, setting the stage for all other national organizations to follow suit. Lorri Jean spoke out in 2001 and 2002 about the dangerous diversions of national resources away from domestic programs that would occur should our country wage wars in the Middle East, leading the Task Force to join the Win without War coalition.

Through a seemingly unending series of ballot initiative campaigns on gay-related issues from 1992 to the present day, LGBT people are smeared with the lie that an inherent immorality in their behavior automatically disqualifies them from full equality under the law. In 2005, the Task Force staff leader Matt Foreman turned this defamation on its head, declaring that "discrimination against lesbian, gay, bisexual and transgender people is immoral" (Forman 2005). Foreman drove this message home in a series of speeches and written opinion pieces, taking on the right-wing anti-LGBT movement that, at least by 2004, had enacted bans on same-sex couples' right to marry in all but a handful of states. By seizing from the anti-LGBT movement its own language of morality, Foreman continued the visionary leadership of the Task Force founders, who, in 1973, dreamed of a world in which sexual orientation and gender identity would no longer disqualify LGBT people from equal protections, social acceptance, and full participation in society.

In 2008, Rea Carey became executive director of NGLTF. In 2013, the Creating Change conference drew more than 4,000 participants. NGLTF is instrumental in helping rural activism, provides accurate information on LGBT issues to legislators, and through the Policy Institute provides rapid-response research to counter the extremist messages generated by the right wing.

Sue Hyde

See also: Activists; Brown, Howard Juniah (1924–1975); Duberman, Martin Bauml (1930–); Kameny, Franklin (1925–2011); Voeller, Bruce (1934–1994).

Further Reading

Cain, Patricia A. 2000. *Rainbow Rights: The Role of Lawyers and Courts in the Lesbian and Gay Civil Rights Movement*. Boulder, CO: Westview.

D'Emilio, John, William B. Turner, and Urvashi Vaid, eds. 2000. *Creating Change: Sexuality, Public Policy, and Civil Rights*. New York: St. Martin's Press.

Foreman, Matt. 2005. "Discimination Is Immoral. Enough Said." NGLTF Press Release. May 11. Available at: http://www.thetaskforce.org/press/releases/pr824_051105. Accessed July 19, 2008.

Hyde, Sue. 2007. *Come Out and Win: Organizing Yourself, Your Community and Your World*. Boston, MA: Beacon Press.

National Gay and Lesbian Task Force. Available at: http://www.thetaskforce.org/.

Riggle, Ellen D.B., and Barry L. Tadlock, eds. 1999. *Gays and Lesbians in the Democratic Process*. New York: Columbia University Press.

Vaid, Urvashi. 1996. *Virtual Equality: The Mainstreaming of Gay and Lesbian Liberation*. New York: Anchor.

National Organization of Gay and Lesbian Scientists and Technical Professionals, Inc.

National Organization of Gay and Lesbian Scientists and Technical Professionals is a professional society that educates and advocates for lesbian, gay, bisexual, transgender, and queer students and professionals in science, technology, engineering, and mathematics. The organization is known by its acronym, NOGLSTP, pronounced "NAW-goal-step." NOGLSTP's mission is twofold:

- empower lesbian, gay, bisexual, transgender, and queer individuals in science, technology, engineering, and mathematics by providing education, advocacy, professional development, networking, and peer support; and

- educate all communities regarding scientific, technological, and medical concerns of lesbian, gay, bisexual, transgender, and queer people (NOGLSTP, 2013)

Like many LGBT advocacy organizations, NOGLSTP was created at the intersection of grassroots equal rights activism and the need to network with colleagues of like-mind. Inspired by Triangle Area Gay Scientists (established 1977) and Los Angeles Gay and Lesbian Scientists (established 1979), the original organizing efforts for a nationwide association of gay and lesbian scientists planted its seeds at the January 1980 American Association for the Advancement of Science (AAAS) annual meeting in San Francisco. At that meeting, a special session was held to discuss problems arising from homophobia in the scientific workplace. Issues were raised that were of concern to all scientists, and the National Organization of Lesbian and Gay Scientists (NOLGS) was created as a grassroots network to organize events and meetings to address those issues (Escoffier et al. 1980).

In those days, most gay people were closeted for fear of stigmatization and social estrangement, which meant that considerable energy that could be spent on scientific creativity and productivity was spent on hiding the truth. Foreign homosexuals were not allowed to enter the United States. That meant foreign LGBT scientists could not attend scientific meetings in the United States. Homosexuals were denied security clearances by some departments of the U.S. government. As such, LGBT scientists and engineers were not eligible to work for these agencies. In the absence of visibility, myths about homosexuals persisted. For example, medical students were not taught about LGBT health care needs, human biology courses did not include accurate information about homosexuality, and science historians ignored or misinterpreted the role of homosexuality in the lives and accomplishments of the some of the world's greatest scientists (Escoffier et al. 1980). Very little funded research about homosexuality existed—either due to disinterest on the part of granting agencies or due to researchers' fears about seeking such funding. This is the climate that the NOLGS organizers sought to expose and address.

NOGLSTP grew out of the informal NOLGS network and was formalized as an organization in August 1983 with a membership structure, a board of directors, and a regular newsletter. "Technical Professionals" was appended to the organization name to indicate a welcoming of engineers, mathematicians, educators, clinicians, and all people who earned a living or were interested in science and technology. Inclusion of "bi" and "trans" were not yet in the naming nomenclature of organizations at the time, although all people were welcomed regardless of gender identity and sexual orientation. By this time, many regional groups for LGBT scientists existed throughout the United States. Some of the groups included Triangle Area Gay Scientists; Los Angeles Gay and Lesbian Scientists; The Humboldt Society; Bay Area Gay and Lesbian Engineers and Scientists; High Tech Gays; Houston Area Gay and Lesbian Scientists; Dallas Area Gay and Lesbian Engineers and Scientists; Gay Association of Technicians, Engineers, and Scientists; Gay and Lesbian Orange County Engineers and Scientists; Gaytek; Natural History Group; New Orleans Area Gay and Lesbian Engineers and Scientists; UFLAGS; and

Washington Area Gay and Lesbian Scientists. The organizers envisioned NOGLSTP serving as a unifying entity for the regional groups as well as a professional society for individuals. For a short time, many of the regional groups affiliated with NOGLSTP in some way but, over the long run, most of the groups went their own way and ultimately evaporated due to leadership attrition. Of these original regional groups, only Los Angeles Gay and Lesbian Scientists is currently a formal NOGLSTP affiliate. Triangle Area Gay Scientists (Chapel Hill, NC), the Humboldt Society (Philadelphia, PA), and the Natural History Group (New York, NY) still thrive thanks to dedicated long-term leadership but are not NOGLSTP affiliates.

NOGLSTP's nascent years focused on identifying and opposing homophobia in the scientific and technical workplace. In the mid-1980s, NOGLSTP received grants from the Chicago Resource Center to produce and distribute the educational pamphlets, "Who Are the Gay and Lesbian Scientists?" (about queer scientists of historical note), "Barriers to Achievement" (about employment discrimination), "Measuring the Gay and Lesbian Population" (about LGBT population demographics), "Security Clearances: Your Rights and the Law", "Sexual Orientation and Computer Privacy" (about data privacy), and "Scientists and AIDS Research: A Gay Perspective." In 1985, NOGLSTP presented its first scientific symposium at an AAAS national meeting, entitled "Homophobia and Social Attitudes: Their Impact on AIDS Research." The symposium was sponsored by the AAAS Office of Opportunities in Science. At the 1989 AAAS annual meeting, NOGLSTP presented a poster entitled "Homophobia in the Scientific Workplace," which summarized the results of a survey of 5,000 employers of scientists and technical professionals. The survey attempted to measure the amount of homophobia in the scientific workplace as part of a broader effort to educate employers about a change in the California State Labor Code that had added sexual orientation to the list of protected classes of people (NOGLSTP 2013). One final educational pamphlet of the Chicago Resource Center grant series was published in 1994: "Beyond Biased Samples: Challenging the Myths on the Economic Status of Lesbians and Gay Men." This pamphlet was a joint effort of NOGLSTP and the Institute for Gay and Lesbian Strategic Studies.

NOGLSTP incorporated in the state of California in 1991 and received its initial 501(c)(3) nonprofit determination from the IRS in 1992. With that in hand, it was only natural for NOGLSTP to leverage its relationship with AAAS into a more formal collaboration. The 1994 AAAS annual meeting was a pivotal event for NOGLSTP. The timely symposium—"Social, Ethical, and Scientific Perspectives of Biological Research on Sexual Orientation"—was presented in response to then "groundbreaking" research findings showing genetic correlation to homosexuality in a subpopulation of gay men. In addition, NOGLSTP was granted affiliate status with AAAS and began regular involvement with organizing timely and newsworthy scientific symposia on topics relevant to LGBT people, presentation of career resources workshops addressing LGBT concerns in science, technology, engineering, and mathematics careers (commonly referred to as STEM careers), and collaboration with the AAAS Section on Societal Impacts of Science and Engineering (NOGLSTP 2013). Some of these symposia included:

- 1997: "Assessing the Health Care Needs of the GLBT Communities"

- 2002: "Scientific & Ethical Perspectives on the Risks of HIV/AIDS Therapeutics"

- 2005: "Defining Male and Female: Biology and the Law"

- 2007: "Electronic Mentoring Programs: Benefits to Minority Communities in Science and Technology"

- 2010: "Targeting HIV/AIDS Prevention: New Research and Future Avenues"

The 1990s was a decade of LGBT activism that resulted in visibility, benefits, and positive change for LGBT people throughout the United States, as well as some disappointments. Corporations lead the nation in workplace equality, yet the Employment Non-Discrimination Act could not get out of committee, and the Defense of Marriage Act was passed. The Government Accounting Office recommended an end to security clearance discrimination, yet the military's Don't Ask Don't Tell policy was established. During this decade, NOGLSTP collaborated with many groups and agencies on the issue of LGBT equality and access in the workplace and in professional societies. LGBT employee support groups throughout the nation were responsible for securing inclusive equal employment opportunity and same-sex partner benefits. The first large firm to offer health benefits to the spousal equivalent of LGBT employees was software company Lotus Development (Spector 1992). Employers of technical professionals—Xerox, Jet Propulsion Laboratory, California Institute of Technology, Apple Computer, Digital Equipment Corporation, IBM—were among the first to adopt nondiscrimination policies, thanks to the efforts of NOGLSTP members and regional groups of LGBT scientists and engineers (Libman 1990). Caucuses of NOGLSTP members formed to represent statisticians, actuaries, sociologists, epidemiologists, chemists, biologists, mathematicians, neuroscientists, astronomers, meteorologists, anthropologists—and more—organized gatherings at their professional society meetings and encouraged their professional societies to include "sexual orientation" in their EEO statements. NOGLSTP assisted the U.S. General Accounting Office prepare a study to document attitudes and experiences of LGBT people involved in the security clearance process. The GAO study resulted in the 1995 report—"Security Clearances: Consideration of Sexual Orientation in the Clearance Process"—which decoupled the (mistakenly presumed) linkage between sexual orientation and vulnerability to blackmail, and recommended positive changes in the security clearance process and policies (Diamond 1995).

In the first decade of the twenty-first century, NOGLSTP continued its scientific symposia and organizational collaborations, and initiated internal programs that would leverage visibility of LGBT scientists, engineers, and other technical professionals nationwide, as well as encourage young LGBT people into the pipeline of technical professions. In 2003, NOGLSTP established a recognition award program to identify, honor, and document the contributions of outstanding queer scientists, engineers, technology professionals, and educators (Burke 2003). This benefitted the technical community and the LGBT community in two ways. First, it engaged allies at the corporate and higher education levels in acknowledgment of their out LGBT colleagues. Second, the growing list of award recipients provided a resource of role models to young LGBT people considering careers in science, technology, engineering, math, and medical sciences (STEMM). In 2005, NOGLSTP established a mentoring program for LGBT students and early career professionals in STEMM by partnering with an existing external organization, MentorNet. Initially focused on mentoring only women and underrepresented minorities in STEMM, MentorNet added LGBT to its outreach mission at very little urging from NOGLSTP. This partnership allowed NOGLSTP members seeking mentors to participate in the MentorNet One-on-One mentoring program, created a place where established career professionals could give back to their community as mentors, and connected LGBT protégés with established professionals and human resources pipelines at top science, engineering, and high-technology companies (Ross 2005). In 2010, NOGLSTP established what has now become its signature program, Out to Innovate, a career summit for LGBT people in STEMM. This biennial summit involves cross-generational sharing and career-centric workshops, keynote speakers that are openly LGBT high-profile STEMM professionals, and career resource opportunities with corporate sponsors and recruiters (Diamond 2010). In 2011, NOGLSTP realized a long-term goal, with the establishment of a competitive scholarship program for LGBT students in STEMM (Diamond 2011).

Over the years, NOGLSTP has become well known across the United States and is a sought-after partner for collaborations with many organizations and agencies in promoting LGBT visibility and equality. With so many employers of technical professionals in the private, public, and academic sectors electing to include sexual orientation and gender expression as protected classes in their employment nondiscrimination policies, NOGLSTP's initial campaign against homophobia in the technical workplace has evolved into championing inclusion of LGBT people in diversity outreach and broadening participation programs in STEMM. NOGLSTP has helped open doors and initiate conversations about equality, supplied resources and information about LGBT people in science, and now provides role models, networking, advocacy and support to young LGBT people pursuing careers in the technical professions.

At the time of writing this encyclopedia, NOGLSTP has five regional affiliates (Los Angeles Gay and Lesbian Scientists, NOGLSTP—Chesapeake Region, NOGLSTP at Purdue, NOGLSTP at Indiana University, and San Diego QuEST) and three professional society affiliates (LGBT Chemists and Allies, Association of Lesbian, Gay, Bisexual and Transgendered Mathematicians, and American Astronomical Society Working Group on LGBTIQ Equality). NOGLSTP is an affiliate of the American Association for the Advancement of Science, a participating professional society in MentorNet Affiliated Partners Plus program, a sustaining member of the National Postdoctoral Association, an endorsing society of National Engineers Week, a founding member of the E-Week Diversity Council, a partner with the Higher Education Recruitment Consortium, and an American Chemical Society Diversity Programs Partner.

Barbara Belmont

See also: Hooker, Evelyn (1907–1996); Kameny, Franklin (1925–2011); Turing, Alan (1912–1954).

Further Reading

Burke, John. 2003. "NOGLSTP Board Announces Annual Awards Program." *NOGLSTP Bulletin*, Spring.

Diamond, Rochelle. 2011. "Battelle and NOGLSTP Establish Scholarship." *NOGLSTP Bulletin*, Spring.

Diamond, Rochelle. 2010. "NOGLSTP Presents 'Out to Innovate.'" *NOGLSTP Bulletin*, Spring.

Escoffier, Jeffrey, et.al. 1980, July. "Homophobia: Effects on Scientists." *Science*, New Series 209 (4454): 340.

Libman, Gary. 1990. "A New Acceptance: Gay Support Groups Are Beginning to Pay Off in the Workplace." *Los Angeles Times*, July 18.

NOGLSTP. 2013. "About NOGLSTP: A Brief History." Available at: http://www.noglstp.org/?page_id=4. Accessed June 30, 2013.

Ross, Amy. 2005. "NOGLSTP Launching Mentoring Program." *NOGLSTP Bulletin*, Fall.

Spector, Barbara. 1992, March. "Gay and Lesbian Scientists Seek Workplace Equality." *The Scientist* 6(5).

Native Americans and LGBTQ Issues

Some Native Americans have begun to use a contemporary term, *two-spirit*, to describe gay, lesbian, bisexual, or transgender Native Americans, Alaskan Natives, and Hawaiians. The specific tribal maintenance of two-spirit traditions is very diverse given differences in histories, languages, gender systems, and geographies: the Alaskan Native Inuit *sipiniq*, for example, refers to sexual change in infancy, while the Aleut *tayagigux* refers to a woman who changes into a man. Some contemporary two-spirits actively honor precolonial transgender categories that could be based on anything from work roles to sexuality to healing abilities. However, because of religious, sexual, and political colonization, many indigenous communities have hidden or forgotten their traditional acceptance of transgendered peoples. Maintenance of two-spirit traditions has sometimes evolved in response to the homophobic practices of Christianized Native Americans and the anti-Indianism of popular gay movements. Two-spirit is a pan–Native American name that creates space to reaffirm both indigenous community relations and queer gender identity.

Natives gathered at designated place to celebrate victory over their enemies, with Chief Holata Outina standing in the foreground with French soldiers, 1588. (Library of Congress)

The evolution of two-spirit histories is complicated by the local differences from one indigenous community to another. On a few reservations, two-spirit traditions have adapted to modern times and continue to be a social, political, and spiritual force in contrast to the majority of places, where they were driven underground. The actual name two-spirit is easier to trace along with the pan-indigenous queer activism that supported its rise. In 1975, Lakota Barbara Cameron and Paiute Randy Burns formed the first official Gay American Indians (GAI) in San Francisco. It was a response to the racism of the largely urban white gay community that was still struggling to free itself of a racial history of segregation and genocidal practices regarding many Native Americans, Alaskan Natives, and Hawaiians. With the onset of the AIDS crisis and the larger gay rights movement, GAI swelled to over a thousand members in the 1980s as it began to manage AIDS services for Native Americans. In similar movements of sexuality and AIDS activism, gay Indian activism and institutions increased throughout the United States. Gays and Lesbians of the First Nations in Toronto, Minnesota American Indian Task Force, the Nations of the Four Directions (San Diego), Nichiwakan (Winnipeg), Tahoma Two-Spirits of Seattle, Vancouver Two-Spirits, We'wha and BarCheeAmpe (New York City) all evolved in the 1980s and 1990s and intensified their practices of cultural difference into the 1990s and new millennium as the gay movement grew and increasingly became fractured by ethnicity and gender differences.

Native youths shooting arrows, throwing balls at a target placed atop a tall pole, and running races, 1588. (Library of Congress)

While white gay authors and communities came to claim the "berdache" or cross-gender indigenous practices as a part of pan-gay history, Native American activists embraced and questioned such histories. *Berdache* as a term used principally by European anthropologists derived from French and other languages that traced its meaning to kept boy, male prostitute, or catamite—clearly derogatory, and not as inclusive in meaning as two-spirit was seen to be. In 1990, at the third American Indian Gay and Lesbian conference in Winnipeg, Canada, the term two-spirit became the preferred pan-Indian identifier and name of that conference. Two-spirit was more gender inclusive than gay and lesbian, and the infusion of spirituality into gender also made the identity change attractive, even though the direct translation back into indigenous languages worked for only a very few. The name allowed a sense of difference from predominantly white gay cultures that were sometimes prone to adopt "berdache" histories as their own. While some Native American scholars feel that the specific roles of indigenous communities do correlate well with same-sex gay cultures, others protested the adoption of gay Indian histories by non-Indians who did not respect contemporary Indian struggles and communities. Two-spirit was a term formed to specifically address the complexity of roles and the necessity of linking contemporary Indians with ancestral ones through family, communal, and ceremonial ties.

Two-spirits actively work to revive and re-create ceremonies after decades or centuries of homophobic oppression. Current practices resonate with once

President Obama signs the Violence against Women Act into law at the Interior Building in Washington, D.C. He is surrounded by members of different organizations that will benefit from its updated groups now included in the act. He addressed the audience before signing the bill citing various women who were instrumental in getting the bill passed which for the first time includes LGBT, Native American, and transgender individuals. (Patsy Lynch/Retna Ltd/Corbis)

openly established two-spirit roles embodied and celebrated by those such as We-wha of the Zuni nation. Cultural ceremonies, healing practices, or gender mediation roles that once required two-spirit presence are now often practiced in greater isolation from the indigenous communities that once benefited from them openly. For example, while strict gender roles accompany most powwow dances, two-spirit powwows allow for a space to cross roles without heterosexist restrictions. Men who would normally dance men's dances in men's regalia are free to wear female regalia such as a shawl or jingle dress. Same-sex couples are encouraged to attend openly, an act that may not

Darren Black Bear, left, and Jason Pickel hold up their marriage license issued by the Cheyenne and Arapaho tribes near Jason's home in Oklahoma City on October 24, 2013. (Nick Oxford/AP/Corbis)

be welcomed by the full community and in other tribal contexts. Two-spirit Southeastern Native American stomp dances are another area open to mixed-gender people. While women usually wear turtle shell rattles and men lead songs, two-spirit stomp dances can feature male lead singers who also wear turtle shell rattles. Female-bodied two-spirits have made cross-gendered statements by choosing to pierce during Plains sun-dance ceremonies, an action more common among adult males. Other two-spirit Plains peoples partake in cross-gender tree ceremonies that relate to the sun dance with the intent to heal the spiritual wounds of indigenous nations and their two-spirit peoples.

While two-spirit peoples may have wildly varying spiritual practices, a sense of honoring past traditions forms a hub of identity. They may differ from Indian gays who identify more with gay communities and emphasize sexual and erotic relationships over their Native American cultures. For urban Indians who have grown up removed from more traditional reservation life, two-spirit practices become more difficult and role models are fewer. Sometimes, two-spirit traditions thrive on reservations so long as identification with tribal relations is maintained. This depends on the extent to which these traditions are passed on. For example, the Lakota have maintained their two-spirit traditions to a much greater extent than their cousins, the Santee Dakota, have.

Both Christian conversion and white secular assumptions about the complete biological differences between all males and females contributed to the decline in two-spirit ways and the oppression of gay Indians. Two-spirit and gay Indian communities often overlap, and members may try one community for a time before returning to the other. The terms gay Indian and two-spirit may be synonymous in some Indian contexts but not others. Social activities at bars and clubs may also be similar for both two-spirits and gay Indians at times, but the ceremonial and family-bound aspects of two-spirits provide healing from bars where addictions tend to take root. Two-spirit organizations may also recruit members from larger gay parades, institutions, and social networks.

Two-spirit women sometimes find greater camaraderie and support in multicultural lesbian-centered networks in urban areas where their numbers are few and sexism is widespread among both Indians and non-Indians alike. Two-spirits and gay Indians do circulate through the white and multicultural gay communities in terms of intimate relations and political alliances when these populations have the chance to meet. While both Native Alaskan and Hawaiian cultures have two-spirit roles, a vigorous gay tourist industry in Hawaii increases the chance of cross-cultural relations compared to what can happen in the more remote villages of Native Alaska. Migrations to and from indigenous land and U.S. or Canadian cities complicate the ways in which both pan-Indian and interracial contact will create new two-spirit identities and experiences.

Gabriel S. Estrada

See also: Allen, Paula Gunn (1939–2008); Historical Overview of Gay Rights and Issues: From Pre-Columbian Times to the 1970s; We'wha (1849–1896).

Further Reading

Brown, Lester, ed. 1997. *Two-Spirit People: American Indian Lesbian Women and Gay Men*. New York: Hawthorn Press.

Gilley, Brian Joseph. 2006. *Becoming Two-Spirit: Gay Identity and Social Acceptance in Indian Country*. Lincoln: University of Nebraska Press.

Jacobs, Sue-Ellen, Wesley Thomas, and Sabine Lang, eds. 1997. *Two-Spirit People: Native American Gender Identity, Sexuality, and Spirituality*. Chicago: University of Illinois Press.

Roscoe, Will, ed. 1989. *Living the Spirit: Gay American Indians*. San Francisco: Beacon Press.

Native Americans and Same-Sex Marriage

So often the controversy surrounding same-sex marriage focuses on international, federal, and state debates. Overlooked are the strides being made with America's First People and their acceptance of same-sex marriages.

There is a long history of First People not only accepting but venerating gender non-conforming people. Many tribes (but not all) located in what would become the United States respected the sexual and gender expressions of their members. If a woman adopted the dress and behaviors of a man, she was allowed to do so. Likewise, if a man adopted the dress and behaviors of a woman, he was allowed to do so. Sometimes the person mixed the dress and behaviors of both genders. The tribal spiritual beliefs accepted that gender and sexuality were gifts of the spirits and were not to be challenged. The tribe needed to accept members who were neither exclusively male nor female as their spiritual expression—what is termed "two-spirit" people. For

Heather Purser, right, and her girlfriend, Rebecca Platter, are shown near their home in Olympia, Washington, on May 7, 2103. Purser, a member of the Suquamish tribe, got her tribal council to vote in favor of gay marriage. (Tony Overman/The Olympian/MCT/Getty Images)

some tribes, being two-spirit was considered special and such persons held the position of counselor, or shaman and teacher for the tribe. For example, we find two-spirit people in Navajo (called *Nadleehe*), Zuni (called *Lhamana*), and Lakota (called *Winkte*) tribes. One such person was We'Wha. She was a two-spirit man-woman from the Zuni tribe who was considered the most intelligent of the tribe with an insatiable thirst for knowledge. She was sent to Washington, D.C., in 1886 to represent the Zuni nation to the U.S. government. We'Wha appeared in native clothing at a number of events including the National Theater, demonstrated Zuni weaving methods at the Smithsonian, and personally met President Grover Cleveland. News reports claim Washington society was thoroughly charmed and accepted her as a woman. There is no indication anyone suspected We'Wha of being a man.

Sometimes two-spirit people would marry and this could be someone of their same or other biological gender. Also, many tribes had friendship ceremonies where two friends would announce to the entire tribe that they had a binding relationship. Sometimes these friendship relationships included sexual behaviors. Together, we see that First People nations often included same-sex relationships that could apply to the discussion of same-sex marriage.

A number of First People nations have formally accepted same-sex marriage. In 2009, the Coquille Tribe (located in Oregon) became the first nation to adopt same-sex marriage. In 2011, the Suquamish Tribe (located in Washington) became the second nation to enact similar regulations. These two tribes reside within states that either have their own same-sex marriage laws or accept same-sex marriages performed elsewhere. As such, there is no conflict between tribal law and state law. In 2013, the Little Traverse Bay Bands of Odawa Indians (LTBB) became the third nation to recognize same-sex marriages. LTBB is located within Michigan, a state that currently does not allow same-sex marriages nor recognizes same-sex marriages performed elsewhere. There is potential conflict between LTBB law and Michigan law.

The United States has expressly recognized tribal nations as separate sovereign nations since the 1831 U.S. Supreme Court case of *Cherokee Nation v. Georgia*. Chief Justice John Marshall wrote that tribal nations were separate political entities capable of managing their own internal affairs. A year later in 1832, the Court in *Worcester v. Georgia* held that Georgia law could not be imposed upon the Cherokee Nation. This separation between state law and tribal law has eroded over the centuries but tribal nations are still considered separate political entities. Furthermore, court opinions in 1897 have upheld tribal nation authority over marriage within its territory.

The Michigan Supreme Court discussed this very matter in *Kobogum v. Jackson Iron Co.* (1889). The court acknowledged that Michigan had no authority of tribal nations' internal affairs and marriage in particular. It is believed that the state of Michigan will not try to nullify marriages performed by the LTBB tribe. However, Michigan will not recognize marriages performed by LTBB as its recently modified constitution defines marriage as a union between one man and one woman and does not consider same-sex marriages performed in other states or nations to be valid.

LTBB has the authority to enact the Waganakising Odawak Statute 2013–003 authorizing same-sex marriages. The statute is consistent with tribal law, customs, and traditions. However, Michigan is not required to recognize same-sex marriages and will not recognize same-sex marriages from LTBB.

As of 2013, other tribes that approve same-sex marriage include Pokagon Band of Potawatomi Indians, the Iipay Nation of Santa Ysabel, the Confederated Tribes of the Colville Reservation, the Cheyenne and Arapaho tribes, and the Leech Lake Band of Ojibwe.

Chuck Stewart

See also: Native Americans and LGBTQ Issues.

Further Reading

Kronk, Elizabeth Ann. 2013, April 16. "One Statute for Two Spirits: Same-Sex Marriage in Indian Country." *JURIST – Forum.* Available at: http://jurist.org/forum/2013/04/elizabeth-kronk-two-spirits.php. Accessed November 18, 2013.

Stewart, Chuck. 2003. *Gay and Lesbian Issues: A Contemporary Resource.* Boulder, CO: ABC-CLIO Publishers.

Navratilova, Martina (1956–)

Martina Navratilova was the number-one ranked tennis player in the world for a number of years and has been one of the few sports personalities who have been open about her homosexuality. Born in Prague, Czechoslovakia, on October 18, 1956, Navratilova was brought up in a sports enthusiast's family. She took up tennis and won tournaments around Czechoslovakia. She visited West Germany in 1969 as part of a tennis club exchange program. It was a revealing experience for her. By age 15, she was touring Czechoslovakia and the Eastern bloc countries; she was better known abroad than at home.

In the early 1970s, she was granted permission to play in the United States in a number of tours, where she was managed by Beverly Hills businessman Fred Barman. In 1975, while participating in the U.S. Open in New York, she contacted the New York office of the Immigration and Naturalization Service through Fred Barman and was granted asylum.

It was during these tours of the United States that she discovered that she was attracted to women. She had a number of relationships over the years, including a three-year affair with her new manager, Sandra Haynie.

In 1978, Navratilova beat Chris Everett at Wimbledon to become the number-one ranked tennis player in the world. That same year she met novelist

Martina Navratilova holds the winner's trophy after she and Bob Bryan won the mixed doubles championship over Kveta Peschke and Martin Damm of the Czech Republic at the U.S. Open tennis tournament in New York on September 9, 2006. (AP Photo/Kathy Willens)

Rita Mae Brown and began a short-lived, intense affair. Brown's divergent opinions concerning sports split the relationship apart. Navratilova learned that celebrity status has a price in a free-press society, as her name often showed up in the tabloids.

Navratilova worried that her homosexuality would affect her career and pending application for U.S. citizenship. However, citizenship was granted without incident in 1981, and tennis sponsors did not withdraw their funding.

Martina Navratilova had a spectacular tennis career, including nine singles wins at Wimbledon, and four U.S. Opens. Her very public affairs with other well-known lesbians made her the most highly visible lesbian sports celebrity in the world.

Navratilova retired twice, first in 1994 after losing in Wimbledon in singles competition. In 2000, she returned to professional competition, playing mainly in doubles contests, including mixed doubles. In July 2006 Navratilova made her final appearance at Wimbledon, when she was nearly 50 years old. She capped her career by winning the mixed doubles title at the 2006 U.S. Open with Bob Bryan and then retired for the second time.

In 2013, the National Gay and Lesbian Hall of Fame in Chicago inducted Navratilova into their first class of inductees. She is also a member of the International Tennis Hall of Fame (1990) and has received numerous awards and accolades.

Chuck Stewart

See also: King, Billie Jean (1943–).

Further Reading

Howard, Johnette. 2005. *The Rivals: Chris Evert vs. Martina Navratilova: Their Epic Duels and Extraordinary Friendship*. New York: Broadway Books.

Navratilova, Martina and George Vecsey. 1986. *Martina*. New York: Fawcett Books.

Overman, S. J. and K. Boyer Sagert. 2012. "Martina Navratilova." In *Icons of Women's Sport*. Santa Barbara, CA: Greenwood.

Wallace, Hannah. 2009. "Martina after 50." *Sarasota Magazine* 31(5): 68–75.

Wolff, Alexander. 1994. "Martina Navratilova." *Sports Illustrated*, September 19. Available at: http://sportsillustrated.cnn.com/vault/article/magazine/MAG1005679/index.htm.

Near, Holly (1949–)

Holly Near was one of the first and probably the most influential lesbian singer to emerge from the women's music movement. Born on June 6, 1949, in Ukiah, California, Near grew up in a musical family. She made her public singing debut when she was seven years old. By her teens, she had appeared in a number of films and television programs. After high school, she traveled to New York, where she landed the lead in the Broadway production of the musical *Hair*.

She was very politically active and campaigned against the Vietnam War. She toured with the controversial Jane Fonda's "Free the Army" show. Throughout the 1970s, Near traveled constantly on the vocal music circuit. Although she was approached by major record companies, she did not take up their offers. She did not want to give up control over material that included lesbian-themed songs. Instead, she established her own record company, Redwood Records.

Redwood released its first album, *Hang in There*, in 1973. By 1979, Redwood had sold more than 155,000 copies of this album, which is considered highly successful for a small independent label. One of her songs, "Singing for Our Lives," with the refrain "We are gay and lesbian people/And we are singing, singing for our lives," was considered by many to be the anthem for the gay civil rights movement.

Another feminist music company to rise in the 1970s was Olivia Records. It was dedicated to women making music for women and operated nonhierarchically as a collective. Its first record was *Meg Christian: I Know You Know*, which included the well-known song "Ode to a Gym Teacher." Its second album was by Cris Williamson, *The Changer and the Changed*. Holly Near also sang for Olivia Records, and the three singers created what is known as the Olivia sound.

Olivia Records flourished throughout the 1970s and early 1980s, but by the mid-1980s was floundering because of financial undercapitalization. Olivia abandoned some of its initial lesbian feminist principles and became more mainstream in its business operations. With the changes at Olivia, Holly Near went on with her solo career and continued playing at college concerts and on the coffeehouse circuit.

In 2004, she performed at the march for Women's Lives in Washington, D.C. She sang "We Are Gentle Angry People" and "Fired Up." "Singing for Our Lives" is used in the official hymnal of the Unitarian Universalists Association under the title "We Are a Gentle, Angry People" (Hymn #170). Although Near is a longtime lesbian activist, she has been in a relationship with a man since 1994. When asked about that relationship and if she identified as bisexual by JD Doyle in 2010 for Queer Music Heritage, Near replied, "I don't know why. Just isn't a handle I relate to. . . . I think my feminism and my ability to love has been highly informed by having had lesbian relationships. The quality of my life has, without question, been elevated. . . . I am going to sing lesbian love songs and support gay rights no matter what. The rest is public relations" (Arenberg 2010). She is well loved and admired by her lesbian followers.

Chuck Stewart

See also: Brown, Rita Mae (1944–).

Holly Near performs at the Clearwater River Revival Festival in 2012. (Brian Cahn/ZUMA Press/Corbis)

Further Reading

Arenberg, Naomi. 2010. Holly Near. Interview at WGBH Boston. Available at: http://www.hollynear.com/art_in terviews.html. Accessed February 14, 2014.

Near, Holly. 1990. *Fire in the Rain, Singer in the Storm: An Autobiography*. New York: W. Morrow.

Ruhlmann, William. 2011. Holly Near/Biography. *Allmusic Biography*. San Francisco: Rovi Corporation.

Obama, Barack, and Support for Same-Sex Marriage

For the first time in U.S. history, a sitting president supported same-sex marriage. In an interview with Robin Roberts on ABC's *Good Morning America*, President Obama stated:

I've always been adamant that gay and lesbian Americans should be treated fairly and equally. . . . I have to tell you that over the course of several years as I have talked to friends and family and neighbors when I think about members of my own staff who are in

Eric Bennett, left, and Trenton Garris, hug as they gathered to show support as President Barack Obama visits the Paramount Theater one day after announcing his support for same-sex marriage, in Seattle on May 10, 2012. (AP Photo/ Kevin P. Casey)

incredibly committed monogamous relationships, same-sex relationships, who are raising kids together, when I think about those soldiers or airmen or Marines or sailors who are out there fighting on my behalf and yet feel constrained, even now that Don't Ask Don't Tell is gone, because they are not able to commit themselves in a marriage, at a certain point I've just concluded that for me personally it is important for me to go ahead and affirm that I think same sex couples should be able to get married. (Stein 2012, Obama)

In prior interviews, Obama stated that his position on same-sex marriage was "evolving" but that he wasn't there yet to endorse full rights for gay and lesbian couples. With the quickly changing political scene in 2012 with same-sex marriage being adopted by so many major states, the president finally embraced full equality for LGBT citizens.

A few days earlier, Vice President Joe Biden made public statements in support of same-sex marriage. In an interview with David Gregory on NBC's *Meet the Press*, Biden stated:

I am vice president of the United States of America. . . . The president sets the policy. I am absolutely comfortable with the fact that men marrying men, women marrying women, and heterosexual men and women marrying another are entitled to the same exact rights, all the civil rights, all the civil liberties. And quite frankly, I don't see much of a distinction—beyond that. (Stein 2012, Biden)

It was Biden's statements that are thought to have encouraged Obama to take the final step and publically support same-sex marriage.

Chuck Stewart

See also: Same-Sex Marriage in the United States.

Further Reading

Stein, Sam. 2012, May 5. "Joe Biden Tells "Meet the Press" He's 'Comfortable' with Marriage Equality." *Huffington Post.* Interview with David Gregory on NBC's Meet the Press. Available at: http://www.huffingtonpost.com/2012/05/06/vice-president-biden-gay-marriage_n_1489235.html. Accessed November 17, 2013.

Stein, Sam. 2012, May 9. "Obama Backs Gay Marriage." *Huffington Post.* Interview by Robin Roberts of *ABC's* "Good Morning America." Available at: http://www.huffingtonpost.com/2012/05/09/obama-gay-marriage_n_1503245.html, Accessed November 17, 2013.

ONE, Incorporated

Door Legg, an early board member of the Mattachine Society and some of his fellow members decided to publish a national monthly newsletter under a new organization, called ONE, Incorporated. Its goals were liberal instead of leftist and it derived its name from a line by the nineteenth-century essayist Thomas Carlyle: "A mystic bond of brotherhood makes all men one" (Blumenfeld and Raymond 1993, p. 293). The newsletter began publication in January 1953 and served as the voice of the homophile movement during its early years. (It is still published today in conjunction with the International Gay and Lesbian Archives located at the University of Southern California.) The members of ONE kept themselves separate from the Mattachine Society, primarily because many Mattachine members were having reservations about the group's secrecy and leftist politics.

In 1954 the Los Angeles postmaster seized copies of *ONE* magazine and refused to mail them on the grounds that they were "obscene, lewd, lascivious and filthy." *ONE* editors challenged the seizure in court. Two lower courts upheld the actions of the postmaster, but, ultimately, the U.S. Supreme Court overturned the lower courts in 1958 (*One, Inc. v. Olesen*). This was a "legal and publishing landmark" (*Gay Almanac* 1996, p. 13). Material containing homosexual themes and information was no longer automatically deemed obscene and could be distributed through the mail service.

ONE, Incorporated and the International Gay and Lesbian Archives merged in the late 1990s. The library moved to the University of Southern California (USC), and in 2010, ONE deposited its extensive collections with the USC Libraries.

Chuck Stewart

See also: Daughters of Bilitis; Mattachine Society.

Further Reading

Blumenfeld, W. J., and D. Raymond, eds. 1993. *Looking at Gay and Lesbian Life*, rev. ed. Boston: Beacon Press.

Gay Almanac, The. 1996. Complied by the National Museum and Archive of Lesbian and Gay History. New York: Berkley Books.

One. National Gay and Lesbian Archives. Available at: http://www.onearchives.org/.

P

Perkins, Will (1928–)

Perkins was an early member and chairman of Colorado for Family Values (CFV), which was responsible for placing Amendment 2 (outlawing antidiscrimination statutes based on sexual orientation) on the Colorado ballot in 1992. Born in Montrose, Colorado, on August 22, 1928, Perkins received his bachelor's degree in business from Colorado College in 1950. While in college, he was a respected athlete and was head baseball

Will Perkins in 1986. (Lyn Alweis/The Denver Post/Getty Images)

coach at Colorado College from 1951 through 1952. Later he played professional baseball for the Chicago White Sox for one year. He worked for many years as a car salesman and eventually became chairman of the board of the Perkins Chrysler Plymouth Company in Colorado Springs. Frustrated with what he perceived as the antifamily gay agenda that was gaining support in many cities throughout the state of Colorado, he became involved with CFV in 1991. He was able to convince a number of city councils to refuse to adopt or to rescind antigay discrimination ordinances. Perkins was successful at obtaining wide support for his efforts and getting Amendment 2 placed on the 1992 statewide ballot. The initiative passed in November 1992 and was immediately challenged in courts. It was eventually ruled unconstitutional in *Romer v. Evans* (1996). Perkins continues to provide expert advice to other conservative organizations battling gay right ordinances, and CFV continues to battle against gay rights laws and ordinances in Colorado.

Chuck Stewart

See also: Robertson, Pat (1930–).

Further Reading

Brewer, Paul R. 2007. *Value War: Public Opinion and the Politics of Gay Rights.* Lanham, MD: Rowman & Littlefield.

Herman, Didi. 1998. *The Anti-gay Agenda. Orthodox Vision and the Christian Right.* Chicago: University of Chicago Press.

Perry, Troy (1940–)

Troy Perry founded the first Christian church in the United States with a special mission to lesbians and gay men. The church's first service was held in Perry's living room in Los Angeles on October 16, 1968, and attracted 12 people. The church, now known as the Metropolitan Community Church, currently has 43,000 members and adherents in almost 300 congregations in 22 countries.

Perry was born in Tallahassee, Florida, on July 27, 1940, the oldest of five boys born to Troy Perry and Edith Allen, whom Perry later described as "the biggest bootleggers in Northern Florida" (Tobin and Wicker 1975, p. 14). Although his parents were not particularly religious, Perry decided at an early age that he wanted to become a minister. His early upbringing occurred within the Baptist and Pentecostal churches, and he soon adopted the strict moral code imposed by the latter denomination. He did not attend movies, dance, or play cards or games involving dice. He claims that he and his dates always knelt and prayed before they went out together, asking to have the strength to avoid temptations.

Although his first homosexual experience was at the age of nine, Perry convinced himself that he was not "that way." He decided that his constant homosexual fantasies were just "different" from what other boys experienced. He had no reservations or doubts, then, when he married a pastor's daughter in 1958 at the age of 18. Two sons resulted from that marriage, which ended in divorce five years later.

In the meanwhile, Perry attended the Midwest Bible College and the Moody Bible Institute in Chicago. In 1962, he was ordained a minister in the Church of God and became a pastor at a small church in Santa Ana, California. He found it increasingly difficult to reconcile his homosexual feelings with his denomination's teachings and his church responsibilities, however, and in 1964, he left the church and took a job with Sears Roebuck.

After a stint in the army, a failed relationship with another man, and an attempted suicide, Perry made a momentous decision—he would start a church with a special mission to the gay and lesbian community. Of the 12 attendees at the first meeting of that church, Perry later said, "Nine were my friends who came to console me and to laugh, and three came as a result of the ad [which he had placed in the gay magazine *The Advocate*]" (Tobin and Wicker 1975, pp. 19–20). This inauspicious beginning gave no hint whatsoever of the spectacular success the Metropolitan Community Church was later to experience.

Perry later wrote about his own life in the book *The Lord Is My Shepherd and He Knows I'm Gay* (Nash Publishing 1972) and its sequel, *Don't Be Afraid Any More* (St. Martin's Press 1990). Perry was the first openly gay person to serve on the Los Angeles County

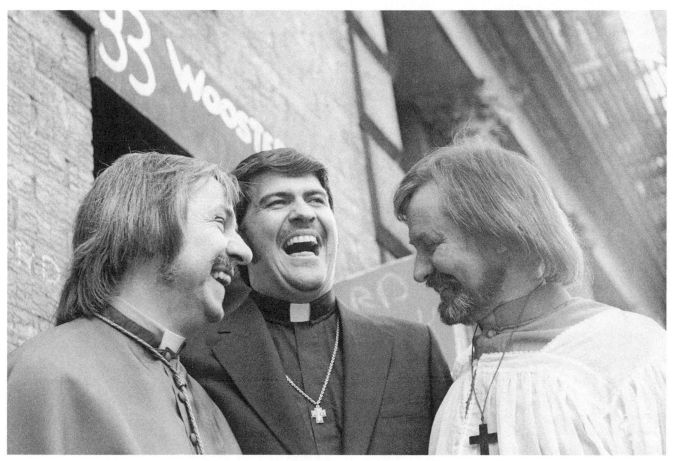

Father Troy Perry, center, who married Father Robert M. Clement, left, and his partner John Noble, right, joke after the wedding at 33 Wooster Street, New York, on July 18, 1971. (AP Photo/Ron Frehm)

Commission on Human Relations. He has been honored with the Humanitarian Awards of the Lesbian and Gay Rights Chapter of the American Civil Liberties Union and of the Gay Press Association. He holds honorary doctorates from Boston's Episcopal Divinity School, Samaritan College of Los Angeles, and Sierra University in Santa Monica, California.

David E. Newton

See also: Soulforce. Documents: Dignity USA's Response to the "Congregation for the Doctrine of Faith—On the Pastoral Care of Homosexual Persons . . ." (1986); A Jewish Rabbi's Acceptance of Gay and Lesbian Rights (1989); Catholic Condemnation of Homosexuality (1994).

Further Reading

Tobin, Kay and Randy Wicker. 1975. *The Gay Crusaders*. New York: Arno Press.

Proposition 8 and the Mormon Church

On November 4, 2008, Californian voters approved the same-sex marriage ban Proposition 8 by a narrow margin. The result of the country's most expensive ballot initiative (Liptak 2010), the constitutional amendment limited the definition of marriage only to those unions between a man and a woman. Besides religious institutions such as the Roman Catholic Church and fundamentalist Christian groups, conservative institutions, and right-wing politicians, the Church of Jesus Christ of Latter-Day Saints (also known as the Mormon Church) became a key player in California's anti same-sex marriage movement. In the months leading to the infamous ballot decision, constituents of the Church of Jesus Christ of Latter-Day Saints not only contributed significantly in terms of community

A protester writes "tax this cult" in chalk on the street in front of the Los Angeles Mormon Temple as hundreds demonstrated against the church's support of Proposition 8, the California ballot measure that banned gay marriage, in the Westwood district of Los Angeles on November 6, 2008. (AP Photo/Reed Saxon)

outreach but also with financial donations, with about half of the contributions in support of Proposition 8 coming from members of the Mormon Church (McKinley and Johnson 2008).

Mormon Teachings: The Law of Chastity as Source of Opposition

The Church of Jesus Christ of Latter-Day Saints' opposition to same-sex activity is largely based on founder Joseph Smith's translation of the Bible as well as the Book of Mormon and the Doctrine and Covenants. One verse critical in understanding the church's opposition to homosexuality in general is Leviticus 20:13, "If a man also lie with mankind, as he lieth with a

woman, both of them have committed an abomination: they shall surely be put to death; their blood shall be upon them." In the law of chastity, specifically, the Church of Jesus Christ of Latter-Day Saints (LDS 2013a) addresses the immorality of sexual relations outside of marriage in general as well as same-sex relations specifically. In the context of same-sex relations, the moral code denounces same-sex activity rather than sexual orientation. Gay, lesbian, and bisexual individuals may not be precluded from their community if they refrain from same-sex activity.

The Proposition 8 Movement

To place the same-sex marriage ban Proposition 8 on the ballot, proponents collected more than 1.1 million signatures. ("Timeline on Same-Sex Marriage" 2013). Despite their vital role in the later campaign, the Mormon Church did not play an active role in qualifying Proposition 8 for the ballot. Rather, it was the activism of Catholic bishop George H. Niederauer that sparked activism within the Mormon community. In June 2008, Niederauer sent a letter to the Church of Jesus Christ of Latter-Day Saints, asking church members for support in the *Yes on 8* campaign (Kuruvila 2008).

In response, the presidency of the Mormon Church sent out a letter to congregations across the state that emphasized supporting the campaign as a means to protect the traditional definition of marriage. The statement further stressed the importance of church members' involvement in the campaign, asking the community to do all they could to "support the proposed constitutional amendment by donating of your means and time to assure that marriage in California is legally defined as being between a man and a woman" (LDS 2008a, June 30, paragraph 5). The statement sparked an uprise in activism among church members in the weeks and months to follow.

According to official estimates, members of the Mormon Church made up almost 90 percent of the volunteer base participating in canvassing efforts in support of Proposition 8. Members of the Church of Jesus Christ of Latter-Day Saints also contributed nearly half of the $40 million raised for the anti same-sex marriage effort (McKinley and Johnson 2008). Direct contributions by the Church of Jesus

Joe Hege, right, of San Francisco holds up a sign during a rally in the Castro district celebrating a federal judge's decision overturning California's same-sex marriage ban in San Francisco on August 4, 2010. Chief U.S. District judge Vaughn Walker made his ruling in a lawsuit filed by two gay couples who claimed the voter-approved ban violated their civil rights. (AP Photo/Eric Risberg)

Christ of Latter-Day Saints totaled about $190,000 in nonmonetary donations. The church's campaign support sparked a controversy after Fred Karger, founder of the organization Californians against Hate, filed a complaint with the Fair Political Practices Commission, accusing the church of misrepresenting campaign donations. After an investigation by the commission, the church had to pay a $5,539 fine (Wollan 2010).

The Aftermath of Proposition 8

On November 4, 2008, Californians voted to approve Proposition 8 by a narrow margin. The decision was the result of the most expensive ballot campaign in the country (Liptak 2010). In a statement responding to the passage, the church reaffirmed its position

and expressed "deep appreciation for the hard work and dedication" of community members (LDS 2008b, November 5, paragraph 11). Moreover, the statement called for respect between proponents and opponents in the continuing same-sex marriage debate.

In the following years, the church responded to several lawsuits challenging the constitutionality of the same-sex marriage ban. In 2010, District Chief Judge Vaughn R. Walker ruled in the decision Perry v. Schwarzenegger that Proposition 8 violated the Due Process and Equal Protection clause of the Constitution. Responding to the decision, the LDS church emphasized its dissatisfaction, pointing out that "California voters have twice been given the opportunity to vote on the definition of marriage in their state and both times have determined that marriage should be recognized as only between a man and a woman. We agree. [. . .]" (LDS 2010, paragraph 2).

After Perry v Schwarzenegger was presented to the U.S. Supreme Court, the church, alongside other congregations of faith, filed an amicus brief defending the same-sex marriage ban based on values of the traditional definition of marriage and family. In response to the Ninth Circuit's argument that Proposition 8 is discriminatory of gay and lesbian couples, the brief countered that "only a demeaning view of religion and religious believers could dismiss our advocacy of Proposition 8 as ignorance, prejudice, or animus" (Brief of National Association of Evangelicals et al. 2013, p. 2). At the same time, the court's challenge to the same-sex marriage ban is considered discriminatory as "reframing the people's considered decision as an attack on civil rights employs a narrative of majority oppression that is powerful, resonant, and wrong" (p. 1). After the Supreme Court's landmark decision to strike down Section 3 of DOMA in June 2013, the Church of Jesus Christ of Latter-Day Saints (2013b, paragraph 4) reaffirmed its opposition based on traditional family values, stating that "regardless of the court decision, the Church remains irrevocably committed to strengthening traditional marriage between a man and a woman, which for thousands of years has proven to be the best environment for nurturing children."

Reaffirming Judge Walker's overturn of Proposition 8, the Supreme Court ruled in June 2013 that "petitioners did not have standing to appeal the District Court's order" (Hollingsworth et al. v. Perry et al., p.1). The Supreme Court further argued that petitioners were not personally harmed by the repeal of the same-sex marriage ban, a reason that may have justified a challenge to the District Court's order. Shortly after, Proposition 8 supporters presented another challenge to California's same-sex marriage law, which was rejected by the California Supreme Court (Dolan 2013), reinstating civil marriage rights for gay and lesbian couples in California.

Andrea M. Hackl

See also: Proposition 8 Legal Analysis and the Impact of Judge Walker's Decision. Document: U.S. Supreme Court Lets Ban against Proposition 8 Stand, Allowing Same-Sex Marriage in California: *Hollingsworth et al. v. Perry et al.*(2013).

Further Reading

Brief of National Association of Evangelicals et al. Amici Curiae Supporting Petitioners, *Hollingsworth v. Perry* (January 29, 2013), (no. 12–144).

The Church of Jesus Christ of Latter-Day Saints. 2008a, June 30. California and Same-Sex Marriage. http://www.mormonnewsroom.org/article/california-and-same-sex-marriage. Accessed July 14, 2013.

The Church of Jesus Christ of Latter-Day Saints. 2008b, November 5. *Church Responds to Same-Sex Marriage Votes*. Available at: http://www.mormonnewsroom.org/ldsnewsroom/eng/news-releases-stories/church-responds-to-same-sex-marriage-votes. Accessed July 8, 2013.

The Church of Jesus Christ of Latter-Day Saints. 2010, August 4. Church Statement on Proposition 8 Ruling. Available at: http://www.mormonnewsroom.org/article/church-statement-on-proposition-8-ruling. Accessed July 9, 2013.

The Church of Jesus Christ of Latter-Day Saints. 2013a. Chapter 39: The Law of Chastity. Available at: http://www.lds.org/manual/gospel-principles/chapter-39-the-law-of-chastity?lang=eng. Accessed July 7, 2013.

The Church of Jesus Christ of Latter-Day Saints. 2013b. Church Responds to Supreme Court Marriage Rulings. Available at: http://www.mormonnewsroom.org/article/church-responds-supreme-court-marriage-rulings. Accessed July 7, 2013.

Dolan, M. 2013, August 14. "California Supreme Court Rejects Bid to Revive Prop. 8." The Los Angeles Times. Available at: http://www.latimes.com/local/lanow/la-me-ln-california-supreme-court-prop-8–20130814,0,1311803.story. Accessed August 20, 2013.

Hollingsworth et al. v. Perry et al., No. 12–144 (2013).

Kuruvila, M. 2008, November 10. "Catholics, Mormons Allied to Pass Prop. 8. SF Gate." Available at: http://www.sfgate.com/news/article/Catholics-Mormons-allied-to-pass-Prop-8–3185965.php. Accessed July 8, 2013.

Liptak, A. 2010, March 22. "Trial in Same-Sex Marriage Case Is Challenged." The New York Times. Available at: http://www.nytimes.com/2010/03/23/us/23bar.html?_r=0. Accessed July 5, 2013.

McKinley, J. and K. Johnson. 2008, November 14. "Mormons Tipped Scale in Ban on Gay Marriage." The New York Times. Available at: http://www.nytimes.com/2008/11/15

/us/politics/15marriage.html?pagewanted=all&_r=0. Accessed July 5, 2013.

Perry v. Schwarzenegger, 704 F.Supp.2d 921 (N.D.Cal. 2010).

Timeline on Same-Sex Marriage. 2013, June 26. SF Gate. Available at: http://www.sf gate.com/default/article/Timeline-on-same-sex-marriage-4624968.php. Accessed July 5, 2013.

Wollan, M. 2010, June 9. "Mormon Church Agrees to Pay Campaign Finance Fine." The New York Times. Available at: http://thecaucus.blogs.nytimes.com/2010/06/09/mormon-church-agrees-to-pay-campaign-finance-fine/. Accessed July 8, 2013.

Proposition 8 Legal Analysis and the Impact of Judge Walker's Decision

Proposition 8 was a California ballot proposition designed to amend the state constitution to prohibit same-sex marriage. A previous attempt was made to ban same-sex marriage in California through the passage of Proposition 22 in 2000. The act added Section 208.5 to the Family Code. As an ordinary statute, it could be deemed in conflict with the state constitution, as it was on May 15, 2008. Prop 8 (as it is informally known) tried to solve the legal issue by amending the constitution. However, Prop 8 was also ruled unconstitutional in 2010, a decision left unchanged by the U.S. Supreme Court in 2013 thereby allowing same-sex marriages to resume in California.

The 2010 decision by Chief Judge Vaughn Walker in the *Perry v. Schwarzenegger* (later renamed *Hollingsworth v. Perry*) was considered by many legal experts to be an exceedingly well-crafted opinion that would have implications for future lawsuits on this topic. Judge Walker ruled that Prop 8 was unconstitutional under both the Equal Protection Clauses of the Fourteenth Amendment and Due Process as the law re-removed rights from a disfavored class only and without a rational basis. The ruling was so clear and concise that the state of California refused to defend the law and appeal his decision.

However, opponents of the law obtained a stay while they appealed the ruling to the U.S. Supreme Court. The Court finally ruled on June 26, 2013, that the proponents of Prop 8 did not possess legal standing in their own right and, as such, had no right to defend the law in federal court. The Court dismissed the appeal and directed the Ninth Circuit to vacate its decision. That left Judge Walker's ruling intact, enabling Governor Jerry Brown to order the resumption of same-sex marriage.

Judge Walker's decision ran for over 50 pages and contained 80 findings of fact (Frank 2010). The decision was crafted similarly to how Justice Kennedy wrote his decision in *Lawrence v. Texas*.

Professor Doug NeJaime of Loyola Law School and John C. Eastman (law professor in support of Prop 8) have suggested that Walker was "speaking" to Kennedy as a strategy to possibly influence the justice (who is commonly the swing vote on the U.S. Supreme Court) in the event that case ever made it to that level (Schwartz 2010; Williams 2010). Similarly, Barry McDonald, a Pepperdine University law professor, admired Walker's strict handling of the case. He believed the meticulous evidence gathering would "make it more difficult for appellate courts to overturn this court's ruling" (Williams 2010).

The Alliance Defense Fund (ADF) defended Prop 8. At the trial, they brought forth only 2 witnesses, whereas those in opposition to the law called fifteen witnesses. Andrew Cohen, legal analyst for CBS, was surprised ADF ceded so much ground and praised Walker's handling of the case. "During the trial, Walker practically begged and cajoled the Prop 8 lawyers to do better for their cause. He asked them written questions to draw them out. He scolded them during closing arguments to make more persuasive arguments. They simply didn't or couldn't or wouldn't respond" (Cohen 2010). The two ADF "expert" witnesses were judged to be of poor quality. David Blankenhorn was judged to be lacking "the qualifications to offer opinion testimony" and Kenneth P. Miller's description of LGBT political power was unsupported (Cohen 2010). Later, in 2012, Blankenhorn changed his opinion coming out in support of same-sex marriage.

Judge Walker delineated the case as a "right to marry." Before Proposition 8, California had implemented a comprehensive domestic partnership statue that granted same-sex couples the same rights as opposite-sex couples but without the use of the word "marriage." Walker rejected domestic partnership arrangement under strict scrutiny analysis since domestic partnerships do not provide the same social meaning as does "marriage" and domestic partnerships were crafted solely to provide benefits to same-sex couples in deference to opposite-sex couples who had the right to marry. As such, Prop 8 was unconstitutional because it did not provide equal protection to same-sex couples under a strict or rational basis of review.

Sometimes it is claimed that allowing same-sex couples to marry somehow threatens "traditional" marriage. That claim was rejected and the Court declared, "it is implausible to think that denying two men or two women the right to call themselves married could somehow bolster the stability of families headed by one man and one woman" (*Perry v. Brown*, 2012, p. 63; Court: Calif. gay-marriage ban unconstitutional, 2013).

At one point during the same-sex marriage debate and court cases, supporters of Prop 8 argued that Judge Walker should have *recused* himself from hearing the case since he was in a long-term relationship with another man (Wood 2011). Furthermore, they claimed, Walker should have made a public statement that he had no interest in marrying his partner in order to distance the personal benefit he would obtain by ruling in favor of same-sex marriage. District Court judge James Ware reviewed and denied the motion in June 2011 and stated: "The presumption that Judge Walker, by virtue of being in a same-sex relationship, had a desire to be married that rendered him incapable of making an impartial decision, is as warrantless as the presumption that a female judge is incapable of being impartial in a case in which women seek legal relief" (Judge being gay a nonissue 2011; Geidner 2011).

The decisions on Prop 8 and Judge Walker's analysis are reverberating throughout the nation. States after state are now accepting same-sex marriage as a logical and constitutional outcome for equality. Ten states alone adopted same-sex marriage in 2013. The legal arguments and analysis contained in Judge Walker's decision upholding Due Process and Equal Protection Clause has provided a roadmap for attorneys in states that do not, at this time, approve same-sex marriage.

Chuck Stewart

See also: Proposition 8 and the Mormon Church.

Further Reading

Cohen, Andrew. 2010, August 6. "The Prop 8 Ruling: Same-Sex Marriage Wins a Sweeping Legal Victory." *Politics Daily*. Available at: http://www.politicsdaily.com/2010/08/04/the-prop-8-ruling-same-sex-marriage-wins-a-sweeping-legal-victo/. Accessed January 4, 2014.

Court: Calif. Gay-Marriage Ban Unconstitutional. 2012, February 7. *CBS News*. CBS/AP. Available at: http://www.cbsnews.com/news/court-calif-gay-marriage-ban-unconstitutional/. Accessed January 3, 2014.

Frank, Adelle. 2010, August 7. "List of 80 Findings of Fact in *Perry v. Schwarzenegger* Decision." *Adelle Frank*. Available at: http://adellefrank.com/blog/review-summary-walker-eighty-findings-of-fact-perry-vs-schwarzenegger. Accessed January 3, 2014.

Geidner, Chris. 2011, June 14. "Motion to Vacate Prop 8 Decision Is Denied." *MetroWeekly*. Available at: http://metroweekly.com/poliglot/2011/06/motion-to-vacate-prop-8-decisi.html. Accessed January 3, 2014.

Hollingsworth v. Perry (formerly *Perry v. Brown* and *Perry v. Schwarzenegger*), 570 U.S. (2013).

Judge Being Gay Nonissue during Prop. 8 Trial. 2010, February 7. *SFGate*. Available at: http://www.sfgate.com/bayarea/article/Judge-being-gay-a-nonissue-during-Prop-8-trial-3201345.php. Accessed January 3, 2014.

Perry v. Schwarzenegger, 704 F.Supp.2d 921 at 940 (N.D. Cal. 2010).

Schwartz, John. 2010, August 4. "In Same-Sex Ruling, an Eye on the Supreme Court." *The New York Times*. Available at: http://www.nytimes.com/2010/08/06/us/06assess.html. Accessed January 3, 2014.

Williams, Carol J. and Maura Dolan. 2010, August 4. "Ruling against Prop. 8 Could Lead to Federal Precedent on Gay Marriage." *Los Angeles Times*. Available at: http://www.latimes.com/news/local/la-me-gay-marriage-california-20100805,0,2696248.story. Accessed January 3, 2014.

Wood, Daniel B. 2011, June 14. "Prop. 8 Ruling: Gay Judge Didn't Need to Recuse Himself." *Christian Science Monitor*. Available at: http://www.csmonitor.com/USA/Justice/2011/0614/Prop.-8-ruling-gay-judge-didn-t-need-to-recuse-himself. Accessed January 3, 2014.

R

Reparative Therapy. *See* Sexual Orientation Change Efforts

Rich, Adrienne (1929–2012)

Adrienne Rich is a major poet and essayist who has been a tremendously influential writer on women's issues and lesbian identity. Rich was born on May 16, 1929, in Baltimore, Maryland. Her father was a professor of medicine and her mother a composer and pianist. In 1951 she graduated from Radcliffe College, and her first collection of poems, *A Change of World*, was chosen for the Yale Younger Poets Award. In 1953 she married Harvard economist Alfred Conrad and lived as a model faculty wife in Cambridge, Massachusetts.

She wrote a number of other books between 1959 and 1966 while trying to balance her traditional female role with her life as a poet. In 1966 she began teaching at City College in New York City. This position brought her into contact with African American poets Alice Walker and Audre Lorde. Rich's 1973 collection of poems, *Diving into the Wreck*, was given a National Book Award. Rich rejected the award as an individual and instead accepted it "in the name of all women whose voices have gone and still go unheard in a patriarchal world" (Russell 1995, p. 184).

Rich became an outspoken radical feminist and lesbian separatist after the suicide of her husband in 1970. Besides publishing her poems in mainstream magazines, she reached out to feminist and lesbian journals. Probably her most influential essay is "Compulsory Heterosexuality and Lesbian Existence." In this essay, Rich argues that "heterosexuality, like motherhood, needs to be recognized and studied as a political institution" (Rich 1980). She believes that women are forced into compulsory heterosexuality by the power wielded by men against women. However, she observes that women have resisted through a number of ways, which she defines as "lesbian continuum." The lesbian continuum is "a range, through each woman's life and through history—of

Poet Adrienne Rich holds her certificate announcing the $25,000 Ruth Lilly Poetry Prize in Chicago, Illinois, in 1986. (AP Photo/Chuck Knoblock)

women-identified experience: not simply the fact that a woman has had or consciously desired genital sexual experience with another woman . . . [but includes] the sharing of rich inner life, the bonding against male tyranny, the giving and receiving of practical and political support. . . . [that far exceeds the] clinical definitions of 'lesbianism'" (Rich 1980).

She taught at City College and Rutgers University in the late 1970s. Later she would teach at Scripps College, San Jose State University, Stanford University, and Cornell University. She published extensively and was awarded a MacArthur Fellowship and Award in 1994 for her work as poet and writer. In 1997, she declined a National medal of Arts to protests the House of Representative's vote to end funding for the National Endowment for the Arts and other policies of the Clinton administration. In the 2000s, she participated in many antiwar activities. In October 2006, she was honored by Equality Forum for her continued support for LGBT issues and the impact her work had on the culture. Rich died March 27, 2012, at the age of 82 in Santa Cruz, California.

Chuck Stewart

See also: Lorde, Audre (1934–1992).

Further Reading

Colby Langdell, Cheri. 2004. *Adrienne Rich: The Moment of Change*. Santa Barbara, CA: Praeger.

Gioia, Dana. 1999. "Midnight Salvage: Poems 1995–1998." *San Francisco Magazine*, January.

Henneberg, Sylvia. 2010. *The Creative Crone: Aging and the Poetry of May Sarton and Adrienne Rich*. Columbia: University of Missouri.

Keyes, Claire. 2008. *The Aesthetics of Power: The Poetry of Adrienne Rich*. Athens: University of Georgia Press.

Rich, Adrienne. 1980. "Compulsory Heterosexuality and Lesbian Existence." *Signs: Journal of Women in Culture and Society* 5 (Summer): 631–60.

Russell, Paul. 1995. *The Gay 100*. New York: Kensington Books.

Shuman, R. Baird. 2002. *Great American Writers: Twentieth Century*. Singapore: Marshall Cavendish.

Yorke, Liz. 1998. *Adrienne Rich: Passion, Politics and the Body*. Thousand Oaks: Sage Publications.

Robertson, Pat (1930–)

Pat Robertson founded the Christian Broadcast Network (CBN) and *The 700 Club* television program and is one of the primary spokespeople against lesbian and gay rights. Born Marion Robertson Gordon on March 22, 1930, in Lexington, Virginia, Robertson grew up in a religious household. He received his bachelor's degree from Washington and Lee University in 1950, a law degree from Yale University in 1955, and a master's degree from the

Christian Coalition founder Pat Robertson addresses a Faith and Freedom celebration on August 1, 2000, in Philadelphia. (AP Photo/Gene J. Puskar)

Rev. Pat Robertson addresses the Christian Coalition Road to Victory '98 conference, Washington, D.C., on September 18, 1998. (AP Photo/Roberto Borea)

New York Theological Seminary in 1959. He was ordained a minister in the Southern Baptist Church in 1961, at the same time founding CBN. The TV program gave him national exposure such that he was able to begin CBN University in 1977. He has hosted *The 700 Club* since its beginnings in 1968 and continues to be active in CBN. He is author or coauthor of a number of books, including *My Prayer for You* (1977), *The Secret Kingdom* (1982), *Beyond Reason* (1984), and *America's Date with Destiny* (1986).

Robertson campaigned for the Republican nomination for president of the United States in 1988. Although not successful, his campaign significantly impacted conservative politics in the United States. From his efforts sprang the Christian Coalition, which sought to transform the United States into a Christian theocratic state.

A national outcry occurred when on *The 700 Club* Pat Robertson agreed with Jerry Falwell that feminists, lesbians and gays, and others were to blame for the destruction of the World Trade Center on

Pat Robertson, the founder of the 700 Club, Regent University, and the Christian Broadcasting Network (CBN), located in Virginia Beach, Virginia, stuck to his earlier statement on July 17, 2003, that the country would be better served by a Supreme Court that consisted of a majority made up of conservatives. (AP Photo/Gary C. Knapp)

September 11, 2001. Robertson often claims God's anger toward sodomy and LGBT people are the cause of natural disasters.

Chuck Stewart

See also: Falwell, Jerry L. (1933–2007).

Further Reading

In Closed-Door Session with Christian Coalition State Leaders, Pat Robertson Unveils Plan to Control GOP Presidential Nomination. 1997, September 18. Americans United for Separation of Church and State.

King, Wayne. 1988. "Pat Robertson: A Candidate of Contradictions." *New York Times*, February 27.

"Pat Robertson: Nuke State Department: Colin Powell Expresses Outrage over Evangelist's Televised Remark." *WorldNetDaily*, 2003, October 10, 2003. Available at: http://www.wnd.com/2003/10/21224/. Accessed February 10, 2014.

Reynolds, John Mark. 2010, January 14. "Pat Robertson on Disasters: Consistently Wrong." *First Things*. Available at: http://archive.is/zTkt. Accessed February 10, 2014.

Romer v. Evans (1996)

In 1987, Boulder citizens approved an antidiscrimination ordinance based on sexual orientation. In 1989, Colorado governor Roy Romer issued an executive order prohibiting discrimination against people with AIDS. In 1991, the Colorado Civil Rights Commission recommended that the state adopt antidiscrimination statues based on sexual orientation.

In response to these progay laws, three religious right activists—David Noebel, Tony Marco, and Kevin Tebedo—formed a new organization, Colorado for Family Values (CFV). Their goal was to repeal the governor's executive order and the antidiscrimination laws already on the books in Aspen, Boulder, and Denver, and to prevent any future efforts to pass antidiscrimination laws aimed at protecting lesbian and gay people elsewhere in the state. They drafted constitutional Amendment 2, which was passed by the voters in 1992 with 53 percent in favor. Nine days later, a group of activists filed a lawsuit in the Colorado District Court for Denver.

At the first hearing, a temporary injunction was granted to the plaintiffs barring the state from implementing Amendment 2. Six months later, the case was heard by the Colorado District Court for Denver, with Judge Jeffrey Bayless presiding the case. The state gave six reasons that Amendment 2 was constitutional. Judge Bayless issued a 16-page ruling adhering closely to the six justifications and the evidence introduced at trial. He rejected all state claims, saying the state failed to demonstrate a compelling reason to abridge the fundamental rights of lesbian and gay citizens.

The Gay, Lesbian, Bisexual, Transgender Community Center of Colorado celebrates the 10th anniversary of the overturning of Amendment 2 on the West Steps of the Colorado State capitol building in 2006. Former Colorado governor Roy Romer, waving to the crowd, appeared as a guest speaker. (Kathryn Scott Osler/The Denver Post via Getty Images)

The state appealed Judge Bayless's decision to the Colorado Supreme Court, asking the court to reverse the fundamental rights analysis. By doing so, the state hoped to lower the burden of proof from a compelling one to a rational interest justification. The court rejected this approach and reiterated its view that Amendment 2's ultimate effect was to infringe on the fundamental rights of the plaintiffs by prohibiting the adoption of laws, regulations, ordinances, and policies against discrimination based on sexual orientation. The court provided a step-by-step analysis similar to that prepared by Judge Bayless.

In 1995, the U.S. Supreme Court agreed to review the Colorado Supreme Court's decision. Besides the two primary parties involved, the Court accepted more than two dozen friend-of-the-court briefs from almost 100 organizations, cities, and individuals. The Court debate was similar to the previous court arguments. The Court characterized Amendment 2 as "unprecedented in our jurisprudence" in that it identified "persons by a single trait and then denies them protection across the board. . . . A law declaring in general that it shall be more difficult for one group of citizens than for all others to seek aid from government is itself a denial of equal protection of the laws in the most literal sense" (p. 637). Also, Amendment 2 "inflicts on [gay people] immediate, continuing, and real injuries that outrun and belie any legitimate justifications that may be claimed for it" (p. 638). The Court ruled (6–1) that Amendment 2 appeared to violate the fundamental right of lesbians, gay men, and bisexuals to participate in the political process on a basis equal to other Coloradans. Justice Kennedy stated, "We conclude that Amendment 2 classifies homosexuals not to further a proper legislative end but to make them unequal to everyone else. This Colorado cannot do. A state cannot so deem a class of persons a stranger to its laws" (p. 639).

Chuck Stewart

See also: Antidiscrimination Statutes; Equal Access Act (EAA).

Further Reading

Eskridge, William M., Jr. 2008. *The Supreme Court's Regime-Shifting Opinion in Romer v. Evans (1996). Dishonorable Passions: Sodomy Laws in America 1861–2003.* New York: Viking, pp. 278–89.

Gerstmann, Evan. 1999. *The Constitutional Underclass; Gays, Lesbians, and the Failure of Class-Based Equal Protection.* Chicago: The University of Chicago Press.

Hasian, Marouf A., Jr. and Trevor Parry-Giles. 1997. "'A Stranger to Its Laws': Freedom, Civil Rights, and the Legal Ambiguity of *Romer v. Evans.*" *Argumentation and Advocacy* 34: 27–42.

Murdoch, Joyce and Deb Price. 2001. "The Constitution 'Neither Knows Nor Tolerates Classes among Citizens." In *Courting Justice: Gay Men and Lesbians v. the Supreme Court,* ed. Joyce Murdoch and Deb Price. New York: Basic Books.

Rustin, Bayard (1912–1987)

Bayard Rustin (1912–1987) was born on March 17, 1912, in West Chester, Pennsylvania, the illegitimate son of Florence Rustin. Florence's parents, Janifer and Julia, raised Bayard in West Chester. Julia Rustin was raised as a member of the Society of Friends or Quakers. Her belief in the Quaker doctrine of pacifism and her social activism in organizations like the National Association for the Advancement of Colored People helped Rustin become a social activist.

While in high school, Rustin began to protest racism. He refused to leave a West Chester restaurant that denied him service. He defiantly sat in the all-white section of the local theater. When traveling as a member of the West Chester High School track team, Rustin threatened not to run unless he and his black teammates were given integrated housing. After high school graduation in 1932, Rustin studied at Wilberforce University and Cheyney State University, but did not graduate. Bored with school, Rustin went to New York City to live with a relative in 1937. He found temporary employment in New York through the Works Progress Administration. In 1938, he enrolled at the City College of New York but again did not graduate because he was performing with the folk group Josh White Singers and folk singer Huddie Ledbetter. Furthermore, Rustin had become a youth organizer for the Young Communist League (YCL). In June 1941, however, after the YCL declared that the fight against fascism was more important than fighting racism, Rustin resigned. He had met the socialist labor union leader A. Philip Randolph while with the YCL, and, when he left the YCL, Rustin went to work for him. Randolph planned a "March on Washington" by thousands of African Americans if President Franklin Roosevelt did not end Jim Crow in the defense industries. Roosevelt gave in to Randolph's demand, issuing an executive order banning discrimination practices by federal defense contractors. Randolph cancelled the march, but Rustin disagreed. It was the first of several rifts between Randolph and Rustin.

In the late summer of 1941, Rustin was hired as race relations secretary for the Fellowship of Reconciliation (FOR), a religious pacifist organization. In FOR, Rustin came under the mentorship of the pacifist A. J. Muste. Muste introduced him to the teachings of Mahatma Gandhi and taught him how to weld Gandhi's philosophy, the organizational skills of the Communist Party, and the pacifism of his Quaker religion into his future life work: civil rights. In 1942, Rustin and others cofounded the Congress for Racial Equality

(CORE). Unlike FOR, which emphasized pacifism, CORE focused on race relations. While still at FOR, Rustin took an additional job as a CORE field secretary. On a bus trip to Nashville, Tennessee, in 1942, Rustin defied the law by sitting in the "whites-only" section. He was arrested but later released. He faced a longer period of incarceration, however, for being a pacifist during World War II. In 1944, Rustin registered as a conscientious objector but refused to report for a physical examination for assignment to a camp for conscientious objectors. As a result, Rustin served 28 months in a federal penitentiary for draft evasion.

After his release from prison in 1946, Rustin worked again with A. Philip Randolph, this time with his Committee against Discrimination in the Armed Forces. Randolph opposed a new federal law requiring universal military training because it sanctioned racial segregation. He put pressure on President Harry Truman to issue an executive order revising the law. Facing reelection in 1948 and desiring

> to keep the black vote, Truman succumbed to Randolph's demand. He issued Executive Order 9981 outlawing discrimination on the basis of race, color, religion, or national origin in the American military. Having succeeded, Randolph wished to disband the committee; however, Rustin and others expressed dissent with Randolph in a national press conference, an action Rustin later regretted.

In 1947, Rustin was part of a group of 16 CORE and FOR activists participating in what may be the earliest known "freedom ride" in the South. The bus trip was officially known as the "Journey of Reconciliation." The purpose of the journey was to test enforcement of the 1946 U.S. Supreme Court decision *Morgan v. Virginia* outlawing discrimination in interstate travel. CORE and FOR riders deliberately sat in segregated sections of buses and trains while traveling through the South. In Chapel Hill, North Carolina, Rustin and three others were arrested and charged with violation of the state's segregation laws. Rustin was sentenced to 30 days of hard labor on a chain gang, but he was released because of good behavior after

Bayard Rustin, deputy director, left, and Cleveland Robinson, chairman of Administrative Committee, right, on August 7, 1963. (Library of Congress)

22 days. Afterward Rustin lectured and wrote about his chain gang experience. Several years later the state of North Carolina abolished chain gangs.

Rustin's work with FOR took on an international dimension in 1951 when he helped organize the Committee to Support South African Resistance, which later became the American Committee on Africa. In 1952, FOR sent Rustin to Africa to meet with two of the leaders of the African independence movement: Kwame Nkrumah of Ghana and Nnamdi Azikiwe of Nigeria. Back in the United States, Rustin was touring to raise money for another African trip when disaster struck. Openly gay, Rustin was arrested on a "moral charge" in Pasadena, California, in 1953 and was sentenced to 60 days in jail. His arrest made national news. In disgrace, Rustin resigned from FOR. He soon found a job with a secular pacifist group: the War

Seated left to right: Bayard Rustin, Andrew Young, Representative William Fitts Ryan, James Farmer, and John Lewis in 1965. (Library of Congress)

Resisters League (WRL). During Rustin's 12 years at WRL, he served as executive director, co-editor of the magazine *Liberation*, and spokesperson for the WRL at international pacifist meetings.

A. Philip Randolph helped Rustin obtain a leave of absence from WRL to assist the Reverend Dr. Martin Luther King Jr. during the Montgomery Bus Boycott in 1956. Dr. King knew of Gandhi's writings but was unclear about how a nonviolent protest should be carried out. Rustin's involvement in the Montgomery Bus Boycott ended when other boycott leaders asked Rustin to leave town for fear that publicity about his past would harm the boycott. Yet Dr. King continued to call on Rustin. In 1957, he asked Rustin to help organize the Southern Christian Leadership Conference (SCLC)'s Prayer Pilgrimage to the Lincoln Memorial

in Washington, D.C. Rustin also organized the National Youth Marches of 1958 and 1959. He was set to organize a SCLC demonstration at the 1960 Democratic Convention until Congressman Adam Clayton Powell threatened to expose him as gay unless he quit the project.

When a March on Washington was proposed in 1963, Rustin and A. Philip Randolph saw an opportunity to do what they dreamed of. Because he originated the idea of a march back in 1942, A. Philip Randolph was selected by the major civil rights leader to be executive director of the march. Randolph, in turn, selected as his deputy director, Bayard Rustin, and it was Rustin who actually coordinated the planning of the event. Planning was going smoothly until South Carolina senator Strom Thumond took the floor of the U.S.

Senate and denounced Rustin as a Communist, a draft dodger, and a homosexual. Although Thurmond's tirade triggered a call by some civil rights leaders for Rustin's resignation, Randolph and Dr. King continued to back Rustin as the march strategist. Rustin's job was anticipating the marchers' needs for housing and transportation, reconciling differences between civil rights and labor groups, lining up speakers and performers, and working with law enforcement officials to ensure a peaceful march. More than 200,000 whites and blacks attended the historic event on August 28, 1963. At the end of the day, the major civil rights leaders met with President John F. Kennedy at the White House. But Rustin was not among them because the other leaders said his presence would embarrass them. Nevertheless, Rustin's accomplishment as strategist of the 1963 March on Washington was the high point of his life.

Rustin and Randolph believed that the 1963 march owed its success to an alliance between organized labor and civil rights groups. Therefore Rustin and Randolph cofounded the A. Philip Randolph Institute, an organization funded by the American Federation of Labor and the Congress of Industrial Organizations (AFL-CIO). The Randolph Institute gave Rustin a formal leadership role in the civil rights movement and an organization promoting the coalition politics Rustin believed in. The Randolph Institute promoted the Recruitment and Training Program designed to increase minority participation in the building and construction trades. It also fostered voter registration and lobbied for labor interests in Congress. Rustin was president of the institute from 1966 to 1979, and co-chairman from 1979 until his death. When he began working at the Randolph Institute, Rustin resigned from his job at the WRL and left the pacifist group, the Committee for Nonviolent Action.

With no time available for the peace movement, Rustin refused to participate in antiwar demonstrations during the 1960s and 1970s. He ridiculed civil rights leaders such as Dr. Martin Luther King Jr., who condemned the Vietnam War, arguing that civil rights and pacifism do not mix. Rustin held this position despite the fact that early in his career he himself was part of both movements. During this period,

Rustin adopted opinions that were controversial in the black community. He opposed black studies and black power because he thought coalition building rather than separatism was the way to gain racial justice. Rustin promoted the tactics of nonviolence while there were riots in many American cities. He urged African Americans to support Israel rather than the Palestinians. Rustin's alienation from other civil rights leaders, the Black Power movement, and the antiwar movement caused one publication to call Rustin "the lone wolf of civil rights." After the 1940s, Rustin wrote many essays, speeches, and editorials that were published in newspapers and magazines. In 1971, Rustin published a number of these writings in a book entitled *Down the Line*. A second book followed in 1976: *Strategies for Freedom: The Changing Patterns of Black Protest*.

During the final decades of his life, Rustin worked with the A. Philip Randolph Institute as well as two international organizations. He was active in the International Rescue Committee (IRC), a group devoted to dealing with refugee problems around the world. With IRC, Rustin traveled to places like Southeast Asia espousing refugee relief in Cambodia, for instance. He was also a representative for Freedom House, traveling to places like Chile, El Salvador, Grenada, Dominican Republic, Pakistan, Zimbabwe, South Africa, and Haiti to monitor elections, protest dictatorships, and promote human rights.

Rustin was in Haiti assisting in setting up democratic elections in 1987 when he suddenly became ill and was rushed back to the United States. He died in New York City on August 24, 1987. His legacy grew after his death and books on his life and work appeared. On January 20, 2003, a documentary entitled *Brother Outsider: The Life of Bayard Rustin* was first broadcasted on educational television. Formerly relegated to the background of the civil rights struggle by his peers and historians, Bayard Rustin is now being recognized as an important figure in the civil rights movement.

Eric Ledell Smith

See also: Navratilova, Martina (1956–); Waddell, Tom (1937–1987).

Further Reading

Anderson, Jervis. 1997. *Bayard Rustin: Troubles I've Seen—A Biography*. New York: HarperCollins Books.

Carbide, Devon W. and Donald Weise, eds. 2003. *Time on Two Crosses: The Collected Writings of Bayard Rustin*. San Francisco: Cleis Press.

D'Emilio, John. 2003. *Lost Prophet: The Life and Times of Bayard Rustin*. New York: Free Press.

Haughton, Buzz. 2000. "Bayard Rustin: An Annotated Bio-Bibliography." *Afro-Americans in New York Life and History* 24(2): 7–56.

Levin, Daniel. 2000. *Bayard Rustin and the Civil Rights Movement*. New Brunswick, NJ: Rutgers University Press.

Rustin, Bayard. 1971. *Down the Line: The Collected Writings of Bayard Rustin*. Chicago: Quadrangle Books.

Rustin, Bayard. 1976. *Strategies for Freedom: The Changing Patterns of Black Protest*. New York: Columbia University Press.

Wilson, Jamie J. 2013. "Biographies of Figures." In *Civil Rights Movement*. Santa Barbara, CA: Greenwood. Available at: http://ebooks.abc-clio.com/reader.aspx?isbn =9781440804274&id= A3496C-639.

S

Same-Sex Marriage in the United States

Considering that the issue of same-sex marriage has been controversial for almost 30 years in the United States, 2013 proved to be a banner year. More states approved gay marriage in 2013 than in all prior years combined.

A number of same-sex couples challenged marriage laws in the 1970s and 1980s without success. All that changed in 1990 when three couples filed suit in Hawaii claiming that the state constitution allowed for same-sex marriage and prohibition against such marriages by local jurisdictions violated the law. The case, *Baehr v. Lewin* (later renamed *Baehr v. Miike*, 1999), was initially dismissed by the first trial court. The plaintiffs appealed to the Supreme Court of Hawaii. The court agreed that denying same-sex couples the right to marry constituted discrimination based on sex and violated the state's equal protection clause. The court remanded it back to the trial court in 1993 to determine if the state could demonstrate denying same-sex couples from marrying met a "compelling state interest." If the state could not make a strong argument for this level of review, then gay marriages would be allowed.

The possibility of Hawaii granting same-sex couples the right to marry sent shock waves through U.S. politics. The Hawaiian legislature quickly crafted law to restrict marriage to opposite-sex couples and formed a Commission on Sexual Orientation and the Law to study the issue. The first commission failed. The second commission issued its report in 1995 that recommended allowing same-sex marriage.

Nationwide, conservatives and the religious right galvanized forces against same-sex marriage and influenced the House Judiciary Committee in 1996 to craft legislation and policy to enable states to: (1) prohibit same-sex marriages, (2) refuse to recognize same-sex marriages legally performed elsewhere, and (3) make same-sex couples ineligible for a host of state and federal rights and benefit. These ideas came together in the Defense of Marriage Act (DOMA) introduced to the House of Representatives on May 7, 1996, by Georgia representative Bob Barr (Republican). "The bill amends the U.S. Code to make explicit what has been understood under federal law for over 200 years; that a marriage is the legal union of a man and a woman as husband and wife, and a spouse is a husband or wife of the opposite sex" (Defense of Marriage Act 5/96). The bill was fast-tracked through Congress and approved with a veto-proof margin. President Clinton signed the bill on September 21, 1996. He refused to hold a traditional signing ceremony or allow photographs to be taken. Although he was not in favor of same-sex marriage at the time (he publicly came out in support for gay marriage in 2009), he thought the political fall-out from vetoing the bill and then being overruled was too great and could become the springboard for an amendment to the Constitution outlawing same-sex marriage (which would be much more difficult to overcome). States also enacted their own form of DOMA. Ultimately 4states passed statutes prohibiting same-sex marriages and 29 states passed amendments to their state constitutions banning same-sex marriages and the recognition of same-sex marriages legally performed elsewhere.

Federal DOMA was important for a number of reasons. Until 1996, the federal government had not

Michael M. Kaiser, left, and John Roberts, right, being married by Justice Ruth Bader Ginsburg, center, at the Kennedy Center on August 31, 2013. (AP Photo/The Kennedy Center, Margot Schulman)

defined marriage leaving it up to individual states to legislate. If a couple was legally married, the federal government accepted it as valid and granted more than 1,138 rights and protections not available to unmarried couples (Defense of Marriage Act: Update to 1997 Report, 2004). But there were constitutional concerns that the federal government did not have the right to pass such legislation. Section 3 of DOMA prevented the federal government from recognizing same-sex marriages. Many legal analysts and government attorneys immediately saw the Federal Act to be in conflict with the Tenth Amendment of the U.S. Constitution and predicted it would fall when challenged. Over the next decade, many suits were filed against DOMA.

Meanwhile, the Hawaii trial court headed by Kevin S. C. Change concluded in 1996 that the state failed to demonstrate a compelling state interest in restricting marriage to opposite-sex couples. He immediately stayed his decision giving the defendants time to appeal to the Hawaii Supreme Court. During these intervening years, conservative groups successfully sponsored a ballot initiative that would amend the state constitution to restrict marriage to one man and one woman. The voters approved the amendment in 1998 before the Hawaii Supreme Court made its ruling. As such, the issue of same-sex marriage in Hawaii became moot and *Baehr v. Mikke* was dismissed in 1999 blocking same-sex couples from marriage.

At the same time, the remnants of sodomy laws came under court scrutiny. Most states had removed ancient sodomy laws from their books during the gradual liberalization of the legal codes in the 1960s, 1970s, and 1980s. The U.S. Supreme Court decision in *Bowers v. Hardwick* in 1986 stopped that process

Dr. Gay Phillips, her partner Sue Barton, and Sharon Baldwin, and her partner Mary Bishop speak with members of the media after leaving court following a hearing at the 10th U.S. Circuit Court of Appeals in Denver on April 17, 2014. (AP Photo/Brennan Linsley)

when the Court upheld the right of states to enforce sodomy provision. In four of the states—Kansas, Missouri, Oklahoma, and Texas—sodomy provisions were applied unequally between same- and opposite-sex couples. In 10 states—Alabama, Florida, Idaho, Louisiana, Michigan, Mississippi, North Carolina, South Carolina, Utah, and Virginia—sodomy laws applied to everyone. By 2002, the sodomy laws had been repealed or overturned in 36 states. The sodomy laws in the other states were rarely enforced or selectively enforced but their existence was often used to justify discrimination against LGBT people. Finally, the U.S. Supreme Court reviewed a case that nullified the remaining sodomy statutes. In *Lawrence v. Texas* (2003), the U.S. Supreme Court struck down the Texas sodomy law stating that private sexual conduct is protected by the due process clause of the U.S. Constitution. The removal of sodomy from the

discussion of same-sex marriage helped legitimatize LGBT relationships.

Many more same-sex couples sued their states over marriage. In Vermont, the court agreed in 1999 that same-sex couples must have the same rights as opposite-sex couples (*Baker v. Vermont*). They threw the problem back to the legislature which then created in 2000 "civil unions" as a way of providing "marriage" to same-sex couples without using the word *marriage*. In the same year, California created a statewide domestic partnership registry—the first in the nation—to provide the benefits of marriage to same-sex couples without calling it marriage. Ironically, Proposition 22 is also passed in California in 2000 that outlawed same-sex marriages.

The world was also changing its attitude concerning same-sex marriage. In 2001, the Netherlands became the first country in the world to approve same-sex marriage. Soon after in 2003, Belgium and two provinces of Canada (Ontario and British Columbia) (eventually all of Canada by 2005) also granted the right of marriage for same-sex couples. By 2014, 16 additional countries and provinces would approve same-sex marriage: Spain (2003), South Africa (2005), Norway (2009), Sweden (2009), Portugal (2010), Iceland (2010), Argentina (2010), Mexico provinces (2010), Denmark (2012), Caribbean Netherlands (2012), Brazil (2013), France (2013), United Kingdom (2013), Uruguay (2013), New Zealand (2013), and the Australian Capital Territory (2013).

Finally, in 2004, Massachusetts became the first state in the United States to approve same-sex marriage. The Massachusetts Supreme Judicial Court ruled in 2003 (*Goodridge v. Department of Public Health*) that same-sex marriages could not be prevented under the Massachusetts constitution and that nothing short of full marriage would fulfill the equality clause of the state constitution. It would take Massachusetts legislature until 2008 to pass legislation recognizing same-sex marriages performed in other jurisdictions.

Months before Massachusetts performed its first same-sex marriage, confusion erupted in California over same-sex marriage. For a brief time in early 2004 same-sex marriages were performed in California. San Francisco mayor Gavin Newsom believed the Equal Protection Clause of the U.S. Constitution overruled the state constitution and allowed him to grant marriage licenses to same-sex couples. He instructed city hall to begin issuing marriage licenses to same-sex couples. Longtime lesbian activists Del Martin and Phyllis Lyon became the first same-sex couple to be legally wed in the United States. Approximately 4,000 same-sex couples obtained their marriage licenses. By August, the California Supreme Court annulled all the same-sex marriages that Newsom authorized. The action caught many people, particularly conservatives and religious groups, off guard and helped galvanized efforts to mount an initiative to block same-sex marriage at the state constitutional level. Although Proposition 22 was passed in 2000 by the electorate adding language to the Family Code (§308.5) to restrict marriage to the union of one man and one woman, it was not tested in the court. Efforts were made by antigay organizations to launch an initiative to place restrictions against same-sex marriages in the state constitution. Eventually this led to Proposition 8—"Eliminates Right of Same-Sex Couples to Marry"—being placed on the ballot in 2008. Much of the financial support against gay marriage came from outside California and from the Mormon Church.

After the brief fiasco created by Mayor Newsom, many couples sued the state. As the cases worked their way through the courts, State Assembly member Mark Leno introduced Assembly Bill 19 that proposed legalizing same-sex marriage. A version of the bill was approved by the state legislature in 2005—making it the first time same-sex marriage was approved by a legislature without being under court order. However, Governor Schwarzenegger vetoed the bill. He claimed that the issue needed to be cleared up by the courts or by the voters, not the legislature. The suits that were filed against Proposition 22 were consolidated into one case—*In re Marriage Cases*. In 2008 the California Supreme Court ruled in a four-to-three decision that Proposition 22 was unconstitutional and that same-sex marriages could resume by June 16, 2008. Although Proposition 8 qualified for the November ballot a short time before this decision, the court refused to stay the ruling. During the months leading up to the November elections, approximately 18,000 same-sex couples were legally married. Proposition 8 passed by a small margin. Immediately, the law was challenged. The California State Supreme Court upheld Proposition 8 as a lawful amendment of the state constitution (in *Strauss v. Horton*) and, surprisingly, upheld the legality of the 18,000 marriages performed before Proposition 8 passed. That put California in the unique position of having thousands of legal marriages that other citizens could no longer obtain the same right. American Foundation for Equal Rights (AFER), opponents of Proposition 8, took the case to federal court to challenge the validity of Proposition 8 under the U.S. Constitution. U.S. District Court for the Northern District of California judge Vaughn R. Walker conducted a full trail beginning in January 2010. Judge Walker ruled Proposition 8 unconstitutional on August 12, 2010, because it violated both the due process and equal protection clauses of the U.S. Constitution (*Perry v.*

Schwarzenegger renamed *Hollingsworth v. Perry*). Neither the governor nor attorney general for California decided to contest Judge Walker's decision and supported same-sex marriage. The motion was stayed by the Ninth Circuit Court of Appeals to allow supporters of Proposition 8 to appeal to the U.S. Supreme Court. Finally, on June 26, 2013, the U.S. Supreme Court ruled the supporters did not have standing for the appeal, ordered the Ninth Circuit to void its stay leaving Judge Walker's decision valid. Same-sex marriage resumed in California on June 28, 2013.

Much happened throughout the country during the 10 years of legal skirmishes in California. In 2008, Connecticut became the second state to approve same-sex marriage. Many more states enacted same-sex marriage laws: Iowa (2009 by judicial decision), Vermont (2009 by legislative action), New Hampshire (2010 by legislative action), district of Columbia (2010 by legislative action), New York (2011 by legislative action), Maine (2012 by ballot initiative), Maryland (2012 by ballot initiative), Washington (2012 by ballot initiative), California (2013 by judicial decision), Delaware (2013 by legislative action), Minnesota (2013 by legislative action; just six months after voters rejected an antigay marriage initiative the legislature passed enabling legislation), Rhode Island (2013 by legislative action), New Jersey (2013 by judicial decision), Illinois (2013 by legislative action taking effect in 2014), Hawaii (2013 by legislative action), a few counties of New Mexico (2013 by judicial action) and Utah (2013 by judicial action). Also, a number of First People nations approved same-sex marriage: Native American nations of Ceara & Little Traverse Bay Bands of Odawa Indians (Michigan), Pokagon Band of Potawatomi Indians (Michigan), Santa Ysabel tribe (California) and the Confederated tribes of the Colville Reservation (Washington).

Importantly, in 2013 the U.S. Supreme Court ruled the Defense of Marriage Act (DOMA) to be unconstitutional (*United States v. Windsor*). The Court decided that Section 3 of DOMA violated the Due Process Clause of the Fifth Amendment. The case clearly demonstrated the inequality DOMA imposed on LGBT citizens. Here, Edith "Edie" Windsor and Thea Spyer,

residents of New York, married in Toronto, Ontario, where same-sex marriages were legal. The women had been together for 40 years and built up significant assets. Spyer died in 2009 and Windsor was required to pay $363,053 in federal estate taxes on her inheritance of her wife's estate. If they had been an opposite-sex couple, there would have been no inheritance tax. The court agreed that Section 3 of DOMA, which specified that the term *spouse* only applied to opposite-sex marriage, denied due process to same-sex couples.

By early 2014, 17 states, the District of Columbia, and eight First People nations had approved same-sex marriages in the United States. By late 2014, legal reviews in Utah, Oklahoma, Virginia and many other states resulted in permanently establishing same-sex marriage rights in more than 30 states. This means a majority of Americans now reside in states that respect marriage equality. Often it is claimed that same-sex marriage is being forced on the American public through activist judges or gay activists influencing legislators and that if it were left up to the people it would be voted down. Yet, public votes in Maine, Maryland, and Washington showed that people vote in favor of same-sex marriage when given the choice. Public polls are showing a shift in American's view in favor of same-sex marriage. For the first time, a sitting president—Barack Obama—voiced his support in 2012 for same-sex marriages. Likewise, for the first time a U.S. Supreme Court judge—Ruth Bader Ginsburg—officiated at a same-sex marriage in 2013. It is expected that these trends will continue and eventually, the U.S. Supreme Court will rule that same-sex marriage must be allowed everywhere and treated equally to opposite-sex marriage.

Chuck Stewart

See also: Native Americans and Same-Sex Marriage; Obama, Barack, and Support for Same-Sex Marriage; Proposition 8 Legal Analysis and the Impact of Judge Walker's Decision. Documents: Same-Sex Marriage in Hawaii: *Baehr v. Lewin* (1993); Same-Sex Marriage Equality: *Baker v. Vermont* (1999); The Threat to Marriage from the Courts (2003); In re Marriage Cases: Opinion (2008) California's Ban on Same-Sex Marriage Is Unconstitutional; In re Marriage Cases: Dissent (2008); Supreme Court Rules That DOMA Is Unconstitutional: *UNITED STATES v. WINDSOR, Executor of the ESTATE OF SPYER, et al.* (2013);

Arizona's Attempted Legislation to Allow Discrimination Based on Religious Freedom: SB1062 (2014).

Further Reading

Baehr v. Lewin, 74 Haw. 530, 852 P.2d 44 (1993), reconsideration and clarification granted in part, 74 Haw. 645, 852 P.2d 74 (1993).

Baehr v. Miike, No. 20371 (Supreme Court of Hawaii 1999–12–09).

Baker v. Vermont, 744 A.2d 864 (Vt. 1999).

Defense of Marriage Act: Update to 1997 Report. (2004). U.S. General Accounting Office.

Defense of Marriage Act 5/96 H.R. 3396 Summary/Analysis. Lectric Law Library. Available at: http://www.lectlaw.com/files/leg23.htm. Accessed January 25, 2014.

Goodridge v. Dept. of Public Health, 798 N.E.2d 941 (Mass. 2003).

Hollingsworth v. Perry (formerly *Perry v. Brown* and *Perry v. Schwarzenegger*), 570 U.S. ___ (2013) (Docket No. 12–144).

In re Marriage Cases, 43 Cal.4th 757 (2008).

Lawrence v. Texas, 539 U.S. 558 (2003)

Strauss v. Horton, 46 Cal.4th 364, 93 Cal.Rptr.3d 591, 207 P.3d 48.

United States v. Windsor, 570 U.S. ___ (2013) (Docket No. 12–307).

Sappho (Sixth Century BCE)

Sappho has been a significant influence on lesbian identity for 2,500 years. Sappho was born on the Aegean island of Lesbos off the coast of Asia Minor, probably in the early sixth century BCE. We know virtually nothing about this woman whose very name has come to signify women who love women. It is believed that she was married to a wealthy merchant, had a daughter named Cleis, and plotted against the tyrant Pittacus. It is also believed that she spent most of her life on Lesbos.

The island of Lesbos in the sixth century was a gathering place for aristocratic women who formed informal societies to compose and recite poetry. Sappho headed one of these societies and wrote mostly about her relationships with other women. Her lyrics are passionate and simple rather than literary. Although no complete poem of hers still exists, with the largest fragment being only 28 lines long, we know that her works were collected into 10 books in the third or second century BCE. These books survived until the Middle Ages, when they were either lost or destroyed. Many writers and religious leaders have attempted to disparage Lesbos and Sappho. Yet the idea of a band of women living with women who were poetic and passionate manages to survive. When American lesbians in the 1950s decided to organize a national organization, they called themselves the Daughters of Bilitis in homage to Sappho's fictitious disciple.

Chuck Stewart

See also: Ancient Greek and Roman Sexuality and Philosophy and Impact on the American Legal System; Daughters of Bilitis; Socrates (469–399 BCE).

Sappho, holding lyre. From *Sappho: a tragedy in five acts;* after the German of Franz Grillparzer, by Edda Middleton. New York: D. Appleton and Company, 1858, frontispiece. (Library of Congress)

Further Reading

Campbell, D.A., ed. 1982. *Greek Lyric 1: Sappho and Alcaeus (Loeb Classical Library No. 142)*. Cambridge, MA: Harvard University Press.

Carson, Anne, trans. 2002. *If Not, Winter: Fragments of Sappho*. New York: Knopf Press; Paris: Virago Press.

Schlafly, Phyllis Stewart (1924–)

Phyllis Schlafly is one of the major conservative voices in the United States and led the successful fight to stop the passage of the Equal Rights Amendment (ERA).

Schlafly was born in 1924 in St. Louis, Missouri. Her family quickly realized how intelligent she was and entered her into college as a young teenager. She graduated at age 20 with a BA from Washington University in St. Louis with honors (Phi Beta Kappa, Pi Sigma Alpha, Final Honors). She received her master's in government from Harvard University the next year (1945). She worked her way through college on the night shift at the St. Louis Ordnance Plant where, as a laboratory technician investigating misfires, tested ammunition by firing rifles and machine guns.

Her appetite for politics was whetted when she worked as the campaign manager for a Republican candidate for Congress in St. Louis in 1946. The campaign was successful which encouraged her to run for an Illinois congressional seat in 1952 and later in 1970. Although she was not successful at these efforts, she later was elected delegate to six different Republican National Conventions beginning in 1956.

In support of Barry Goldwater's 1964 presidential campaign, she wrote *A Choice, Not an Echo*. It became a best seller and put Schlafly on the conservative map as author and speaker. She began in 1967 to publish a regularly syndicated column—*The Phyllis Schlafly Report*—which continues today in 100 newspapers and with radio commentaries heard daily on

Activist Phyllis Schlafly wearing a Stop ERA badge, demonstrating with other women against the equal rights amendment in front of the White House in Washington, D.C., on February 4, 1977. (Library of Congress)

460 stations. Mainstream press seeks her conservative, profamily, prolife, and antigay comments and she has testified before more than 50 congressional and state legislative committees. She also wrote a monthly article for the ultraconservative *Daughters of the American Revolution* magazine from 1977 to 1995.

In the 1970s, she started the Eagle Forum, a conservative think tank and political action organization. At the same time, she launched the Stop ERA campaign. Schlafly was the major force behind the defeat of the Equal Rights Amendment. She believes a constitutional amendment should be passed to put prayer back into the schools, "but to the real God, the Christian God, the one referred to on our currency. Don't let the atheists and the communists run this country. Put it back in the hands of good, Christian, white males. That's my opinion" (Schlafly 1998).

She has authored more than 20 books and was selected the 1992 Illinois Mother of the Year. She and her late husband are the parents of six children. Her oldest son, John, is gay. He was outed by Queer World in 1992. At age 41, he still lived with his mother. Schlafly conceded that she knew from John's earliest years that he was homosexual, but thought that the issue was introduced to embarrass her. The National Gay and Lesbian Task Force assailed her as one of the "top five most powerful anti-gay forces in the country").

Chuck Stewart

See also: Bryant, Anita (1940–); Helms, Jesse (1921–2008).

Further Reading

Felsenthal, Carol. 1981. *The Sweetheart of the Silent Majority: The Biography of Phyllis Schlafly*. Garden City: Doubleday.

Mansbridge, Jane J. 1986. *Why We Lost the ERA*. Chicago: University of Chicago Press.

Schlafly, Phyllis. 1998. "None Dare Call It Reason." *Phyllis Schlafly Report* 31(8) (March): 1. Available at www.mattneuman.com/schlafly.htm.

Sexual Orientation Change Efforts

Many persons and organizations within the religious right promote the idea that homosexual feelings can be changed to heterosexual through a number of intervention techniques. It is often stated that the therapies can "repair" homosexuals of their "broken" sexual urges. So-called reparative therapy and the call to change homosexual sexual orientations to heterosexual orientation is also a source of revenue for many conservative churches, organizations, and politicians.

From the earliest days of the modern gay movement (often pinpointed to the Stonewall Riot of 1969), there have been calls by religious leaders for homosexuals to change their ways and, in particular, become heterosexual. In 1973, Frank Worthen, John Evans, and Kent Philpott launched an ex-gay ministry named Love in Action (LIA) (renamed *Restoration Path* in 2012) targeting homosexuals in Marin County (near San Francisco). Exodus International grew from this ministry as a nonprofit worldwide organization focused on helping people (mostly men) limit their homosexual desires. Exodus was an umbrella organization including over 270 ministries worldwide and asserted that it could help reorient a persons' sexual orientation from homosexual to heterosexual.

During this same time period, prominent academic researchers and professional organizations were normalizing homosexuality. By 1973, the American Psychiatric Association had removed homosexuality from the *Diagnostic and Statistical Manual of Mental Disorders* (*DSM*) as a mental disorder. Dr. Robert Spitzer spearheaded the effort, and the changes to the *DSM* resulted from an approval from an overwhelming majority of APA's 15,000 members. Still, there were a handful of therapists who clung to the belief that homosexuality was a mental disorder and that therapists had a responsibility to help those clients desiring a change to heterosexuality.

Paul Drummond Cameron became central to the fight to keep homosexuality pathologized. As a psychologist and sex researcher at a number of American universities, he conducted research and wrote articles that made outrageous claims about homosexuals. Many of the other academic researchers he quoted in his works demanded that he retract his papers since they misconstrued their findings. Likewise, his personal research methodologies violated academic protocols and statistical scrutiny. He came under investigation by the APA for ethics violations in 1983. The Nebraska Psychological Association issued a public statement in 1984 disassociating themselves from his work. Judge Buchmeyer of the U.S. District Court of Dallas in *Baker v. Wade* (1985) commented on Cameron's affidavits submitted to the court to be fraudulent and misrepresentations. In 1986, the American Sociological Association publically stated that Paul Cameron was not a sociologist. Later in 1996, the Board of Directors of the Canadian Psychological Association publicly stated that Cameron work on sexuality consistently misrepresented the academic work of other respected researchers.

The more Cameron was discredited, the more the religious right held him up as a martyr and cited his work. Cameron co-founded the Institute for Scientific Investigation of Sexuality (ISIS) in Lincoln, Nebraska in 1982. Money poured in and the institute was renamed the Family Research Institute (FRI) and moved to Washington, D.C., for greater access to political lobbyists. Cameron and FRI have published many antigay pamphlets and reports. Currently, the Southern Poverty Law Center has classified FRI as a hate group.

There were, however, considerable problems with the organizations and people involved with the efforts to change homosexuals into heterosexuals. Many of the organizations experienced public scandals when board members or leaders were discovered to be hiding homosexual behaviors. For example, two of the founders of Exodus International left the organization after falling in love and publicly announced to the world their relationship. Later, Alan Chambers, president of Exodus International, told the Gay Christian Network in 2012 that virtually all efforts to change sexual orientation were failures and that the efforts were potentially harmful.

There were many reports of absolute failure to change sexual orientation and emotional and psychological harm perpetrated in the efforts—some leading to suicide. For example, Jack McIntyre, friend of John Evans (one of the founders of Love in Action) committed suicide due to his inability to change his sexual orientation after years of trying. Evans left Love in

Bob Davis, director of Exodus International, speaks during the opening meeting of Exodus '99 on July 26, 1999, in Wheaton, Illinois. Exodus International is a Christian referral and resource network whose primary purpose was to proclaim freedom from homosexuality through faith in Jesus Christ. (AP Photo/Stephen J. Carrera)

Action and stated in a 1993 interview with *Wall Street Journal*, "They're destroying people's lives. If you don't do their thing, you're not of God, you'll go to hell. They're living in a fantasy world" (Ybarra 1993).

To lend support to the sexual orientation change efforts (SOCE) of Exodus International, Paul Cameron and FRI, and many others, the National Association for Research & Therapy of Homosexuality (NARTH) was founded in 1992 by Benjamin Kaufman, Charles Socarides, and Joseph Nicolosi in Encino, California, to provide clinically based sexual orientation conversion therapies. NARTH's research papers use standard academic format and give the impression of being legitimate reports. Their work was often cited by FRI, Exodus, and other groups—thus, central to supporting the veneer of SOCE legitimacy.

Alan Chambers, left, president of Exodus International, sits with his wife, Leslie, in their home in Winter Park, Florida, in 2006. The president of the country's best-known Christian ministry dedicated to helping people repress same-sex attraction through prayer is trying to distance the group from the idea that gay people's sexual orientation can be permanently changed or cured. (AP Photo/Phelan M. Ebenhack)

Mainstream therapists reported seeing more and more clients distressed over their experiences with reparative therapies. Not only did clients fail to become heterosexual but feelings of failure and low self-esteem were endemic. There were reports of suicide and young teens being forced to attend SOCE camps and facilities. A very public controversy occurred when Zach Stark, a 16-year-old Tennessee boy posted on his Myspace site in 2005 a blog entry about his coming-out and being forced to attend a fundamentalist Christian program designed to change his sexual orientation. His parents sent him to a camp known as Refuge run by Love in Action. Several legal scholars have argued that forcing underage children into reparative therapy is a form of child abuse (Cohan 2002;

Talbot 2006). The Tennessee Department of Children's Services were made aware of the situation and investigated. Although no specific evidence of child abuse was found, the Tennessee Department of Mental Health determined that Refuge was operating as an unlicensed mental health living facility and directed Refuge to stop accepting the mentally ill and dispensing medications, which it did. The negative media led Love in Action to discontinue the Refuge program by 2009. A documentary—*This Is What Love in Action Looks Like*—was filmed by director Morgan Jon Fox detailing Zach's and other teenagers' experience in these camps.

California state senator Ted Lieu was made aware of the considerable emotional toll SOCE was taking

Witnesses for both sides of House Bill 1330 wait to deliver testimony to the Senate Committee at the capitol on April 2, 2007. Kathy Glass, age 75, representing the League of Women Voters (for) and Paul Cameron, PhD, representing the Family Research Institute (against) sit next to each other. (Brian Brainerd/The Denver Post/Getty Images)

on his state's citizens and, in particular, its teenagers. In 2012 he authored a bill to prohibit the use of reparative therapies on children under 18 years of age. SB-1172: *Sexual orientation change efforts*—passed both the state Assembly and Senate by large margins and signed into law by Governor Jerry Brown. While signing the bill, Governor Brown stated, "These practices have no basis in science or medicine, and they will now be relegated to the dustbin of quackery" (Shapiro 2013).

Immediately, the conservative nonprofit Pacific Justice Institute representing family therapist Donald Welch, psychiatrists Dr. Anthony Duk, and psychology student Aaron Bitzer challenged the bill in court. They claimed the bill violated Californian's right to privacy, due process, and freedom of religion. NARTH also filed its own lawsuit against the state. However, NARTH was fighting its own image crisis. The Internal Revenue Services had revoked NARTH's nonprofit tax status in 2012 for failure to file reports. At the same time, the California Board for Behavioral Sciences removed their certification granting them the ability to offer continuing education credits. And, to add insult to injury, one of its board members, George Rekers, resigned the same year when he was discovered to have hired a gay male escort to provide nude sexual massages. The year 2012 was also a pivotal year for Exodus International. It officially acknowledged its failure to change sexual orientation in any of its members over decades of operation and apologize for the years of undue judgment

Attorney Peter Drake, executive director of the Coming Out into Light Foundation, right, speaks about his negative experiences while receiving a controversial form of psychotherapy aimed at making gay people straight, while testifying in favor of a bill to ban the therapy during a hearing at the capitol in Sacramento, California, on May 8, 2012. The bill, SB1172, by state senator Ted Lieu (D-Torrence), left, prohibited so-called reparative therapy for minors and obligate adults to sign a release form stating that the counseling is ineffective and possibly dangerous. (AP Photo/Rich Pedroncelli)

and pain against gays and lesbians. In 2013, Exodus officially disbanded.

While the NARTH case challenging the California law to prohibit sex change orientation efforts waited to be heard, psychiatrist Dr. Robert Spitzer published in *The Archives of Sexual Behavior* (April 2012) a letter apologizing to the gay community and, in particular, victims of reparative therapy for a study conducted in 2001 (published in 2003) that claimed some "highly motivated" homosexuals could change

their sexual orientation (Carey 2012). Many academic researchers were critical of Spitzer's findings. For almost a decade he reflected on his work and heard the parade of legitimate researchers who found SOCE to be emotionally damaging and hurtful—sometimes leading to suicide in gay patients. Finally, in 2012, Spitzer, then in his 80s, issued a formal retraction and apology of his research and wrote:

> You know, it's the only regret I have; the only professional one . . . and I think, in the history of psychiatry, I don't know that I've ever seen a scientist write a letter saying that the data were all there but were totally misinterpreted. Who admitted that and who apologized to his readers? (Carey 2012)

Spitzer, considered by many to be the "grandfather" of modern psychiatry and instrumental in having the American Psychiatric Association remove homosexuality as a mental disorder from the *DSM* in1973, was considered above reproach and unbiased. Not surprisingly, his 2003 findings had been appropriated by SOCE advocates as proof their methods could change homosexuals into heterosexuals. His admission that sexual orientation cannot be changed and that his 2003 study was flawed was a major blow to SOCE advocates.

The California law was to take effect January 1, 2013, but it was placed on hold pending a ruling. A three-judge panel of the Ninth Circuit Court of Appeals heard arguments in April 2013. Opponents of the law claimed the law was breathtakingly broad since it would prohibit therapists from even mentioning to minors the possibility of changing one's sexual orientation and that would be a violation of free speech and freedom of religion. Chief Judge Alex Kozinski, a Ronald Reagan appointee to the court, asked: "Why can't the Legislature say, 'We looked into it, we think it is harmful, we think it causes harm to minors . . . and we the Legislature are going to protect them" (Dolan 2013). Deputy Attorney General Alexandra Robert Gordon supported the state's contention that reparative therapy causes emotional harm citing the reports and position papers of the largest and most respected mental health organizations in the country.

On August 29, 2013, the Ninth Circuit Court of Appeals lifted the injunction against SB 1172. The court unanimously ruled that the ban on SOCE does not violate essential rights and that the state has the right to regulate medical providers. New Jersey Legislature passed a similar law, A3371, in June 2013, which was signed into law by Governor Chris Christie in August 2013. The law was challenged in court but U.S. District Court judge Freda Wolfson, an appointee of former president George W. Bush, quickly upheld the law in November (Court upholds N.J. ban 2013). Similar legislation is being considered by the District of Columbia and other states. The National Center for Lesbian Rights is the primary organization spearheading the national effort to ban SOCE.

Chuck Stewart

See also: Africa's Gay Punishment Legislation: Involvement from U.S. Christian Factions; Exodus International; Proposition 8 Legal Analysis and the Impact of Judge Walker's Decision.

Further Reading

Bailey, Sarah Pulliam. June 20, 2013. "Ex-Gay Group Exodus International Shuts Down, President Apologizes." Religion News Service. Available at: http://www.religionnews.com/2013/06/20/exodus-international-to-shut-down-after-presidents-apology-to-gay-community/.

Baker v. Wade 563 F.Supp 1121 (N.D. Tex. 1982), rev'd 769 F.2nd 289 (5th Cir. 1985) (en banc) cert denied 478 US 1022 (1986).

Carey, Benedict. 2012. "Psychiatry Giant Sorry for Backing Gay 'Cure'." *New York Times*, May 18.

Cohan, J. 2002. "Parental Duties and the Right of Homosexual Minors to Refuse 'Reparative' Therapy." *Women's Law Journal*, 67.

Court upholds N.J. ban on "ex-gay" therapy. 2013, November 9. *Washington Blade*. Available at: http://www.washingtonblade.com/2013/11/09/court-upholds-n-j-ban-ex-gay-therapy/. Accessed January 2, 2014.

Dolan, Maura. 2013, April 17. "9th Circuit Hears Arguments on the Therapy Aimed at Converting Gays." *Los Angeles Times*. Available at: http://articles.latimes.com/2013/apr/17/local/la-me-ln-gay-therapy-20130417. Accessed January 2, 2014.

Morgenstein, Mark. 2012, October 4. "'Gay Cure' Therapists, 'Cured' Student Sue California Over New Law." *CNN*. Available at: http://www.cnn.com/2012/10/04/us/california-gay-therapy/index.html. Accessed January 1, 2014.

Shapiro, Lila. 2013, June 25. "Straight Talk: How Mathew Shurka and His Conversion Therapist Renounced the 'Gay Cure.'" *Huffington Post*. Available at: http://www.huffingtonpost.com/2013/06/25/mathew-shurka-conversion-therapy_n_3466943.html. Accessed January 1, 2014.

Talbot, T. 2006. "Reparative Therapy for Homosexual Teens: The Choice of the Teen Should Be the Only Choice Discussed." *Journal of Juvenile Law* 27: 33–46.

Ybarra, Michael J. 1993, April 21. "Going Straight: Christian Groups Press Gay People to Take a Heterosexual Path; Pentecostal Ministries Claim Successes in Some Cases, but the Road Is Difficult Torments of Failed Attempts." *The Wall Street Journal*. Available at: http://www.skeptictank.org/hs/gaycurg.htm. Accessed January 1, 2014.

Signorile, Michelangelo (1960–)

Michelangelo Signorile launched the newsmagazine *Outweek*, which outed public figures. Signorile was born in Brooklyn, New York, in 1960 to a tight-knit Roman Catholic family. He did not enjoy baseball but instead played with dolls and his female cousin. He was called a sissy and faggot and queer in school and fought back. He later wrote, "I became a queer-basher to prove I wasn't queer" (Signorile 1993, p. 23).

He had his first sexual experience when he was 12 years old with a 35-year-old male neighbor. He felt insurmountable guilt and was physically ill for days. In an attempt to "cure himself," he took up football and became very athletic. However, he discovered other Italian boys his own age along the Franklin D. Roosevelt boardwalk at South Beach with whom he could have sex.

SiriusXM OutQ host and Editor-at-Large of Huffington Post Gay Voices, Michelangelo Signorile talks to voters/listeners across the country on election day at SiriusXM Studios on November 6, 2012 in New York City. (Cindy Ord/Getty Images)

He attended a prestigious high school where he played football and continued to queer-bash. He was called in by his principal to explain his violent behavior. He replied that he got into fights because the other boys called him faggot or queer.

He tried Brooklyn College for a short time but was dissatisfied. He transferred to Syracuse University to study journalism. There, he was able to come out of the closet. He reported, "I was the happiest I had ever been" (Signorile 1993, p. 34).

He graduated from Syracuse, moved to New York City, and began working for a public relations firm that placed celebrity gossip in the news. Signorile noticed that everything was fair game in the gossip trade except homosexuality. He saw this as a vast conspiracy of silence.

He began to attend ACT UP meetings as one friend after another became HIV-positive or died of AIDS. His friend Gabriel Rotello asked him in 1989 to start a controversial gay and lesbian publication named *Outweek*. Its purpose was to publicly identify and disclose closeted gay and lesbian public figures. *Outweek* garnered a large readership of not only those who approved of his methods but also of those who were offended. Signorile was accused of engaging in McCarthyism and invasion of privacy.

It was *Outweek* that revealed that Malcolm Forbes, one of the wealthiest men in the United States and owner of the business magazine *Forbes*, was homosexual. *Outweek* folded in 1991 but firestorm over the Forbes revelation was nothing compared to what occurred in 1991 when Signorile revealed in *The Advocate* that Pete Williams, senior civilian Department of Defense spokesman and a protégé of Secretary of Defense Dick Cheney, was gay. Signorile saw this as the greatest hypocrisy: the U.S. military, which regularly discharged homosexual personnel, had as its spokesperson a gay man. Signorile came under much abuse for the revelation. In 1993, Signorile presented his case for outing in his book *Queer in America: Sex, the Media, and the Closets of Power*.

Signorile wrote for *The Advocate* for many years and then as a columnist for *Out* magazine. There he addressed issues of unsafe sex in as well as coming out. He released his second book—*Life Outside: The Signorile Report on Gay Men: Sex, Drugs, Muscles and the Passages of Life*—in 1997, which quickly rose to be a bestseller. With a change in management at *Out* magazine, Signorile was asked to "tone down" his activist-style writing. He refused and abruptly quit. For the next decade he wrote for *The Advocate* and other magazines, and hosted a number of radio programs including *The Michelangelo Signorile Show* on Sirius XM Radio's OutQ.

David E. Newton

See also: Activists; Historical Overview of Gay Rights and Issues: From the 1980s to the Present.

Further Reading

Gross, Larry. 1993. *Contested Closets: The Politics and Ethics of Outing.* Minneapolis: University of Minnesota Press.

Gross, Larry and James Woods. 1999. *The Columbia Reader on Lesbians & Gay Men in Media, Society, and Politics.* New York: Columbia University Press.

Johansson, Warren and William A. Percy. 1994. *Outing: Shattering the Conspiracy of Silence.* New York: Harrington Park Press.

Signorile, Michelangelo. 1993. *Queer in America: Sex, the Media, and the Closets of Power.* Madison: The University of Wisconsin Press.

Socrates (469–399 BCE)

Socrates was one of the earliest Western philosophers to promote same-sex love. Socrates was born in 469 BCE in the Greek city-state of Athens. Very little known about his childhood, but he served as a foot soldier in the Athenian Army during the Peloponnesian War. In his adult life, Socrates spent much of his time sitting under the shade of olive trees discussing philosophical questions of justice, virtue, and the soul with well-born youths. He was a teacher and lover of young men and embodied the Athenian institution of *paiderasteia*, or "boy love."

The Great Oracle at Delphi declared Socrates to be the wisest among men. He held no firm philosophical doctrines of his own but asked students a series of questions and then directed them to examine the implications of their answers. This became known as the Socratic method. Socrates criticized Athenian politics and religious institutions. He was arrested, tried, convicted of corrupting the morals of Athenian youths and speaking religious heresy, and sentenced to death.

Socrates by J. C. Lavater, 1788–1799. (Wellcome Library, London)

He fulfilled the sentence by drinking hemlock, a poison prescribed by law.

None of Socrates's writings has survived. Instead, we have the writings of his famous student Plato with which to better understand this man and his influence. Plato's *Symposium* and *Phaedrus* have had the greatest impact on gay thought. Socrates discussed how the love between an older man and a beautiful boy begins as erotic passion, then evolves as the older man becomes a teacher, as well as lover, of the beautiful boy. This is the essence of what is known as platonic love.

Chuck Stewart

See also: Ancient Greek and Roman Sexuality and Philosophy and Impact on the American Legal System; Sappho (Sixth Century BCE).

Socrates, seated, holding a cup of hemlock, 1750. (Library of Congress)

Further Reading

Dover, Kenneth J. 1978. *Greek Homosexuality*. Cambridge: Harvard University Press.

Hubbard, Thomas K. 2003. *Homosexuality in Greece and Rome*. Berkeley: University of California Press.

Percy, William A. 1996. *Pederasty and Pedagogy in Archaic Greece*. Champaign: University of Illinois Press.

Taylor, C. C. W., R. M. Hare, and J. Barnes.1998. *Greek Philosophers—Socrates, Plato, and Aristotle*. New York: Oxford University Press.

Verstraete, Beert C. and Vernon Provencal, eds. 2005. *Same–Sex Desire and Love in Greco-Roman Antiquity and in the Classical Tradition of the West*. Binghamton: Haworth.

Vlastos, Gregory. 1991. *Socrates, Ironist and Moral Philosopher*. Ithaca: Cornell University Press.

Soulforce

The mission of Soulforce is relentless nonviolent resistance to religious and political oppression of lesbian, gay, bisexual, and transgender people. Soulforce is a social justice organization that works directly at the difficult intersections of injustice that are born out of religious fundamentalism, patriarchy, and white supremacy. Simply put, Soulforce is in the business of stopping stigma about LGBT people that the church and society stimulate and sanction through misinterpretation and misuse of scripture. At its worst, the Church is a perpetrator of violence and exclusion against LGBT people in those 76 countries where it remains illegal to be openly "gay" (Smith 2012). At its best, the Church can, in a moment, choose to right its grievous treatment of sexual minorities and women. (See "Erasing 76 Crimes.")

Tommy Atz, right, is joined by other protesters at the final stop of the Soulforce Equality Ride outside the main gate of the U.S. Military Academy at West Point in Highland Falls, New York, on April 26, 2006. Twenty-one protesters were arrested during their protest of the "Don't Ask, Don't Tell" policy regarding homosexuality in the military. (AP Photo/ Keith Ferris)

Soulforce is unceasing in its efforts to help both Church and state choose higher ground. In the first half of its life cycle as a nonprofit organization, Soulforce was focused on the lives of lesbian, gay, bisexual, and transgender people and the Church's broken relationships with them. Over time, Soulforce more deeply invested in the "roots" rather than the "shoots" of this brokenness, recognizing that in every instance that the Church subjugated women, LGBT people suffered, people of color suffered, and a host of others. This meant Soulforce began to address fundamentalism in the places where it brought harm to all kinds of people.

The Early Days

Soulforce was established in 1998 by Rev. Mel White and his partner, Gary Nixon, soon after White "came out" as a gay man and was fired from his job as Rev. Jerry Falwell's ghost writer. White was ejected from his church and his lucrative religious film production business. He had already spent years trying to "cure" himself of being gay and when those efforts proved futile, he told his wife (who is supportive of him) and started his life anew.

Deeply wounded and feeling adrift without his vocation, his church, and friends, White spent a year studying the philosophies of Mahatma Gandhi and Rev. Dr. Martin Luther King and their practice of non-violent resistance. He began to use the name Soulforce to represent the "truth force" about which Gandhi spoke. Recognizing that he needed a constructive way to deal with his own grief and to channel his talents, he decided to establish a nonprofit organization committed to changing the hearts and minds of religious leaders like Jerry Falwell. White felt people like Falwell and James Dobson, founder of the Christian fundamentalist group, Focus on the Family, were misinformed about the real truth of scripture in their lives and that acts of nonviolent resistance could prove catalytic in helping them change their views.

In 1998 when he felt ready, White told Jerry Falwell he was going to bring 5,000 people to Falwell's church in Lynchburg, Virginia, and pray and hold a vigil for a transformation of their hearts. Furthermore, White said that they wanted to have a meal with congregants at the church so people could get to know gay people and start breaking down the stereotypes and homophobia and stigma.

Following intense negotiations, the mealtime was set, but not before Falwell whittled down the number of Soulforce volunteers who could be present from 5,000 to 200. He brokered the meeting to take place inside the church away from television camera crews and reporters. He restructured the outside arrival area for congregants so they wouldn't see the protesters.

In some ways it appears that Falwell agreed to what was an easy out for him. Falwell agreed to break bread with Rev. White and his 200 volunteers. Falwell thought he had won but the art of nonviolent resistance is not about winning or losing but rather about transforming. Rev. White was disappointed about the smaller number who would meet Falwell. He conceded because the important thing wasn't the numbers but rather the interaction.

On the day of the planned event, Falwell withdrew his offer to eat with Rev. White and volunteers saying he could not eat with sinners in accordance with a scripture in the New Testament. It was a limited interpretation because in Luke 14:21b-23 and Matthew 22:9–10, Jesus told the story of a man receiving guests. He had prepared a dinner and sent his servants out to invite the guests. They all made excuses why they could not come. The servant told his master, "The people whom you have invited to dinner have asked to be excused." The master said to his servant, "Go out on the streets and bring back whomever you find to have dinner. Bring the poor and maimed and blind and lame." The servant did and then told the master that "there was still room." He said, "Go to the highways and hedges—go under the bridges and the overpasses and to the shelters and the Red Light District and bring them all so my house will be filled." And they did and the hall was filled with guests. Imagine the scene. Anyone next to anyone, female next to male, free next to slave, socially high next to socially low and ritually pure next to ritually impure. The host broke all the rules that day, rejecting patriarchy, sexism, racism, and classism. Some say that this parable of the inclusive host speaks directly to God's promise—there is enough room, enough God, enough love for all of us. And, the parable also speaks to the greatest commandment in Christian scripture—love one another.

Denominational Protests and Arrests

From 1998 to 2006, Soulforce leaders and volunteers focused the majority of their efforts on denominations whose policies, practices, and polity discriminated against LGBT people. Almost no religious organizations in the United States and, indeed the Vatican, were exempt from a visit by Soulforce. The honor roll of denominations and churches that were fully inclusive and affirming of LGBT people could be counted on one hand at the time.

There are hundreds of stories that Soulforce volunteers tell about their actions at Southern Baptist, Presbyterian, Episcopal, Methodist, and other Protestant and Christian mega-church gatherings. Most of them involve a nonviolent vigil or peaceful demonstration resulting in the arrest of Soulforce volunteers.

Breaking Through: Focus on the Family

In 2012, for the first time, Focus on the Family (a conservative evangelical para-church organization) leaders did not call the police, demanded no arrests, and accepted Soulforce Equality Riders into their facilities in Colorado Springs for a daylong dialogue. The history of this relationship illustrates the principle of relentlessness in nonviolent resistance. For more than eight years, Soulforce knocked on the door of Focus and was rejected. In 2007, Soulforce launched "Focus on the Facts," an ongoing campaign of nonviolent direct action and civil disobedience which aimed to intervene in James Dobson and Focus on the Family's inflammatory and negative characterizations of lesbian and gay families. During the inaugural action, Dotti Berry and Robynne Sapp of Blaine, Washington, entered the Focus on the Family building and refused to leave until the organization's founder, James Dobson, agreed to cease his misleading statements about lesbian and gay parents. They were arrested and escorted from the building.

In the months that followed, Soulforce organizers kept nonviolent pressure on Dobson's Colorado headquarters through a variety of means, including a telephone press conference featuring social science researchers who detailed Dobson's misrepresentation of their research on same-sex families; vigil outside Focus on the Family; a sit-in featuring Soulforce Q youth activists; and a tour of Dobson's headquarters with members of the Denver LGBT community, led by Denver-based musician James Roy.

Marriage Equality

In September 2007, Focus on the Facts expanded its purview to include direct action for marriage equality. Kate Burns and Sheila Schroeder of Englewood, Colorado, entered the Denver Clerk and Recorder Office to request an application for a marriage license. After being denied on the basis of state and federal law, Burns and Schroeder refused to leave, insisting that discriminatory marriage laws are an example of religion-based oppression and undermine America's tradition of religious pluralism protected by the U.S. Constitution. The two were arrested, cited for trespassing, and released without bail. Soulforce remained relentless in its work to achieve not only marriage equality for LGBT people but also the end of denominational restrictions on clergy who wish to marry same-sex couples and on clergy who are LGBT and partnered.

In recognition of Soulforce's long-tenured work to reverse denominational resistance to equal marriage, on March 2013, the executive director of Soulforce, Rev. Dr. Cindi Love, was asked to lead the closing benediction for the rally of thousands of equal marriage supporters in Washington, D.C., at the end of the DOMA hearings by the Supreme Court. A few days later, President Barack Obama invited her to the White House Easter Prayer Breakfast where she was seated next to some of the most conservative religious figures in the United States including Richard Land, (Ret.) President of the Southern Baptist Convention's Ethics & Religious Liberty Commission; and Bishop T. D. Jakes of Potter's House. Rev. Land is the person who publicly stated that gays should not be allowed to join the Boy Scouts because, "gays will jeopardize the ability of the organization to 'protect children' and consequently 'human tragedies will follow'" (Tashman 2013). Jakes appeared on *Oprah's Next Chapter* television program and stated unequivocally that scripture condemns homosexuality (Menzie 2012). In keeping with the principles of nonviolence, Rev. Love was able to join these passionate opponents, break bread. and talk about the possibility of a "third way" where LGBT people can pray with their adversaries for healing of our nation and world.

Ex-Gay Therapy

The trailer for *Sole Journey* (a documentary film covering the 2005 and 2006 actions at Focus on the Family) was included in the DVD release of *Shock to the System*—a *Here! Movie* starring Soulforce supporter Chad Allen. The movie was a fictional account of an investigation into the world of "gay conversion therapy"—a mix of psychology and religion designed to turn homosexuals "straight" (Sole Journey 2008).

Soulforce hosted three national conferences from 2006 through 2012 to raise awareness about the dangers of ex-gay, reparative, or conversion therapy. More than 1,000 therapists, ex-gay survivors, ministers, public officials. and students participated in training and designed their own local projects to demise ex-gay therapy in their communities.

In 2013, Alan Chambers announced the closing of Exodus International, the largest ex-gay organization in the world. Soulforce was at the announcement and presented Alan with a public statement and list of proposed restorative justice actions he could take. Alan thanked Rev. Mel White and the chair of Soulforce, Chuck Phelan, for being available to help him on the day he dismantled his organization.

The Catholic Church

In December 2008, France introduced a *Declaration to Decriminalize Homosexuality* at the United Nations Assembly in New York City. The statement condemned violence, harassment, discrimination, exclusion, stigmatization, and prejudice based on sexual orientation and gender identity. It also condemned killings, executions, torture, arbitrary arrest, and deprivation of economic, social, and cultural rights noting that in 76 member countries, homosexuality is illegal; 7 countries declaring it punishable by death.

Almost immediately following the Declaration's introduction, the Holy See issued a statement opposing it and suggesting that it could lead to same-gender marriage acceptance (Glatz 2008). In response, Soulforce pulled together a team to confront the Holy See and begin a dialogue on the destructive nature of homophobia and heterosexism. The Soulforce team decided to hold a vigil at the Holy See's embassy in late April. For two days, the Holy See's response was to shut down the embassy (a very unusual move). Several weeks later, as Soulforce persisted in trying to meet with the ambassador for the Holy See, he agreed to meet. In that session, the ambassador indicated that he would be discussing the statement with the UN when they met in Switzerland in the summer of 2008. This meeting was significant. Soulforce spent eight years trying to negotiate with the hierarchy of the Roman Catholic Church and this was the first time a high-ranking representative of the Holy See agreed to meet face to face.

The Evangelical Lutheran Church in America (ELCA)

In April 2010, after 25 years of deliberation and multiple visits by Soulforce to protest their anti-gay policies, the Evangelical Lutheran Church in America (ELCA) Church Council abolished its anti-gay policies, effective immediately. The ELCA now allowed people in same-sex relationships to serve as rostered leaders. Lesbian, gay, bisexual, transgender, and queer (LGBTQ) human beings are no longer considered abominations but blessed church members with full standing. Same-sex partners and families can now fully participate in the ELCA Pension Plan. Furthermore, the ELCA reinstated people who were removed from ministry positions because they were truthful and came out of the closet, as well as those who conducted holy unions for non-heterosexual couples.

Soulforce is particularly grateful to the ELCA for adding restoration to its reforms. Soulforce board member Rev. Paul W. Egerston faithfully pastored and served as bishop in the Lutheran church for 31 years. He resigned one month before the end of his term in 2001 after he ordained a lesbian as a pastor and took a public stand for justice in opposition to the official antigay policy of the ELCA. The ELCA might be viewed as a beta test site for a process through which a very traditional faith community can reverse its thinking and policies.

The Equality Ride, Delegates and Solandres

In 2006, Rev. White authorized the start of the *Soulforce Equality Ride*. Fashioned after the Freedom Rides of the Civil Rights Movement, Jake Reitan and co-director Haven Herrin took up the banner of nonviolent resistance on Christian colleges and universities throughout the United States. There are 211 affiliated institutions of higher education in the CCCU (Council for Christian Colleges & Universities). From 2006 through 2012, young adult volunteers, all under 35 years of age, boarded buses and attempted to enter these campuses to discuss the Bible and homosexuality as well as the climate for LGBT students. Most were arrested. A documentary, *Equality U*, about the first Ride in 2006 was produced and has been viewed by aspiring young activists and wary administrators trying to "block and tackle" Soulforce visitors.

When an Equality Ride visits a campus, the riders respectfully request that the administrators of these colleges to eliminate all antigay policies and practices from their student codes of conduct and communities including bullying or harassment. Furthermore, no ex-gay therapy should be required of students who "come out" no disciplinary action for telling the truth about sexual orientation and gender expression, and no more establishing policies such as "don't ask, don't tell" on campuses.

Most recently, Soulforce started the *Delegate Program*, which recruits and appoints local representatives for Soulforce in college communities. These individuals help build sustainable and relentless strategies to ensure safe campus climates, open communities and dialogue. For example, a Soulforce delegate, Delfin Bautista, recently led a delegation of young people to the World Youth Day in Brazil. He was interviewed by the BBC and expressed his hope that Pope Francis would open up the Church to LGBT people. When a physical presence is not possible at an event or in a community, young people can join the new Soulforce *Solandres* online community to obtain resources, share strategies, and support one another in developing campus and community-based safe space.

The First Amendment

University administrators rightly say that the First Amendment protects their private church-related college community rights to freely believe what they wish—to teach these beliefs in their colleges and to say them out loud without fear of reprisal. However, when the First Amendment is used to create cloisters of discrimination and bullying, the "religious freedom" argument is just a cover-up for oppression done in the name of Jesus that Soulforce continues to overcome.

In 2011, the executive director of Soulforce, Rev. Dr. Cindi Love was invited by the National Religious Broadcasters to a Public Policy Debate with Joe Dallas, moderated by Janet Parshall. Mark DeMoss, principal of the largest PR/Media firm for the religious right, characterized the event as "a beautiful debate on gay marriage . . . one of the most beautiful things I've ever seen on something that is very divisive. It took a lot of courage for this woman from Soulforce to accept this invitation" (De Groote 2011).

Soulforce continues its never-ending efforts to stimulate a dialogue in the public square, in classrooms, in sanctuaries of every type, and in the homes of families of LGBT people.

Cynthia H. Love

See also: Africa's Gay Punishment Legislation: Involvement from U.S. Christian Factions; Exodus International; Falwell, Jerry L. (1933–2007); Sexual Orientation Change Efforts.

Further Reading

Council for Christian Colleges & Universities. n.d. About CCCU. Available at: http://www.cccu.org/about. Accessed August 29, 2013.

Erasing 76 Crimes. n.d. "The Human Toll of 76 Countries' Anti-Gay Laws. The Struggle to Repeal Them." Available at: http://76crimes.com/tag/spirit-of-76-worldwide/. Accessed August 30, 2013.

Glatz, Carol. 2008, December 2. "Vatican Makes Clear Its Opposition to U.N. Homosexuality Declaration." *Catholic News Service*. Available at: http://www.catholicnews.com/data/stories/cns/0806042.htm. Accessed August 30, 2013.

Groote, Michael. 2011, May 22. "Gay Marriage Issue, National Elections Lead to Civility Fight." *Deseret News*, 12:31 a.m. MDT. Available at: http://www.deseretnews.com/article/700137770/Gay-marriage-issue-national-elections-lead-to-civility-fight.html?pg=all. Accessed August 30, 2013.

Menzie, Nicola. 2012, April 17. "TD Jakes: Scripture Condemns Homosexuality; Not My Job to Give Opinions." *The Christian Post*. Available at: http://www.christianpost.com/news/td-jakes-scripture-condemns-homosexuality-not-my-job-to-give-opinions-73330/. Accessed August 30, 2013.

Smith, David. 2012, March 15. "Ugandan Group Sues Anti-Gay Pastor in US." *The Guardian*. Available at: http://www.theguardian.com/world/2012/mar/15/uganda-gay-group-sues-us-pastor. Accessed August 30, 2013.

Sole Journey. 2008. Available at: http://www.klondykepictures.com/Soulforce website. Soulforce.com. Accessed August 30, 2013.

Tashman, Brian. 2013, February 27. "Richard Land Explains How to Tell Your Gay Friends They Can't Join the Boy Scouts." *Right Wing Watch*. Available at: http://www.rightwingwatch.org/content/richard-land-explains-how-tell-your-gay-friends-they-cant-join-boy-scouts. Accessed October 20, 2013.

Universal Decriminalization of Homosexuality a Human Rights Imperative—Ban. (2008). United Nations News Centre. Available at: http://www.un.org/apps/news/story.asp?NewsID=37026#.UiFTjOBGWMk. Accessed August 30, 2013.

Stonewall Riot

The riot at Stonewall Inn in New York's Greenwich Village marks the beginning of the modern gay activists' movement. On the night of June 27, 1969, officers from the Public Morals Section of the New York City Police Department attempted to shut down this small local bar. The bar was a favorite meeting place for drag queens, street kids, dope heads, speed freaks, and other marginal people. As people were dismissed by the police and allowed to leave, they gathered across the street. Each time someone appeared in the doorway whom the crowd knew, they applauded, which encouraged the brassy individual to pose and make some flippant remark. This only infuriated the police even more. When the paddy wagon came to take away the drag queens, bar owner, and bartender, a cry went up from the crowd to overturn the paddy wagon. The wagon drove off, but then the crowd exploded by throwing bottles and stones at the police. The police had to retreat into the bar. A battle cry was heard throughout the Village and hundreds came out to participate. A small fire began in the window of the Stonewall. Soon after, more police arrived and the crowd scattered.

For the next couple of nights, street demonstrations took place that were more political in nature.

A crowd attempts to impede police arrests outside the Stonewall Inn on Christopher Street in Greenwich Village on June 28, 1969. (NY Daily News Archive/Getty Images)

Groups of people milled around the streets yelling "gay power," holding hands, and kissing in public. A group of gay cheerleaders were heard singing "We are the Stonewall girls/We wear our hair in curls/We have no underwear/We show our pubic hairs" (Marotta 1981, p. 75). After the first two days of disturbances, the Mattachine Society of New York handed out flyers in the Village christening the "Christopher Street Riots" as the "Hairpin Drop Heard around the World" (Marotta 1981, p. 77).

Before Stonewall, approximately a dozen gay organizations existed. Within three months of the riot, more than 50 lesbian and gay organizations formed throughout the United States. These organizations became more radical, with many cities hosting marches and festivals in June to commemorate the anniversary of the Stonewall Riots. It is these events more than any others that help bring unity to the gay community and influence their political and legal progress.

See also: Historical Overview of Gay Rights and Issues: From Pre-Columbian Times to the 1970s; Mattachine Society.

Chuck Stewart

Further Reading

Carter, David. 2004. Stonewall: *The Riots That Sparked the Gay Revolution*. New York: St. Martin's Press.

Duberman, Martin. 1993. *Stonewall*. New York: Penguin.

Franke-Ruta, Garance. 2013, January 24. "An Amazing 1969 Account of the Stonewall Uprising." *The Atlantic*. Available at: http://www.theatlantic.com/politics/ar

Revelers celebrate in front of the Stonewall Inn in Manhattan's west village following the passing of the same-sex marriage bill by a vote of 33–29 on June 24, 2011, in New York. (AP Photo/Louis Lanzano)

Secretary of the Interior Sally Jewell speaks to the media in front of the Stonewall Inn announcing a new National Park Service initiative intended to identify places and events associated with the civil rights struggle of lesbian, gay, bisexual, and transgender (LGBT) Americans on May 30, 2014, in New York City. The initiative is part of the Obama administration's effort for the National Park Service to join other agencies in helping to better explain the complex story of the people and events responsible for building this nation. (Spencer Platt/Getty Images)

chive/2013/01/an-amazing-1969-account-of-the-stonewall-uprising/272467/.

Marotta, T. 1981. *The Politics of Homosexuality*. Boston: Houghton Mifflin.

Mohr, R. D. 1988. *Gay Justice—A Study of Ethics, Society, and the Law*. New York: Columbia University.

The Stonewall Riot and Its Aftermath. 2011. (Guest Curator Ken Harlin, Starr East Asian Library, Columbia University) Available at: http://www.columbia.edu/cu/lweb/eresources/exhibitions/sw25/case1.html.

Symonds, John Addington (1840–1893)

John Symonds is credited with writing the first essay to review all existing research on homosexuality and to show that same-sex love was admirable and normal. Born in Bristol, England, on October 5, 1840, Symonds came from the family of a physician. He attended Balliol College and earned high honors in classics. He suffered from many health problems and began to travel extensively in hopes of finding a climate where he could live.

He married a woman while on a visit to Italy in 1864 and had four daughters. He was still in poor health and devoted himself to a literary life. Over the next three decades, he produced many volumes of literary works, travel articles, biographies, and translations. Modern scholars are mostly interested in his essay entitled "A Problem in Greek Ethics," an essay not listed in his official biography. He had 50 copies of it printed at his own expense and distributed it in 1891. In the essay, he systematically reviewed all that was known about homosexuality and took the position that same-sex love was both normal and admirable.

Although Symonds was married, he had homosexual feelings throughout his life. While in high school he fell in love with a boy three years younger than himself, and he referred to this as his "birth," an experience similar to what could be construed in modern life as coming out.

Symonds wrote extensively to Walt Whitman. This concerned Whitman so much that he abruptly discontinued corresponding with Symonds. Symonds formed relatively long-lasting homosexual relationships with other men. Upon his death, he left his autobiography and papers in the hands of Horatio Brown—a longtime friend whose house Symonds stayed at while in Venice, Italy. Brown wrote an expurgated biography in 1895 of Symonds life. Fellow writer and editor Edmund Grosse further stripped any reference to homoeroticism from the biography before its publication. Grosse came into possession of Symonds' papers in 1922 and burned everything except the memoirs, to the consternation of Symonds' granddaughter.

Chuck Stewart

See also: Carpenter, Edward (1844–1929); Whitman, Walt (1819–1892); Wilde, Oscar (1854–1900).

Further Reading

Amigoni, David and Amber K. Regis, eds. 2013. "Reading John Addington Symonds." Special Issue of *English Studies* 94:2.

Davis, Whitney. 2010. *Queer Beauty*, Chapter 4 "Double Mind: Hegel, Symonds, and Homoerotic Spirit in Renaissance Art." Columbia University Press.

Grosskurth, Phyllis., ed. 1984. *The Memoirs of John Addington Symonds*. London: Hutchinson.

John Addington Symonds, n.d. (Wellcome Library, London)

T

Title VII

Title VII is the section of the 1964 Civil Rights Act that prohibits discrimination in employment based upon race, color, religion, sex, and national origin.

There have been numerous court cases initiated by lesbians, gay men, transsexuals, and intersexuals claiming discrimination under Title VII. Courts have consistently held that sex, gender, and sexual orientation are distinctive characteristics, and that Title VII applies only to sex discrimination (*Holloway v. Arthur Anderson Co.*, 1977). Some gay males have complained that they were discriminated against because they do not

President Johnson signing the 1968 Civil Rights Bill on April 11, 1968. Johnson was seated at a table surrounded by members of Congress. (Library of Congress)

President Lyndon B. Johnson reaches to shake hands with Dr. Martin Luther King Jr. after presenting the civil rights leader with one of the 72 pens used to sign the Civil Rights Act in Washington, D.C. in 1964. (AP Photo)

conform to gender role expectations or because they were "effeminate." Courts have rejected these claims under Title VII (see, for example, *Smith v. Liberty Mutual Insurance Co.*, 1978; *DeSantis v. Pacific Telephone & Telegraph Co.*, 1979). Furthermore, a federal district court stated, "The term 'sex' in Title VII refers to an individual's distinguishing biological or anatomical characteristics, whereas the term 'gender' refers to an individual's sexual identity," or socially constructed characteristics (*Dobre v. Amtrak*, 1993, p. 76).

However, in the year 2000, the Ninth Circuit Court of Appeals reanalyzed Title VII in a case entitled *Schwenk v. Hartford*. Judge Stephen Reinhardt believed that sex and gender had been collapsed into one category—gender identity—in the 1989 Supreme Court decision in *Price Waterhouse v. Hopkins*. *Hopkins* dealt with a woman who did not conform to

traditional feminine norms. Ann Hopkins was a successful senior manager and a candidate for partnership at Price Waterhouse. When her nomination came up, many partners at Price Waterhouse reacted negatively and accused her of being "macho," said she "overcompensated for being a woman," and that she needed to take a "course in charm school." To improve her chances of becoming a partner she was told to "walk more femininely, talk more femininely, dress more femininely, wear makeup, have her hair styled, and wear jewelry." Hopkins sued and prevailed with the courts. The U.S. Supreme Court stated:

An employer who objects to aggressiveness in women but whose positions require this trait places women in an intolerable and impermissible Catch 22: out of a job if they behave aggressively and out of a job if they do not. Title VII lifts women out of this bind. . . . She had proved discriminatory input into the decisional process, and had proved that participants in the process considered her failure to conform to the stereotypes credited by a number of decisionmakers had been a substantial factor in the decision. (p. 257)

Using the logic in *Price Waterhouse v. Hopkins*, Reinhardt stated, "The Supreme Court held that Title VII barred not just discrimination based on the fact that Hopkins was a woman, but also discrimination based on the fact that she failed 'to act like a woman'—that is, to conform to socially constructed gender expectations" (*Schwenk v. Hartford*, p. 16). Thus, it follows that transsexuals and others not conforming to gender

expectations are afforded federal protection from discrimination in employment under Title VII. This was a radical ruling and is sure to be challenged.

Chuck Stewart

See also: Federal Employment Nondiscrimination Order; Gender-Motivated Violence Act (GMVA).

Further reading

U.S. Equal Employment Opportunity Act. Title VII of the Civil Rights Act of 1964. Available at: http://www.eeoc.gov/laws/statutes/titlevii.cfm.

Transgender Children

Recent legislative events, such as the passage of the School Success and Opportunity Act, AB 1266

Jonas Maines, left, and his transgender sister, Nicole Maines, stand outside the Penobscot Judicial Center on June 12, 2013, in Bangor, Maine. The siblings were born as identical twins boys. (AP Photo/Robert F. Bukaty)

Dr. Norman Spack, of Children's Hospital Boston, in 2011. Spack authored a report in the *Journal of Pediatrics* about teens and children who insist they were born the wrong sex and are requesting body-altering treatments. (AP Photo/Childrens Hospital Boston)

in California, that took effect on January 1, 2014, have seen greater focus on the rights—and the very existence—of trans* children and adolescents. (Note: the * next to trans signifies all the variations of trans such as transsexual, transgender, transvestite, genderqueer, non-gendered, two-spirit, trans man, trans woman, and others.) This brings up the question, "How can children know they are transgender?" which can lead to another, more provocative question, "How young is too young?" The children and adolescents faced with these choices and experiences deserve to live in a society that addresses such valid questions with reason and thought.

Gender, comprised of several intersecting components running along infinite spectra, includes assigned sex, physiology, identity, expression, and others' perception. These components combine to form a person's total multi-modal, multifaceted gender (separate though interconnected, "sexual attraction/orientation" runs along its own spectrum). The first, not a spectrum but two fixed points, represents assigned sex, or birth gender, without regard for physiological diversity such as intersex and congenital conditions, nor internal gender development. The next, physiological gender, refers to infinite physical diversity that has come to possess gendered meaning, for example, penile/clitoral length and size, hair length, internal and external reproductive organs, height, baseline testosterone/estrogen and neurochemical levels, karyotype, genotype, visible and hidden intersex conditions, disability, and so forth. The third component, identity, refers to infinite gender identities that run the spectrum, but also leap off the page entirely. The fourth, expression, attempts to encompass the different ways one can externally express gender without necessitating a direct one-to-one relationship between gender identity and gender expression, for example, the difference between "male" and "masculine" and "female" and "feminine." A particular presentation does not necessarily correspond with gender identity, gender expression, or sexuality. The fifth component describes how others' perceptions of an individual's gender, while not as valuable as that individual's own identity and internal gender configuration, do contribute to an individual's lived experience of gender and may interplay with one's self concept. The sixth and seventh subcomponents attempt to describe from mono to multiple and from fixed to fluid gender identities, experiences, and expressions.

The above demonstrates only a few of the myriad components of gender and can vary depending on the model, which evolve and change as understanding changes. Given these components, how can an individual, especially a young child, have the self knowledge, resources, and awareness to come to the realization that his or her gender may not correspond with that which was assigned to him or her at birth? Studies consistently show that an individual's gender, whatever that may be, comes to a stable place between three and four years of age, before the age when most children enter kindergarten and the socialization that comes with structured education. The expression and realization of that gender will take a lifetime, much like how tissues, organs, and finally a fully formed organism develop from the coding embedded in DNA.

Expression of gender difference in children can mean a number of things, from simple play to indicators of future trans*/gender diversity, sexual diversity (e.g., gay, lesbian, bisexual, pansexual, and/or queer), or something else entirely. What does this mean for parents, teachers, caregivers, and anyone who works with children? Parents, teachers, and other adults can nurture gender expression among children as manifested,

for example, through attire, toys, drawings, choice of playmates, activities, mannerisms, and speech, knowing that these forms of self-expression, regardless of the gender(s) or sexual identity now or in the future, all have a place in the world, as do the infinite varieties of genders and sexualities represented by each and every Being. Parents and teachers must nurture and allow the development and expression of whatever gender(s) a child possesses, rather than punishing, discouraging, or invalidating him or her. Weigh the damage inflicted (e.g., which can manifest as depression or suicide) when family members or significant adults in a child's life vilify and extricate a natural, normal, and inherent part of a person such as gender as a foreign

Sylvia Guerrero, middle, mother of slain teen Eddie Araujo speaks to supporters next to her attorney Gloria Allred, left, and sister Imelda Guerrero, right, outside Newark Memorial High School in Newark, California, on November 8, 2002. The rally coincided with the opening of the school's production of "The Laramie Project," a play about the murder of Mathew Shepard in Wyoming. Araujo, who often dressed as a girl, was killed after attending a party in Fremont on October 3, 2002, in an apparent hate crime. (AP Photo/Marcio Jose Sanchez)

or immoral component, versus any potential damage suffered from the discrimination, intolerance, and lack of societal infrastructure to accommodate diversity. If a trans*/gender-diverse child does happen to change his or her mind later in life and comes to realize a different gender expression and identity, or, if an individual who begins to express gender difference at an early age should grow into a gender diverse and/or sexually diverse adult, that child will remember loving parents and adaptive and understanding teachers who accepted and nurtured ALL of himself or herself, including his or her gender, expression, and sexuality. The confidence imbued from such a solid base will carry that person into later life and the process of growing and changing, including any evolution of gender.

Trans* and gender diverse children and adolescents of any age and gender expression and identity have several similarities. Children develop a sense of the idea of gender usually by the age of one, and a child can begin to express gender difference as early as age two. Additionally, individuals who do discover their gender difference during the window between developing a basic understanding of gender as a concept (age one) and the formation of gender (age four) share traits with those who develop self-awareness of gender during the pre-adolescent and adolescent years, such as adopting attire, names, pronouns, and age-appropriate activities of (a) gender(s) other than that assigned at birth. The age at which a child or adult begins to realize, acknowledge, and express his or her gender does not in any way diminish his or her actual gender, nor does it invalidate or make "less real" the person's true gender(s) and expression.

The way in which an individual comes to understand and express his or her very real gender difference does differ depending on age. A very young child, for example, a four-year old, may express that gender by choosing a different name and telling family members to call him or her by that name, identifying directly as a boy, girl, or other gender, choosing hair lengths and styles that feel more comfortable and natural for him or her, indicating distress when dressed in clothes of what to him or her will be experienced as the wrong gender, specifying clothes which do feel more right, and drawing himself or herself in depictions of family as his or her true gender. Pre-adolescents and adolescents, in addition to "cross-gender" activities, adopting a different name and/or pronoun, and changing attire, hairstyle, and speech, may also express discomfort at existing or future pubescent changes. Parents can address this discomfort and validate their child's personhood by offering their child puberty suppression through an understanding and experienced medical provider. Puberty suppression (e.g., androgen blockers) provides relief from discomfort and dysphoria, a trusting relationship between parents and child, greater confidence and self-esteem, and other potential benefits, without any permanent changes or negative side effects.

Children and adolescents can, indeed, truly know that they are trans* and/or gender diverse, just as individuals whose genders align with their assignment at birth know who they are, without needing any justification or experimentally derived evidence. The anxiety experienced by adults over trans* and gender-diverse individuals, especially children and youth, reflects their own anxiety about themselves, the dark places of their psyche, their own socialization, gender role, sexuality, and internalized oppressions. The question of whether a child can know his or her gender opens the discussion to how anyone of any age can assert their gender. Rather than asking "How can children know they are transgender?" or "How young is too young?" a better question might be to ask, "What kind of privilege do gender-normative and heteronormative people possess that they can demand that people of trans* and gender-diverse experience, especially the most vulnerable among them—children—somehow "prove" or verify what gender-normative people take as undeniable fact when applied to themselves?" Or perhaps, "What kind of unconscious, unrecognized internalized oppressions and self-hatred do gender-normative people refuse to examine to the detriment of those who dare to do the work of self-reflection?" These questions, and not the ones which began this discussion, deserve more attention, thought, and deliberation.

Alexander Yoo

See also: We'wha (1849–1896). Documents: Illinois Indian Transgender (1677); Pirates in the Caribbean (1724), Spanish Priests Condemn Transgendered Yuma Indians (1775);

Brandon Teena Murder Trial (1996); Transsexual Name Change: *In re McIntyre* (1998); Transgender Rights and the ACLU (2000); Transsexual Rights: *Schwenk v. Hartford* (2000).

Further Reading

Ackerman Institute for the Family. The Gender and Family Project. 2014. Available at: http://www.ackerman.org/posts/view/142-the-gender-and-family-project.

Brill, Stephanie A. and Rachel Pepper. 2008. *The Transgender Child: A Handbook for Families and Professionals*. San Francisco: Cleis Press.

Green, Jesse. 2012, May 27. "S/He." *New York Magazine*. Available at: http://nymag.com/news/features/transgender-children-2012–6/.

Turing, Alan (1912–1954)

Alan Turing developed the basic theories used for creating the computer. Turing was born in London on June 23, 1912. His parents were British civil servants stationed in India. He and his brother were placed with an English family to attend school at Sheborne, one of England's oldest public schools. There, the headmaster characterized Turing as being "antisocial." Turing developed a deep, affectionate relationship with one of the boys in the school and was devastated when the lad died at the age of 18.

Turing was only 23 and studying mathematical logic at King's College, Cambridge, when in 1938 he wrote the article "On Computable Numbers, with an Application to the *Entscheidungsproblem*." The theories presented in the article about unsolvable problems became the basis for the development of computer theory. Turing conceived of a universal machine—a Turing machine—that eventually became what we now know as a digital computer.

Turing came to the United States in 1938, where he received his doctoral degree in mathematics from Princeton University. He returned to England at the

Alan M. Turing and colleagues working on the Ferranti Mark I Computer in 1951. (SSPL/Getty Images)

A four-rotor Enigma machine, right, once used by the crews of German U-boats in World War II to send coded messages, which British World War II code-breaker mathematician Alan Turing was instrumental in breaking, is widely thought to have been a turning point in the war. (AP Photo/Alex Dorgan Ross)

beginning of World War II and worked with the British Code and Cipher School. He is credited with inventing the machines that broke the German code, otherwise known as Enigma, and contributed directly to the defeat of Germany by the Allies.

Turing helped design and construct the Automatic Computing Engine and became director of Manchester Automatic Digital Machine. His far-ranging theories about mathematics, machines, and intelligence led to the development of the computer and were the beginnings of research into the field of artificial intelligence.

Immediately after the war, Turing's top-secret clearance was revoked because of his known homosexuality. In 1952, a burglary of his apartment by a former lover resulted in the police charging him with "gross indecency" for being a homosexual. In exchange for going to prison, he was subjected to "chemical castration" by means of hormone injections that left him physically and emotionally scarred. On June 7, 1954, he committed suicide by eating an apple dipped in cyanide. In the following years, public opinion against his treatment by the British government increased, and in 2009, Prime Minister Gordon Brown made a public apology on behalf of the government for the "horrifying" treatment he received (Fitzsimmons 2013). In December 2013, he received a posthumous royal pardon from Queen Elizabeth.

Chuck Stewart

See also: Historical Overview of Gay Rights and Issues: From Pre-Columbian Times to the 1970s.

Further Reading

Cooper, S. Barry and Jan van Leeuwen, eds. 2013. *Alan Turing: His Work and Impact*. Waltham, MA: Elsevier Science.

Fitzsimmons, Emma G. 2013, December 24. "Alan Turing, Enigma Code-Breaker and Computer Pioneer, Wins Royal Pardon." *New York Times*. Available at: http://www.nytimes.com/2013/12/24/world/europe/alan-turing-enigma-code-breaker-and-computer-pioneer-wins-royal-pardon.html.

Hodges, Andrew and Alan Turing. 1983. *The Enigma*. New York: Simon & Schuster.

U

U.S. Department of Housing and Urban Development's Office of Fair Housing

After decades of LGBT people reporting overt housing discrimination to governmental agencies, the U.S. Department of Housing and Urban Development (HUD) developed rules to reduce discrimination in Federal Housing Administrations (FHA) programs. The proposed rules sought to ensure equal access to federal housing by prohibiting discrimination based on sexual orientation and gender identity.

The HUD website gives three examples of "typical" forms of discrimination that LGBT experience:

- A gay man is evicted because his landlord believes he will infect other tenants with HIV/AIDS. That situation may constitute illegal disability discrimination under the Fair Housing Act because the man is perceived to have a disability, HIV/AIDS.

- A property manager refuses to rent an apartment to a prospective tenant who is transgender. If the housing denial is because of the prospective tenant's non-conformity with gender stereotypes, it may constitute illegal discrimination on the basis of sex under the Fair Housing Act.

- An underwriter for an FHA-insured loan is reviewing an application where two male incomes are being used as the basis for the applicants' credit worthiness. The underwriter assumes the applicants are a gay couple and, as a result, denies the application despite the applicants' glowing credentials. This scenario may violate HUD regulations, which prohibit FHA-insured lenders from taking actual or perceived sexual orientation into consideration in determining adequacy of an applicant's income. (Examples n.d.)

Importantly, the HUD regulations apply to *all* organizations that operate HUD-assisted or HUD-insured housing facilities—including religious-based organizations. When the rules were proposed in 2011, the U.S. Conference of Catholic Bishops wrote to HUD claiming that the new rules would be at "odds" with the 1996 Defense of Marriage Act and, as such, put religious organizations such as the Catholic Bishops at risk. Furthermore, they claimed the rules would put religious organizations in the difficult position of either accepting HUD funds or upholding their beliefs. Regardless of the position of church officials, surveys of American Catholics found that a majority support marriage rights for same-sex couples and gay-inclusive employment nondiscrimination laws (Williams 2011). HUD secretary Shaun Donovan called the proposed rules as a fundamental issue of fairness.

The new rules came into effect in 2012. Besides preventing discrimination, the rules broaden the definition of "eligible families" by including those who are gay, lesbian, bisexual, or transgender. Donovan further stated, "We will make clear that a person's eligibility for federal housing programs is, and should be, based on their need and not on their sexual orientation or gender identity" (Thompson 2012).

Equal Access to Housing in HUD Programs Regardless of Sexual Orientation or Gender Identity

—Department of Housing and Urban Development, 24 CFR Parts 5, 200, 203, 400, 570–574, 882, 891, and 982

Through this final rule, HUD implements policy to ensure that its core programs are open to all eligible individuals and families regardless of sexual orientation, gender identity, or marital status. This rule follows a January 24, 2011, proposed rule, which noted evidence suggesting that lesbian, gay, bisexual, and transgender (LGBT) individuals and families are being arbitrarily excluded from housing opportunities in the private sector. Such information was of special concern to HUD, which, as the Nation's housing agency, has the unique charge to promote the federal goal of providing decent housing and a suitable living environment for all. It is important not only that HUD ensure that its own programs do not involve discrimination against any individual or family otherwise eligible for HUD-assisted or -insured housing, but that its policies and programs serve as models for equal housing opportunity.

See also: Equal Access Act (EAA).

Chuck Stewart

Further Reading

Equal Access to Housing in HUD Programs Regardless of Sexual Orientation or Gender Identity. 2012. Department of Housing and Urban Development, 24 CFR Parts 5, 200, 203, 400, 570–574, 882, 891, and 982.

Examples. n.d. HUD.GOV: U.S. Department of Housing and Urban Development. *Ending Housing Discrimination against Lesbian, Gay, Bisexual and Transgender Individuals and Their Families.* Available at: http://portal.hud.gov/hudportal/HUD?src=/program_offices/fair_housing_equal_opp/LGBT_Housing_Discrimination. Accessed November 17, 2013.

Thompson, Ian S. 2012, January 28. "New HUD Rule Delivers for LGBT Americans." *ACLU.* Available at: https://www.aclu.org/blog/content/new-hud-rule-delivers-lgbt-americans. Accessed November 17, 2013.

Williams, Steve. 2011, March 24. "Majority of American Catholics Support Gay Rights and Civil Marriage. *Care2 Make a Difference.* Research from Public Religion Research Institute (http://publicreligion.org/research/. Available at: http://www.care2.com/causes/majority-of-catholics-support-gay-rights-and-civil-marriage.html. Accessed November 17, 2013.

Ulrichs, Karl Heinrich (1825–1895)

Karl Ulrichs is sometimes regarded as the first person in modern European history to publicly acknowledge his attraction to other men. Over a period of more than a decade, he wrote extensively about the nature of homosexuality and worked continuously to educate the general public on the subject and to have the laws dealing with same-sex acts in Germany abolished. Ulrich's first effort in this area was a 12-volume work published under the pseudonym Numa Numantius in 1864. He then wrote another dozen books in the next six years, all published under his own name. In 1867, he tried to bring the issue of civil rights for gay men and lesbians to the attention of the Congress of German Jurists, but he was shouted down and prevented from speaking on the subject.

Ulrichs was born in Hannover, Germany, on August 28, 1825. He studied law and theology at Göttingen University in 1846 and history at Berlin University from 1846 to 1848. After completing his studies, Ulrichs was given a position as a lawyer in the Hannoverian government. Four years later he was promoted, but two years after that he was dismissed from his position because of his sexual activities with other men.

In his many books, Ulrichs developed many fundamental ideas about homosexuality and civil rights for gay men and lesbians. He suggested the notion that homosexuals constituted a third sex, intermediary between male and female, that he called *uranian*. Since homosexuality was an inborn, natural condition, he argued, society could not call the condition sinful, perverted, or depraved.

Many of Ulrichs's ideas, primitive as they were, are reflected in ideas still to be found in the modern gay and lesbian rights movement. For example, a common theme in the movement today is that sexual orientation is an inborn, genetic trait, similar to skin color or sex, and that, as such, it is unreasonable to discriminate against people with a homosexual orientation.

Ulrichs's spurt of creative energy during the 1860s apparently exhausted him. He left Germany for Italy in 1870, where he lived in Naples and then for the last 12 years of his life in Aquila, where he died on July 14, 1895. Ulrichs had virtually no impact on mainstream social or political thought in Germany. However, many of his ideas were eventually incorporated into medical thought on the subject of homosexuality. He is remembered today in an annual award presented by the International Lesbian and Gay Law Association, the Karl Heinrich Ulrichs Award.

David E. Newton

See also: Carpenter, Edward (1844–1929); Historical Overview of Gay Rights and Issues: From Pre-Columbian Times to the 1970s.

Further Reading

Kennedy, Hubert. 2002. *Karl Henrich Ulrichs: Pioneer of the Modern Gay Movement*. San Francisco: Peremptory Publications.

Ulrichs, K.H. 1994. *The Riddle of Man-Manly Love*. Trans. Michael Lombardi-Nash. Prometheus Books.

Karl Heinrich Ulrichs, n.d. (Appeared originally in *Jahrbuch fur sexuelle Zwischenstufen*, vol. 1 (1899), p. 35.)

V

Vaid, Urvashi (1958–)

Urvashi Vaid has served as media director and executive director of the National Gay and Lesbian Task Force (NGLTF) and as director of the organization's Policy Institute, the nation's primary think tank for gay and lesbian issues. She presently serves as director of the Engaging Tradition Project at the Center for Gender and Sexuality Law at Columbia Law School, Columbia University.

Vaid was born in New Delhi, India, on October 8, 1958. In 1966, she moved with her family to Potsdam, New York, and became politically involved at an early age. Among her first activities was participation in a number of protests against the Vietnam War at the age of 11. A bright and eager student, Vaid graduated from high school in three years and entered Vassar College, from which she received her bachelor's degree in English in 1979. It was at Vassar that Vaid first met a group of out lesbians, confirming her own long-held feelings that she was more attracted to women than to men.

After leaving Vassar, Vaid enrolled at Northeastern University in Boston, from which she received her law degree in 1983. At Northeastern she focused on legal issues faced by gay men, lesbians, and women in general. She was also cofounder of the Boston Lesbian/Gay Political Alliance. Her first job after leaving Northeastern was as a staff attorney for the American Civil Liberty Union's National Prisons Project (ACLU-NPP) in Washington, D.C. In 1984, she initiated the ACLU-NPP's program for prisoners who had contracted the human immunodeficiency virus (HIV).

In 1986, Vaid was appointed director of public information at NGLTF, where she also served on the organization's board of directors. In 1989, she was promoted to executive director at NGLTF, a post she held until 1992. She then left the organization for a period of five years during which she worked on her book, *Virtual Equality: The Mainstreaming of Gay*

Urvashi Vaid and Kate Clinton during 18th Annual GLAAD Media Awards. (M. Von Holden/WireImage for GLAAD/ Getty Images)

From left, Urvashi Vaid, Lynn Mahafey-Boudreau, Rabbi Sharon Kleinbaum, and Rev. Mel White sing to open the National Religious Leadership Roundtable on August 23, 1999, in downtown Colorado Springs, Colorado. The roundtable, which was sponsored by the National Gay and Lesbian Task Force Policy Institute and Equal Partners in Faith, was a two-day conference comprised of national leaders of faith, spiritual, and religious organizations who affirm gay, lesbian, bisexual, and transgender equality. (AP Photo/David Zalubowski)

and Lesbian Liberation (Anchor Books, 1996). In the book, Vaid reviews the history of the gay and lesbian rights movement in the United States, analyzes the movement's shift toward conservatism, and discusses the options facing the movement in coming years.

In 1997, Vaid returned to the Task Force as executive director of its Policy Institute. During her four years in that position, she coedited (with John D'Emilio and Bill Turner) an anthology on the history of gay, lesbian, bisexual, and transgender public policy issues entitled *Creating Change: Public Policy, Sexuality and Civil Rights* (St. Martin's Press, 2000). In 2001, Vaid left NGLTF again to take a position as deputy director of the Governance and Civil Society Unit of the Ford Foundation, where she remained until 2005. She then accepted an appointment as executive director of the Arcus Foundation, headquartered in Kalamazoo, Michigan.

In 2012, Urvashi Vaid founded LPAC, the first lesbian political action committee. She serves on the board of directors of the Gill Foundation, dedicated to achieving equal opportunity for all, regardless of sexual orientation and gender identity. She is founder of the Vaid Group, a consulting practice that advises individuals and organizations working to achieve social justice in a wide range of fields. She continues to be a leader in LGBT and social justice movements.

David E. Newton

See also: D'Emilio, John (1948–); National Gay and Lesbian Task Force.

Further Reading

D'Emilio, John, William B. Turner, and Urvashi Vaid, eds. 2000. *Creating Change: Sexuality, Public Policy, and Civil Rights*. New York: St. Martin's Press.

Vaid, Urvashi. 2012. *Irresistible Revolution: Confronting Race, Class and the Assumptions of LGBT Politics*. Bronx, NY: Magnus Books.

Voeller, Bruce (1934–1994)

Bruce Voeller coined the term *acquired immune deficiency syndrome* (AIDS). Voeller was born in Minneapolis, Minnesota, on May 12, 1934. He experienced homosexual feelings as early as junior high school, but a school counselor and minister assured him he was not gay because, unlike sick perverts, he "was emotionally healthy, a good athlete and not effeminate" (Newton 1994, p. 90).

He graduated Reed College with a bachelor's degree in 1956 and received his Ph.D. in biology in 1961 from the Rockefeller Institute in New York City. He became a research assistant, assistant professor, and then associate professor at Rockefeller.

He met and married a woman from graduate school and fathered three children. His life seemed to be following a traditional academic and personal path, but he could no longer ignore his homosexual feelings. He left his academic life and marriage in 1971 to concentrate full-time on the growing gay liberation movement.

He became president of the New York Gay Activists Alliance (GAA) and soon found that it was too limited in scope. Sitting at his kitchen table in October 1973 with four other friends, they drew up plans for a new national organization called the National Gay Task Force (later known as the National Gay and Lesbian Task Force).

Voeller worked for the task force until 1978, by which time it had achieved most of its early goals including establishing contacts with more than 2,000 local gay groups throughout the country and building a national membership of more than 10,000.

Voeller moved to California and became president of the Mariposa Foundation, an organization devoted to sex research and education. As a biological researcher and gay activist, he felt the term *gay related immune defense disorder* continued to stigmatize homosexuals. He coined the term *acquired immune deficiency syndrome* (AIDS) and wrote more than 60 scholarly papers on the topic. Voeller died from AIDS in California on February 13, 1994.

Chuck Stewart

See also: AIDS History Project; National Gay and Lesbian Task Force.

Further Reading

Saxon, Wolfgang. 1994. "Dr. Bruce Voeller Is Dead at 59; Helped Lead Fight against AIDS." *New York Times*, February 24.

Stewart, Chuck. 2003. *Gay and Lesbian Issues*. Santa Barbara, CA: ABC-CLIO, pp. 168–9.

Waddell, Tom (1937–1987)

Tom Waddell founded the Gay Games. He was born Tom Flubacher on November 1, 1937, in Paterson, New Jersey. At an early age he befriended Gene Waddell, who was a vaudevillian acrobat, and his wife, Hazel Waddell, who was a dancer. They fueled Tom's interest in sports. Tom's closeness with the Waddells eventually led to his decision to change his name to Waddell. As a child he studied ballet. In secondary school he took up athletics, but he dropped athletics while in college to pursue a medical degree which he completed to become a physician.

Passionately opposed to the Vietnam War, Waddell avoided fighting by excelling in military athletics. As a 33-year-old, he trained for the 1968 Olympic Games in Mexico City and placed sixth in the decathlon. It was at this Olympics that two African American athletes gave the Black Power salute during the U.S. national anthem. Waddell supported their actions and was threatened with court-martial by his commanding officers.

In 1980, Waddell proposed the idea for a gay Olympics that would be inclusive rather than exclusive. He intended that anyone, regardless of sex, age, sexual orientation, race, national origin, or athletic ability, be allowed to participate. As a committed Socialist, he believed the Gay Olympics should promote equality and universal participation.

When the U.S. Olympic Committee (USOC) heard about the Gay Olympics, its members were outraged. Just 19 days before the first Gay Olympics were to take place in 1982, the committee filed a court action claiming that it had exclusive use of the word *Olympic*. The Gay Olympics therefore changed its name to the Gay Games.

Tom Waddell, of the U.S. Army from Washington, D.C., has his feet off the ground as he starts his vault in the Olympic decathlon finals at Echo Summit at South Lake Tahoe, California in 1968. (AP Photo)

The first Gay Games (1982) were held in San Francisco, with 1,300 female and male athletes competing. Two years later, a lien was placed against Waddell's house by the USOC in an attempt to recover $96,000 in legal fees it had spent in the court case against the Gay Olympics.

At the next Gay Games (1986), more than 3,000 athletes competed. Sadly, Waddell was diagnosed with AIDS-related pneumocystis carninii pneumonia. He still competed and won, but the disease was taking its toll. He was forced to resign his position as chief physician at San Francisco's Central Emergency Facility. His last few years were spent fighting the USOC's lawsuit. A month before his death, the U.S. Supreme Court upheld USOC's legal authority "to bar homosexual rights group from using the generic word *Olympic* in the names of its games" (Russell 1995, p. 328).

Thomas Waddell died on July 11, 1987, at his home. His last words were, "Well, this should be interesting" (Dick Schaap 1998). Just three years after his death, in 1990, the Gay Games in Vancouver attracted more than 7,000 athletes from around the world. The Gay Games have become the largest amateur sporting event in the world.

Chuck Stewart

See also: Historical Overview of Gay Rights and Issues: From Pre-Columbian Times to the 1970s; Voeller, Bruce (1934–1994).

Further Reading

Russell, Paul. 1995. *The Gay 100.* New York: Kensington Books.

Schaap, Dick. 1987. "The Death of an Athlete." *Sports Illustrated*, July 27.

Schaap, Dick. 1998. *Gay Olympian; The Life and Death of Dr. Tom Waddell.* New York: Knopf.

We'wha (1849–1896)

We'wha was a Zuni Two-Spirit who became the toast of Washington, D.C., society and whose legacy has had an impact on our modern understanding of transgenderism. We'wha was born at Anthill at the Middle of

We'wha, a Zuni berdache. (NARA)

the World, of the Pueblo of Zuni (near the present-day border of New Mexico and Arizona), in 1849. His parents died from smallpox brought by white American settlers passing through. His father's sister adopted him and his brother. In matrilineal Zuni society, this would mean that he retained membership in his mother's clan, the Badger People, while also maintaining lifelong ties to his father's clan, the Dogwood People. We'wha's adoptive family was very powerful within the pueblo.

As a child, perhaps as early as three or four, We'wha showed signs of being a woman. The Zuni saw gender as an acquired trait, not something inborn. Biological sex was not the determining factor as to whether someone was male or female. Thus, We'wha was identified as a *lhamana* (what anthropologists refer to as two-spirited) and trained in the customs and skills of a woman.

During We'wha's childhood, there was great intertribal conflict between the Zunis and the neighboring Navajos and Apaches. The U.S. Army defeated the Navajos in 1864 and forced their removal to distant reservations. Peace brought increasing contacts between the Zunis and white people. Mormon missionaries converted hundreds of Zunis in 1876 and set up a mission. Presbyterians moved in two years later, hoping to run the Mormons out. It was then that anthropologist Matilda Stevenson discovered We'wha and assumed him to be a Zuni "girl."

A friendship developed between Stevenson and We'wha. In 1885, We'wha, along with Stevenson and several others Zunis, went to Washington, D.C. We'wha quickly learned English and soon became the toast of the town. People did not know that he was not a woman. He was introduced as an Indian princess, and receptions were held in his honor. On June 23, 1886, We'wha shook hands with President Grover Cleveland.

We'wha returned to his pueblo. There were conflicts between the Zuni leaders and the U.S. military. We'wha was arrested along with five of the Zuni leaders. We'wha was charged with engaging in witchcraft and served a month in prison.

While participating in the annual Sha'lako festival in December 1896, We'wha died from heart failure at the age of 47. His death was viewed as a great "calamity" and disrupted the calm of the clan. Some Zuni took to their horses and raided nearby lands. This provided the U.S. government with an excuse to exert complete authority over the Zunis. Understanding We'wha's place in Zuni culture sheds light on how gender is constructed in Western societies.

Chuck Stewart

See also: Historical Overview of Gay Rights and Issues: From Pre-Columbian Times to the 1970s; Native Americans and LGBTQ Issues.

Further Reading

Gilley, Brian Joseph. 2006. *Becoming Two-Spirit: Gay Identity and Social Acceptance in Indian Country*. Lincoln: University of Nebraska Press.

Roscoe, Will. 1991. *The Zuni Man-Woman*. (see pp. 29–52 for an account of We'wha's life). Albuquerque: University of New Mexico Press.

White, Dan (1946–1985)

Dan White was born Daniel James White on September 2, 1946, in Los Angeles County, California. White grew up in San Francisco and was one of 10 children. His parents were working-class people who practiced the Roman Catholic religion. White was expelled from Riordan High School during his junior year because he had committed acts of violence. He eventually graduated from Woodrow Wilson High School where he was a star athlete and valedictorian of his class (Geluardi 2008).

In 1965, White joined the U.S. Army and achieved the rank of sergeant. He was a veteran of the Vietnam War and was honorably discharged from military service in 1972. White then returned to his hometown of San Francisco where he was hired as a police officer. When White filed a report against another police officer for beating an African American who was handcuffed, White had no choice but to resign his position because it was an unspoken rule that police officers did not file complaints against each other (Geluardi 2008).

In 1974, White entered the fire academy where he earned a reputation for assisting African Americans who were struggling and helped them pass the written examinations. White graduated at the top of his class from the fire academy and was eventually hired as a firefighter by the city of San Francisco. While serving as a firefighter, White participated in the dramatic rescue of a mother and her baby from a seventh floor apartment. The local media began to refer to White as "the all-American boy" (Geluardi 2008).

In 1977, White won a seat on the board of supervisors representing the eighth district in San

Francisco. White's constituents were mostly white and middle-class citizens who were opposed to the increasing number of homosexuals in the city. White created an image for himself as a family man with religious values who viewed gays and drug users with contempt.

During his time on the board of supervisors, White was at odds over policy matters with members such as Harvey Milk, an openly gay supervisor, and the liberal mayor of San Francisco, George Moscone. On November 10, 1978, White resigned as a city supervisor, citing the corruption within city politics and the financial difficulties of providing for a wife and three children on a supervisor's salary of $9,800 per year. Four days later, however, White changed his mind after his conservative supporters persuaded him to seek a reappointment from Moscone because his departure would have tilted the balance of power in favor of the liberal progressives on the board (Law Library 1979).

After White was denied his reappointment, he shot and murdered Moscone and supervisor Harvey Milk at the San Francisco City Hall on November 27, 1978. White was convicted by a jury on a reduced charge of manslaughter in a controversial trial in which defense attorneys argued that he did not intend to commit the murders. Instead, White's attorneys maintained that he had experienced severe depression, which created a mental state of diminished capacity. As a result, White served only five years of a seven-year and eight-month sentence and was released from the Soledad State prison on January 6, 1984 (Law Library 1979).

After his release from prison, White admitted to a San Francisco homicide inspector that he had planned the murders of Moscone and Milk and also had wanted to murder two other city officials, Carol Ruth Silver and Willie Brown (Weiss 1998). On October 21, 1985, White committed suicide when he died from carbon monoxide poisoning after running his car engine inside of his garage. He was 39 years old at the time of his death (Geluardi 2008).

In 2008, White was portrayed by actor Josh Brolin in the film *Milk*, which highlighted the political career

and assassination of Harvey Milk. Brolin received an Academy Award nomination for his performance in the best-supporting-actor category (Ernst 1979).

Scott P. Johnson

See also: Historical Overview of Gay Rights and Issues: From Pre-Columbian Times to the 1970s; Milk, Harvey (1930–1978); Moscone, George (1929–1978); White (Dan) Trial (1979).

Further Reading

Ernst, Cindi. 1979. "The Dan White (Harvey Milk Murder) Trial: Selected Links & Bibliography." *Famous Trials*. Available at: http://www.law.umkc.edu/faculty/projects/ftrials/danwhitelinks.html.

Geluardi, John. 2008. "Dan White's Motive More about Betrayal than Homophobia." *San Francisco Weekly*, January 29.

Law Library–American Law and Legal Information. "Dan White Trial: 1979—Double Execution, Unique Defense." *Notable Trials and Court Cases—1973 to 1980*. Available at: http://law.jrank.org/pages/3303/Daniel-James-White-Trial-1979.html.

Weiss, Mike. 1998. "Killer of Moscone, Milk Had Willie Brown on List." *San Jose Mercury News*. September 18, A1.

White (Dan) Trial (1979)

The Dan White trial was a powerful reminder of the discrimination and unequal treatment directed toward gays in American society. After White murdered two public officials, including the first openly gay man elected to a citywide position, defense attorneys used a controversial strategy to argue that White did not intend to commit the murders, even though his actions were clearly premeditated. The strategy proved effective as a jury returned a conviction on a reduced charge, which provided a relatively light punishment for double murder. The conservative jurors were apparently influenced by the fact that one of the murder victims was homosexual and the defendant was a local politician who had opposed gay rights. In the aftermath of the verdict, the supporters of civil rights for homosexuals argued that the American criminal

Dan White (directly beneath Fraud sign), a then-suspect in the killing of San Francisco mayor George Moscone and Supervisor Harvey Milk, is led by police officers toward a jail elevator at the Hall of Justice in California. (Bettmann/Corbis)

justice system had sent a dangerous message that the life of a gay man was worth less than a heterosexual man who represented traditional values (Law Library 1979).

On November 27, 1978, Dan White shot and murdered the mayor of San Francisco, George Moscone, and a city supervisor, Harvey Milk, at the San Francisco City Hall. White was a 32-year-old politician and former police officer who had recently resigned as a city supervisor because he was frustrated by the lack of support for conservative policies. Moscone was a liberal mayor, and Milk was a gay activist who had been successful at securing civil rights for homosexuals in the city of San Francisco (Law Library 1979).

On the day of the murders, White had gone to the city hall to ask Mayor Moscone to reinstate him as a city supervisor. When the mayor refused to reappoint him, White fired four bullets into the body of Moscone with a .38 Smith and Wesson revolver. After shooting Moscone, White reloaded his weapon and sought out Harvey Milk, the political rival who had opposed his reappointment. After finding Milk in his office, White shot him five times with his weapon. White had been able to bring the weapon into the city hall because he had entered the building through a basement window in order to avoid metal detectors (Law Library 1979).

White was charged with two counts of first-degree murder and was eligible for the death penalty under a new law in California that required a defendant to be given the gas chamber if he assassinated a public official in the performance of his governmental duties (Shilts 2008, p. 306). The trial of Dan White on double murder charges began on April 25, 1979, in San Francisco, California, in front of Judge Walter F. Calcagno. Thomas F. Norman served as the lead prosecutor, while White was defended by two lawyers, Douglas Schmidt and Stephen Scherr (Law Library 1979).

The jury selection process was a critical phase in the trial as White's defense lawyer, Douglas Schmidt, strategically excluded potential jurors who admitted to supporting homosexual rights. Schmidt was also successful at seating a number of jurors who were working-class citizens with Catholic backgrounds. As a result, the jury of seven women and five men turned out to be ideologically conservative and less likely to have sympathy for a murder victim who had lived the controversial lifestyle of a homosexual (Shilts 2008, pp. 308–9).

Throughout the trial, White was guarded closely by police who feared that the supporters of Harvey Milk, a gay activist, would seek revenge against White. In fact, White and his defense lawyers as well as the prosecution, judge, and jury sat behind a bullet-proof shield that separated the participants of the trial from the large crowd of people who attended the proceedings (Shilts 2008, p. 310).

In his opening statement for the prosecution, Thomas Norman presented the facts of the case to the jury as premeditated and deliberate murder. Therefore, White's assassination of the two public officials qualified as first-degree murder. Norman explained to the jury how White had brought his weapon and additional ammunition to city hall for the purpose of committing the murders. He snuck into the building through a basement window to avoid security and coolly murdered his two victims by firing his weapon nine times. Norman argued that White clearly deserved the death penalty for committing the double murder of Moscone and Milk (Shilts 2008, p. 311).

During his opening statement, White's defense attorney, Douglas Schmidt, skillfully presented an argument that distracted the jury away from the double murder charges and called attention to the personal trauma experienced by Dan White in the time period leading up to the double murder. Schmidt told the jury that White was a good person with traditional American values. However, he had a history of manic depression. As a result, White had a chemical imbalance in his brain that caused him to lose complete control of his behavior. Therefore, Schmidt argued for "diminished capacity" in the case of Dan White. Diminished capacity is a legal term that means a defendant did not intend to commit a crime but instead recklessly committed an offense because of mental impairment. In contrast to a plea of "not guilty by reason of insanity," a diminished capacity plea simply allowed for a defendant to be convicted of a lesser offense with a reduced punishment (Lippman 2009, p. 289).

The prosecution's first witness was Boyd Stephens, the medical coroner, who testified about the deaths of the two victims and emphasized that blood spatters on the wall where Milk was shot indicated that White had fired his weapon with such accuracy that he could not have been mentally unstable at the time of the shooting. Other witnesses documented for the jury the 10-minute period during which White shot and murdered the two public officials (Shilts 2008, pp. 311–12). Next, the prosecution called several witnesses who discussed the series of events leading up to the double murder. A key witness was the newly elected mayor of San Francisco, Diane Feinstein, who testified about White's frustrations in local politics and his inability to bring about conservative policies. Feinstein maintained that White's experiences within the political environment of San Francisco had caused him severe emotional trauma. On cross-examination, Douglas Schmidt was successful in getting Feinstein to admit that White had acted out of character when he shot and killed Moscone and Milk. Feinstein conceded that she never would have thought that White was the type of person who could commit murder (Law Library 1979).

Finally, the prosecution called its last witness, Frank Falzon, the police investigator who had recorded White's confession on a tape recorder roughly one hour after the murders. Falzon was asked to play the taped confession for the jury, which was to serve as a critical part of the prosecution's case against White (Shilts 2008, pp. 312–13). However, the taped confession seemed to garner sympathy for White from the jury. White was heard on the tape discussing the various struggles in his life such as his financial problems, family matters, and the frustrations in his political career. Any discussion of the murders was not mentioned in the confession, and the prosecution was surprised to see four of the jurors crying and seemingly interested in White's story of a good man pushed beyond his limits by political corruption and personal struggles (Law Library 1979).

During the cross-examination provided by the defense, Falzon spoke of his friendly relationship with White and how the two men had first met in Catholic grade school. Falzon described White as a great athlete who won the most valuable player award in a police softball league. Falzon added that he had offered his support to White during his political career and had great respect for him as "a man among men." When asked if White was a person who was capable of murder, Falzon replied that White was a man who rarely lost his temper. Falzon concluded by stating that the man who committed the murders was a completely different person from the friend that he had known for many years. In a strange turn of events, Falzon, a key witness for the prosecution, had proved to be an impressive character witness for White, who was presented as a man incapable of premeditated murder. The prosecution failed miserably with its presentation of the taped confession and ended its case against White after only three days without discussing the history of political grudges that had existed between White and Milk or emphasizing the fact that White had assassinated two public officials who were attempting to perform their duties under the law (Shilts 2008, pp. 312–13).

In making their case for diminished capacity, the defense attorneys continued to build their case before the jury that White's mental condition had deteriorated to the point where he was not in control of his actions on the day of the murders. A number of psychiatrists testified that White never intended to commit the murders and attempted to justify White's actions before and during the murders. One psychiatrist maintained that White only took his gun to the city hall because he felt threatened by his political opponents. Another psychiatrist told the jury that White entered the city hall through the basement window because he didn't want to embarrass the security officer at the front door, who would be required to deal with a politician who was in possession of a gun. In other words, White did not want to hurt the security officer's feelings. Finally, a psychiatric expert testified that White had an extremely high amount of sugar in his blood from eating junk food, which exacerbated his manic depression and caused him to behave irrationally (Shilts 2008, pp. 316–17). The so-called Twinkie Defense was sensationalized by the media as a critical part of the White trial but, in actuality, it was a very minor part of the defense strategy in seeking a lesser charge for the defendant (Pogash 2003).

The defense attorneys had presented an effective argument before the jury that White was a family man with traditional values who was involved in a battle beyond his control. White was portrayed as a martyr who was trying to save San Francisco from the crime and corruption that had become commonplace within the city. In addition to his fight against a corrupt political system that included a militant gay activist, Harvey Milk, White had personal troubles that caused him to break down emotionally and mentally. The "Twinkie Defense" provided the last bit of the equation that apparently caused White to commit the two murders (Pogash, "Myth of the 'Twinkie Defense'").

Perhaps the most successful part of the defense's strategy was its repeated attempts to introduce the issue of homosexuality into the proceedings. Douglas Schmidt raised the issue throughout the trial as a subtle reminder to the conservative jurors that Harvey Milk had lived a controversial life as a homosexual while White's lifestyle reflected the traditional values of America. Schmidt consistently referred to White's distinguished background as a Vietnam veteran and former police officer and fireman who had saved people's lives (Shilts 2008, pp. 310–18).

During his closing statement, Thomas Norman repeated for the jury the details of the murders and argued that a mentally ill person would not have been able to plan and successfully commit the two murders. Norman's summation lasted for four hours, and he clearly bored the jurors with his attention to detail (Shilts 2008, p. 321).

In his closing statement, Douglas Schmidt argued that there was nothing unusual about White carrying a gun on the day of the murders because he was a former law enforcement officer. In addition, Schmidt reminded the jurors of the psychiatrist who testified that White entered the city hall through the basement window in order to avoid embarrassing the security officer in the building (Law Library 1979). In contrast to the prosecution, Schmidt provided a shorter and more exciting presentation for the jury by dramatically referencing God several times. He noted that White was a good man who would eventually be punished by God. However, circumstances beyond White's control caused a reasonable man to act impulsively with great passion. In utilizing the diminished capacity argument, Schmidt begged the jury to find White guilty of a reduced charge of manslaughter, instead of the first-degree murder charge (Schilts 2008, p. 322).

On May 21, 1979, after three days of deliberations, the jury concluded that Dan White was guilty of the reduced charge of voluntary manslaughter in the deaths of George Moscone and Harvey Milk. Judge Calcagno sentenced White to a maximum of seven years and eight months in prison. However, White would be able to gain parole in five years if he demonstrated good behavior. The jury's verdict caused a riot in San Francisco as thousands of people demonstrated in front of San Francisco's city hall (Law Library 1979).

In the early 1980s, California voters passed statewide propositions to ban the use of diminished capacity in criminal trials (Ernst 1979). Despite protests from the gay community, White was released from prison in 1984 less than five years after his conviction on murder charges. Less than two years after his release from prison, White committed suicide on October 21, 1985. Today, the Dan White trial and the "Twinkie Defense" have taken on a mythical quality in American popular culture (Law Library 1979). While most Americans believe that White was given a reduced sentence because junk food caused him to commit the murders, the outcome of the trial was based largely upon the political environment of San Francisco and intolerance to homosexuality (Pogash 2003).

Scott P. Johnson

See also: Milk, Harvey (1930–1978); Moscone, George (1929–1978); White, Dan (1946–1985).

Further Reading

Ernst, Cindi. 1979. "The Dan White (Harvey Milk Murder) Trial: Selected Links & Bibliography." *Famous Trials.* Available at: http://www.law.umkc.edu/faculty/projects/ftrials/danwhitelinks.html.

Law Library–American Law and Legal Information. "Dan White Trial: 1979—Double Execution, Unique Defense." *Notable Trials and Court Cases—1973 to 1980.* Available at: http://law.jrank.org/pages/3303/Daniel-James-White-Trial-1979.html.

Lippman, Matthew. 2009. *Contemporary Criminal Law: Concepts, Cases, and Controversies.* Thousand Oaks, CA: Sage.

Pogash, Carol. 2003. "Myth of the 'Twinkie Defense.'" *San Francisco Chronicle.* November 23, D1.

Shilts, Randy. 2008. *The Mayor of Castro Street: The Life and Times of Harvey Milk.* New York: Macmillan.

Whitman, Walt (1819–1892)

Walt Whitman was an influential poet of early America whose homosexual themes encouraged closeted gay men and women. Born in Huntington, New York, on May 31, 1819, Whitman began working in a printing shop at 11 years of age and continued in the publishing business for the next 24 years. He met his heart's companion, Peter Doyle, an 18-year-old streetcar conductor, in 1865 and depicted their relationship in the collection of poems *Leaves of Grass.* The section called "Calamus" contained overtly homosexual poems. During the Civil War, Whitman volunteered to visit soldiers in hospitals and was appreciated for his ability to bring cheer and boost the men's spirits in the camps.

In 1873, Whitman had a stroke that partially paralyzed him. He moved to Camden, New Jersey, leaving Doyle behind. While there he met an 18-year-old boy named Harry Stafford. Their relationship lasted a number of years, but Whitman finally disengaged himself from the boy.

By 1884, the Philadelphia edition of *Leaves of Grass* brought financial rewards that enabled him to

Walt Whitman in 1887. (Library of Congress)

Walt Whitman with Peter Doyle. (Library of Congress)

purchase a house in Camden, New Jersey. However, another stroke in 1888 left him very incapacitated. He died at home on March 26, 1892.

Chuck Stewart

See also: Carpenter, Edward (1844–1929); Historical Overview of Gay Rights and Issues: From Pre-Columbian Times to the 1970s; Symonds, John Addington (1840–1893).

Further Reading

Callow, Philip. 1992. *From Noon to Starry Night: A Life of Walt Whitman*. Chicago: Ivan R. Dee.

Kaplan, Justin. 1979. *Walt Whitman: A Life*. New York: Simon and Schuster.

Loving, Jerome. 1999. *Walt Whitman: The Song of Himself.* Oakland: University of California Press.

Miller, James E., Jr. 1962. *Walt Whitman*. New York: Twayne Publishers, Inc.

Reynolds, David S. 1995. *Walt Whitman's America: A Cultural Biography*. New York: Vintage Books.

Stacy, Jason. 2008. *Walt Whitman's Multitudes: Labor Reform and Persona in Whitman's Journalism and the First Leaves of Grass, 1840–1855*. New York: Peter Lang Publishing.

Wilde, Oscar (1854–1900)

Oscar Wilde was a famous British writer and playwright who was arrested and convicted in a very public trial for his "love that dare not speak its name." Born on October 16, 1854, in Dublin, Ireland, Wilde came from a professional family. His father was a famous eye and ear surgeon, and his mother was a folklorist and poet. He graduated with honors in 1878 from Oxford University. He had a reputation as a serious classic scholar, but he was also an aesthete who favored gorgeously decorated rooms and gaudy clothing.

Acting as the advance agent for London's Gilbert and Sullivan touring companies, he was able to lecture in more than 70 U.S. cities on arts and literature. He became a celebrity hound and was well known for being well known. Although he married and had two sons, he led a double life with a widening circle of available young men.

In 1891, Wilde completed his novel *The Picture of Dorian Gray*. It caused a storm of indignation for

Novelist and playwright Oscar Wilde. (Library of Congress)

its "purple patches" and thinly veiled allusions to homosexual life. At the same time, Wilde was introduced to Lord Alfred Douglas. The beauty of this 21-year-old stunned Wilde. Within the year they were reckless lovers and Wilde was completely in love. Personal letters between them found their way to Douglas's father, the marquis of Queensberry. The father left a card with a scrawled insult at Wilde's hotel. Douglas egged on Wilde, who sued Queensberry for criminal libel. When the case came to court, the tables were turned, and Wilde was placed on trial for sodomy. Wilde was convicted and sentenced to two years of hard labor. After his release from prison, Wilde moved to France and was reunited with Douglas. Wilde died November 30, 1900, at the age of 46, destitute, in Paris.

Chuck Stewart

See also: Carpenter, Edward (1844–1929); Historical Overview of Gay Rights and Issues: From Pre-Columbian Times to the 1970s; Symonds, John Addington (1840–1893).

Further Reading

Beckson, Karl E. 1998. *The Oscar Wilde Encyclopedia.* AMS Studies in the Nineteenth Century, no. 18. New York: AMS Press. Detailed reference work on Wilde.

Holland, Merlin, ed. 2003. *Irish Peacock and Scarlet Marquess: The Real Trial of Oscar Wilde.* London: Fourth Estate.